A to Z神秘案件

中英双语

第二辑

THE KIDNAPPED KING

被绑架的国王

[美]罗恩·罗伊 著

[美]约翰·史蒂文·格尼 绘 杨琼琼 译

CNS
湖南少年儿童出版社
HUNAN JUVENILE & CHILDREN'S PUBLISHING HOUSE
小博集
BOOKY KIDS
·长沙·

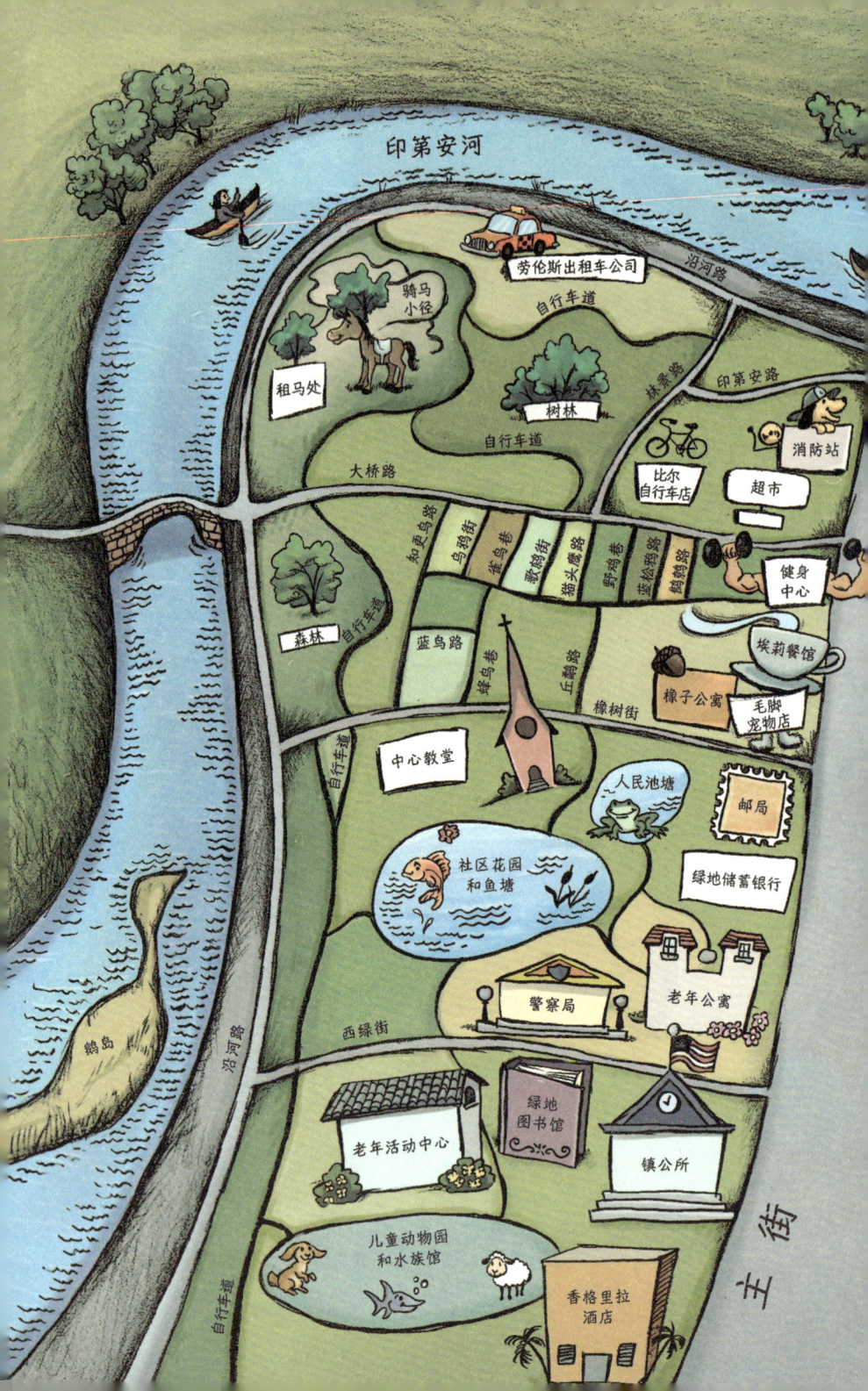

人物介绍

三人小组的成员，聪明勇敢，喜欢读推理小说，紧急关头总能保持头脑冷静。喜欢在做事之前好好思考！

丁丁

三人小组的成员，活泼机智，喜欢吃好吃的食物，常常有意想不到的点子。

乔希

三人小组的成员，活泼开朗，喜欢从头到脚穿同一种颜色的衣服，总是那个能找到大部分线索的人。

露丝

哥斯达拉国的王子，来美国后暂住在丁丁家。

萨米尔·本·奥兹

丁丁的妈妈。

邓肯太太

萨米尔的指导老师。

琼·克林克尔

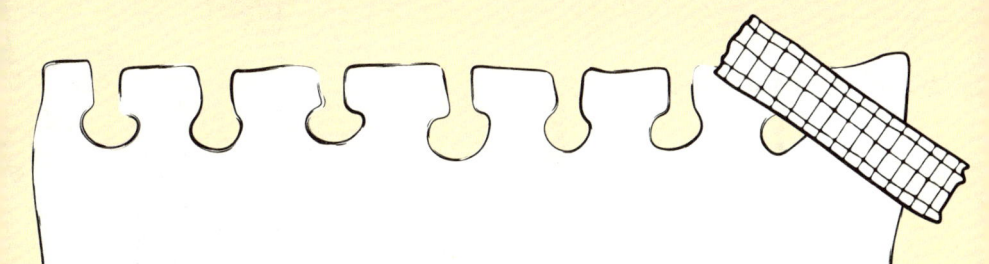

字母 K 代表 kidnapped，绑架……

"萨米尔？"丁丁叫了一声，同时扫视着空荡荡的房间。"他去哪儿了？"丁丁下楼的时候心里想。

"妈妈，萨米尔不在房间里。"丁丁说。

丁丁的妈妈舀了一勺做煎饼的面糊，正要放进煎锅，她停下来问："他不在房间？他去哪儿了？"

"我不知道，妈妈。"丁丁猛地推开后门，向院子里四处张望了一下。"也不在这里。"他说。

丁丁关门的时候，他的手碰到了某样尖锐的东西。

"妈妈，快来看这个！"他大叫起来。

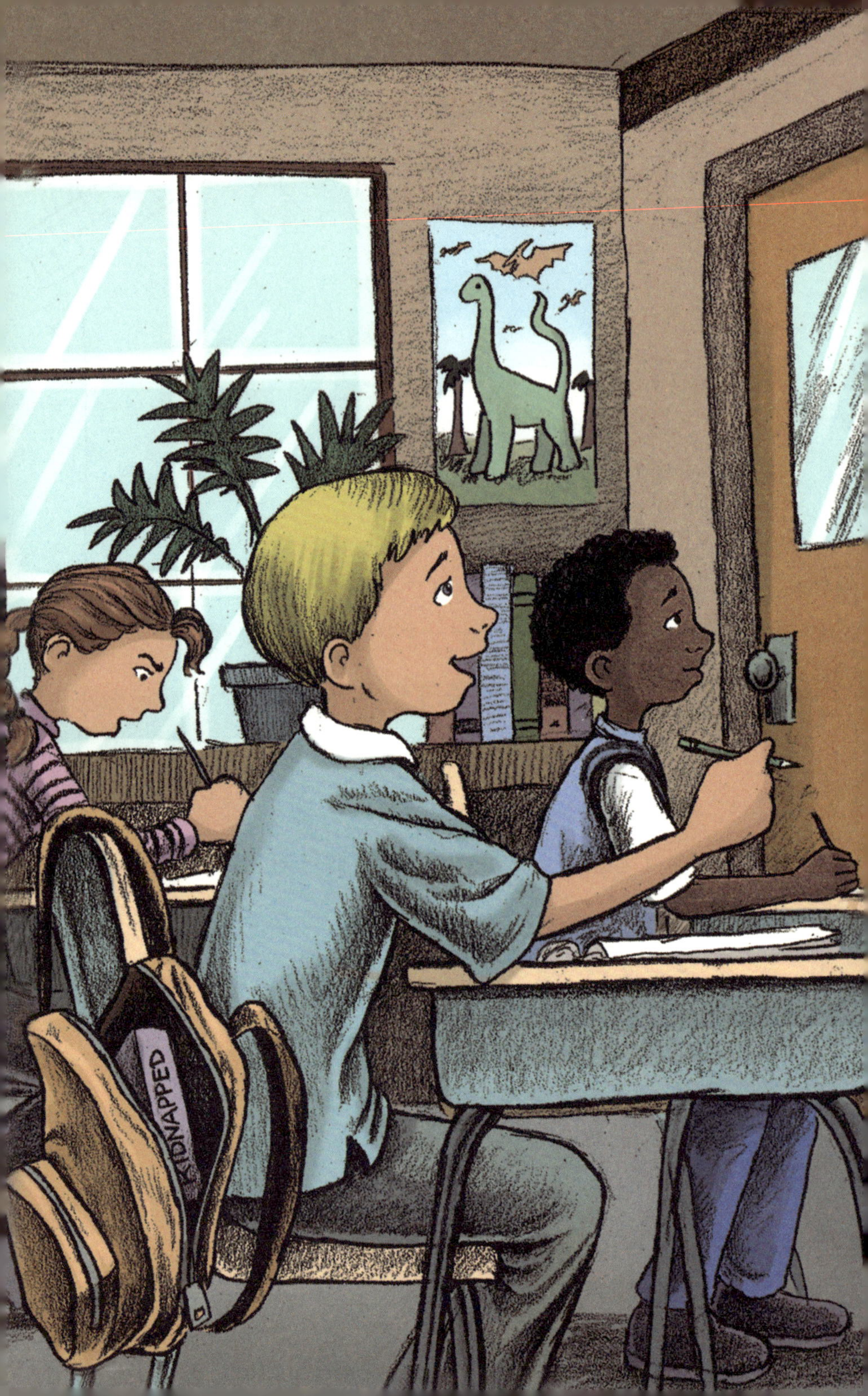
KIDNAPPED

第一章

"做完了!"丁丁心里这样想着,脸上露出了笑容。做完数学试卷上的最后一道题后,他在试卷上端写下了"唐纳德·D.邓肯",然后抬头看了看教室里的时钟:两点十五分。再过二十分钟,就要放春假啦!

"同学们,请准备,'DEAR 时间'到了!"伊格尔夫人说,"请拿出你们的书,找一个舒服的地方去阅读,直到下课铃响。"

DEAR 是 Drop Everything and Read(放

下手头的事情享受阅读）的缩写,这是一天中丁丁最喜欢的时间。

丁丁阅读的书是由罗伯特·路易斯·史蒂文森写的《绑架》。他已经看过电影了,但还是喜欢读读故事。于是,他拿着书走到阅读角,"扑通"一声坐在豆袋椅上。

乔希和露丝来到丁丁的旁边,拿着书躺在地毯上阅读。教室里变得十分安静,只能听见时钟的嘀嗒声和书页的翻动声。

突然,教室里的电话响了。伊格尔夫人接完电话,走到阅读角。"丁丁,"她小声说,"狄龙先生让你去他的办公室。"

乔希对丁丁笑了一下,扬了扬眉毛。"你惹麻烦了!"他说。

"狄龙先生找我?"丁丁问,"为什么?"

伊格尔夫人耸了耸肩,小声说:"快去快回。"

丁丁放下书,离开了教室。

走过安静的走廊,丁丁心里琢磨着校长为什么要找他。他实在想不出自己做错了什么!

在狄龙先生的办公室外面,丁丁深吸了一口

气，然后走了进去。校长秘书沃特斯夫人正坐在校长办公室外的办公桌前。她对丁丁笑了笑。"你好，唐纳德，快进去吧，别畏畏缩缩的。"她说，"狄龙先生又不会吃孩子！"

丁丁笑了，然后打开了通向狄龙先生办公室的门，他第一眼看到的人竟然是自己的妈妈！

看见妈妈拍了拍她旁边的空椅子，丁丁走过去，坐了下来。

办公室里还有其他三个人：狄龙先生，一个黄头发的女人，还有一个和丁丁年龄相仿的孩子。

那个孩子穿得像电影里的人物——身上穿着一件深蓝色的长袍，脚上穿着一双凉鞋。

"你好，唐纳德！"狄龙先生说。他胖乎乎的，像个足球；头发理得很短；在灯光的照射下，他的眼镜片闪闪发亮。

"我来介绍一下，"他说着，向黄头发的女人点了点头，"这是琼·克林克尔女士，这位是，"他微笑地看着那个男孩，"萨米尔·本·奥兹。"

丁丁含糊地说了声"你好"，然后就盯着这个男孩看。

他的体型和丁丁差不多大，头发是黑色的，皮肤也是黑色的。他的眼睛是亮黄色的，如同蜂蜜的颜色。

"萨米尔来自哥斯达拉，"狄龙先生说，"那是印度洋上的一个小岛国，他是来美国学英语的。"

"我早就会说英语了。"那个男孩说。

他声音轻柔，说话时带着口音。丁丁觉得，那个男孩的表情和声音都透露着忧伤。

"实际上，萨米尔会在这里待一年。"琼·克

林克尔说,"我是他的指导老师。他的父母让他来这里学习美国的风俗习惯。"

狄龙先生看着丁丁。"萨米尔将和你一起上三年级。我们觉得你会愿意带他到处看看。"他说。

所有人都看着丁丁,他感觉自己的脸变红了。妈妈捏了一下他的手,解释道:"萨米尔要和我们一起生活几周,丁丁。"

"你叫丁丁?"萨米尔问。

丁丁向男孩点了点头。

"丁丁,"萨米尔重复了一遍,"和思考、粉色以及臭味押韵。"[1]

"联想同韵的单词可以帮助萨米尔记忆新单词。"他的指导老师解释道。

"萨米尔可以住客房。"丁丁的妈妈说,"你爸爸出差了,家里有个客人住挺好的。我希望萨米尔能和你、乔希、露丝成为好朋友。"

萨米尔咯咯地笑起来:"露丝和脚趾、鼻子押韵。"[2]

丁丁也笑了。他心想:"等着瞧乔希和露丝见到他会怎么样吧。"

---

1. 丁丁的英文是 Dink,思考、粉色、臭味的英文分别是 think、pink、stink,四个词同韵。——编者
2. 露丝的英文是 Rose,脚趾和鼻子的英文分别是 toes(复数)、nose,三个词同韵。——编者

第二章

丁丁回到班级后,交给伊格尔夫人一张字条。马上要放假了,狄龙先生准许丁丁提前放学。

丁丁收拾好书包,将刚才发生的事小声地告诉了乔希和露丝。

丁丁的妈妈开车带着他和萨米尔回家——他们家在林荫街。萨米尔安静地坐在车里,不断地扭头,透过后车窗往外看。

"克林克尔老师说,过一会儿,她会把你的行李送过来。"丁丁的妈妈对萨米尔说,"丁丁会帮你安顿下来,而我会给你们做点吃的。"

"非常感谢你,邓肯太太。"萨米尔说。丁丁的妈妈把车停在林荫街的停车道上。

丁丁下车时,背上的书包发出"咚"的一声。

"你的房间就在我的隔壁。"他一边对萨米尔说,一边领着他上楼。

丁丁带萨米尔来到了客房。客房里面有一张床、一个梳妆台,地板上铺着编织地毯,床边的床头柜上放着一个阅读灯。

萨米尔静静地打量着这间屋子。"这里不错。"他说。

"快来,我要让你看看我的房间。"丁丁说。他和萨米尔穿过卫生间,来到另一头的丁丁的卧室。

丁丁一走进房间,洛蕾塔就开始吱吱叫,在笼子里乱跑。

"那是什么?"萨米尔大叫着躲在丁丁身后。

"是我养的豚鼠。"丁丁说,"洛蕾塔很友好。你想抱抱它吗?"

"我对皮毛过敏!"萨米尔一边往笼子里瞄一边说,"别放它出来。"

"好吧,不放它出来。"丁丁说。

被绑架的国王

"丁丁!"妈妈在楼下喊道,"你和萨米尔可以下来吃点东西了吗?"

"你饿不饿?"丁丁问萨米尔。

萨米尔努努鼻子问:"我们吃什么?"

丁丁假装想了一会儿,然后说:"和平常一样——老鼠耳朵薄脆饼干。"

萨米尔盯着丁丁说:"你是在开玩笑吧?"

"没错,我在开玩笑。"丁丁说,"走吧,我们去楼下。"

丁丁的妈妈在餐桌上放了一盘花生酱小甜饼和一夸脱[1]牛奶。萨米尔打量着那些小甜饼,然后挑了一块。

"你对小甜饼不过敏,对吧?"丁丁问。

萨米尔摇摇头,咬了一小口。

这时,门铃响了。丁丁打开门,看到乔希和露丝站在门口台阶上,帕尔——乔希的短腿长耳猎犬——蹲在他们的脚边。

---

1. 夸脱:英美制体积单位。计量液体体积时,1英夸脱合 1.137 升,1 美夸脱合 0.946 升。——编者

"我们来看看你和萨米尔想不想出来玩。"露丝说。她手里拿着一个 NERF[1] 牌的橄榄球,橄榄球的颜色与她身上的紫色的牛仔裤和运动衫十分相配。

---

1. NERF:孩之宝公司所拥有的玩具品牌,品牌为 Non-Expanding Recreational Foam 的缩写,意思是"非膨胀娱乐海绵"。——编者

"嘿，伙伴们！进来吧！"丁丁说。

乔希直接走向那盘小甜饼，帕尔跟在他后面，伸出粉红色的长舌头。

萨米尔一下跳上椅子。"赶它走！"他大叫，"我会过敏！"

丁丁的妈妈把一只手放到萨米尔肩上，说："没事的，萨米尔。——乔希，能让帕尔在走廊里待着吗？"

"当然，邓肯太太。——来吧，伙计。"乔希说着，领着帕尔出了屋子。

"随便吃，孩子们。"丁丁的妈妈一边说，一边倒了四杯牛奶。

乔希回来了，他抓了两个小甜饼。"你为什么穿浴袍啊？"他问萨米尔。

A to Z 神秘案件

"我们国家的人都穿这样的衣服。"萨米尔说着,抿了一口牛奶。

"我觉得这样穿很漂亮,"露丝说,"我也想有一件这样的长袍。"

这时,门铃又响了。萨米尔的指导老师琼·克林克尔来了。她是乘出租车来的,带着萨米尔的小提箱。丁丁帮司机把小提箱提到了门厅里。

"你好,萨米尔。"指导老师说,"你喜欢这座房子吗?"

"这里有动物!"萨米尔说,"我对皮毛过敏,你知道的。"

"很抱歉,我们养了一只豚鼠。"丁丁的妈妈说。

"嗯,而且我刚才看见门廊上有一只狗。"琼·克林克尔说,"但愿萨米尔的过敏不会给你们带来太多麻烦。"

丁丁的妈妈微笑着。"我相信我们会处理好的。"她说。"丁丁,你们先帮萨米尔把行李提到楼上他的房间去,然后再一起出去玩,好吗?"

"我也一起去,可以吗?"琼·克林克尔问,"我想看看萨米尔住的房间,你不介意吧?"

"哪儿的话。丁丁会领着你去看。"

丁丁和乔希拖着小提箱上楼,然后"扑通"一声,把小提箱放在萨米尔的床上。露丝走在他们身后,萨米尔和指导老师紧跟在她身后。

琼·克林克尔在房间里走了一圈,查看了窗户,试了试锁。她"咔嗒咔嗒"地拧了拧卫生间和大厅的门把手。"这些门都有锁吗?"她问丁丁。

"嗯,有的,但是我们从来不用。"他回答。

"有夜灯吗?"她问。

丁丁用手指了指墙上的电源插座,上面插着一个小小的蓝色的灯。

琼·克林克尔点了点头。"我想这样是可以的。"她说,"现在,我可以看看萨米尔的卫生间吗?"

丁丁领着琼看了他和萨米尔要共用的卫生间。

这位女士检查了卫生间里的所有东西,然后瞥了一眼另一头的丁丁的房间。"谁住这儿?"她问。

"是我。"丁丁说,"我爸爸妈妈在楼下住。"

"他们在楼下有自己的卫生间吗?"琼问。

丁丁点了点头。他们一起回到了萨米尔的房间。

琼·克林克尔对丁丁笑了笑。"这里太完美

了！"她轻轻拍了拍萨米尔的头说:"一会儿再见,好吗?"

萨米尔看着她,脸上露出紧张的神色:"你要去哪儿?"

"去我住的酒店房间。"琼说,"吃完晚饭后我就来给你上法语课。"她又看了一眼萨米尔的房间,然后离开了。

"你们国家玩NERF的橄榄球吗?"露丝问萨米尔。

萨米尔摇摇头:"NERF是什么?"

"就是这个。"乔希把那个泡沫球抛向萨米尔。泡沫球撞在萨米尔身上,弹开后落在了地上。

"嗯,你要不要换衣服?"丁丁问萨米尔。

萨米尔盯着他的小提箱。"你妈妈说她会帮我打开箱子收拾的。"他说。

"她会的。"丁丁说,"但是,你现在可以穿我的衣服。走,去我的房间。"

四个孩子一个接一个地穿过卫生间去到丁丁的房间。洛蕾塔开始在笼子里欢蹦乱跳。

丁丁在他的衣橱里找出一件运动裤和一件运

被绑架的国王

动衫。"这两件应该适合你。"他对萨米尔说。

萨米尔看了看衣服,没有伸手接。

"谁给我穿衣服?"他问。

第三章

丁丁、乔希和露丝全都盯着萨米尔。

"嗯……你说的话是什么意思?谁给你穿衣服?"丁丁问。

"在我的国家,仆人给我穿衣服和脱衣服。"萨米尔说。

"啊,没错。"乔希微笑着说,"我还有仆人帮我做作业呢!"

"你真的有仆人吗?"露丝问萨米尔。

萨米尔点点头:"我有五个仆人,我父亲有二十个仆人。"

被绑架的国王

"二十个仆人!"乔希大叫,"你们家很有钱吗?"

萨米尔坐到丁丁的床上。"我们非常富有。"他说,"我爸爸是……"

萨米尔没有往下说,而是突然痛哭起来。

"好了,乔希,你把他弄哭了。"丁丁说。

"我没有!我只是问他是不是很有钱。"

露丝坐到萨米尔旁边。"你为什么哭啊?"她问。

萨米尔没有回答。大颗大颗的泪珠顺着他的脸颊流下。

丁丁把运动衫扔到床上,去卫生间拿来一卷纸。"给你。"他说。

萨米尔接过纸,擦了擦眼泪。

"你是想你的爸爸妈妈了吗?"露丝问萨米尔,"你是因为这个哭吗?"

萨米尔深深吸了一口气,擦了擦眼泪。"我不知道我的父母在什么地方。"他说,"他们上周被人绑架了。"

"被绑架了!"三个孩子大叫道。

萨米尔点了点头:"我父亲的敌人偷偷溜进王宫,绑架了他和我母亲。"

A to Z 神秘案件

"王宫?"乔希说,"你们住在王宫?你是什么人?是王子之类的人吗?"

萨米尔点了点头:"是的,我父亲是哥斯达拉的国王,我是萨米尔·本·奥兹王子。有一天我会成为国王。"

萨米尔又哭了起来。

大家都没有说话,连洛蕾塔都不在笼子里乱

被绑架的国王

跑了。

　　丁丁盯着萨米尔。"你真的是一位王子?"最后他问,"我妈妈知道这些吗,萨米尔?我的意思是,她知道你的家人被绑架以及其他的事情吗?"

那个男孩摇了摇头。"只有我的指导老师知道。"他说。"我父母是夜里被绑架的,那时我正在睡觉。为了不遇到危险,第二天,我就被悄悄带出王宫,送到了这里。"

"不遇到什么危险?"露丝问。

萨米尔看着她,眼眶红红的,流着鼻涕。"被绑架的危险。"他说。

就在这时,帕尔在前面的门廊上狂吠起来。

"他们来了。"萨米尔哭叫着。他跳下床,跑进了卫生间。

丁丁看了看窗外,看到帕尔正对着一辆车狂吠,那是一辆出租车。丁丁看到车转过拐角,不见了。

"出来吧,萨米尔。"丁丁说,"那不过是你的指导老师乘车离开了。"

萨米尔从卫生间里走了出来,眼睛里满是恐惧。"对不起。"他小声说。

"没事。"丁丁说,"我们一起下楼去玩吧?"

丁丁指着床上的运动服,说:"你真的需要别人给你穿衣服吗?"

被绑架的国王

萨米尔深深吸了一口气,笑着说:"不,我现在在美国,我要学会自己穿衣服。"

萨米尔换衣服时,其他孩子走出屋子,在丁丁家的后院里玩起橄榄球来,他们将橄榄球抛来抛去。

"当王子肯定很酷。"乔希说,"想想看,你可以对身边那些仆人发号施令。"

丁丁用橄榄球砸了他一下。

"乔希,萨米尔根本不在乎那种东西。"丁丁说,"他想念他的父母。"

"我知道。"乔希说,"但我还是会想,他打个响指就可以在半夜享用冰激凌。"

这时,萨米尔穿着丁丁的运动服走了出来。

帕尔被拴在一棵树上,萨米尔经过时,它试图舔萨米尔的脚。

萨米尔远远地跳开了。"它会咬我吗?"他问。

乔希大声笑了。"不,它在跟你打招呼,说'你好'呢!"他说,"帕尔连只蚂蚁都不会伤害。去吧,摸摸它。"

萨米尔走近帕尔,在它的脑袋上摸了摸,接

29

着，他打了一个喷嚏。

"我喜欢它。"萨米尔说，"但是，我还是会过敏。"

孩子们教给萨米尔玩橄榄球的规则。他们一直玩到丁丁的妈妈叫他们回屋吃东西。

乔希答应明天早晨会再过来，然后就解开狗绳，带帕尔回家了。

"再见，萨米尔！"露丝说。她穿过树篱，回到隔壁自己的家。

"你的朋友们真好。"萨米尔说，"你们每天都在一起玩吗？"

"当然。"丁丁说，"你在哥……哥……就是你来的地方，也和朋友们一起玩吗？"

萨米尔摇摇头："我没有朋友，我待在王宫里，跟着我的指导老师学习。"

没有朋友？丁丁盯着萨米尔。他不敢想象没有乔希和露丝陪自己玩的生活。

"我们最好上去洗洗手。"丁丁看着自己脏兮兮的手说，"但愿你喜欢汉堡包和炸薯条。"

"Burgersandfries[1]?"萨米尔问,"那是什么?"

丁丁笑着说:"就是汉堡包和炸薯条。炸薯条是一根根很细的土豆条,你要蘸着番茄酱吃。"

萨米尔叹了口气,说:"好吧,我会尝尝你们吃的东西。谁为我试菜呢?"

"试菜?"丁丁问,"为什么?"

"在我们国家,"萨米尔解释道,"我父亲的敌人有时候会尝试毒害他,所以他有一个专门的仆人试菜,以确保食物安全。"

丁丁冲萨米尔笑着说:"我妈妈的厨艺不错,她下的毒不多。"

萨米尔的眼睛瞪得溜圆:"你在开玩笑,对吗?"

"对。"丁丁说,"但是,我们最好把你的情况告诉我妈妈,好吗?"

"为什么?"萨米尔问。

"因为这是我们做事的方式。"丁丁说,"别担心,你在这里很安全。在绿地镇,没有人会绑架你。"

---

1. 即上文丁丁说的汉堡包和薯条(burgers and fries),英文全称是 hamburgers and French fries。萨米尔将两种食物误当成了一种。——编者

第四章

吃晚餐的时候，丁丁和萨米尔对丁丁的妈妈说了萨米尔来美国的真正原因。

"哦，萨米尔，"丁丁的妈妈说，"我真的为你感到难过。谢谢你告诉我这些。"

吃过冰激凌，丁丁和他的妈妈帮助萨米尔收拾行李。丁丁的妈妈拿起一个长长的镶嵌了黄金的木盒子。"这个盒子很重，萨米尔，里面装了什么？"她问。

萨米尔打开盒盖，拿出一个金光闪闪的万花筒。金色的筒壁上镶满了珠宝。

"这个万花筒在我们家族中传很多年了，"萨米尔解释说，"这是我太爷爷的太爷爷留下的，现在归我父亲所有。"

"太有意思了！"丁丁的妈妈说，"这个万花筒有一天会传给你吗？"

"等我过十五岁生日的时候，父亲就会把这个万花筒传给我。"萨米尔说着，皱起眉头，"至

A to Z 神秘案件

少他本来会这样做，但是现在……我不知道接下来会发生什么。"

丁丁替萨米尔感到难过。他不敢想象，如果父母被绑架了，自己会是什么感觉。

丁丁的妈妈坐到萨米尔旁边，拉起他的手。"萨米尔，我相信，你的父母很快就会被找到。"她说，"你不是对我们说过，你父亲的朋友正在你们的国家到处找你的父母吗？"

萨米尔点了点头。"但是他的敌人很狡猾，"他说，"他们可能把我父母带到远离哥斯达拉的地方了。"

丁丁的妈妈拥抱了一下萨米尔，然后把他的睡衣和拖鞋放到他的床上。睡衣是红色丝绸的，拖鞋是紫色法兰绒的，拖鞋上面缀着松垂的金黄色流苏。

"太华丽了！"丁丁笑着对萨米尔说，"我通常穿旧T恤衫和短裤睡觉。"

就在这个时候，前门门铃响了，丁丁的妈妈离开了房间。

"看。"萨米尔跪在地板上说。他拧开万花筒较粗的一端，倒出里面所有的玻璃片。他们把红色、黄色和蓝色的玻璃片分别在地毯上堆成一堆。

"万花筒被拆开了！"丁丁说。他捡起一些玻璃片，薄薄的玻璃片摸起来滑滑的。

有人敲萨米尔房间的门。琼·克林克尔探进头。"你好，萨米尔！"她说。

萨米尔笑了笑，将玻璃片收拾起来。"我在给丁丁看我的万花筒。"他说。丁丁帮着萨米尔把万花筒装回盒子。

"很好，萨米尔。"琼说着，看了看手表，"现在快八点了，上一小节法语课怎么样？"

她把一本黄色的书放在萨米尔的床上，对丁丁说："你能过一会儿再来找萨米尔吗？"

"能让丁丁留下来吗？"萨米尔问，"他可以和我一起上课。"

琼·克林克尔看了看丁丁，然后说："当然可以，为什么不呢？"

"好极了！"丁丁说。他挨着萨米尔坐在地板上。琼斜倚在床上，打开了那本黄色的书。

"首先，学习关于颜色的词。"琼说。她指了

A to Z 神秘案件

指丁丁的衬衫:"蓝色,用法语说是 bleu。跟我说,萨米尔。"

萨米尔说:"bleu。"丁丁觉得这个词听起来几乎和英语 blue 一样。

琼指了指丁丁:"现在,请你说一下。"

"bleu。"丁丁尽量模仿萨米尔。

"不错!"琼把一只手放在折叠好了的萨米尔的睡衣上。"红色。"她说。

"rouge。"萨米尔说。

对丁丁来说,这个词听起来像 rooj,因此他就那样说了。

琼·克林克尔拿起了黄色的书。"jaune。"她说,"Le livre est jaune,这本书是黄色的。"

她指了指丁丁:"你能说 jaune 吗?"

丁丁脸红了,最后说成了 Joan。

"不对,Joan 是我的名字。"指导老师说。

丁丁又试着读了一下:"zhone。"

萨米尔哈哈大笑起来。"这已经很好了。"他说,"我花了一个月的时间学说 jaune。"

"现在我们要学点数字了。"琼说。

半个小时后,她合上了那本黄色的书。"今天晚上就学这些,"她说,"我们明天继续。"

她检查了萨米尔房间的窗户的锁,卫生间的锁,通向客厅的门的锁,然后转身微笑着说:"晚安,萨米尔。"

"晚安,老师。"萨米尔回应。

琼离开后,丁丁站起来打了个哈欠:"晚安,萨米尔。我会叫你吃早餐的。"

丁丁走到卫生间刷牙。他对着镜子里的自己笑了笑。他下定决心,明天要学会用法语说"我的牙刷是紫色的"这句话。

第五章

第二天早上,丁丁洗漱后去敲萨米尔卧室的门。

"快点起床啦!"丁丁说,"我们早餐吃煎饼和香肠!"

房间里没人回应他。丁丁打开门,探头往里看,萨米尔的床上一片凌乱,但他不在房间里。

"萨米尔?"丁丁叫了一声,同时扫视着空荡荡的房间。"他去哪儿了?"丁丁下楼的时候心里想。

"妈妈,萨米尔不在房间里。"丁丁说。

丁丁的妈妈舀了一勺做煎饼的面糊,正要放

被绑架的国王

进煎锅,她停下来问:"他不在房间?他去哪儿了?"

"我不知道,妈妈。"丁丁猛地推开后门,向院子里四处张望了一下。"也不在这里。"他说。

丁丁关门的时候,他的手碰到了某样尖锐的东西。

"妈妈,快来看这个!"他大叫起来。

门锁周围的木头被撬碎了,参差不齐的木头碴子露了出来,丁丁脚边的地上还有一些木头碎片。

"啊,我的天!"他的妈妈说,"有人撬门进来了。"

她连忙转身,顺着大厅的楼梯跑上楼去。丁丁跟在妈妈身后也去了客房。

"萨米尔?"丁丁的妈妈大声呼唤,"萨米尔,请回应我!如果你藏起来了,就出来吧。"

但是萨米尔没有回应。

"我去给法伦警官打电话。"丁丁的妈妈说,"还要给琼·克林克尔打电话!你为什么不去邻居家看看,看看露丝家里的人有什么发现?"

丁丁冲下楼梯,跑到屋外。他飞快地跑到露丝家的院子,用拳头重重地敲她家的门。

39

露丝打开门。她正津津有味地嚼着一片烤面包。

"你看到萨米尔了吗?"丁丁气喘吁吁地问。

她摇了摇头:"怎么啦?他不见了吗?"

"是的。"丁丁说,"有人弄坏了我家的门进来了……萨米尔不见了。"

"什么?"露丝大叫道,"你的意思是,萨米尔被绑架了吗?"

突然,丁丁听到了警笛声。他告别了手里还

拿着烤面包的露丝,跑回了自己家的前院。

一辆鸣着警笛的警车从拐角处开过来,直接停在了丁丁家门前的车道上。警笛声一停,法伦警官和基恩警官就从车上走了下来。

丁丁的妈妈飞一般地跑出房子,脸色苍白。"谢天谢地,你们来了。"她对警官们说,"我想住在我家的房客被绑架了!"

就在这时,一辆黄色的出租车停在了丁丁家的前面。车后门一下子打开了,琼·克林克尔下了车。

"萨米尔怎么啦?"她叫喊着,飞快地跑过前院。

"我们不清楚。"丁丁的妈妈说,"他不在房子里,而且我家后门被人撬开过。"

琼·克林克尔用手捂住嘴巴,身体摇晃了一下。她站立不稳,差点摔倒在地,基恩警官扶住了她。

"把她扶到家里来。"丁丁的妈妈说着,跑向前门。

"到周围找找。"法伦警官对基恩警官说。然后,他帮丁丁的妈妈把琼·克林克尔扶进了屋。

露丝拨开隔开两家院子的树篱,来到了丁丁家的院子。她身上穿着蓝色背带裤、蓝色衬衫,脚上穿的是一双蓝色的高帮运动鞋。

"萨米尔真的不见了吗?"她问丁丁,"这不是在开玩笑吧?"

丁丁摇了摇头。他口干舌燥,连唾沫都咽不下去。"我想这是真的。"他说着,心里想起萨米尔对他们讲述过的他父亲的敌人的事。

"但是怎么会有人能进入房子把他带走呢?"露丝问。

"我们家后门的锁被撬坏了。"丁丁说,"他们一定是从那里进来的。"

丁丁解释的时候,露丝的爸爸妈妈也来到了丁丁家。

"我们都去街上找找。"露丝的爸爸提议。然后他就去组织邻居们帮忙了。

这时,乔希和他的狗来了。"发生什么事了,丁丁?"他问,"为什么这里有警车?"

"萨米尔不见了。"丁丁说,"我们认为他被人绑架了!"

被绑架的国王

乔希的嘴巴不知不觉张大了,然后他笑着说:"这是在开玩笑吧?"

丁丁摇了摇头:"快进来,我让你们看看被绑匪撬开的厨房门。"

丁丁把他们带到前门台阶处,正要开门,门打开了,丁丁的妈妈和琼·克林克尔从里面走了出来。

"你确定没事了吗，琼？"丁丁的妈妈问，"你不再多待一会儿吗？"

琼·克林克尔摇了摇头。"我需要打一些电话。"她小声地说，然后很快上了出租车，走了。

"可怜的女士。"丁丁的妈妈说着，走回厨房。

丁丁走上门廊台阶的时候，看到了一个闪闪发亮的东西。

他弯下腰，捡起一小片黄色的玻璃。

"那是什么？"露丝问。

丁丁盯着那个黄色的玻璃片。他记得在哪里看到过类似的东西。

"这是从萨米尔的万花筒里掉出来的！"他说。

第六章

在丁丁家里,法伦警官仔细端详那个玻璃片。"如果这是从那个男孩的万花筒里掉出来的,玻璃片怎么会到了你们家前门的台阶上?"他问。

"是万花筒的一端被拧开了。"丁丁解释,"萨米尔喜欢把玻璃片倒出来。"

乔希和露丝静静地站在丁丁家的厨房里,帕尔躺在乔希的脚边打盹。丁丁、丁丁的妈妈和法伦警官坐在桌旁。基恩警官早就离开房子去组织人员找人了。

法伦警官叹了口气,把玻璃片放到桌子上,

然后站了起来。

"绿地镇地方不大,"他说,"我们会找到那个男孩的。我保证每条可能通往镇子以外的路都会被检查。请别担心,好吗?"

丁丁的妈妈抓起车钥匙。"我想开车到处转转,去找萨米尔。"她说。

"我们也一起去,可以吗?"丁丁问。

妈妈摇了摇头,说:"你们就守在家帮忙吧。"她看着法伦警官问:"你觉得绑匪会打电话到这里来吗?"

法伦警官点了点头:"他们可能会联系你们。但是绑匪通常会等上几天再打电话。他们喜欢让人质的家庭成员担惊受怕,这样,他们就能索要更多的赎金了。"

丁丁看着妈妈和法伦警官离开,听到前门锁上的声音。

"你们看这个。"丁丁说着,带着乔希和露丝去看损坏了的后门。

"天啊,这真够吓人的!"乔希说。

"可怜的萨米尔。"露丝说,"他一定吓坏了!"

"我们去看看他的房间,"丁丁说,"也许我们能找到更多线索。"

孩子们匆匆跑上楼梯。帕尔跟着他们来到了萨米尔的房间,它的长耳朵扫着地板。

萨米尔的床单和毯子缠在一起,十分凌乱,还有半截垂在床边。丁丁走向书桌,书桌上放着装万花筒的盒子和两小堆彩色玻璃片,两堆玻璃片的颜色不同。

"这就是那个万花筒。"丁丁一边说,一边把万花筒从盒子里拿了出来,"看,他把所有的玻璃片都倒出来了。"

乔希摸了摸镶嵌在万花筒筒壁上的宝石。"这些是真的宝石吗?"他问。

"萨米尔说是真的。"丁丁回答。

露丝仔细观察那堆玻璃片。"怎么没有黄色的玻璃片呢?"她问。

"你这么问是什么意思?"丁丁问。

"我们找到的玻璃片是黄色的,"她说,"但是这里都是红色的玻璃片和蓝色的玻璃片,没有黄色的。"

"真奇怪。"丁丁说,"我们在周围再找找。"

孩子们开始在萨米尔的房间里找黄色的玻璃片,帕尔摇摇摆摆地在房间里走来走去,边走边用鼻子嗅嗅这儿,闻闻那儿。

丁丁在卫生间里找,乔希在衣橱里翻衣服,露丝则扑在地上往床底下找。

"唉,即使这个房间里有黄色的玻璃片,我也找不到。"乔希说着,从衣橱边走开了。

"别动!"露丝大声叫道。乔希在原地站着

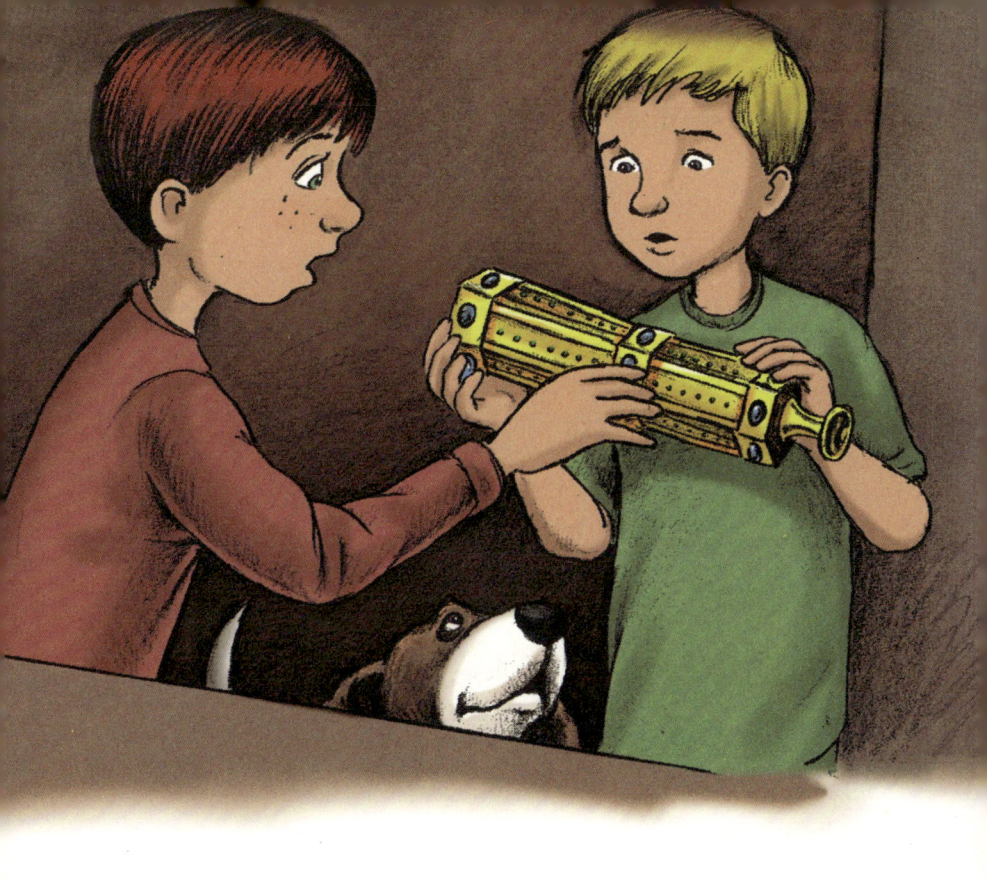

不动了。

她一把从乔希刚要踩到的地毯上抓起一个东西，原来是另一个黄色的玻璃片。

就在这时，电话响了。

丁丁跑下楼，在电话响第三声的时候抓起电话听筒。

"你好！"

丁丁听了一会儿电话，然后朝楼上喊："嘿！伙伴们，是法伦警官打过来的电话，他想知道，萨米尔的睡衣和拖鞋在房间里吗？你们能看一下吗？"

他等待了一会儿，露丝跑到楼梯口说："房间里没有睡衣和拖鞋。"

丁丁对着电话说："我们没有找到睡衣和拖鞋。"

过了一会儿，丁丁挂断电话，爬上楼梯，来到了萨米尔的房间。

"他的拖鞋怎么啦？"乔希问。

"罗恩·平科夫斯基在他的鱼饵店附近的河边发现了一条金黄色的流苏。"丁丁说，"萨米尔的拖鞋上有金黄色的流苏。"

"但是——"

"还有，平科夫斯基先生家的一条小船也不见了。"丁丁打断乔希。

丁丁盯着他的两个朋友说："法伦警官认为，绑匪用一条小船把萨米尔带走了。"

第七章

"什么样的小船?"乔希问,"印第安河里的水不是很深。"

"但是在里面摇桨划艇是可以的。"露丝说。

丁丁想着罗恩鱼饵店旁边的那条河。他们以前都蹚过那条河,水只不过到他们的膝盖。

"是的。"丁丁说,"也许他们就是用小船带着萨米尔顺流而下。等到达水深的地方,他们可能会换更大的船……"

"……然后把他带到大海上!"露丝补充道。

孩子们你看看我,我看看你。丁丁想着可怜

的萨米尔,他非常害怕嘈杂声和动物,如今还被绑架在某条小船里。

"我们一定要做些什么,伙伴们。"丁丁说,"我们去鱼饵店看看,看能不能找到更多线索。"他跑下楼梯,来到厨房里。

露丝匆匆跟在他后面,乔希和帕尔跟在露丝后面。

"你妈妈让我们留在家里不走的。"乔希提醒丁丁。

"我知道,乔希。"丁丁边说边在便笺簿上写下潦草的文字,"我正在给我妈妈留言,告诉她我们要去哪儿,也许她看到便笺前我们就回来了。我们快点行动吧!"

孩子们穿过餐厅,直接走向后门。

突然,帕尔狂吠起来,开始用力拽狗绳。它一直拽,直到乔希放开了狗绳。帕尔跑向了客厅,孩子们跟在它后面。

"我想它嗅到了什么东西。"乔希说。帕尔的鼻子贴在地毯上,嗅着一个发亮的小东西。

"又一个玻璃片!"乔希说。他从帕尔的鼻

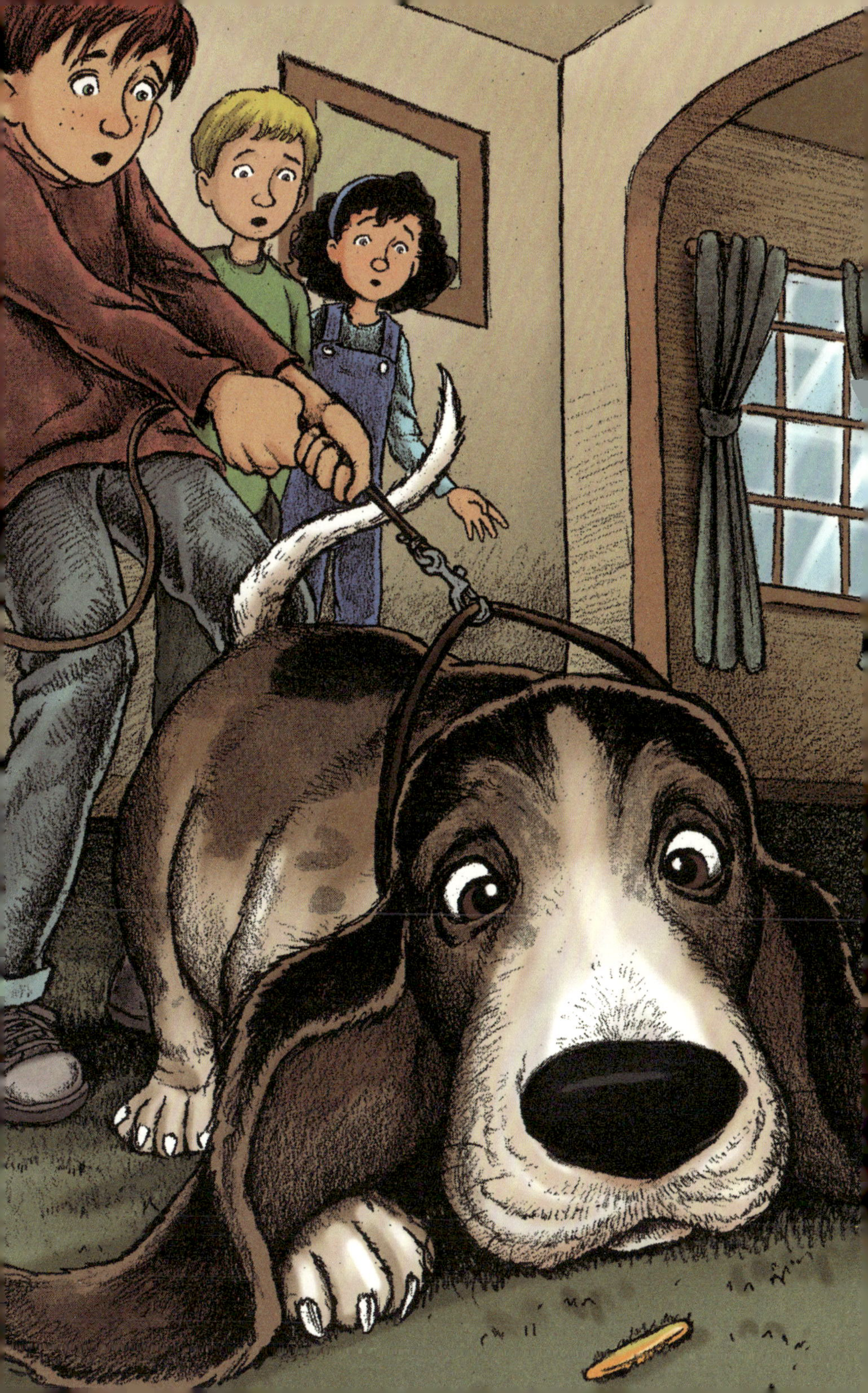

子底下迅速捡起了玻璃片。

"这是第三个玻璃片。"丁丁说着,看向通向卧室的楼梯,"萨米尔在自己的卧室丢了一个玻璃片,在这儿丢了一个,另外一个被丢在前门的台阶上……"

"萨米尔给我们留下了线索。"露丝突然大喊道。

"我想你是对的。"丁丁说,"绑匪一定是把他拖下了楼梯,然后从前门出去的。来吧,我们一起去找更多线索。"

孩子们走出前门,来到了前院。帕尔一路用鼻子嗅着,而孩子们则用眼睛搜寻着。

"没有线索了。"过了一会儿,丁丁小声说,"线索在这儿断了。"

突然,帕尔猛地拽了一下狗绳。

"哇!狗狗乖。"乔希说。

但是帕尔还是继续拽绳子,拖着乔希来到路边。帕尔把鼻子伸到了路边的排水沟里。

"瞧!"乔希嚷道。他捡起了第四个黄色的玻璃片。

丁丁和露丝跑过去。"萨米尔一定是在绑匪把他拖上车时丢下了玻璃片。"露丝说。

"我敢肯定,在河边也能发现线索。"丁丁说,"我们走!"

孩子们沿着林荫街飞快地跑,帕尔迈着大步跟在后面。他们经过小学,穿过鸭子步行道,朝河边走去。

在鱼饵店里,罗恩·平科夫斯基正在往一个大水箱里扔银色小鱼鱼饵。

"嘿!我听说一个男孩失踪了。"罗恩看到孩子们走进来,说道。

"不是失踪。"乔希说,"他被绑架了!"

罗恩点了点头:"法伦警官是那样说的。他们还偷了我一条划艇呢!"

"你能带我们看看那条划艇原来在什么地方吗?"丁丁问。

"当然,跟我来。"罗恩把孩子们带到了室外。"就在那儿。"他说着,用手指向河岸边一排底朝上的划艇,其中的两条划艇之间有一个空位。

"他们撬开了挂锁,还拿走了一对全新的桨。"

"谢谢你,平先生。"丁丁说。

孩子们匆匆跑到那一排船边找黄色玻璃片。帕尔在地上嗅了嗅,然后"扑通"一声趴在树下,闭上了眼睛。

孩子们仔细查看了划艇原来在的地方,完全没找到玻璃片。"我们到车道上去找一下。"丁丁说。

他们走回路上,然后沿原路回到船边。

乔希发现了一枚镍币,但没有找到黄色的万花筒玻璃片。

"太奇怪了。"丁丁说,"既然萨米尔在我家留下了线索,为什么他到了这儿就没有留下玻璃

片了呢？"

"也许他没有玻璃片了。"乔希说。

露丝摇了摇头，说："怎么会呢。他拿走了所有黄色的玻璃片，还记得吗？"

"我跟你们说，"丁丁说，"有关黄色玻璃片的事情让我感到困惑，萨米尔为什么留下黄色的玻璃片作为线索，而不是红色的或蓝色的呢？"

"这个嘛，他把玻璃片分成了不同颜色的小堆，"乔希说，"所以，也许他只是抓了离他最近的那堆黄色的玻璃片。"

罗恩·平科夫斯基朝他们走了过来。"孩子们，在找什么？"他问。

丁丁解释了黄色玻璃片的事情。"你在这里没有发现黄色的玻璃片吗？"

"没有。我只发现了那条流苏，已经把它交给法伦警官了。"

"你昨天晚上听到了汽车的声音吗？"露丝问。

罗恩笑着说："你是说类似我睡觉打鼾的声音吗？我晚上睡觉的时候，即使一辆坦克开过来，我也会因为酣然入睡而听不见的。"

"我们回去看看我妈妈回家了没有。"丁丁说，"她也许会有些发现。谢谢你，平先生。"

孩子们带着帕尔很快回到了丁丁家。丁丁的妈妈正在打电话，看上去一副忧心忡忡的样子。她边打电话边示意孩子们坐下。

孩子们坐了下来，帕尔卧在他们脚边。片刻后，丁丁的妈妈挂断了电话。

"是法伦警官打来的电话。"她说，"警察正在到处搜寻，他们搜查了火车站、飞机场，还有河上的每条船，但是到目前为止，没有找到任何

蛛丝马迹。"

丁丁的妈妈看着孩子们,眼神中充满焦虑。

"怎么一个男孩就这样不留痕迹地消失了呢?"她问。

第八章

"萨米尔留了线索，妈妈。"丁丁说。

"他留了什么线索？"

丁丁给妈妈解释了黄色玻璃片的事情。

"哦，我的天！"丁丁的妈妈急忙抓起电话拨号，然后把听筒递给了丁丁。"告诉法伦警官这件事。"她说。

法伦警官听着丁丁讲述。"可是，我们到罗恩的鱼饵店就找不到玻璃片了。"丁丁对着电话说。

丁丁点了点头，说："嗯，好。"然后，他挂断了电话。

"法伦警官想看看我们找到的所有玻璃片。"丁丁说着,从口袋里掏出了那四个玻璃片。

丁丁的妈妈拿起电话。"我觉得我应该去看看琼·克林克尔。"她说,"她一个人在酒店,一定急坏了。"

丁丁的妈妈拨打了另一个电话号码。"喂,是琼吗?我是丁丁的妈妈,邓肯太太。"她对着电话说,"你需要人陪陪吗?我可以过去吗?"

丁丁不能听到琼说了什么,但是他看见妈妈脸上露出了笑容。"好的,好的,我五分钟后就到。"说完,她挂断了电话。

丁丁的妈妈照了一下镜子,然后就往门口走去。"我们要去埃莉餐馆见面,喝咖啡。"她说,"哦,把那些玻璃片给我吧,和琼见面后我就把它们送到警察局去。"

丁丁把黄色玻璃片放到妈妈的手中。丁丁的妈妈冲着孩子们无力地笑了一下,然后很快走出后门,离开了。

丁丁盯着后门,在想着什么。

"别发呆了,丁丁。"乔希说着,在丁丁面前打了个响指。

丁丁摇了摇头,说:"妈妈说的话让我想起了别的什么,可是我现在忘了!"

"你忘了你妈妈说的话,还是忘了你妈妈说的话让你想起的什么?"露丝问。

"都忘记了。"丁丁说完看向乔希:"我正要想起来的时候,你却在我面前打起了响指。"

"对不起。"乔希说,"我们为什么不一起吃点东西呢?也许吃点冰激凌你就能想起来了。"

露丝哈哈大笑说:"丁丁,找点东西给他吃,你知道他肚子饿的时候是什么样子。"

丁丁叹了一口气。"我们昨天晚上把冰激凌吃完了。"他走向厨房的时候说。打开冰箱后,丁丁说:"但是,冰箱里还有冰奶油和樱桃果冻。"

他端出一碗递给乔希:"给你,你要……"

这时,丁丁没有往下说,他的眼睛盯着碗里的樱桃果冻。"我想起来了!"他大叫道,"是黄色的。"

乔希摇了摇头,说:"丁丁,这是红色的果冻,

被绑架的国王

不是黄色的。"

"不,我的意思是……是的,我知道是红色

的。但是看到果冻,我就想起了黄色[1]!"丁丁说。

"你说话的时候,我能吃果冻吗?"乔希问。

丁丁拿来了碗和勺子,把它们放到餐桌上。然后,他继续说:"你们昨天离开后,萨米尔的指导老师来了,她还给我和萨米尔上了一节法语课。"

乔希笑着说:"说两句法语听听。"

"吃你的,乔希,听我把话说完。"

"对不起。"乔希一边说,一边用勺子舀了一团奶油到果冻上,然后让帕尔舔他的勺子。

"还记得几分钟前,我妈妈说她要去见萨米尔的指导老师吗?"丁丁问,"我妈妈称呼她'琼',对吧?"

乔希和露丝都点了点头。

"这让我想起了昨天上的法语课。琼教我说法语单词'黄色','黄色'的法语是 jaune,但是我发音时却念成了她的名字 Joan。"

"嗯,丁丁,"乔希说,"这和其他事情有关系吗?"

---

1. 果冻英文为 jello,黄色英文为 yellow,发音相似。——编者

"难道你们不明白吗?"丁丁说,"我的意思是'黄色'的法语听起来很像Joan,那是萨米尔指导老师的名字。萨米尔本可以留下红色或蓝色的玻璃片,但是他选择留下黄色的玻璃片,我觉得萨米尔就是想告诉我们——是琼干的!"

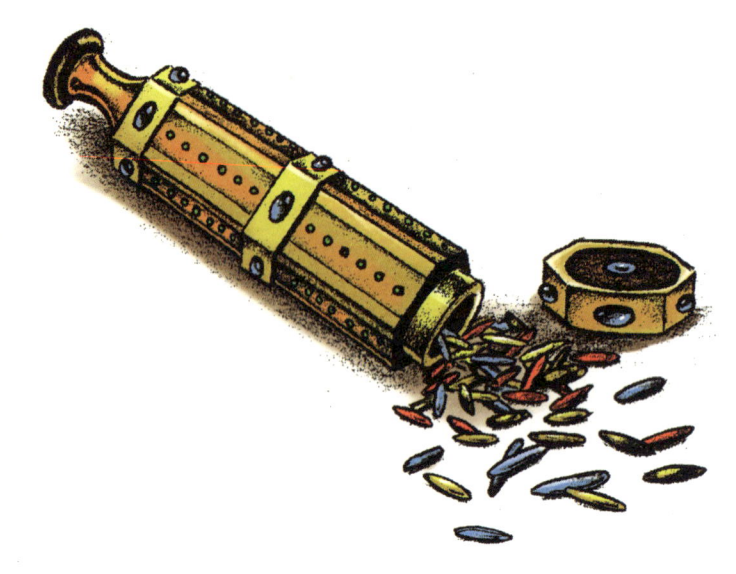

第九章

"也许萨米尔认为琼知道谁是绑匪。"露丝说。

"也许吧。"丁丁说,"或者,琼就是绑匪。"

乔希和露丝正吃着果冻,听到这句话,他们都抬起了头看着丁丁。

乔希的鼻子上沾了奶油。"他的指导老师?"他问。

"想想看,"丁丁接着说,"萨米尔是半夜醒过来的。有人进入了他的房间,他认出了琼,于是他抓起了一堆玻璃片。他选择的是黄色的玻璃片,那是因为他记得琼的名字听起来就像法语中

被绑架的国王

的'黄色',萨米尔知道我清楚这一点。"

"可是,她怎么会是绑匪呢?"露丝问,"她是萨米尔的朋友,她到这里来是为了帮助萨米尔。"

"没错。你也看到了,今天早上听到这件事后,琼有多伤心。"乔希说,"那不可能是装出来的。我还是认为,萨米尔只不过是在黑暗中,用手抓了离他最近的那堆玻璃片。"

露丝站了起来。"有一个办法可以看出琼是不是绑匪。"她说,"我们去酒店找她谈谈。"

"好。"丁丁说,"但是,琼现在不在酒店,我妈妈说琼要去埃莉餐馆和她见面。"

"很好!"乔希说着,吞下了碗里的最后一口果冻,"交谈的时候,我还可以买一个冰激凌吃。"

孩子们带着帕尔很快就来到了主街上的埃莉餐馆。丁丁透过窗户往里看,但是没有看到琼·克林克尔和他的妈妈。

"我想知道她们去了哪里。妈妈的车也没有停在这里。"丁丁说着往主街四周看。

"我们问问埃莉吧。"露丝说。

乔希推开门,孩子们走进了餐馆。餐馆里面

67

只有两个少年正在吃炒蛋,卡座和柜台边的座位都没有其他客人。

"嘿,孩子们!"埃莉说,"嘿,狗狗!"她弯下腰拍了拍帕尔,然后用手捋了捋狗狗的耳朵。"要三份甜筒冰激凌吗?"她问。

丁丁摇了摇头,说:"不了,谢谢。我在找我妈妈。"他说,"你见过她吗?不久前,她应该在这儿见过一个人。"

埃莉摇了摇头,说:"没有,我好多天没有看到你妈妈了。"

"也许她们在酒店里。"露丝说。

丁丁点了点头。"我觉得我们要去酒店看看。"他说。

他们谢过埃莉,然后朝香格里拉酒店走去——沿着主街走两个街区就到了。

"我们为什么不能买了甜筒冰激凌再走呢?"乔希问。他夸张地把一只手放在额头上,说:"我感觉我要晕过去了。"

"以后买。"丁丁说,"我们找到萨米尔后再买。"他说。"或者等我们找到我妈妈后买。"他心

里想。

三分钟后,他们走进了酒店。林克莱特先生正坐在酒店大堂的一把椅子上,吃着甜甜圈,小口抿着咖啡。

"嘿,你们好!"看到三个孩子朝他走来的时候,他招呼道。他看了一眼帕尔,说:"乔希,我想你的狗……嗯……已经受过大小便训练,不会在室内大小便,对吗?"

看到帕尔"扑通"一声卧在林克莱特先生脚边的时候,乔希笑着说:"对,它受过训练,也不会在酒店里大小便。"

林克莱特先生拧起眉毛,说:"好吧,那么今天需要我帮什么忙呢?"

"我在找我妈妈。"丁丁说,"她本来应该在埃莉餐馆和琼见面的,但是她们不在那儿,你见到她们了吗?"

林克莱特先生放下手里的咖啡杯,说:"我没有看见你妈妈,但是不久前,我看到克林克尔女士离开了酒店。"

"她告诉你她去哪儿了吗?"

林克莱特先生摇了摇头:"她一句话也没说。"

丁丁扫视了一下酒店大堂。他的妈妈去了哪里呢?要是计划有变,她一定会让他知道的,她一贯如此。

"她没有留下字条什么的吗?"

"不好意思,唐纳德,"林克莱特先生说,"也许她已经回家了,你要打个电话给她吗?"

丁丁突然觉得很难受,他强忍着泪水。一定是出了什么问题。首先是萨米尔失踪,现在自己的妈妈也不见了。她可是拿着黄色玻璃片去见琼·克林克尔的!

林克莱特先生用餐巾纸擦了擦手指,站了起来。"来吧,你可以用我的电话。"他说。他把丁丁带到柜台前,帕尔跟着林克莱特先生,不停地嗅他的脚后跟。

丁丁拨打了电话,等着听电话另一头传来妈妈的声音,但是没有人接听电话。

丁丁放下电话听筒,抬头看着林克莱特先生。"她会去哪儿呢?"丁丁问。

第十章

就在这个时候,帕尔开始狂吠,撕咬着林克莱特先生左脚的鞋子。

"怎么回事?"林克莱特先生一边说,一边试着抽走左脚。

但是帕尔不罢休,它试图用爪子和牙齿把林克莱特先生脚上锃亮的黑色皮鞋脱下来。

"乔希!"林克莱特先生说,"管管你的狗,让它懂点礼貌。"

"快脱掉鞋!"露丝突然说。

林克莱特先生低头看着露丝,问:"你说什么?"

A to Z 神秘案件

"我想我知道帕尔想要做什么,"露丝说,"请你脱掉鞋。"

林克莱特先生长叹了一口气。"好吧,如果那样做狗就不会狂吠的话,我就脱鞋。"

这个高个子男人弯下身子,脱掉左脚的鞋子。他把鞋子拿给帕尔看。"好了,满意了吧?"他问。

被绑架的国王

帕尔立即用嘴咬着鞋子,把它丢在乔希的脚边。

"我猜对了!"露丝大叫。她拿起鞋子,将它翻了过来。

粘了一团口香糖的鞋底下有一个闪闪发光的黄色玻璃片。

"这只狗在找一团恶心的口香糖吗?"林克莱特先生问。

"不。"丁丁说,"那个玻璃片是萨米尔万花筒里的东西!这意味着,绑匪把萨米尔带进了酒店。"

"唐纳德,你真让我伤脑筋。"林克莱特先生说着,拿回了他的鞋。他抠掉鞋底的口香糖,然后重新穿上了鞋。"萨米尔是谁?什么绑匪?"

丁丁把萨米尔从床上失踪的事情告诉了林克莱特先生,然后,他又讲了琼·克林克尔上的法语课,萨米尔的万花筒,还有黄色玻璃片的事情。

"现在我妈妈也不见了。"丁丁说,"我想,是琼·克林克尔绑架了他们两个人,她可能把他们绑在了她的酒店房间里。"

"啊,丁丁你说什么呢?"乔希说,"法伦警官说萨米尔是被一条船带走的,他怎么能既在酒店里又在船上呢？"

"这我就不知道了。"丁丁说，"但是我还是想看看琼·克林克尔的房间，你鞋底的那个玻璃片证明萨米尔来过这里！"

林克莱特先生叹了一口气，放下他吃了一半的甜甜圈。"好吧，"他说，"琼·克林克尔的房间号是301，我会带你们上去，但是你们一定要保持安静。我们的客人不喜欢一群小孩在走廊里跑。"他低头看了看帕尔，"而且这只狗一定要留在这里，香格里拉酒店不允许宠物到楼上去。"

"但是它嗅觉灵敏，"乔希说，"我们需要它的帮助。"

林克莱特先生看着帕尔褐色的大眼睛，说："哦，好吧！再破一次例吧。"

孩子们和帕尔跟在林克莱特先生后面进了电梯。

电梯停在三楼，他们都走出电梯，快速走向301房间。一个穿白色制服的男人正推着满满一车织物，沿着走廊朝拐角走去。

林克莱特先生打开门锁，推开了门。

琼·克林克尔的床铺得很整齐，地板上放着

被绑架的国王

两只手提箱。

"快去嗅嗅。"乔希对着帕尔的耳朵小声说。

帕尔转了一个大圈,在地毯上嗅了嗅。突然,它径直向衣橱跑去,并开始用爪子挠衣橱的门。

乔希打开衣橱门,帕尔跑了进去。

丁丁看到衣橱是空的,琼·克林克尔已经打包了所有东西。

"伙计,那里面有什么?"乔希趴下身子问帕尔。

帕尔和乔希搜查衣橱底板的时候,丁丁和露丝在查看床底和卫生间。

突然,乔希从衣橱里退了出来。"看看帕尔找到了什么!"他手里拿着一个小小的黄色玻璃片,大叫道。

"你说得对,丁丁。"露丝说,"萨米尔肯定来过这个房间。"

就在这个时候,帕尔一边用鼻子在地上嗅,一边快速跑出了房间。接着,他们就听到了帕尔的叫声,它的叫声疯狂又响亮。

大家都跟在它后面,刚好看到帕尔扑向那辆装满白色织物的推车。它咬着推车的一侧,想要把推车往回拉。

穿着白色制服的男人把车推向相反的方向。

"滚开,笨狗!"那个男人大叫着,用脚去踢帕尔。

但那不是个好主意,帕尔用牙齿咬住那个男人的裤角,开始撕咬、扭动和狂吠。

"帕尔,不可以!"乔希大叫道。他把帕尔拉开,但是这只猎狗仍然对着那个男人狂吠。

林克莱特先生看着那个男人问:"你是谁?"

"我是收换洗织物的。"那个男人说着,瞪向帕尔。

林克莱特先生指向男人衬衫上绣的字。"可是我们酒店没有用过王牌洗衣服务。"他说。

突然,那个男人朝电梯飞奔过去,但是他被帕尔的狗绳绊住,脸朝下摔倒了。

林克莱特先生敏捷地跑过去,坐在了那个男人的背上。"你在这里干什么?"他质问道。

"我不会说的。"那个男人的脸贴在地毯上,咕哝着。

"帮帮我,伙伴们。"丁丁抓着推车的一侧说

道。孩子们猛地一拉,推车翻了。

一大堆床单和毛巾掉在了地板上。

萨米尔躺在推车底部,他被捆绑得紧紧的,嘴巴也被塞得严严实实。

第十一章

  三个孩子把萨米尔从推车里弄出来,轻轻地放到地上。丁丁和乔希解开捆绑他的绳子,露丝拿走塞在他嘴巴里的东西。

  萨米尔还没来得及说话,帕尔就摇摇摆摆地走过去,用湿湿的舌头舔他的脸。

  萨米尔给了帕尔一个大大的拥抱,然后,他就打起了喷嚏。

  电梯门突然打开了,他们全都吓了一跳。

琼·克林克尔从电梯里走了出来。她看到萨米尔和地上的男人时,脸变得像床单一样惨白。

"你……你们找到萨米尔了!"琼说着,跑到了萨米尔的身边。

"别装了!"地上的男人说,"好了,我不能一个人背黑锅。她谋划了这一切,我们一起干的。"

"你在胡说什么?"琼说。"我……我从未见过这个男人。"

那个男人冷笑了一声,说:"你这样说你的丈夫真是太坏了。"

正在这时,电梯门又一次打开了,丁丁的妈

妈和法伦警官走到了走廊里。

"好啦，好啦。"法伦警官说，"还好我带来了两副手铐。"

一个小时过后，琼·克林克尔和她的丈夫尼克都被送进了监狱。

林克莱特先生要回去继续吃他剩下的甜甜圈。

丁丁、乔希、帕尔、露丝、萨米尔和丁丁的妈妈，跟着法伦警官一起到了警察局。

"你很聪明，留下黄色的玻璃片作为线索。"法伦警官对萨米尔说。

"谢谢。"萨米尔说，"我当时希望丁丁记得'黄色'的法语读起来像'琼'。"

"我当然记得。"丁丁说，"但是大部分玻璃片是乔希的狗发现的。"

乔希脸上泛红，轻轻地拍了拍帕尔的脑袋，说："乖狗狗。"

"哎呀，克林克尔女士和她的丈夫真是夫唱妇随。"法伦警官说，"他们精心谋划了这一切，把萨米尔藏在了楼上的衣橱里后，又把萨米尔拖

鞋上的一条流苏扔到了河边,好让线索中断。"

"我听到了他们在车里的谈话。"萨米尔说,"他们要把我带回哥斯达拉。我本来会像我父母那样失踪的,那样的话,我父亲的敌人就会夺走我们的国家。"

丁丁看着妈妈。"你怎么知道我们去了酒店?"他问。

"哦,我在埃莉餐馆外面碰到了琼。"丁丁的妈妈说,"她说她很高兴从酒店里走出来,提议我们一起走走。很自然,我们谈到了绑架的事情,她提到在河边的拖鞋流苏被发现了。"

"她本来不应该知道这件事,对吗?"露丝说。

丁丁的妈妈笑了:"对的,当我提到黄色玻璃片的线索时,她就突然急匆匆地走开了。她说她在酒店里有重要的事情要处理。所以,我就来到这里找法伦警官。"

法伦警官朝三个孩子微笑着说:"但是我们到达酒店的时候,你们三个就已经控制住整个局面啦!"

就在这个时候,法伦警官的电脑发出一条语

音提示:"你有新邮件。"

"哈哈,我一直在等这封邮件呢!"他说。

他移动电脑鼠标,点击了两下,然后微笑着说:"你们都应该听听这个,我大声读啦。"

"哥斯达拉的国王和王后已经被找到了,多谢你的提示!他们安然无恙。请转告王子,他的父母爱他,希望他立刻回家。"

办公室里的每个人都开始鼓掌欢呼。萨米尔一时呆住了,然后他绽开了笑容。

"你们是怎么找到他们的?"萨米尔问法伦警官。

"绑架你的绑匪说漏了嘴,"法伦警官说,"绑架你父母的绑匪雇了他们。他们告诉了我对方的姓名和地址,于是,我就给哥斯达拉的警方发了一封电子邮件。"

第二天,丁丁、乔希、帕尔和露丝向萨米尔道别,每个孩子都送了他一个包装精美的礼物。帕尔给萨米尔的礼物就是用它那又湿又大的舌头在他的脸颊上舔了舔。

萨米尔笑了,然后开始打喷嚏。

三周后,丁丁家收到了一个大包裹。包裹是

被绑架的国王

从哥斯达拉邮寄过来的,是给三个孩子的。

"酷酷的邮票归我啦!"乔希说。

丁丁打开包裹,看到里面有四个小包裹,上面分别写着丁丁、乔希、露丝和帕尔。

丁丁和乔希的包裹里都是金制的小万花筒,万花筒筒壁上用红宝石镶嵌着他们的名字。

"他给你寄了什么?"乔希问露丝。

"哦,我的天!"露丝激动得尖叫了一声。她手里拿着一件深蓝色的袍子,那袍子和萨米尔的一模一样。

亲爱的朋友们:

我想你们啦!我父亲说你们可以来这里玩,你们甚至可以带上帕尔。

你们的朋友
萨米尔·本·奥兹

"这里有一张照片和一张便条。"丁丁说着,大声读了起来。

照片上,萨米尔穿戴着孩子们送给他的礼物:露丝送的运动衫、乔希送的牛仔裤和丁丁送的棒球帽。

突然,帕尔叫了一声。"它想要我们帮它打开包裹。"乔希说。

乔希帮帕尔撕掉包裹的包装纸,包裹里装着一件紫色的天鹅绒小狗毛衣,毛衣上用金线绣着"乖狗狗"三个字。

A to Z Mysteries®

THE KIDNAPPED KING

by Ron Roy

illustrated by
John Steven Gurney

INDIAN RIVER
LAWRENCE TAXI
RIVER ROAD
HORSE TRAILS
HORSES FOR RENT
BIKE PATH
WOODS
WOODVIEW ROAD
INDIAN WAY ROAD
FIRE STATION
BILL'S BIKES
SUPER MARKET
BRIDGE LANE
ROBIN ROAD
CROW ST
FINCH LA
THRUSH CT
OWL RD
PHEASANT LA
BLUE JAY WAY
WREN DR
FITNESS CENTER
WOODS
BIKE PATH
BLUE BIRD WAY
HUMMINGBIRD LA
WOODCOCK CROSS
ELLIE'S DINER
ACORN APTS
FURRY FEET PET SHOP
OAK STREET
CENTER CHURCH
BIKE PATH
PEOPLE'S POND
POST OFFICE
COMMUNITY GARDEN AND FISH POND
GREEN LAWN $ SAVINGS BANK $
POLICE STATION
ELDERLY HOUSING
GOOSE ISLAND
RIVER ROAD
WEST GREEN ST
MAIN STREET
SENIOR COMMUNITY CENTER
GREEN LAWN LIBRARY
TOWN HALL
BIKE PATH
CHILDREN'S PETTING ZOO AND AQUARIUM
SHANGRI-LA HOTEL

WELCOME TO
GREEN LAWN
HOME OF THE
A to Z Mysteries
N
W
E
S
RIVER ROAD
BOAT LAUNCH
SQUAW ISLAND
GREEN LAWN MIDDLE SCHOOL
BOAT RENTAL
RON'S BAIT
DUCK WALK WAY
EAGLE LANE
FARM LANE
JOSH
MEADOW ROAD
GREEN LAWN ELEMENTARY SCHOOL
DINK
RUTH ROSE
TREE TOP CIRCLE
FOX LANE
QUAIL RUN ROAD
SILVER CIRCLE
WOODY STREET
PLEASANT STREET
THISTLE COURT
WILDFLOWER WAY
BAND SHELL
ROSE GARDEN
CENTER PARK
ROSE STREET
SWAN POND
GREEN LAWN HIGH SCHOOL
PLAYING FIELDS
GYM + POOL
BOXWOOD LANE
HOWARD'S BARBER-SHOP
BOOK NOOK
GAS STATION
CRYSTAL POND
MYSTIC GREENHOUSE
DOG KENNEL + VETERINARIAN
RIVER ROAD
EAST GREEN STREET
TOWN TENNIS COURTS
TOWN SWIMMING POOL
KIDDIE POOL
TOWN BASEBALL FIELD
TO THE BLUE HILLS

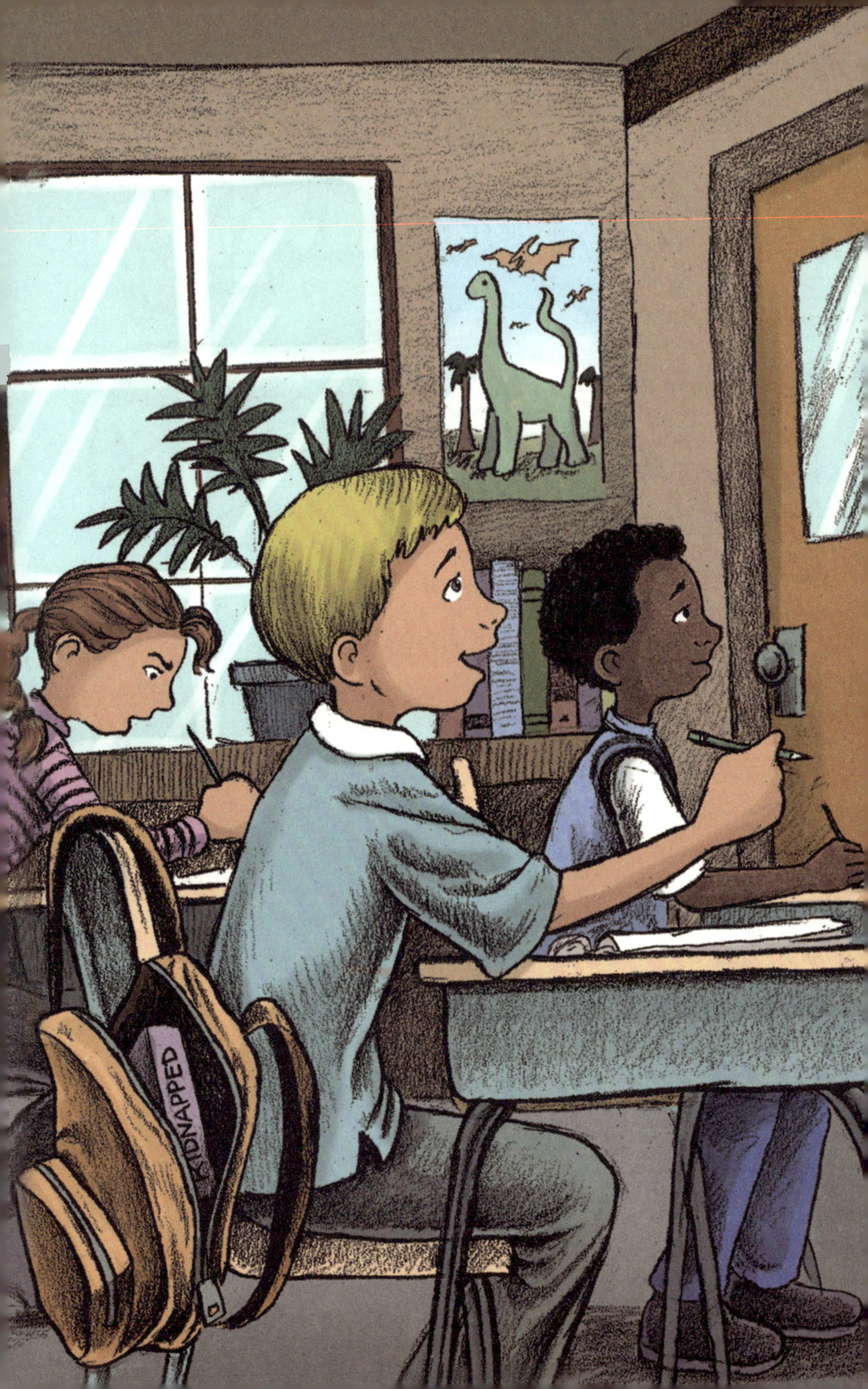
KIDNAPPED

CHAPTER 1

"Done!" Dink said to himself, smiling. He had solved the last problem on his math paper. He wrote Donald D. Duncan at the top, then glanced up at the classroom clock: two-fifteen. In just twenty minutes, spring vacation would begin!

"Class, please get ready for DEAR time," Mrs. Eagle said. "Take out your books and find a cozy place to read until the bell rings, please."

DEAR stood for Drop Everything and Read.

This was Dink's favorite time of the day.

Dink was reading Kidnapped by Robert Louis Stevenson. He had seen the movie, but he still loved the story. He took the book to the reading corner and flopped onto a beanbag chair.

Josh and Ruth Rose joined him, sprawling on the carpet with their books. The classroom grew quiet, except for the clock's ticking and the sound of pages being turned.

Suddenly, the room phone rang. Mrs. Eagle

answered it, then walked to the reading corner. "Dink," she said quietly, "you're wanted in Mr. Dillon's office."

Josh grinned at Dink and raised his eyebrows. "You're in trouble!" he said.

"Mr. Dillon wants me?" Dink asked. "Why?"

Mrs. Eagle shrugged. "Hurry back," she whispered.

Dink put down his book and left the room.

Walking down the quiet hall, Dink tried to figure out why the principal wanted to see him. He couldn't think of anything he'd done wrong!

Outside Mr. Dillon's office, Dink took a deep breath, then walked in. Mrs. Waters, the principal's secretary, was sitting at her desk outside his door. She smiled. "Hi, Donald. You can go right in. And don't look so scared!" she said. "Mr. Dillon doesn't eat children!"

Dink grinned, then opened the door to Mr. Dillon's office. The first person he saw was his mother!

She patted the empty chair next to hers, and Dink slid into it.

There were three other people in the room: Mr. Dillon, a woman with yellow hair, and a kid about Dink's age.

The kid was dressed like someone in a movie. He had on a long dark blue robe and sandals.

"Hi, Donald," Mr. Dillon said. Mr. Dillon was shaped like a football. His hair was cut short and his eyeglasses gleamed under the lights.

"Let me introduce my guests," he said. He nodded at the woman with yellow hair. "This is Ms. Joan Klinker. And this," he added, smiling at the boy, "is

Sammi Bin Oz."

Dink mumbled, "Hi," then stared at the boy.

He was about Dink's size and had black hair and dark skin. His eyes were the color of honey.

"Sammi is from Costra," Mr. Dillon said, "a small island country in the Indian Ocean. He's come to the United States to learn English."

"I already speak English," the boy said.

He had a soft voice and an accent. Dink thought he looked and sounded kind of sad.

"Actually, Sammi will live here for a year," Joan Klinker said. "I am his tutor. His parents want him to learn American customs."

Mr. Dillon looked at Dink. "Sammi will be in third grade with you. We thought you might want to show him around the school," he said.

Everyone looked at Dink. He felt himself blushing. His mother gave his hand a squeeze. "And Sammi will be staying with us for a few weeks, Dink," she explained.

"Your name is Dink?" Sammi asked.

Dink nodded at the boy.

"Dink," Sammi repeated. "That rhymes with think and pink and…stink!"

"Making rhymes helps Sammi remember new words," his tutor explained.

"Sammi can have the spare room," Dink's mother said. "With Daddy away on business, it'll be nice to have a guest in the house. I hope Sammi will be friends with you and Josh and Ruth Rose."

Sammi giggled. "Rose rhymes with toes and nose!"

Dink grinned. Wait'll Josh and Ruth Rose meet him, he thought.

CHAPTER 2

Dink went back to class and handed a note to Mrs. Eagle. Since school was almost out, Mr. Dillon had given him permission to leave early.

Dink filled his book bag, then whispered what was going on to Josh and Ruth Rose.

Dink's mother drove him and Sammi home to Woody Street. Sammi was quiet in the car. He kept turning around and looking out the rear window.

"Ms. Klinker said she'd bring your luggage over in a little while," Dink's mother told Sammi. "Dink will help you get settled, then I'll make you both a snack."

"Thank you very much, Mrs. Duncan," Sammi said as Dink's mom pulled into the driveway on Woody Street.

Dink climbed out of the car with his book bag clunking against his shoulders.

"Your room is next to mine," he told Sammi, leading the way upstairs.

Dink took Sammi into the guest room. There was a bed, a dresser, and a braided rug on the floor. A reading lamp stood on the table next to the bed.

Sammi looked at the room quietly. "This is very nice," he said.

"Come on, I'll show you my room," Dink said. He and Sammi passed through the bathroom. On the other side was Dink's bedroom.

As soon as Dink stepped into his room, Loretta began squeaking and running around in her cage.

"What is that?" Sammi shouted, hiding behind Dink.

"Just my guinea pig," Dink said. "Loretta's real friendly. You want to hold her?"

"I am allergic to fur!" Sammi said, peering into the cage. "Don't let it out!"

"Okay, I won't," Dink said.

"Dink!" his mother called from downstairs. "Are you and Sammi ready for a snack?"

"Are you hungry?" Dink asked Sammi.

Sammi wrinkled his nose. "What are we having?"

Dink pretended to think, then said, "Just the usual-rats' ears on crackers."

Sammi stared at Dink. "You are joking?"

"Yeah, I'm joking," Dink said. "Come on downstairs."

Dink's mother put a plate of peanut butter cookies and a quart of milk on the counter. Sammi inspected the cookies, then selected one.

"You're not allergic to cookies, are you?" Dink asked.

Sammi shook his head and took a small bite.

The doorbell rang, and Dink opened the door. Josh and Ruth Rose stood on the steps. Pal, Josh's basset hound, sat at their feet.

"We came to see if you and Sammi want to come out and play," Ruth Rose said. She held a purple Nerf football in her hand. The ball matched her purple jeans and sweatshirt.

"Hi, guys. Come on in," Dink said.

Josh made a beeline for the plate of cookies. Pal padded along behind him. His long pink tongue hung out of his mouth.

Sammi jumped onto a chair. "Keep it away!" he yelled. "I am allergic!"

Dink's mother put her hand on Sammi's shoulder. "It's okay, Sammi. Josh, can Pal wait on the porch?"

"Sure, Mrs. D. Come on, boy," Josh said as he led Pal out of the room.

"Help yourselves, kids," Dink's mom said, pouring four glasses of milk.

Josh came back and grabbed two cookies. "Why're you wearing your bathrobe?" he asked Sammi.

"It is what we wear in my country," Sammi said, sipping his milk.

"I think it's beautiful," Ruth Rose said. "I wish I had one."

The doorbell rang again. This time it was Joan Klinker, Sammi's tutor. She had come in a taxi with Sammi's suitcases. Dink helped the driver carry them into the hallway.

"Hi, Sammi," she said. "How do you like this house?"

"There are animals here!" Sammi said. "I am allergic, you know."

"I'm afraid we have a guinea pig," Dink's mother said.

"Yes, and I saw the dog on the porch," Joan Klinker said. "I hope Sammi's allergies won't be too much trouble."

Dink's mother smiled. "I'm sure we'll make out fine," she said. "Dink, why don't you kids take Sammi's luggage up to his room before you go out to play?"

"May I come, too?" Joan Klinker asked. "I'd like to look at the room where Sammi will stay. Do you mind?"

"Not at all. Dink will show you the way."

Dink and Josh lugged the suitcases up the stairs, then plopped them down on Sammi's bed. Ruth Rose followed, with Sammi and his tutor right behind.

Joan Klinker walked around the room. She inspected the windows and tested the locks. She rattled the handles on the doors to the bathroom and hallway. "Do these doors have locks?" she asked Dink.

"Um, yeah, but we never use them," he answered.

"Is there a night-light?" she asked.

Dink pointed to a small blue light sticking from a wall socket.

Joan Klinker nodded. "I guess this will do," she said. "Now may I see Sammi's bathroom?"

Dink showed Joan the bathroom he and Sammi would share.

The woman checked out everything in the bathroom, then peeked into Dink's room on the other side. "Who sleeps in here?" she asked.

"Me," Dink said. "My parents' room is downstairs."

"Do they have their own bathroom down there?" Joan asked.

Dink nodded as they walked back into Sammi's room.

Joan Klinker smiled at Dink. "This will be perfect!" she said. She patted Sammi on the head. "I'll see you later, okay?"

Sammi looked at her nervously. "Where are you going?"

"To my hotel room," Joan said. "But I'll come back after dinner for your French lesson." She took one more look around Sammi's room, then left.

"Do you play Nerf ball in your country?" Ruth Rose

asked Sammi.

Sammi shook his head. "What is Nerf?"

"This," Josh said, tossing the foam ball to Sammi. It bounced off him and fell to the floor.

"Um, do you want to change?" Dink asked Sammi.

Sammi stared at his suitcase. "Your mother said she'd unpack for me," he said.

"She will," Dink said. "But for now, you can wear some of my stuff. Come on in my room."

The four kids trooped through the bathroom and into Dink's room. Loretta began running around her cage.

Dink found a pair of sweatpants and a sweatshirt in his closet. "These should fit," he told Sammi.

Sammi looked at the clothes but didn't take them from Dink.

"Who is going to dress me?" he asked.

CHAPTER 3

Dink, Josh, and Ruth Rose stared at Sammi.

"Um, what do you mean, who's gonna dress you?" Dink asked.

"In my country, my servants dress me and undress me," Sammi said.

"Yeah, right," Josh said, grinning. "And my servants do my homework for me!"

"Do you really have servants?" Ruth Rose asked Sammi.

Sammi nodded. "I have five servants of my own. My father has twenty!"

"Twenty servants!" Josh yelled. "Are you guys rich?"

Sammi sat on Dink's bed. "We are very rich," he said. "My father is…"

Sammi didn't finish what he was going to say. Instead, he burst into tears.

"Great, Josh, you made him cry!" Dink said.

"I did not! I just asked him if he was rich!"

Ruth Rose sat next to Sammi. "Why are you crying?"

被绑架的国王

she asked.

Sammi didn't answer. Big tears rolled down his cheeks.

Dink tossed the sweat clothes onto the bed. Then he ran into his bathroom and came out with a wad of tissues.

"Here," he said.

Sammi took the tissues and wiped his eyes.

"Do you miss your mom and dad?" Ruth Rose asked Sammi. "Is that why you're crying?"

Sammi took a deep breath and wiped at his tears. "I don't know where my parents are," he said. "They were kidnapped last week."

"KIDNAPPED!" the three other kids yelled.

Sammi nodded. "My father's enemies snuck into the palace and took him and my mother."

"Palace?" Josh said. "You live in a palace? What are you, a prince or something?"

Sammi nodded. "Yes. My father is the king of Costra. I am Prince Samir Bin Oz. I will be king someday."

Sammi started crying again.

No one said anything. Even Loretta stopped running around in her cage.

Dink stared at Sammi. "You're a prince?" he finally asked. "Does my mom know all this, Sammi? I mean, about your folks being kidnapped and everything?"

The boy shook his head. "Only my tutor knows," he said. "My parents were kidnapped at night. I was sleeping. The next day I was snuck out of the palace and sent here so I would be safe."

"Safe from what?" Ruth Rose asked.

Sammi looked at her. His eyes were red and his nose dripped. "From the kidnappers," he said.

Just then, Pal started barking from the front porch.

"They're here!" Sammi cried. He jumped off the bed and ran into the bathroom.

Dink looked out the window. Pal was barking at a car. It was a taxi. Dink watched it turn the corner and disappear.

"Come on out, Sammi," Dink said. "It was just your tutor leaving."

Sammi stepped out of the bathroom. His eyes looked scared. "I am sorry," he whispered.

"No problem," Dink said. "Why don't we go down and play?"

He pointed to the sweat clothes on the bed. "Do you really need help getting dressed?"

Sammi took a deep breath and grinned. "No. I am in America now. I will learn to dress myself."

While Sammi changed, the other kids went outside and tossed the Nerf ball in Dink's backyard.

"It must be so cool to be a prince!" Josh said. "Just imagine ordering all those servants around!"

Dink bopped him with the Nerf ball.

"Josh, Sammi doesn't care about all that stuff," he said. "He misses his parents."

"I know," Josh said, "but still, just think. He could get ice cream in the middle of the night by snapping his fingers!"

Sammi came out dressed in Dink's sweat clothes.

Pal, tied to a tree, tried to lick Sammi's foot as he walked by.

Sammi jumped out of reach. "Is he trying to bite me?" he asked.

Josh laughed. "Naw, he's just saying hi," he said. "Pal wouldn't hurt a flea. Go ahead, pet him."

Sammi stepped closer and gave Pal a pat on his head. Then he sneezed.

"I like him," Sammi said. "But I am still allergic."

The kids taught Sammi the rules of touch football. They played until Dink's mother called them in to eat.

被绑架的国王

Promising to come over the next morning, Josh untied Pal and headed for home.

"Bye, Sammi!" Ruth Rose said. She cut through the hedge to her house next door.

"Your friends are nice," Sammi said. "Do you play together every day?"

"Sure," Dink said. "Don't you play with your friends in Co…in that place you come from?"

Sammi shook his head. "I have no friends. I stay in the palace and study with my tutors."

No friends? Dink stared at Sammi. He couldn't imagine not having Josh and Ruth Rose to hang out with.

"We better go wash up," Dink said, looking at his dirty hands. "I hope you like burgers and fries."

"Burgersandfries?" Sammi said. "What is burgersandfries?"

Dink grinned. "Hamburgers and French fries. French fries are skinny little potato slices. You dip them in ketchup."

Sammi let out a sigh. "Okay, I will try your food. Who will taste it for me?"

"Taste it?" Dink asked. "Why?"

"In my country," Sammi explained, "my father's enemies sometimes try to poison him. He has a servant taste our food to make sure it is safe."

Dink grinned at Sammi. "My mom's a real good cook. She doesn't use much poison at all!"

Sammi's eyes bugged out. "You are making a joke, right?"

"Yeah," Dink said. "But we have to tell her the truth about you, okay?"

"Why?" Sammi asked.

"Because it's the way we do things," Dink said. "Don't worry. You're safe here. Nobody will get you in Green Lawn."

CHAPTER 4

During supper, Dink and Sammi told Dink's mom the real reason why Sammi was in the United States.

"Oh, Sammi," Dink's mom said. "I am so sorry. Thank you for telling me."

After they all had some ice cream, Dink and his mother helped Sammi unpack. Dink's mother held up a long wooden box decorated with gold. "This is heavy, Sammi. What's inside?" she asked.

Sammi opened the lid and took out a shiny

kaleidoscope. Its golden sides were encrusted with jewels.

"This kaleidoscope has been in my family for many years," Sammi explained. "It belonged to my grandfather's grandfather and his grandfather! Now it is my father's."

"What a lovely idea!" Dink's mother said. "Will the kaleidoscope belong to you someday?"

"On my fifteenth birthday, my father will give this

to me," Sammi said. He frowned. "At least he would have, but now…I don't know what will happen."

Dink felt badly for Sammi. He couldn't imagine what he would feel like if his parents ever got kidnapped.

Dink's mother sat on the bed next to Sammi. She took his hand. "Sammi, I'm sure your parents will be found soon," she said. "Didn't you tell us that your father's friends are searching every corner of your country?"

Sammi nodded. "But his enemies are clever," he said. "They may have taken my parents far away from Costra."

Dink's mother gave Sammi a hug. Then she laid his pajamas and slippers on his bed. The pj's were red silk, and the slippers were purple velvet with floppy gold tassels.

"Pretty snazzy," Dink said, grinning at Sammi. "I usually sleep in an old T-shirt and shorts!"

Just then, the front doorbell rang. Dink's mother left the room.

"Watch," Sammi said, kneeling on the floor. He unscrewed the large end of the kaleidoscope and poured out all the pieces of glass. They made a red, yellow, and blue mound on the rug.

"It comes apart!" Dink said. He picked up some of the glass. The thin pieces felt smooth in his fingers.

A knock came at the door to Sammi's room. Joan Klinker poked her head in. "Hi, Sammi," she said.

Sammi smiled and scooped up the glass. "I'm showing Dink my kaleidoscope," he said. Dink helped Sammi put the kaleidoscope back in its box.

"Fine, Sammi," Joan said, looking at her watch. "It's almost eight. How about a short French lesson?"

She dropped a yellow book on Sammi's bed. "Will you excuse Sammi for a little while?" she said to Dink.

"Can't he stay?" Sammi asked. "Dink can have a lesson with me!"

Joan Klinker looked at Dink for a moment, then said, "Sure. Why not?"

"Great!" Dink said. He sat next to Sammi on the floor. Joan perched on the bed and opened the yellow book.

"First, some colors," Joan said. She pointed at Dink's

shirt. "Blue. But in French, we say *bleu*. Repeat, Sammi."

Sammi said, "*Bleu.*" To Dink, it sounded almost the same as "blue."

Joan pointed at Dink. "Now you, please."

"*Bleu,*" said Dink, trying to imitate Sammi.

"Good!" Joan put a hand on Sammi's folded pajamas. "Red," she said.

"*Rouge,*" said Sammi.

To Dink, it sounded almost like "rooj," so that's what he said.

Joan Klinker held up the yellow book. "*Jaune,*" she said. "*Le livre est jaune.* The book is yellow."

She pointed at Dink. "Can you say *jaune*?"

Dink blushed. "Joan," he finally said.

"No, Joan is my name," the tutor said.

Dink tried again. "Zhone," he said.

Sammi laughed. "That's okay," he said. "It took me a month to learn to say *jaune*."

"Now we will do some numbers," Joan said.

A half hour later, she closed the yellow book. "That's all for tonight," she said. "Tomorrow we will continue."

She checked the locks on Sammi's window, his bathroom door, and the door out into the hall. Then she turned and smiled. "*Bonsoir*, Sammi."

"*Bonsoir, madame*," Sammi answered.

After Joan left, Dink stood up and yawned. "Night, Sammi. I'll wake you up for breakfast."

Dink headed into the bathroom and brushed his teeth. He smiled at his reflection in the mirror. Tomorrow, he decided, he'd learn how to say "My toothbrush is purple." In French!

CHAPTER 5

The next morning, Dink washed his hands and face, then tapped on Sammi's bedroom door.

"Rise and shine!" Dink said. "We're having pancakes and sausages for breakfast!"

There was no answer. Dink opened the door and peeked in. Sammi's bed was mussed, but he wasn't in it.

"Sammi?" Dink said, glancing around the empty room. Where could he be? Dink wondered as he headed down the stairs.

"Mom, Sammi's not in his room," Dink said.

Dink's mother stopped spooning pancake batter into a frying pan. "He's not? Where is he?"

"I don't know, Mom." Dink shoved open the back door and looked around the yard. "Not out here either," he said.

As Dink pulled the door shut again, his hand struck something sharp.

"Mom, look at this!" he yelled.

The wood around the door lock was shattered. Jagged slivers of wood stuck out. A few wood splinters lay on the floor under Dink's feet.

"Oh, my goodness!" his mother said. "Someone forced the door open!"

She turned and hurried up the hall stairs. Dink followed his mom into the guest room.

"Sammi?" his mom called. "Sammi, please answer! If you're hiding, please come out."

But Sammi did not answer.

"I'm calling Officer Fallon," Dink's mother said. "And Joan Klinker! Why don't you run next door and find out if Ruth Rose's family saw anything?"

Dink charged down the stairs and out of the

house. He tore into Ruth Rose's yard and banged his fist on her door.

Ruth Rose opened it, munching on a piece of toast.

"Have you seen Sammi?" Dink asked, out of breath.

She shook her head. "Why, is he missing?"

"Yes!" Dink said. "Someone broke in…Sammi's gone!"

"WHAT?" Ruth Rose yelled. "You mean he was kidnapped?"

Suddenly, Dink heard a siren. He left Ruth Rose with the toast in her hand and raced back to his front yard.

A police cruiser roared around the corner and whipped into his driveway. As the siren died, Officers Fallon and Keene burst out of the car.

Dink's mom came flying out of the house. Her face was white. "Thank goodness you came," she told the officers. "I think our house guest has been kidnapped!"

Just then, a yellow taxi pulled up in front of Dink's house. The rear door flew open, and Joan Klinker climbed out.

"What has happened to Sammi?" she called, running across the front yard.

"We don't know," Dink's mother said. "He's not in the house, and the lock on our back door has been forced open."

Joan Klinker put her hand to her mouth. She swayed, then started to topple. Officer Keene caught her just before she fell.

"Bring her inside," Dink's mother said, running for

the front door.

"Take a look around," Officer Fallon told Officer Keene. Then he helped Dink's mother take Joan Klinker into the house.

Ruth Rose appeared through the hedge that separated their yards. She was dressed in blue bib overalls, a blue shirt, and blue high-top sneakers.

"Is Sammi really gone?" she asked Dink. "This isn't a joke, is it?"

Dink shook his head. His mouth was so dry he could hardly swallow. "I think it's real," he said, remembering what Sammi had told them about his father's enemies.

"But how could anyone just walk in and take him?" Ruth Rose asked.

"Our back door lock is busted," Dink said. "They must have gotten in that way."

Ruth Rose's mom and dad joined them as Dink explained.

"Let's all search the street," Ruth Rose's dad suggested. He went to organize the neighbors.

Just then, Josh arrived with his dog. "What's going

A to Z 神秘案件

on, Dinkus?" he asked. "Why's the cruiser here?"

"Sammi is gone," Dink said. "We think he's been kidnapped!"

Josh's mouth dropped open. Then he grinned. "This is a joke, right?"

Dink shook his head. "Come on, I'll show you where the kidnappers broke the kitchen door."

Dink started for the front steps. But before he

reached the door, it opened. Joan Klinker and Dink's mother stepped out.

"Are you sure you're all right, Joan?" Dink's mother asked. "Won't you stay for a while?"

Joan Klinker shook her head. "I have to make some phone calls," she muttered. Then she hurried into the cab and it pulled away.

"That poor woman," Dink's mom said, heading back to the kitchen.

As Dink climbed the porch steps, something shiny caught his eye.

He bent down and picked up a small piece of yellow glass.

"What's that?" Ruth Rose asked.

Dink stared at the yellow sliver. He remembered where he'd seen others just like it.

"This came out of Sammi's kaleidoscope!" he said.

CHAPTER 6

Inside the house, Officer Fallon examined the piece of glass. "If this came out of the boy's kaleidoscope, how'd it get to your front steps?" he asked.

"The top unscrews," Dink explained. "Sammi likes to take the glass out."

Josh and Ruth Rose stood silently in Dink's kitchen. Pal lay at Josh's feet, snoozing. Dink was sitting at the table with his mom and Officer Fallon. Officer Keene had left to organize a search.

Officer Fallon sighed. He left the piece of glass on the table and stood up.

"Green Lawn isn't that big," he said. "We'll find the boy. I'll make sure every possible way out of town is checked. Try not to worry, okay?"

Dink's mother grabbed her car keys. "I'm going to drive around and look for him," she said.

"Can we come, too?" Dink asked.

His mother shook her head. "You can help by staying by the phone," she said. She looked at Officer Fallon. "Do you think the kidnappers would telephone here?"

Officer Fallon nodded. "They might try to make contact. But kidnappers usually wait a few days before calling. They like to get the family worried so they'll hand over more ransom money."

Dink watched his mother and Officer Fallon leave. He heard the front door lock click into position.

"Look at this," Dink said. He showed Josh and Ruth Rose the damaged back door.

"Boy, this is creepy!" Josh said.

"Poor Sammi," Ruth Rose said. "He must be so scared!"

"Let's go check out his room," Dink said. "Maybe

we'll find some more clues."

The kids hurried toward the stairs. Pal followed them into Sammi's room, his long ears brushing the floor.

Sammi's sheet and blanket were tangled, half off the bed. Dink walked over to the bureau. There was the kaleidoscope box and two small mounds of colored glass. Each mound was a different color.

"This is the kaleidoscope," Dink said, removing it from the box. "See, he took all the glass out."

Josh touched the jewels that decorated the kaleidoscope. "Are these real?" he asked.

"Sammi said they were," Dink answered.

Ruth Rose was examining the pieces of glass. "Where are the yellow pieces?" she asked.

"What do you mean?" Dink asked.

"The piece we found is yellow," she said. "But all I see here is red and blue. No yellow."

"That's weird," Dink said. "Let's look around."

The kids began to search Sammi's room for the

yellow glass. Pal waddled around, sniffing everything.

Dink checked in the bathroom while Josh went through the clothes in the closet. Ruth Rose got down on her hands and knees and looked under the bed.

"Well, if there's yellow glass in this room, I don't know where it is," Josh said. He stepped away from the closet.

"WATCH OUT!" Ruth Rose yelled, stopping Josh in his tracks.

She snatched something from the carpet where Josh was about to step. It was another piece of yellow glass.

Just then, the phone rang.

Dink ran down the stairs and grabbed the phone on its third ring.

"Hello?"

Dink listened for a minute, then yelled up the stairs, "Hey, guys, it's Officer Fallon. He wants to know if Sammi's pajamas and slippers are in his room. Can you look?"

He waited. Ruth Rose came to the top of the stairs. "No pj's or slippers," she said.

Dink spoke into the phone. "We can't find them."

After a minute, Dink hung up the phone. He climbed the stairs to Sammi's room.

"What's up with the slippers?" Josh asked.

"Ron Pinkowski found a gold tassel near the river by his bait shop," Dink said. "Sammi's slippers had gold tassels on them."

"But what—"

"And one of Mr. Pinkowski's boats is missing," Dink interrupted.

He stared at his two friends. "Officer Fallon thinks the kidnappers took Sammi away in a boat!"

CHAPTER 7

"What kind of boat?" Josh asked. "The water in Indian River isn't very deep."

"But it's deep enough for a rowboat," Ruth Rose said.

Dink thought about the river near Ron's Bait Shop. They'd all waded there before. The water was only up to their knees.

"Yeah," he said. "Maybe they took Sammi downriver in a small boat. When they got to the deep part, they could have put him in a bigger boat …"

" …and taken him out to sea!" Ruth Rose added.

The kids stared at each other. Dink thought about poor Sammi, afraid of noises and animals, tied up in some boat.

"We have to do something, guys," he said. "Let's go see if we can find more clues at the bait shop." He ran down the stairs to the kitchen.

Ruth Rose hurried after him, with Josh and Pal right behind her.

"Your mom told us to stay put," Josh reminded Dink.

"I know, Josh." Dink was scribbling on a pad. "I'm telling her where we're going," he said. "We'll probably be back before she sees this. Come on!"

The kids cut through the dining room and headed for the back door.

Suddenly, Pal barked and began straining on his leash. He pulled until Josh let him have his way. Pal headed for the living room, and the kids followed.

"I think he smells something," Josh said. Pal had his nose on the rug, sniffing at something small and shiny.

"It's another piece of glass!" Josh said, snatching it

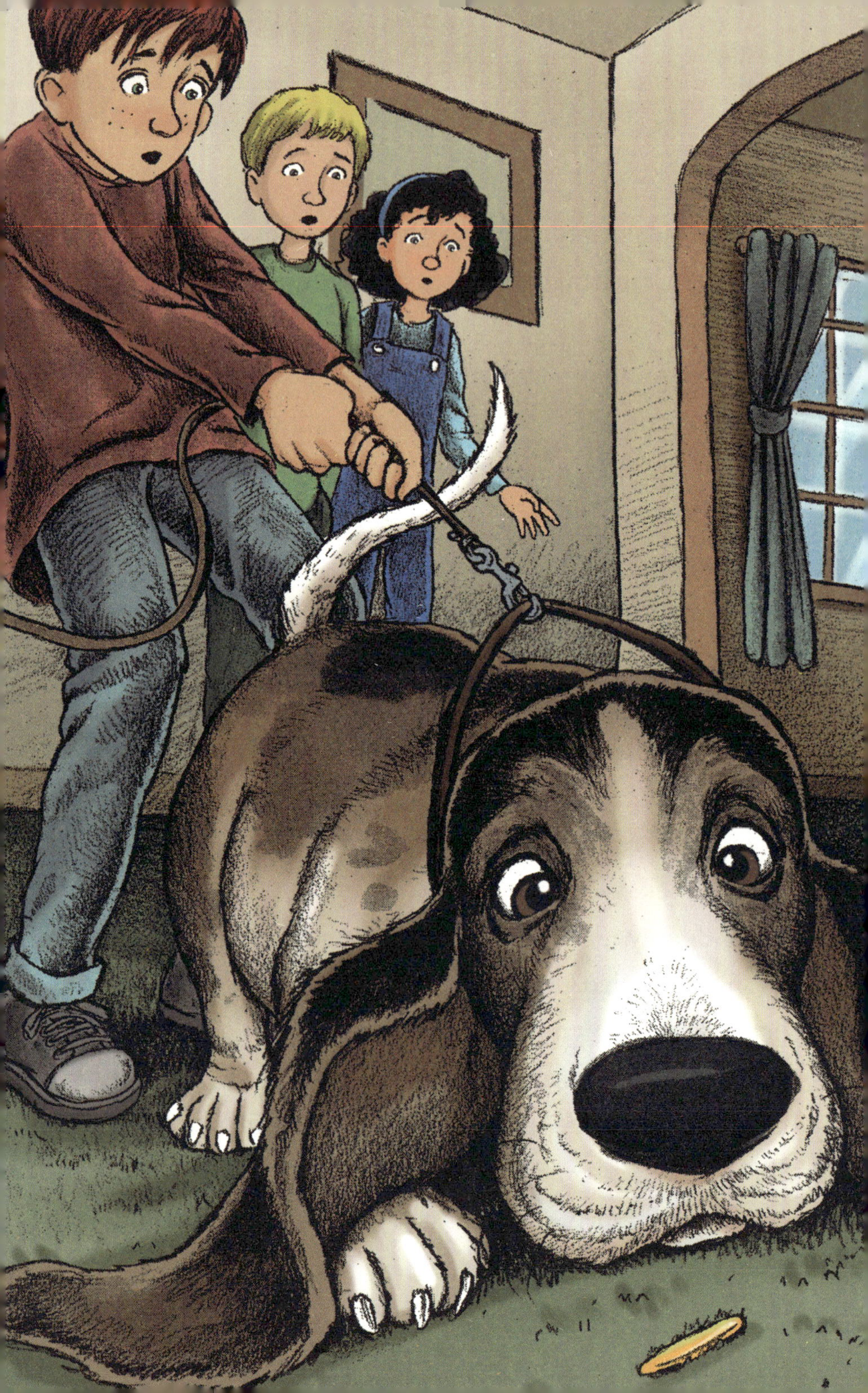

away from the dog's nose.

"This is the third one," Dink said. He looked at the stairs going up to the bedrooms. "Sammi dropped one in his room, one down here, and another one on the front steps …"

"SAMMI LEFT US A TRAIL!" Ruth Rose suddenly yelled.

"I'll bet you're right," Dink said. "The kidnappers must have brought him down the stairs and out the front door. Come on, let's look for more!"

The kids hurried out the door and into the front yard. Pal snuffled with his nose along the ground while the kids searched with their eyes.

"Nothing," Dink muttered after a few minutes. "The trail ends here."

Suddenly, Pal yanked on the leash.

"Whoa, doggie," Josh said.

But Pal kept pulling. He dragged Josh to the road. At the curb, Pal's nose went right into the gutter.

"Look!" Josh said. He held up a fourth piece of yellow glass.

Dink and Ruth Rose ran over. "Sammi must've

dropped it when the kidnappers loaded him into a car," Ruth Rose said.

"And I bet the trail picks up again down at the river," Dink said. "Let's go!"

With Pal loping along behind them, the kids hurried down Woody Street. They cut past the elementary school, then crossed Duck Walk Way toward the river.

Inside his shop, Ron Pinkowski was feeding the bait shiners in one of his huge tanks.

"Hey, I heard about that boy disappearing," Ron said when he saw the kids.

"He didn't disappear," Josh said. "He was kidnapped!"

Ron nodded. "That's what Officer Fallon said. And they stole one of my rowboats!"

"Can you show us where the boat was?" Dink asked.

"Sure, come on." Ron took the kids outside. "Right over there," he said, pointing to a line of upside-down boats along the riverbank. There was an empty space between two of the boats.

"They broke my padlock and took a pair of my brand-new oars, too."

"Thanks, Mr. P." Dink said.

被绑架的国王

The kids hurried over to the row of boats and searched for yellow glass. Pal sniffed the ground for a few seconds, then flopped under a tree and closed his eyes.

The kids examined the ground where the boat had been. They didn't find any glass at all. "Let's look in the driveway," Dink suggested.

They walked back to the road, then worked their way down to the boats again.

Josh found a nickel, but there wasn't a piece of yellow kaleidoscope glass anywhere.

"That's weird," said Dink. "If Sammi left a trail back at my house, why didn't he drop another piece of glass when he got here?"

"Maybe he ran out of glass," Josh said.

Ruth Rose shook her head. "How could he? He took all the yellow glass, remember?"

"You know," Dink said, "something about the yellow glass is bugging me. Why did Sammi leave a yellow trail? Why not red or blue?"

"Well, he had the colors in separate little piles," Josh said. "So maybe he just grabbed the closest pile

135

and it was yellow."

Ron Pinkowski walked over. "What're you kids looking for?" he asked.

Dink explained about the trail of yellow glass. "You didn't see any, did you?"

"Nope. Just that tassel thing, and I gave it to Officer Fallon."

"Did you hear a car last night?" Ruth Rose asked.

Ron grinned. "The way I snore? A tank could drive down here and I'd snooze right through it!"

"Let's go back and see if my mom is home," Dink

said. "She might have found out something. Thanks, Mr. P."

The kids and Pal hurried back to Dink's house. His mom was on the phone, looking worried. She made a motion for the kids to sit.

They did, with Pal at their feet. A minute later, Dink's mother hung up the phone.

"That was Officer Fallon," she said. "The police are searching everywhere. They're checking the train station, the airport, and every boat on the river, but so far, they aren't having any luck."

Dink's mother looked at the kids with concern in her eyes.

"How could a boy just disappear without a trace?" she asked.

CHAPTER 8

"Sammi left a trail, Mom," Dink said.

"He what?"

Dink explained about the pieces of yellow glass.

"Oh, my goodness!" Dink's mother grabbed the phone, dialed quickly, and handed the phone to Dink. "Tell Officer Fallon," she said.

Dink talked and Officer Fallon listened. "But when we got to Ron's Bait Shop, we didn't find any more glass," Dink said into the phone.

He nodded, said, "Uh-huh," then hung up.

"Officer Fallon wants all the glass we found," Dink

said. He pulled the four little pieces out of his pocket.

His mother picked up the phone. "I think I'll go visit Joan Klinker," she said. "She must be frantic, and she's all alone there at the hotel."

She dialed another number. "Hello, Joan? This is Dink's mom, Mrs. Duncan," she said into the phone. "Would you like some company? May I come over?"

Dink couldn't hear Joan's answer, but his mother smiled. "Okay, fine. I'll be there in five minutes," she said before hanging up.

She glanced into the mirror, then headed for the door. "We're meeting for coffee at Ellie's," she said. "Oh, let me have the pieces of glass. I can take them to the police station after I meet Joan."

Dink dropped the yellow glass into his mother's hand. She smiled weakly at the kids, then hurried out the back door.

Dink stared at the door, thinking.

"Earth to Dink," Josh said, snapping his fingers in front of Dink's nose.

Dink shook his head. "Something my mother said made me think of something else, but now I forgot!"

"You forgot what your mother said, or you forgot what it made you think of?" Ruth Rose asked.

"Both!" Dink said, giving Josh a look. "I was just getting it when you snapped your fingers!"

"Sorry," Josh said. "Why don't we have a snack? Maybe your memory needs some ice cream."

Ruth Rose laughed. "Better feed him, Dink. You know how he gets when his tummy is empty."

Dink sighed. "We finished the ice cream last night," he said, heading for the kitchen. He pulled open the refrigerator. "But we've got Cool Whip and cherry Jell-O."

He grabbed the bowl and handed it to Josh. "Here, are you…"

Then Dink stopped. He stared at the bowl of Jell-O. "That's it!" he yelled. "It's yellow!"

Josh shook his head. "Dinkus, this is red Jell-O, not yellow Jell-O."

"No—I mean, yes, I know. But Jell-O made me think of yellow!" Dink said.

"Can I eat while you talk?" Josh asked.

Dink got bowls and spoons and put them on

the table. Then he continued. "After you guys left yesterday, Sammi's tutor came over and gave me and Sammi a French lesson," he said.

Josh grinned. "Say something in French," he said.

"Just eat, Josh, and let me finish!"

"Sorry," Josh said, plopping a gob of Cool Whip onto his Jell-O. He let Pal lick his spoon.

"Remember a few minutes ago when my mom said she was going to see Sammi's tutor?" Dink asked. "She called her Joan, remember?"

Josh and Ruth Rose nodded.

"That made me think of the French lesson yesterday. She taught me to say yellow in French. The word for yellow is *jaune*, only I pronounced it 'Joan,' like her name."

"Um, Dinkus?" Josh said. "What's this got to do with anything?"

"Don't you guys see?" Dink said. "The French word for yellow sounds just like 'Joan.' That's Sammi's tutor's name. Sammi could have left a trail of red or blue, but he chose the yellow glass. I think Sammi was trying to say 'Joan'!"

CHAPTER 9

"Maybe Sammi thinks Joan knows who the kidnappers are," Ruth Rose said.

"Maybe," Dink said. "Or maybe Joan is the kidnapper!"

Josh and Ruth Rose looked up from their Jell-O.

Josh had Cool Whip on his nose. "His tutor?" he asked.

"Think about it," Dink went on. " Sammi wakes up in the middle of the night. Someone's in his room. He recognizes Joan and grabs a pile of glass. Yellow glass, because he remembers how much her name sounds like the French word for yellow. And he knows I know that!"

"But how could she be the kidnapper?"Ruth Rose asked."She's Sammi's friend. She came here to help him."

"Yeah, and you saw how upset she was this morning,"Josh said."That couldn't be an act. I still think Sammi just grabbed the first pile of glass his hand landed on in the dark."

Ruth Rose stood up."There's one way to find out,"she said."Let's go to the hotel and talk to her."

"Okay,"Dink said."But she's not at the hotel. My mom said she was meeting Joan at the diner."

"Good!"Josh said, gulping down the last of his Jell-O."I can get an ice cream while we talk!"

The kids took Pal and hurried to Ellie's Diner on Main Street. Dink glanced through the window, but he didn't see Joan Klinker or his mom.

"I wonder where they are. Mom's car isn't here either,"Dink said, looking up and down Main Street.

"Let's ask Ellie,"Ruth Rose suggested.

Josh pushed the door open and the kids stepped

inside. Two teenagers were eating scrambled eggs, but no one else sat in the booths or at the counter.

"Hey there, kids," Ellie said. "Hi, cute poochie!" She bent down and patted Pal, then stroked his ears. "Shall I scoop up three cones?" she asked.

Dink shook his head. "No, thanks, I'm looking for my mom," he said. "Have you seen her? She was supposed to meet someone here a little while ago."

Ellie shook her head. "Nope, haven't seen your mother in a few days," she said.

"Maybe they're at the hotel," Ruth Rose said.

Dink nodded. "I guess it's worth a try," he said.

They thanked Ellie and headed for the Shangri-la Hotel, two blocks up Main Street.

"Why couldn't we at least get cones to go?" Josh asked. He placed one hand dramatically across his forehead. "I think I feel faint."

"Later," Dink said. "After we find Sammi." And after we find my mom, he thought.

Three minutes later, they walked into the hotel. Mr. Linkletter was sitting on one of the lobby chairs, eating a doughnut and sipping coffee.

"Well, hello there," he said when the trio approached him. He glanced at Pal. "Joshua, I assume your dog is, um, house-trained?"

Josh grinned as Pal flopped down at Mr. Linkletter's feet. "Yep, and he's hotel-trained, too!"

Mr. Linkletter twitched an eyebrow. "Well, then," he said, "how can I be of service today?"

"I'm looking for my mom," Dink said. "She was supposed to meet Joan Klinker at Ellie's, but they're not there. Have you seen them?"

Mr. Linkletter set his coffee down. "I didn't see your mom, but Ms. Klinker left the hotel a short while ago."

"Did she say where she was going?"

Mr. Linkletter shook his head. "Not a word."

Dink glanced around the hotel lobby. Where could his mother be? She always let him know if she had to change her plans. Always!

"She didn't leave a note or anything?"

"I'm sorry, Donald," Mr. Linkletter said. "Perhaps she's gone back home. Would you like to call her?"

Suddenly, Dink felt sick. He blinked back tears. Something was wrong! First Sammi disappeared, and

147

now his mother was gone! And she'd been on her way to see Joan Klinker with the yellow glass!

Mr. Linkletter wiped his fingers on his napkin and stood up."Come, you can use my phone,"he said. He took Dink over to the counter. Pal followed Mr. Linkletter, sniffing at his heels.

Dink dialed and listened for his mother's voice on the other end. But no one answered.

He set the phone down and looked up at Mr. Linkletter."Where could she be?"he asked.

CHAPTER 10

Just then, Pal began growling and biting at Mr. Linkletter's left shoe.

"What on earth? "Mr. Linkletter said, pulling his foot away.

But Pal wouldn't give up. Using his paws and teeth, he tried to pull Mr. Linkletter's shiny black loafer right off his foot.

"Joshua! "Mr. Linkletter said. "Please teach your dog some manners!

"Take it off!"Ruth Rose suddenly said.

Mr. Linkletter glanced down at Ruth Rose."I beg

your pardon?"

"I think I know what Pal wants," she said. "Please take off your shoe!"

Mr. Linkletter let out a big sigh. "Very well. If that will bring peace!"

The tall man leaned over and removed his left shoe. He showed it to Pal. "There, satisfied?" he asked.

Pal grabbed the shoe in his mouth and dropped it

at Josh's feet.

"I WAS RIGHT!" Ruth Rose yelled. She picked up the shoe and held it upside down.

On the sole, stuck to a wad of gum, was a piece of shiny yellow glass.

"The dog was after a nasty piece of gum?" Mr. Linkletter asked.

"No," Dink said. "That piece of glass is from Sammi's kaleidoscope! This means the kidnappers brought Sammi here, to the hotel!"

"Donald, you're giving me a headache," Mr. Linkletter said, taking his shoe back. He pulled the gum off and slipped the loafer back on his foot. "Who is Sammi? What kidnappers?"

Dink told Mr. Linkletter about Sammi's disappearing from his bed. Then he explained about Joan Klinker's French lesson, Sammi's kaleidoscope, and the trail of yellow glass.

"Now my mom's missing, too, "Dink said. "And I think Joan Klinker kidnapped them both! She might be keeping them up in her room!"

"Um, Dink?" Josh said. "Officer Fallon said Sammi

was taken away in a boat. How could he be in the hotel and in a boat at the same time?"

"I don't know," Dink said. "But I still want to check out Joan Klinker's room. That piece of glass on your shoe proves Sammi was here!"

Mr. Linkletter sighed and set down his half-eaten doughnut. "Very well," he said. "Ms. Klinker has room 301. I'll take you up there, but you must be very quiet. Our guests don't expect crowds of children parading about the halls. "He looked down at Pal. "But the hound has to stay down here. The Shangri-la does not permit animals upstairs!"

"But he can smell stuff," Josh said. "We need him!"

Mr. Linkletter looked at Pal's big brown eyes. "Oh, all right. What's one more broken rule?"

The kids and Pal followed Mr. Linkletter into the elevator.

When it stopped on the third floor, they all walked quickly to room 301. A man in a white uniform was pushing a cart full of linens down the hall and around the corner.

Mr. Linkletter unlocked the door and pushed it

open.

Joan Klinker's bed was made and two suitcases stood on the floor.

"Do your thing," Josh whispered into Pal's ear.

Pal walked in a wide circle, sniffing the carpet. Suddenly, he made a beeline for the closet and began scratching at the door.

Josh opened the closet door and Pal rushed in.

Dink noticed that the closet was empty. Joan Klinker had packed everything.

"What's in there, boy?" Josh asked, getting down on his hands and knees.

While Pal and Josh searched the closet floor, Dink and Ruth Rose looked under the bed and in the bathroom.

Suddenly, Josh backed out of the closet. "Look what Pal found!" he cried. In his hand, he held a small piece of yellow glass.

"You were right, Dink," Ruth Rose said. "Sammi must have been in this room!"

Just then, Pal raced from the room with his nose to the floor. The next thing they heard was Pal barking and growling.

Everyone followed him, just in time to see Pal attack the white linen cart. He bit at the side of the cart and tried to pull it back along the floor.

The man in the white uniform pushed the cart in the other direction.

"Get outta here, mutt!" the man yelled, kicking at the dog.

That wasn't a good idea. Pal grabbed the man's pants cuff in his teeth and began thrashing and growling.

"Pal, no!" Josh shouted. He pulled Pal away, but the hound was still barking at the man.

Mr. Linkletter looked at the man. "Who are you?" he asked.

"Just collectin' the laundry," the man said, glaring at Pal.

Mr. Linkletter pointed to the words stitched into the man's shirt. "But we don't use Ace Laundry Service," he said.

Suddenly, the man bolted for the elevator. But he tripped over Pal's leash and fell on his face.

被绑架的国王

Mr. Linkletter moved spryly and sat on the man's back. "What are you doing in this building?" he demanded.

"I ain't talkin'!" the man mumbled with his face in the carpet.

"Help me, guys," Dink said, grabbing the side of the cart. With a solid yank, the kids toppled it over.

A mountain of sheets and towels piled out onto the floor.

In the bottom of the cart lay Sammi, tied and gagged.

CHAPTER 11

The three kids slid Sammi out of the cart and laid him gently on the floor. While Dink and Josh worked on the knots, Ruth Rose pulled away his gag.

Before Sammi could speak, Pal waddled over and covered his face with wet dog kisses.

Sammi gave Pal a big hug. Then he sneezed.

They all jumped when the elevator door slid open and Joan Klinker stepped out. When she saw Sammi and the man on the floor, her face turned as white as the sheets.

"You—you've found Sammi!" Joan said, rushing to his side.

"Ain't that cute!" the man on the floor said. "Well, I ain't taking this rap alone! She's the one planned the whole thing! We done it together."

"What are you talking about?" Joan said. "I—I've never seen this man in my life!"

The man let out a cackle. "What a lousy thing to say about your own husband!" he said.

Just then, the elevator door slid open again. Dink's

mother and Officer Fallon stepped into the hallway.

"Well, well," Officer Fallon said. "Good thing I brought two pairs of handcuffs!"

An hour later, Joan Klinker and her husband, Nick, were in jail.

Mr. Linkletter went back to finish eating his doughnut.

Dink, Josh and Pal, Ruth Rose, Sammi, and Dink's mom joined Officer Fallon in the police station.

"You were pretty clever to leave that trail of yellow glass," Officer Fallon told Sammi.

"Thank you," Sammi said. "I hoped Dink would remember that the French word for yellow sounds like 'Joan.'"

"I did remember," Dink said. "But Josh's dog was the one who found most of the glass."

Josh beamed and patted Pal's head. "Good dog," he said.

"Well, Ms. Klinker and her husband sang like little birds," Officer Fallon said. "They planned this thing carefully. After they stashed Sammi in the closet upstairs, they brought one of his slipper tassels to the river to throw us off the trail."

"I heard them talking in the car, "Sammi said."They were going to take me back to Costra. I would have disappeared, just like my parents. Then my father's enemies would have taken over our country."

Dink looked at his mom."How did you know we were at the hotel?"he asked.

"Well, I met Joan outside Ellie's," Dink's mother said."She said she was happy to be out of the hotel and suggested we go for a walk. Naturally, we talked about the kidnapping, and she mentioned Sammi's slipper tassel being found at the river."

"Which she shouldn't have known about, right?" said Ruth Rose.

Dink's mother smiled."Right. And when I happened to mention the trail of yellow glass, she suddenly hurried away. She said she had something important to do at the hotel. So I came right here to see Officer Fallon."

Officer Fallon smiled at the three kids."But by the time we got to the hotel, you three had everything under control."

Just then, Officer Fallon's computer said, "You've got mail!"

"Ah, I've been waiting for this e-mail," he said.

He moved his computer mouse, clicked twice, and smiled. "You should all hear this, so I'll read it aloud."

"The king and queen of Costra have been found, thanks to your tip. They are alive and well. Both send love to their son. Want him to come home immediately."

Everyone in the office cheered. Sammi looked shocked, and then he beamed.

"But how did you find them?" he asked Officer Fallon.

"Your kidnappers spilled the beans," he said. "They were hired by the same guys who kidnapped your parents. They gave me names and places, so I just e-mailed the Costran police."

The next day, Dink, Josh, Pal, and Ruth Rose said good-bye to Sammi. Each of the kids gave him a wrapped gift. Pal's gift for Sammi was a big, wet lick on the cheek.

Sammi smiled, then sneezed.

Three weeks later, a large package arrived at Dink's house. It was from Costra and addressed to all three kids.

"Dibs on the cool stamps!" Josh said.

Dink opened the parcel and found four smaller packages labeled DINK, JOSH, RUTH ROSE, and PAL.

Dink and Josh found small gold kaleidoscopes in their packages. Their names were spelled on the sides with tiny rubies.

"What'd he send you?" Josh asked Ruth Rose.

"OH, MY GOSH!" she screamed and held up a dark blue robe just like Sammi's.

"Here's a picture and a note," Dink said. He read the note aloud.

The picture showed Sammi wearing the gifts the kids had given him-Ruth Rose's sweatshirt, Josh's jeans, and Dink's baseball cap.

Suddenly, Pal let out a woof. "He wants us to open his package," Josh said.

Dear friends,
I miss you. My father says you can come here and visit someday. You can even bring Pal!
Your friend,
Sammi Bin Oz

He helped Pal rip off the paper. Inside, they found a purple velvet doggy sweater. GOOD DOG had been stitched into the velvet with gold thread.

Text copyright © 2000 by Ron Roy
Illustrations copyright © 2000 by John Steven Gurney
All rights reserved under International and Pan-American Copyright Conventions.
Published in the United States by Random House, Inc., New York,
and simultaneously in Canada by Random House of Canada Limited, Toronto.

本书中英双语版由中南博集天卷文化传媒有限公司与企鹅兰登（北京）文化发展有限公司合作出版。

"企鹅"及其相关标识是企鹅兰登已经注册或尚未注册的商标。
未经允许，不得擅用。
封底凡无企鹅防伪标识者均属未经授权之非法版本。

©中南博集天卷文化传媒有限公司。本书版权受法律保护。未经权利人许可，任何人不得以任何方式使用本书包括正文、插图、封面、版式等任何部分内容，违者将受到法律制裁。

著作权合同登记号：字18-2023-258

图书在版编目（CIP）数据

被绑架的国王：汉英对照 /（美）罗恩·罗伊著；
（美）约翰·史蒂文·格尼绘；杨琼琼译. -- 长沙：湖
南少年儿童出版社，2024.10. -- （A to Z神秘案件）.
ISBN 978-7-5562-7818-3

Ⅰ. H319.4

中国国家版本馆CIP数据核字第2024AK4751号

A TO Z SHENMI ANJIAN BEI BANGJIA DE GUOWANG
A to Z神秘案件 被绑架的国王
［美］罗恩·罗伊 著　［美］约翰·史蒂文·格尼 绘　杨琼琼 译

责任编辑：唐 凌　李 炜	策划出品：李 炜　张苗苗　文赛峰
策划编辑：文赛峰	特约编辑：杜佳美
营销编辑：付 佳　杨 朔　周晓茜	封面设计：霍雨佳
版权支持：王媛媛	版式设计：马睿君
插图上色：河北传图文化	内文排版：霍雨佳

出 版 人：刘星保
出　　版：湖南少年儿童出版社
地　　址：湖南省长沙市晚报大道89号
邮　　编：410016
电　　话：0731-82196320
常年法律顾问：湖南崇民律师事务所　柳成柱律师
经　　销：新华书店

开　本：875 mm×1230 mm　1/32	印　刷：三河市中晟雅豪印务有限公司
字　数：89千字	印　张：5.125
版　次：2024年10月第1版	印　次：2024年10月第1次印刷
书　号：ISBN 978-7-5562-7818-3	定　价：280.00元（全10册）

若有质量问题，请致电质量监督电话：010-59096394　团购电话：010-59320018

A to Z 神秘案件

中英双语

第二辑

The Lucky Lottery
被偷走的彩票

[美]罗恩·罗伊 著
[美]约翰·史蒂文·格尼 绘　刘巧丽 译

湖南少年儿童出版社　小博集

·长沙·

印第安河
劳伦斯出租车公司
沿河路
骑马
小径
自行车道
租马处
树林
林景路
印第安路
消防站
自行车道
大桥路
比尔
自行车店
超市
知更鸟路
乌鸦街
雀鸟巷
歌鹤街
猫头鹰路
野鸡巷
蓝松鸦路
鹤鹑路
健身
中心
森林
自行车道
蓝鸟路
蜂鸟巷
丘鹬路
埃莉餐馆
橡子公寓
毛脚
宠物店
橡树街
自行车道
中心教堂
人民池塘
邮局
社区花园
和鱼塘
绿地储蓄银行
老年公寓
警察局
西绿街
鹅岛
沿河路
老年活动中心
绿地
图书馆
镇公所
儿童动物园
和水族馆
香格里拉
酒店
自行车道
主街

欢迎来到绿地镇
一起解开A to Z神秘案件
北
南
西
东
码头
沿河路
少女岛
租船处
罗恩鱼饵店
鸭子步行道
绿地中学
老鹰巷
牧场路
乔希家
绿地小学
银环路
丁丁家
露丝家
林荫街
林梢弯道
牧场路
狐狸小道
鹌鹑路
音乐台
玫瑰园
宜人街
蓟花街
玫瑰街
野花路
中心公园
天鹅池
绿地高中
运动场
体育馆+游泳馆
黄杨木巷
霍华德理发店
角落书店
加油站
清水塘
奇妙温室
狗舍+兽医
东绿街
沿河路
镇网球场
儿童游泳池
镇游泳池
镇棒球场
去往蓝山镇

人物介绍

三人小组的成员,聪明勇敢,喜欢读推理小说,紧急关头总能保持头脑冷静。喜欢在做事之前好好思考!

丁丁

三人小组的成员,活泼机智,喜欢吃好吃的食物,常常有意想不到的点子。

乔希

三人小组的成员,活泼开朗,喜欢从头到脚穿同一种颜色的衣服,总是那个能找到大部分线索的人。

露丝

幸运儿的爷爷，会给孩子们买彩票当圣诞礼物。

赫克托·奥利里

和赫克托·奥利里住在同一个老年公寓里，和赫克托·奥利里有过节。

塞尔达·祖特

幸运儿奥利里

幸运儿，是丁丁、乔希和露丝的朋友。

字母 L 代表 lost，丢失……

"每年，我爷爷都会给我们这些孩子寄一张圣诞贺卡，里面有七张彩票。每年，他都用我们的生日作为彩票号码……"

…………

幸运儿指着壁炉架上的一排圣诞贺卡。"今年，一个小偷闯进来，偷走了他寄的贺卡。我甚至还没打开信封！"

"我爷爷今天早上给我打电话，他很激动。他说他看了周日的报纸，看到中奖的彩票号码是我的生日！但是当我赶到这里拿贺卡的时候，贺卡不见了。"

…………

"嗯……那张彩票中了多少钱呢？"丁丁问。

幸运儿瘫坐在椅子上。"是七开头的呢。"他说。

"七千美元？"乔希激动得尖声说道。

"不，"幸运儿说着，摇了摇头，"是七百万美元。"

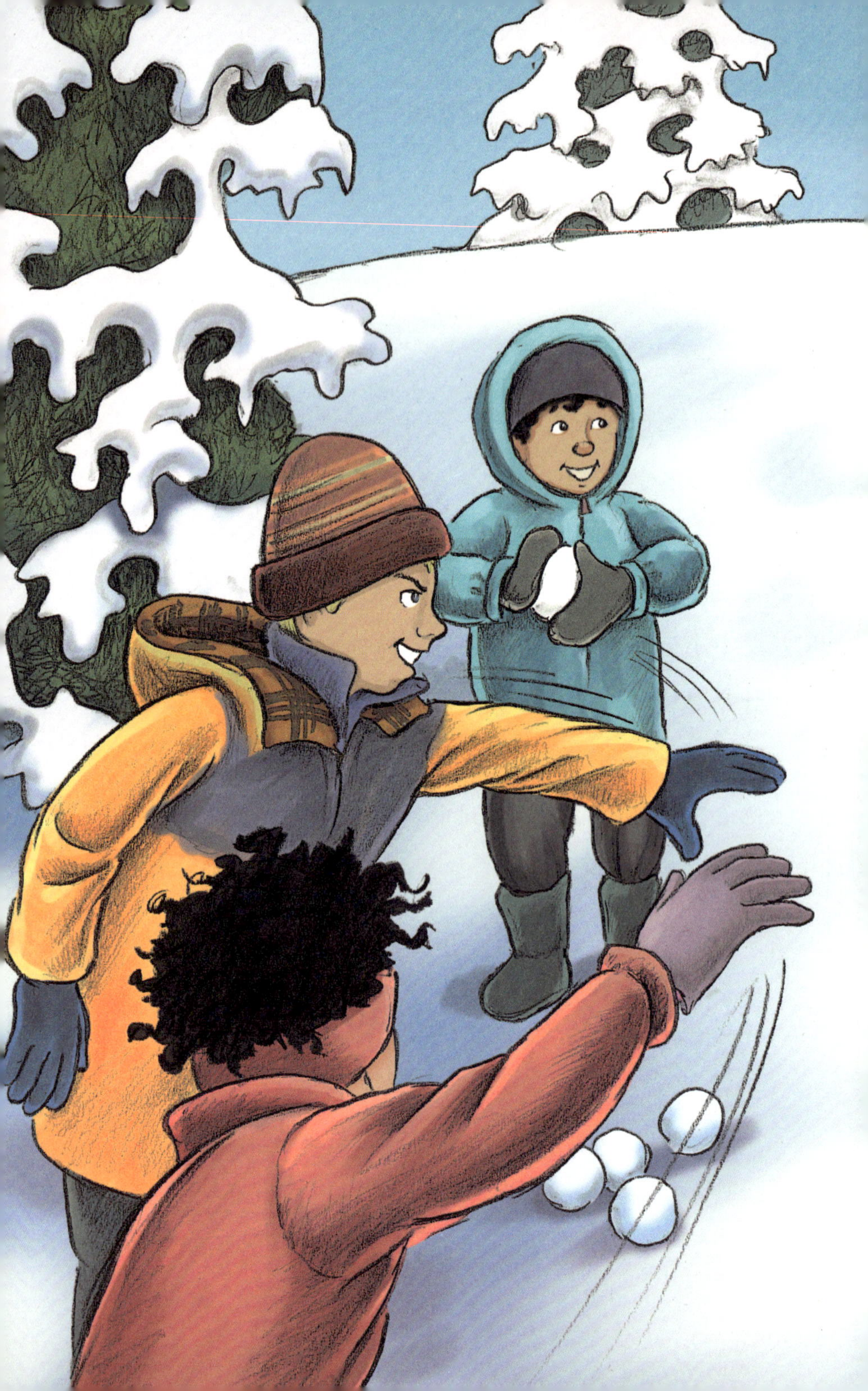

第一章

"准备,瞄准,发射!"露丝大声叫道。

她和丁丁朝着乔希堆起的堡垒扔雪球。

乔希咧着嘴笑了起来。"还差得远呢!"他大喊道,"露丝,你扔雪球像个女孩子!"

"我就是个女孩子!"露丝大声回复。她又扔出一个雪球,这次正好砸到乔希的脸上。

两边的人数是不对等的,但是没有人在乎这个。丁丁、露丝和她的小弟弟纳特对战乔希和他的狗狗帕尔。

纳特负责给他的姐姐和丁丁做雪球。帕尔则一边跑来跑去,一边狂吠着,试图叼住飞来的雪球。

9

更多的雪球向乔希的堡垒飞去。突然，丁丁大叫一声："快停下！"

两个穿着厚厚防雪服的小孩走进了丁丁家的后院。

"他们是谁？"露丝问。

丁丁耸耸肩。他和露丝放下雪球，向那两个小孩走去。

较高的那个是男孩。他穿着一件深蓝色的派克服，戴着一顶绿色的滑雪帽。较矮的是一个女孩。她的红色头发衬着蓝色眼睛和粉嘟嘟的脸颊。

"你们好，"丁丁说，"你们是谁？"

"我是约瑟芬！"女孩说。

"我是本。"男孩说，"我们的大哥有封信给你们。"

乔希从他的堡垒里面爬出来，走了过去。"你们的大哥是谁？"他问。

"幸运儿奥利里！"约瑟芬说。

"哦，现在我认出你了。"露丝说，"你们住在知更鸟路那边。"

本·奥利里拉开派克服口袋的拉链，掏出一

张皱巴巴的字条。"给你,幸运儿说让你们现在就看。"他把字条递给丁丁。

丁丁展开那张字条。

朋友们,我需要你们。
马上来我家。十万火急!
幸运儿

"幸运儿说是什么事了吗?"丁丁问。

"这是个秘密!"约瑟芬说。她的眼睛瞪得大大的。

丁丁、乔希和露丝你看看我,我看看你。

"我们走吧!"露丝说。她朝弟弟指了指他们的房子。"纳特,去陪妈妈吧。告诉她,我要去执行一项秘密任务!"

丁丁、乔希和露丝跟在本和约瑟芬后面。在帕尔的陪同下,他们朝绿地镇的西边走去。

眼下正值圣诞节假期,主街上的商店橱窗里都装饰着白色的小灯。大雪覆盖了草地,但车行道和人行道上的雪已被清理干净。

11

"你哥哥从大学回来了吗?"丁丁问本。

本点了点头说:"他几天前就回来了。"

"我们买了圣诞树和礼物!"约瑟芬说。

孩子们穿过主街,向大桥路走去。他们向左转,停在了知更鸟路33号。

房子很高,外墙是蓝色的。孩子们的玩具和运动用品散落在院子里和前廊上。

五个孩子迈着沉重的步子走上台阶。约瑟芬推开前门,步履蹒跚地走进大厅,地板上留下了雪脚印。

丁丁和其他孩子抖了抖靴子上的雪,然后走了进去。乔希让帕尔在前廊等着。

"幸运儿就在厨房里。"本一边说着,一边在前面带路。

幸运儿正在为他的六个弟弟妹妹做午餐。操作台上一字排开六份烤奶酪三明治、牛奶和香蕉。

"我们把他们带来了!"约瑟芬说。她和本把外套挂起来后,和其他兄弟姐妹一起坐了下来。

幸运儿跟上次丁丁见到的样子相比,长高了许多,头发也长长了许多。

被偷走的彩票

"嘿。"幸运儿说着,向丁丁、乔希和露丝点了点头。他对他的弟弟妹妹们说:"好了,你们吃午饭吧。乖乖的,不要打架!本,你来管着他们。"

"为什么是他来管?"约瑟芬尖声问道。

"因为我说他来管就是他来管。"幸运儿说,然后他对约瑟芬笑了笑,"你可以做本的助手,好吗?"

幸运儿招呼着丁丁、乔希和露丝跟他走。他们跨过足球、连指手套、书和曲棍球的球棒,跟着幸运儿走进了客厅。

一棵高高的圣诞树立在一个角落里,才装饰了一半。地板上满是装饰品和一串串的灯。

幸运儿一屁股坐到椅子上,摸了摸自己的头顶。"有人偷了我们的东西。"他说。

丁丁环顾了一圈。"他们拿走了什么?"丁丁问。

"彩票。"幸运儿说,"每年,我爷爷都会给我们这些孩子寄一张圣诞贺卡,里面有七张彩票。每年,他都用我们的生日作为彩票号码。每个圣诞节的早晨,我们都会在他的陪伴下一起打开贺卡。这是我们家的一项重要仪式。从来

没有人中奖，但爷爷总是乐在其中。"

　　幸运儿指着壁炉架上的一排圣诞贺卡。"今年，一个小偷闯进来，偷走了他寄的贺卡。我甚至还没打开信封！"

　　"但是小偷是怎么知道那里面有彩票的呢？"

乔希问。

"我不知道。"幸运儿说,"我爷爷今天早上给我打电话,他很激动。他说他看了周日的报纸,看到中奖的彩票号码是我的生日!但是当我赶到这里拿贺卡的时候,贺卡不见了。"

"这么说,小偷一定是在你爷爷之前知道中

奖号码的。"露丝说。

幸运儿点了点头。"每周六晚上，电视上会宣布彩票中奖者。"他说，"小偷肯定是那个时候知道的。"

"所以他是昨晚偷偷溜进来的，"乔希说，"在电视上看到这个消息后。他有打破窗户或者其他东西吗？"

"没有必要。"幸运儿说，"后门的锁已经坏了好几年了，那家伙可以直接走进来！"

"嗯……那张彩票中了多少钱呢？"丁丁问。

幸运儿瘫坐在椅子上。"是七开头的呢。"他说。

"七千美元？"乔希激动得尖声说道。

"不，"幸运儿说着，摇了摇头，"是七百万美元。"

第二章

丁丁盯着幸运儿。没有人动,也没有人说话。厨房里传来咯咯的笑声和吃午饭的声音。

"七百……百万美元!"乔希终于发出了声音。

幸运儿点了点头。"爷爷高兴得几乎说不出话来。"他说,"但当我告诉他贺卡不见了的时候,我想他都要哭了吧。"

坐在椅子里的幸运儿猛地探向前。"你们能找到那个小偷,把我的彩票拿回来吗?我不能离开家,因为我还要照看这些孩子。"

"要是太迟了怎么办?"露丝问,"也许小偷已经把彩票兑换了!"

幸运儿摇了摇头。"他还兑换不了。今天是周日,兑奖的地方不开门。但他可以在明天早上那里开门的时候去兑奖。"

就在这时,他们听到厨房里传来撞击声,撞击声过后是一阵窃窃私语声,接着又是一阵咯咯的笑声。

"我想我最好还是回到厨房。"幸运儿说,"我答应他们午饭后带他们去滑雪。所以你们能帮我吗?"

"我们当然会帮忙了!"丁丁说。

幸运儿咧嘴一笑:"那太好了,我——"

一个三英尺[1]高的红发男孩激动地走进房间。"斯图尔特把我的香蕉弄烂了!"那孩子哭着说,"我什么也没对他做!"

"别哭了,弗雷迪。我们会让斯图[2]把香蕉清理干净的。"幸运儿说。他拉着弗雷迪的手向厨房走去。"给我打电话,好吗?"他回过头说。

---

1. 英尺:英美制长度单位。1英尺 = 0.3048米。——编者
2. 斯图:斯图尔特的昵称。——编者

被偷走的彩票

孩子们便自己出去了。帕尔在前廊上睡着了,发出轻微的鼾声。

"所以我们怎么才能找到这个小偷呢?"乔希问,"我们从哪里开始找?"

站在门廊上,丁丁向前院看去。奥利里家的孩子们玩耍过的地方,积雪都被踩踏了。

"如果那个小偷昨晚来了这里,也许他会留下痕迹。"丁丁说,"我们去后面看看。"

孩子们绕到房子后面。奥利里家的孩子们只在前院玩耍过,所以后院的雪没有被破坏,十分平整。院子四周都是高大的松树。

"看!"乔希说。只见一串脚印从院子那头通向后门。

"那家伙一定是从树林里出来的!"丁丁说。

"然后他原路返回了。"露丝说,"这些脚印是双向的。"

孩子们顺着脚印走进了树林。脚印向右偏去,孩子们也跟着脚印向右边走去。

帕尔把鼻子伸进雪里,嗅着每一个脚印。突然,它叫了一声。

乔希弯下腰,从雪地里捡起一个闪闪发亮的东西。

"这是什么?"露丝问。

乔希伸出戴着连指手套的手。他手里拿着一张被拧成小领结形状的锡纸。

"你们觉得这是小偷掉的吗?"乔希问。

"留着吧。"丁丁说,"这是我们的第一条线索。"

几分钟后,他们走出树林,来到大桥路。

"没有脚印了。"乔希说着,朝小路左右看了看,"小偷可以从这里走到任何地方。"

"或者开车。"露丝说,"也许那家伙把车停在这里,然后徒步进了树林。"

天越来越冷了。大片的雪花开始飘落。三个孩子冻得脸颊通红,开始流鼻涕。

"我们去埃莉餐馆喝点热巧克力吧。"丁丁建议道,"然后我们再计划下一步该怎么做。"

沿着大桥路走一小段路就到了主街上的埃莉餐馆。孩子们推门而入,在埃莉的橡胶垫上跺了跺脚。帕尔摇摇晃晃地跟在乔希后面。

"你们好,孩子们。你好,帕尔。你们要来点

什么?"埃莉在柜台后面问。

孩子们闪身进入一个隔间。"热巧克力。"乔希一边说,一边挣扎着脱下羽绒服,"上面再加一层厚厚的鲜奶油!"

他们等待的时候,丁丁思考着幸运儿告诉他们的话。

"朋友们,周六晚上看电视的人都知道中奖

21

号码,对吧?"他说,"但是小偷怎么知道中奖的彩票在幸运儿的圣诞贺卡里?"

就在这时,埃莉走了过来。"热巧克力来了!"她说着,把三个高高的马克杯放在桌上。每杯热巧克力上面的鲜奶油都堆得像个小山,上面还点缀着巧克力屑。

"可别把你那可爱的鼻子烫伤了,乔希。"埃莉转身时说。

乔希的脸顿时红了起来,接着,他舔了舔鲜奶油的顶部。

丁丁吹着他的热巧克力。"有人有思路了吗?"他问。

"不知怎么回事,小偷知道幸运儿的爷爷把彩票寄给了幸运儿。"乔希说。

"但是他是怎么知道的呢?"露丝问。

"也许小偷认识幸运儿的爷爷,"乔希说,"也许他们是朋友!"

"这个思路不错,乔希!"露丝说,"我们为什么不跟幸运儿的爷爷谈谈呢?"

丁丁从口袋里摸出一枚二十五美分的硬币。

"我先出去一下，朋友们。"他说，"我要打电话给幸运儿。"

丁丁从乔希的腿上爬过。"快喝吧，"丁丁说，"但别把你那可爱的鼻子烫伤了！"

第三章

"好了。"几分钟后,丁丁回来说,"幸运儿的爷爷是赫克托·奥利里。他住在叫'心房'的老年公寓。我们去看看他吧。"

"我妈妈说喝东西太快不好。"乔希咕哝着。他舔了舔嘴上的奶油,闪身出了隔间。"喝太快容易打嗝。"说完,他便打了一个嗝。

孩子们朝主街走去。雪不停地下,人行道渐渐变白了。当雪花从帕尔的鼻子边落下时,帕尔试图叼住它们。

老年公寓的窗户上装饰着花环。大门的牌子上写着:

被偷走的彩票

欢迎来到"心房"
为好人提供
好的生活

大厅里,一棵圣诞树立在中央的地板上。CD机播放着圣诞颂歌。

"我能帮你们什么吗?"一位坐着轮椅的白发妇人转着轮子向他们而来。

"我们是来找奥利里先生的。"丁丁说。

妇人笑了。"赫克托在那里。"她指着一边说,"穿过旋转门,找一个戴黄色棒球帽的人,那就是他了。但你的狗必须在这里等,我会替你照看它的。"

"谢谢。"乔希说着,把狗绳递给她,"它叫帕尔,它真的很友好。"

妇人俯下身来,拍了拍帕尔的头。"我一看它就知道了。"她说。

孩子们朝旋转门走去。门上贴着一张字条,上面写着:"不要让鸟出来!"

"鸟?"乔希说,"什么鸟?"

丁丁耸了耸肩。他推开一扇沉重的木门,孩

子们进入了房间。

房间里又暖和又潮湿,像热带雨林一样。阳光透过玻璃天花板和玻璃墙照进来。在一角,喷泉从光滑的石堆间喷涌而出。孩子们目之所及都是植物。大多数植物被放在吊盆里,但也有一些被放在大盆里。一棵树正好从地板上的一个裂缝里长出来,它的枝叶像一把巨大的绿伞。

许多长尾小鹦鹉在植物间飞来飞去。它们长着绿色、蓝色和黄色的羽毛,看起来就像会飞的珠宝。

"这太棒了!"当一只长尾小鹦鹉从他头顶飞过时,乔希一边说一边躲了起来。他脱下羽绒夹克、帽子和连指手套。

丁丁脱下外套,环视着房间。老爷爷老奶奶们有些在喂鸟,有些在打牌,还有些只是在打盹。他看见一个人头上落着一只长尾小鹦鹉!

"我看到那顶黄色的帽子了。"露丝指着站在工作台前的一个人说。孩子们走了过去。

赫克托·奥利里穿着宽松的运动衫和旧牛仔裤。他正在给一个小鸟窝钉屋顶。孩子们走近时,他抬起头。

"嘿,大家好!"赫克托说,"你们在卖糖果吗?我每样都买一个!"

丁丁摇了摇头。"我们是幸运儿的朋友。"丁丁说,"关于你寄给他的彩票的事,他都告诉我们了。"

老人友好的眼神突然变得充满怒气。"我气得都要吐口水了!"他说,"这是个什么世道,小偷连圣诞贺卡都偷!如果我抓到那个小偷,我会让他后悔见过赫克托·弗朗西斯·奥利里[1]!"

"幸运儿拜托我们帮忙找出是谁偷走了它。"露丝说,"我们能问你几个问题吗?"

---

1. 赫克托·弗朗西斯·奥利里:赫克托·奥利里的全名,弗朗西斯是他的中间名。——编者

"好吧。"赫克托说着，放下他的锤子。"跟我来。"

幸运儿的爷爷带着他们来到一圈椅子旁，椅子中间是一张矮桌子。一只蓝色的长尾小鹦鹉立在桌子上，嘴里还叼着一个小钉子。

"喂，你从哪儿弄来的钉子？"赫克托拿起钉子放进口袋里。"蓝小子[1]喜欢任何闪闪发光的东西。"他说，"好了，你们问吧。"

"有人知道你把彩票寄到了幸运儿的家里。"丁丁说，"我们想知道你有没有把这件事告诉别人，比如你的朋友。"

"嗯……我当然告诉过别人！"赫克托说，他向房间里的其他人挥了挥手，"我告诉了所有人！"

---

1. 蓝小子：叼着钉子的蓝色长尾小鹦鹉的名字。——编者

第四章

乔希看了看周围的老人。"他们当中会有小偷吗?"他低声说道。

赫克托点点头,然后把一根手指放在嘴唇上。"看到那个织毛衣的女人了吗?"他朝一个坐在沙发上的白发妇人扬了扬下巴。

"她是塞尔达·祖特。"他低声说,"她是个真正的窥探者!她想要了解这里每个人的情况。我知道她偷拿过零食车上的饼干!"

被偷走的彩票

孩子们顺着赫克托的目光望去。塞尔达·祖特是一位祖母般慈祥的老妇人,她的膝盖上放满了粉红色的纱线和闪闪发亮的编织针。

"塞尔达讨厌我。"他接着说,"因为我把她

偷饼干的事告诉了厨师。如果这个地方有人想报复我的话,那就是塞尔达。"

丁丁试着想象这位老妇人穿过雪地去偷幸运儿家的东西的画面,但他想象不出来。

"我会看着她的。"赫克托小声说,"如果她开始表现得很有钱,我会告诉你们的!"

蓝小子突然飞到露丝的头顶,开始轻轻地啄她的红发带。

"它喜欢鲜艳的颜色。"赫克托解释道。

乔希从口袋里掏出一支铅笔。"你可以借我几张纸吗?"他问,"我得把露丝头上有只鸟的样子画下来!"

赫克托咯咯地笑了,起身去拿纸。

"别动,露丝。"乔希低声说。

"它在上面干什么?"露丝问。

"我想它在筑巢。"丁丁笑着说。

赫克托拿着一张纸回来了。乔希开始画画,露丝则像雕像一样坐着,一动不动。

乔希忙着画画时,丁丁在想赫克托告诉他们的话。心房里的任何一个居民都可能是小偷,但丁丁不这么认为。

"奥利里先生，你能告诉我们你是在哪里买的彩票吗？"丁丁问道。

"当然。"赫克托说着，把椅子朝丁丁拉近了一点，"我周五早上在超市买的。"

"你买的时候旁边还有其他顾客吗？"

赫克托闭上眼睛，然后猛地睁开。"是的，我现在想起来了。有一群人站在那里聊雪的事。有些人要买糖果和口香糖，有些人排在我后面等着买彩票。"

"会不会有人看到了你选的号码？"

"有可能。"赫克托说，"我把我所有孙子孙女的生日都写了下来，递给了店员。然后，她把号码输入彩票机，七张彩票就蹦了出来。任何人都可以看到我写下的数字。"

丁丁想了一会儿："你有没有提到你要把它们送给你的孙子孙女们？"

突然，赫克托的脸变得惨白。"我想我提到过吧。"他说，"当我在信封上写上地址，并把彩票放进去的时候，我没想过这会有什么害处，因为我从没想过彩票会中奖。"

赫克托叹了口气,摇了摇头:"我和我的这张大嘴巴啊!我只是忍不住要炫耀一下。我在他们家吃晚饭,幸运儿在大学里的表现,诸如此类的事。"

蓝小子离开露丝的头,飞快地穿过房间,落在一个吊盆上。

"糟了。"乔希咕哝,"我还没开始画呢。"

"让我看看。"露丝一边说,一边伸手去拿画纸。

乔希咧嘴一笑,把画对折,塞进了口袋。"不行,等我画完再看。"

丁丁站了起来。"非常感谢,奥利里先生。"他说,"我想我们应该去和卖彩票的工作人员谈谈。你知道她的名字吗?"

"当然知道了。"赫克托说,"她叫多萝西。她是新来的,但她会记得我的。如果你们抓住了偷彩票的人,今年你们的圣诞袜里就会有一份额外的礼物!"

"太好了!"乔希说,"我通常只得到一些毫无新意的内衣内裤!"

被偷走的彩票

孩子们说完再见，离开了房间。帕尔正在一盆棕榈树下睡觉，狗绳就在它的爪子上。乔希把它叫醒，孩子们又穿上了外套，戴上了帽子。

公寓外面的主街上，风雪向孩子们迎面吹来。

"你们觉得塞尔达·祖特是小偷吗？"乔希问，"她看起来像我奶奶！"

"如果心房的老人们知道赫克托每年圣诞节都会给他的孙子孙女们寄彩票的话，"露丝说，"那他们都有嫌疑！"

"朋友们，"丁丁说，"你们也听到赫克托说的话了。他喜欢谈论他的孙子孙女们。绿地镇的任何一个人都可能是小偷！"

孩子们在主街上步履蹒跚地走着。两分钟后，他们匆匆走进超市，朝彩票柜台走去。

"跟我来。"乔希告诉帕尔。帕尔摇摇晃晃地走在他旁边。

"我想那就是多萝西。"露丝指着柜台后面的一个年轻的金发女人说。她头顶的墙上挂着一个小型的安全摄像头。

丁丁走近柜台。"打扰一下，"他说，"请问你

35

是多萝西吗?"

那女人抬起头来,嘴里还嚼着一块口香糖。"我是。"她指着自己的名牌,上面写着"多萝西·卡尔姆"。

"人们都叫我多特。你们是谁?"

"我是丁丁。"他说,"这是乔希和露丝。"

多特·卡尔姆吹了一个粉色的小泡泡,等它爆开后继续咀嚼着口香糖。"很高兴见到你们。"她说。

被偷走的彩票

"我们想知道你是否记得,周五上午你卖过一堆彩票的事。"露丝说。

女人笑了:"孩子们,我每天都能卖出几百张彩票。"

"一共是七张彩票。"丁丁解释道。关于幸运儿的爷爷,以及彩票是如何从幸运儿的家里被偷走的事,他都告诉了多特。

多特盯着丁丁看了一会儿,然后亲切地笑了。"是的,我记得他。"她说,"一位不错的老绅士,喜欢说一些杂七杂八的话。他告诉了我有关他孙子孙女的一切,以及他每年都给他们寄彩票的事。"

"你还记得他买彩票的时候,都有谁在周围闲逛吗?"乔希问。

多特打开一块口香糖,把它塞进嘴里。她咀嚼了几秒钟,然后说:"很多人都站在周围。"

"你注意到有谁离得很近,近到可以听到奥利里先生说的话吗?"露丝问。

多特眯起眼睛,望向远方。"是的,"最后她说,"我记得有一个人很特别。"她颤抖着说:"他长得很吓人。"

"你能描述一下他的样貌吗?"露丝问。

多特笑了。"我不仅能描述他的样貌。"她说,"我还知道他的名字!"

第五章

"你知道他是谁?"丁丁问。

"只知道他的名字。"多特说,"他穿着一件保龄球衫,球衫口袋上绣着'乔'。"

"现在我们终于有进展了!"乔希说。

"我想,他把球队的名字印在了他的球衫后面。"多特补充道,"他离开的时候我才注意到这一点,但他走得太远了,我没看清。"

乔希拿出铅笔,翻过赫克托给他的那张画纸。"如果你告诉我他长什么样,我可以把他画出来。"乔希说。

"你可以吗?"多特问,"好吧,让我想想。他的头发是黑色的，有点蓬松。他留着小胡子，很稀疏的小胡子。他的两颗门牙之间还有一道缝。"

"他大概多大年龄？"乔希画画时，露丝在一边问道。

多特闭上眼睛，啪啪地吹着口香糖。"我想大概二十五岁左右。"她最后说道。

"他有伤疤、文身之类的吗？"丁丁看着小偷的脸在乔希的纸上逐渐成形，问道。

多特摇了摇头："我记得没有。"

乔希举起他的画，好让多特看到。"这看起来像那个人吗？"他问。

"是的，差不多。"她说，"但是你把他的下巴画得太方了。他的下巴有点尖。"

乔希擦去男人的下巴，又用铅笔画了几下，然后再次给多特看。

"就是他！"她说，"孩子，你可以靠画画谋生了！"

乔希脸红了："谢谢，这就是我长大后想做的事情。"

露丝看着丁丁和乔希。"我们应该把这个带

被偷走的彩票

到警察局,给法伦警官看。"她说。

"好主意。"丁丁说。

孩子们谢过多特·卡尔姆,就准备离开了。

"嘿,我刚想到一件事。"她在他们身后喊道,"乔说如果他有足够的钱,他打算搬到加利

福尼亚去。"

"谢谢。"丁丁说,"我们会告诉法伦警官的。"他们匆匆走出了超市。

雪还在下,风把雪花吹到他们的脸上,雪花落在他们的睫毛上。乔希把他的画塞进羽绒服里,以免它被淋湿。

过了一会儿,他们到了警察局,敲了敲法伦警官的门。

"进来吧。"法伦警官说,"要吃点圣诞点心吗?"他拿出一盘饼干。

"我们想举报一起犯罪。"丁丁说着,拿起一块饼干,坐在办公室的一把椅子上。

乔希和露丝每人拿了一块饼干,坐在丁丁旁边。乔希把饼干掰成两半,给了帕尔一半。

法伦警官靠着自己的胳膊肘。"我听着呢。"他说。

丁丁告诉了他幸运儿家彩票被偷的事。

当丁丁说到"七百万美元"时,法伦警官轻轻地吹了一声口哨。

露丝接着告诉法伦警官他们去拜访了幸运儿

的爷爷。最后,乔希复述了他们和多特·卡尔姆的谈话。他从羽绒服里抽出那幅画,给法伦警官看。"她告诉我们这个人叫乔。"他说。

"这画画得相当不错,乔希。"法伦警官一边说,一边研究那幅画,"你知道,这张脸看起来很眼熟。"

"你觉得我们能在明天之前找到他吗?"丁丁问道。

法伦警官扬起一条眉毛。"在不知道他姓什么的情况下,我无法追踪他。"他说,"为什么这么急?"

"因为明天他就可以去兑换幸运儿的彩票了。"露丝说。

"而且卖彩票的那位女士说这家伙要去加利福尼亚!"乔希说。

法伦警官站了起来。"我会尽力的。乔希,我能留着这张画吗?"

"好吧,我还打算画完露丝呢。"他说,"我在背面还画了一幅画。"

法伦警官把纸翻过来。他朝露丝咧嘴一笑:

"这是有只鸟在你头上吗?"

"是一只长尾小鹦鹉。"露丝说完,向他介绍了蓝小子。

丁丁把塞尔达·祖特的事也告诉了法伦警官。"赫克托说她偷过饼干。"他补充道。

"我们会查一查她的。"法伦警官说着,朝复印机走去。

他把乔希的画放在机器上,复制了一份,然后把原件还给了乔希。

"我会把这张画发出去,看看会有什么发现。"他说。

"如果没有及时找到那个小偷怎么办?"丁丁问道。

"嗯,这倒是个问题。"法伦说,"据我所知,谁出示了中奖的彩票,谁就能得到这笔钱,不会被问任何问题。"

"即使彩票是他们偷的?"乔希说,"这不公平!"

"我知道这不公平。"法伦说,"但彩票中心的人员必须把钱付给持票人。"

法伦警官想了一会儿。"我想,如果他们有证

被偷走的彩票

据证明彩票是偷来的,他们就会扣下这笔钱。"他看着孩子们,"但是你们没有确凿的证据。你的朋友不能证明彩票是他的爷爷买了寄给他们的。"

丁丁站了起来。"那我们就去找证据!"他说。

第六章

孩子们谢过法伦警官后离开了。"咱们去我家商量一下吧。"丁丁说。他们走到外面,走进不停飘落的雪花中间。

"还商量,你可真是个笨蛋。"乔希气急败坏地说,"我得吃午饭了!那半块饼干让我饿了!"

丁丁笑了:"好吧,那我们一边吃饭一边想想下一步该怎么做。"

到达丁丁家的前门时,他们看起来就像三个小雪人。他们在大厅里脱下外套和靴子,摘掉帽子和连指手套,然后朝厨房走去。

帕尔小跑进来,立刻在暖气片旁"扑通"一

声坐下。

丁丁在桌上发现了他妈妈写的一张字条。

丁丁：

我得把车送去换上雪地轮胎。你先用微波炉加热一下汤，然后做花生酱三明治吃吧。我很快就回来。

爱你的妈妈

"我来做三明治。"乔希一边说一边在橱柜里翻着。

丁丁热了一些番茄汤，孩子们把午餐拿进了书房。"有人想看录像带吗？"丁丁问道。

"录像！"露丝突然说，"就是这个！"

"就是哪个？"乔希问。

"彩票柜台上有一个摄像头。"露丝说，"如果乔所在的保龄球队的名字印在他的衣服后面，摄像头也许会拍到！"

"好主意！"丁丁说，"我最好把这件事告诉法伦警官。"

他拿起电话打给警察局。丁丁告诉法伦警官关于摄像头的事后,他拨通了信息台的电话,询问了超市的号码。然后丁丁又拨通电话,要求转给彩票柜台的多特接听。

丁丁问多特,赫克托买七张彩票的那天,摄像头是否开着。他听完对方的答复,说了声谢谢,然后挂断了电话。

"她会让她的老板去查看录像带的。"丁丁说,"如果乔所在的保龄球队的名字出现了,多特的老板就会打电话给法伦警官。"

"我在想,这个叫乔的家伙会不会在健身中心打保龄球。"乔希说。

"好想法,乔希。"丁丁说,"我们可以吃完饭去看看。"

"这是什么?"露丝突然叫了起来。有什么东西从她的头发里掉了下来,落在了她的汤里。

乔希咯咯笑了:"也许是虱子。"

"不,乔希,这不是虱子!"露丝说着,用汤勺捞起一个亮晶晶的东西,"又是一个锡纸做的领结!"

被偷走的彩票

乔希从口袋里掏出之前那个领结。除了番茄汤里的那个被弄湿了之外,这两个锡纸领结一模一样。

露丝看着丁丁和乔希。"这个东西是怎么跑到我头发里的?"她问道。

孩子们面面相觑。"蓝小子!"他们同时喊道。

"它落在你头上的时候,嘴里一定叼着这东西。"丁丁说,"它把这锡纸领结藏在你的头发里了!"

"是的,但是它从哪儿弄来这个领结的呢?"乔希问。

"肯定来自心房。"丁丁说,"那些长尾小鹦鹉从来没有出去过。"

"那么小偷也一定在心房!"露丝说,"也许就是塞尔达·祖特!"

"也有可能是乔。"乔希说,"他可能去过心房,向人询问赫克托的孙子住在哪里。"

就在这时,丁丁的妈妈快步走了进来。"路太难走了,而且外面还在下雪!"她说。

她脱下大衣和靴子,解开围巾,说:"今晚很适合拿着一大碗爆米花好好享受享受。"

A to Z 神秘案件

"我们滑完雪一般都会这样做。"露丝说。

"你会滑雪?"乔希问。

"当然了。我们一家人几年前就学会了越野滑雪。"露丝说,"嘿,不如我来教你们滑雪吧?这样我们在镇里到处走动就容易多了。"

"这是个好主意。"丁丁的妈妈说,"但是你们

被偷走的彩票

要远离车行道。扫雪车已经全力出动了。"

孩子们收拾好餐具,穿上羽绒服,走到隔壁的露丝家。

露丝从车库里拿了三套越野滑雪装备(滑雪板和滑雪杖),然后教丁丁和乔希如何把滑雪板固定在靴子上。

"好啦,现在就可以滑了。"她说,"在雪地上滑动,用雪杖保持平衡。"

"小菜一碟。"乔希说着,往前迈了一步。

然后,他摔进了雪堆。

第七章

很快，丁丁和乔希就可以跟着露丝在后院滑行而不摔跟头了。

"你们学得很快。"她说，"我们为什么不滑着去健身中心呢？可以在保龄球馆给人看看乔希画的画。"

孩子们从学校附近滑过。帕尔在他们后面蹦蹦跳跳，在雪地里跳得很高。

滑到主街时，他们等一辆扫雪车经过，然后滑到街道的另一边。

他们在大桥路和主街交叉的拐角处停了下来。一个男人带着一个看起来很重的包和一双雪

鞋从健身中心走了出来。

男人对孩子们笑了笑。"今天可真是个外出滑雪的好天气。"他说。

"我们刚学会滑雪。"乔希说。

那个人把他的雪鞋扔到积雪的人行道上,然后试图把它们系在靴子上。

"我帮你拿包好吗?"丁丁问道。

"谢谢。"那人说,"可别砸到你的脚趾头,包里是我的保龄球。"

"你是保龄球队的吗?"乔希问。

"是的。我在绿地镇巨人队打保龄球。"他说,"怎么了,你们想加入儿童保龄球队吗?"

"不是,但我们想知道你是否认识这个人。"乔希拿出他画的乔给那人看。

"嗯……"那人边说边研究那幅画,"他不是我们队的,但他看起来很眼熟。"

"他叫乔。"露丝说。

那人摇了摇头,咂了咂舌头。"我很确定我见过这张脸。"他说,"你们为什么不去里面问问呢?"

"谢谢,我们这就去。"丁丁说。

那个人穿好雪鞋,拿回他装保龄球的包。"谢谢你的帮助。"他说完,迈着沉重的步子沿主街走去。

孩子们拂去长凳上的雪,坐下来取下滑雪板。他们带着滑雪板和滑雪杖走进健身中心,顺着一段楼梯向下走。帕尔紧紧地跟在他们后面。

两条长长的保龄球道占据了地下室的大部分空间。一群人在打保龄球,有些人穿了口袋上印着名字的衬衫。

角落里有一辆手推车,一个女人在那里卖热狗和苏打水。

乔希和帕尔停了下来,盯着那辆手推车。"我们为什么不吃个午饭?"乔希问。

"我们吃过午饭了,记得吗?"丁丁一边说一边环顾四周。

被偷走的彩票

"你看见乔了吗?"露丝问。

丁丁摇了摇头。没有一个人长得像乔希画上的人。

"让我们问问有谁认识他。"乔希说。

孩子们把滑雪板和滑雪杖放在一个角落里,让帕尔看管。他们开始把乔希的画给旁边不打保龄球的人看。

有几个人说乔看起来像他们见过的人。

一个女人说乔长得像她的丈夫乔治。

一个男人说乔的脸很像他在邮局的通缉令上看到的银行抢劫犯。

但是没有人说他们认识乔。

"好吧,真是浪费时间。"乔希咕哝着。

在走出地下室的路上,孩子们路过了热狗摊。乔希打开他的画。"你见过这个人吗?"他问卖热狗的女人。

那个女人笑了。"你是在逗我吗,小家伙?"

"你这话是什么意思?"乔希问。

"我的意思是,"女人用一根手指点着画说,"这上面画的是你,只是年纪比你现在大一点。"

孩子们仔细看了看那幅画。

"她说得对!"露丝说,"除了胡子,这看起来确实像乔希。"

"这就是为什么每个人都说这家伙看起来很眼熟。"丁丁说,"他长得和你很像!"

乔希盯着他的画:"这么说,根本就没有乔这个人?"

手推车后面的女人一直在听他们说话。"听起来你们是白费力气了。"她说。

"可是多特为什么要让我们去找一个根本不存在的人呢?"乔希问,"我不明白。"

丁丁耸了耸肩。"我也不知道。"他说,"我们为什么不去问问她呢?超市就在街对面。"

第八章

孩子们带着雪具，穿过大桥路，走进了超市。在这个下雪的周日下午，这家超市几乎空无一人。

"看！"丁丁指着贴在彩票机上的一张小字条。

因暴雪打烊
请您明日再来

就在这时，一个少年走过来。他拿着一把扫帚和一个簸箕。他衬衫上的名牌上写着"埃里克"。

"酷狗狗。"他笑着对帕尔说。

"请问多特还在不在?"露丝问。

"不在。"那少年说,"她走了有一会儿了,走的时候还非常高兴。她说:'圣诞快乐,埃里克!'然后塞给我二十美元。我说:'哇,谢谢你,多特!'"

埃里克走到柜台后面。

"多特把这儿弄得真是一团乱。"他一边打扫一边咕哝着。

"嗯……多特的老板在不在?"丁丁说,"我们能和那位男士谈谈吗?"

埃里克蹲在柜台后面。"老板是位女士,不是男士。"他说着,站了起来,"老板是米尔克太太。不过她好像生病了,这一周都在感冒。"

"感冒?"丁丁说,"可是多特告诉我,她会跟——"

突然,帕尔叫了一声。它在埃里克扫出来的一堆垃圾里嗅了嗅。

"你发现了什么?"乔希问。"给我吧,小狗。"乔希掰开帕尔的嘴,掏出了一个东西。

"看,伙计们!"乔希拿出一个小小的锡纸领结。

露丝从乔希手里拿过领结，然后从口袋里掏出另外两个。这三个锡纸领结完全一样。

孩子们弯下身子，看向柜台里——地板上满是小小的锡纸领结。

A to Z 神秘案件

突然间,一切都说得通了。丁丁从乔希和露丝脸上的表情看出来,他们也想通了。

"快走!"丁丁低声说。他抓起滑雪板和滑雪杖,匆匆奔向出口。

乔希和露丝也带着滑雪板和滑雪杖跟在后面。"走吧,帕尔。"乔希对他的狗说。

"你们想的和我想的一样吗?"露丝一出门就问道。

"是的。"丁丁说,"天啊,我们真是笨蛋!我们回到埃莉餐馆去吧。"他们艰难地穿过雪地,挤进餐馆。

埃莉抬起头。"一天来两次?"她说,"再来三杯热巧克力吗?"

"谢谢你,埃莉。"丁丁说。孩子们闪身进入一个隔间,帕尔"扑通"一声趴在他们脚边。

"这么说,多特就是那个小偷,对吧?"乔希说。

"是的。"丁丁说,"多特把彩票卖给赫克托后,一定留下了赫克托写下孩子们生日的那张纸。所以她才知道幸运儿的彩票中了奖。"

"但她不知道幸运儿住在哪里。"露丝说,"所以她不得不去心房打听。她不想和赫克托对话,所以她可能问了别人。她一定是在偷偷打听的时候弄丢了一个领结!"

"然后她去了幸运儿的家,偷走了贺卡……"丁丁补充道。

"并且在雪地里又弄丢了一个领结。"乔希说。

"然后她编了一个关于乔的故事来迷惑我们。"露丝说。

丁丁看着乔希:"我敢打赌,她按照你的脸来描述是因为你画画的时候,她正好盯着你看。"

"是的。我太笨了,甚至没有注意到那是我。"乔希说。

"来吧,孩子们。"埃莉把热巧克力端到桌子上,"这些算我请大家喝的,还有招待小帕尔的一点食物。"

埃莉把一碗切碎的汉堡放在帕尔跟前。帕尔抬起头,对着埃莉眨了眨它那棕色的大眼睛,然后把鼻子扎进了碗里。

"非常感谢你,埃莉。"乔希说,"也代帕尔说声谢谢。"

露丝一直在喝她的热巧克力。"你们知道的,朋友们,"她说,"我们无法证明是多特偷了彩票。我们知道是她干的,但法伦警官会说:'证据在哪里?'"

丁丁点点头:"是啊,他肯定会这么说。"

"好吧,我们得找到证据。"乔希说,"不然对幸运儿一家来说,这个圣诞节肯定会过得很糟糕——七百万美元泡汤了。"

孩子们喝着热巧克力,闷闷不乐,桌子下面却传来快乐的咀嚼声。

第九章

丁丁邀请乔希和露丝来家里过夜。他们在丁丁的圣诞树前展开睡袋。帕尔爬进了乔希的睡袋里,开始打鼾。

外面雪还在不停地下。孩子们在想办法证明是多特偷了幸运儿的彩票。

"要是我们有证人就好了。"露丝躺在睡袋里说。

"可惜她没有留下写着她名字的东西。"乔希说着,把脚放在帕尔的身上暖了暖。

"那事情就太容易解决了。"丁丁咕哝着。他爬进睡袋,闭上眼睛。

然后丁丁进入了梦乡,但这不是一个圣诞前夜应有的快乐的梦。

这是一场噩梦。梦里,丁丁不知道在外面的哪个地方,他在雪地里挣扎着。他光着脚,没有戴手套,浑身发冷。当他试图找到回家的路时,却发现他的脚印交错着……

丁丁大叫着坐了起来。在乔希的睡袋里,帕尔呜咽了一声。

"没事的。"丁丁低声说。他坐着想了一会儿,从睡袋里爬出来。他踮着脚,拿着闹钟走了下来。在大厅里,丁丁打了一个电话,小声地留了言,然后回到客厅。

他把闹铃定到六点钟,并把闹钟放在睡袋底部,然后,他爬回睡袋里继续睡觉。

当闹铃响时,丁丁用脚趾按下了关闭按钮。他从睡袋里钻了出来,摇了摇乔希和露丝。"醒醒。"他低声说,"小点声!"

乔希打了个哈欠,露丝眨了眨眼睛。他们静静地看着丁丁穿上靴子。

丁丁咧嘴一笑。"走吧,朋友们,"他说,"厨

房见!"

"最好是有早餐吃。"乔希嘀咕着。

过了一会儿,三个孩子喝着橙汁,吃着烤面包。乔希和帕尔分享了他的面包,然后帕尔回到了乔希温暖的睡袋里。

丁丁把他的噩梦讲给乔希和露丝听。"我只能看到自己在雪地上的脚印。"他说,"当我醒来的时候,我想起了乔希说过的话——他希望多特能留下写着她名字的东西。"

他咧嘴一笑:"我知道怎么证明幸运儿的爷爷确实买了那张彩票了。"

"怎么证明?"乔希说,"而且你为什么要在大半夜告诉我们这些?"

"指纹。"丁丁说,"那张被偷的彩票上会有谁的指纹呢?"

"如果是多特偷的,那上面肯定会有她的指纹。"露丝说。

"但她的指纹无论如何都会出现在彩票上,因为是她把彩票卖给了幸运儿的爷爷。"乔希说,"这能证明什么呢?"

"不能证明什么。"丁丁说,"但是那张彩票上不仅有多特的指纹……"

乔希和露丝盯着他。"你说得对!"露丝说,"彩票上也有赫克托的指纹!"

"他们能从彩票上提取指纹吗?"乔希问。

丁丁点了点头。"我想可以的。我在电视上看过一个关于指纹的节目。"他说,"人的手指是油性的,我们一碰到纸,纸上就会留下油渍。"

"我们应该把这件事告诉法伦警官。"露丝说。

丁丁点点头:"我在他的语音信箱里留言了,让他在蓝山镇的彩票总部和我们见面。"

"可是那儿离这儿有两英里[1]呢!"乔希说着,朝窗外看了一眼,"而且外面还很黑。"

"我们可以滑雪去,很快就能到。"丁丁说,"到那里的时候,太阳就出来了。"

"那里会开门吗?"露丝问,"我敢打赌,因为下雪,今天很多地方都会关门。"

"我早就想到了。"丁丁一边说着,一边把杯

---

1. 英里:英美制长度单位。1 英里 =1.6093 千米。——编者

被偷走的彩票

子放到水池里,"如果那里不开门,多特就不能兑换彩票;但如果那里开门,我们就能当场抓住她!"

"那么幸运儿就会成为百万富翁了!"乔希说,"再乘七!"

"走吧。"丁丁说,"如果我们沿着河边滑,就能以最快的速度到蓝山镇。"

丁丁匆匆地写了张字条给父母,然后孩子们回到客厅,穿好衣服。

突然,乔希的睡袋动了。一大团东西朝睡袋的开口处扭动。帕尔把鼻子探了出来。它看着乔希,发出了好奇的声音。

"它想和我们一起去。"乔希抚摸着帕尔光滑的耳朵,低声说。

孩子们抓起滑雪板和滑雪杖走了出去。

一轮圆月悬挂在绿地镇上空,把雪染成了银色。孩子们滑出丁丁家的院子,经过露丝家的时候,他们看到自己呼出的热气。他们一路向南,顺着沿河路向蓝山镇滑去。

孩子们一找到节奏,就飞快地向前滑去。河

边，太阳慢慢地出现了。夜色渐渐退去，银色的光也变成了金色的。

被偷走的彩票

帕尔高兴地小跑着,它呼出的热气变成了朵朵小云。

第十章

丁丁看到雪堆里立着的牌子上写着：欢迎来到蓝山镇。

孩子们停下来，挂着滑雪杖。阳光照在云杉树上，将被白雪覆盖的树枝染成了金色。

"现在应该离镇里不远了。"丁丁说着，看了看表，"快八点了。"

"能休息一会儿吗？"乔希问，"我想躺在雪地里。"

"休息可以。"丁丁说，"但如果多特趁我们休息的时候把彩票兑换了怎么办？"

"可能她现在还躺在床上，"乔希抱怨道，

被偷走的彩票

"就像我们本来也应该躺在床上。"

露丝笑了:"乔希,如果你中了彩票,你还会赖在床上吗?快来,我和你比赛!"

丁丁和乔希跟在露丝后面滑行,过了一会儿,他们来到了蓝山镇的主街。

"我们去问问兑奖的地方在哪里。"露丝指着一个加油站说。

孩子们滑到加油站的办公室,眯起眼睛往窗户里看。丁丁看见一个人在一边看报纸,一边喝咖啡。

丁丁敲了敲窗户。那人站了起来,打开门。"滑雪板!"那人说,"我怎么没想到呢?今天早上,我那可怜的旧卡车差点滑进印第安河里!"

他蹲下来拍了拍帕尔:"这家伙肯定也希望自己有滑雪板。"

"你能告诉我们怎么去兑彩票的地方吗?"丁丁问道。

"当然可以。"那人说。他走到外面,关上了身后的门。"看到那个闪光的灯了吗?那是中街。到那里右转,再往前走大约半英里,你就会看到

73

兑彩票的标志。那是一栋红砖建筑。"

他瞥了孩子们一眼："你们中有人中奖了吗？"

"不，但我们的一个朋友中了奖！"露丝说。

那人看了看表。"那个地方肯定刚开门。"他说。

"谢谢你，先生。"丁丁说完，他们便在安静的白色街道上滑了起来。

彩票总部前的停车场里停着两辆车。其中一辆车停在一个写着"员工停车区"的牌子旁边；另一辆车就停在入口的正前方。乔希扒着车窗往里看。

"朋友们，快看！"他低声说。

丁丁和露丝滑了过来，朝车里看了看，口香糖包装纸被扭成了银色领结，散落在地上和座位上。

"多特一定在里面！"露丝说，"快点，我们进去吧！"

孩子们取下滑雪板，把滑雪板和滑雪杖放在门外。乔希让帕尔留下看守。

丁丁打开门，孩子们走了进去。房间里有几把椅子、一个柜台和一排文件柜。

被偷走的彩票

架子上的收音机里传出了一首圣诞歌曲。同一个架子上还放着一台摄像机，镜头对准了柜台。一个小牌子上写着：为了你的安全，所有的彩票交易都将被全程录像。

一个男人背对着孩子们站在柜台前。他穿着蓬松的羽绒服，戴着滑雪帽，帽子被拉下，遮住了一头黑发。丁丁只能看到对方胡子的一端。

"那家伙看起来像我画的乔！"乔希在丁丁耳边小声说。

那个男人把手伸进口袋。当他把手抽出来时，一样东西掉到了地上——又是一个银色领结！

就在这时，一位工作人员走近柜台。她微笑着对孩子们说："早上好。我马上就来接待你们。"

那个男人转过身来，惊得丁丁倒吸了一口气。那人根本不是男人，是戴着假发、贴着假胡子的多特！

多特认出了孩子们。她惊讶地睁大了眼睛，然后迅速转向那位工作人员。

"这是彩票。"她说，"现在请给我七百万美元

75

A to Z 神秘案件

的支票。"

店员点了点头,把一张纸递过柜台:"只要你

被偷走的彩票

签了这个——"

"住手!"丁丁喊道,"她是个骗子,那张彩票是她偷来的!"

店员张大了嘴:"你说的是什么意思?你是谁?"

"我们是这张彩票真正主人的朋友。"露丝说。

"是的,我们可以证明它是被偷来的!"乔希插嘴道。

多特冲孩子们冷笑:"这张彩票是我周五买的,没人能证明我没有买。"

"是吗?"丁丁反驳道,"那为什么彩票上面有我朋友的指纹?"

"一派胡言。"贴着假胡子的多特说。

"而且你偷圣诞贺卡的地方——壁炉架——上面还有你的指纹!"露丝指着多特说。

多特笑了:"你们疯了,孩子们。我当时戴着手……"

店员拿起电话。"我要报警了。"她说。

突然,多特朝门口冲去。她猛地打开门,冲

到外面的雪地里。

乔希追在她后面,大声喊着:"出击,帕尔!"

当孩子们追到外面的时候,多特已经倒在雪地里,她被滑雪板和滑雪杖绊住了。帕尔正坐在小偷的背上,汪汪地叫着。

突然,两辆警车呼啸着开进停车场。法伦警官从其中一辆车上走了下来,另一辆车上下来的是基恩警官。

"怎么回事?"法伦警官问。

"她偷了幸运儿的彩票。"丁丁指着多特说,"我们有证据!彩票上有幸运儿爷爷的指纹。"

乔希把帕尔拉开,法伦警官把多特扶了起来。她的脸上都是雪。当她把雪擦掉时,她的胡子也被擦掉了。

"什么……这是谁?"法伦警官问。

"她叫多特·卡尔姆。"丁丁说,"她戴着假发呢!"

法伦警官伸手揪了揪多特的假发,假发掉了下来,多特的金发露出来了。

被偷走的彩票

"你还有什么要说的吗，小姐？"法伦警官说。

多特摇了摇头。

"那就伸出你的手。"法伦警官给她戴上了手铐。基恩警官把多特带到了他的巡逻车上。

就在这时，工作人员拿着彩票急急忙忙地走出办公室。"我该怎么办呢？"她说道，"这可是七百万美元的奖！"

法伦警官看了看丁丁、乔希和露丝。"孩子们，你们想搭车去幸运儿的家吗？"他问。

五分钟后，警车停在了知更鸟路33号的门前。孩子们和帕尔从车里拥出，法伦警官紧随其后。

幸运儿和他的六个弟弟妹妹正在他们的前院堆雪人。他们都跑向警车。

"你是来抓我们的吗？"约瑟芬问道。她的脸颊和鼻子冻得和她的连指手套一样红。

法伦警官拍了拍约瑟芬的头："不是。不过，丁丁有东西要给你哥哥。"

丁丁咧嘴一笑，把那张中了七百万美元的彩

79

A to Z 神秘案件

票递给幸运儿。

"圣诞节快乐!"丁丁说。

幸运儿看了一眼彩票,然后倒在了雪地里。

被偷走的彩票

"叠罗汉！"本·奥利里大叫一声，然后六个红发小孩都跳到了幸运儿的身上。

A to Z Mysteries®

The Lucky Lottery

by Ron Roy

illustrated by
John Steven Gurney

INDIAN RIVER
LAWRENCE TAXI
RIVER ROAD
HORSE TRAILS
HORSES FOR RENT
BIKE PATH
WOODS
INDIAN WAY ROAD
WOODVIEW ROAD
FIRE STATION
BIKE PATH
BRIDGE LANE
BILL'S BIKES
SUPER MARKET
ROBIN ROAD
CROW ST
FINCH LA
THRUSH CT
OWL RD
PHEASANT LA
BLUE JAY WAY
WREN DR
FITNESS CENTER
WOODS
BIKE PATH
BLUE BIRD WAY
HUMMINGBIRD LA
WOODCOCK CROSS
ELLIE'S DINER
ACORN APTS
FURRY FEET PET SHOP
OAK STREET
BIKE PATH
CENTER CHURCH
PEOPLE'S POND
POST OFFICE
COMMUNITY GARDEN AND FISH POND
GREEN LAWN SAVINGS BANK
GOOSE ISLAND
RIVER ROAD
POLICE STATION
ELDERLY HOUSING
WEST GREEN ST
SENIOR COMMUNITY CENTER
GREEN LAWN LIBRARY
TOWN HALL
BIKE PATH
CHILDREN'S PETTING ZOO AND AQUARIUM
SHANGRI-LA HOTEL
MAIN STREET

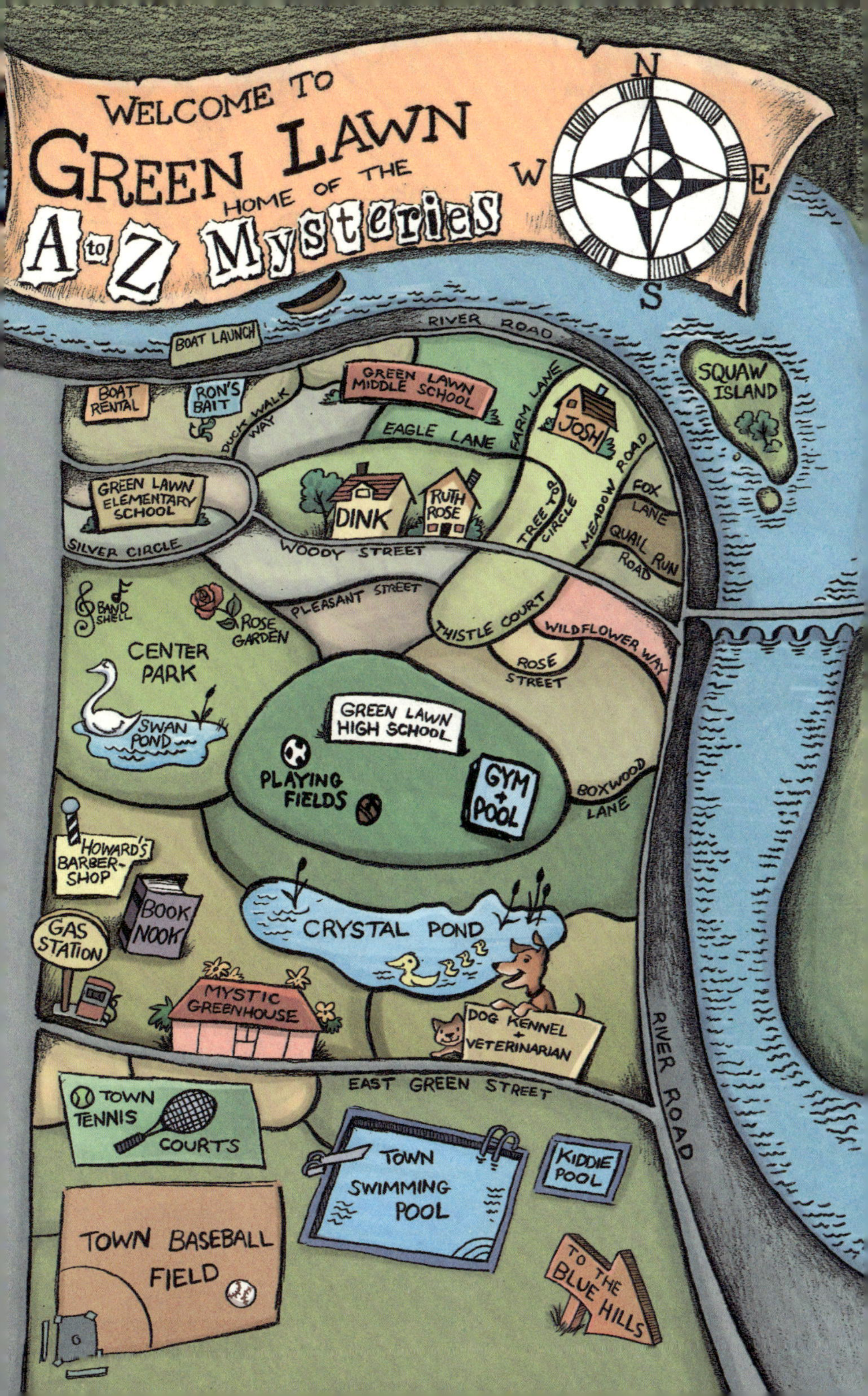

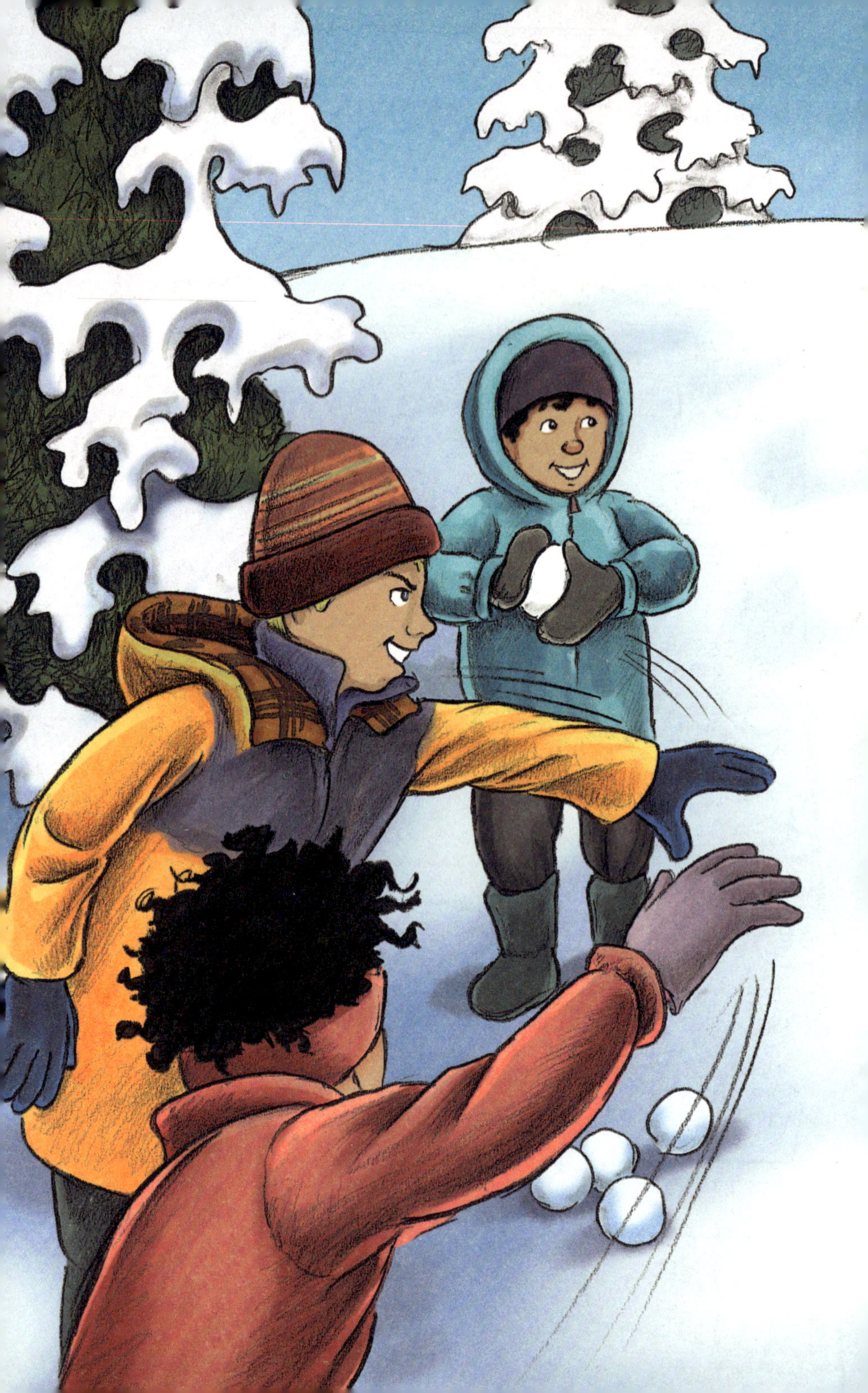

CHAPTER 1

"READY, AIM, FIRE!" yelled Ruth Rose.

She and Dink hurled snowballs at Josh's fort.

Josh's grinning face popped up. "Missed by a mile!" he yelled. "You throw like a girl, Ruth Rose!"

"I am a girl!" Ruth Rose yelled back. She whipped another snowball, catching Josh in the face.

The sides were uneven, but no one cared. It was Dink, Ruth Rose, and her little brother, Nate, against Josh and his dog, Pal.

Nate was in charge of making snowballs for his sister and Dink. Pal raced around barking and trying to catch the snowballs in his mouth.

More snowballs flew at Josh's fort. Suddenly, Dink yelled, "Stop!"

Two little kids in lumpy snowsuits had wandered into Dink's backyard.

"Who're they?" asked Ruth Rose.

Dink shrugged. He and Ruth Rose dropped their snowballs and walked over to the newcomers.

The taller one was a boy. He wore a dark blue parka and a green ski hat. The shorter one was a girl. Her red hair framed blue eyes and pink cheeks.

"Hi," Dink said. "Who're you?"

"I'm Josephine!" the girl said.

"And I'm Ben," the boy said. "We brought you a message from our big brother."

Josh climbed out of his fort and walked over. "Who's your brother?" he asked.

"Lucky O'Leary!" Josephine said.

"Oh, now I recognize you," Ruth Rose said. "You live over on Robin Road."

Ben O'Leary unzipped his parka pocket and pulled out a crumpled note. "Here, Lucky said to read it right now." He handed the note to Dink.

被偷走的彩票

Dink flattened out the paper.

> Guys, I need you.
> Come to my house now. Urgent!
> Lucky

"Did Lucky say what this is about?" Dink asked.

"It's a secret!" Josephine said, her eyes wide.

Dink, Josh, and Ruth Rose looked at each other.

"Let's go!" Ruth Rose said. She pointed her brother toward their house. "Nate, please go stay with Mom. Tell her I had to go on a secret mission!"

Dink, Josh, and Ruth Rose followed Ben and Josephine. With Pal at their side, they headed for the west side of Green Lawn.

It was Christmas vacation, and the store windows on Main Street were decorated with tiny white lights. Snow covered the grass, but the streets and sidewalks had been cleared.

"Is your brother home from college?" Dink asked Ben.

Ben nodded. "He came home a couple days ago."

89

"We bought a Christmas tree and presents!" Josephine added.

The kids crossed Main Street and headed up Bridge Lane. They turned left and stopped at 33 Robin Road.

The house was tall and blue. Kids' toys and sports stuff were scattered across the yard and front porch.

The five kids tromped up the steps. Josephine threw open the front door and clumped down the hall, leaving snow tracks on the floor.

Dink and the rest of the kids knocked the snow off their boots before stepping inside. Josh told Pal to wait on the front porch.

"Lucky's in the kitchen," Ben said, leading the way.

Lucky was making lunch for his six brothers and sisters. Lined up on the counter were six grilled-cheese sandwiches, six glasses of milk, and six bananas.

"We brought 'em!" Josephine said. She and Ben hung up their jackets and sat at the table with the rest of their sisters and brothers.

Lucky had grown taller since Dink had last seen him. His hair was longer, too.

"Hey," Lucky said, nodding at Dink, Josh, and

被偷走的彩票

Ruth Rose. To his brothers and sisters, he said, "Okay, you guys eat your lunches. Be good, and no fighting! Ben's in charge."

"Why does he get to be in charge?" Josephine piped up.

"Because I said so," Lucky said. Then he smiled at Josephine. "You can be Ben's assistant, okay?"

Lucky beckoned for Dink, Josh, and Ruth Rose to follow him. Stepping over soccer balls, mittens, books, and hockey sticks, they trailed after Lucky into the living room.

A tall Christmas tree stood in one corner, half decorated. Ornaments and strings of lights covered the floor.

Lucky threw himself into a chair and rubbed the top of his head. "Someone robbed us," he said.

Dink looked around the room. "What did they take?" he asked.

"Lottery tickets," Lucky said. "Every year, my grandfather sends us kids a Christmas card with seven lottery tickets inside. Every year, he uses our birthdays for the numbers. And every Christmas morning, we open the card while he's here. It's a big ritual in my family. Nobody ever wins, but Gramps gets a kick out of it."

Lucky pointed to a row of Christmas cards propped up on the fireplace mantel. "This year, a burglar got in here and stole his card. I hadn't even opened the envelope!"

"But how did the burglar know there were lottery tickets inside?" Josh asked.

"I don't know," Lucky said. "My grandfather called me this morning, all excited. He said he'd been reading his Sunday newspaper and saw that the winning lottery number was my birthday! But when I ran in here to get the card, it was gone."

"So the burglar must have learned the winning number before your grandfather did," Ruth Rose said.

Lucky nodded. "Lottery winners are announced on TV every Saturday night," he said. "The crook must've heard about it then."

"So he snuck in here last night," Josh said, "after he saw it on TV. Did he break a window or anything?"

"Wouldn't have to," Lucky said. "The back-door lock hasn't worked in years. The guy walked right in!"

"Um, how much was the ticket worth?" Dink asked.

Lucky drooped lower into his chair. "Seven big ones," he said.

"Seven thousand dollars?" Josh squeaked.

"No," Lucky said, shaking his head. "Seven million."

CHAPTER 2

Dink stared at Lucky. No one moved or spoke. Giggling and eating-lunch noises came from the kitchen.

"Seven m-million dollars!" Josh said, finally finding his voice.

Lucky nodded. "Gramps was so happy he could hardly talk," he said. "But when I told him the card was gone, I thought he was going to cry."

Lucky scooted forward in his chair. "Do you guys think you can find the crook and get my ticket back? I can't leave the house because I have to watch the kids."

"What if it's too late?" Ruth Rose asked. "Maybe the thief cashed in the ticket already!"

Lucky shook his head. "He can't. Today's Sunday, so the lottery place is closed. But he could do it when they open again tomorrow morning."

Just then they heard a crash from the kitchen. Whispering followed the crash, then a chorus of giggling.

"Guess I better get back in there," Lucky said. "I promised I'd take them sledding after lunch. So do you think you can help?"

"Sure we'll help!" Dink said.

Lucky grinned. "Great, I— "

A three-foot-tall redhead whirled into the room. "Stuart mushed my banana!" the kid wailed. "And I didn't do nothin' to him!"

"Don't cry, Freddie. We'll make Stuie clean up that mushy banana," Lucky said. He took Freddie by the hand and headed for the kitchen. "Call me, okay?" he said over his shoulder.

The kids let themselves out. Pal was asleep on the front porch, making little snoring sounds.

被偷走的彩票

"So how are we supposed to find this crook?" Josh asked. "Where do we even start?"

From the porch, Dink looked over the front yard. The snow had been trampled where the O'Leary kids had been playing.

"If the crook was here last night, maybe he left a trail," Dink said. "Let's check out back."

The kids tramped around to the back of the house. The O'Leary kids had played only in the front yard, so the snow in the back was fresh and smooth. The yard was surrounded by tall pine trees.

"Look," Josh said. A trail of footprints led to the back door from across the yard.

"The guy must've come out of those trees!" Dink said.

"And gone back the same way," Ruth Rose said. "These footprints go in both directions."

The kids followed the tracks into the trees. The footprints veered off to the right, and the kids went with them.

With his nose in the snow, Pal sniffed each footprint. Suddenly, he let out a woof.

97

Josh stooped down and picked something shiny out of the snow.

"What is it?" Ruth Rose asked.

Josh held out his mitten. He was holding a piece of tinfoil that had been twisted into the shape of a small bow tie.

"Do you suppose the burglar dropped this?" Josh

asked.

"Keep it," Dink said. "It's our first clue."

A few minutes later, they walked out of the woods onto Bridge Lane.

"No more footprints," Josh said, glancing up and down the lane. "The thief could've walked anywhere from here."

"Or driven," Ruth Rose said. "Maybe the guy parked a car here, then hiked into the woods."

The day was growing colder. A few big snowflakes started to fall. All three kids had pink cheeks and runny noses.

"Let's get some hot chocolate at Ellie's," Dink suggested. "Then we can plan what to do next."

It was a short hike down Bridge Lane to Ellie's Diner on Main Street. The kids pushed through the door and stomped their snowy boots on Ellie's rubber mat. Pal waddled along at Josh's heels.

"Hey, kids. Hey, Pal. What'll it be?" Ellie asked from behind her counter.

The kids slid into a booth. "Hot chocolate," Josh said, struggling out of his down jacket. "With about a mile of whipped cream on top!"

While they waited, Dink thought about what Lucky had told them.

"Guys, anyone watching TV Saturday night would know the winning numbers, right?" he said. "But how did the thief know that the winning ticket was inside Lucky's Christmas card?"

Just then Ellie came over. "Hot stuff!" she said, setting three tall mugs on the table. Each was topped with a small mountain of whipped cream and dotted with chocolate sprinkles.

"Don't burn that cute nose, Josh," Ellie added as she turned away.

Josh blushed, then licked the top of his whipped cream.

Dink blew on his hot chocolate. "Anyone got an idea?" he asked.

"Somehow, the thief knew Lucky's grandfather mailed that ticket to Lucky," Josh said.

"But how?" asked Ruth Rose.

"Maybe the thief knows Lucky's grandfather," said Josh. "Maybe they're friends!"

"That's a great idea, Josh!" Ruth Rose said. "Why

don't we talk to Lucky's grandfather?"

Dink fished in his pocket for a quarter. "Let me out, guys," he said. "I'm gonna call Lucky."

Dink climbed over Josh's legs. "Drink fast," he said, "but don't burn that cute nose!"

CHAPTER 3

"Got it," Dink said when he returned a few minutes later. "Lucky's grandfather is Hector O'Leary. He lives at Atrium, the elderly-housing building. Let's go see him."

"My mom says it's not good to drink too fast," Josh muttered. He licked his whipped-cream mustache and slid out of the booth. "Makes you burp," he added with a burp.

The kids headed down Main Street. Snow was falling steadily, and the sidewalk was turning white. Pal tried to bite the flakes as they fell past his nose.

The windows of the elderly-housing building were

decorated with wreaths. A sign on the door said:
WELCOME TO ATRIUM—
GOOD LIVING
FOR GOOD PEOPLE

Inside the lobby, a Christmas tree stood in the center of the floor. Christmas carols came from a CD player.

"Can I help you?" A white-haired woman in a wheelchair came wheeling up to them.

"We're here to see Mr. O'Leary," Dink said.

The woman smiled. "Hector's in the atrium," she said, pointing. "Just go through the swinging doors and look for a guy wearing a yellow baseball cap. But your doggy has to wait here. I'll watch him for you."

"Thanks," Josh said, handing over the leash. "His name's Pal, and he's real friendly."

The woman leaned down and patted Pal's head. "I could tell that just by looking at him," she said.

The kids headed for the swinging doors. A note on one door said DON'T LET THE BIRDS OUT!

"Birds?" Josh said. "What birds?"

Dink shrugged. He pushed open one of the heavy

wooden doors, and the kids entered the atrium.

The room felt warm and moist, like a tropical rain forest. Sunlight poured in through the glass ceiling and walls. In one corner, a fountain bubbled over smooth stones. Everywhere the kids looked they saw plants. Most were in hanging pots, but others stood in large tubs. One tree grew right through an opening in the floor. Its branches and leaves were like a huge green umbrella.

Among the plants flew scores of parakeets. With their green, blue, and yellow feathers, they looked like flying jewels.

"This is awesome!" Josh said, ducking as a parakeet flew past his head. He took off his jacket, hat, and mittens.

Dink removed his coat as he looked around the room. Elderly men and women were feeding the birds, playing cards, or just snoozing. He saw one man with a parakeet on his head!

"I see a yellow cap," Ruth Rose said, pointing to a man standing at a workbench. The kids walked over.

Hector O'Leary wore a baggy sweatshirt and old jeans. He was nailing the roof onto a small birdhouse. He looked up when the kids approached.

"Well, hello there!" Hector said. "Are you selling candy? I'll buy one of each!"

Dink shook his head. "We're friends of Lucky's," Dink said. "He told us about the lottery ticket you sent him."

The man's friendly eyes suddenly turned fiery. "I'm so mad I could spit!" he said. "What's this world coming to when burglars steal Christmas cards! If I get my hands on that gangster, he'll wish he never met Hector Francis O'Leary!"

"Lucky asked us to try to find out who stole it," Ruth Rose said. "Can we ask you some questions?"

"Okey-dokey," Hector said, laying down his hammer. "Follow me."

Lucky's grandfather led them to a circle of chairs around a low table. A blue parakeet landed on the table, carrying a small nail in his beak.

"Now, where did you get that?" Hector took the nail and put it in his pocket. "Blue Boy loves anything shiny," he said. "Okey-dokey, ask away."

"Someone knew that you sent lottery tickets to

Lucky's house," Dink said. "We were wondering if you told anyone, like a friend."

"Well, of course I told someone!" Hector said. He waved his arm toward the other people in the atrium. "I told everyone!"

CHAPTER 4

Josh glanced around at the old folks. "Could one of them be the thief?" he whispered.

Hector nodded, then put his finger to his lips. "See that woman knitting?" He dipped his chin toward a white-haired woman sitting on a sofa.

"That's Zelda Zoot," he whispered. "She's a real snoop! Has to know everyone's business around here. I know for a fact that she snitches cookies off the snack cart!"

The kids followed Hector's gaze. Zelda Zoot was

被偷走的彩票

a grandmotherly woman with a lap full of pink yarn and flashing knitting needles.

"Zelda hates me," he went on, "'cause I told the chef about the cookies. If anyone in this place wants to get even with me, it's Zelda."

Dink tried to picture this elderly woman tromping through the snow to burglarize Lucky's house. He couldn't do it.

"I'll keep an eye on her," Hector whispered. "If she starts acting rich, I'll let you know!"

Blue Boy suddenly flew to the top of Ruth Rose's head. He began pecking gently at her red headband.

"He likes bright colors," Hector explained.

Josh pulled a pencil out of his pocket. "Do you have some paper I could borrow?" he asked. "I have to draw a picture of Ruth Rose with a bird on her head!"

Hector chuckled and got up to get some paper.

"Don't move, Ruth Rose," Josh whispered.

"What's it doing up there?" Ruth Rose asked.

"I think he's making a nest," Dink said, grinning.

Hector came back with a sheet of paper. Josh began drawing while Ruth Rose sat like a statue.

While Josh was busy sketching, Dink thought about what Hector had told them. Any one of the Atrium's residents could be the thief, but Dink didn't think so.

"Mr. O'Leary, can you tell us where you bought the lottery tickets?" Dink asked.

"Sure," Hector said, dragging his chair closer to Dink. "I got 'em at the supermarket Friday morning."

"Were there any other customers around?"

Hector closed his eyes, then snapped them open again. "Yep, I remember now. A bunch of people were standing around gabbing about the snow. Buying candy and gum. Some were behind me in line to buy lottery tickets."

"Could one of them have seen the numbers you picked?"

"I suppose it's possible," Hector said. "I wrote all my grandkids' birthdays down and handed the slip to the clerk. Then she typed the numbers into the lottery machine, and out popped the seven tickets. Anyone could have seen the numbers as I wrote them down."

Dink thought for a minute. "And did you mention that you were going to send them to your grandkids?"

Suddenly, Hector's face turned white. "I guess maybe I did," he said, "while I was addressing the envelope and putting the tickets inside. Never thought it would do any harm 'cause I never expected them to win."

Hector sighed and shook his head. "Me and my big mouth! I just can't help bragging about 'em. How I eat supper at their house, how Lucky's doin' in college, stuff like that."

Blue Boy left Ruth Rose's head and zipped across the room. He landed on one of the hanging pots.

"Rats," Josh muttered. "I hardly got started."

"Let me see," Ruth Rose said, reaching for the paper.

Josh grinned and folded the drawing in half, then slipped it into his pocket. "Nope. Not till it's done."

Dink stood up. "Thanks a lot, Mr. O'Leary," he said. "I think we'll go talk to the lottery clerk. Do you know her name?"

"Sure do," Hector said. "It's Dorothy. She's new, but she'll remember me. And if you catch the snake who stole those tickets, there'll be something extra in your Christmas stockings this year!"

"Great," Josh said. "I usually just get boring underwear!"

The kids said good-bye and left the atrium. Pal

被偷走的彩票

was sleeping under a potted palm tree with his leash on his paws. Josh woke him up, and the kids got back into their hats and coats.

Outside on Main Street, the wind blew snow into the kids' faces.

"Do you guys think Zelda Zoot is the thief?" Josh asked. "She looks like my grandmother!"

"If the old folks at the Atrium know that Hector sends lottery tickets to his grandkids every Christmas," Ruth Rose said, "they're all suspects!"

"Guys," Dink said, "you heard what Hector said. He likes to talk about his grandkids. Anyone in Green Lawn could be the thief!"

The kids trudged up Main Street. Two minutes later, they bustled into the supermarket and headed toward the lottery counter.

"Heel," Josh told Pal, who waddled along next to him.

"I wonder if that's Dorothy," Ruth Rose said. She pointed at a young blond woman behind the counter. On the wall above her head hung a small security camera.

Dink approached the counter. "Excuse me," he

said. "Are you Dorothy?"

The woman looked up, chomping on a wad of gum. "That's me," she said, pointing to her name tag. It said DOROTHY CALM.

"People call me Dot. Who are you?"

"I'm Dink," he said, "and this is Josh and Ruth Rose."

Dot Calm blew a small pink bubble, let it pop, and then continued chewing. "Nice to meetcha," she said.

"We were wondering if you remember selling a bunch of lottery tickets on Friday morning," Ruth Rose

said.

The woman laughed. "Kiddo, I sell hundreds of tickets every day."

"This was seven tickets together," Dink explained. He told Dot Calm about Lucky's grandfather, and how the tickets had been stolen from Lucky's house.

Dot stared at Dink for a moment, then smiled fondly. "Yeah, I remember him," she said. "Nice old gent, loves to blah, blah, blah. He told me all about his grandkids and how he sends them lottery tickets every year."

"Do you remember who was hanging around here when he bought the tickets?" Josh asked.

Dot Calm unwrapped a piece of gum and popped it into her mouth. She chewed for a few seconds, then said, "Lots of people were standing around."

"Did you notice anyone real close who could have overheard what Mr. O'Leary was saying?" Ruth Rose asked.

Dot Calm squinted and looked into the distance. "Yeah," she said finally. "There was one guy I remember special." She shuddered. "He was pretty creepy-looking."

"Can you describe him?" Ruth Rose asked.

Dot Calm smiled. "I can do better than that," she said. "I know his name!"

CHAPTER 5

"You know who he is?" Dink asked.

"Just his first name," Dot Calm said. "He was wearing a bowling shirt with 'Joe' stitched over the pocket."

"Now we're getting somewhere!" Josh said.

"I think the name of his team was printed on the back of his shirt," Dot added. "I noticed it when he left, but he was too far away to read it."

Josh pulled out his pencil and flipped over the piece of drawing paper Hector had given him. "I can sketch him if you tell me what he looked like," he said.

"You can?" Dot asked. "Okay, let me see. His hair

was dark and kind of floppy. He had a little mustache, too, a skinny one. And he had a space between his two front teeth."

"About how old was he?" Ruth Rose asked as Josh sketched.

Dot closed her eyes and snapped her bubble gum. "I'd say about twenty-five or so," she said finally.

"Did he have any scars or tattoos or anything?" Dink asked, watching the thief's face take shape on Josh's paper.

Dot shook her head. "Not that I can remember."

Josh held up his drawing so Dot Calm could see it. "Does that look like the guy?" he asked.

"Yeah, pretty much," she said. "But you drew his chin too square. He had kind of a pointy chin."

Josh erased the man's chin, made a few more pencil marks, and then showed her the drawing again.

"That's him!" she said. "Boy, you could make a living as an artist!"

Josh blushed. "Thanks, that's what I want to do when I grow up."

被偷走的彩票

　　Ruth Rose looked at Dink and Josh. "We should take this to the police station and show it to Officer Fallon," she said.

　　"Good idea," Dink said.

　　The kids thanked Dot Calm and started to leave.

　　"Hey, I just thought of something," she called

after them. "Joe said he was thinking of moving to California if he ever got enough money."

"Thanks," Dink said. "We'll tell Officer Fallon." They hurried out of the supermarket.

Snow was still falling. The wind blew it into their faces, and flakes caught on their eyelashes. Josh slipped his drawing inside his jacket to keep it dry.

A few minutes later they tapped on Officer Fallon's door inside the police station.

"Come on in," he said. "How about a Christmas goody?" He held out a paper plate of cookies.

"We want to report a crime," Dink said, taking a cookie and sitting on one of the chairs in the office.

Josh and Ruth Rose each took one, then sat next to Dink. Josh broke his cookie in half and gave a chunk to Pal.

Officer Fallon leaned on his elbows. "I'm listening," he said.

Dink told him about the lottery tickets stolen from Lucky's house.

Officer Fallon let out a low whistle when Dink said "seven million dollars."

被偷走的彩票

Ruth Rose continued, telling Officer Fallon about visiting Lucky's grandfather. And Josh finished by telling about their talk with Dot Calm. He slid his drawing out from under his jacket and showed it to Officer Fallon. "She told us his name is Joe," he said.

"Pretty good artwork, Josh," Officer Fallon said, studying the drawing. "You know, this face looks familiar."

"Do you think we can find him before tomorrow?" Dink asked.

Officer Fallon raised one eyebrow. "I can't trace him without knowing his last name," he said. "Why the rush?"

"Because tomorrow he can cash in Lucky's lottery ticket," Ruth Rose said.

"And the lottery lady said the guy is heading for California!" Josh added.

Officer Fallon stood up. "I'll do my best. Josh, can I keep this sketch?"

"Well, I was planning to finish drawing Ruth Rose," he said. "I started a picture on the back."

Officer Fallon flipped the paper over. He grinned

at Ruth Rose. "Is that a bird on your head?"

"It's a parakeet," Ruth Rose said, then explained about Blue Boy.

Dink told Officer Fallon about Zelda Zoot. "Hector said she steals cookies," he added.

"We'll check her out," Officer Fallon said, heading for the copying machine.

He placed Josh's drawing on the machine, made a copy, and handed the original back to Josh.

"I'll circulate the sketch and see what turns up," he said.

"What happens if you don't find the crook in time?" Dink asked.

"Well, that's a problem," Officer Fallon said. "As far as I know, whoever presents a winning lottery ticket gets the money, no questions asked."

"Even if they stole it?" Josh said. "That's not fair!"

"I know it isn't fair," Officer Fallon said. "But the lottery people have to award the money to the ticket holder."

Officer Fallon thought for a minute. "I suppose if they had proof that the ticket was stolen, they would

被偷走的彩票

hold back the money." He looked at the kids. "But you have no real proof. Your friend can't prove his grandfather bought the tickets or sent them."

Dink stood up. "Then we'll get proof!" he said.

CHAPTER 6

The kids thanked Officer Fallon and left. "Let's go to my house and talk," Dink said as they stepped outside into the falling snow.

"Talk, schmuck," Josh sputtered. "I've gotta eat lunch! That half a cookie made me hungry!"

Dink laughed. "Okay, we'll eat while we figure out what to do next."

By the time they reached Dink's front door, they looked like three kid-sized snowmen. They left their jackets, boots, hats, and mittens in the hall and headed for the kitchen.

Pal trotted in and immediately flopped down next

to the radiator.

Dink found a note from his mom on the table.

Dink,

I had to take the car in for snow tires. Heat up the soup in the microwave and make peanut butter sandwiches. I'll be home soon.

Love, Mom

"I'll make the sandwiches," Josh said, pawing through the cupboard.

Dink heated some tomato soup, and the kids carried their lunches into the den. "Anyone want to watch a video?" Dink asked.

"Video!" Ruth Rose said suddenly. "That's it!"

"What's it?" Josh asked.

"There was a video camera at the lottery counter," Ruth Rose said. "If Joe's bowling team is on the back of his shirt, maybe it'll show up on the tape!"

"Good idea!" Dink said. "I'd better tell Officer Fallon."

He picked up the phone and called the police

station. After Dink told Officer Fallon about the video camera, he dialed information and asked for the phone number of the supermarket. Dink dialed again and asked to be transferred to Dot Calm at the lottery counter.

Dink asked Dot if the camera was turned on the day Hector bought the seven tickets. He listened, said

被偷走的彩票

thank you, and then hung up.

"She's gonna ask her boss to check the tape," Dink said. "If the name of Joe's bowling team shows up, Dot's boss will call Officer Fallon."

"I wonder if this Joe guy bowls at the fitness center," Josh said.

"Good thinking, Josh," Dink said. "We can check

it out after we eat."

"What's this?" Ruth Rose suddenly cried. Something had fallen out of her hair and landed in her soup.

Josh giggled. "Maybe it's a cootie."

"No, Joshua, it's not a cootie!" Ruth Rose said. She lifted something shiny onto her soup spoon. "It's another tinfoil bow tie!"

Josh dug the other bow tie out of his pocket. Except that one was wet from tomato soup, the two tinfoil bow ties were the same.

Ruth Rose looked at Dink and Josh. "How did that thing get in my hair?" she asked.

The kids stared at each other. "Blue Boy!" they shouted at the same time.

"He must've had it in his beak when he landed on your head," Dink said. "He buried it in your hair!"

"Yeah, but where did he get it?" Josh asked.

"The bow tie had to be in the atrium," Dink said. "Those parakeets never go outside."

"Then the crook must have been in the atrium, too!" Ruth Rose said. "Maybe it is Zelda Zoot!"

"It could still be Joe," Josh said. "He might've gone to

被偷走的彩票

the atrium to ask someone where Hector's grandkids live."

Just then Dink's mother burst into the house. "The roads are awful, and it's still snowing!" she said.

She slipped off her coat, scarf, and boots. "This will be a goodnight to curl up with a big bowl of popcorn."

"That's what we do after skiing," Ruth Rose said.

"You know how to ski?" Josh asked.

"Sure. My family learned to cross-country-ski a couple years ago," Ruth Rose said. "Hey, why don't I teach you guys? We can get around town a lot easier that way."

"That's a nice idea," Dink's mother said. "Just keep out of the streets. The snowplows are out in full force."

The kids cleaned up their lunch things, got into their jackets, and walked next door to Ruth Rose's house.

She took three sets of cross-country skis and poles from the garage. Then she showed Dink and Josh how to strap them onto their boots.

"Okay, now just glide," she said. "Slide your skis along the snow and use the poles to keep your balance."

"Piece of cake," Josh said, taking a step.

He fell into a snowbank.

CHAPTER 7

Soon Dink and Josh could follow Ruth Rose across her backyard without falling.

"You guys learned fast," she said. "Why don't we ski to the fitness center? We can show Josh's picture around in the bowling alley."

The kids skied around the school. Pal bounded after them, leaping high in the snow.

When they reached Main Street, they waited for a snowplow to pass, then skied across to the other side.

They stopped near the corner of Bridge Lane and Main. A man carrying a heavy-looking satchel and a pair of snowshoes came out of the fitness center.

The man smiled at the kids. "Nice day to be out in the snow," he said.

"We just learned how to ski," Josh said.

The man flopped his snowshoes onto the snowy sidewalk and tried to strap them onto his boots with one hand.

"Can I hold your bag for you?" Dink asked.

"Thanks," the man said. "Don't drop it on your toe, it's my bowling ball."

"Do you belong to a bowling team?" Josh asked.

"Yep. I bowl with the Green Lawn Giants," he said. "Why, you thinking of joining a kids' league?"

"No, but we were wondering if you know this guy." Josh pulled out his drawing of Joe and showed it to the man.

"Hmmm," the man said, studying the picture. "He's not on our team, but he looks familiar."

"His name is Joe," Ruth Rose said.

The man shook his head and clicked his tongue. "I'm pretty sure I've seen this face before," he said. "Why don't you ask inside?"

"Thanks, we will," Dink said.

The man finished strapping on his snowshoes and took back his bowling bag. "Thanks for your help," he said, then clomped down Main Street.

The kids brushed the snow off a bench and sat to remove their skis. They carried the skis and poles into the fitness center and walked down a set of stairs. Pal trotted right behind them.

Two long bowling lanes took up most of the basement. A bunch of men and women were bowling. Some of them wore shirts with names over the pockets.

There was a cart in one corner where a woman sold hot dogs and sodas.

Josh and Pal stopped and stared at the cart. "Why

被偷走的彩票

don't we get some lunch?" Josh asked.

"We ate lunch, remember?" Dink said, glancing around.

"Do you see Joe anywhere?" Ruth Rose asked.

Dink shook his head. Not one of the men looked like Josh's sketch.

"Let's ask if anyone knows him," Josh said.

The kids leaned their skis and poles in a corner and left Pal in charge. They began showing Josh's picture to anyone who wasn't bowling.

A few people said Joe looked like someone they'd seen.

One woman said Joe resembled her husband, George.

A man said Joe had a face like a bank robber he'd seen on a MOST WANTED sign at the post office.

But no one said they knew Joe.

"Well, that was a big waste of time," Josh muttered.

On the way out of the basement, the kids passed the hot dog stand. Josh unfolded his drawing. "Have you seen this guy?" he asked the woman.

She laughed. "Are you trying to be cute with me, sonny boy?"

135

"What do you mean?" Josh asked.

"I mean," the woman said, tapping the drawing with one finger, "this is a picture of you, only older."

The kids took a closer look at the sketch.

"She's right!" Ruth Rose said. "It does look like Josh, except for the mustache."

"That's why everyone said this guy looks familiar," Dink said. "He looks just like you!"

Josh stared at his drawing. "So there is no Joe?"

The woman behind the cart had been listening. "Sounds like you've been sent on a wild-goose chase," she said.

"But why would Dot have us looking for some guy who isn't even real?" Josh asked. "I don't get it."

Dink shrugged. "I don't, either," he said. "Why don't we ask her? The supermarket is right across the street."

CHAPTER 8

The kids carried their skis across Bridge Lane and into the supermarket. The store was almost empty on this snowy Sunday afternoon.

"Look," Dink said, pointing to a small sign taped to the lottery machine:

> CLOSED FOR THE STORM.
> SEE YOU TOMORROW.

Just then a teenager walked by. He was carrying a broom and a dustpan. The name tag on his shirt said ERIC.

"Cool pooch," he said, smiling at Pal.

"Do you know if Dot is still here?" Ruth Rose asked.

"Nope," the kid said. "She left a while ago, all happy. She goes, like, 'Merry Christmas, Eric!' and slips me twenty bucks. I go, like, 'Wow, thanks, Dot!'"

Eric walked behind the counter.

"What a mess Dot left back here," he mumbled as he began sweeping.

"Um, do you know if Dot's boss is around?" Dink said. "Can we talk to him?"

Eric crouched down behind the counter. "It's a her, not a him," he said, standing up. "The boss is Mrs. Milk. She's, like, out sick, though. She's had the flu all week."

"The flu?" Dink said. "But Dot told me she'd talk to— "

Suddenly, Pal let out a howl. He buried his nose in the pile of dust Eric had swept up.

"What did you find?" Josh asked. "Let me have it, boy." Josh pried open Pal's mouth and pulled something out.

"Look, guys!" Josh held out a small tinfoil bow tie.

Ruth Rose took it from Josh, then pulled the other two out of her pocket.

The three were exactly the same.

The kids leaned over the counter. The floor was littered with tiny tinfoil bow ties.

Suddenly, it all made sense. Dink could tell by

the looks on their faces that Josh and Ruth Rose had figured it out, too.

"Come on," Dink muttered. He grabbed his skis and poles and hurried toward the exit.

Josh and Ruth Rose followed with their skis and poles. "Let's go, Pal," Josh told his dog.

"Are you guys thinking what I'm thinking?" Ruth Rose asked once they were outside.

"Yeah," Dink muttered. "Boy, have we been dopes! Let's go back to Ellie's." They trudged through the snow and piled into the diner.

Ellie looked up. "Twice in one day?" she said. "Three more hot chocolates?"

"Thanks, Ellie," Dink said. The kids slid into a booth while Pal flopped down at their feet.

"So Dot Calm is the crook, right?" Josh said.

"Right," Dink said. "After Dot sold Hector his tickets, she must have kept the paper he wrote the kids' birthdays on. That's how she knew Lucky's ticket was the winner."

"But she didn't know where Lucky lived," Ruth Rose said, "so she had to go to the Atrium to find out.

She wouldn't want to talk to Hector, so she probably asked someone else where his grandkids lived. She must've dropped a bow tie while she was snooping!"

"Then she went to Lucky's house and stole the card…," Dink added.

"…and dropped another bow tie in the snow," Josh said.

"Then she made up that story about Joe to throw us off her trail," Ruth Rose said.

Dink looked at Josh. "I bet she described your face because she was looking right at you when you were drawing him."

"Yeah, and I was so dumb I didn't even notice it was me," Josh said.

"Here we go, kids." Ellie brought their hot chocolates to the table. "These are on me, and a little treat for Pal."

Ellie set a bowl of chopped-up hamburger in front of Pal's nose. Pal raised his head, blinked his big brown eyes at Ellie, and stuck his nose in the bowl.

"Thanks a lot, Ellie," Josh said. "Pal says thanks, too."

Ruth Rose had been sipping her hot chocolate. "You know, guys," she said, "we can't prove Dot stole the tickets. We know she did it, but Officer Fallon will say, 'Where's the proof?'"

Dink nodded. "Yeah, that's exactly what he'll say."

"Well, unless we find the proof," Josh said, "this sure is going to be a lousy Christmas for Lucky's family. Seven million bucks down the drain."

The kids drank their hot chocolate with glum expressions on their faces.

From beneath the table came the sound of happy chomping.

CHAPTER 9

Dink invited Josh and Ruth Rose to spend the night. They unrolled their sleeping bags in front of Dink's Christmas tree. Pal crawled inside Josh's bag and started snoring.

While it snowed outside, the kids tried to figure out how to prove that Dot Calm had stolen Lucky's lottery ticket.

"If only we had a witness," Ruth Rose said from her sleeping bag.

"Too bad she didn't drop something with her name on it," Josh offered, warming his feet on Pal's body.

"That would be too easy," Dink mumbled. He crawled into his sleeping bag and closed his eyes.

Then Dink was dreaming. But it wasn't a happy, the-night-before-Christmas-Eve kind of dream.

This was a nightmare. Dink was outside somewhere, floundering in the snow. He was barefoot, without gloves, and freezing. His tracks crisscrossed each other as he tried to find his way home.

Dink yelled and sat up. From inside Josh's sleeping bag, Pal whimpered.

"It's okay," Dink whispered. He sat and thought for a minute, then crawled out of his bag. He tiptoed up the stairs and came down with his alarm clock. In the hall, Dink made a phone call, left a quiet message, and returned to the living room.

He set the alarm for six o'clock and put the clock in the foot of his sleeping bag. Then Dink climbed back in and went to sleep.

When the alarm buzzed, Dink pressed the off button with his toes. He slipped out of his bag and shook Josh and Ruth Rose. "Wake up," he whispered.

"And be quiet!"

Josh yawned and Ruth Rose blinked her eyes. Silently, they watched Dink pull on his boots.

Dink grinned. "Come on, you guys," he said. "Meet me in the kitchen."

"There better be breakfast," Josh mumbled.

Within minutes, the three kids were drinking orange juice and eating toast. Josh shared his bread with Pal, who then went back to Josh's warm sleeping bag.

Dink told Josh and Ruth Rose about his nightmare. "All I could see was my footprints in the snow," he said. "When I woke up, I thought about what Josh said about wishing Dot had left something with her name on it."

He grinned. "I know how we can prove Lucky's grandfather really did buy that ticket."

"How?" Josh said. "And why'd you have to tell us this in the middle of the night?"

"Fingerprints," Dink said. "Whose fingerprints would be on that stolen ticket?"

"Dot's would be, if she stole it," Ruth Rose said.

145

"But her prints would be on the ticket anyway, since she sold it to Lucky's grandfather," Josh said. "So what does that prove?"

"Nothing," Dink said. "But Dot's fingerprints aren't the only ones on that ticket … "

Josh and Ruth Rose stared at him. "You're right!" Ruth Rose said. "Hector's fingerprints are on the ticket, too!"

"Um, can they get prints off lottery tickets?" Josh asked.

Dink nodded. "I think so. I saw a program about fingerprints on TV," he said. "Fingers are oily, and the oil stains paper when we touch it."

"We should tell Officer Fallon," Ruth Rose said.

Dink nodded. "I left a message on his voice mail asking him to meet us at the lottery headquarters in Blue Hills."

"But that's two miles from here!" Josh said. He glanced out the window. "And it's still dark out."

"We can get there fast on skis," Dink said. "And by that time, the sun will be up."

"Are they even open?" Ruth Rose asked. "I bet a

被偷走的彩票

lot of places are closed today because of the snow."

"I thought of that," Dink said, setting the glasses in the sink. "If the place is closed, Dot Calm won't be able to cash in the ticket. But if it's open, we'll catch her in the act!"

"Then Lucky will be a millionaire!" Josh said. "Times seven!"

"Let's get going," Dink said. "We can get to Blue Hills fastest if we ski along the river."

Dink scribbled a note to his parents, and then the kids went back to the living room and finished dressing.

Suddenly, Josh's sleeping bag moved. A big bump wriggled toward the opening, and Pal poked his nose out. He looked at Josh and woofed.

"He wants to come with us," Josh whispered, rubbing Pal's silky ears.

The kids grabbed their skis and poles and stepped outside.

A full moon hung over Green Lawn, turning the snow to silver. The kids saw their breath as they skied out of Dink's yard and past Ruth Rose's house. They

147

followed River Road south toward Blue Hills.

Once they found their rhythm, the kids zipped along. Over the river, the sun slowly appeared. Silver became gold as night turned to day.

被偷走的彩票

Pal trotted happily along, his breath making small clouds.

CHAPTER 10

Dink read the sign sticking out of the snowbank: WELCOME TO BLUE HILLS.

The kids stopped and leaned on their ski poles. The sun shone on the spruce trees, turning their snowy branches to gold.

"The town can't be far now," Dink said. He looked at his watch. "It's almost eight."

"Can we rest for a while?" Josh asked. "I feel like lying right down in the snow."

"We could," Dink said, "but what if Dot cashes in the ticket while we're resting?"

"She's probably still in bed," Josh grumbled, "where

we should be."

Ruth Rose laughed. "Josh, would you still be in bed if you had a winning lottery ticket? Come on, I'll race you!"

Dink and Josh skied after Ruth Rose, and a few minutes later they were on Main Street in Blue Hills.

"Let's ask where the lottery place is," Ruth Rose said, pointing to a gas station.

The kids skied up to the office and peeked in the window. Dink saw a man reading a newspaper and sipping from a coffee mug.

Dink tapped on the window, and the man got up and opened the door. "Skis," the man said. "Why didn't I think of that? My poor old truck nearly skidded into Indian River this morning!"

He knelt and patted Pal. "Bet this fella wishes he had some skis, too."

"Can you tell us how to get to the lottery place?" Dink asked.

"Sure can," the man said. He stepped outside and closed the door behind him. "See that flashing light? That's Middle Street. Hang a right there, and about a half mile up, you'll see the sign. Red-brick building."

He glanced at the kids. "One of you a winner?"

"No, but a friend of ours is!" Ruth Rose said.

The man looked at his watch. "Place must be just opening," he said.

"Thanks a lot, mister," Dink said, and they skied up the quiet white street.

There were two cars in the parking lot in front of lottery headquarters. One of the cars had pulled in next to a sign that said EMPLOYEE PARKING. The other car was right in front of the entrance. Josh peeked through the windows.

"Guys, take a look," he whispered.

Dink and Ruth Rose skied over and looked into the car. Gum wrappers twisted into silver bow ties littered the floor and seats.

"Dot must be inside!" Ruth Rose said. "Hurry up, let's get in there!"

The kids took off their skis and left them and their poles outside the door. Josh told Pal to stay.

Dink opened the door, and the kids stepped inside. The room had a few chairs, a counter, and a

被偷走的彩票

row of filing cabinets.

A Christmas song was coming from a radio on a shelf. On the same shelf was perched a video camera. The lens was aimed at the counter. A small sign read: ALL LOTTERY TRANSACTIONS ARETAPED FOR YOUR SAFETY.

A man was standing at the counter with his back to the kids. He was wearing a puffy down coat. A ski hat was pulled down over dark hair, and Dink could just see one end of a mustache.

"That guy looks like my picture of Joe!" Josh hissed in Dink's ear.

The man reached a hand into his pocket. When he pulled his hand out, something dropped to the floor. It was another silver bow tie!

Just then a clerk approached the counter. She smiled at the kids and said, "Good morning. I'll be right with you."

The man turned around, and Dink gasped. It wasn't a man at all. It was Dot Calm wearing a wig and fake mustache!

Dot Calm recognized the kids. Her eyes widened

153

A to Z 神秘案件

in surprise, and then she turned quickly back to the clerk.

"Here's the ticket," she said. "Now I'll take my check for seven million, please."

The clerk nodded and slid a paper across the counter. "If you'll just sign this…"

"Stop!" Dink yelled. "She's a crook, and she stole that lottery ticket!"

The clerk's mouth dropped open. "What do you mean? Who are you?"

"We're friends of the ticket's real owner," Ruth Rose said.

"Yeah, and we can prove it's stolen!" Josh threw in.

Dot Calm sneered at the kids. "I bought this ticket Friday, and nobody can prove I didn't."

"Yeah?" Dink retorted. "Then why are my friend's fingerprints on it?"

"Baloney," Dot Calm said through her fake mustache.

"And your fingerprints are on the mantel where you stole the Christmas card!" Ruth Rose said, pointing at Dot Calm.

Dot Calm laughed. "You're crazy, kid. I was wearing glov…"

The clerk picked up the telephone. "I'm calling the police," she said.

Suddenly, Dot Calm charged toward the door. She flung it open and hurtled out into the snow.

"Josh ran after her, screaming, "Attack, Pal!"

When the kids got outside, Dot Calm was lying in the snow with her feet tangled in skis and ski poles. Pal was sitting on the thief's back, barking.

Suddenly, two police cruisers roared into the parking lot. Officer Fallon stepped from one of them, Officer Keene from the other.

"What's going on?" Officer Fallon asked.

"She stole Lucky's lottery ticket," Dink said, pointing to Dot Calm. "And we have proof! Lucky's grandfather's fingerprints will be on the ticket."

Josh pulled Pal away, and Officer Fallon helped Dot Calm to her feet. Her face was covered with snow. When she wiped the snow away, the mustache fell off.

"What…who is this character?" Officer Fallon asked.

"Her name is Dot Calm," Dink said. "She's wearing a wig!"

Officer Fallon reached over and pulled at the wig. It came off, revealing Dot Calm's blond hair.

被偷走的彩票

"Anything to say for yourself, miss?" Officer Fallon said.

Dot Calm shook her head.

"Then hold out your hands." Officer Fallon snapped on a pair of handcuffs. Officer Keene led Dot Calm to his cruiser.

Just then the clerk came bustling out of the office holding the lottery ticket. "What should I do with this?" she asked. "It's the seven-million-dollar winner!"

Officer Fallon looked at Dink, Josh, and Ruth Rose. "Would you kids like a ride to Lucky's house?" he asked.

Five minutes later, the cruiser pulled up in front of 33 Robin Road. The kids and Pal piled out, followed by Officer Fallon.

Lucky and his six brothers and sisters were building snow people in their front yard. They all came running over to the cruiser.

"Are you gonna' rest us?" Josephine asked. Her cheeks and nose were as red as her mittens.

Officer Fallon patted Josephine on her head. "No,

A to Z 神秘案件

but Dink has something to give your big brother."

Dink grinned and handed the seven-million-dollar winning ticket to Lucky.

"Merry Christmas!" he said.

被偷走的彩票

Lucky took one look at the ticket, then fell over in the snow.

"Pig pile!" Ben O'Leary yelled, and all six redheads leaped on top of Lucky.

Text copyright © 2000 by Ron Roy
Cover art copyright © 2015 by Stephen Gilpin
Interior illustrations copyright © 2000 by John Steven Gurney
All rights reserved. Published in the United States by Random House Children's Books,
a division of Random House LLC, a Penguin Random House Company, New York.
Originally published in paperback by Random House Children's Books, New York, in 2000.

本书中英双语版由中南博集天卷文化传媒有限公司与企鹅兰登（北京）文化发展有限公司合作出版。

"企鹅"及其相关标识是企鹅兰登已经注册或尚未注册的商标。
未经允许，不得擅用。
封底凡无企鹅防伪标识者均属未经授权之非法版本。

©中南博集天卷文化传媒有限公司。本书版权受法律保护。未经权利人许可，任何人不得以任何方式使用本书包括正文、插图、封面、版式等任何部分内容，违者将受到法律制裁。

著作权合同登记号：字18-2023-258

图书在版编目（CIP）数据

被偷走的彩票 ：汉英对照 /（美）罗恩·罗伊著 ；
（美）约翰·史蒂文·格尼绘 ；刘巧丽译. -- 长沙 ：湖
南少年儿童出版社，2024.10. --（A to Z神秘案件）.
ISBN 978-7-5562-7818-3

Ⅰ. H319.4

中国国家版本馆CIP数据核字第2024HW9523号

A TO Z SHENMI ANJIAN BEI TOUZOU DE CAIPIAO

A to Z神秘案件 被偷走的彩票

[美] 罗恩·罗伊 著　　[美] 约翰·史蒂文·格尼 绘　　刘巧丽 译

责任编辑：唐 凌　李 炜	策划出品：李 炜　张苗苗　文赛峰
策划编辑：文赛峰	特约编辑：杜佳美
营销编辑：付 佳　杨 朔　周晓茜	封面设计：霍雨佳
版权支持：王媛媛	版式设计：马睿君
插图上色：河北传图文化	内文排版：霍雨佳

出 版 人：刘星保
出　　版：湖南少年儿童出版社
地　　址：湖南省长沙市晚报大道89号
邮　　编：410016
电　　话：0731-82196320
常年法律顾问：湖南崇民律师事务所　柳成柱律师
经　　销：新华书店
开　　本：875 mm × 1230 mm　1/32　　印　刷：三河市中晟雅豪印务有限公司
字　　数：87千字　　　　　　　　　　　印　张：5
版　　次：2024年10月第1版　　　　　　印　次：2024年10月第1次印刷
书　　号：ISBN 978-7-5562-7818-3　　　定　价：280.00元（全10册）

若有质量问题，请致电质量监督电话：010-59096394　团购电话：010-59320018

A to Z 神秘案件

中英双语

第二辑

The Missing Mummy
失踪的木乃伊

[美] 罗恩·罗伊 著
[美] 约翰·史蒂文·格尼 绘　叶雯熙 译

湖南少年儿童出版社　小博集
·长沙·

马萨诸塞州
哈特福德镇
罗得岛州
纽约州
绿地镇
康涅狄格州
弗蕾达姨妈的
美味薯条
主街
银行
禁止停车
北
西
东
南
公共汽车

欢迎来到**康涅狄格州**的哈特福德镇

一起解开 A to Z 神秘案件

小路

金鱼池

沃兹沃思博物馆

墓室

储藏室

珍宝室

人物介绍

三人小组的成员，聪明勇敢，喜欢读推理小说，紧急关头总能保持头脑冷静。喜欢在做事之前好好思考！

丁丁

三人小组的成员，活泼机智，喜欢吃好吃的食物，常常有意想不到的点子。

乔希

三人小组的成员，活泼开朗，喜欢从头到脚穿同一种颜色的衣服，总是那个能找到大部分线索的人。

露丝

是博物馆的讲解员，懂得木乃伊相关知识。

哈里斯·特威德博士

在薯条店里工作。

短发女人

薯条店的主人，有炸薯条的秘方。

弗蕾达姨妈

字母 M 代表 missing，缺失……

孩子们盯着这三具木乃伊。每具木乃伊身上都包裹着一种布，这种布因年代久远而泛着黄色。丁丁想起特威德博士的话，博士说得没错，木乃伊根本就没有臭味。

"每一具木乃伊都用亚麻布条包裹好了。"特威德博士说，"在这层布的下面……"

突然，一个有着金色长发、穿着宽松衣服的女人冲了进来。她抢走了那具小木乃伊，跑出了陵墓。

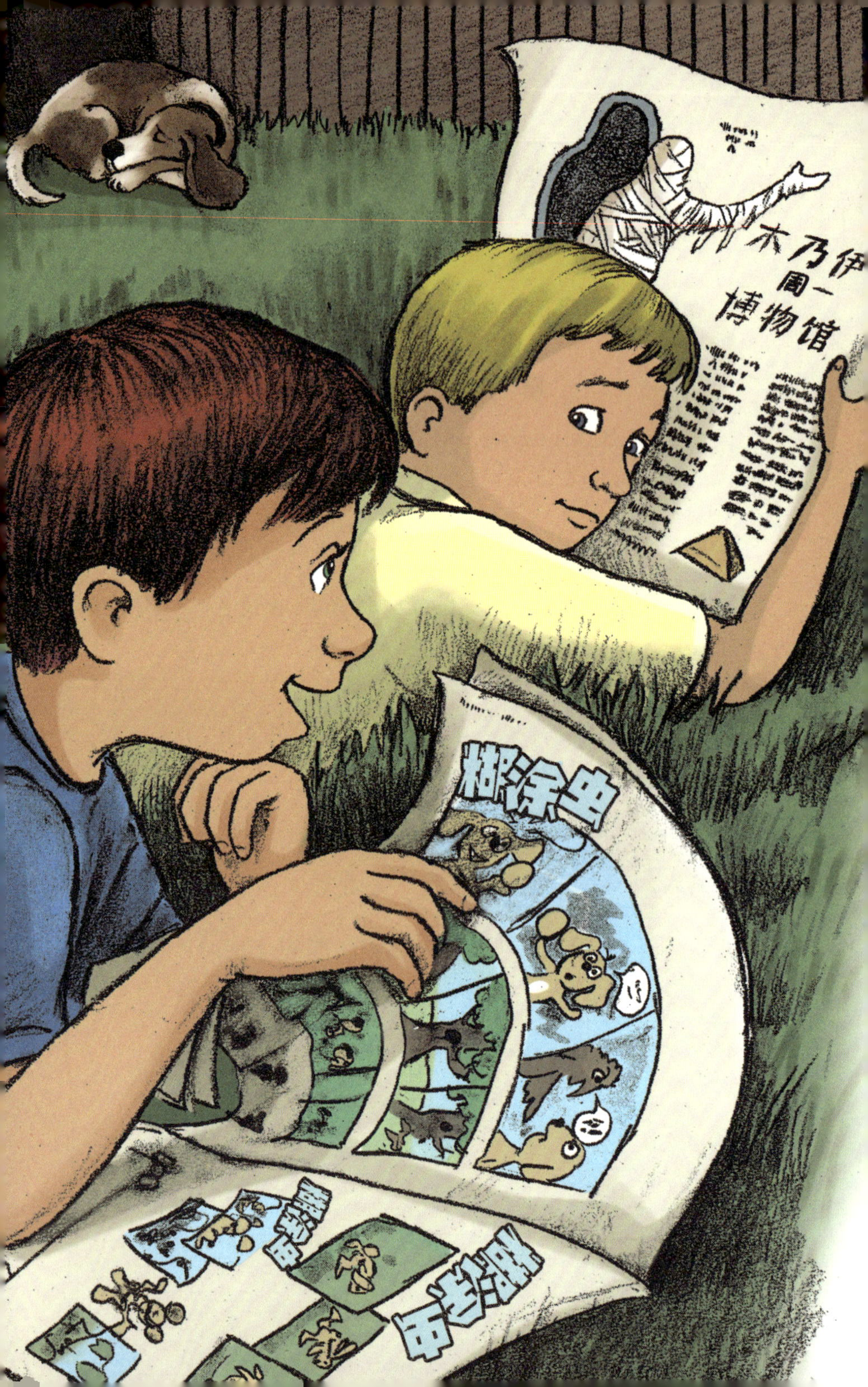
木乃伊
周一
博物馆
糊涂虫
糊涂虫

第一章

"周一博物馆会举办木乃伊日?"丁丁正在读周日的报纸。乔希从他的身后瞟了一眼问:"那周二是什么日,肚子日[1]?"

现在正值暑假,丁丁、乔希和露丝正躺在丁丁家后面的草坪上。乔希的那只名叫帕尔的狗则在树下打瞌睡。

露丝拿起报纸,快速读完这篇文章。"不,乔希,第二天是关于恐龙的,"她说,"叫周二霸

---

1. 肚子日:木乃伊英文为 mummy,肚子英文为 tummy。
——编者

王龙日。"

"博物馆这一周都在为孩子们举办活动。"丁丁解释道。

"那么周三有什么活动呢?"乔希问。

"组织孩子们去康涅狄格河研究植物和动物。"露丝说,"叫作周三湿地日。"

丁丁从露丝那里拿回报纸,说:"接下来,他们会安排你拍一部恐怖电影,那是周四惊悚日。最后一天是周五青蛙日,每个孩子都可以分到一只青蛙来研究。"

"我们报名吧!"乔希说,"报名费多少?"

丁丁翻看了这份报纸。"每个项目一美元。"他看着乔希和露丝说,"五天一共是五美元。"

"我没有五美元。"露丝说。

"我也没有。"乔希说,"但我知道怎么可以挣到钱。"

"怎么挣?"丁丁问。

"我爸爸一直想把牲口棚打扫干净。"他说,"我敢保证,如果我们帮他把牲口棚打扫干净了,他一定会给我们钱的。"

"好主意!"丁丁说。

孩子们跑到乔希家,把周日剩下的时间都用来做打扫。乔希的两个弟弟——布赖恩和布拉德利,则帮忙照看小狗帕尔。

乔希的爸爸给了每个孩子七美元,作为他们辛勤工作的报酬。第二天午饭后,丁丁、乔希和露丝坐上了一辆去哈特福德市的巴士。十五分钟后,他们在沃兹沃思博物馆前的主街下了车。

街对面是一家银行。银行入口处的数字屏幕显示:周一,七月十日,八十二华氏度[1]。随即,屏幕上显示出时间——已经快两点了!

"快点,朋友们。"丁丁说,"我们的报名时间只剩几分钟了。"

他们跑上博物馆前的台阶,穿过大门进入博物馆。装有空调的博物馆十分安静,地面铺着大理石,白色墙壁上挂着一张张挂毯和大幅油画。

"欢迎参加周一木乃伊日。"一位站在柜台后面的女士说。

---

1. 华氏度:非法定计量单位中的华氏温度单位。八十二华氏度相当于约二十八摄氏度。——编者

在大厅的另一边,一群孩子和几位大人已经在等待了。露丝从门后的架子上拿了一张地图,然后大家走上前,加入了这个队伍。

他们每人向柜台后面的女士付了一美元。

"我想知道他们把那些木乃伊放哪儿了。"乔希低声说。

两点整,柜台后面的一扇门开了,一位高个子男士走了出来。他穿着棕褐色夹克和短裤,脚上穿着及膝的袜子和系带靴子,头上戴着白色头盔。

"我是哈里斯·特威德博士,"这位男士说,"今天,我将带你们踏上古埃及之旅。"

特威德博士的脸、手和膝盖都被晒得黝黑。丁丁心想:"他到底在埃及的沙漠里生活了多长时间啊。"

"准备好跟我进入陵墓了吗?"特威德博士问。他微笑着,露出洁白的牙齿,这使他黝黑的脸看起来更黑了。

"我们居然要去陵墓里面吗?"乔希低声道,"我想要回我的一美元!"

"嘘!"丁丁低声道。

失踪的木乃伊

特威德博士的眼睛眯成了一条缝:"如果你害怕木乃伊,要抓紧时间说出来。"

"嘿!"一个红发女孩说,"木乃伊会不会闻

起来臭臭的？"

"今天，你们正好可以学习一下为什么木乃伊不会散发臭味。"特威德博士说，"现在，请跟随我进入陵墓！"

大厅的里侧有一个拱门，他们走了过去。拱门后面是一个房间，里面有一排排长凳，长凳后面是一堵空白石墙。这堵墙是由扁平的巨石堆砌而成的，它们被严丝合缝地堆在一起。丁丁感到很惊讶，他好奇博物馆的工作人员是怎么把那些巨石搬进来的。

"陵墓，包括木乃伊，就在这面墙的后面。"特威德博士说，"在我们进去之前，我想讲解一下这些人是如何死亡并变成木乃伊的。"

他指着长凳说："请坐。"

"我们坐在前面吧。"丁丁一边说，一边朝长凳走去。

大家都坐下后，特威德博士压低声音说："闭上眼睛，想象你正站在四千年前的尼罗河河岸上。感受你背后的阳光，看着在你身旁流动的河水，聆听牛在田间劳作时发出的哞哞声。"

失踪的木乃伊

大家都安静了下来。

"突然，地面晃动起来，地震了！"特威德博士提高声音。

丁丁猛地睁开了眼睛，胳膊上起了一层鸡皮疙瘩。所有的孩子都睁开了眼睛，盯着特威德博士。

"之后，"他继续说，"幸存者准备埋葬死者。我们今天要参观的，就是在那次地震中丧生的三个人。"

特威德博士走到墙边，按下了一块石头。此时，墙壁缓缓滑开了。

丁丁往门里看，看到一个昏暗的房间。部分石头地面上覆盖着沙子和砾石。

"你们看到的就是那时的陵墓。"特威德博士轻声地说，"进来吧，但请小声说话，不要碰任何东西。"

"真不可思议！"大家朝里面走去时，露丝低声说。

陵墓里温度很低，丁丁被冻得瑟瑟发抖。旧罐子和农具散落在地上。墙上画着奇怪的符号。

墙边放着三个石棺。

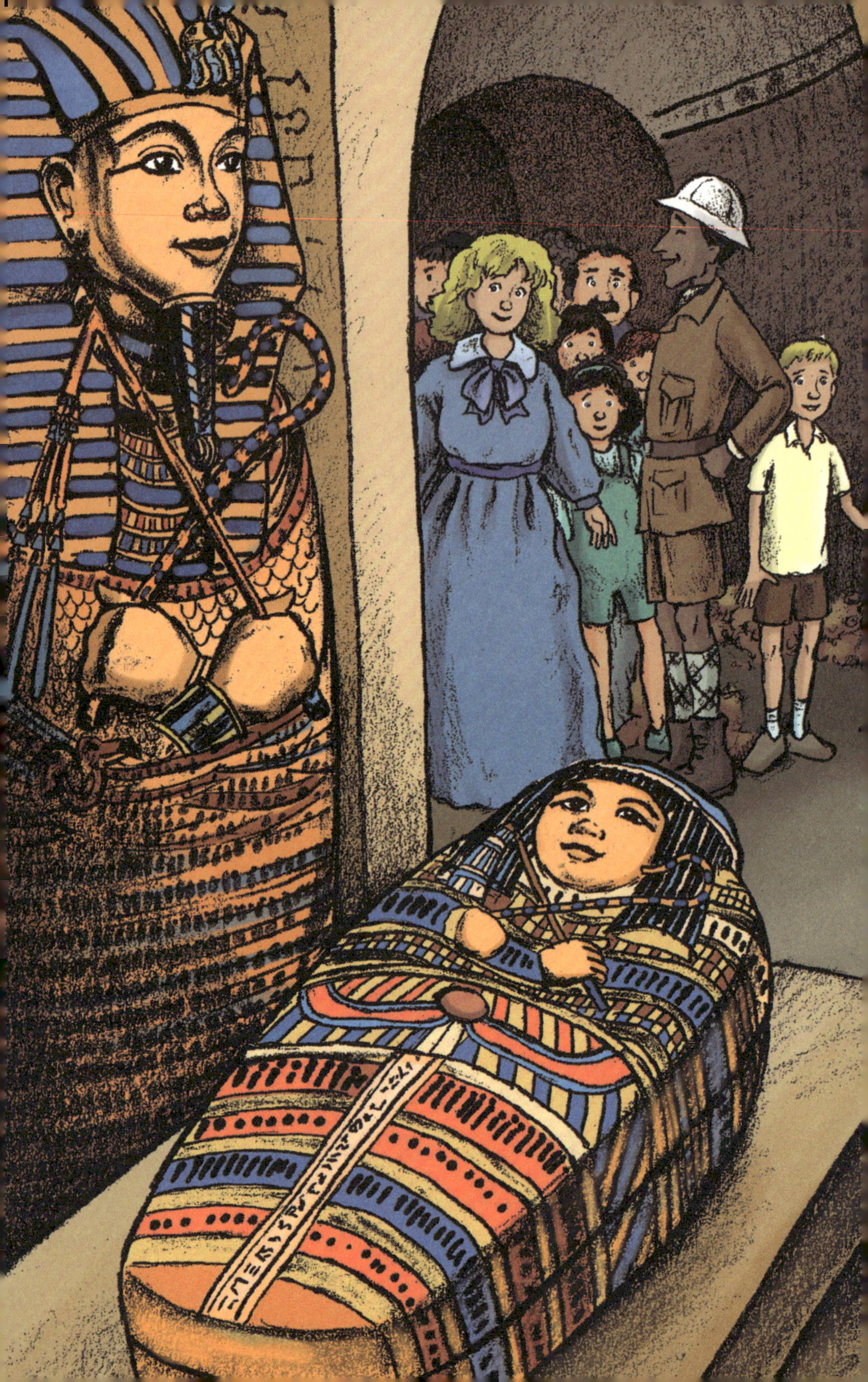

第二章

其中一个石棺被放在一张石桌上,另外两个则分别立在两边的墙壁前。丁丁发现桌子上的石棺比另外两个小。

"你们所站的地方是一个真正的埃及陵墓。"特威德博士压低声音说,"它是被拆分后带到这里,然后再按照原样组建的。"

他指着石棺说:"古埃及人的棺椁被称为石棺,每个石棺里都放有一具木乃伊。过一会儿,我会打开棺盖。但在那之前,让我们先欣赏一下这些精美的艺术品。"

每个棺盖上都有一个由珠宝和金子打造的面

具。丁丁觉得这些面具上的表情看上去很平静，甚至可以说是开心。

"埃及人认为死者来生也会需要钱，"特威德博士说，"所以有钱人死后常常会有很多陪葬品。"

他指向一个拱门后的另一个房间。"那就是珍宝室。"他说，"看完这些木乃伊，你们有机会进那里看看。"

露丝举起手。"为什么其中一个石棺这么小？"她问。

特威德博士走向桌子上的石棺。"这个石棺里面是一具小孩子的木乃伊。"他解释道，"这个小男孩和他的父母一起去世了，他的父母现在永远守护在他的身边。"

特威德博士把手放在一个立着的石棺上。"这是男孩的母亲。"他说着，用双手把棺盖打开了。

"还有他的父亲。"特威德博士打开了另一个立着的石棺。

然后他沉默着，将最小的石棺的棺盖移开，让它靠在墙边。

孩子们盯着这三具木乃伊。每具木乃伊身

失踪的木乃伊

上都包裹着一种布,这种布因年代久远而泛着黄色。丁丁想起特威德博士的话,博士说得没错,木乃伊根本就没有臭味。

"每一具木乃伊都用亚麻布条包裹好了。"特威德博士说,"在这层布的下面……"

突然,一个有着金色长发、穿着宽松衣服的女人冲了进来。她抢走了那具小木乃伊,跑出了陵墓。

"站住!"特威德博士大声喊,紧追那个女人。

房间里立刻炸开了锅。孩子们不知道接下来要怎么办。这时,特威德博士急忙回到陵墓里。"请安静,"他说,"嗯……看来周一木乃伊日要推迟了。我们明天继续。"

"但是明天是周二霸王龙日!"有人说。

特威德博士看上去很慌张,他黝黑的脸已经变得煞白,一只眼皮正在抽搐着。"是的,你说得对。"他说,"我会在下周再安排一次木乃伊日,现在你们得离开陵墓了。我很抱歉。"

孩子们一边向外走着,一边咕哝着"这不公平"。特威德博士靠边站了站,让大家出去。

"为什么有人要偷木乃伊呢?"乔希、丁丁和露丝跟在其他孩子后面往外走时,乔希问。

"我在某个地方读到过,木乃伊里包裹着金子和珠宝。"露丝说,"也许那个木乃伊里包有贵重的东西。"

"你的意思是,那个女人会打开木乃伊?"乔希说,"真恶心!"

丁丁、乔希和露丝是最后出陵墓的。过了一会儿,特威德博士从他们身旁匆匆走过。在孩子们身后,陵墓的门重重地关上了。

"这也太不可思议了。"乔希说,"我们现在只能回家了吗?"

"我得先去趟洗手间。"露丝说。

孩子们在拐角处找到了洗手间。女洗手间的门打开了,一位穿着得体,有着黑色短发的女士走了出来。她拿着手提箱,正在用手机通话。

"我们在这里等你。"露丝闪身走进洗手间时,丁丁说。

"我想知道小偷会怎么处置那具木乃伊。"乔希说,"我的意思是,她根本无法将它带到大街上!"

失踪的木乃伊

突然，洗手间的门砰的一声打开了。露丝站在门口，那表情像是看见了鬼。

"露丝，怎么了？"丁丁说。

"把……把特威德博士叫来。"她回答，"它在洗手间里！"

"什么在洗手间里？"乔希问。

露丝深吸了一口气。"那具失踪的木乃伊！"她说。

第三章

　　特威德博士正站在前门处与两名警官交谈。丁丁冲向他们。"打扰一下。"他突然不知道该怎么说话。

　　"需要帮忙吗?"其中一名警官问道。她衬衫上的名牌上写着"S.华盛顿"。

　　"我的朋友在女洗手间里发现了木乃伊!"丁丁说。

　　"我们去看看。"另一名警官说。他的名牌上写着"P.彼得斯"。

　　乔希和露丝站在洗手间外,大家匆匆赶了过来。

　　"你能和我一起进去吗?"华盛顿警官问露丝。

失踪的木乃伊

露丝和华盛顿警官走进了洗手间。几秒钟后,她们俩出来了。

"特威德博士,请你跟我来一下,好吗?"华盛顿警官说。

特威德博士跟着华盛顿警官进了洗手间。

"那具木乃伊放在哪儿?"乔希问露丝。

"你知道那种桌子吗?就是父母给婴儿换尿布的那种,"她说,"它就在那个桌子上!"

"就在那种一览无余的地方?"丁丁问。

露丝点了点头:"起初我以为那是个大玩偶,直到我凑近看了一眼……"

"好恶心!"乔希说。

洗手间的门又开了,华盛顿警官走了出来,特威德博士在她身后,怀里抱着那具小木乃伊。

"看起来这具木乃伊并没有损坏。"特威德博士说,"但是我得在我的办公室里再检查一下。"

特威德博士和两名警官穿过大厅,走到柜台后面的那扇门后。

"我想我们还是回家吧。"丁丁说。

"糟糕的周一木乃伊日。"露丝抱怨道。

"看，那儿有一家自助餐厅。"乔希说，"我们去买点喝的吧。"

孩子们走进餐厅，买了一些冷饮，围坐在圆桌旁。

"我好奇的是，小偷把木乃伊留在洗手间后去了哪里。"露丝一边说着，一边小口喝着柠檬水。

"什么意思？"丁丁问。

"里面没有窗户，所以她不可能从窗户出去。"露丝说，"可是，如果她从门口出来，她一定会碰到我们。"

"确实有个女人从门口出来了。"乔希说，"还

记得吗？她当时正在打电话。"

"对，但是她看上去和抢走木乃伊的女人不一样。"露丝说。

"也许她是乔装的。"丁丁说，"也许抢走木乃伊的女人在洗手间里换了衣服！"

"可能她把换下来的衣服藏在手提箱里了。"乔希说，"可能那头金发也是假发。"

"伙计们，我刚刚意识到一些事情。"露丝说，"那个女人离开洗手间后，向陵墓走去，也许她回去偷别的东西了。"

孩子们放下饮料，跑到陵墓前。

"芝麻开门！"乔希说。他按了石头，门砰的一声开了。

墓室顶部的小灯闪出微光，在地上投下光影。

小木乃伊的石棺里空无一物，它的棺盖仍然靠在墙边。另外两个木乃伊如守卫般立在房间里。

露丝抓住了丁丁和乔希，让他们看向珍宝室。三个人没有说话，踮着脚走到那个拱门处。

珍宝室和墓室一样，部分石头地面上覆盖着沙子和砾石。墙壁也是石头砌成的，没有窗户。

"她不在这里。"丁丁低声说。他瞥了一眼珍宝室昏暗的角落，手臂上突然起了鸡皮疙瘩。

"是啊，但是你们看这些金子！"乔希说。他的鼻子紧紧抵在一个玻璃展柜上。

珍宝室中有六个展柜，其中四个摆满了陶器和农具，另外两个则装满了金饰和珠宝。

"如果有人想偷东西，"丁丁说，"目标肯定是这些宝贝，而不是木乃伊。"

"这些展柜是锁着的，还安装了警报器。"露丝说。她指了指每一个柜子边缘都有的细细的灰

失踪的木乃伊

色电线。

突然，丁丁听到一声闷响。"什么声音？"他问。

"听起来像墓门发出的声音！"露丝说。

孩子们跑回陵墓，正好看到大门缓缓关上。

乔希跑到墙边，试图用手指强行把门打开。然后他转过身，脸色变得煞白。

"我们被锁在里面了。"他说。

第四章

"一定有办法从这里打开门。"露丝说,"我们去找找看,有没有开关之类的东西。"

孩子们在靠近门的墙壁上摸了半天,没有发现能打开门的东西。

"但门为什么会关上呢?"乔希问。

"你碰这个柜子的时候,可能触发了警报。"露丝说。

"如果露丝是对的,"丁丁说,"有人会听到警报,并且进来查看谁在这里。我们要做的就是等待。"

"那我们就在这里等着?"乔希尖叫道。

失踪的木乃伊

"不会太久的。"丁丁说,"做好准备,那扇门随时会再次打开。"

"好吧,那我们在珍宝室里等着吧。"乔希低声说,"那些木乃伊太吓人了。"

"它们只是骸骨。"露丝说。

"但它们都是死人的骸骨!"乔希说着,走进珍宝室。

孩子们坐在地上,靠着墙。房间里静悄悄的,天花板上的小灯投下一道柔和的光,照在展柜里的金子上。

"我一直梦想着被关在一个装满金子的房间里。"乔希说,"现在梦想已经实现了,但我宁愿待在家里。"

几分钟过去了,然后又过了几分钟。没有人来营救他们。陵墓的石门一直紧闭着。

"没有人知道我们在这里。"乔希嘟囔道,"我们可能永远出不去了。我们会死掉,然后变成木乃伊的!"

"我们的父母都知道我们在博物馆。"露丝说,"如果我没有回家吃晚饭,我爸爸会打电话来的。"

"但那个时候，博物馆都关门了。"乔希继续说，"没有人会接电话的！"

"那我的父母会开车到这里来。"露丝说。

"或者他们会报警。"丁丁说。"我们要做的就是坐在这里，冷静下来。"

"我已经很冷了。"乔希低声说，"这地方给人的感觉像一个冰箱。"

丁丁咧嘴笑了："哎哟，乔希，我以为你很愿意待在冰箱里呢。"

"真好笑，丁丁！"乔希低声说道，"再说了，我还坐在碎石子上呢。他们怎么不像一般人那样在里面铺个地毯呢？"

露丝站起来，拍了拍短裤上的砾石和沙子。"乔希说得对，让我们看看能不能找个舒服的地方坐。"她说。

"找个像家一样舒服的地方。"乔希说。

"或者这种！"露丝说。她打开了一扇嵌在石墙里的小门。

"这是一个壁橱。"丁丁朝里面看了看说。

"埃及人可不用壁橱。"乔希说。孩子们看到

了折叠椅、清洁用品和一堆地毯。

"这些方形地毯应该是给小孩子坐的。"露丝说,"我们把它们铺在地上吧。"

孩子们将从壁橱中拿出的地毯在地上铺好,然后躺下。

"这更像我的梦了。"乔希舒舒服服地躺着,

A to Z 神秘案件

"如果现在有人给我带一些比萨和一杯苏打水,我会非常开心。"

"你愿意和这些木乃伊分享美食吗?"露丝问乔希。

"不愿意。"

又过了一段时间。丁丁打了个哈欠,眼皮开始打架。他把壁橱的门关上,小房间一下变得昏暗。然后他躺下来,三个人都沉沉地睡去。

突然,巨大的爆炸震动了房间。折叠椅在震动中散落一地,清洁用品也从架子上掉了下来。

丁丁、乔希和露丝从沉睡中醒了过来。

"怎么回事?"乔希说,"听起来像炸弹爆炸了!"

"我闻到烟味了!"露丝在黑暗中说。

丁丁把门开了一条缝,然后又关上了。"外面全是烟尘。"他揉着眼睛说。

"出什么事了?"露丝问。

就在这时,丁丁听到了动静。

"有人在外面,"乔希说,"我们获救了!"

"别说话!"丁丁低声说,"不会有人为了救我们而炸了这个地方的。"

失踪的木乃伊

丁丁将门打开一条小缝，透过飘浮的烟尘向外望，然后突然缩了回来。

两个穿着深色衣服的人在壁橱外闪过，离孩子们的鼻头只有几英寸[1]远。两个人都背着黑色的健身包。

孩子们看见这两个人分别停在两个玻璃展柜前。丁丁听到玻璃被打碎的声音，然后一阵刺耳的警报声响了起来。

"能装多少装多少，然后赶紧离开！"其中一个闯入者说。

"他们不是来救我们的。"丁丁低声说，"他们是来偷木乃伊的金子的！"

---

1. 英寸：英美制长度单位。1 英寸 = 2.54 厘米。——编者

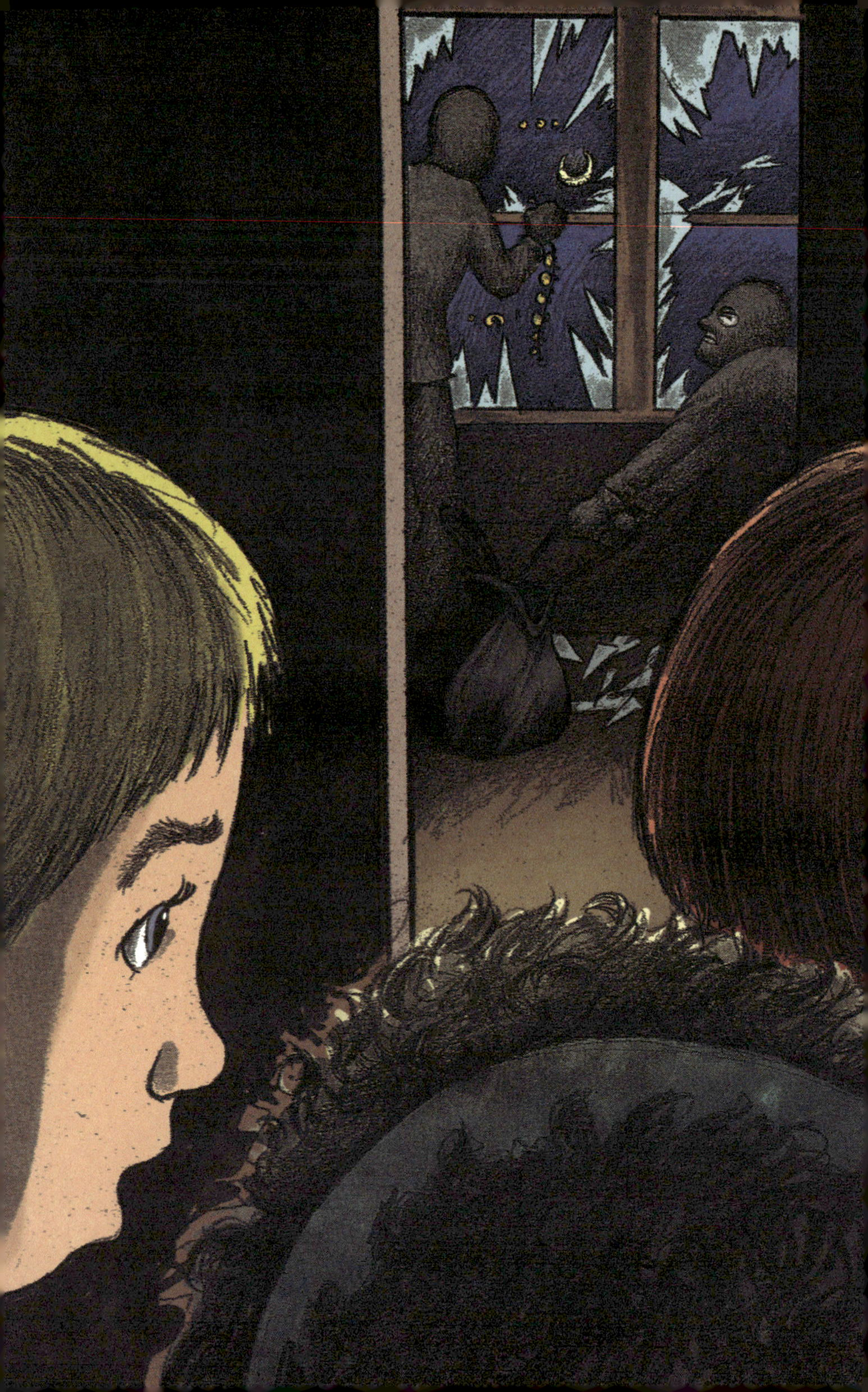

第五章

小偷们行动迅速。从门缝里,丁丁看着这两个人将他们的包里装满了金子。

"天啊,这东西真够沉的。"其中一个人咕哝着。他们拖着沉重的包往外走。

丁丁努力记下他们衣服的颜色、头上的滑雪面罩和手提包的样式。当小偷们经过壁橱时,他注意到,其中一个人的腰和膝盖之间似乎有一道白色条纹。

两个人离开后,珍宝室变得静悄悄的。

丁丁等了几秒钟，然后把壁橱的门完全推开。

金子不见了，两块大石头躺在碎玻璃上，房间里到处都是灰尘。

丁丁、乔希和露丝从壁橱里走出来，警报声戛然而止，和之前一样突然。

"他们到哪儿去了?"乔希在安静的房间里低声问。

丁丁还没来得及回答,他们就听到陵墓门打开的声音。随即,彼得斯警官和华盛顿警官冲进了珍宝室。

"不许动!"彼得斯警官大喊。随后他定睛

一看，说："怎么是……孩子们！"

特威德博士出现在两名警官后面。"请解释一下你们在这里的原因。"他说。特威德博士一只眼睛的眼皮跳个不停。

"我们想要找到那个带走木乃伊的女人，"露丝说，"然后门就自己关上了。"

"我们在壁橱里睡着了。"乔希说，"几分钟前，我们听到砰的一声。两个人进来把金子偷走了！"

特威德博士跨过破碎的玻璃，看了看被破坏的柜子。"什么都没有了，"他说，"无价之宝都被偷走了。"

"我们检查一下这堵墙吧。"彼得斯警官说。

大家跟着他进入陵墓。其中一堵墙被炸开了一个巨大的、边缘不规则的洞。通过这个洞，丁丁可以看到博物馆后面又高又密的灌木丛。

洞周围散落着大块的石头，但两具立着的木乃伊看起来并没有受损。

桌子上，小木乃伊的石棺已经被盖上了。

棺盖上的面具平静地"望"着天花板。

"哦，谢天谢地！"有人喊道。丁丁转过身，

失踪的木乃伊

是他的父母跑进了陵墓。

接着,露丝的父母也来了。很快,乔希的家人也跟了进来。

"你们这些孩子在这里经历了什么?"丁丁的妈妈一边抱着丁丁,一边问。"这几个小时我们一直在打电话,几乎走遍了哈特福德镇!"

"我们被困在这里了。"乔希说,"当时我们正在找偷走木乃伊的人!"

"什么木乃伊?"露丝的妈妈问。

"我们回家再聊这件事。"丁丁的爸爸建议道,"这些孩子一定饿坏了。"

"是啊!"乔希说。

第二天上午十点,彼得斯警官和华盛顿警官来到丁丁家中。丁丁叫来乔希和露丝,一群人坐在后院里。

"我希望你们昨晚睡了个好觉。"彼得斯警官微笑着说,"我们刚和你们的父母谈过,他们同意我们询问你们几个问题。"

"如果你们不介意的话。"华盛顿警官补充道。

孩子们点点头。

彼得斯警官瞥了一眼他的笔记本。"我们认为偷木乃伊的女人是想把所有人都引出陵墓。"他解释道,"混乱中,有人把一小枚炸弹藏在了墙边。"

"我们已经和特威德博士谈过了。"华盛顿警官补充道,"现在,我们想听听你们的经历。"

孩子们讲述了被爆炸惊醒前经历的一切。

"有时候,"华盛顿警官说,"人在情绪激动时会忘记一些小事。现在我想让你们回想一下,你们看到那两个小偷进入珍宝室时是怎样的情景。告诉我你们记得的所有事情,哪怕是最小的细节。"

丁丁最先开口:"好吧,他们都穿着深色的衣服,脸上应该都戴着滑雪面具。"

"其中一个人说了话。"露丝说,"他说——"

"是男人的声音吗?"彼得斯警官打断了她。

露丝闭上眼睛回忆了一分钟,然后说:"我想是的。他的声音很低沉,他说:'能装多少装多少,然后赶紧离开!'"

"另一个人说什么了吗?"华盛顿警官问。

露丝想了一会儿。"我记得他们中的一个说,他们要带走的东西很沉。"她补充道。

彼得斯警官点了点头,做了记录。

"我记得闻到了某种味道。"乔希说。

两位警官都看着他。

"我不知道那是什么,但是……"乔希停了下来,表情尴尬。

"我们洗耳恭听。"华盛顿警官说,"你闻到了……"

"我觉得是食物的味道。"

彼得斯警官微笑着看乔希。

"什么食物?汉堡包?比萨?"

乔希摇摇头:"对不起,我不记得了。"

"我记得别的事!"丁丁突然说,"其中一个人的衣服上有一道白色条纹。"

"白色条纹?"彼得斯警官重复道,"我以为他们穿的是深色衣服。"

丁丁点点头。"是的,但我看见他在这里有一道白色条纹。"

他站起来,在膝盖上方比画了一下。

"你看到了他的正面还是背面呢?"华盛顿警

官问。

"都看到了。"丁丁说,"但只有前面有条纹。"

警官们记了下来,然后合上他们的笔记本。

"孩子们,你们帮了大忙。"华盛顿警官说。她看着乔希说:"如果你想起了那个味道,就给我打电话。"她递给他一张名片。

乔希接过名片。"嗯……我们能去博物馆吗?"他问,"今天是周二霸王龙日!"

"当然。"华盛顿警官说,"不过你们要小心它们的大牙齿!"

第六章

下午一点半，巴士把孩子们送到博物馆前。银行门口上方的电子屏上显示着温度为九十华氏度[1]。

"还有半个小时，"乔希说，"我可以吃点零食。"

"乔希，我们刚吃完！"露丝说，"我觉得你有点饿狼血统。"

乔希吼叫着，挤了挤他的眉毛。

"天气太热了，吃不下。"丁丁说，"我们去阴凉处坐几分钟吧。"

---

1. 相当于约三十二摄氏度。——编者

A to Z 神秘案件

孩子们沿着博物馆一侧的一条石子路走着，旁边是乔木、灌木和花圃。在博物馆的拐角处，他们发现了一座金鱼池和几条长凳。胖乎乎的金鱼游到水面上，好像在等待着投喂。

"看！"乔希指着博物馆的后墙说，"那一定

失踪的木乃伊

是炸弹爆炸的地方。"

　　一大块胶合板盖住了被炸开的洞,水泥和空心砖就堆放在附近。

乔希说:"小偷逃跑的时候,一定经过了这些长凳。"

孩子们在长凳处坐了下来,从他们的位置可以看到主街上银行的钟。

"我想知道他们往哪儿去了。"丁丁说,"他们带着那些金子,不可能跑很远。"

露丝从她后口袋里拿出博物馆的地图。地图的一面是博物馆内部展室的示意图,另一面是小公园、博物馆和主街的地图。

乔希指着主街。"也许他们有车在那里接应。"他说。

露丝摇了摇头:"博物馆前面是不允许停车的。如果小偷们把车停在那里,警察会注意到的。"

"博物馆附近也没有其他街道可供他们停车。"丁丁一边观察,一边研究地图。

乔希看了看四周的乔木和灌木。"那么他们把金子拿到哪里去了?"他低头看着地上,"也许他们把金子埋了!"

丁丁摇摇头。"他们时间紧迫,没有时间挖洞。"他说着,看了看银行前面的电子屏,"我们

失踪的木乃伊

还是先进去吧,快两点钟了。"

孩子们起身离开,沿着小路走到了博物馆的前面。

"好香啊,我闻到了好吃的东西。"正当他们急忙跑上台阶时,乔希说。

"你总能闻到好吃的东西。"露丝说。

他们走进博物馆,把钱付给柜台后面的女士。大厅的中央有一只充气的橡胶霸王龙。它的牙齿上挂着一个指示牌,上面写着"请随箭头方向走"。

一分钟后,孩子们发现特威德博士站在一扇敞开的门外。

"你们好。"他说,"进来吧,我们就要开始了。"

一群孩子围坐在几张桌子旁。丁丁、乔希和露丝闪身进去,在三个空座位上坐下。桌子中间有一具巨大的恐龙骨架,它的大脑袋几乎要顶到天花板啦!

"我敢肯定,你们中的大多数人都认识霸王龙。"特威德博士说。

丁丁抬头盯着那具骨架。他努力想象着它活

着的时候会是什么样子。

"今天,"特威德博士继续说,"我们打算研究这种史前的食肉动物——"。

一个坐在前排的男孩举起了手。"你把木乃伊找回来了吗?"他问。

"是的,我们的一位客人在女洗手间里找到了它。"特威德博士说,"现在,正如我所说的——"

"我在电视上看到有人破门而入,偷走了财宝。"一个女孩说。

特威德博士叹了口气。"没错。小偷仍逍遥法外,财宝也不知踪迹。但是我们今天到这里是来讨论恐龙的。"

他打开一个橱柜,拿出一根长长的骨头。"这是霸王龙的腿骨化石。"他说,"这只恐龙生活在我们现在所知的犹他州,它也是在那里死去的。你们可以摸摸这根骨头,但请轻一点。"

孩子们围了上来,在特威德博士旁边摸摸化石。

"关于霸王龙,我们知道些什么呢?"特威德博士问。

孩子们立马给了回答：

"它们的牙齿很大！"

"它们吃其他恐龙！"

"它们会下蛋！"

"很好。"特威德博士说，"你们知道霸王龙有惊人的嗅觉吗？它能闻到数百码[1]之外的食物的味道。"

"就像乔希一样。"丁丁低声说。

"并且霸王龙的脑袋相较它的体形来说很小。"特威德博士继续说。

"就像丁丁一样。"乔希低声说。

特威德博士将灯光调暗，开始放幻灯片。孩子们学习了恐龙是如何生活的，它们吃什么东西，还有它们是如何养育幼崽的。

幻灯片放映结束后，特威德博士把灯重新打开。他拉开一个橱柜的门说："现在你们可以来做自己的恐龙了。"他让志愿者们将黏土、木头和铁丝等材料分发给孩子们。

---

1. 码：英美制长度单位。1 码 =0.9144 米。——编者

"你们做的恐龙要立在木板上。你们可以用铁丝来固定恐龙的腿和尾巴。"

很快,二十多双小手便开始制作微型霸王龙。

"真好玩。"乔希说,"没准以后我不做画家了,改做雕塑家。"

露丝看了看乔希的那堆黏土。"乔希,"她说,"我们是来做恐龙的。你做的看起来像一颗土豆。"

"有意思。"乔希说。然后他瞪大了眼睛:"就是它!"

"什么意思?"露丝问。

"我昨晚在壁橱里闻到的就是它的味道!"

"土豆?"丁丁问。

乔希摇摇头,他闭上眼睛,吸了吸鼻子。"炸薯条!"他说。

第七章

丁丁给他的恐龙做了一条尾巴,说:"我只闻到炸弹爆炸引起的烟尘味。你怎么能闻到炸薯条的味道?"

乔希一边给他的霸王龙做牙齿一边说:"因为我有惊人的嗅觉。"

"时间快到了,"特威德博士说,"你们可以多带一些黏土回去,在家里完成你们的雕塑作品。"

他给孩子们发了纸箱,用来装这些黏土恐龙。

"谢谢你们的到来。"大家快要离开时,特威德博士说,"明天是周三湿地日,我没有时间陪伴大家,但我的一位同事会来接替我。记得一定

A to Z 神秘案件

要穿短裤和旧运动鞋,并且带上你们父母准许你们参加活动的证明。"

几分钟后,丁丁、乔希和露丝拿着他们的箱子站在了博物馆门口。

"我们的巴士几点来?"乔希问。

"巴士半个小时一趟。"露丝望着街对面银行的钟说,"现在是三点半,我们刚好错过了一辆。"

失踪的木乃伊

乔希咧嘴笑了:"那太好啦,我们有时间吃点零食啦。"

丁丁翻了个白眼："乔希，我的爸爸妈妈还在因为之前的炸弹袭击担惊受怕呢。我答应他们今天博物馆活动一结束就回家。我们到阴凉处等着吧。"

他们走到金鱼池边，坐在长凳上。金鱼立刻游过来索要食物。

突然，乔希站了起来，用鼻子嗅了嗅。"我又闻到那个味道了！"他转动着脑袋，像潜望镜在寻找敌人的船只。

"那儿！"他一边说着，一边指向身后那条伸向主街的公园小路。一家小餐馆就在银行旁边。

餐馆橱窗上写着"弗蕾达姨妈的美味薯条"。

"别嘴馋了，乔希。"丁丁说，"下一辆巴士很快就到了。"

乔希坐回长凳上。

"我冤枉。"他说，"我只是想弄清楚那些金子的情况。"

"好吧。"丁丁说，"说说看。"

"好。"乔希说，"昨晚，我闻到了炸薯条的味道，那味道闻起来和街对面那家炸薯条店里散发的味道一样。所以小偷们可能在那家店工作，也许他们把金子藏在了那里！"

"我看到那些小偷是拖着金子走的。"丁丁说，"他们不可能一路拖着那些金子去那家餐馆。"

露丝看着丁丁。"不过，也许乔希说得对，小偷们有可能就在那里工作。"她说，"也许我们应该过去看看。"

"但是我们的巴士……"

"来吧，丁丁。"乔希站起来说，"我们赶下一趟。"

"好吧，但我依然觉得这就是你的把戏。"丁丁说，"为了一盘薯条，你什么都愿意做。"

孩子们带着他们的箱子穿过公园和主街，走进了餐馆。

他们坐在窗边的一个卡座上。头顶的吊扇嗡嗡作响，自动唱机播放着猫王的歌曲。

六个年轻人刚走，留下的脏盘子和玻璃杯堆成了小山。

一位矮胖的妇人拿着三杯冰水从活动门里走了出来。她头发灰白，系着一条白色围裙。

"欢迎来到弗蕾达姨妈的店。"她说,"我是弗蕾达姨妈。你们一定去过博物馆了,对吗?"

"你怎么知道的?"露丝问。

这位妇人指着露丝的小箱子,箱子侧面有

失踪的木乃伊

"沃兹沃思博物馆"的字样。

"我们用黏土做了恐龙。"乔希说。

"哦,那应该是特威德博士组织的。"弗蕾达姨妈说,"他是我这里的常客。好了,今天你们要吃点什么呢?"

"炸薯条和一杯柠檬水。"乔希说。

"你们会喜欢我的炸薯条的。"弗蕾达姨妈说,"这是哈特福德最美味的薯条!"

"我和他一样。"露丝说。

丁丁也要了一样的东西,弗蕾达姨妈便匆匆走去厨房了。

乔希向前探身,低声说:"也许弗蕾达姨妈就是其中一个小偷!"

丁丁咧嘴笑了。"她看起来不像。"他说。

"而且,那两个小偷更高更瘦。"露丝说。

弗蕾达姨妈端着薯条、饮料、番茄酱和餐巾纸回来了。"回头告诉我你们觉得这薯条怎么样。"她说,"这是我的秘密配方!"

孩子们一起蘸着番茄酱,狼吞虎咽地吃了起来。

几分钟后,一个有着黑色短发的女人从厨房

A to Z 神秘案件

里走了出来。她系着围裙,拿着一个大塑料盆。

那个女人走到杯盘狼藉的桌子旁,开始打扫。当她费力地将装有盘子的塑料盆拖进厨房时,丁

失踪的木乃伊

丁听到了她小声的抱怨。

"怎么了?"见丁丁还盯着那个女人,露丝问。

乔希拿着一根炸薯条在丁丁的面前挥了挥:"怎么眼睛瞪这么大,丁丁?"

"那个女人……"他说,"她拖着那堆盘子的样子……让我想起了昨晚的一个小偷。"

"哎哟!"乔希说,"终于有人认同我了!"

露丝转身朝厨房看去。"你们看,她的黑发很短,我找到木乃伊之前,就看到一个这样的女人从洗手间出来。"

三个孩子盯着厨房。

"而且她身上有炸薯条的味道!"乔希说。

第八章

弗蕾达姨妈走到他们的卡座处。"天啊,你们把薯条全部吃完啦!"她说,"还需要再来一点吗?"

"不用了,谢谢——"丁丁说。

"要的!"露丝打断道,"你能告诉我们你是怎么做出如此美味的薯条的吗?我们这位朋友唐纳德对烹饪很感兴趣。"

"我对烹饪感兴趣吗?"丁丁心里想。

弗蕾达姨妈看着丁丁,笑容满面。"当然,亲爱的,快到厨房来。"她说。

露丝轻推着丁丁,大家都跟在了弗蕾达姨妈

A to Z 神秘案件

后面。

门里,炸薯条的味道在空气中肆意弥漫。

墙上有一排排架子,上面放着各种锅碗瓢盆、烹饪香料和烹饪书。一箱箱未加工的土豆堆在墙边。

那个有着黑色短发的女人正在台面上切土豆片。她戴着耳机,似乎没有注意到孩子们。

丁丁盯着那个女人。当她弯下腰去拿土豆时,丁丁想象着她弯下腰从展柜里拿金子的样子。

弗蕾达姨妈打断了他的想象。"过来。"她说着,领着孩子们走向一台油炸机。

她压低了声音。"这是我的秘密配方,我在橄榄油里放了一点大蒜和醋。"她眨着眼睛说,"可以答应我不告诉别人吗?"

丁丁点点头。"我答应你。"他说,"天啊,炸薯条的过程真是有趣极了!"

丁丁瞥见乔希从厨房的地板上捡了个东西,随后塞进了自己的口袋。

露丝戳了一下丁丁。她抬了抬下巴,示意他看后门的衣架。一件黑色的夹克挂在衣架的一个

失踪的木乃伊

钩子上。地上还放着一个黑色的健身包。

"你们还想知道什么吗?"弗蕾达姨妈问。

"没有了,谢谢你。"露丝微笑着说,"我们想知道的已经都知道啦。"

弗蕾达姨妈跟着孩子们离开了厨房。孩子们付了钱,向门口走去。

突然,弗蕾达姨妈一把抓住了丁丁的胳膊。"等等!"她一边说一边在她围裙的口袋里掏着什么,"伸出手来!"

孩子们伸出了手,弗蕾达姨妈在每个人的手里放了一颗糖。"祝你们玩得开心。"弗蕾达姨妈说着,为他们打开了门。

孩子们一边把糖果塞进嘴里,一边急急忙忙地回到巴士站。

"你看见那件夹克了吗?"露丝说,"如果那个女人把它穿在围裙外面,白色的围裙边就会露出来。你昨晚看到的就是这个吗,丁丁?"

"有可能。"丁丁说,"还有那个健身包,看上去很像小偷们提着的那个。"

乔希摇摇头。"你们太不专业了。"他说,"任何人都可以有那样一件夹克。并且在哈特福德，有黑色健身包的人多了去了。"

他把手伸进口袋："我找到了真正的线索！"

他拿出一块巧克力豆大小的光滑的小石头。

"这是什么？"丁丁问。

"来，我来告诉你们。"乔希朝博物馆的台阶走去。

丁丁和露丝跟着乔希穿过大厅。在陵墓前，他们看见了一个告示牌，上面显示木乃伊展览已经结束。告示牌后面的大门紧闭着。

乔希走到墙边，按下了那块石头。随着一阵隆隆声，墙上的门打开了。

乔希向里面探了探身子，从地上抓起一把砂石，然后将门关上了。

"看，它们是一样的。"乔希说着，亮出刚抓起的砂石和在薯条店中发现的小石头。

"我不明白。"丁丁说。

"我在弗蕾达姨妈的厨房地上发现了这个小石头。"乔希解释道，"它和陵墓里的砂石是一样的。砂石从陵墓的地上跑到弗蕾达姨妈厨房的地上的

失踪的木乃伊

唯一解释，就是它粘在了小偷的一只鞋上！"

"好吧。"露丝说。"但这仍然不能告诉我们金子在哪里。"

"以及第二个小偷是谁。"丁丁补充道。

"也许确实不能。"乔希说，"但那家餐馆里的气味有点不对劲！"

第九章

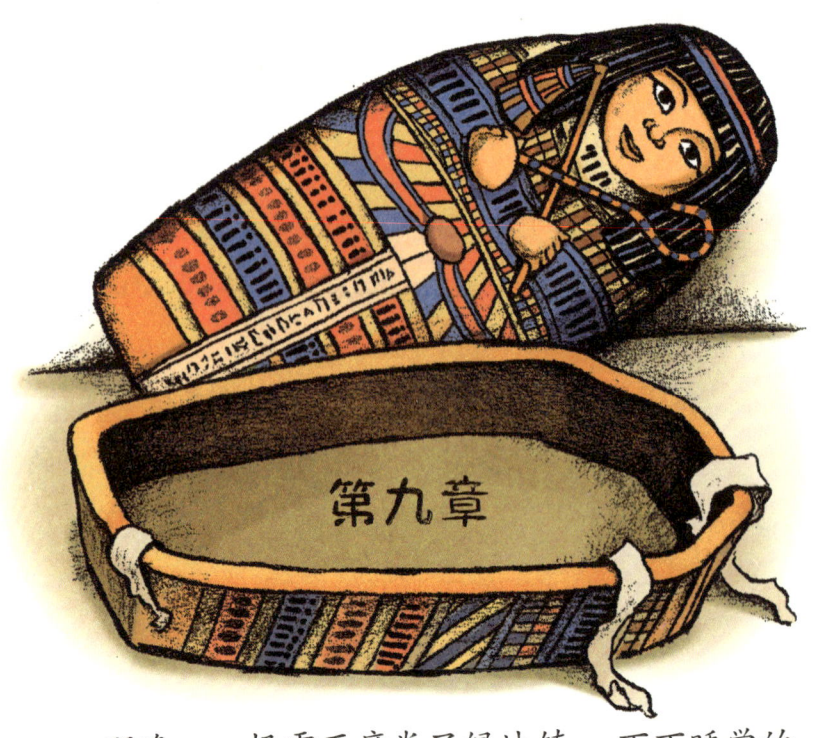

那晚,一场雷雨席卷了绿地镇。丁丁睡觉的时候,卧室的窗外电闪雷鸣。

丁丁做了个噩梦,梦见他又被困在陵墓里了。这次,他是独自一人。

两个靠墙的木乃伊依次睁开了眼。它们一个接一个地走出石棺,向他走来。

它们从小木乃伊的石棺旁走过,小木乃伊的棺盖紧闭着,棺盖上的面具望着天花板。

"这是因为那具木乃伊不在里面。"丁丁想,"但为什么——"

就在这时,丁丁感觉有一只冰冷的手触碰了

失踪的木乃伊

他的肩膀。他想逃跑，但腿却无法动弹。包裹木乃伊的布散开了，像触手一样缠绕着他的身体。

丁丁大叫着醒了过来，发现原来自己被床单缠住了。当意识到自己是在床上，而不是陵墓里时，他又躺了下来。

他试着再次睡去，但睡不着。这似乎是因为他的噩梦，或者是那座陵墓。到底因为什么呢？

他躺着，试图再一次回想陵墓中的场景。炸弹爆炸前，三个石棺的棺盖都被打开了。那个小石棺是空的，因为那具木乃伊还在特威德博士的办公室里。

但爆炸后，那个小木乃伊的石棺被盖上了。

然后丁丁回忆起当时小偷拖着两袋沉重的金子的场景。他笑了起来，闭上眼睛，再次进入了梦乡。

早餐后，丁丁给乔希打了电话。乔希赶了过来，然后他们去了隔壁的露丝家。露丝正坐在门前的台阶上，膝盖上放着一盘烤面包。

丁丁坐在台阶的底部。"我昨晚想明白了。"他告诉他们，"我知道小偷把金子藏在哪里了。"

乔希伸手去拿露丝的烤面包，但被露丝打了手。

"你难道不知道分享是一种美德吗？"乔希问。

"你难道不知道事先询问也是一种美德吗？"露丝说。不过她还是递给了乔希一些烤面包。"告诉我们到底是怎么回事吧，丁丁。"

"昨晚我做了个噩梦。"丁丁说，"我被困在陵墓里。两口大石棺被打开了，木乃伊在追赶我。但那个小木乃伊的石棺却紧闭着。"

他看着乔希和露丝说："醒来后，我想起了一件事。我们被困在陵墓之前，小石棺是打开的，还记得吗？但当我们在炸弹爆炸后回到那里时，小石棺的棺盖被盖上了！"

"我不明白你的意思。"乔希一边说一边舔着手指上的果酱。

"你马上就会明白了。"丁丁说，"昨晚我睡不着，便开始想，是谁盖上了那个小石棺？突然，我灵光一动。如果小偷们没有接应的车，如果金子太重，他们无法将它带到很远的地方，也许他们就把它藏在小石棺里了！"

失踪的木乃伊

乔希说:"那么这个小偷必须是一个能够回到陵墓去拿金子的人。"

"特威德博士!"露丝喊道。

"我也是这么想的。"丁丁说,"弗蕾达姨妈说特威德博士是她的常客。我想是他和那个留着短发的女人策划了这一切。"

"她有那个健身包。"露丝说,"而且她只要走到街对面就可以了。"

"她身上都是炸薯条的味道!"乔希补充道。

露丝问:"但是是谁藏的炸弹呢?"

"我觉得是特威德博士。"丁丁说,"还记得我们走后,他在陵墓里待了几分钟吗?"

"那女人为什么要抢走木乃伊呢?"乔希问。

"为了把我们引出去。"丁丁说,"特威德博士必须一个人在陵墓里,才可以安放炸弹。"

丁丁笑着对乔希和露丝说:"并且石棺空了,正好可以用来藏金子!"

"我的天!"露丝喊道,"特威德博士跟我们说,他今天不会参加周三湿地日。我打赌他一定会拿着金子逃跑!"

她跳起来，跑进屋子。丁丁和乔希跟了上去。露丝打电话给警察局，找到法伦警官。

第十章

法伦警官开车带着丁丁、乔希和露丝来到了哈特福德。

他给彼得斯警官和华盛顿警官打了电话。两辆警车在博物馆前会和了。

"华盛顿警官会抓住餐厅里那个年轻女子。"彼得斯警官对法伦警官说,"你和我去博物馆。孩子们,跟我们走。"

丁丁、乔希和露丝在两名警官的护送下穿过主街,进入了安静的博物馆。他们沿着走廊一直走到了特威德博士的办公室门口。

彼得斯警官让孩子们跟在他的身后,然后他

A to Z 神秘案件

敲响了房门。没有人应答。他转动门把手,打开了门。"他不在这里。"彼得斯警官说。

失踪的木乃伊

　　法伦警官和孩子们朝办公室里看了看,看见小木乃伊被放在桌子上。

　　彼得斯警官看向丁丁、乔希和露丝。"我们去检查一下那个陵墓。"他说。

　　孩子们和两位警官往回走,穿过大厅,在紧闭的墓门前停了下来。

　　"我们怎么进去?"法伦警官问。

　　"我知道!"乔希说着,按下了那块石头,门

打开了。特威德博士正站在小石棺前。

特威德博士猛地转身,死死捂住胸前一个鼓鼓囊囊的健身包。在石棺里,丁丁看到了一堆金子。

特威德博士眨着一直抽搐的眼睛。

"你好。"法伦警官说,"这是要去旅行吗?"

特威德博士冲向被胶合板盖住的大洞,双手一挥,把健身包砸向板子。板子被击中,向外倒下,特威德博士从洞口冲了出去。

出去后,他被一袋水泥绊倒了,掉进了金鱼池,健身包也沉到了水底。

这池塘的水很浅,特威德博士扑腾几下就坐起来了,吐了吐嘴里的水。睡莲的叶子挂在他的耳朵上,黏糊糊的水藻顺着他的眉毛往下滴水。

"我需要打电话给我的律师。"他结结巴巴地说着。

正好华盛顿警官押着餐馆的那个女人走进了公园,那个女人戴着手铐。

"她认罪了吗?"彼得斯警官问他的搭档。

"认罪了。他们两个人原本计划在几分钟后就乘坐出租车去机场。"华盛顿警官说,"他们的下一站是欧洲,他们想在那里卖掉赃物。"

"把她带走,"彼得斯警官说,"过几分钟我就把她那浑身湿漉漉的朋友带过去。"

华盛顿警官领着她抓捕的犯人走出了公园。

彼得斯警官走进池塘,扶起特威德博士,把浑身湿透的特威德博士按在一棵树上,将手铐铐在他滴水的手腕上。

法伦警官脱下鞋袜进入池塘,将健身包从池

失踪的木乃伊

塘里拖了出来。健身包里面装满了古埃及的宝物和池塘里的水。

"谢谢你的帮助。"彼得斯警官对法伦警官说,

"我晚点联系你。"

彼得斯警官拿起那个沉重的健身包,推着特威德博士向前走,离开了公园。他们进了水的鞋子一直发出呱唧呱唧的声音。

丁丁、乔希和露丝正坐在长凳上,法伦警官在他们旁边坐了下来,拧着滴水的裤腿。

"干得好,孩子们!"他对他们说。

然后,他拿出他的便签簿,翻开新的一页,开始做记录。突然,他停了下来。

"我实在是太激动了,"法伦警官说,"忘了今天是周几了。"

孩子们你看看我,我看看你,咧嘴笑了。

"今天是'湿的周三'!"乔希说。

A to Z Mysteries®

The Missing Mummy

by Ron Roy

illustrated by
John Steven Gurney

MA
HARTFORD
RI
NY
GREEN LAWN
CONNECTICUT
AUNT FREDA'S FABULOUS FRIES
MAIN STREET
NO PARKING
BANK
N
W
E
S
BUS ST

Welcome to
A to Z Mysteries
on Location at
HARTFORD, CONNECTICUT
PATH
POND
TOMB
WADSWORTH MUSEUM
CLOSET
TREASURE CHAMBER

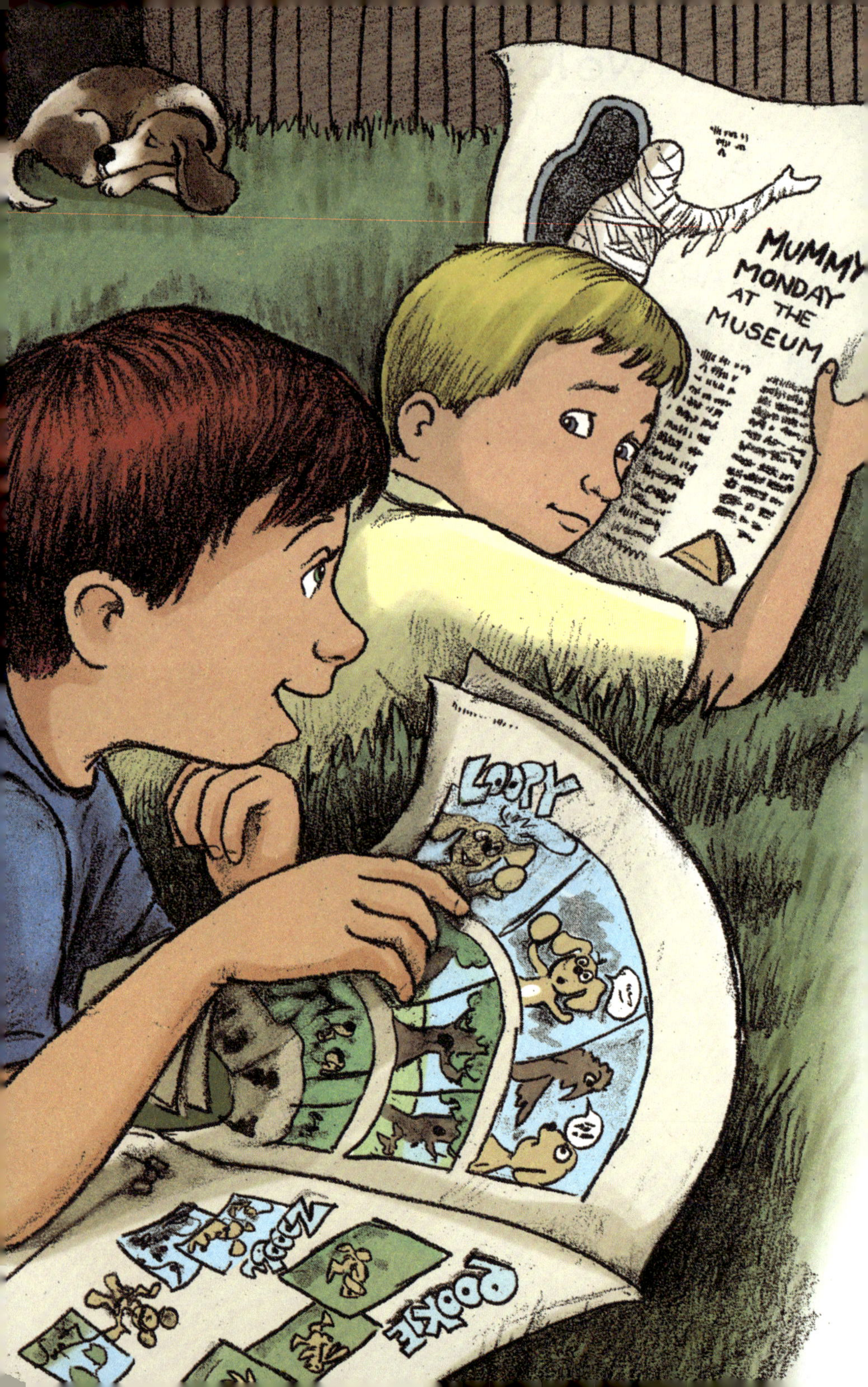
MUMMY MONDAY AT THE MUSEUM
LOOPY

CHAPTER 1

"Mummy Monday at the museum?" Josh said. He peered over Dink's shoulder at the Sunday newspaper. "So what's the next day, Tummy Tuesday?"

It was summer vacation, and Dink, Josh, and Ruth Rose were lying on the lawn behind Dink's house. Josh's dog, Pal, was snoozing under a tree.

Ruth Rose took the paper and read the article quickly. "No, Josh, the next day is about dinosaurs," she said. "It's called Tyrannosaurus Tuesday."

"The museum is having programs for kids all week," Dink explained.

"So what happens on Wednesday?" Josh asked.

"Kids go to the Connecticut River and study plant and animal life," Ruth Rose said. "It's called Wet Wednesday."

Dink took the newspaper back from Ruth Rose. "And the next day, you get to make a horror movie—that's Thrilling Thursday. The last day is Frog Friday. Each kid gets to study a frog."

"So let's sign up!" Josh said. "How much does it cost?"

Dink scanned the page. "A dollar for each program," he said. He looked at Josh and Ruth Rose. "That's five dollars for all five days."

"I don't have five bucks," Ruth Rose said.

"Me neither," said Josh. "But I know how we can earn it."

"How?" Dink asked.

"My dad's been trying to get the barn cleaned out," he said. "I bet he'd give us the money if we did it for him."

"Great idea!" Dink said.

The kids ran to Josh's house and spent the rest of Sunday working. Brian and Bradley, Josh's two little brothers, helped by playing with Pal.

失踪的木乃伊

Josh's dad gave each of the kids seven dollars for their hard work.

After lunch the next day, Dink, Josh, and Ruth Rose got on a bus to Hartford. Fifteen minutes later, the bus dropped them off on Main Street, in front of the Wadsworth Museum.

Across the street was a bank. A digital sign over the bank's entrance said MONDAY, JULY 10, 82 DEGREES. Then the sign flashed the time:It was nearly two o'clock!

"Come on, guys," Dink said. "We only have a few minutes to sign up."

They ran up the museum's front steps and through the wide doors. Inside, the museum was air-conditioned and quiet. The floor was made of marble. Tapestries and large paintings covered the white walls.

"Welcome to Mummy Monday," said a woman standing behind a counter.

Across the lobby, a bunch of other kids and a few grownups were already waiting. Ruth Rose took a map from a rack just inside the door. Then the kids walked over to join the group.

They each gave the woman behind the counter a dollar.

"I wonder where they keep the mummies," Josh whispered.

At exactly two o'clock, a door behind the counter opened and a tall man walked out. He was wearing a tan jacket and shorts, knee socks, laced boots, and a white helmet.

"I'm Dr. Harris Tweed," the man said. "Today, I will take you on a journey to ancient Egypt."

Dr. Tweed's face, hands, and knees were deeply tanned. Dink wondered how much time he had spent in the Egyptian desert.

"Who's ready to follow me into a tomb?" Dr. Tweed asked. He smiled, showing big white teeth that made his tanned face even darker.

"We're going in a tomb?" Josh muttered. "I think I want my dollar back!"

"Shh," Dink whispered.

Dr. Tweed's eyes narrowed. "If you're afraid of mummies, now's the time to speak up."

"Ugh!" a girl with red hair said. "Won't the mummies smell?"

"Today, you will learn precisely why mummies don't

smell," said Dr. Tweed. "Now please, follow me to the tomb!"

They walked to an arch at the rear of the lobby. Through the arch was a room with rows of benches facing a blank stone wall. The wall was built of large, flat rocks fitted closely together. Dink wondered how the museum people got those huge rocks inside.

"The tomb—and the mummies—are on the other side of this wall," Dr. Tweed said. "Before we go inside, I want to tell you a little about how these people died, and how they became mummies."

He pointed to the benches. "Please be seated."

"Let's sit in front," Dink said, heading for a bench.

When everyone was seated, Dr. Tweed began speaking in a deep voice. "Close your eyes and imagine you are standing on the bank of the River Nile four thousand years ago. Feel the sun on your back. See the river as it flows by. Hear the oxen bellow as they labor in the fields."

A hush fell over the group.

"Suddenly, an earthquake shakes the ground!" Dr. Tweed shouted.

失踪的木乃伊

Dink's eyes popped open as goose bumps crept up his arms. All the kids opened their eyes and stared at Dr. Tweed.

"Later," he continued, "the survivors prepare the dead for burial. Three of the people who died in that earthquake are with us today."

Dr. Tweed walked over to the wall and pressed his hand against one of the stones. Immediately, the wall slid open.

Through the opening, Dink could see a dim room. The stone floor was partly covered with sand and gravel.

"What you see is the burial tomb," Dr. Tweed said quietly. "Come in, please, but speak only in whispers and touch nothing."

"This is so great!" Ruth Rose whispered as they entered the tomb.

The tomb was cold, and Dink shivered. Old pots and farming tools were scattered around the floor. Strange-looking symbols were painted on the walls.

Off to one side were three stone coffins.

89

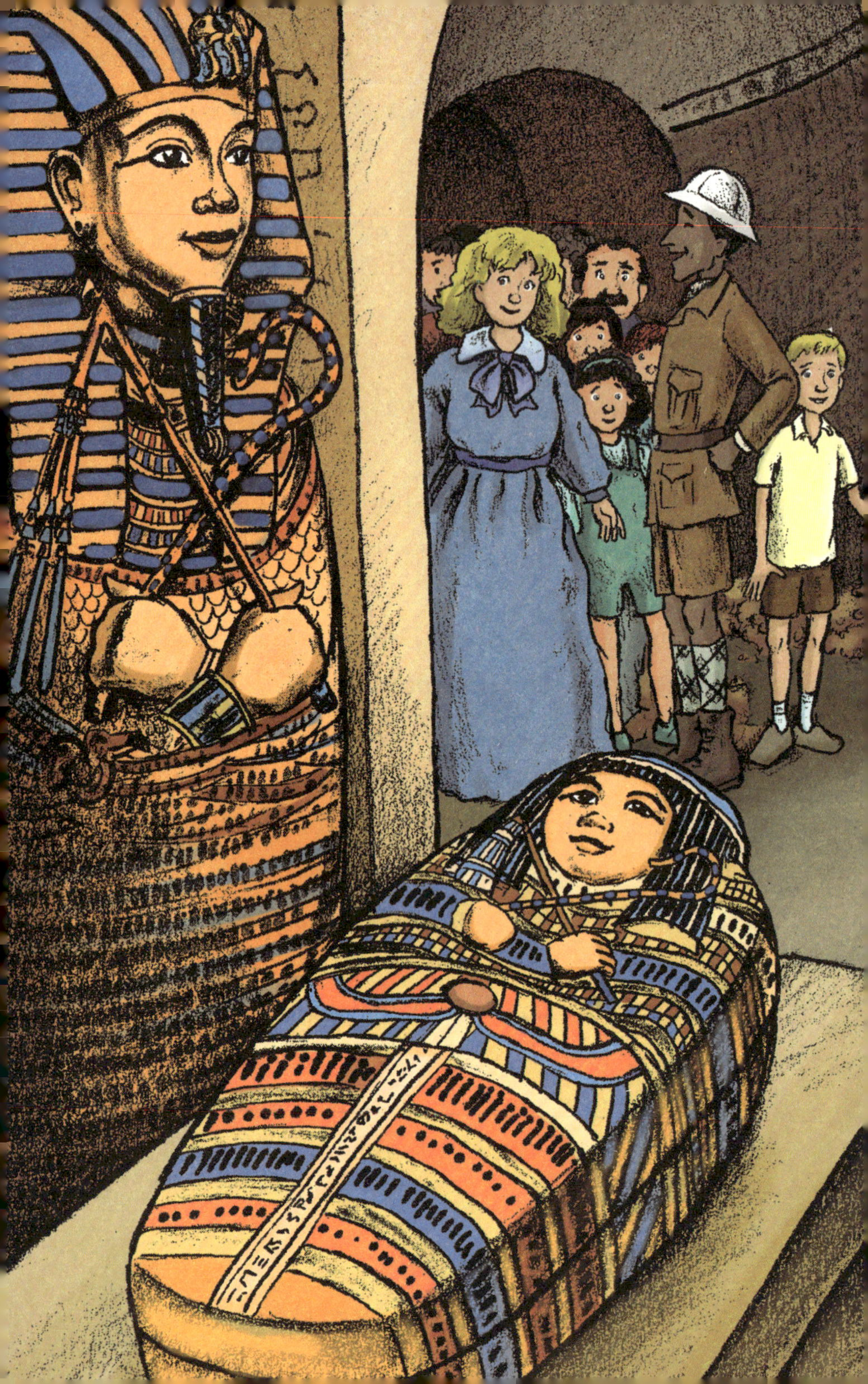

CHAPTER 2

One of the coffins was lying on a stone table. The other two were leaning upright against the walls to either side. Dink noticed that the coffin on the table was smaller than the other two.

"You are standing in an actual Egyptian tomb," Dr. Tweed said in a hushed voice. "It was brought here in pieces and then reconstructed."

He pointed at the coffins. "An ancient Egyptian coffin is called a sarcophagus. Each sarcophagus holds a mummy. In a moment, I will open the lids. But first, take a moment to appreciate the fine artwork."

On each lid, jewels and gold had been used to

create a mask. The faces look peaceful, almost happy, thought Dink.

"The Egyptians believed that people who died would need their money in the next life," Dr. Tweed said. "So rich people were often buried near their wealth."

He pointed through an arch into another room. "That is the treasure chamber," he said. "You'll get a chance to look in there after we view the mummies."

Ruth Rose raised her hand. "How come one of the coffins is so small?" she asked.

Dr. Tweed walked over to the sarcophagus on the table. "This sarcophagus contains a child mummy," he explained. "The little boy died with his parents, who now stand beside him for eternity."

Dr. Tweed placed his hand on a standing sarcophagus. "This is the boy's mother," he said. Using both hands, he swung the lid open.

"And the father." Dr. Tweed opened the other standing sarcophagus.

Without saying another word, here moved the lid of the smallest sarcophagus and leaned it against the wall.

失踪的木乃伊

The kids stared at the three mummies. Each was covered with some kind of cloth, yellowed with age. Dink realized that Dr. Tweed was right—there was no smell at all.

"Each mummy is wrapped in strips of linen," Dr. Tweed said. "Beneath the cloth— "

Suddenly, a woman with long blond hair who was wearing a baggy dress darted forward. She snatched the child and raced out of the tomb.

"Stop!" Dr. Tweed shouted, bolting after the woman.

Everyone in the room began talking at once. Before the kids could figure out what to do, Dr. Tweed hurried back into the tomb. "Quiet, please," he said. "Um, it seems Mummy Monday will have to be postponed. We'll have it tomorrow."

"But tomorrow is Tyrannosaurus Tuesday!" someone said.

Dr. Tweed looked flustered. His tanned face had turned pale, and one of his eyelids was twitching. "Yes, of course, you're right," he said. "I'll schedule another mummy day for next week. Now you'll have to leave the tomb. I'm very sorry."

93

Kids mumbled, "No fair" as they filed out. Dr. Tweed stepped aside to let them pass.

"Why would anyone steal a mummy?" Josh asked as he, Dink, and Ruth Rose followed the other kids.

"I read somewhere that gold and jewels were wrapped up with the bodies," Ruth Rose said. "Maybe that mummy has valuable stuff inside the cloth."

"You mean that woman is gonna unwrap the mummy?" Josh asked. "Gross!"

Dink, Josh, and Ruth Rose were the last kids out of the tomb. A moment later, Dr. Tweed hurried past. Behind them, the tomb door closed with a rumble.

"This is so bogus," Josh said. "Should we just go home?"

"I have to use the rest room first," Ruth Rose said.

The kids found the rest rooms around the corner from the tomb. The door to the ladies' room opened, and a smartly dressed woman with short dark hair stepped out. She was carrying a briefcase and talking on a cell phone.

"We'll wait for you here," Dink said as Ruth Rose slipped into the rest room.

失踪的木乃伊

"I wonder what the thief did with the mummy," Josh said. "I mean, she couldn't exactly carry it down Main Street!"

Suddenly, the rest room door crashed open. Ruth Rose stood there looking as if she'd seen a ghost.

"Ruth Rose, what's the matter?" Dink said.

"G-get Dr. Tweed," she answered. "It's in the rest room!"

"What's in the rest room?" Josh asked.

Ruth Rose took a deep breath. "The missing mummy!" she said.

Chapter 3

Dr. Tweed was standing by the front doors talking with two police officers. Dink dashed over to them. "Excuse me," he said, his mouth suddenly dry.

"Can we help you?" one of the officers asked. The name tag on her shirt read S. WASHINGTON.

"My friend found the mummy in the ladies' room!" Dink said.

"Show us," said the other officer. His name tag read P. PETERS.

Everyone rushed over to where Josh and Ruth Rose were standing outside the rest rooms.

"Will you come inside with me?" Officer

Washington asked Ruth Rose.

Ruth Rose and the officer walked into the rest room. A few seconds later, they both came out again.

"Dr. Tweed, will you step in with me, please?" Officer Washington said.

Dr. Tweed followed the officer back inside the rest room.

"So where was it?" Josh asked Ruth Rose.

"You know those tables they have so parents can change a baby's diaper?" she said. "It was right there on the table!"

"In plain sight?" Dink asked.

97

Ruth Rose nodded. "At first I thought it was a big doll, so I took a closer look..."

"Yuck!" Josh said.

The rest room door opened again. Officer Washington walked out, with Dr. Tweed behind her. He was carrying the child mummy in his arms.

"The mummy seems to be undamaged," Dr. Tweed said. "But I'll have to examine it in my office."

Dr. Tweed and the two police officers crossed the lobby and disappeared through the door behind the counter.

失踪的木乃伊

"I guess we might as well go home," Dink said.

"Some Mummy Monday," Ruth Rose grumbled.

"Look, there's a cafeteria," Josh said. "Let's get something to drink."

The kids entered the large room, paid for cold drinks, and sat at a round table.

"I wonder where the thief went after she left the mummy in the restroom," Ruth Rose said as she sipped her lemonade.

"What do you mean?" Dink asked.

"There weren't any windows in there, so she couldn't have gotten out that way," Ruth Rose said. "And if she'd come through the door, she would have bumped right into us."

"But a woman did come out," Josh said. "Remember, she was talking on a cell phone?"

"Yeah, but she looked totally different," Ruth Rose said.

"Maybe she was in disguise," Dink said. "Maybe the mummy snatcher changed clothes in the rest room!"

"She might've hidden her dress in the briefcase," Josh said. "And the blond hair could've been a wig."

99

"Guys, I just realized something," Ruth Rose said. "When that woman came out of the rest room, she walked toward the tomb. Maybe she went back to steal something else!"

The kids left their drinks on the table and ran to the tomb.

"Open, sez me!" Josh said. He pressed the stone and the door rumbled open.

Tiny lights shone from the tomb ceiling, casting shadows on the floor.

The child mummy's sarcophagus lay empty. Its lid still leaned against the wall. The other two mummies stood guard over the room.

Ruth Rose grabbed Dink and Josh and pointed them toward the treasure chamber. Without speaking, the three tiptoed under the arch.

The treasure chamber, like the tomb, had a stone floor partly covered with sand and gravel. The walls were also stone, with no windows.

"She's not here," Dink whispered, glancing into the chamber's dim corners. His arms suddenly bristled with goose bumps.

失踪的木乃伊

"Yeah, but look at all the gold!" Josh said, pressing his nose up against a glass display case.

There were six cases in the chamber. Four were filled with pottery and farming equipment. The other two held gold carvings and jewelry.

"You'd think if someone wanted to steal something," Dink said, "it'd be this treasure, not a mummy."

"These cases are locked, and they have alarms," Ruth Rose said. She pointed to thin gray wires running along the edges of each case.

Suddenly, Dink heard a low rumbling noise. "What's that?" he asked.

"It sounds like the tomb door!" Ruth Rose said.

The kids ran back into the tomb. They were just in time to see the wall slide shut.

Josh ran to the wall and tried to force it open with his fingers. When he turned around, his face was white.

"We're locked in!" he said.

CHAPTER 4

"There must be a way to open the door from in here," Ruth Rose said. "Let's look for a switch or something."

The kids searched the walls near the door but found nothing that would open it.

"But why did the door close in the first place?" Josh asked.

"You might have set off an alarm when you touched the case," Ruth Rose said.

"If she's right," Dink said, "someone will hear the alarm and come to see who's in here. All we have to do is wait."

103

"Wait in here?" Josh squeaked.

"It won't be for long," Dink said. "Any second now, that door will slide open again."

"Yeah, well, let's wait in the treasure chamber," Josh muttered. "Those mummies are creeping me out."

"They're just dust," Ruth Rose said.

"But they're dead dust!" Josh said, heading into the chamber.

The kids sat on the floor and leaned against a wall. The room was silent. The ceiling lights cast a soft glow onto the gold inside the cases.

"I've always dreamed of being locked in a room full of gold," Josh said. "But now that I am, I'd rather be home."

Minutes passed, then more minutes. No one came to rescue them. The stone door in the tomb remained solidly shut.

"No one knows we're in here," Josh muttered. "We could be trapped forever. We'll die and become mummies!"

"Our parents all know we're at the museum," Ruth Rose said. "If I'm not home for supper, my dad will call."

"But by then the museum will be closed," Josh insisted. "No one will answer the phone!"

"Then my folks will drive here," Ruth Rose said.

"Or they'll call the police," Dink said. "All we have to do is sit here and chill out."

"I'm already chilled," Josh mumbled. "This place feels like the inside of a refrigerator."

Dink grinned. "Gee, Joshua, I thought you'd be happy inside a refrigerator."

"Very funny, Donald!" Josh muttered. "Plus, I'm sitting on gravel. Why can't they have carpets like normal people?"

Ruth Rose stood up and wiped gravel and sand off her shorts. "Josh is right. Let's see if we can find someplace more comfortable to sit," she said.

"Like home," Josh said.

"Or like this!" Ruth Rose said. She had opened a small door cut into the stone wall.

"It's some kind of closet," Dink said, peering inside.

"Egyptians didn't have closets," Josh said. The kids saw folding chairs, cleaning supplies, and a stack of

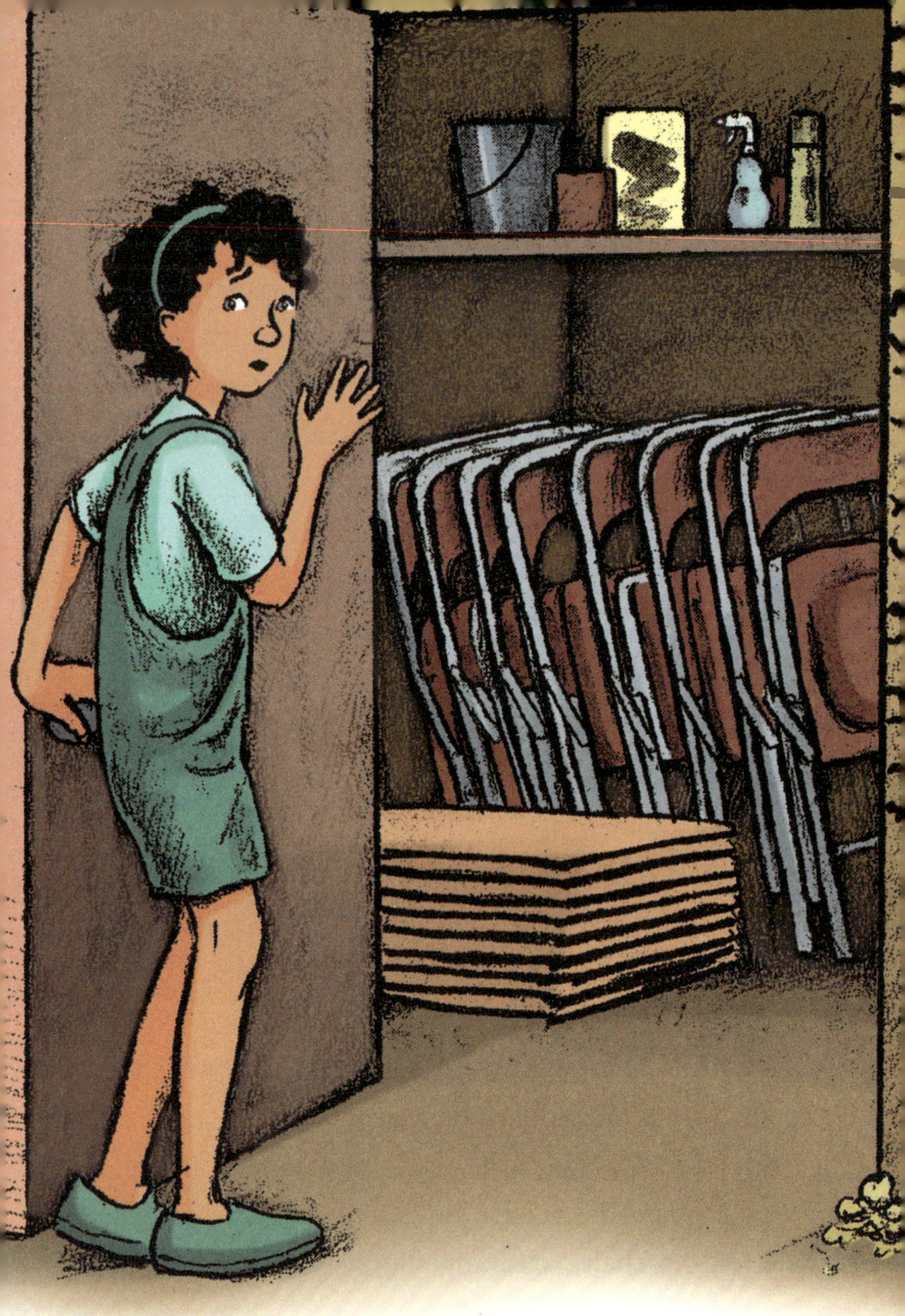

失踪的木乃伊

carpet pieces.

"The carpet squares must be for kids to sit on," Ruth Rose said. "Let's spread them out."

The kids covered the closet floor with carpet squares, then lay down.

"This is more like it," Josh said, making himself comfortable. "Now if someone would just bring me some pizza and a soda, I'd be happy."

"Would you share it with the mummies?" Ruth Rose asked Josh.

"Nope."

More time passed. Dink yawned, and his eyes grew heavy. He pulled the closet door shut, darkening the small room. Then he lay down, and they all drifted off to sleep.

Suddenly, a huge blast shook the room. The folding chairs fell over with a crash, and a box of cleaning stuff flew off a shelf.

107

Dink, Josh, and Ruth Rose bolted up out of a sound sleep.

"What the heck was that?" Josh said. "It sounded like a bomb!"

"I smell smoke!" Ruth Rose said in the dark.

Dink opened the closet door a crack, then pulled it shut again. "The place is filled with dust," he said, wiping his eyes.

"What happened?" Ruth Rose asked.

Just then Dink heard voices.

"Someone's out there," Josh said. "We're rescued!"

"Quiet!" Dink whispered. "They wouldn't bomb the place to rescue us."

Dink nudged the door open a crack. He peered through the floating dust, then suddenly scooted back.

Two shapes in dark clothing slipped past the closet, inches from the kids' noses. Both carried black gym bags.

As the kids watched, the two figures separated, stopping in front of two of the glass cases. Dink heard glass breaking, and then a piercing alarm bell sounded.

"Grab as much as you can. Then we're outta here!" one of the intruders said.

"They're not here to rescue us," Dink whispered. "They're here to steal the mummies' gold!"

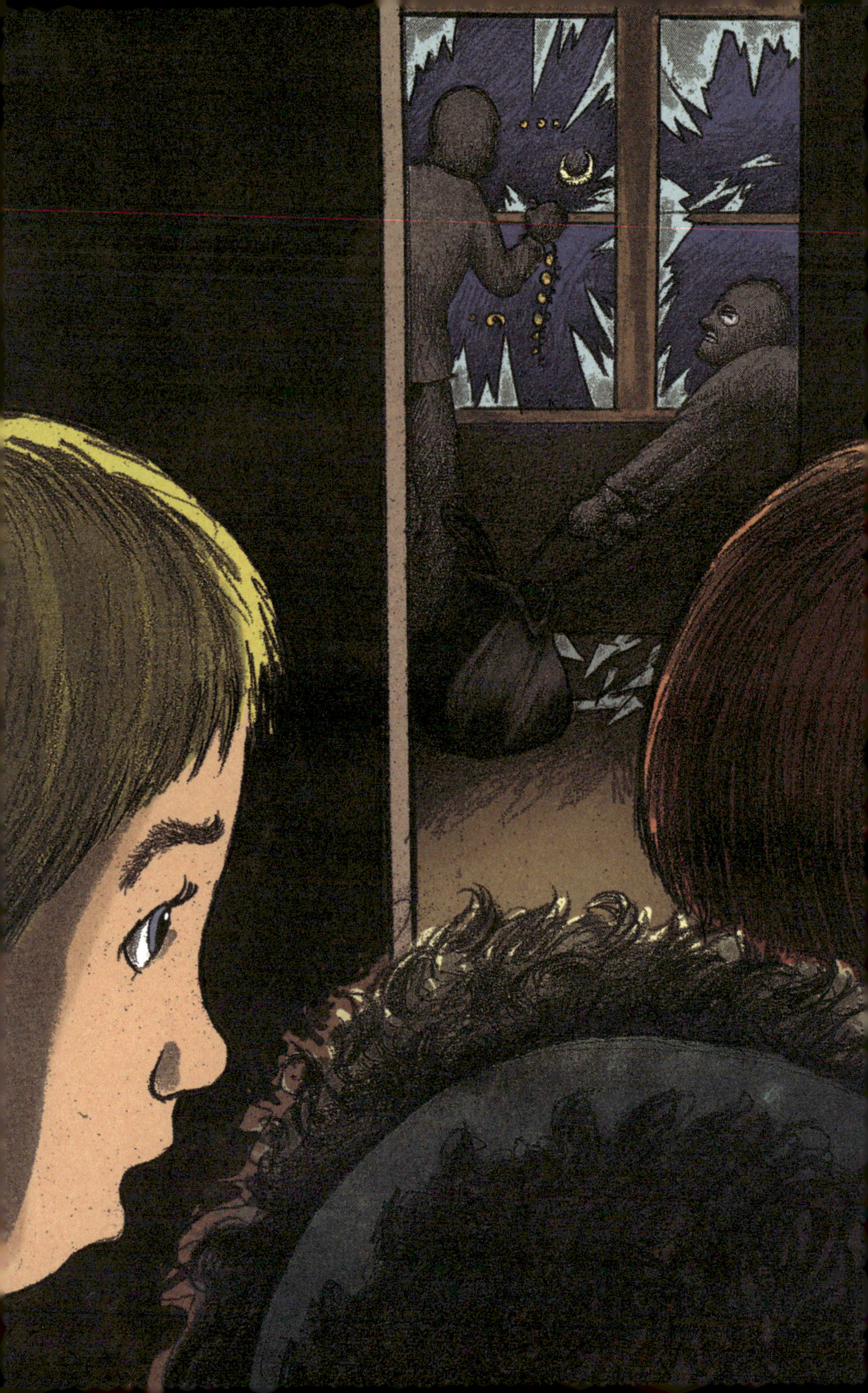

CHAPTER 5

The thieves worked fast. Through the door crack, Dink watched the two dark forms fill their satchels with the gold.

"Jeez, this stuff is heavy," one of them grunted. The crooks dragged the heavy satchels across the floor.

Dink tried to memorize the black clothing, the thieves' ski masks, and the satchels. As the crooks passed the closet, he noticed that one of them seemed to have a white stripe between his waist and knees.

Then both were gone, and the treasure chamber was quiet.

Dink waited several seconds, then pushed the closet door all the way open.

The gold was gone. Two large hunks of stone lay

on top of broken glass. Dust covered everything.

As Dink, Josh, and Ruth Rose stepped out of the closet, the alarm bell stopped as suddenly as it had started.

"Where did they go?" Josh whispered in the now silent room.

113

Before Dink could answer, they heard the tomb door slide open. A second later, Officers Peters and Washington stormed into the treasure chamber.

"Freeze!" Officer Peters shouted. Then he took a second look. "What...it's the kids!"

Dr. Tweed appeared behind the two officers. "Please explain why you're in here," he said. One of Dr. Tweed's eyes was twitching.

"We were trying to find the woman who took the mummy," Ruth Rose said. "Then the door closed all by itself."

"We fell asleep in the closet," Josh said. "A few minutes ago, we heard a loud bang. Then two guys came in and stole the gold!"

Dr. Tweed stepped over broken glass and examined the shattered cases. "Nothing is left," he said. "A priceless treasure has been stolen."

"Let's check out the wall," Officer Peters said.

Everyone followed him into the tomb. A large, jagged hole had been blown through one of the walls. Through it, Dink could see the tall, thick shrubbery behind the museum.

失踪的木乃伊

The floor around the hole was littered with chunks of stone, but the two standing mummies didn't look damaged. On the table, the child mummy's coffin was closed. The mask on its lid stared peacefully up at the ceiling.

"Well, thank goodness!" someone shouted. Dink turned around. His parents ran into the tomb.

Ruth Rose's parents came in next, quickly followed by Josh's folks.

"What happened to you kids?" Dink's mom asked, giving him a hug. "We've been calling practically the whole city of Hartford for hours!"

"We got locked in," Josh said. "We were trying to find the mummy snatcher!"

"What mummy?" Ruth Rose's mom asked.

"Let's save the story till we get home," Dink's dad suggested. "You kids must be starving."

"I am!" Josh said.

At ten the next morning, Officers Peters and Washington stopped by Dink's house. Dink called Josh and Ruth Rose, and they all sat in the backyard.

"I hope you got a good night's sleep," Officer Peters said, smiling. "We just talked to your parents, and they said it would be okay if we asked you some questions."

"If that's okay with you," Officer Washington said.

The kids nodded.

Officer Peters glanced at his notes. "We think the woman who stole the mummy wanted to get everyone to leave the tomb," he explained. "In all the confusion, someone hid a small bomb near the wall."

"We've had a chat with Dr. Tweed," Officer Washington added. "Now we'd like to hear your part of the story."

The kids explained everything that had happened up until they had been awakened by the bomb blast.

"Sometimes," Officer Washington said, "in the excitement of the moment, we forget small things. I'd like you to think back to the point when you saw the two thieves enter the treasure chamber. Tell me everything you remember, even the smallest detail."

Dink went first. "Well, they were both wearing dark clothes. I think they had ski masks over their faces."

"One of them talked," Ruth Rose said. "He said—"

失踪的木乃伊

"It was a man's voice?" interrupted Officer Peters.

Ruth Rose closed her eyes for a minute. "I think so. It was a low voice," she said. "He said, 'Let's grab as much as we can and get out of here.'"

"Did the other one say anything?" asked Officer Washington.

Ruth Rose thought for a minute. "I think one of them said whatever they were carrying was heavy," she added.

Officer Peters nodded and made a note.

"I remember smelling something," Josh said.

Both officers looked at him.

"I don't know what it was, but..." Josh stopped, looking embarrassed.

"We're listening," said Officer Washington. "You smelled..."

"It was something to eat, I think."

Officer Peters smiled at Josh.

"What, hamburgers, pizza... ?"

Josh shook his head. "Sorry, I can't remember."

"I remember something else!" Dink said suddenly. "One of the guys had a white stripe on his clothes."

117

"A white stripe?" Officer Peters repeated. "I thought they were dressed in dark clothes."

Dink nodded. "They were, but I saw a white stripe right here."

He stood up and drew an imaginary line just above his knees.

"Did you see him from the front or back?" Officer Washington asked.

"Both," Dink said. "But the stripe was just in front."

The officers took notes, then closed their pads.

"You've been very helpful, kids," Officer Washington said. She looked at Josh. "If you remember that smell, give me a call." She handed him a card.

Josh took the card. "Um, can we go back to the museum?" he asked. "Today is Tyrannosaurus Tuesday!"

"Sure," Officer Washington said. "Just be careful of those big teeth!"

CHAPTER 6

At one-thirty that afternoon, the bus dropped the kids off in front of the museum. The digital sign over the bank said 90 DEGREES.

"We've still got a half hour," Josh said. "I could use a snack."

"Josh, we just ate!" Ruth Rose said. "I think you're part wolf."

Josh growled and wiggled his eyebrows.

"It's too hot to eat, anyway," Dink said. "Let's go sit in the shade for a few minutes."

The kids followed a gravel path around the side of the museum. They passed trees, shrubs, and flower

119

beds. At the corner of the building, they found a goldfish pond and a few benches. Fat goldfish came to the surface, as if expecting food.

"Look!" Josh said, pointing at the back wall of the museum. "That must be where the bomb blew up."

失踪的木乃伊

A large sheet of plywood covered the blasted-out hole. Bags of cement and a stack of cinder blocks stood nearby.

"The crooks must have run right past this bench," Josh said.

The kids sat down. From their bench, they could see the bank clock on Main Street.

"I wonder where they went," Dink said. "They couldn't have carried that gold far."

Ruth Rose pulled the museum map from her back pocket. On one side was a drawing of the rooms inside the museum. On the other side was a map showing the little park, the museum, and Main Street.

Josh pointed at Main Street. "Maybe they had a getaway car waiting," he said.

Ruth Rose shook her head. "Parking isn't allowed in front of the museum. If the crooks had left a car there, the police would have noticed it."

"And there are no other streets near the museum where they could have parked," Dink observed, studying the map.

Josh glanced around at the trees and shrubs. "So where did they take the gold?" He looked down at the ground. "Maybe they buried it!"

Dink shook his head. "They were in a hurry. I

失踪的木乃伊

can't see them taking the time to dig a hole," he said. He checked the digital sign in front of the bank. "Anyway, we'd better get inside. It's almost two o'clock."

The kids left, following the path back around to the front of the museum.

"Yum, I smell something good," Josh said as they hurried up the front steps.

"You're always smelling something good," Ruth Rose said.

They entered and paid the woman behind the counter. An inflated rubber tyrannosaur stood in the center of the lobby. In its teeth, it held a sign that said FOLLOW THE ARROWS.

A minute later, the kids found Dr. Tweed standing outside an open door.

"Hello again," he said. "Come on in. We're just about to start."

A bunch of kids were sitting in a circle of desks. Dink, Josh, and Ruth Rose slid into three empty seats. In the middle of the circle stood a giant dinosaur skeleton. Its huge head almost touched the ceiling!

"I'm sure most of you recognize Tyrannosaurus

123

rex," Dr. Tweed said.

Dink stared up at the skeleton. He tried to picture what the massive dinosaur would have looked like when it was alive.

"Today," Dr. Tweed went on, "we are going to study this prehistoric carnivore— "

A boy in the front row raised his hand. "Did you get the mummy back?" he asked.

"Yes, one of our guests found it in the ladies' room," Dr. Tweed said. "Now, as I was say—"

"I saw on TV that someone broke in and stole the treasure," a girl said.

Dr. Tweed sighed. "Yes, that is true. The thieves are still at large, and the treasure is missing. But we are here to discuss dinosaurs today."

He opened a cupboard and pulled out a long bone. "A tyrannosaur leg fossil," he said. "This dinosaur lived and died in what we now know as Utah. You can touch the bone, but please be gentle."

The kids crowded around Dr. Tweed to touch the fossil.

"What do we know about the tyrannosaur?" Dr.

Tweed asked.

Answers came swiftly:

"They had big teeth!"

"They ate other dinosaurs!"

"They laid eggs!"

"Good," Dr. Tweed said. "Did you also know that Tyrannosaurus rex had an amazing sense of smell? It could smell its food from hundreds of yards away."

"Like Josh," Dink whispered.

"And T. rex also had a very small brain for his size," Dr. Tweed went on.

"Like Dink," Josh mumbled.

Dr. Tweed dimmed the lights and showed slides. The kids learned how the dinosaur lived, what it ate, and how it raised its young.

When the slide show was over, Dr. Tweed turned the lights up again. He pulled open a cupboard. "Now you can construct your own dinosaur." He asked for volunteers to pass out clay, wood, and wire.

"Your creation will stand on the wood. Use the wire to help shape the legs and tail."

Soon twenty pairs of hands were building

miniature tyrannosaurs.

"This is fun," Josh said. "Maybe I'll be a sculptor instead of a painter."

Ruth Rose looked at Josh's pile of clay. "Josh," she said, "we're supposed to make dinosaurs. Yours looks like a potato."

"Very funny," Josh said. Then his eyes opened wide. "That's it!"

"That's what?" Ruth Rose asked.

"That's what I smelled last night when we were in the closet!"

"Potatoes?" Dink asked.

Josh shook his head. He closed his eyes and sniffed. "French fries!" he said.

CHAPTER 7

Dink shaped a tail for his dinosaur. "All I smelled was dust from the bomb. How could you smell French fries?"

Josh was making a row of teeth for his tyrannosaurs. "Because I have an amazing sense of smell," he said.

"I'm afraid we've run out of time," Dr. Tweed said. "You may take extra clay and finish your sculptures at home."

He handed out cardboard boxes for carrying the clay dinosaurs.

"Thank you all for coming," Dr. Tweed said as everyone got up to go. "Tomorrow is Wet Wednesday.

A to Z 神秘案件

I will be away, but one of my colleagues will be here in my place. Be sure to wear shorts and old sneakers, and bring permission slips from your parents."

A few minutes later, Dink, Josh, and Ruth Rose stood in front of the museum holding their boxes.

"What time does our bus come?" Josh asked.

"They run every half hour," Ruth Rose said,

失踪的木乃伊

glancing across the street at the bank clock. "It's three-thirty now. We must have just missed one."

Josh grinned. "Good, we have time to get a snack."

Dink rolled his eyes. "Josh, my folks are still freaked about the bomb. I promised I'd get right home after the museum today. Let's just go wait in the shade."

They walked around to the little pond and sat on a bench. Immediately, the goldfish came up for handouts.

Suddenly, Josh stood up and stuck his nose in the air. "I smell it again!" he said. He swiveled his head, like a periscope looking for enemy ships.

"There!" he said, pointing back along the park path toward Main Street. A small restaurant stood next to the bank.

A sign in the window said AUNT FREDA'S FABULOUS FRIES.

"Forget your stomach, Josh," Dink said. "The next bus will be here soon."

Josh slumped back on the bench.

"I'm being falsely accused," he said. "All I'm trying to do is figure out what happened to that gold."

"Okay," Dink said. "So tell us."

"Okay," Josh said. "I smelled French fries last night.

They sell French fries across the street. So maybe the robbers work there. Maybe that's where they took the gold!"

"I saw those crooks dragging the gold," Dink said. "There's no way they carried it all the way to that restaurant."

Ruth Rose looked at Dink. "Still, Josh might be right about the thieves working there," she said. "Maybe we should go over and check it out."

"But our bus…"

"Come on, Dinkus," Josh said, standing up. "We'll catch the next one."

"Okay, but I still think it's just a trick," Dink said. "You'd do anything for a plate of fries."

The kids carried their boxes through the park, across Main Street, and into the restaurant.

They sat in a booth by the window. Overhead, a ceiling fan hummed, and a jukebox played an Elvis song.

Six teenagers were just leaving. They left behind a small mountain of dirty dishes and glasses.

A roly-poly woman came through a swinging

door with three glasses of ice water. She had gray hair and wore a white apron over her dress.

"Welcome to Aunt Freda's," she said. "I'm Aunt Freda. I'll bet you've been to the museum, right?"

失踪的木乃伊

"How did you know?" asked Ruth Rose.

The woman pointed to Ruth Rose's small box. WADSWORTH MUSEUM was printed on the side.

"We made dinosaurs out of clay," Josh said.

"Oh, that would be Dr. Tweed," Aunt Freda said. "He's one of my regular customers. So, what can I get you today?"

"Fries and a lemonade, please," said Josh.

"You'll love my fries," Aunt Freda said. "The best in Hartford!"

"I'll have the same," Ruth Rose said.

Dink made it three, and Aunt Freda bustled away to the kitchen.

Josh leaned forward and whispered, "Maybe Aunt Freda was one of the robbers!"

Dink grinned. "She doesn't exactly look like a robber," he said.

"Plus, the crooks were taller and thinner," Ruth Rose said.

Aunt Freda returned with their fries, drinks, ketchup, and napkins. "Let me know how you like my fries," she said. "It's my secret recipe!"

133

A to Z 神秘案件

The kids dug in, sharing the ketchup.

A few minutes later, a woman with short dark hair came out of the kitchen. She was wearing an apron and carrying a large plastic tub.

失踪的木乃伊

The woman walked over to the table with the dirty dishes and began cleaning up. Dink heard her grunt as she lugged the loaded dish container into the kitchen.

"What's the matter?" Ruth Rose asked Dink, who was staring after the departing woman.

Josh waved a French fry in front of Dink's face. "Why the big eyes, Dink?"

"That woman," he said. "The way she was lugging that pile of dishes... she reminded me of one of the robbers last night."

"Hot diggety," Josh said. "At last someone agrees with me!"

Ruth Rose turned and looked toward the kitchen. "You know, she has short dark hair just like the woman who came out of the rest room before I found the mummy."

The three kids stared at the kitchen door.

"And she smells like French fries!" Josh said.

CHAPTER 8

Aunt Freda walked over to their booth. "My, you did a good job on those fries," she said. "Anything else?"

"No, thank—" Dink started to say.

"Yes!" Ruth Rose interrupted. "Could you show us how you make your fabulous fries? Donald here is really interested in cooking."

I am? thought Dink.

Aunt Freda beamed at Dink. "Of course, dearie. Come on back to the kitchen," she said.

Ruth Rose nudged Dink, and they all followed Aunt Freda.

On the other side of the swinging door, the smell

137

of frying potatoes hung heavy in the air.

A row of wall shelves held pots and pans, cooking spices, cookbooks, and a bunch of bottles and jars. Against one wall stood a pile of crates bulging with raw potatoes.

The woman with short dark hair was standing at a counter, slicing potatoes. She was wearing earphones and didn't seem to notice the kids.

Dink stared at the woman. As she stooped over a pile of potatoes, Dink imagined her stooped over a case of Egyptian gold.

Aunt Freda interrupted his thoughts. "Come over here," she said, leading the kids to a deep-fry machine.

She lowered her voice. "Here's my secret. I put a little garlic and vinegar right in the olive oil," she said, then winked. "Promise you won't tell?"

Dink nodded. "Promise," he said. "Boy, cooking potatoes is really interesting!"

From the corner of his eye, Dink saw Josh scoop something off the kitchen floor and shove it in his pocket.

Then Ruth Rose poked Dink. She pointed her chin

失踪的木乃伊

at a coatrack by the back door. A black jacket hung from one of the pegs. On the floor sat a black gym bag.

"Anything else you want to know?" Aunt Freda asked.

"No, thanks," Ruth Rose said, smiling. "We've seen everything we need."

The kids left the kitchen, with Aunt Freda following them. They paid for their food and started for the door.

Suddenly, Aunt Freda put her hand on Dink's arm. "Wait!" she said, digging into the pocket of her apron. "Put out your hands!"

The kids obeyed, and she dropped a candy into each palm. "Have a nice day," Aunt Freda said, then opened the door for them.

The kids popped the candies into their mouths as they hurried back to their bus stop.

"Did you see that jacket?" Ruth Rose said. "If that woman put it on over her apron, the white edge would show. Is that what you saw last night, Dink?"

"It could be," Dink said. "And that gym bag looked like the ones the robbers were carrying."

Josh shook his head. "You guys are such amateurs," he said. "The jacket could belong to anyone, and there

139

are a million black gym bags in Hartford."

He reached into his pocket. "But I found a real clue!"

He held out a smooth pebble the size of an M&M.

"What's that?" Dink asked.

"Come on, I'll show you." Josh headed for the museum steps.

Dink and Ruth Rose followed Josh through the lobby. In front of the tomb, they found a sign announcing that the mummy exhibit was closed. Behind the sign, the sliding door was shut.

Josh walked over to the wall and pressed the stone. With a rumble, the wall slid open.

Josh leaned inside and scooped a handful of the gravel off the floor. Then he closed the door again.

"See, they're the same," Josh said, holding up the gravel and the pebble he'd found at Aunt Freda's.

"I don't get it," Dink said.

"I found this pebble on the floor in Aunt Freda's kitchen," Josh explained. "It matches the pebbles in the tomb. The only way it could have gotten from the tomb floor to Aunt Freda's floor was on the bottom of one of the crook's shoes!"

"Okay," Ruth Rose said. "But that still doesn't tell us where the gold is."

"Or who the second crook is," Dink added.

"Maybe not," Josh said, "but something in that restaurant smells!"

CHAPTER 9

That night, a thunderstorm blew through Green Lawn. While Dink slept, lightning flashed and thunder boomed outside his bedroom window.

Dink had a nightmare. He was trapped in the tomb again. This time he was alone.

One by one, the two mummies leaning against the wall opened their eyes. One by one, they stepped out of their coffins and shuffled toward him.

They passed the child's coffin. Its lid stayed shut, the child's mask staring up at the ceiling.

Because the mummy's not in there, Dink thought. But then why—

失踪的木乃伊

Just then Dink felt a cold hand on his shoulder. He tried to run, but his legs wouldn't budge. The mummies' cloth wrappings had come loose and were encircling his body, like tentacles.

Dink bolted awake with a yell, tangled in his sheet. When he realized that he was in his bed and not the tomb, he lay back down.

He tried to go back to sleep, but something kept him awake. It was something in his nightmare, in the tomb. What was it?

He lay there trying to picture the tomb again. Before the bomb went off, all three sarcophagus lids had been open. The small sarcophagus was empty because the mummy was still in Dr. Tweed's office.

But after the blast, the smallest coffin—the one for the child—was closed.

Then Dink remembered the robbers dragging those two heavy bags of gold. He smiled, closed his eyes, and went back to sleep.

After breakfast, Dink called Josh. He came over, and they walked next door to Ruth Rose's house. She was sitting on her front steps with a plate of toast on her knees.

Dink sat on the bottom step. "I figured it out last night," he told them. "I know where the crooks hid the gold."

Josh reached for a piece of Ruth Rose's toast, but she slapped his hand.

"Don't you know it's nice to share?" he asked.

"Don't you know it's nice to ask first?" Ruth Rose said. But she passed Josh a section of her toast. "Tell us, Dink."

"I had an awful dream last night," Dink said. "I was trapped in the tomb. The two big coffins were open, and the mummies were chasing me. But the little coffin, the one for the kid, was closed."

He looked at Josh and Ruth Rose. "After I woke up, I remembered something. When we were in the tomb just before we got locked in, the little coffin was open. Remember? But when we went back into the tomb after the bomb went off, the coffin lid was closed!"

"I don't get it," Josh said, licking jam from his fingers.

"You will in a minute," Dink said. "I couldn't get back to sleep last night, so I started wondering: Who closed that little coffin? Then it hit me. If the robbers didn't have a car waiting, and if the gold was too heavy to carry far, maybe they hid it there!"

"Then the crook has to be someone who can get back into the tomb later and get the gold," Josh said.

"DR. TWEED!" Ruth Rose yelled.

"That's what I think, too," Dink said. "Aunt Freda said Dr. Tweed was a good customer. I figure he and the woman with the short dark hair planned it together."

"She had that gym bag," Ruth Rose said. "And all she had to do was walk across the street."

"And she smelled like a walking French fry!" Josh added.

"But which one hid the bomb?" Ruth Rose asked.

"Dr. Tweed, I think," Dink said. "Remember how he stayed in the tomb for a few minutes after we all left?"

"But why did the woman grab the mummy?" asked Josh.

"To get us out of there," Dink said. "Dr. Tweed had to be alone in the tomb so he could plant the bomb."

Dink grinned at Josh and Ruth Rose. "And that left the sarcophagus empty for the gold!" he said.

"OH MY GOSH!" Ruth Rose yelled. "Dr. Tweed told us he wouldn't be at Wet Wednesday today. I'll bet he's gonna take the gold and leave!"

She jumped up and ran into the house. Dink and Josh were right behind her.

Ruth Rose called the police station and asked for Officer Fallon.

CHAPTER 10

Officer Fallon drove Dink, Josh, and Ruth Rose to Hartford.

He had called Officers Peters and Washington. The two cruisers met down the street from the museum.

"Officer Washington will nab the young woman in the restaurant," Officer Peters told Officer Fallon. "You and I will take the museum. Kids, you come with us."

Dink, Josh, and Ruth Rose—flanked by the two officers—crossed Main Street and entered the quiet museum. They followed the hallway until they came

147

A to Z 神秘案件

to Dr. Tweed's office door.

With the kids standing behind him, Officer Peters

失踪的木乃伊

knocked. When there was no answer, he turned the knob and opened the door. "Not here," he said.

Officer Fallon and the kids peered into the office. They saw the little mummy lying on a table.

Officer Peters looked at Dink, Josh, and Ruth Rose. "Let's check that tomb," he said.

The kids and the two officers walked back through the lobby. They stopped in front of the closed tomb door.

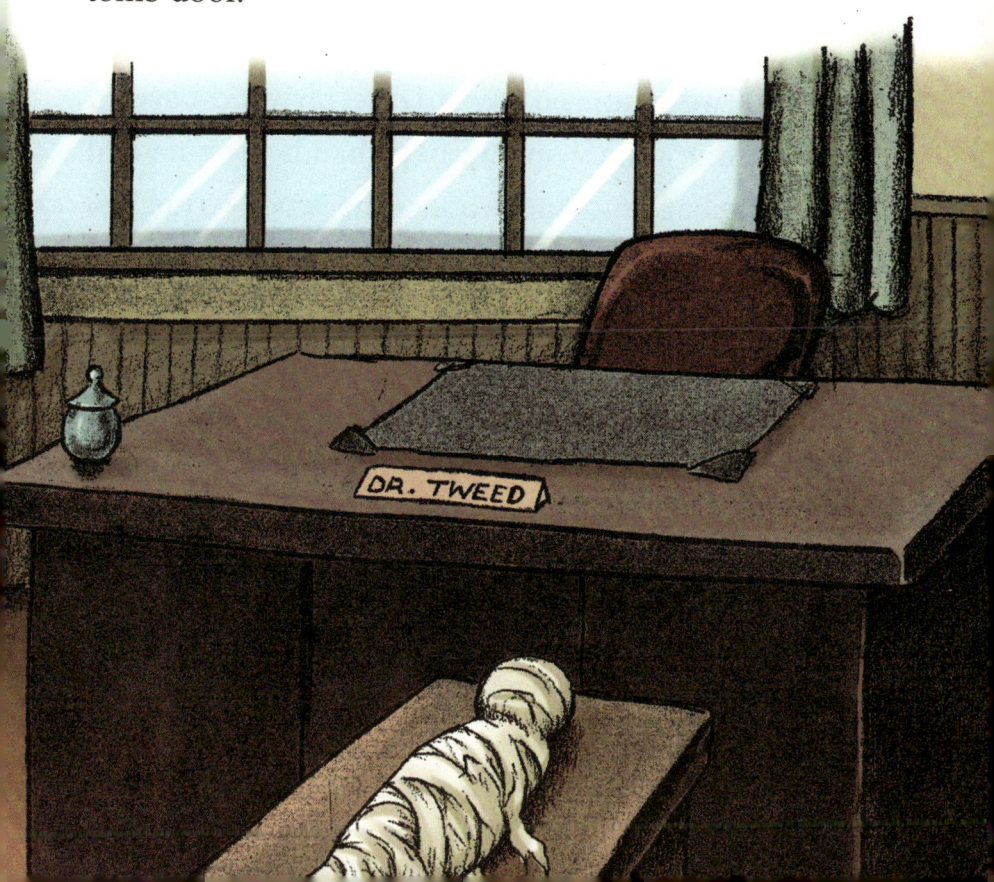

"How do we get in?" Officer Fallon asked.

"I know!" said Josh. He pressed the secret stone, and the door slid open. Dr. Tweed was standing in front of the small sarcophagus.

He whipped around, clasping a lumpy gym bag to his chest. In the sarcophagus, Dink saw a pile of gold objects.

Dr. Tweed's eyes were blinking and twitching at the same time.

"Hello there," Officer Fallon said. "Taking a trip?"

Dr. Tweed lunged toward the plywood-covered hole in the wall. Swinging both hands, he smashed the gym bag into the wood. The wood crunched and fell outward, and Dr. Tweed leaped through the opening.

Outside, he tripped over a bag of cement and plunged into the goldfish pond. The gym bag sank to the bottom.

Dr. Tweed flopped around in the shallow pond, then sat up, spitting out water. Lily pads hung from his ears and slimy algae dripped from his eyebrows.

"I need to call my lawyer," he sputtered.

失踪的木乃伊

Just then Officer Washington walked into the park. She was leading the woman from the restaurant, who wore handcuffs.

"So she talked?" Officer Peters asked his partner.

"Yep. These two were supposed to take a taxi to the airport in a few minutes," Officer Washington said. "Their next stop was Europe, where they hoped to sell the treasures."

"Take her away," Officer Peters said. "I'll bring our wet friend along in a few minutes."

Officer Washington led her prisoner out of the park.

Officer Peters stepped into the pond and helped Dr. Tweed to his feet. He leaned the wet thief against a tree and snapped handcuffs onto his dripping wrists.

Officer Fallon pulled off his shoes and socks and waded into the pond. He lugged out the gym bag, filled with Egyptian treasure and pond water.

"Thanks for your help," Officer Peters told Officer Fallon. "I'll call you later."

Officer Peters picked up the heavy gym bag with a grunt. He nudged Dr. Tweed forward, and the two left

151

the park. Their sopping shoes made squishing noises as they walked.

Officer Fallon sat on a bench next to Dink, Josh, and Ruth Rose. He wrung pond water from his dripping pant legs.

152

"Good job, kids," he told them.

Then he pulled out his pad, opened to a fresh page, and began writing. He paused.

"In all the excitement," Officer Fallon said, "I've forgotten what day this is."

153

A to Z 神秘案件

The kids grinned at each other.
"It's Wet Wednesday!" Josh told him.

Text copyright © 2001 by Ron Roy
Illustrations copyright © 2001 by John Steven Gurney
All rights reserved under International and Pan-American Copyright Conventions.
Published in the United States by Random House, Inc., New York,
and simultaneously in Canada by Random House of Canada Limited, Toronto.

本书中英双语版由中南博集天卷文化传媒有限公司与企鹅兰登（北京）文化发展有限公司合作出版。

"企鹅"及其相关标识是企鹅兰登已经注册或尚未注册的商标。
未经允许，不得擅用。
封底凡无企鹅防伪标识者均属未经授权之非法版本。

©中南博集天卷文化传媒有限公司。本书版权受法律保护。未经权利人许可，任何人不得以任何方式使用本书包括正文、插图、封面、版式等任何部分内容，违者将受到法律制裁。

著作权合同登记号：字18-2023-258

图书在版编目（CIP）数据

失踪的木乃伊：汉英对照 /（美）罗恩·罗伊著；
（美）约翰·史蒂文·格尼绘；叶雯熙译. -- 长沙：湖
南少年儿童出版社，2024.10. --（A to Z神秘案件）.
ISBN 978-7-5562-7818-3

Ⅰ. H319.4
中国国家版本馆CIP数据核字第2024VP1207号

A TO Z SHENMI ANJIAN SHIZONG DE MUNAIYI

A to Z神秘案件 失踪的木乃伊

[美]罗恩·罗伊 著　　[美]约翰·史蒂文·格尼 绘　　叶雯熙 译

责任编辑：唐　凌　李　炜	策划出品：李　炜　张苗苗　文赛峰
策划编辑：文赛峰	特约编辑：杜佳美
营销编辑：付　佳　杨　朔　周晓茜	封面设计：霍雨佳
版权支持：王媛媛	版式设计：马睿君
插图上色：河北传图文化	内文排版：霍雨佳

出 版 人：刘星保
出　　版：湖南少年儿童出版社
地　　址：湖南省长沙市晚报大道89号
邮　　编：410016
电　　话：0731-82196320
常年法律顾问：湖南崇民律师事务所　柳成柱律师
经　　销：新华书店
开　　本：875 mm×1230 mm　1/32
字　　数：83千字
版　　次：2024年10月第1版
书　　号：ISBN 978-7-5562-7818-3

印　　刷：三河市中晟雅豪印务有限公司
印　　张：4.875
印　　次：2024年10月第1次印刷
定　　价：280.00元（全10册）

若有质量问题，请致电质量监督电话：010-59096394　　团购电话：010-59320018

A to Z 神秘案件

中英双语

第二辑

The Ninth Nugget
第九块金子

[美] 罗恩·罗伊 著
[美] 约翰·史蒂文·格尼 绘　高榕 译

湖南少年儿童出版社
HUNAN JUVENILE & CHILDREN'S PUBLISHING HOUSE
小博集 BOOKY KIDS

·长沙·

惠特农场地图

- 小溪
- 淘金区
- 池塘
- 空房
- 篝火区
- 克莱德夫妇的小木屋
- 空房
- 小路
- 埃德的小木屋
- 孩子们的小木屋
- 菲奥娜的小木屋
- 办公室
- 主屋
- 餐厅
- 草坪
- 花园
- 惠特农场
- 北 / 南 / 西 / 东

欢迎来到**惠特农场**
一起解开 **A to Z** 神秘案件

大拇指的小木屋

通往天堂草场的小路

畜棚

马厩

畜栏

蒙大拿州博兹曼

康涅狄格州绿地镇

美国

人物介绍

三人小组的成员，聪明勇敢，喜欢读推理小说，紧急关头总能保持头脑冷静。喜欢在做事之前好好思考！

丁丁

三人小组的成员，活泼机智，喜欢吃好吃的食物，常常有意想不到的点子。

乔希

三人小组的成员，活泼开朗，喜欢从头到脚穿同一种颜色的衣服，总是那个能找到大部分线索的人。

露丝

惠特农场的老板的儿子,帮父母照料农场的生意。

惠特·尤德

惠特农场的帮工,性格有些古怪,有一只手缺少了一根手指。

大拇指

埃德·盖茨

从纽约来牧场度假的魔术师,正在努力成为一名演员,不过还没接到多少工作。

字母 N 代表 nugget，天然金块……

"看我找到了什么！"乔希说着，伸出他的另一只手。

丁丁瞪大了眼睛。乔希手里拿着一块跟土豆差不多大的金子。

"乔希，你可真厉害！"丁丁大喊。他和露丝都跟乔希击掌庆祝，其他人也围了过来。

"这是到目前为止我见过的最大的一块金子。"尤德惊叹道。

这块金子有乔希的手掌那么大，几乎跟手一样平。有些沙砾和泥巴嵌在这块金子上，但其余部分都是纯金。

接客区 进站

第一章

傍晚时分,丁丁、乔希和露丝目送一架小型飞机升上天空。此时,他们刚刚抵达蒙大拿州的博兹曼市,接下来的一周,他们将在西部惠特牧场度过假期。

孩子们在机场外等人来接,这时天空已经变成了淡紫色,太阳也慢慢地滑到了山的后面。

"现在几点了?"乔希问,"他们说五点就有人来接我们。"

露丝看了看手表说:"已经过了二十分钟了。"

丁丁把手放在眼睛上方遮挡阳光,看向远方,说道:"有可能是那个人。"

一辆脏兮兮的旅行车慢慢减速,停了下来。一个高高瘦瘦、面带微笑的男人纵身从驾驶座上跳了下来,问道:"孩子们,你们是从康涅狄格州来的吗?"

丁丁点点头说:"你是来自惠特牧场的吗?"

"是的,欢迎来到蒙大拿!"那人说,"抱歉我迟到了。我是尤德·惠特。"

丁丁说:"我叫丁丁,这是我的朋友乔希和露丝。"

尤德看起来二十岁左右,有一双大长腿。他穿着牛仔裤和牛仔衬衫,脚上穿着一双破旧的牛仔靴。

"我来帮你们拿行李吧。"尤德说完就抓起孩子们的背包,从后车窗扔进了车里。

"快上车吧,我们出发啦!"他说。

露丝和乔希坐在前排座位上,丁丁坐在后排,旁边放着几个背包、一堆杂乱的马具,还有一副马鞍。

"车里是什么味道啊?"乔希问。

尤德哈哈大笑:"有些是马的味道,有些是皮

革的味道,还有我身上的味道。"说话间,车已经开到了主干道上。

乡村公路上只有零星几辆小轿车和卡车在行驶。透过车窗,丁丁看到了大片平坦的土地,整齐有序的栅栏里圈养着数百万头牛。

"孩子们,你们这周想去骑马吗?"尤德问。

"嗯,可我以前从没骑过马。"乔希回答。

"没关系。"尤德说,"我们的大多数客人都没骑过。我会教你们怎么骑马。"

"你在惠特牧场是做什么工作的呢?"露丝问尤德。

"什么都做一点，小姑娘。"尤德回答，"这个牧场是我父母的，我从小就在这里长大。今年秋天本来我要回大学读书，但现在我必须要留下来帮忙。因为牧场最近生意不太好，没赚到什么钱。"

"那你在大学里面学什么呢？"丁丁问尤德。

"我想成为一名教师。"尤德说，"比起跟牛待在一起，我还是更喜欢和孩子们待在一起。"

尤德把车停在一个加油站前。"得给车加满油，我马上就好。"他一边说，一边从车上下来。

孩子们看着尤德给车子加油。随后他跑向收银台窗口，从后面的口袋里拿出钱包。

"我希望他能带些糖果回来。"乔希说，"我快饿死了！"

丁丁笑着说："你在飞机上吃了可能有二十袋花生，怎么还说饿？"

尤德迈着重重的步子走了回来，又重重地坐在驾驶座上。

"真没想到！"他说，"我刚才打开钱包付钱，结果里面空空如也，什么也没有！我几乎可以肯定，今天下午的时候，里面还有两张二十美元的钞票。"

尤德摇了摇头，然后笑着说："不过，幸好我有信用卡，不然我们就只能走路回家了！"

尤德开着车，穿过更广阔的乡村。丁丁从来没有见过这么多田地！他把车窗摇了下来，一阵热烘烘的风迎面吹来！

"看，那儿有一只雄鹰！"乔希突然喊道。

"它正在寻找一只肥美的田鼠当晚餐。"尤德说。

就在这时，乔希的肚子咕咕叫了起来，声音大极了。

"看来还有其他人也肚子饿了。"尤德笑着说，"再过几分钟就到了。孩子们，你们怎么会碰巧选中我们家的牧场？"

"不是我们选的。"丁丁回答，"这次旅行是一个朋友送给我们的礼物。"

尤德对着后视镜笑了笑，说："那你们这位朋友人可真好！"

"他的彩票被偷了，我们帮他找回来了。"露丝解释说。

"你的意思是那张彩票中奖了?"尤德问。

"是的,"乔希补充说,"他中了七百万美元呢!"

尤德吹了个口哨,说:"七千美元就能帮我家的农场走出现在的困境呢。"几分钟后,车子穿过一扇大门,转入一条土路。大门上挂着一块牌子,上面写着"惠特牧场"。

正前方是一个红色的畜棚和畜栏。往左边一瞧,丁丁看到一栋白色的大房子。房子后面有一个池塘,四周环绕着树木和小木屋。鸭子和小鸡在车道边的草地上啄食。

"这里也太美了吧!"露丝感叹道,"我可以喂小鸡吗?"

"当然可以,小姑娘。"尤德说完就在房子前面停下了车。

门廊上有一男一女,坐在两张木制摇椅上。男人头发花白,看起来像老版的尤德,女人的黑发间也夹杂着灰白的头发。两人都穿着靴子、牛仔裤和法兰绒衬衫。他们一笑起来,黝黑的脸上就布满了皱纹。

尤德向孩子们介绍:"这是我的爸爸妈妈,大家都叫他们惠特妈妈和惠特爸爸。"

尤德的父母赶忙走下门廊的台阶。"欢迎你们来到惠特牧场!"惠特妈妈说,"你们一定是丁丁、乔希和露丝吧。"

"你们好!"惠特爸爸也跟孩子们打了招呼。

就在这时,纱门砰的一声打开了。一个反戴棒球帽、身材壮实的女人大步走了出来。她里面

A to Z 神秘案件

穿着牛仔裤和西式牛仔衬衫,外面套着一条白色长围裙。

"这是露露,蒙大拿最好的厨师。"尤德一边说,一边把孩子们的背包放到了门廊上。

露露朝孩子们微笑,问道:"他们在飞机上给

你们吃什么东西了吗?"

乔希回答:"只给了一些花生,我现在好饿啊!"

"十五分钟后晚餐就准备好啦。注意听铃声。"露露指着门廊屋檐下挂着的一个三角铁说。

"我带你们去小木屋。"一个低沉的声音从后面传来。

丁丁、乔希和露丝扭头一看,一个男人走到他们身后,汗渍斑斑的牛仔帽下露出蓬乱的头发,他的皮肤看起来就像起皱的皮革。

"我叫大拇指。"那人说。当他伸手去拿孩子们的背包时,丁丁看到他的手上缺了一根大拇指。

第二章

孩子们跟着大拇指走上一条两边铺着石子的狭窄小路。小路通向三间小木屋,小木屋后面,池塘在阳光下闪闪发光。

丁丁注意到沿着小路的更远处还有几间小木屋,便问:"那几间小木屋是谁在住?"

"除了一间有人住,其余都是空的。"大拇指咕哝着说。他在中间的小木屋前停了下来。

"这间是你们的。那边那间住着一位女士。"大拇指一边说,一边朝他们右边的小木屋抬了抬下巴,"另一间住着一个纽约来的小伙子,还有一对已婚夫妇住在池塘对面那间小木屋。"

这些小木屋都带有烟囱,前面有狭窄的门廊,屋子的两侧和正面都有窗户,正中间是一道门。

"要是天气变冷了，惠特妈妈会另外拿毯子给你们的。"大拇指说着，把孩子们的背包都放在了台阶上，"洗手间里有毛巾。"

他朝孩子们点了点头，然后迈着沉重的脚步走下门廊，沿着小路往回走。

"这家伙有点吓人。"乔希说，"你们觉得他的大拇指是怎么没的？"

"也许是被熊咬掉的。"丁丁说着冲露丝使了个眼色。

"也可能是美洲狮。"露丝说，尽量憋住不笑出声来。

乔希哼了一声，说："别想吓唬我，外面除了鸡和鸭，什么都没有。"

孩子们把背包拿进小木屋。屋里有一张双层床靠着里面那堵墙，对面还有一张单人床。

双层床和小洗手间之间有一个石头做的壁炉。除此之外，室内陈设只有一张编织地毯、几把椅子和一张桌子。

"我真想永远住在这里！"露丝感叹道。她把背包扔在单人床上，看着窗外的畜棚。

"我要睡上铺!"乔希说着就把背包扔了上去。

丁丁把背包放在了下面的床铺上,这时一声响亮的铃声从主屋那边传来。

"终于可以吃饭啦!"乔希说。他们跑出小木屋,差点撞上一个瘦骨嶙峋、胡子拉碴的男人。

"哎哟!"男人笑着说,"不用着急,食物很充足。你们一定是新来的吧。"

"我们刚到这儿。"丁丁说。

"我是埃德·盖茨,昨天刚从纽约来到这里。"他说着冲孩子们转了转手指,"我是一个魔术师。我正在努力成为一名演员,不过我还没接到多少工作。"

埃德的手臂很长,双手修长,手指纤细。

"太酷了!"乔希说,"那你会变魔术吗?"

埃德点点头说:"以后变给你看。"

他们走回大房子,接着走进餐厅。餐厅里有一个宽大的壁炉,上方挂着一个麋鹿头。墙上还挂着套索、马刺、马鞍座毯和缰绳,都是一些装饰物。

壁炉前摆着一张长桌,几把长凳。尤德、大

第九块金子

拇指和另外三人都已经坐下了,露露正在往桌子上摆放食物。

惠特妈妈和惠特爸爸从厨房走出来。惠特妈妈招呼他们:"嘿,孩子们,快坐下来吧。"

惠特爸爸用勺子敲了敲玻璃杯,说:"大家跟来自康涅狄格州的丁丁、乔希和露丝打个招呼吧。"

一个身穿西式衬衫和牛仔裤的女人说:"你们好,我是菲奥娜·尼皮特。"

"我们是塞斯·克莱德和邦妮·克莱德。"坐在一位金发美女旁边的男人说。

露露端着一大盘沉甸甸的食物从厨房里快步走出来,说:"趁热吃吧!现在不吃完的话,明天就要吃剩饭了!"

大家互相传递着一盘盘炸鸡、土豆泥和热气腾腾的蔬菜。

十二个人坐在一张桌子上吃饭,肯定免不了嘈杂。

孩子们了解到,菲奥娜在芝加哥当护士,克莱德夫妇刚刚在佛罗里达州登记结婚,决定在牧

场度蜜月。

只有大拇指没有加入餐桌上的闲聊。其他人都在聊天，他只是埋头吃东西。

甜品时间到了，露露端上了苹果派，上面还放了冰激凌。饱餐一顿后，大家都在揉肚子。

惠特爸爸站起身来，说："天差不多黑了。尤德会在屋后给我们生起篝火。要是我没猜错的话，大拇指肯定会跟你们讲附近有灰熊四处游荡的事。"

乔希看向大拇指，问道："这儿真的有灰熊吗？"

大拇指眨了眨眼，举起他那只缺了大拇指的手，无声地回答了乔希的问题。

大家一起帮忙把餐具收拾到厨房。桌子清理干净后,孩子们走到外面,沿着小路往前走,看到尤德和大拇指正在往一个用树桩围成的圆圈里堆放柴火。

天几乎已经完全黑了。丁丁看到池塘附近的灌木丛里有几只萤火虫在闪烁。

"请坐。"尤德指着树桩示意孩子们坐下。他们和菲奥娜、埃德和克莱德夫妇坐在了一起。

大拇指在自己的皮带扣上划了一根火柴,跪在地上,点燃了树枝下的一些干松针。很快,木头就被点着了,升起的火焰把周围的每一张脸都笼罩在阴影中。

"这也太棒了！"乔希说，"朋友们，我真希望我不是只在这里待一周。"

"我也是。"丁丁说。

这时，惠特妈妈、惠特爸爸和露露也过来了。"大拇指，有什么要跟我们聊聊的吗？"惠特爸爸问。

大家齐齐看向大拇指，火焰把他帽檐下的双眼映得通红。他开始用嘶哑的声音低声讲了起来：

"我永远不会忘记那个夜晚。那是一个干燥的夏天，那天下了一场大雷雨，一道闪电引发了火灾，山上的树林开始燃烧。我们当时就像现在一样坐在这里，突然，一只灰熊从树林里跑了出来。那是一只灰熊幼崽，就一丁点大。看得出来，它被烧伤了。它呜咽着，看起来非常痛苦。于是我们抓住灰熊，把它带进屋里，露露帮它在烧伤处涂了一些黄油。"

说到这儿，大拇指停了下来。此时只有火堆中的木头在噼啪作响。

丁丁瞥了一眼坐在露丝旁边的乔希，只见乔希张大了嘴，眼睛也睁得大大的。

第九块金子

"那只灰熊幼崽怎么样了?"露丝问道。

大拇指看向露丝,眼睛通红。他继续说:

"第二天一早，我们把这只可怜的灰熊幼崽带去了兽医那里。它痊愈后，兽医把它送到了加利福尼亚州的某个动物园。"

"太好了！"乔希说。

大拇指把目光转向乔希，说："简直糟透了！那天晚上，灰熊妈妈来了。它摧毁了这里的一切，大声呼喊着它的孩子。那只灰熊大概有七百磅[1]重。小木屋的门被砸得稀碎，畜棚上被撕开了一个大洞，于是我们不得不躲进露露的地窖里。"

"那灰熊妈妈后来还回来过吗？"乔希问。

大拇指咯咯笑了起来："孩子，灰熊妈妈每年夏天至少会来我们这里两三次。它就像一阵毛茸茸的龙卷风一样席卷而来，几乎摧毁了它所到之处的一切东西。"

他看着自己缺了大拇指的那只手，说："那个可怜的妈妈想找回自己的孩子，已经过去两年了，它还在四处寻找。"

大拇指把那只手放在乔希的肩膀上。"那只

---

1. 磅：英美制质量或重量单位，1磅=0.4536千克。——编者

第九块金子

灰熊幼崽和你差不多大,孩子。"说完他就走进了茫茫夜色中。

第三章

大拇指离开后,大家都没作声,一个接一个站起来,打着哈欠离开了这里。

"别忘了,明天的早餐是酪乳煎饼。"露露一边说,一边向主屋走去。

孩子们留了下来,一起帮尤德用池塘里的水浇灭了篝火。

"这儿真的有熊吗?"乔希问尤德,"他刚才一定是在开玩笑,对吧?"

"我当时在上大学,不在家,所以我也不确定。"尤德说,"但我从没见过大拇指开玩笑。"

"这个故事可能是真的。"露丝说,"我看过一本关于灰熊的书。母熊会保护小熊幼崽,直到它们长大。"

丁丁搂住乔希的肩膀。"别担心，熊就算饿了也不会咬你，你都骨瘦如柴了。"

"孩子们，需要我送你们回小木屋吗？"尤德问道。

"不用！"乔希回答，"我才不怕这些熊呢。而且，我敢打赌大拇指是在骗我们。尤德，他的大拇指到底是怎么没的？"

尤德笑了起来，说："那你得去问他了。睡个好觉，别被小动物们给咬了！"

丁丁、乔希和露丝向那三间小木屋走去。漫天星斗将柔和的光倾泻在小路两旁的石头上。

菲奥娜和埃德的小木屋亮着灯，但中间的小木屋一片漆黑。

"我记得我留了一盏灯。"露丝说。

"我也记得你留了。"丁丁告诉她。

"我就知道我肯定没关灯！"露丝说。然后她跳到乔希的背上，大声尖叫道："那只灰熊肯定就在我们的小屋里！"

"露丝，这可真是有趣极了！"乔希说，"等熊真的来了，看我会不会保护你！"

大家都躺上床后,丁丁把床边的灯关掉了。他翻了个身,侧向一边,望着窗外。

萤火虫四处飞舞。

池塘里的青蛙和蟋蟀发出悦耳的叫声。

露丝睡在房间的另一侧,说:"晚安,朋友们!"

"晚安,露丝。晚安,灰熊。"丁丁说。

"我不要跟你们任何一个人说话了。"躺在上铺的乔希说。

丁丁在他的铺位上笑了起来。乔希真的很容易被吓到。丁丁想着想着,就陷入了梦乡。

突然,丁丁一下子清醒过来。他觉得自己听到小木屋外有什么东西砰的一声响。

他坐了起来,透过露丝床边的窗户朝外望去。露丝此刻还在被窝里,睡得香极了。

丁丁不知道现在是几点,但他觉得自己应该没睡多久。乔希还在打呼噜。

也许是一颗松果掉在了门廊上,丁丁心里这样想着。是啊,松果从大树上掉下来的时候会发出很大的响声。

丁丁又躺下了,闭上眼睛,试图强迫自己重

新入睡。

随即丁丁听到外面传来更嘈杂的声音。门廊上有什么重物在动来动去，那可不是松果！

突然，一个黑影出现在窗前。丁丁吓得一抖，倒在了枕头上。不管外面的东西是什么，都大得足以遮住星光。

丁丁听到了剐蹭声，然后那个黑影就移开了。星光又透过窗户照进了房间。

丁丁把被子拉到下巴下面，感觉心脏在胸口怦怦跳动。他告诉自己：冷静点，这不会是那只孤独的灰熊妈妈吧，应该不会吧？

丁丁真希望自己没有在乔希害怕灰熊的时候取笑他，想着想着，丁丁终于又进入了梦乡。

第二天早上，早餐铃声把孩子们从睡梦中唤醒。乔希从上铺跳下来，差点落到丁丁身上。

趁丁丁和乔希还在穿衣服，露丝冲进了洗手间。三分钟后，三人走在通往主屋的路上。

"听着，伙伴们，"丁丁说，"我知道你们不会相信我说的话，但昨晚屋外的门廊上有东西。"

"什么东西?"露丝问,"它有皮毛和大爪子吗?"

"又来了。"乔希嘀咕道。

"是真的,真的有东西在外面。"丁丁继续说,"我听到了砰砰的声音,露丝,然后有东西挡住了你那边的窗户,还有爪子的剐蹭声。"

乔希笑着说:"你们真是太逊了,搞不好是一只浣熊呢!"

"如果你说的是对的,那我们可得给《吉尼斯世界纪录大全》打电话了!"丁丁说,"不管那扇窗前站着什么东西,都有大概六英尺[1]高呢!"

"我才不在乎窗外是不是有怪物在偷看我们呢。"乔希一边说,一边冲向主屋,"我要去吃煎饼啦!"

孩子们冲进餐厅,这时大家都已经坐好了。

"早上好!"惠特妈妈边说边给大家倒果汁,"希望你们昨晚睡得很好,今早醒来都已经饿了吧!"

一盘盘炒鸡蛋、香肠和薄煎饼摆在桌子中

---

1. 英尺:英美制长度单位,1 英尺 = 0.3048 米。——编者

间,每个人都大快朵颐。

等大家都吃得差不多了,丁丁就向大家说起昨晚小屋门廊上传来的奇怪声音,还有黑影。

"奇怪的声音?"惠特爸爸说,"我什么也没听到。尤德,你听到了吗?"

"爸爸,可没有什么声音能把我吵醒。"尤德说,"你听到什么了吗,妈妈?"

惠特妈妈摇摇头说:"大拇指,你听到什么奇怪的声音了吗?"

大拇指咧嘴笑了,摇摇头说:"没有,但今天早上我走过来的时候,我好像闻到了熊身上的味道。"

第四章

除了乔希，大家都哈哈大笑起来。然后惠特爸爸请埃德给大家表演一个魔术。

埃德站起身来，向观众展示他的手里什么东西都没有，两手空空。接下来，他把餐巾盖在一只手上，小声嘀咕了几句咒语。当他唰的一下把餐巾扯下来后，一枚鸡蛋竟然在他的手心。

大家都在鼓掌，这时大拇指站起来说："露露，早餐非常美味。我们要去淘金了，你们要是想去可以一起去。"

二十分钟后，七位客人跟着大拇指和尤德，沿着池塘另一侧的石子路徒步往前走。一条小溪顺着小路流过，在岩石上溅起水花，潺潺流淌。在离开主屋之前，尤德给每个人发了一个大大的

第九块金子

平底淘金盘。

几分钟后,大拇指在小溪边的一片沙岸上停了下来,说:"就是这里了。"

"我没看到哪里有金子呀。"乔希向水中望去,瞧了好几眼。

尤德笑了起来,说:"光靠眼睛看是看不到的。"他指了指小溪上游的群山。

"那些山上才有金子。"他解释说,"每次下暴风雨的时候,金子就会被冲到下游。大拇指,教教他们怎么淘金子吧。"

大拇指蹲了下来,把淘金盘浸入水中,说:"不要站在小溪里,不然就会搅乱泥浆。"他轻轻一抬手腕,连水带沙端起了一盘。

"金子比沙砾重,"大拇指继续说,"所以金子会沉淀在盘底。"

大拇指轻轻地来回晃动盘子,沙砾和水都晃动了起来。接着他把盘子倾斜,让水和沙砾滑到盘子边缘。

"看这里!"大拇指一边说,一边把他的淘金盘举了起来。盘底有几块暗淡的鹅卵石,但在这

35

些鹅卵石中，有粒豌豆大小的金子在闪闪发光。

"那是金子吗？"丁丁问。

"当然！"大拇指说。他把金子挑出来，向大家展示了一番。

"这粒金子值多少钱？"乔希问。

大拇指把金子放进衬衫口袋里。"这个大小的吗？那可不值多少钱。"他抬起下巴，冲着远处的群山说，"要想找到真正的金子，还是得上山去。"

"我们现在可以试试吗？"露丝问。

大拇指从溪边退了回来，说："自己选个地方

第九块金子

试试吧，记住，不要下水。"

于是大家都跪在小溪边开始淘金。

尤德和孩子们一起把淘金盘浸入水中。"我从小时候起就开始淘金了。"他说，"有一年，有一位客人找到了一块高尔夫球那么大的金子。我听说他把它卖掉了，给自己买了一辆新的吉普车！"

"太酷了！"乔希说，"我也想要一辆吉普车！"他跪在沙地上，将盘子浸入水中。

大家纷纷行动起来。有一阵子，只能听到沙砾与金属碰撞的声音。

丁丁很快就掌握了其中的诀窍。他喜欢一次

次把盘子浸入水中时，阳光照耀后背的感觉。

突然，菲奥娜大喊了一声："我找到了一粒！"她笑着举起一粒金子，比大拇指找到的还要大一点。

尤德说："太好了！现在让我们看看其他人能不能找到。"

在接下来的半个小时里，其他人包括尤德，都大叫着举起自己找到的金子。大家一共找到了八颗小金粒。到最后，只有乔希没有从小溪里捞到金子。

"得赶紧收拾一下回去了。"大拇指催促大家，"如果我们吃饭迟到了，露露就会变得跟熊一样不好惹。"

"我打算换个地方试试，这里已经没有金子了。"乔希说。

"你要去哪儿？"露丝问。

乔希用淘金盘指了指上游，说："我要去那边的山上，去真正有金子的地方。"

丁丁看着乔希踩着岩石和树枝，小心翼翼地沿着小溪往上游走去。

露丝说："我真希望他能找到一块金子，不

第九块金子

然，整个一周他都会闷闷不乐的！"

丁丁把自己淘到的金子举到太阳底下，那颗小金粒跟玛氏巧克力豆差不多大。他问："你觉得我可以用这个换一辆自行车吗？"

突然，他们听到了乔希的叫喊声，紧接着是水花飞溅的声音。他们向上游看去，原来乔希跌坐在水里了！

丁丁和露丝跑过去帮忙，但尤德比他们先赶到了。"你还好吗？"尤德伸手去抓乔希。

乔希抓住尤德的手，跌跌撞撞地从小溪里站了起来。他腰部以下都湿透了，但脸上却绽放着灿烂的笑容。

"看我找到了什么！"乔希说着，伸出他的另一只手。

丁丁瞪大了眼睛。乔希手里拿着一块跟土豆差不多大的金子。

第五章

"乔希,你可真厉害!"丁丁大喊。他和露丝都跟乔希击掌庆祝,其他人也围了过来。

"这是到目前为止我见过的最大的一块金子。"尤德惊叹道。

这块金子有乔希的手掌那么大,几乎跟手一样平。有些沙砾和泥巴嵌在这块金子上,但其余部分都是纯金的。

"好了,朋友们,"大拇指在队伍后面说,"咱们该回去了。"

大家一边祝贺乔希,一边往回走。乔希穿着湿透了的运动鞋,走起路来嘎吱作响。大家直接前往主屋吃午餐。

乔希把找到的大金块砰的一下放在自己餐盘

旁边的桌子上。

"我打赌,我可以让它消失。"埃德笑着说。

"不用不用,谢谢!"乔希说。

"你真是个幸运的孩子。"惠特爸爸对乔希说,"但我劝你别把金子带在身边,你肯定不想把它弄丢吧!"

"为什么不把它放在我们家的保险箱里呢?"尤德问,"明天我们就可以把金子拿去镇上估价。"

"估价是什么意思?"乔希问。

"就是专家会鉴定一下这块金子,然后告诉你它值多少钱。"尤德解释说,"如果你愿意,就可以把它卖掉。"

"好呀,那可太好了!"乔希说。

午餐过后,孩子们跟着尤德去了办公室。牧场的办公室很小,里面到处都积满了灰尘。大部分空间都被一张巨大的橡木桌子占据了,一面墙上挂着一张棕色的牛皮。开着黄色小花的植物摆放在窗台上,排成一行。

桌子旁边放着一个黑色的老式保险箱,上面还摆着一瓶干花。尤德蹲在保险箱前,孩子们都看着他。他把密码锁来回转了几圈，然后打开了保险箱的门。

尤德笑着说："该你了，乔希。放心，你的金子放在我们的保险箱里一定会很安全的。"为了腾出空间，他移开了一些文件和一本绿色的账簿。

乔希走上前去，把金子放在了账簿的上面。随后，尤德把保险箱门关上，锁好了密码锁。

"你们都准备好去骑马了吗？"一个声音从乔希的身后传来。他转过身来，发现大拇指站在那里，嘴边叼着一根牙签。

"当然！"尤德说，"准备好了吗，孩子们？"

"我已经给马套上了马鞍。"大拇指说着离开了办公室。

菲奥娜、埃德和克莱德夫妇，还有孩子们，都跟着尤德和大拇指一起来到畜棚。

九匹马都套好了马鞍，绑在畜栏上。马鞍座毯上还绣着每匹马的名字。

惠特爸爸和惠特妈妈开着一辆绿色的旧卡车停了下来。惠特妈妈说："祝你们骑马骑得尽兴！我们要进城去了。"

第九块金子

大家挥了挥手跟他们告别，卡车开走了，扬起了一片灰尘。

"我能骑一匹温顺点的马吗？"丁丁问。

尤德笑了笑，说："我们所有的马都很温顺，你可以骑这匹马，它叫扳机，它可喜欢小孩子了。"

扳机是一匹淡金色的马，长着白色的鬃毛。它用一双温和的棕色眼睛看着大家。

"有小一点的马吗？"乔希问，"我害怕那些比我高的动物！"

"巴尼是我们这里最小的马，"尤德回答，"它跑得可好了，不过它喜欢停下来吃路边的野花野草。"

"那让乔希骑这匹马真是再合适不过了！"露丝说。

乔希轻轻拍了拍巴尼柔软的鼻子。"好好表现，我等会儿偷偷给你吃一些甜点。"

"有母马吗？"露丝问尤德。

"当然有！"尤德说，"你可以骑雪球。它非常可爱，而且是这些马里面步态最轻柔的。"

雪球又白又胖，有着长长的睫毛。当露丝抚

43

摸它的身体时，它就会发出轻轻的嘶鸣声。

尤德很快就给埃德、菲奥娜和克莱德夫妇也挑好了马。"好了，各位，该上马了。"尤德站在一匹银白色的马旁边，那匹马很高大，名叫子弹。尤德说："大家看我，我来教你们怎么骑。"

尤德用左手握住马鞍头，将左脚的靴尖伸进脚镫。然后他纵身一跃，把右腿甩到马鞍上，就上了马。"大家学会了吗？有没有谁需要帮忙？"

"我需要帮忙！"丁丁说。

大拇指把三个孩子扶上了马鞍，给他们示范了一下怎么握住缰绳，还根据他们的腿长调整了一下脚镫。

就在这时，埃德大叫了一声："哎哟！"只见他的身体半跨在马鞍上，右脚悬在脚镫外，姿势非常别扭。

尤德跳下马，跑过去帮埃德从马上下来，问道："你还好吗？"

"我也不清楚。"埃德说。他走了一步，疼得龇牙咧嘴，脸色发白。"好疼啊，我想可能是扭伤了！"

"你最好别用那只脚踝发力。"菲奥娜建议，

第九块金子

"过来吧,我扶你回小木屋。"

埃德说:"不用,菲奥娜,你继续骑吧。我不会有事的。"

菲奥娜说:"别瞎说!反正我本来也不是很想骑马,我去找露露拿些冰块吧。"

菲奥娜扶着一瘸一拐的埃德,两人慢慢走回小木屋。

"大拇指,你能留下来给埃德和菲奥娜的马卸一下马鞍吗?"尤德问,"到时候你可以来草地上跟我们会合。"

大拇指点了点头,开始给菲奥娜的马卸鞍。

"我们骑成一列吧,"尤德对其他人说,"每匹马都要跟在前面那匹马的后面。"

"那谁骑在最前面?"乔希问。

"你来吧。"尤德说,"巴尼喜欢带队。只要用你的脚后跟轻轻碰一下它的肚子,它就会往前走了。"

乔希用脚后跟轻轻地碰了碰马肚子,说:"好啦,乖小马,快走吧!"

巴尼抖了抖鬃毛,扭头看了看乔希,耳朵抽

动了一下，但一步也没往前走。

"请？"乔希说。

巴尼哼了一声，然后踏着轻快的步子离开了畜棚。

"可简单了！"乔希对丁丁和露丝说，"但你们要记得说'请'！"

其余五匹马跟在巴尼身后。很快，他们就骑到了一条被灌木丛和树木包围的狭窄小道上。马队走过一座横跨小溪的木桥，嘚嘚的马蹄声回荡在空中。

一行人穿过树林后，牧场很快就消失在众人的身后。

第六章

马儿依旧排成一列,嘚嘚地往前走。巴尼似乎早就知道要去哪里,其他马儿也跟在后面。尤德骑着子弹,一直在队伍末尾。

很快,大家就来到一片草地。池塘掩映在一片野花丛中,池水清澈透蓝。乔希的马儿没有继续往前走,而是停在一棵松树下,低头吃着树下的野草。

"让马儿在这儿吃一会儿草吧。"尤德说。他扶着孩子们从马上下来,大家各自把马拴在它可以吃到草的树荫底下。

"这里真是太美了!"乔希说。

"当地的人们都叫它'天堂草场'。"尤德说,

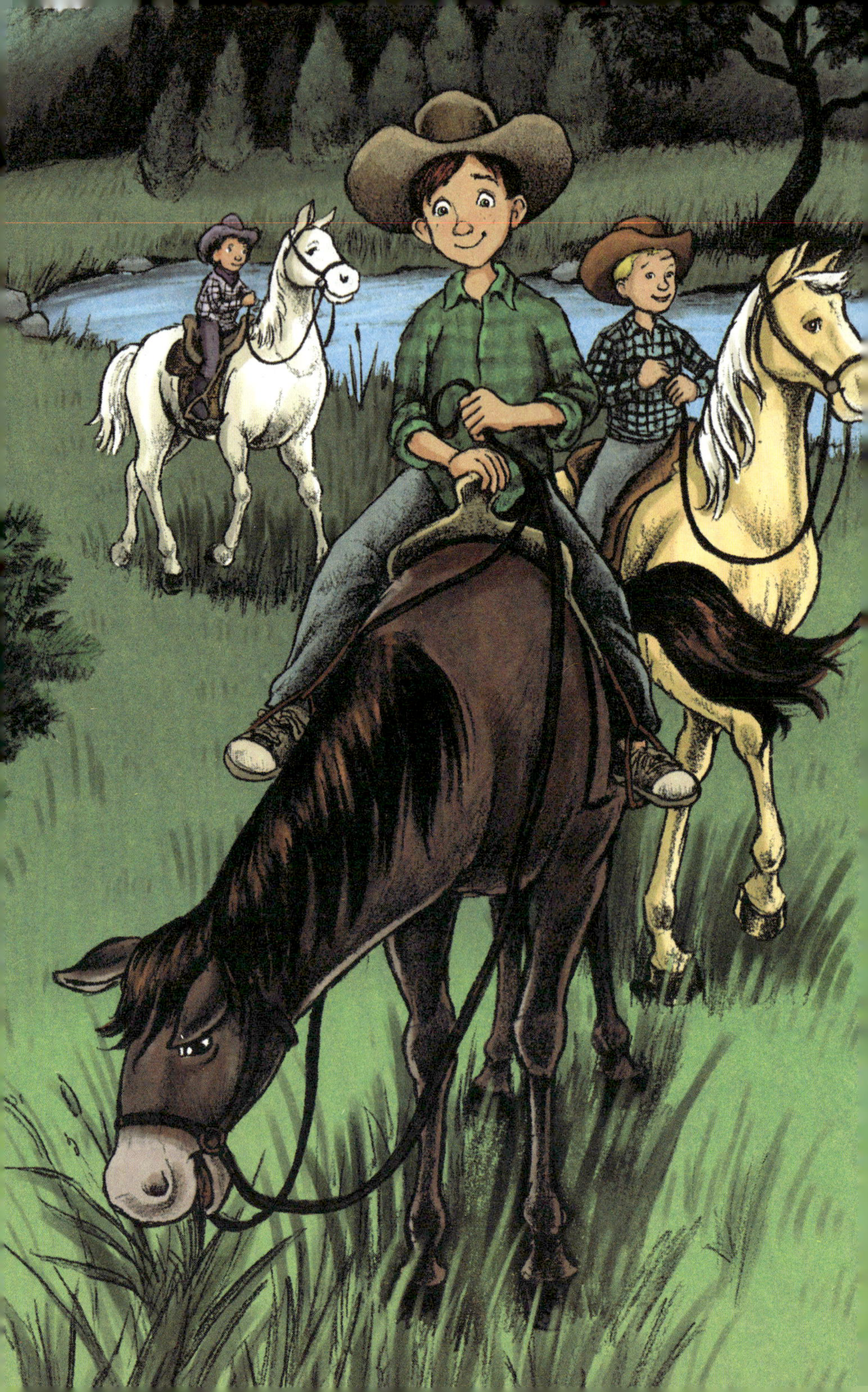

第九块金子

"如果你想喂鱼,池塘里还有肥美的鳟鱼。"

他从鞍袋里掏出一袋午餐时吃剩的面包屑。"只要把面包屑洒在水面上,鱼儿就会浮上来。"

"你能教我抛套索吗?"乔希问尤德。

"等大拇指来了,你可以问问他。"尤德说,"他可是套索专家。"

尤德仰头望着天空,只见几朵乌云夹杂在白云中间。

"快要下雨了。"他担忧地说,"万一下雨了,你们的鞍袋里有雨披。山脚下的暴风雨可是说来就来!"

邦妮问尤德:"这里所有的花你都认识吗?"

尤德笑着说:"我都认识。谁要是愿意,我可以带你们去野外散散步。"

"我们乐意至极!"邦妮说。

尤德看着孩子们问:"你们想一起去,还是在这里等大拇指?"

"我想去喂鱼。"露丝说。

"我也是。"丁丁说着,伸手去拿那袋面包屑。

"我能借你的套索用用吗?"乔希问道,"搞

49

不好我还可以套住一条鱼呢！"

尤德把套索递给乔希。

"用不了多久，大拇指就能让你成为牛仔竞技比赛的明日之星。"尤德说，"我们不会走远的。"

尤德、塞斯和邦妮向草地的另一边走去。孩子们走到池塘边上。丁丁脱掉运动鞋，蹚入水中，露丝在往池塘里扔面包屑。一群鳟鱼立刻就围了过来，争着吃面包屑。

"看这个！"乔希说。他用尤德的套索绕了个圈，朝一个树桩扔了过去。套索在半空中缠在了一起，一下子就掉在了地上。

"那些牛仔是怎么做到的？"乔希喃喃自语，捡起套索准备再试一次。

就在这时，孩子们身后响起了马蹄声。他们转过身来，看到大拇指骑着一匹高大的黑马来到草地上。

"嘿，大拇指！"丁丁和露丝一起打了个招呼。

大拇指点了点头，但没说话。他下了马，把马拴在其他马儿附近。

"你打算让他教你抛套索吗？"露丝问乔希。

"我不知道。"乔希低声说,"我总感觉他有点吓人。"

"别傻了!"露丝对乔希说。然后她走到大拇指身边,说:"乔希想让你教他抛套索。"

大拇指朝她身后瞥了一眼,乔希正在试图把套索卷起来。

"我想也许我可以教他。"大拇指回答道,接着用他那乌黑的眼睛环视了一下草场,"大家都去哪儿了?"

"尤德带克莱德夫妇去野外散步了。"丁丁说。

大拇指咕哝了一声,然后他走到乔希身边,拿起套索,迅速绕出一个大圈。他在头顶上方挥了三圈,然后把套索抛了出去。套索在空中呼啸而过,一下就套住了树桩。

"你是怎么做到的?"乔希问。

"全靠手指和手腕发力。"大拇指说。他正教乔希如何抓住套索,这时尤德和克莱德夫妇回来了。

"暴风雨来得比我预期的要快。"尤德说,"我们最好还是回牧场去。朋友们,抱歉,骑马的时间缩短了。"

头顶上,几朵乌云已经形成了一片雷暴云,从北面一路飘来,在草场上投下了阴影。

几分钟后,他们都骑上了马,穿着黄色连帽雨披。这次大拇指带头,尤德殿后。

先前还是晴天,现在就已经刮起了风,天气陡然转凉,突如其来的雨拍打着树林。丁丁感觉脑袋和肩膀上都淋到了雨,还能听到淅淅沥沥的雨滴声。

半小时后,七匹湿漉漉的马驮着它们的主人回到了畜棚。

"我来给小黑卸马鞍吧。"尤德对大拇指说,"你去告诉露露说我们回来了,让她给大家准备一些热巧克力和饼干。"

大拇指跳下马,把小黑的缰绳交给尤德,然后跑向主屋。

雨差不多已经停了,一阵强风把云朵吹跑了。大家都下了马,把马牵进畜棚。

突然,晚餐的铃声响了起来。

"露露怎么现在就敲响了铃声?"尤德疑惑地

说,"离晚餐时间还早着呢!"

铃声还在叮当作响,尤德冲出了畜棚。

第七章

克莱德夫妇和三个孩子在后面追赶尤德。他们穿过院子,牧场的卡车这时刚好停在了车道上。

惠特妈妈和惠特爸爸拎着几袋食品杂货跳下车。"发生什么事了?"惠特爸爸问尤德。

"有人敲响了铃声!"尤德说着,纵身一跃,跳上了门廊的台阶。

门廊上空无一人,但挂着的三角铁仍然在摇晃作响。

"尤德!快进来!"大拇指在屋里喊道,"我在办公室。"

尤德穿过纱门，飞奔进去，其他人紧随其后。

九个人都挤在狭小的办公室里。大拇指半跪在露露面前，露露被绑在椅子上，嘴也被堵上了。

大拇指帮露露解开绳结，惠特妈妈帮露露把堵住嘴的东西拿了下来。惠特爸爸正在给警长打电话。

"露露，发生什么事了？"惠特妈妈担心地问。

"保险箱！"露露指着保险箱喊道。

A to Z 神秘案件

保险箱的门敞开着,里面放着一沓文件和一本绿色的账簿,只有乔希的金子消失不见了。

"他们偷走了我的金子!"乔希大喊道。

"能给我点水喝吗?"露露问。她揉了揉手腕,上面有被绳子勒出的红印。

邦妮跑去拿水,露露向大家讲述了事情的经过。

"我当时就在这儿给植物浇水,"露露说,"突然有人一把抓住我,把我推到椅子上。我刚要喊,他就用东西堵住了我的嘴,把我绑了起来。"

惠特爸爸问:"这是谁干的?你认出他是谁了吗?"

露露摇摇头说:"他穿着一身黑衣服,脸上还戴着黑色面罩,没跟我说一句话。"

"欸?菲奥娜和埃德在哪儿呢?"尤德问,"他们应该跟我们一样,都听到了铃声。"

"菲奥娜让埃德躺下休息了,"露露说,"还给他包扎了脚踝。我给他拿了一副拐杖,本来还想叫医生,但埃德说自己吃了阿司匹林就能好。"

尤德跑出门,孩子们也跟了出来。"菲奥娜住在哪间小木屋?"尤德转身问道。

"那间。"丁丁指着离主屋最近的那间小木屋说。

第九块金子

尤德以迅雷不及掩耳之势跳上台阶,敲响了门:"菲奥娜?我是尤德。你还好吗?"

没人回答,尤德打开门,冲了进去。"噢,天哪……快去把惠特妈妈叫来,快!"尤德转身大喊。露丝冲出门廊,向主屋跑去。

丁丁越过尤德向屋里扫了一眼。菲奥娜被绑在椅子上,嘴也被堵住了,跟露露被绑的情形一模一样。

丁丁抓住乔希的胳膊,喊道:"我们快去看看埃德!"

丁丁和乔希跑向埃德的小木屋。丁丁问:"盖茨先生?你还好吗?"

没人应声,丁丁就打开了门。只见埃德躺在床上,一条头巾堵住了他的嘴,他的双手背在身后。

丁丁解开头巾,扔到一旁。

埃德说:"太感谢了!我还以为我得在这里待一整天呢!"

他朝衣橱抬了抬下巴:"衣橱里有一个运动包,包里放着一个小盒子,里面有一把钥匙。那家伙用我自己的手铐铐住了我!"

57

乔希找到了那把钥匙。埃德坐了起来,丁丁和乔希看到他的双手都被铐在了铁制床板上。乔希转动钥匙,手铐啪的一下打开了。

"发生什么事了?"丁丁说,"他们还把菲奥娜和露露也绑起来了!"

"是啊,那个卑鄙小人还偷走了我的金子!"乔希愤愤地说。

丁丁注意到,埃德的一只脚上缠了很多圈绷带,一副拐杖靠在床边。

"我正拿着手铐把玩,准备在晚餐时给你们表演一些魔术。"埃德说,"突然,一个穿黑衣服的人冲了进来。我还没来得及动,他就把我铐在了床上,用头巾堵住了我的嘴。"

埃德晃了晃手,揉着手腕说:"哎哟,绑得真紧!"

"你还能走路吗?"丁丁问道,"惠特爸爸已经给警长打了电话。我们估计都要去办公室会合。"

埃德靠没受伤的那只脚撑着站了起来。乔希把拐杖递给埃德,埃德把拐杖放在腋下,撑着那只缠着绷带的脚,单脚点地,一步一步往前跳。

"我们走吧!"埃德说,"不要离我太近,万一我摔倒了,我可不想倒在你们身上。"

丁丁和乔希走在前头,埃德走在后面,三人沿着小路向主屋走去。露丝、惠特妈妈和菲奥娜正与一名男子站在门廊上。

车道上停着一辆绿白相间的汽车,车门上印着"警长"两个字,几只鸡正在啄轮胎。

第八章

所有人都挤在狭小的办公室里。警长在本子上做记录，露露把她的遭遇复述了一遍。菲奥娜和埃德时不时插嘴，补充一些细节。

"所以我的理解是，"警长说，"某个穿黑衣服的男人或女人把你们三个人都绑了起来，然后打开保险箱，偷走了一大块金子，是这样吗？"

"会不会是哪个碰巧路过这里的陌生人干的？"惠特妈妈问。

露露摇摇头说："相信我，方圆一英里[1]以内，我没有看到一个陌生人。"

"也许是有路人躲在树林里。"惠特爸爸说，

---

1. 英里：英美制长度单位，1英里合1.609千米。——编者

第九块金子

"一定是个陌生人,盗贼不可能是这个房间里的任何一个人!"

丁丁迅速扫视了一下办公室,发现每个人都在看向其他人,大家面面相觑。

惠特妈妈问:"露露,你有注意到那个盗贼是怎么打开保险箱的吗?"

"我没看到他的动作。"露露说,"他蹲下身

子，背对着我，但我看到他手上戴着手套。"

警长走到保险箱前，说："所以我们甚至无法获取指纹。我想保险箱已经锁上了，有谁知道密码吗？"

"嗯，我当然知道。"惠特爸爸说，"还有惠特妈妈，也就是我的妻子惠特太太，以及我们的儿子尤德，就我们几个人知道。"

警长向大家道谢，然后向门口走去。临走时他递给惠特妈妈一张名片，说："如果你们有谁想起什么线索，请务必打电话给我。"

警长看着乔希，说："孩子，很遗憾你的金子丢了，我会尽我所能帮你找回来。"

乔希喃喃地说："谢谢。"

孩子们跟着警长走出了主屋。警长挥手告别，开着警车飞快地驶离了车道。

大家茫然地走回各自的小木屋。孩子们坐在门廊前的台阶上。

"这个盗贼真聪明。"露丝说。

"什么意思？"乔希问道。他把套索绕了一圈，瞄准门廊的栏杆抛了过去，但没套中。

"我的意思是,这个盗贼让牧场里的每个人看起来都不像是盗贼。"露丝说,"我们七个人在骑马,对吧?所以不可能是我们中的任何一个人。露露、埃德和菲奥娜被绑起来了,所以也不可能是他们。惠特妈妈和惠特爸爸去买东西了,我们回来的时候他们也刚好回来了。我们十二个人都有充分的不在场证明。那谁是那个盗贼?没剩谁了!"

乔希叹了口气,把套索卷了起来,说:"你很接近真相了,露丝。但你忘了一件小事。只有六个人在骑马——我们三个,还有塞斯、邦妮和尤德。"

"那大拇指呢?"丁丁问道,"他和我们在一起——"

"噢,我的天哪!"露丝喊道,"丁丁,乔希说得对!大拇指最后是跟我们一起骑马回来的,但一开始他没跟我们一起!"

乔希笑着说:"是的。他有可能在卸下菲奥娜和埃德的马鞍后,去把他们绑了起来。然后他把露露也绑了起来,偷走了金子,接着又匆匆赶到草场。"

"但大拇指实际上可以说是惠特家族的一员。"丁丁说,"他为什么要在牧场里抢劫呢?"

"为了他见过的最大的一块金子。"乔希一边说,一边想用套索套住丁丁的脚。

但他还是没有套中。

第九章

孩子们坐在那里，思考着大拇指到底是不是盗贼。

"我知道你不喜欢大拇指，"丁丁对乔希说，"但我不相信他会抢劫惠特一家。而且你们还记得吗？他不知道密码是什么。"

"谁说的？"乔希问道，"他在这里工作了很多年，很可能早就在惠特一家不知情的情况下知道了密码。"

丁丁捡起几块鹅卵石扔到小路上，说："就像惠特妈妈说的那样，也许是某个陌生人干的。"

"我一直在想他们被绑起来并堵住嘴的事。"露丝说，"不管是谁干的，都是在冒很大的风险。如果我们中途回来了怎么办？"

乔希说:"这也是我认为盗贼是大拇指的另一个原因。他知道我们一时半会儿不会回来,也知道惠特爸爸和惠特妈妈至少会离开一个小时。你们有没有注意到,他总是偷偷跟在别人后面?"

过了片刻,丁丁说:"伙伴们,我想知道,为什么盗贼用绳子绑住了菲奥娜和露露,却用手铐铐住了埃德。"

乔希说:"埃德跟我们说,他把手铐拿出来是为了练习一下魔术。盗贼看到了之后就决定用手铐铐住他。"

"也许吧。"丁丁说。

"难道你觉得那个盗贼是埃德吗?"乔希笑着说,"我只能想象他一瘸一拐地走来走去,把人绑起来,然后挂着拐杖打开保险箱的样子。"

"除非他是假装的。"露丝说。

"假装什么?"乔希问。

露丝转过身,盯着丁丁和乔希说:"如果埃德的脚踝没有真的受伤呢?如果他是装的,那他不就可以顺理成章地留在这里抢劫保险箱了吗?"

"露丝,埃德被手铐铐住了,嘴也被堵住了。"

第九块金子

乔希分析道,"他总不可能自己铐住自己,还用头巾堵住嘴吧?"

"哎呀,他还是个魔术师呢,不是吗?"

"而且,菲奥娜一直和他待在一起。"乔希继续说,"除非你认为她和埃德是犯罪同伙。"

"嗯,这是有可能的,不是吗?"露丝问道。

"我觉得他们任何一个人都有可能。"丁丁说,"但我们该如何证明呢?"

过了一分钟,乔希说:"我还是认为盗贼是大拇指。他对套索很了解,而且我打赌,那个盗贼戴着手套是为了不让别人看到他缺失的拇指。"

"乔希,很多人都知道怎么打绳结,"丁丁说,"而且所有计划抢劫保险箱的人都会戴上手套,这样就不会留下指纹。"

"法伦警官常说'要找到证据',"露丝说,"那我们为什么不去他们几个人的小木屋里找找呢?"

"找什么?"丁丁问。

"找线索呀,"露丝说,"比如找盗贼穿的黑色衣服。"

"还有我的金子!"乔希说,"不管是谁拿走了金子,都有可能会把它藏在自己的房间里。"

"那不就是破门而入吗?"丁丁问。

露丝说:"只是进入罢了,所有的门都没锁,我们压根不用破门而入。"

就在这时,晚餐铃声响了起来。

乔希放下手中的套索,站起来说:"我们去吃饭吧。肚子一饿,我的大脑就无法思考了。"

他们赶到餐厅。吃饭的时候,大人们在谈论抢劫案,孩子们埋头吃饭,静静地听着。

丁丁环视了一下在场的所有人。真是令人难以置信,要是这些人中真有一个人可能犯了罪,那这个人怎么还能坐在这里装模作样呢?

丁丁暗自想,盗贼不可能是惠特一家或克莱德夫妇中的任何一个人,那就只剩下埃德、菲奥娜、大拇指和露露了。

丁丁瞥了一眼坐在桌子另一边的埃德。他把拐杖靠在墙上,正在用一根绳子给菲奥娜和尤德表演魔术。

菲奥娜穿着一件黑色的高领衫和一条黑色牛仔裤。丁丁可以看到她手腕上的红色绳痕。她会是那个穿黑衣服的盗贼吗？

露露在厨房和餐厅之间来来回回地忙碌着。无论如何，丁丁都无法想象她会把人绑起来并打开保险箱。不过，她可能跟大拇指一样，早就知道密码是什么了。

丁丁顺着桌子朝大拇指平时坐的位置看去。他的位置是空的！

突然，丁丁感觉到有人在桌子底下用脚踢了踢他，原来是乔希。

丁丁瞪着他，乔希朝空椅子抬了抬下巴，竖起大拇指，挑了挑眉毛。

丁丁低声说："我知道他不在这儿！冷静点。"

"发生什么事了？"露丝问。

丁丁还没来得及回答，乔希就向惠特妈妈问起大拇指在哪里："他……他答应晚餐后教我一个套索技巧。"

惠特妈妈说："哎呀，乔希，这我也不清楚，他可能是去镇上了。"

惠特爸爸用勺子轻轻敲了敲水杯，说："今天真是糟糕的一天。要不晚餐后大家留在这里打打牌？埃德，你可以给我们多表演几个魔术。"

饭桌上的大人们似乎都很赞成惠特爸爸的提议。

乔希把丁丁和露丝拉到一边，低声说："太好了！我们可以趁他们都在这里的时候去小木屋里看看。"

"但是如果我们就这样离开，不会显得很奇怪吗？"露丝问。

乔希眨了眨眼，然后走到惠特妈妈身边，跟她说了些什么。一分钟后他回来了，说："搞定了，我们现在就走吧。"

"你跟惠特妈妈说了什么？"丁丁问。

"说了一个小小的谎言。"乔希说着就朝门口走去。

丁丁和露丝紧随其后。"什么样的谎言？"露丝站在门廊上问。

乔希沿着小路朝小木屋走去。"我告诉她，我们有一项学校要求一定要完成的暑假作业。"

丁丁笑着问："什么作业？"

乔希抬头看了一眼天空，说："研究星座。"

第九块金子

"可是我们对星座一无所知!"露丝说。

"我知道。"乔希说,"但这只是我们的掩护。如果有人发现我们在黑暗中东奔西跑,他们会认为我们只是在观星!"

第十章

"我们应该先去哪间小木屋?"乔希问。

"我去埃德的小屋。"丁丁说。

"我去菲奥娜那儿。"露丝说,"你们注意到了吗?她今晚穿的是黑色的衣服。"

丁丁说:"注意到了。而且,埃德在用绳子表演魔术。乔希,要不你去大拇指的小木屋看看吧?就在畜棚后面。不过你要小心,他可能会在那儿!"

乔希说:"没问题,我先看看牧场的卡车和旅行车在不在。如果其中一辆不在,那大拇指肯定也出去了。"

孩子们分头行动起来。丁丁蹑手蹑脚地走上埃德屋前的台阶,一踩上去,木板就嘎吱作响。

第九块金子

丁丁很紧张，尽管他知道此时埃德还在主屋里。

他推开纱门，走了进去，埃德床头的小灯还亮着。

埃德并不是一个很爱干净的人，衣服随处乱扔，床上放着一个运动包和行李袋，只收拾了一半。

丁丁迅速检查了一下梳妆台的抽屉。他找到了一本名为《让魔术变简单》的书，还有几条彩色头巾。他还发现了几根绳子，但看起来并不像之前绑菲奥娜和露露的那种绳子。

丁丁还在洗手间里看到了一瓶阿司匹林、一些剃须用品和一把紫色牙刷。毛巾架上还挂着一根黑色橡胶管。起初，丁丁没有认出这是什么，后来他才意识到这是一个听诊器。丁丁心想，这可能是埃德表演魔术的道具。

从洗手间出来后，丁丁检查了一下墙上的挂钩。挂钩上挂着衬衫和裤子，但没有一件衣服是黑色的。

在别人的房间里四处探寻，丁丁对此感到有些愧疚，好在他没有弄坏任何东西，也没有偷窃。

他瞄了一眼行李袋和运动包，里面都装着衣

服，还装了几本书。丁丁感到有些奇怪，为什么埃德只收拾了一半行李呢？

突然，丁丁听到门廊上传来脚步声！

他僵住了，然后一个箭步钻到床底。他躺在那里，祈祷纱门不会被打开。

片刻之后，丁丁笑了起来，那肯定是乔希或露丝在各自小木屋的门廊上走动的声音！小木屋之间只隔大约二十英尺左右，窗户又都开着。

丁丁站了起来，往窗外悄悄看去。只见乔希和露丝就在隔壁，正透过窗户在跟他招手！

丁丁也跟他们招了招手，然后赶紧跑到隔壁。"伙伴们，你们吓到我了！"他说。

"你发现什么了吗？"乔希问他。丁丁扑通一声躺在床上，说："只发现了一本关于魔术的书和一些变魔术的道具，没有黑色衣服，也没有金子。很抱歉，乔希。"

露丝说："菲奥娜有很多黑色衣服，还有一大堆悬疑推理小说！"

"有关于盗窃保险箱的吗？"丁丁问。

"没有，但我仔细检查了她被绑时坐的那把

椅子。"露丝说,"我搞不明白她是怎么把自己绑起来的。她可以自己把脚绑起来,但她的手被绑在背后!"

"她没有把自己绑起来。"乔希说,"是大拇指绑的她。对了,旅行车已经开走了。我真希望大拇指不是开车进城去卖我的金子了!"

"他的小屋是什么样的?"丁丁问。

"屋里放满了东西。"乔希说,"我妈妈会喜欢这家伙的,他太整洁了!他的床铺得整整齐齐,所有衣服都挂好了。"

"乔希,先别管他有多整洁。你找到什么线索了吗?"露丝问道。

乔希笑着说:"找到了,他有黑色手套、黑色牛仔裤和黑色滑雪面罩!他还有一堆绳子。还有,看看这个,他有电视和录像机,猜猜他在看什么影片?"

丁丁和露丝盯着他。

"西部著名抢劫案!"乔希说,"我看到录像带的盒子了。"

"但这并不能证明他就是那个盗贼呀。"丁丁说，"事实上，我们看到的东西都不能证明什么。"

"而且我们还是不知道我的金子到底在哪里。"乔希说着，把套索放在膝盖上一圈一圈地绕，"我差点就要发财了！"

就在这时，孩子们听到外面传来拖着脚走路的声音。透过纱门，他们看到埃德拄着拐杖一瘸一拐地从小屋门前走过。

他走得很慢，缠着绷带的脚悬在空中。他走上前面的台阶时，就用没受伤的那只脚保持平衡，然后打开了门溜了进去。

"乔希，我知道你现在很沮丧。"露丝说，"我不怪你，但也许警长会找到那个盗贼呢。"

乔希推开纱门，走到门廊上。他坐在台阶上，把套索搭在膝盖上，喃喃自语："到了明天，那个盗贼就会把金子卖掉，他会得到一大笔钱，然后远走高飞，没有人会抓住他。"

丁丁和露丝陪着乔希一起坐在门廊上。天渐渐黑了，萤火虫在灌木丛中闪烁。主屋那边传来阵阵笑声。

丁丁坐在乔希旁边，试图把乔希的注意力从

丢失的金子上转移，问道："想去池塘边走走吗？"

乔希只是耸了耸肩，继续凝望着夜色。

露丝说："好吧，我们去吧，但我要先去拿防蚊喷雾。"

她转身要回小屋，可她突然停了下来。从她站的地方可以看到埃德的小屋侧面的那扇窗户。

"朋友们，快看！"

"看什么？"丁丁抬起头问。

A to Z 神秘案件

　　丁丁和乔希也站到露丝那里一起看,只见埃德拿着东西在小屋里走来走去。
　　"他在干什么?"丁丁问。
　　露丝说:"他看起来像是在收拾行李,好像准备要离开这里了!"

第十一章

"有点奇怪。"乔希说。他蹑手蹑脚地走下门廊,猫着腰飞快地走到埃德的小屋边上。丁丁和露丝跟在他身后,三个人蹲在窗户下面。他们慢慢抬起头,直到能看到屋内。

运动包和行李袋的拉链都已经拉上了,放在门边,拐杖扔在地上。

埃德坐在床上,正在解绷带,绷带在地毯上堆成一团。埃德一把扯下袜子,把袜子倒过来,这时,乔希的金子滚落了出来。

"原来他就是那个盗贼!"乔希低声说。

埃德飞快地将金子塞进口袋,接着向门外走去。他的腿根本没瘸!

"他要逃走了。"丁丁低声说,"我们该怎么办?"

A to Z 神秘案件

露丝说:"我去敲响铃声,你们拦住他!"
说完露丝就冲向了主屋。

"我想到了一个办法!"乔希说完就跑到了埃德的小屋后面。

小屋的灯熄灭了,丁丁听到了前门打开的声音。当埃德拿着运动包走到门廊上时,丁丁弯腰躲了起来。

埃德环视了一下四周,伸手从门缝里去拿行李袋。他一只手提着一个袋子,走下门廊。

突然,晚餐的铃声响了起来。

埃德停下了脚步。这时,乔希用套索套住了他的肩膀。随即套索一紧,埃德踉跄了一下,然后砰的一声摔

倒在了地上。

"抓到了！"乔希站在屋顶上大喊。随后他把套索的另一端绑在了烟囱上。

"发生了什么事？"惠特爸爸和尤德沿着小路跑了过来。

"我抓住了盗贼！"乔希站在屋顶上喊道，"我的金子就在他的口袋里！"

第二天吃早餐时，餐桌旁有一个座位空着。埃德已经被关进了博兹曼监狱，乔希也拿回了自己的金子。

"埃德根本没有扭伤脚踝。"尤德说，"他知道金子放在保险箱里之后，就假装受伤留在了牧场。我总觉得他也从我的钱包里偷了钱。"

乔希说："他肯定是把露露和菲奥娜绑起来

后，把自己的嘴堵住，又给自己铐上了手铐。"

"我敢打赌，他是用那个听诊器来听保险箱的锁，找出密码的。"丁丁说。

"应该就是这样。"惠特爸爸说着，拿起桌上的一份传真，"这是警长刚发过来的。看来我们这位盖茨先生在纽约也犯了罪。他就是一个专门撬保险箱的盗贼，还是一个扒手呢。"

尤德说："要不是有这三个孩子在，他早就逃之夭夭了。半夜就有一列火车驶离博兹曼。"

大拇指顺着长桌看向乔希，说："孩子，你之前以为我才是那个盗贼，对吧？"

乔希的脸色活像他那碗麦片粥上的草莓，红得不得了。"我……我们……你怎么知道？"

"昨天晚上，我听到了你们三个孩子的计划。"大拇指说，"我特意躲开，这样你们就可以搜查我的小屋了。然后我就坐在那里，等着看你们会发现什么。"

就在这时，他们都听到厨房里传来一声吼叫。大家还没来得及站身起，一个毛茸茸的身影就咆哮着冲进了餐厅，大喊道："你们对我的小熊宝宝做了什么?"

"露露,你会把这些孩子吓坏的!"惠特妈妈说。

露露从毛皮下面探出头来,笑着说:"希望我那天晚上没有吓坏你们。"

"露露,原来是你啊!"丁丁震惊地说。

露露说:"是我,不过那天是大拇指让我吓你们的。"

大拇指眨了眨眼睛,说:"实在是没忍住,想吓你们一下。"

乔希的金子就放在他盛麦片的碗旁边,在白色桌布的映衬下闪闪发光。

"这块金子应该能换一大笔钱。"尤德说着,朝乔希一笑,"吃完早餐我就带你到镇上去把金子卖掉。"

"谢谢,但是不用了。"乔希说,"我已经决定了,把金子留给牧场。我希望你们能把它卖掉,用这笔钱带牧场走出困境。"

一桌子人都安静了下来,安静到丁丁只能听到自己的心跳声。

"乔希,你确定吗?"尤德问,"那你的新车怎么办?"

"我想我只能再找一块金子了。"乔希说完看了看大拇指,"我要给你展示一下我的淘金技巧。"

大拇指哈哈大笑:"那我可迫不及待了!"

"我们该怎么报答你呢?"惠特妈妈问乔希。

乔希的脸红了起来。

"我知道该怎么做。"露丝在桌子底下轻轻踢了丁丁一下,"乔希喜欢被别人亲!"

惠特妈妈站了起来。"哎呀,这可太简单了!"说着她就把头伸到乔希那边。

"我也觉得!"露露说着撅起嘴唇,从桌子的另一边向乔希伸过头去。

乔希尖叫着冲出了餐厅,不知道的还以为他背后有一只熊在追他呢。

A to Z Mysteries®

THE NINTH NUGGET

by **Ron Roy**

illustrated by
John Steven Gurney

STREAM
GOLD-PANNING AREA
BONFIRE AREA
EMPTY
POND
CLYDES
EMPTY
PATH
ED
KIDS
FIONA
PATH
OFFICE
MAIN HOUSE
DINING ROOM
N
W
E
S
LAWN
FLOWER GARDEN
WHEAT ω RANCH

Welcome to A to Z Mysteries on Location at Wheat Ranch
THUMBS'S CABIN
TRAIL TO PARADISE MEADOW
BARN
HORSE STALLS
CORRAL
BOZEMAN, MONTANA
GREEN LAWN, CONNECTICUT
USA

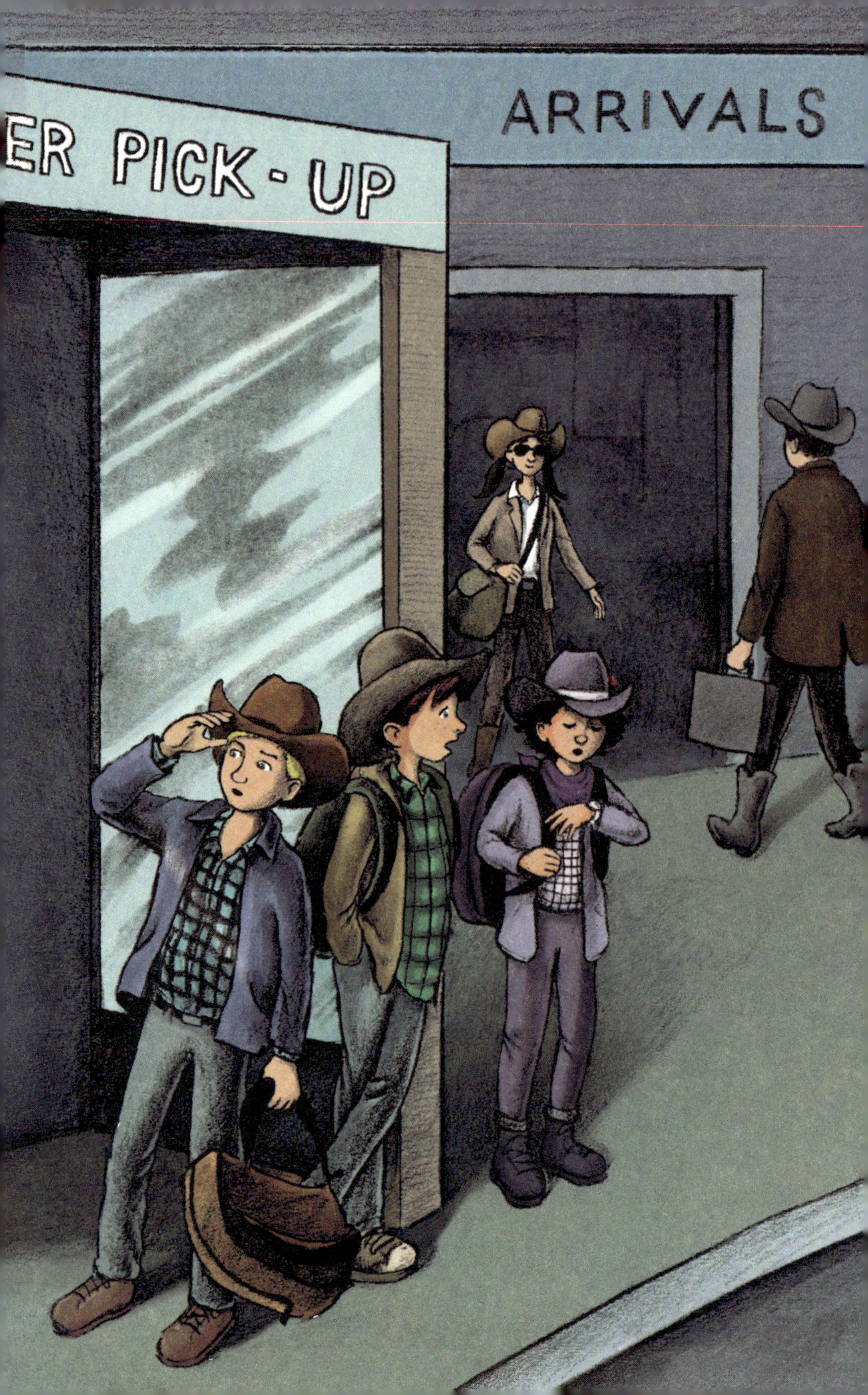
ER PICK-UP
ARRIVALS

CHAPTER 1

Dink, Josh, and Ruth Rose watched the small airplane rise into the late afternoon sky. They'd just arrived in Bozeman, Montana, for a week's vacation at the Western Wheat dude ranch.

As the kids waited outside the airport for their ride, the sky turned purple. The sun slipped slowly behind the mountains.

"What time is it?" Josh asked. "They said someone would pick us up at five o'clock."

Ruth Rose checked her watch. "It's twenty past," she said.

Dink shielded his eyes against the setting sun.

"This might be him," he said.

A dusty station wagon pulled up and stopped. A lanky, smiling guy swung out of the driver's seat. "Are you the kids from Connecticut?" he asked.

Dink nodded. "Are you from Wheat Ranch?"

"You betcha, and welcome to Montana!" the man said. "Sorry I'm late. I'm Jud Wheat."

"I'm Dink, and these are my friends Josh and Ruth Rose," Dink said.

Jud was long-legged and looked about twenty years old. He wore jeans, a western shirt, and scuffed cowboy boots.

"Let me get your stuff," Jud said. He grabbed the

第九块金子

kids' backpacks and slung them into the car through a rear window.

"Hop in and let's ride!" he said.

Ruth Rose and Josh rode up front with Jud. Dink sat behind them with the backpacks, a jumble of harnesses, and a saddle.

"What's that smell?" Josh asked.

Jud laughed. "Some of it's horse, some of it's leather, and the rest is me," he said as he pulled onto the main road.

Only a few other cars and trucks shared the country road. Through his window, Dink saw plenty of flat land and millions of cows behind neat fences.

"You kids looking forward to riding horses this week?" Jud asked.

"Um, I never rode a horse before," Josh said.

"No problem," Jud said. "Most of our guests haven't. I'll show you all you need to know."

"What do you do at the ranch?" Ruth Rose asked Jud.

"A little of everything, miss," he answered. "My folks own the place, and I grew up there. I was supposed to go back to college this fall, but I have to stay on to help out. The ranch isn't earning much money these days."

"What are you going to college for?" asked Dink.

"I want to be a teacher," Jud said. "I'd rather spend my days with kids than cows."

Jud pulled up in front of a gas station. "Gotta fill up," he said, stepping out of the car. "I'll just be a minute."

The kids watched as Jud pumped gas into the wagon. Then he loped toward the cashier's window, reaching into his back pocket for his wallet.

"I hope he brings back a few candy bars," Josh said. "I'm starving."

Dink laughed. "After eating about twenty bags of peanuts on the plane?"

Jud stomped back to the car and flung himself into the driver's seat.

"Can you beat that?" he said. "I go into my wallet to pay, and it's totally empty! I'm almost positive I had two twenties in there this afternoon ."

Jud shook his head, then grinned. "Well, good

thing I had my credit card. Otherwise, we'd be walking!"

Jud drove through more countryside. Dink had never seen so much land! He rolled down his window and felt a hot, dry breeze.

"Look, a hawk!" Josh suddenly yelled.

"He's looking for a nice fat mouse for his supper," Jud said.

Just then Josh's stomach let out a loud growl.

"Someone else is hungry," Jud said, grinning. "We'll be there in a few minutes. How'd you kids happen to pick our dude ranch?"

"We didn't pick it," Dink answered. "A friend of ours gave us this trip as a gift."

Jud grinned into the rear view mirror. "Nice friend," he said.

"His lottery ticket was stolen, and we got it back for him," Ruth Rose explained.

"You mean the ticket was a winner?" asked Jud.

"Yeah," Josh added. He got seven million bucks!"

Jud whistled. "Seven thousand bucks would help the ranch," he said. Minutes later, he turned through a gate into a dirt driveway. A sign hanging over the gate said WHEAT RANCH.

Straight ahead was a red barn and corral. To the left, Dink saw a large white house. Behind it was a pond surrounded by trees and cabins. Ducks and chickens pecked in the grass bordering the driveway.

"This is so beautiful!" Ruth Rose said. " Can I feed the chickens?"

"Sure can, missy," Jud said. He stopped in front of the house.

On the porch sat a man and a woman in two wooden rocking chairs. The man had white hair and looked like an older version of Jud. The woman had black hair turning gray. They both wore boots, jeans, and flannel shirts. Their tanned faces were covered with smile wrinkles.

"Those are my folks," Jud said. "Everyone calls'em Ma and Pa."

Jud's parents hurried down the porch steps. "Welcome to Wheat Ranch!" Ma Wheat said. "You must be Dink, Josh, and Ruth Rose."

"Howdy!" said Pa Wheat.

Just then the screen door banged open. A stout woman wearing a backwards baseball cap strode onto the porch. Over her jeans and western shirt, she wore a long white apron.

"And that's Lulu, the best cook in Montana," Jud said as he dumped the kids' backpacks onto the porch.

Lulu smiled at the kids. "They feed you anything

97

on the plane?" she asked.

"Just peanuts," Josh said. "I'm starving!"

"Supper will be ready in fifteen minutes. Listen for the bell," Lulu said, pointing at an iron triangle hanging from the porch roof.

第九块金子

"I'll take you to your cabin," a deep voice said.

Dink, Josh, and Ruth Rose whipped around. A man had walked up behind them. Wild hair poked out from under a sweat-stained cowboy hat. His skin looked like wrinkled leather.

"I'm Thumbs," the man said. As he reached for the kids' backpacks, Dink saw that one of the man's thumbs was missing.

CHAPTER 2

The kids followed Thumbs down to a narrow path lined with stones. The path led to three small cabins. Behind the cabins, the sun sparkled off the pond.

Dink noticed other cabins farther along the path. "Who's in those?" he asked.

"They're all empty 'cept one," Thumbs grumbled. He stopped in front of the middle cabin.

"This here's yours. There's a lady in that one," Thumbs said, nodding at the cabin to their right. "Some New York feller in the other. Married couple got one of those across the pond."

They were log cabins with chimneys and narrow front porches. There were windows on the sides and in front, where they framed the door.

"Ma Wheat' ll give you extra blankets if it turns cold," Thumbs said, clumping up the steps with the backpacks. "You'll find towels in the bathroom."

He nodded at the kids, then clumped off the porch and headed back along the path.

"That guy creeps me out," Josh said. "What do you think happened to his thumb?"

"Maybe a bear bit it off," Dink said, winking at Ruth Rose.

"Could've been a mountain lion," Ruth Rose added, trying not to laugh.

Josh snorted. "Don't try to scare me," he said. "There's nothing out here but chickens and ducks."

The kids carried their packs into the cabin. A set of bunk beds stood against the far wall, and a single bed was opposite the bunks.

A stone fireplace nestled between the bunk beds and a small bathroom. The only other furnishings were a braided rug, a few chairs, and a table.

"I want to live here forever!" Ruth Rose said. She tossed her backpack on the single bed and looked out her window at the barn.

"I've got upper," Josh said, slinging his pack onto the top bunk.

Dink set his pack on the bunk beneath it as a loud clanging came from the main house.

"Food at last!" Josh said. They ran out of the cabin, nearly colliding with a skinny, bearded man.

"Whoa," the man said, smiling. "No need to rush. There's plenty of food. You must be the newcomers."

"We just got here," Dink said.

"I'm Ed Getz," the man said. "I came in yesterday from New York." He wiggled his fingers at the kids. "I'm a magician. I'm trying to be an actor, but there's not much work."

Ed Getz had long arms, tapered hands, and thin fingers.

"Cool!" Josh said. "Can you do tricks?"

Ed nodded. "I'll show you some later."

They walked to the main house, then into the dining room. A moose head hung over a wide fireplace. Lassos, spurs, saddle blankets, and bridles decorated the walls.

In front of the fireplace stood a long table and

benches. Jud, Thumbs, and three others were already seated. Lulu was placing food on the table.

Ma and Pa Wheat came out of the kitchen. Ma said, "Hi, kids, take a seat."

Pa tapped a spoon against a glass. "Say howdy to Dink, Josh, and Ruth Rose from Connecticut," he said.

A woman wearing a western shirt and jeans said, "Hello, I'm Fiona Nippit."

"And we're Seth and Bonnie Clyde," said a man sitting next to a pretty woman with long blond hair.

Lulu bustled out of the kitchen carrying a heavy tray of food. "Eat while it's hot!" she said. "What you don't eat now is leftovers tomorrow!"

Everyone began passing platters of fried chicken, mashed potatoes, and steaming vegetables.

With twelve people at the table, it got pretty noisy.

The kids learned that Fiona was a nurse from Chicago. The Clydes had just gotten married in Florida and decided to spend their honeymoon at a dude ranch.

Only Thumbs didn't join in the dinner table chatter. While everyone else talked, he just ate.

For dessert, Lulu served apple pie with ice cream on top. By the end of the meal, they were all rubbing their stomachs.

Pa stood up. "It's almost dark. Jud'll build us a bonfire out back. And unless I miss my guess, Thumbs will tell you about the grizzly bear that roams these parts."

Josh shot a look at Thumbs. "Are there really grizzlies here?" he asked.

For an answer, Thumbs winked and held up his hand with the missing thumb.

Everyone helped carry stuff into the kitchen. When the table was cleared off, the kids went outside and walked down the path. They found Jud and Thumbs arranging firewood inside a circle of tree stumps.

It had grown almost completely dark. Dink saw a few fireflies in the bushes near the pond.

"Have a seat," Jud told the kids, motioning toward the stumps. They were joined by Fiona, Ed, and the Clydes.

Thumbs struck a match on his belt buckle. He knelt and lit some dry pine needles under the branches, and soon the wood caught. The flames cast each face around the fire into shadow.

"Is this great or what?" Josh said. "Man, I wish I

could stay here longer than a week."

"Me too," Dink said.

Then Ma, Pa, and Lulu came outside. "Got something to tell us, Thumbs?" Pa asked.

Everyone looked at Thumbs. The reflection from the flames made his eyes appear red under his hat brim. He began to speak in a hoarse whisper.

"I'll never forget that night," Thumbs said. "It was a dry summer. There was a lightning storm, and one of the strikes caused a fire. The woods in the hills began to burn. We was sittin' here, just like now. Suddenly, a bear cub came a-runnin' out of the trees. It was a young'un, just a bitty thing. You could tell it had been burned. It was whimpering, like in pain. We caught the cub, took it inside. Lulu put some butter on the burns."

Thumbs paused. The only sound was wood crackling in the fire.

Dink glanced over at Josh, sitting next to Ruth Rose. Josh's mouth and eyes were wide open.

"What happened to the cub?" Ruth Rose asked.

Thumbs's red eyes turned to Ruth Rose. "Next

第九块金子

morning, we took the poor critter to the vet's office," he continued. "When the little thing was all healed up, the vet sent it to a zoo someplace in California."

"Good!" Josh said.

Thumbs swung his gaze back at Josh. "Bad," he said. "The momma grizzly came later that night. She tore through here, howling for her young'un. Probably weighed seven hundred pounds, that grizzly did. Smashed cabin doors, ripped a hole in the barn, sent us all a-hidin' down in Lulu's root cellar."

"D-did she ever come back?" Josh asked.

Thumbs let out a laugh that was more like a cackle. " Sonny, that grizzly pays us a visit at least two, three times every summer. She tears through here like a hairy tornado, destroyin' nearly everythin' in her path."

Thumbs looked at his thumbless hand. "That poor momma wants her baby back. It's been two years now, and she still comes around lookin' for it."

Thumbs placed the thumbless hand on Josh's shoulder. "That cub would be just about your size, sonny," he added, then walked into the night.

CHAPTER 3

No one talked after Thumbs left. One by one, they stood, yawned, and left the circle.

"Remember, buttermilk pancakes for breakfast," Lulu called as she walked toward the main house.

The kids stayed behind to help Jud douse the fire with pond water.

"Was there really a bear?" Josh asked Jud. "He was kidding, wasn't he?"

"I was away at college, so I don't know for sure," Jud said. "But I've never known Thumbs to be a kidder."

"It could be a true story," Ruth Rose said. "I read a book about grizzly bears once. The mother bears protect their young until they're all grown up."

Dink slung his arm around Josh's shoulders. "Don't worry, even a hungry bear wouldn't want you. You're too skinny."

"Want me to walk you kids back to your cabin?" Jud asked.

"Nope," Josh said. "I'm not afraid of any old bear. Besides, I bet Thumbs was fooling us. How did he really lose his thumb, Jud?"

Jud laughed. "You'll have to ask him," he said. "Sleep tight and don't let the critters bite!"

Dink, Josh, and Ruth Rose walked toward the three cabins. The stars cast a soft glow over the stones that lined the path.

Light came from Fiona's and Ed's cabins, but the cabin in the middle was pitch-black.

"I thought I left a light on," Ruth Rose said.

"I thought you did, too," Dink told her.

"I know I did!" Ruth Rose said. Then she jumped on Josh's back and screamed, "THE GRIZZLY BEAR'S IN OUR CABIN!"

"Very funny, Ruth Rosebush," Josh said. "See if I protect you when the bear really comes!"

When they were all in their beds, Dink turned out the light next to his bunk. He rolled onto his side and gazed out the window.

Fireflies flickered everywhere.

Frogs and crickets made a sweet racket from the pond.

"Good night, you guys," Ruth Rose said from the other side of the room.

"Good night, Ruth Rose. Good night, grizzly bear," Dink said.

"I'm not speaking to either one of you," Josh said from the top bunk.

Dink smiled in his bunk. Josh is so easy to scare, he thought as he drifted off to sleep.

Suddenly, Dink was wide awake. He thought he'd heard something thump outside the cabin.

He sat up and peered through the window over Ruth Rose's bed. She was a sleeping lump under her blankets.

Dink didn't know what time it was, but he didn't think he'd been sleeping for long. Josh was snoring.

Maybe a pine cone fell on the porch, Dink said to

himself. Yeah, pine cones can make big thumps when they fall from tall trees.

Dink lay back down and closed his eyes. He tried to force himself back to sleep.

Then he heard more noises. Some thing heavy was moving around on the porch, and it was no pine cone!

Suddenly, a dark shape stepped in front of the window. Dink shuddered and fell back on his pillow. Whatever was out there was large enough to shut out the starlight.

Dink heard a scraping noise, and then the shape moved away. Starlight once more flowed through the window.

Dink pulled his covers up under his chin. He could feel his heart thumping in his chest. Calm down, he told himself. It couldn't be that lonely mother grizzly bear. Could it?

Wishing he hadn't teased Josh about the bear, Dink finally went to sleep.

The next morning, the breakfast bell woke the

kids. Josh leaped off the top bunk, nearly landing on Dink.

Ruth Rose dashed into the bathroom while the boys were getting dressed. Three minutes later, they were on the path to the main house.

"Um, guys," Dink said, "I know you're not gonna believe me, but something was on our porch last night."

"What kind of something?" Ruth Rose asked. "Did it have fur and big claws?"

"Here we go again," Josh muttered.

"Honest, something was out there," Dink continued. "I heard these thumps; then something blocked your window, Ruth Rose. There was a scratching noise, too."

Josh laughed. "You guys are so lame. It was probably a raccoon."

"If you're right, we'd better call *The Guinness Book of World Records*," Dink said. "Whatever stepped in front of that window was about six feet tall!"

"I don't care if Frankenstein was peeking in our window," Josh said, racing toward the main house. "I need pancakes!"

The kids hurried into the dining room. Everyone was already seated.

"Good morning," Ma Wheat said as she poured juice. "Hope you slept well and woke up hungry!"

Platters of scrambled eggs, sausages, and pancakes filled the middle of the table. Everyone dug in.

When most of the food was gone, Dink told everyone about the noises and the shape on their cabin porch.

"Strange noises?" Pa said. "I didn't hear anything. How' bout you, Jud?"

"Nothin' could have woke me up, Pa," Jud said. "You hear anything, Ma?"

Ma shook her head. "You hear any strange noises, Thumbs?"

Thumbs grinned and shook his head. "Nope," he said, "but I thought I smelt bear when I walked over here this morning."

CHAPTER 4

Everyone had a good laugh—everyone except Josh. Then Pa asked Ed Getz to do a magic trick.

Ed stood up and showed his audience that his hands were empty. Next, he draped his napkin over one hand and mumbled a few magic words. When he yanked the napkin away, an egg was sitting in his hand.

Everybody clapped, and then Thumbs stood up. "Fine breakfast," Lulu, he said. "Those of you who want to, we're gonna pan for gold."

Twenty minutes later, all seven guests hiked with Thumbs and Jud along a gravel path on the other side of the pond. A stream followed the path, splashing and gurgling over rocks. Before leaving the main house, Jud had given everyone a wide, flat pan.

"This is it," Thumbs said a few minutes later, stopping at a sandy bank on the stream.

"I don't see any gold," Josh observed, peering into the water.

Jud laughed. "You won't see it," he said. He pointed farther upstream, toward the mountains.

"There's gold in those hills," he explained. "Every time it storms, nuggets get washed downstream. Show 'em how to find gold, Thumbs."

Thumbs squatted and dipped his pan into the water. "Don't step in the stream or you'll disturb the

第九块金子

mud," he said. With a flick of his wrist, he brought up a panful of water and gravel.

"Gold is heavier than the gravel," Thumbs went on, "so it'll settle on the bottom of my pan."

Thumbs shook his pan gently back and forth, swishing the gravel and water. Then he tipped the pan and let the water and gravel slide over the edge.

"Lookee here," Thumbs said, holding his pan up. In the bottom lay a few dull pebbles. But among the pebbles was a shiny golden nugget the size of a pea.

"Is that gold?" Dink asked.

"Sure is," Thumbs said. He picked out the nugget

and let everyone have a look at it.

"How much is it worth?" Josh asked.

Thumbs dropped the nugget into his shirt pocket. "This size? Not much." He pointed his chin toward the distant hills. "To find the real gold, you'd have to go up there."

"Can we try panning now?" Ruth Rose asked.

Thumbs backed away from the stream. "Pick yourself a spot, and remember, don't get in the water."

The seven guests knelt along the stream .

Jud joined the kids and dipped his pan into the water. "I've been doing this since I was a kid," he said. "One year a guest found a nugget the size of a golf ball. I heard he sold it and bought himself a new Jeep!"

"Cool!" Josh said. "I need a Jeep!" He knelt in the sand and dipped his pan into the water.

Everyone began dipping. For a while, all you could hear was the sound of gravel swishing against metal.

Dink soon got the hang of it. He liked the feel of the sun on his back as he dipped his pan over and over.

第九块金子

Suddenly, Fiona Nippit let out a yell. "I found one!" she said. Grinning, she held up a gold nugget a bit larger than the one Thumbs had found.

"Great!" Jud said. "Now let's see if everyone else can find one."

Over the next half hour, others began to shout and hold up small nuggets, even Jud. Eight nuggets were found. Finally, only Josh hadn't brought up any gold from the stream.

"Gotta pack up soon," Thumbs announced. "Lulu's a bear if we're late for her meals."

"I'm gonna try a different place," Josh announced. "There are no more nuggets here."

"Where are you going?" Ruth Rose asked.

Josh pointed his pan upstream. "Up there," he said, "where the real gold is."

Dink watched Josh pick his way along the stream, tramping over rocks and branches.

"I hope he finds one," Ruth Rose said. "Otherwise, he'll be grumpy all week!"

Dink held his nugget up to the sun. It was the size of an M&M. "Do you suppose I can get enough money for this to buy a bike?" he asked.

Suddenly, they heard Josh yelling, then a big splash. They looked upstream and saw Josh sitting in the water!

Dink and Ruth Rose ran to help, but Jud reached him first. "Are you okay?" Jud asked, reaching for Josh's hand.

Josh grabbed Jud's hand and stumbled out of the stream. He was soaked from the waist down, but grinning.

"Look what I found!" Josh said, sticking out his other hand.

Dink's eyes bugged out. Josh was holding a chunk of gold the size of a potato.

CHAPTER 5

"Way to go, Josh!" Dink cried. He and Ruth Rose gave him a double high five while everyone else crowded around.

"That's the biggest nugget I've ever seen," Jud marveled.

The nugget was as large as Josh's hand and almost as flat. Particles of rock and dirt were embedded in the lump, but the rest was pure gold.

"Okay, folks," Thumbs said from behind the group. "It's time to get a move on."

Still congratulating Josh, the group trekked back to the ranch. Josh's wet sneakers squished as he walked. Everyone headed to the main house for lunch.

Josh plunked his huge nugget on the table next to his plate.

"I bet I can make that disappear," Ed said, grinning.

"No thanks!" Josh said.

"You're a lucky boy," Pa told Josh. "But I wouldn't carry that around with you. You don't want to lose it!"

"Why don't you put it in our safe?" Jud asked. "Tomorrow we can take it to town and get it appraised."

"What's 'appraised' mean?" Josh asked.

"That's when an expert examines the gold and tells you its value," Jud explained. "Then you can sell it if you want."

"Okay, that'd be great," Josh said.

After lunch, the kids followed Jud to the office. The ranch office was small and dusty. Most of the floor space was taken up by a giant oak desk. A brown cowhide hung on one wall. Plants with tiny yellow blossoms were lined up on the windowsill.

Next to the desk stood an old black safe with a vase of dried flowers on top. As the kids watched, Jud hunkered down in front of the safe. He spun the combination lock back and forth a few times, then

第九块金子

pulled the safe door open.

"There you go, Josh. Your gold will be safe in our safe," Jud said, grinning. He moved some papers and a green accounts book to make room.

Josh stepped forward and placed his nugget on top of the book. Then Jud slammed the door shut and twirled the lock.

"You all ready for that trail ride?" came a voice over Josh's shoulder. He turned to find Thumbs standing there with a toothpick sticking out one side of his mouth.

"Sure thing," Jud said. "Ready, kids?"

" 1 saddled the horses," Thumbs said as he left the office.

Fiona, Ed, and the Clydes followed Jud, Thumbs, and the kids to the barn.

Nine horses were saddled and tied to a corral rail. Each horse's name was stitched into its saddle blanket.

Pa and Ma pulled up in an old green truck. "Have a good ride!" Ma called. "We're going into town."

Everyone waved, and the truck raised dust as it pulled away.

123

"Can I have a nice gentle horse?" Dink asked.

Jud smiled. "All our horses are gentle," he said. "You can ride Trigger here. He really likes kids."

Trigger was pale gold with a white mane. He looked at the crowd with mild brown eyes.

"Do you have any small horses?" Josh asked. "I'm afraid of animals that look down at me!"

"Barney is our smallest horse," Jud said. "He's a good ride, but he likes to stop and eat the wildflowers."

"Perfect for Josh!" Ruth Rose said.

Josh patted Barney's soft nose. "Be a good horse and I'll sneak you some dessert later," he said.

"Do you have any girl horses?" Ruth Rose asked Jud.

"Sure do," he said. "You can take Snowball. She's a real sweetie and has the softest gait in the bunch."

Snowball was fat and white with long eyelashes. She nickered when Ruth Rose rubbed her side.

Jud soon matched horses with Ed, Fiona, and the Clydes. "Okay, everyone, time to saddle up," he said, standing next to Bullet, a tall silver-colored horse. "Watch how I do it."

Holding the saddle horn with his left hand, Jud slid his left boot toe into Bullet's stirrup. Then he hoisted himself up and swung his right leg over the saddle . "Okay? Anyone need help?"

"I do!" Dink said.

Thumbs helped all three kids into their saddles and showed them how to hold the reins. He adjusted the stirrup straps to the length of their legs.

Just then Ed yelled, "Ouch!" He was half in and half out of his saddle. His right foot was hanging out of the stirrup in an awkward position.

Jud jumped off Bullet and ran over to help Ed get his foot untangled. "Are you all right?" he asked.

"I don't know," Ed said. He took a step, then winced. His face was white with pain. "That really hurts! I think I sprained something."

"You'd better get off that ankle," Fiona suggested. "Come on, I'll help you back to your cabin."

"No, you go ahead, Fiona," Ed said. "I'll be fine."

"Nonsense. I didn't really want to ride anyway," Fiona said. "I'll get some ice from Lulu."

With Ed limping beside her, Fiona walked slowly

toward the cabins.

"Thumbs, would you mind staying behind to unsaddle Ed's and Fiona's horses?" Jud asked. "Then you can join us in the meadow."

Thumbs nodded and began unsaddling Fiona's horse.

"We'll ride in a line," Jud told the others. "Your horse will follow the one in front of him."

"Who goes first?" Josh asked.

"You do," Jud said. "Barney loves to lead the pack. Just touch his sides with your heels and he'll move."

Josh gently poked his heels into Barney's sides. "Okay, nice horsey," he said. "Giddyup!"

Barney shook his mane and turned his head to look at Josh. His ears twitched, but he didn't take a single step.

"Please?" Josh said.

Barney snorted, then started to walk briskly away from the barn.

"This is easy!" Josh called to Oink and Ruth Rose. "But you gotta say please!"

The other five horses fell in line behind him. Soon

第九块金子

they were on a narrow trail surrounded by shrubbery and trees. The horses thudded over a wooden bridge that crossed a stream.

As the group moved through the trees, the ranch quickly disappeared.

CHAPTER 6

The horses clip-clopped along in single file. Barney seemed to know where he was going, and the others followed. Jud, riding Bullet, was last in line.

Soon the riders entered a meadow. A blue pond nestled among the wildflowers. Josh's horse stopped under a pine tree and began nibbling a patch of weeds.

"We can let 'em graze here," Jud said. He helped the kids dismount, and the riders tied their horses where they could reach grass and shade.

"This is awesome," Josh said.

"Folks around here call it Paradise Meadow," Jud said. "There's fat trout in the pond if you'd like to feed them."

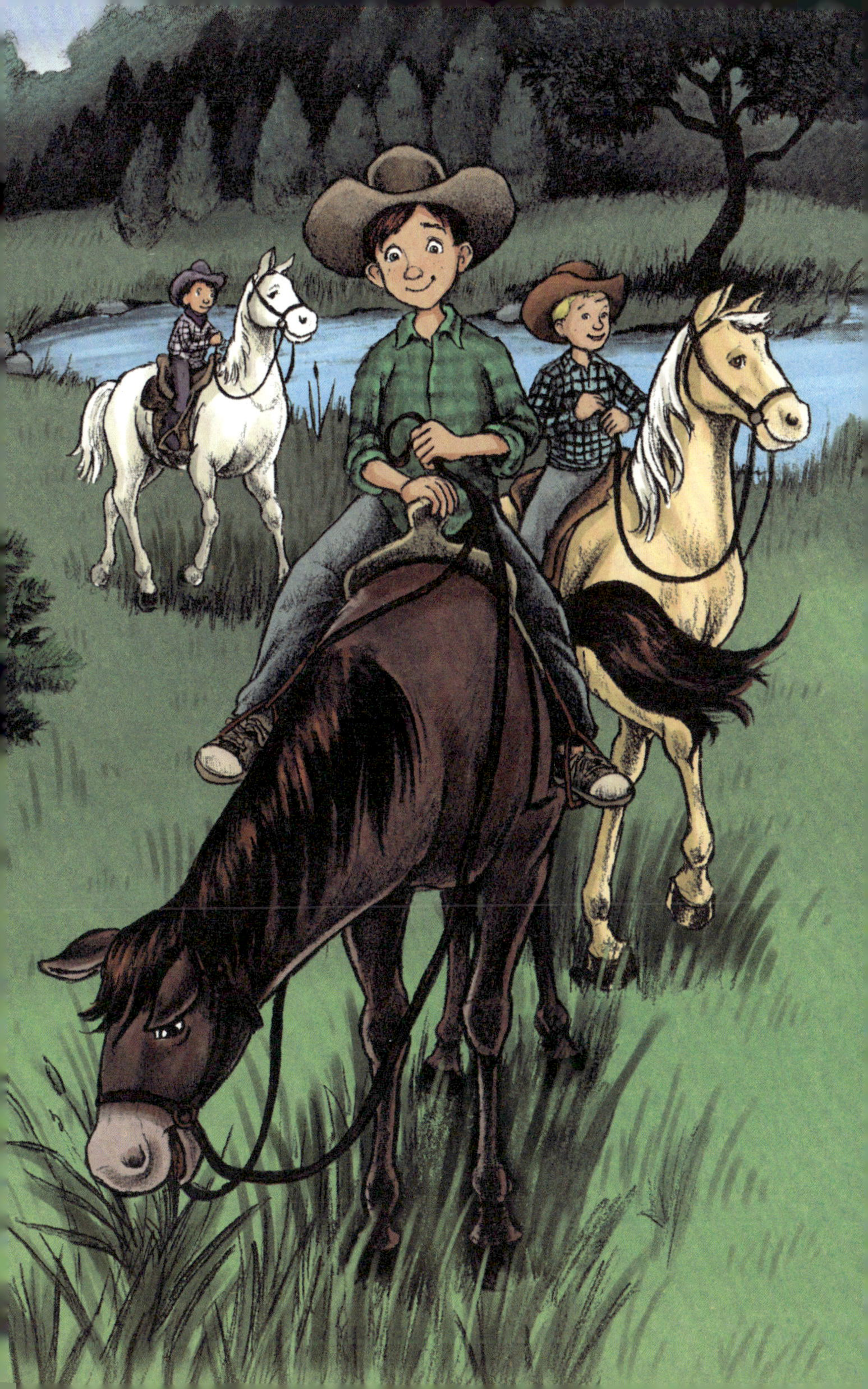

From his saddlebag pocket, he pulled a bag of bread crumbs from lunch. "Just sprinkle it on the surface and they'll come."

"Will you teach me to throw a lasso?" Josh asked Jud.

"Ask Thumbs when he gets here," Jud said. "He's the rope expert."

Jud tipped his head back and looked at the sky. A few dark clouds were mixed with white ones.

"There's rain coming," he said. "You'll find ponchos in your saddlebags, just in case. Storms come up pretty fast in these foothills."

"Can you identify any of these flowers?" Bonnie asked.

Jud grinned. "All of 'em. Tell you what, I'll take whoever wants to on a little nature hike."

"We'd enjoy that," said Bonnie.

Jud looked at the kids. "You want to come along or wait here for Thumbs?"

"I want to feed the fish," Ruth Rose said.

" Me too," said Dink, reaching for the bag.

"Can I borrow your rope?" Josh asked. "Maybe I'll lasso a fish!"

第九块金子

Jud handed Josh his rope.

"Thumbs'll make you a rodeo star in no time," he said. "We won't be far off."

Jud, Seth, and Bonnie hiked toward the other end of the meadow. The kids walked to the edge of the pond. Dink yanked off his sneakers and waded in the water while Ruth Rose tossed crumbs. Almost immediately, trout gathered and gobbled them up.

"Watch this!" Josh said. He made a loop in Jud's lasso and tossed it at a tree stump. The loop crumpled in midair and flopped to the ground.

"How do the cowboys do it?" Josh muttered, gathering in the rope to try again.

Just then hoofbeats sounded behind the kids. They turned to see Thumbs riding into the meadow on a big black horse.

"Hi, Thumbs," Dink and Ruth Rose said together.

Thumbs nodded but didn't answer. He dismounted and tied his horse near the others.

"Are you going to ask him to show you how to use that lasso?" Ruth Rose asked Josh.

"I don't know," he whispered. "There's something

creepy about him."

"Don't be silly," Ruth Rose said. She walked over to Thumbs and said, "Josh wants you to show him how to throw a lasso."

Thumbs glanced behind her, where Josh was trying to coil the rope.

"I suspect maybe I can," Thumbs answered. His dark eyes swept the meadow. "Where's everyone at?"

"Jud took Mr. and Mrs. Clyde on a nature hike," Dink said.

Thumbs grunted. Then he walked over to Josh, took the rope, and quickly formed a large circle. He swung the loop over his head three times, then let it fly. The lasso whistled through the air and landed around the stump.

"How'd you do that?" Josh asked.

"It's all fingers and wrist," Thumbs said. He showed Josh how to hold the rope just as Jud and the Clydes appeared.

"Storm's moving in faster than I thought it would," Jud said. "We'd better head back to the ranch. Sorry to cut this short, folks."

Overhead, the few dark clouds had formed a wall of thunderheads. They were blowing out of the north, casting moving shadows over the meadow.

Within minutes they were all saddled up, wearing yellow hooded ponchos. Thumbs led this time, with Jud at the back of the line.

The sunny day had turned windy and cool. Sudden rain splattered through the trees. Dink felt and heard the drops as they splashed on his head and shoulders.

Thirty minutes later, seven wet horses carried their riders into the barn.

"I'll unsaddle Blackie for you," Jud told Thumbs. "Why don't you let Lulu know we're back so she can rustle us up some hot chocolate and cookies."

Thumbs jumped to the ground, handed Blackie's reins to Jud, and jogged toward the main house.

The rain had almost stopped and a stiff wind was blowing the clouds past. Everyone dismounted and led the horses into the barn.

Suddenly, the dinner bell began to peal.

"Why's Lulu ringing now?" Jud said. "It's nowhere near suppertime."

When the clanging didn't stop, Jud ran toward the barn door.

CHAPTER 7

The Clydes and the three kids hurried after Jud. As they ran across the yard, the ranch truck pulled into the driveway.

Ma and Pa hopped out carrying bags of groceries. "What's going on?" Pa asked Jud.

"Someone rang the bell," Jud answered, leaping up the porch steps.

There was no one on the porch, but the bell was still swinging.

"Jud! Get in here!" Thumbs yelled from inside the house. "I'm in the office."

Jud sprinted through the screen door, with everyone else following.

Nine people crowded into the small office. Thumbs was kneeling on the floor in front of Lulu, who was gagged and tied to a chair.

While Thumbs untied the knots, Ma removed the gag. Pa was already on the phone, calling the sheriff.

"What happened to you?" Ma asked.

"The safe!" Lulu cried, pointing.

第九块金子

The safe door was wide open, revealing a stack of papers and one green accounts book. The only thing missing was Josh's nugget.

"They got my gold!" Josh yelled.

"Can I have some water?" Lulu asked. She rubbed her wrists, which had red marks on them from the rope.

Bonnie ran to get water while Lulu told her story.

"I was in here watering the plants," she said, "when someone grabbed me and shoved me into this chair. I started to yell, so he gagged me, then tied me up.

"Who was it?" Pa asked. "Did you recognize him?"

Lulu shook her head. "He was dressed all in black, with a black hood over his face. Never said a word to me."

"Say, where are Fiona and Ed?" Jud asked. "They should've heard the bell like everyone else."

"Fiona made Ed lie down," Lulu said. "She wrapped his ankle, and I got him a pair of crutches. I offered to call a doc, but he said he'd take aspirin and be fine."

Jud ran out the door, and the kids followed .

137

"Which cabin is Fiona's?" he asked over his shoulder.

"That one," Dink said, pointing to the cabin closest to the main house.

Jud thundered up the steps and banged on the door. "Fiona? It's Jud Wheat. Are you all right?"

When he heard no answer, Jud opened the door and stepped inside. "Oh my... someone go get Ma, quick!" Jud yelled over his shoulder. Ruth Rose barreled off the porch and raced toward the main house.

Dink peeked past Jud. Fiona was tied in a chair with a gag tied over her mouth, just like Lulu.

Dink grabbed Josh's arm. "Let's go check Ed!" he cried.

Dink and Josh ran to Ed's cabin. "Mr. Getz?" Dink called. "Are you okay?"

When no answer came, Dink opened the door. Ed Getz was lying on his bed. A scarf was covering his mouth. His hands were behind his back.

Dink untied the scarf and pulled it away.

"Thanks!" Ed said. "I thought I'd be here all day!"

He nodded toward his closet. "There's a gym bag

in there. Look for a small box. Inside is a key. The guy used my own handcuffs on me!"

Josh found the key. When Ed sat up, Dink and Josh saw that his hands had been cuffed to the iron bed board. Josh used the key, and the handcuffs popped open.

"What happened?" Dink said. "They tied up Fiona and Lulu, too!"

"Yeah, and the rat stole my gold nugget!" Josh said.

Dink noticed that Ed's foot was tightly wrapped in a bandage. A pair of crutches was leaning against the bed.

"I was fooling around with my handcuffs, preparing to show you guys some tricks at dinner," Ed said. "All of a sudden, someone dressed in black burst in here. Before I could move, he cuffed me to the bed and tied this scarf around my face."

Ed shook his hands and rubbed his wrists. "Boy, those things were tight!"

"Can you walk?" Dink asked. "Pa called the sheriff. We should probably all meet in the office."

Ed propped himself up and stood on his good foot. Josh handed Ed the crutches, which he slid under his arms. Holding his bandaged foot off the floor, he took a hop, then another.

"Let's go," Ed said. "Don't walk too close to me. If I fall, I don't want to land on you."

With Dink and Josh leading, the three of them moved down the path toward the main house. Up ahead, Ruth Rose, Ma Wheat, and Fiona were standing with a man on the porch.

In the driveway, a few chickens were pecking the tires on a green-and-white car. The word SHERIFF was printed on the door.

CHAPTER 8

Everyone crowded into the office. While the sheriff took notes on a pad, Lulu repeated her story. Fiona and Ed broke in to add details.

"So the way I understand it," the sheriff said, "some man or woman dressed in black tied each of you up. Then he or she opened the safe and stole a hunk of gold. Is that about it?"

"Could it have been some stranger, someone just passing through?" Ma Wheat asked.

Lulu shook her head. "You can see a mile in any direction from here, and believe me, I didn't see a soul."

"Maybe some passerby was hiding in the trees," Pa said. "It had to be a stranger-the robber sure couldn't

A to Z 神秘案件

be anyone in this room!"

Dink quickly glanced around the office. Everyone was doing the same thing, looking at everyone else.

"Lulu," Ma said, "did you happen to notice how this character got the safe open?"

"I couldn't see what he was doing," Lulu said. "He was crouched down with his back to me, but I did see

第九块金子

that he was wearing gloves."

The sheriff walked over to the safe. "So we can't even get fingerprints. I assume the safe was locked. Who knows the combination?"

"Well, I do, of course," Pa said. "And Ma—Mrs. Wheat—and our son, Jud. That's it."

The sheriff thanked everyone and headed for the door. He handed Ma Wheat a card. "If any of you think of anything, please call my office."

The sheriff looked at Josh. "Sorry you lost your gold, son. I'll do my best to get it back for you."

Josh mumbled, "Thanks."

The kids followed the sheriff out of the main house. He waved good-bye and sped down the drive in his cruiser.

Everyone wandered back to their cabins in a daze. The kids sat down on their front porch.

"This crook was pretty clever," Ruth Rose said.

"What do you mean?" Josh asked. He formed a loop in his rope and aimed for the porch rail post. He missed.

"I mean the crook made it look like nobody on

the ranch could be the robber," Ruth Rose said. "Seven of us were riding, right? So it couldn't be any of us. Lulu, Ed, and Fiona were tied up, so it couldn't be them, either. Ma and Pa went shopping and got back when we did. That's twelve people with good alibis. So who was the robber? Nobody's left!"

Josh sighed and coiled his rope. "You're close, Ruth Rose," he said. "But you forgot one little thing. There were only six of us riding—us three, Seth and Bonnie, and Jud."

"What about Thumbs?" Dink asked. "He was with us—"

"OH MY GOSH!" Ruth Rose yelled. "Dink, Josh is right! Thumbs was with us at the end of the ride, but not at the beginning!"

Josh grinned. "Yep. He could've tied up Fiona and Ed after he unsaddled their horses. Then he did the same to Lulu, grabbed the gold, and hotfooted it up to the meadow."

"But Thumbs is practically one of the Wheat family," Dink said. "Why would he rob the ranch?"

"For the biggest hunk of gold he's ever seen," Josh

said, tossing his loop at Dink's foot.
　　He missed.

CHAPTER 9

The kids sat and thought about Thumbs as the thief.

"I know you don't like Thumbs," Dink said to Josh, "but I can't believe he'd rob the Wheats . Besides, he didn't know the combination, remember?"

"Who says?" Josh asked. "If he worked here for years, he could've learned it without the Wheats knowing."

Dink picked up some pebbles and tossed them into the path. "Maybe it was some stranger," he said, "like Ma suggested."

"I keep thinking about them being tied up and gagged," Ruth Rose said. "Whoever did it was taking a real chance. What if we all came back from riding in the middle of it all?"

"That's another reason I think it was Thumbs," Josh said. "He knew we wouldn't be back for a while. And he knew Ma and Pa would be gone at least an hour. Have you guys noticed how he's always sneaking up behind people?"

"Guys," Dink said after a moment, "I wonder why the robber used ropes on Fiona and Lulu but he handcuffed Ed."

"Ed told us," Josh said. "He had the handcuffs out to practice some tricks. The robber saw the handcuffs and decided to use them."

" Maybe," Dink said.

"What, do you think Ed was the robber?" Josh asked, grinning. "I can just see him hobbling around, tying up people and cracking safes on crutches."

"Unless he was faking," Ruth Rose said.

"Faking what?" Josh asked.

Ruth Rose turned and stared at Dink and Josh. "What if Ed didn't really hurt his ankle? What if he pretended so he could stay here to rob the safe?"

"Ruth Rose, Ed was handcuffed and gagged," Josh

commented. "He couldn't do that to himself, could he?"

"Well, he is a magician, isn't he?"

"Plus," Josh went on, "Fiona stayed with him. Unless you think she and Ed are partners in crime."

"Well, it's possible, isn't it?" Ruth Rose asked.

"I guess it could be any of them," Dink said. "But how do we prove it?"

"I still say it was Thumbs," Josh said after a minute. "He knows a lot about ropes, and I bet he wore gloves so no one would see his missing thumb."

"Josh, a lot of people know how to tie knots," Dink said, "and anyone planning to rob a safe would wear gloves so he wouldn't leave fingerprints."

"Officer Fallon would say, 'Find the proof,'" Ruth Rose said. "So why don't we look in their cabins?"

"For what?" Dink asked.

"Clues," Ruth Rose said. "Like the black clothing this guy was wearing."

"And my gold!" Josh said. "Whoever took the nugget might've hidden it in his room."

"Wouldn't that be breaking and entering?" Dink asked.

148

第九块金子

"Just entering," Ruth Rose said. "All the doors are unlocked, so we wouldn't be breaking in."

Just then the dinner bell clanged.

Josh dropped his rope and stood up. "Let's go eat. My brain can't think when my stomach is empty."

They hurried to the dining room. While the adults talked about the robbery, the kids ate, kept quiet, and listened.

Dink looked around the table at the guests and staff. It seemed unbelievable that one of these people was probably guilty. How could that person sit here and pretend?

It can't be any of the Wheats or the Clydes, Dink reminded himself. That leaves Ed, Fiona, Thumbs, and Lulu.

Dink glanced at Ed, sitting on the other side of the table. His crutches were leaning against the wall. Ed was showing Fiona and Jud a trick using a piece of string.

Fiona was wearing a black turtleneck shirt over black jeans. Dink could see the red rope marks on her wrists. Was she the thief in black?

Lulu was bustling back and forth between the kitchen and dining room. Somehow, Dink couldn't picture her tying people up and cracking safes. But, like Thumbs, she might have learned the combination.

Dink looked down the table toward the seat Thumbs usually occupied.

His chair was empty!

Suddenly, Dink felt someone's foot kicking him under the table. It was Josh.

When Dink glared at him, Josh nodded toward the empty chair. Josh held up his thumb and wiggled his eyebrows.

"I know he's not here!" Dink whispered. "Cool it."

"What's going on?" Ruth Rose said.

Before Dink could answer, Josh asked Ma Wheat where Thumbs was. "He...he promised to teach me a rope trick after supper."

"Why, I don't know, Josh," Ma said. "Perhaps he's gone to town."

Pa tapped his spoon against his water glass. "It's been a bad day at the ranch," he said. "Why don't we all stay here after supper and play some cards? Ed, you can show us more of your magician tricks."

The adults at the table seemed to think Pa's idea was great.

Josh pulled Dink and Ruth Rose aside. "This is great!" he whispered. "We can check out the cabins while they're all here."

"But won't it seem weird if we just leave?" Ruth Rose asked.

Josh just winked, then walked off to talk to Ma Wheat. He came back a minute later. "It's all set," he said. "We're outta here."

"What did you tell her?" Dink asked.

"Just a little lie," Josh said, heading for the door.

Dink and Ruth Rose followed. "What kind of lie?" Ruth Rose asked on the front porch.

Josh headed down the path toward the cabins. "I told her we had a summer project we had to work on for school."

Dink laughed. "So what's the project?"

Josh glanced up at the sky. "Studying the constellations," he said.

"But we don't know anything about stars!" Ruth Rose said.

"I know that," Josh said. "But it's our cover. If anyone spots us running around in the dark, they'll think we're just stargazing!"

CHAPTER 10

"Which cabin should we do first?" Josh asked.

"I'll do Ed's," Dink said.

"I'll take Fiona's," Ruth Rose said. "Did you guys notice she was wearing black tonight?"

"Yeah, and Ed was doing knot tricks," Dink said. "Josh, why don't you check out Thumbs's cabin? It's out behind the barn. But be careful, he might be there!"

"No problem," Josh said. "I'll look for the truck and the station wagon. If one of them is gone, he's gone, too."

The kids separated and Dink crept up the steps of Ed's cabin. The wood creaked under his feet. Dink was nervous, even though he knew Ed was still in the main house.

He pushed open the screen door and stepped inside. The small light over Ed's bed was on.

Ed Getz wasn't very neat. Clothes were tossed around the room. A gym bag and duffel lay on the bed, half packed.

Dink quickly checked the dresser drawers. He found a book called *Magic Made Easy* and a few colored scarves. He also discovered a couple of pieces of rope, but they didn't look like the ones Fiona and Lulu had been tied with.

In the bathroom, Dink saw a bottle of aspirin, shaving stuff, and a purple toothbrush. A black rubber tube hung from the towel rack. At first, Dink didn't recognize it. Then he realized it was a stethoscope. He probably uses it in a magic trick, thought Dink.

Back in the main room, Dink checked the wall hooks. Shirts and pants were hanging there, but none of the clothing was black.

Dink felt guilty about poking around in some other person's room. But he wasn't hurting anything, and he wasn't stealing.

第九块金子

He peeked inside the duffel and gym bags. Each held clothing and a few books. Dink wondered why Ed hadn't finished unpacking.

Suddenly, Dink heard footsteps on the porch!

He froze, then dove behind the bed. He lay there praying the screen door wouldn't open.

Then Dink smiled. Of course! It was Josh or Ruth Rose walking on their own cabin porch! The cabins were only about twenty feet apart, and the windows were all open.

Dink stood up and peeked out Ed's window. Josh and Ruth Rose were next door waving through the window!

Dink waved back, then hurried next door. "Boy, you guys scared me!" he said.

"What'd you find?" Josh asked him. Dink flopped on his bed. "A book about magic and some stuff to do tricks, " Dink said. "No black clothing, and no gold. Sorry, Josh."

"Fiona has a lot of black clothes, "Ruth Rose said. "And she has a ton of mystery books!"

"Anything about safecracking?" Dink asked.

155

"Nope, but I did check out that chair she was tied in," Ruth Rose said. "I don't see how she could have tied herself. She could have done her feet, but her hands were tied behind her back!"

"She didn't tie herself," Josh said. "It was Thumbs. By the way, the station wagon is gone. I sure hope he didn't drive to town to sell my gold!"

"What's his cabin like?" Dink asked.

"Filled with stuff," Josh said. "My mother would love this guy, he's so neat! His bed was made and all his clothes were hung up."

"Josh, never mind how neat he is. Did you find any clues?" Ruth Rose asked.

Josh grinned. "Yup. He owns black gloves, black jeans, and a black ski mask! A bunch of ropes, too. And check this out—he has a TV and VCR, and guess what movie he's watching?"

Dink and Ruth Rose just stared at him.

"*Famous Robberies of the West*!" Josh said. "I saw the box it came in."

"That doesn't prove he's the robber," Dink said. "In fact, none of the stuff we saw proves anything."

"And we still don't know where my gold is," Josh said, coiling his lasso on his lap. "I was almost rich!"

Just then the kids heard a scuffling noise out front. They looked through their screen door and saw Ed hobble past the cabin on his crutches.

He moved slowly, holding his bandaged foot in the air. Once he made it up his front steps, he balanced on his good foot while he opened the door. Then he slipped inside.

"Josh, I know you're bummed out," Ruth Rose said. "I don't blame you. But maybe the sheriff will find the robber."

Josh shoved open the screen door and walked out onto the porch. He sat on the step with his lasso draped over one knee. "By tomorrow, the guy will sell the gold," Josh muttered. "He'll get a bunch of money and take off and no one will ever catch him."

Dink and Ruth Rose joined Josh on the porch. It was growing dark, and fireflies were beginning to flicker in the bushes. Sounds of laughter came from the main house.

Dink sat next to Josh. "Want to walk down to the pond?" he suggested, trying to get Josh's mind off his lost gold.

Josh just shrugged and continued staring into the night.

"Okay, let's go," Ruth Rose said, "but let me get my bug spray."

She turned to go back in the cabin, then stopped. From where she was standing, she could see right into Ed's side window. "Guys, look," she said.

第九块金子

"What?" Dink asked, looking up from where he was sitting.

Dink and Josh joined Ruth Rose. They could see Ed Getz moving around the cabin, carrying stuff.

"What's he doing?" Dink asked.

"It looks like he's packing," Ruth Rose said . " Like he's getting ready to leave!"

CHAPTER 11

"Something's weird," Josh said. He tiptoed down off the porch and scooted over to the side of Ed's cabin. Dink and Ruth Rose followed him, and the three crouched under the window. They slowly raised their heads till they could see inside.

The gym bag and duffel bag were zipped and standing next to the door. The crutches were lying on the floor.

Ed was sitting on the bed, unwrapping his bandage. When the bandage was in a pile on the rug, Ed pulled off his sock. He tipped it upside down, and out tumbled Josh's nugget.

"That rat!" Josh whispered.

Ed quickly jammed the nugget into his pocket.

Then he walked toward the door. He wasn't limping at all!

"He's leaving," Dink whispered. "What should we do?"

"I'll go ring the bell," Ruth Rose said. "You guys stop him!"

Ruth Rose dashed toward the house.

"I've got an idea," Josh said, and ran behind Ed's cabin.

The cabin light went off, and Dink heard the front door open. He ducked down as Ed stepped onto the porch with his gym bag.

Ed looked around, then reached back through the doorway for the duffel bag. Carrying one bag in each hand, he stepped off the porch.

Suddenly, the dinner bell began to clang.

Ed Getz stopped in his tracks. At that moment, a rope loop fell over his shoulders. The rope tightened. Ed stumbled, then fell to the ground with a thud.

"Gotcha!" Josh yelled down from the cabin roof. He wrapped the other end of the rope around the chimney.

"What's goin'on out here?"

It was Pa and Jud, running down the path.

"I caught the crook!" Josh yelled from the roof. "My gold is in his pocket!"

The next morning, there was one empty seat at breakfast. Ed Getz had been taken to the Bozeman jailhouse, and Josh had his gold back.

"That sprained ankle was faked," Jud said. "After he knew the gold was in the safe, he pretended to be hurt so he could stay back at the ranch. I have a feeling he stole money out of my wallet, too."

"He must've gagged and handcuffed himself after he tied up Lulu and Fiona," Josh said.

"I'll bet he used that stethoscope to listen to the safe's lock and figure out the combination," Dink said.

"Seems that way," said Pa. He picked up a fax off the table. "This came in from the sheriff a while ago. Seems our Mr. Getz got himself into trouble in New York, too. He was a safecracker and a pickpocket."

"Hadn't been for these three kids," Jud said, "he'd have been long gone. There's a train out of Bozeman at midnight."

Thumbs looked down the long table at Josh. "You thought it was me, didn't you, sonny?"

Josh turned the color of the strawberries lying on top of his cereal. "I...we...how did you know?"

"I heard you three kids makin' your plans last night," Thumbs said. "I made myself scarce so's you could search my cabin. Then I just sat and waited to see what you'd find."

Just then they all heard a loud roar from the kitchen. Before anyone could stand up, a fur-covered shape came running into the dining room, growling.

"What have you done with my baby bear?" it cried.

"Lulu, you'll scare these kids half to death!" Ma said.

Lulu stuck her head out from under the cowhide and grinned. "Hope I didn't frighten you too much the other night," she said.

"It was you!" Dink said.

"Yeah," she said, "but Thumbs put me up to it."

Thumbs winked. "Couldn't resist," he said.

Josh's huge nugget sat next to his cereal bowl, gleaming against the white tablecloth .

"That should bring in a tidy sum," Jud said, grinning at Josh. "I'll take you to town to sell it after breakfast."

"No thanks," Josh said. "I've decided to leave the gold here. I want you to sell it and use the money to save the ranch."

第九块金子

The table becaine so quiet all Dink could hear was his own heartbeat.

"Josh, are you sure?" Jud asked. "What about your new car?"

"Guess I'll just have to find another nugget," Josh said. He looked at Thumbs. "I'll show you my method."

Thumbs laughed. "I'm eager to learn, sonny."

"How can we ever repay you?" Ma asked Josh.

Josh just blushed.

"I know how, " Ruth Rose said, giving Dink a little kick under the table. "Josh loves to be kissed!"

Ma stood up. "Well, that's easy," she said, heading down the table toward Josh.

"Me too!" Lulu said, puckering up her lips. She came at Josh from the other side of the table.

Josh charged out of the dining room, screaming as if a bear were after him.

165

Text copyright © 2001 by Ron Roy
Illustrations copyright © 2001 by John Steven Gurney
All rights reserved under International and Pan-American Copyright Conventions.
Published in the United States by Random House, Inc., New York,
and simultaneously in Canada by Random House of Canada Limited, Toronto.

本书中英双语版由中南博集天卷文化传媒有限公司与企鹅兰登（北京）文化发展有限公司合作出版。

"企鹅"及其相关标识是企鹅兰登已经注册或尚未注册的商标。
未经允许，不得擅用。
封底凡无企鹅防伪标识者均属未经授权之非法版本。

©中南博集天卷文化传媒有限公司。本书版权受法律保护。未经权利人许可，任何人不得以任何方式使用本书包括正文、插图、封面、版式等任何部分内容，违者将受到法律制裁。

著作权合同登记号：字18-2023-258

图书在版编目（CIP）数据

第九块金子：汉英对照 /（美）罗恩·罗伊著；
（美）约翰·史蒂文·格尼绘；高榕译. -- 长沙：湖南
少年儿童出版社，2024.10. --（A to Z神秘案件）.
ISBN 978-7-5562-7818-3

Ⅰ．H319.4
中国国家版本馆CIP数据核字第2024LT8234号

A TO Z SHENMI ANJIAN DI-JIU KUAI JINZI

A to Z神秘案件 第九块金子

[美]罗恩·罗伊 著　　[美]约翰·史蒂文·格尼 绘　　高榕 译

责任编辑：唐凌 李炜	策划出品：李炜 张苗苗 文赛峰
策划编辑：文赛峰	特约编辑：张晓璐
营销编辑：付佳 杨朔 周晓茜	封面设计：霍雨佳
版权支持：王媛媛	版式设计：马睿君
插图上色：河北传图文化	内文排版：霍雨佳

出版人：刘星保
出　版：湖南少年儿童出版社
地　址：湖南省长沙市晚报大道89号
邮　编：410016
电　话：0731-82196320
常年法律顾问：湖南崇民律师事务所　柳成柱律师
经　销：新华书店
开　本：875 mm × 1230 mm　1/32
字　数：91千字
版　次：2024年10月第1版
书　号：ISBN 978-7-5562-7818-3

印　刷：三河市中晟雅豪印务有限公司
印　张：5.25
印　次：2024年10月第1次印刷
定　价：280.00元（全10册）

若有质量问题，请致电质量监督电话：010-59096394　团购电话：010-59320018

A to Z 神秘案件 中英双语
第二辑

THE ORANGE OUTLAW
橙色怪盗

[美]罗恩·罗伊 著
[美]约翰·史蒂文·格尼 绘 史芷溪 译

湖南少年儿童出版社　小博集
·长沙·

主卧	入口	餐厅	厨房 橙子
浴室			
浴室	书房 名画	客厅	阳台
客房			

沃伦伯伯的公寓

沃伦伯伯的家

街区聚会

第110街区

欢迎来到纽约市
一起解开 A to Z 神秘案件

通往绿地镇

纽约州
康涅狄格州
哈得孙河
奥西宁
拉奇蒙特
新泽西州
纽约市
长岛

北 东 南 西

人物介绍

三人小组的成员，聪明勇敢，喜欢读推理小说，紧急关头总能保持头脑冷静。喜欢在做事之前好好思考！

丁丁

三人小组的成员，活泼机智，喜欢吃好吃的食物，常常有意想不到的点子。

乔希

三人小组的成员，活泼开朗，喜欢从头到脚穿同一种颜色的衣服，总是那个能找到大部分线索的人。

露丝

训练动物表演杂耍的人，傲慢自大，被三人组怀疑是偷盗名画的嫌疑人。

哈维

非常称职的警察，负责调查名画失窃案。尊重孩子们的意见，和孩子们一起抓住了偷盗名画的盗贼。

弗兰克·科斯特洛警探

科尔内留斯夫人

公寓的住户，曾经是百老汇的女演员，报警说看到自己家的阳台上有人。因为一些巧合，被三人组怀疑是偷走名画的嫌疑人。

字母 O 代表 observe，观察……

在离杂耍者不远的地方，孩子们注意到一个戴着帽子、穿着背心的男人正牵着一匹小马绕着环形场地走着。突然，一只打扮成小丑的猩猩跳上了小马。当小马奔驰得越来越快的时候，猩猩便在马背上开始表演倒立。

在大家欢呼的同时，一个同样戴着帽子、穿着背心的女士正在分发传单，丁丁便拿了一张塞进口袋里。

表演完毕，那个男人拍了拍手，小马便跳上拖车，马背上还背着猩猩。

乔希沿着街道往前走去，突然说："看那个大木头！"

"跟你一样木呆呆的！"丁丁咧嘴笑着对乔希说。

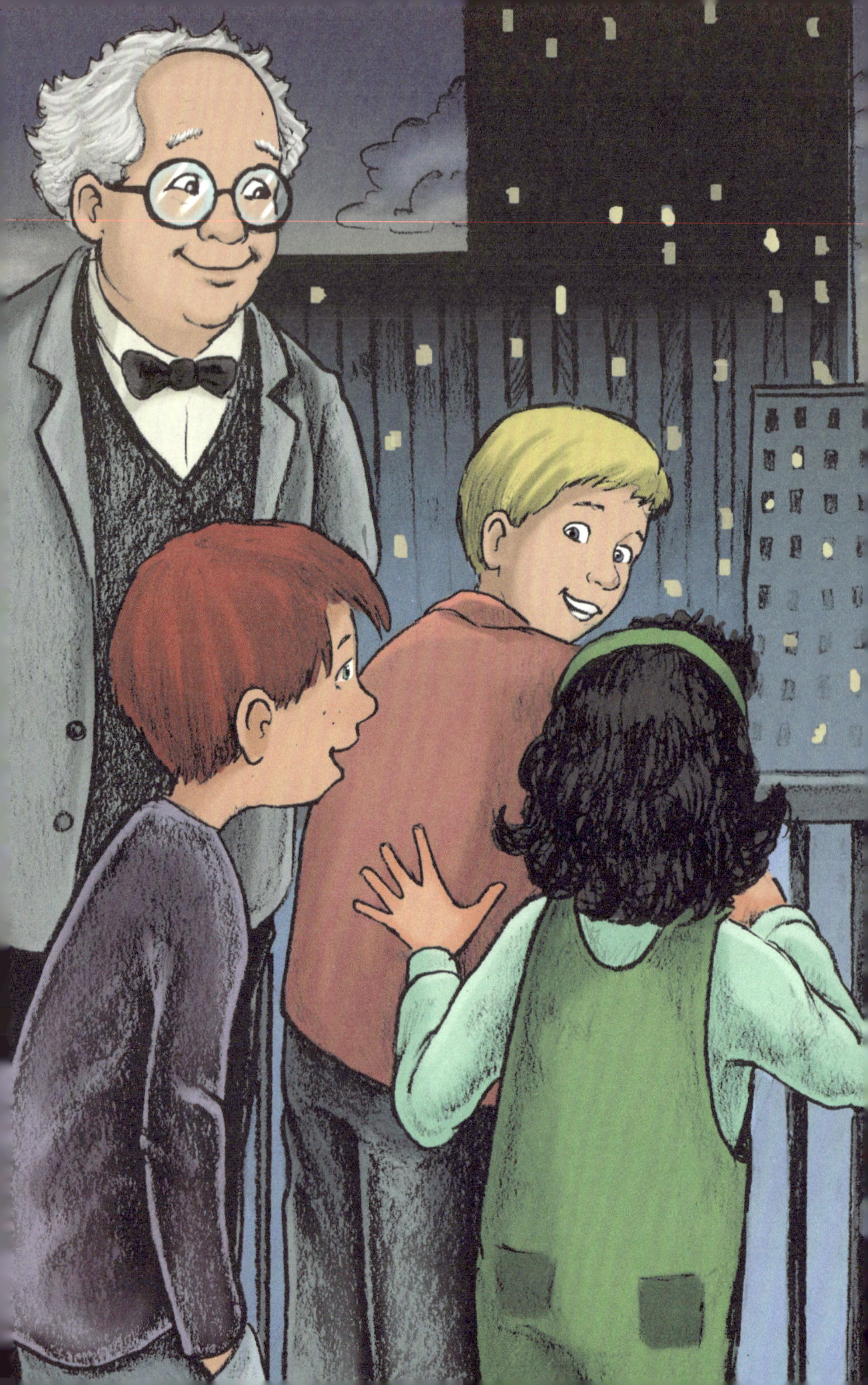

第一章

丁丁、乔希和露丝·罗斯站在沃伦伯伯家的阳台上。九层楼以下,纽约市的私家车、公共汽车和出租车呼啸而过。随着夜幕降临,城市的灯光开始闪烁,人们漫步到餐馆和剧院。

丁丁的伯伯走到阳台上,说:"好美的夜色啊,不是吗?"

丁丁回答道:"太美了!在这里,我感觉自己像一只老鹰!"

"谢谢您邀请我们一起过周末。"乔希对他说。

"非常欢迎你们。"沃伦伯伯说。

"还要谢谢您邀请我们参加您的街区聚会。"露丝说,"我以前从未去过。"

A to Z 神秘案件

乔希咯咯地笑了笑，说："我的弟弟们总是举办'积木'[1]聚会，他们会把积木拿到沙地里，然后互相扔对方。"

沃伦伯伯被逗笑了，他解释道："在纽约市，我们经常举办聚会，并邀请住在这个街区里的每个人。今晚我们计划为中央公园的动物园募捐。"

"为什么动物园需要钱？"露丝问道。

"有些动物需要更大的栖息空间。"沃伦伯伯说。

"他们能从一次聚会上筹集那么多钱吗？"乔希凝视着街道问。

"今晚只是一个开始。"沃伦伯伯说，"动物园至少需要一年的时间来筹集资金。"

他看了看手表，说："我们该出发了，但在此之前，我想给你们看一样东西。"

孩子们跟着丁丁的伯伯穿过客厅，来到公寓

---

1. 英文中单词 block 既有街区又有积木的含义，这里乔希弄混了二者的含义。——译者

后面的一间小书房。这间书房里有一张桌子、一把椅子和一些堆满书的高高的书架。桌子上放着一幅画,画的是一艘漂浮在池塘中的带桨的小船。

"你们喜欢这幅画吗?"沃伦伯伯问。

"太漂亮了。"露丝说,"我喜欢水中的那些花。"

"那些是睡莲。"沃伦伯伯说,"这是很久以前一位叫克劳德·莫奈的人画的,这幅画价值连城。"

"这幅画是您的吗?"丁丁问道。

"我希望是我的,唐尼。"沃伦伯伯说,"我

11

A to Z 神秘案件

的朋友福雷斯特·埃文斯在法国度假时刚买了它,并把它运给我保管。几天后他回到纽约,就会取走这幅美丽的画作。"

沃伦伯伯看了看手表,又说:"是时候下楼了,帮我把灯关了吧。"孩子们便分头行动了起来。

"把厨房餐桌上面的那盏灯留着!"沃伦伯伯喊道。

厨房里,一盏吊灯照在一个盛满橙子的木碗

上。丁丁很想吃一个,但还是决定晚些时候再吃。

他们离开了公寓,沃伦伯伯锁好了门。接着他们穿过走廊,挤进了小电梯,丁丁按下了标着"大堂"的按钮。

"当你们举办街区聚会时,那些来往的车辆该怎么办呢?"乔希在电梯下行时问。

"警察会封锁街道的。"沃伦伯伯向他解释,"你待会儿就知道了。"

不一会儿,他们出了电梯,穿过大堂,朝着公寓楼的大门走去。

"你们好啊,孩子们。"门卫罗杰说,"街区聚会已经吸引了很多人!"他穿着利落的制服,留着尖尖的胡子,看起来活像个皇室成员。

"你会去吗?"露丝问他。

他摇了摇头,说:"恐怕不行,小姐。我必须待在门口,但从这里我也可以看到很多聚会的场景。玩得开心!我听说会有很多美食可以吃。"

"太棒了!"乔希揉着肚子说。

"你还没吃饱吗,乔希?"沃伦伯伯问,"我没有让你吃饱吗?"

乔希咧嘴笑了:"那都是两个小时前的事了!"

露丝说:"乔希就像一头小狼,他一天需要吃十顿饭。"

孩子们跟着沃伦伯伯走到了大街上,六月的夜晚十分温暖,街上挤满了人,空气中弥漫着音乐声、交谈声和食物的香气。

"这太酷了,沃伦伯伯。"丁丁说,"我们就站在平时小汽车和公共汽车行驶的地方!"

"是的。"沃伦伯伯说,"明天早上,这里就会恢复原样。"

"晚上好,邓肯先生。"他们身后的一位女士对他们说。这位女士有些驼背,她的脸上布满了皱纹,还有着一头乱蓬蓬的橙色短发。

"你好,布克小姐。"沃伦伯伯说,"你还没见过我的侄子唐尼和他的朋友吧?孩子们,布克小姐是公寓的管理员。"

孩子们一一向布克小姐问好,并和她握手。尽管今天天气晴朗,她还是穿着雨衣。

"很高兴认识你们,祝你们聚会愉快。"这位女士说完,转身走进了大楼。透过玻璃门,丁丁

看到她和罗杰交谈了一阵。过了一会儿,她走向了电梯。

乔希问:"公寓管理员是干什么的?"

"要做很多事情。"沃伦伯伯说,"她负责修理漏水的水龙头,联系电工,并确保大楼保持清洁。她甚至会把包裹送到我家门口,这样罗杰就不用离开他的岗位了。"

"她和你一样住在这里吗?"露丝问道。

A to Z 神秘案件

沃伦伯伯点了点头,说道:"布克小姐在地下室有一间小公寓。"

突然,乔希停下了脚步。"你们不会相信的。"他说,"但我刚刚看到一个会飞的西瓜!"

第二章

乔希带领大家走向一个正在表演水果杂耍的男人，都是大水果！一个西瓜、一个葡萄柚、一个哈密瓜和一个菠萝正在这个男人头顶盘旋。

"我妈妈会告诉他不要玩食物。"乔希轻声说。

一个比丁丁高一点的男孩站在那个男人的面前，问他："准备好了吗，爸爸？"男人点了点头，这个男孩便把一串香蕉抛向空中。当香蕉加入空中水果的阵营时，所有观看的人都惊呼出声："哇哦！"

在离杂耍者不远的地方，孩子们注意到一个戴着帽子、穿着背心的男人正牵着一匹小马绕着环形场地走着。突然，一只打扮成小丑的猩猩跳

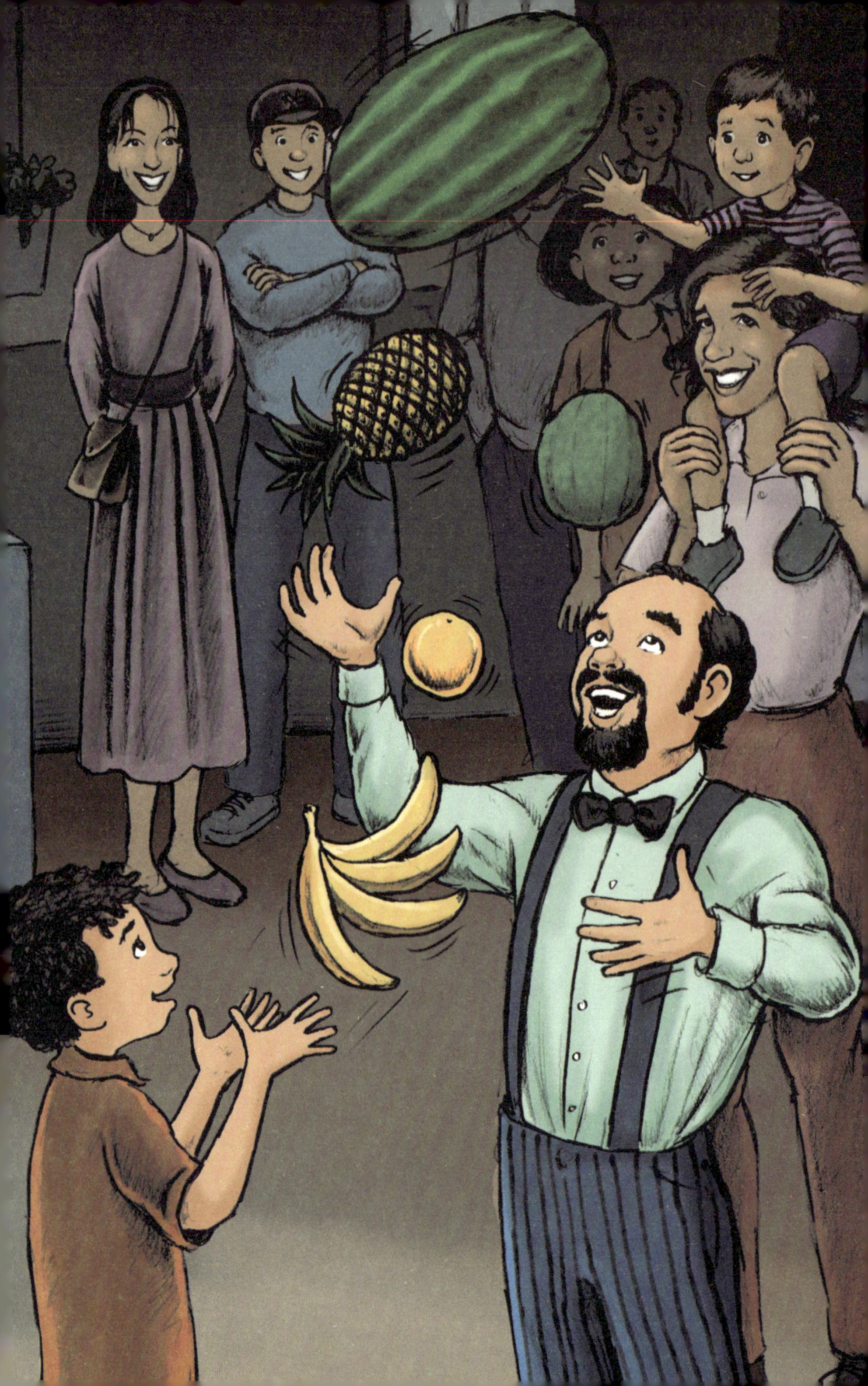

上了小马。当小马奔驰得越来越快的时候，猩猩便在马背上开始表演倒立。

在大家欢呼的同时，一个同样戴着帽子、穿着背心的女士正在分发传单，丁丁便拿了一张塞进口袋里。

表演完毕，那个男人拍了拍手，小马便跳上拖车，马背上还背着猩猩。

乔希沿着街道往前走去，突然说："看那个大木头！"

"跟你一样木呆呆的！"丁丁咧嘴笑着对乔希说。

"我想他说的是那个木偶吧。"露丝说。

前面有一个小舞台，上面坐着一个男人，他的腿上放着一个木偶，他和木偶正在交谈。

"我饿了！"木偶说。

它说话时嘴巴会一张一合，明亮的眼睛也会左右转动。

"去睡觉吧。"男人用更加低沉的声音回答。

"喂我食物，否则我就告你虐待木偶！"木偶说。

"他们是怎么做到的？"乔希问。那个男人

的声音似乎是从木偶的嘴里传出来的。

男人从他脚下一个打开的袋子里拿出一块饼干,他对着观众笑了笑,吃了起来。

"嘿,给我一块!"他的木偶嚷嚷着。

"不行。"

"可以！"

"不行。"那人说，"你已经吃过甜点了。"

"给我一块饼干，否则我就不说话了。"木偶说。

这一幕惹得观众哈哈大笑起来。

男人叹了口气，还翻了个白眼，说："唉，好吧！但只给你一块。"

男人便伸手从袋子里又拿出一块饼干，把它放进木偶的嘴里："给你，现在你高兴了吧？"

木偶咀嚼着把这块饼干吞了下去，还打了个响嗝，这一幕再一次让观众们忍俊不禁。木偶对男人说："谢谢你。"

"不客气。"男人回答完就把木偶抱在怀里，站起来鞠了一躬。

"嘿，先生！饼干去哪儿了？"乔希大声询问。

男人微笑着对乔希说："钻进他的木头肚子里啦！"

乔希笑了，他转身对丁丁、露丝和沃伦伯伯说："这个木偶的表演让我也感到饿了。"

"来点比萨怎么样？"沃伦伯伯问，"我注意到附近有一个卖比萨的小贩。"

四人便走到比萨摊，买了几块比萨，他们把比萨拿在手里，一边吃一边继续享受街区聚会的乐趣。

当丁丁开始打哈欠时，他的伯伯带着大家回到了公寓大楼，罗杰依然站在大堂门口。

"你们玩得开心吗？"罗杰问道。

"好极了！"丁丁说。

"我认为今天的晚会非常成功。"沃伦伯伯说，"晚安，罗杰。"

"那是肯定的。"罗杰说，"晚安，邓肯先生。"

沃伦伯伯按下电梯按钮，片刻后，他们便回到了他的公寓。

"孩子们快点做好睡觉前的准备工作吧，然后我们就可以看看电视上有什么好看的节目了！"他建议道，随后径直走向书房。

露丝刚拿起自己的背包，他们就听到沃伦伯伯大叫了一声。

孩子们急匆匆地穿过走廊，差点撞到沃伦伯伯。他的脸色苍白，看起来很不舒服。

"沃伦伯伯，怎么了？"丁丁问道。

"那…那幅画，"沃伦伯伯结结巴巴地说，"有人偷了福雷斯特的画！"

第三章

丁丁从他的伯伯身边望向书房,那幅画真的不见了。

"我必须报警。"沃伦伯伯说完,匆匆走向厨房,把孩子们留在走廊里。

"谁偷走了它?"露丝问。

"还有,他是怎么偷走的呢?"乔希百思不得其解,"门可是锁着的。"

"孩子们,快来!"沃伦伯伯在公寓另一端的厨房喊道。

他们立刻沿着走廊往回跑进了厨房。

"看那儿!"沃伦伯伯指着厨房的桌子说。

桌面上散落着橙汁和果皮,盛水果的碗被倒

扣在桌子上,地板上到处都是果皮和果汁。

"哎哟,全都变得黏糊糊的!"乔希说着,小心翼翼地避开地上的一摊污渍。

"太可怕了!"沃伦伯伯一边报警一边说。

"伙计们,快看!"露丝指着阳台附近的一块橙子皮。

孩子们上前,露丝打开了阳台的门。"门把手上也有果汁。"她一边说,一边在牛仔裤上擦了擦手。

他们在阳台上发现了更多的橙子皮。

"这家伙一定饿坏了。"乔希说。

丁丁俯身从阳台栏杆上往下看,问道:"小偷就是从这儿进来的吗?"

"怎么进?"乔希问,"难不成从滑翔伞上下来的?丁丁,你难道忘了我们在十楼?"

沃伦伯伯也来到了阳台,对孩子们说:"有一个警探很快就会赶过来。"随后,他注意到阳台上到处都是橙子皮,喊道:"天哪!"

孩子们开始捡阳台上的橙子皮。

沃伦伯伯说:"别捡,警察说了不要碰现场的任何东西。"

于是他们便回到客厅坐着,等待警察的到来。

"福雷斯特肯定会崩溃的。"沃伦伯伯说,"谢天谢地,还好他给这幅画买了保险!至少他还能把钱拿回来。"

突然,罗杰的声音从门旁边的小对讲机里传来:"邓肯先生,有个警探来找您。请问我可以让他上去吗?"

沃伦伯伯跳起来跑向门口,按下对讲机上的"对话"按钮,迫不及待地说:"谢谢你,罗杰。"然后他打开门,走进走廊。

孩子们坐在沙发上盯着大门口,过了一会

儿,他们听到电梯门开了,还听到沃伦伯伯说:"这儿!就是这里,我是沃伦·邓肯。"

沃伦伯伯走回屋内,身后跟着一个穿着深色西装、打着领带的高个子男人。

"孩子们,这位是弗兰克·科斯特洛警探。"沃伦伯伯向大家介绍道。

那个高个子男人朝孩子们点了点头,然后环视了一下房间。他有一双黑色的眼睛,乌黑的向后梳的头发,鼻子看起来好像断了。

"那幅画之前在哪里?"科斯特洛警探问道。

"在后面。"沃伦伯伯说,并领着他穿过走廊走向书房。

"我们去和罗杰谈谈吧!"露丝说。

28

"为什么?"乔希问。

"也许他看到过鬼鬼祟祟的人。"她回答道。

"好主意。"丁丁说完便抓起一本便笺簿,留了一张潦草的字条给他的伯伯,"行了,我们走吧。"随后,他和乔希跟着露丝来到电梯。

在大堂里,他们发现罗杰在大门口附近的桌子旁。透过玻璃,丁丁可以看到街区聚会正趋于尾声。

"又准备出门吗?"罗杰问孩子们。

丁丁摇了摇头,说:"有人从我伯伯的公寓里偷走了一幅珍贵的画!"

罗杰从座位上跳了下来,惊讶地说:"我们大楼里发生了盗窃案?我简直不敢相信!"

"事情发生在我们逛街区聚会的时候。"乔希说,"那个卑鄙的家伙还吃了所有的橙子!"

"我们想知道你有注意到什么奇怪的人吗?"露丝插话道。

罗杰摇了摇头,说:"我一直守在这里,只看到了住在这里的人,绝对没有其他人……"

罗杰闭上眼睛,然后慢慢睁开,说道:"我刚想起来,大约一个小时前,九楼的科尔内留斯夫人打来电话,说她看到她的阳台上有人。我主动提出上去帮忙查看,但她说不用了。"

"她的阳台在沃伦伯伯的阳台正下方吗?"露丝问道。

罗杰点了点头,说道:"大楼后面的所有阳台都在彼此的正上方或正下方。"

露丝看着丁丁和乔希说:"也许她看到了那个贼!"

第四章

丁丁告诉罗杰,他们在沃伦伯伯的阳台上发现了很多橙子皮。

然而罗杰却摇了摇头,问道:"可是这个盗贼要怎么爬上去呢?"

乔希建议道:"我们为什么不到大楼外面看看呢?也许我们会发现一些线索。"

罗杰说:"孩子们,现在已经很晚了,你们应该等明天早上再——"

"我们只出去一小会儿!"丁丁打断道。

"好吧。"罗杰便领着他们来到了电梯旁拐角处的一扇金属门前。

丁丁滑开一个长长的门闩,推开了门。他们走进大楼后面一个光线充足的狭小空间。除了一条通往街道的小巷外,这里被完全封闭了,大楼旁边的阴影中还放着一个大垃圾桶。

露丝盯着这个大垃圾桶说:"我在想,如果盗贼爬到这个大垃圾桶的上面,他是不是就可以爬进一楼阳台呢?"

丁丁抬头看了看,说:"前两层没有阳台。再说了,即使有这个大垃圾桶,我也看不出来这个盗贼是怎样爬上去再爬下来的。"

"所以他必须从前门走进去。"乔希说,"但如果罗杰没看见他……"

就在他们谈话的时候,黑暗中传来了一个愤怒的声音:"你们在这儿干什么?这可是私家产业!"

"谁?谁在那儿?"丁丁问。

一个人影从黑暗中走了出来,是布克小姐,她看起来对他们的出现感到很不高兴。

"是我们。"丁丁说,"我的伯伯是邓肯先生,我们今晚早些时候在街区聚会上见过您。"

布克小姐在离孩子们几英尺[1]远的地方停了

---

1. 英尺:英美制长度单位,1英尺 = 0.3048米。——编者

下来,她的手塞在外套的口袋里,帽子压得低低的,遮住了她橙色的头发。她问道:"你们这些孩子在这里做什么?"

"在我伯伯的公寓里发生了一起盗窃案。"丁丁说。

布克小姐点了点头,说:"我知道,罗杰刚刚告诉我了。"

露丝说:"我们认为盗贼可能是从这里爬上去的。"

"对。"乔希说,"除非他长了一双翅膀。"

布克小姐抬头看向大楼的侧墙,伸出一根长长的手指触碰了一下墙砖,说:"几年前,我还能不费吹灰之力从这儿爬上去。"

孩子们听完惊讶地盯着布克小姐。

布克小姐笑了,告诉他们:"在我像你们这么大的时候,我的父亲和母亲经营着一个游艺团。我的兄弟们负责表演高空走钢丝的节目,他们被称为'飞翔布克小子',而我就是表演空中飞人的女孩。"

"哦,那您在巷子里看到过其他人吗?"丁丁问。

布克小姐摇了摇头。"小巷当时是被挡住了的。"

"挡住了？怎么挡住的？"露丝问。

"我带你们去看看吧。"孩子们便跟着布克小姐沿着小巷向大楼前面走去。

"就在这儿。"布克小姐一边说，一边在小巷与街道相接的地方停了下来。"街区聚会期间，有一辆拖车停在这里。"

"拖车？"丁丁问道，并努力回想着当时的场景。

就在这时，罗杰打开大门，探出头来说："唐纳德[1]，你伯伯想让你和你的朋友上楼。"

"好的，我们马上就来。"丁丁说，"晚安，布克小姐，也许我们明天会再见的。"

"也许吧。"女人答道，随后她转过身，沿着黑暗的小巷往回走。

---

1. 丁丁的全名是唐纳德·戴维·邓肯。——编者

第五章

当孩子们走出电梯时,沃伦伯伯正在走廊里等着,并说:"谢谢你给我留了一张字条,但现在已经过了你的就寝时间了,唐尼。"

"警探还在吗?"丁丁问。

"不,他几分钟前就走了。"沃伦伯伯说,"他检查了指纹,并提取了橙子皮和橙子汁的样本。"

他们走进厨房,橙子皮已经打扫干净了,但地板还是黏糊糊的。白色指纹粉残留在餐桌和吧台上,留下了一块块污点,盛水果的空碗则被放在水槽里。

"你认识科尔内留斯夫人吗?"丁丁问他的伯伯。

沃伦伯伯笑了:"很多人都认识科琳娜·科尔

内留斯,许多年前,她是百老汇的一名女演员。她就住在我们楼下,我们经常在一起喝茶。你问这个干什么?"

丁丁告诉他的伯伯,他们在罗杰那儿打听到了什么:"科尔内留斯夫人可能从她的阳台上看到了盗贼,也许她能告诉我们他长什么样!"

"唐尼,科尔内留斯夫人很老了。"他的伯伯说,"恐怕她的视力已经大不如前了。"

沃伦伯伯环顾了厨房一周,叹了口气,说:"我应该收拾一下,但我已经筋疲力尽了,明天早上再收拾这个烂摊子吧。孩子们,现在你们该上床睡觉了。"

露丝说:"我们明天会帮您一起打扫的。"

"谢谢你们,亲爱的。祝你们做个好梦。"沃伦伯伯一边说,一边轻手轻脚地走向他的卧室。

"我不知道你们怎么样。"露丝说,"但是我现在一点也睡不着。"

"我也是。"丁丁说。于是,三人便向客厅走去,露丝和丁丁并排坐在沙发上,乔希扑通一声坐到了地毯上。

露丝说:"我一直在想,有多少人知道你伯伯的家里放着一幅价值连城的画呢?"

丁丁说:"罗杰可能早就知道了。"

乔希猛地坐直了:"当然了!他就是那个盗贼!"

丁丁说:"可是他整晚都在看大门啊。"

露丝说:"这只是他告诉我们的,他也有可能撒谎了。罗杰有这套房子的钥匙吗?"

丁丁反对道:"伙伴们,我伯伯和罗杰是朋友。再说了,他在这栋大楼里工作很多年了。"

乔希眉飞色舞地说:"你都不看电视吗?就是管家——我是说,就是门卫干的!"

丁丁被他逗笑了,说:"你疯啦!罗杰是不可能偷偷溜到这里偷走那幅画的。"

乔希起身走进厨房,丁丁听到冰箱门被他开了又关的声音。

露丝问:"好吧,还有没有其他人知道这件事?"

"布克小姐算不算?"乔希一边说着话,一边拿着一串葡萄回来了,"她跟我们说过她曾经是'空中飞人',也许就是她从大楼外面爬了上来,而且她还知道我们在街区聚会的时候没人

A to Z 神秘案件

在家。"

露丝点点头,说:"她还是大楼的管理员,所以我敢打赌她有所有公寓的钥匙,她甚至不必从大楼外面爬上来!"

丁丁问:"但是她怎么会知道我伯伯有这幅画?"

"丁丁,我记得你伯伯提到过布克小姐的职

责之一是送快递?"露丝问道,"也许这幅画的包裹就是她派送的,你伯伯可能在签收的时候告诉了她这个包裹里装的是什么。"

乔希说:"她可能还告诉了罗杰。见鬼,也许他们是一起干的,罗杰可以在她偷这幅画的时候帮她放哨!"

丁丁说:"然后再把橙子皮扔得到处都是?那不是有点愚蠢吗?"

露丝说:"也许她是故意这么做的,把橙子皮丢在阳台上,看起来像盗贼爬下了大楼。"

乔希说:"没错,那会让我们认为盗贼是一个没有钥匙的人。"

"好吧,那怎么解释厨房里到处都是果汁呢?"丁丁问道,"布克小姐为什么要那样做?"

"很简单。"乔希说,"她想迷惑警察。"

丁丁打了个哈欠,然后站起来伸了个懒腰,说:"好吧!不管是谁干的好事,都成功地把我搞糊涂了!"

他走到阳台上,抬头看着星星。他辨认出高空中闪烁的光点来自一架飞机,他的思绪飞到了这架飞机是从哪里起飞的这个问题上。

乔希和露丝走了过来,站在他的身旁。

露丝说:"我想到了一个可能知道这幅画的事情的人。"

"谁?"丁丁问。

"科尔内留斯夫人。"她回答道。

丁丁难以置信地看着她说:"但是她年纪很大了,而且视力不好,我伯伯刚刚才告诉我们这一点了。"

露丝说:"他还告诉我们她曾经是一名演员呢。"

乔希补充道:"另外,偷画可不需要一双千里眼。"

"但是如果科尔内留斯夫人是这个盗贼,为什么她还会告诉罗杰她看到了有人在她的阳台上?"

露丝说:"也许她这样做是为了不让任何人怀疑她。"

丁丁沉思了一会儿后,说:"好吧,但她是怎么进入我伯伯的公寓的?难道你想说她可以像人猿泰山一样在藤蔓上荡来荡去吗?"

乔希哈哈大笑,说:"我不知道,说不定她在

这里喝茶时偷了一把备用钥匙呢。但是我认为我们明天早上可以去找科尔内留斯夫人聊聊。"

第六章

"乔希，起床啦。"

丁丁摇了摇乔希的肩膀，然后猛地拉开他身上的被子，对他说："快起来吧，在我伯伯起床之前帮我一起打扫厨房。"

乔希嘟囔了几句，并把被子拉了回来。

"他给我们做了早餐……"丁丁说。

还没等丁丁说完，乔希就从床上跳了起来，冲进厨房时还被自己的运动鞋绊倒了。

露丝已经在那里洗盛水果的碗了。

"我没看到任何食物。"乔希抱怨道。

丁丁告诉他："现在没有，但等我们把这一片狼藉收拾干净之后，你会看到的，蓝莓煎饼可是我伯伯的拿手菜。"

乔希倒在椅子上，嘟囔着："我上当了。"

"来吧，乔希。"丁丁说，"如果我们一起努力，可以在十分钟内完成这项工作。"

"我来拖地。"露丝一边从壁橱里拿出拖把一边说。

丁丁递给乔希一块湿海绵，并说："刚好你坐在那儿，就擦一下椅子和桌面吧。"

"我以为我们今天早上要和科尔内留斯夫人谈谈呢。"乔希说着，并快速地擦了一下桌子。

"是啊。"丁丁说完便打开了他伯伯的通讯录，接着说："我现在就给她打电话。"

当丁丁打给科尔内留斯夫人的电话被接通时，他进行了自我介绍，并询问她几分钟后他们是否可以去拜访她，随后他道了谢，并挂断了电话。

丁丁说："我们打扫完就可以去拜访她了，快开始干活吧！"

丁丁把收音机的音量开得很低，他们一边听着乡村音乐一边打扫卫生。

"嘿！瞧我发现了什么！"乔希手里拿着一根长长的橙色头发说，"它卡在椅背上了。"

A to Z 神秘案件

丁丁和露丝走了过去,仔细研究了一下这根头发。露丝说:"看起来像你的头发呢,乔希。"

乔希说:"才不是呢!我的头发是红色的,才不是这种橙色,而且我的头发干净多了!"

露丝接过头发,把它举到灯前仔细观察,说:"布克小姐就有一头橙色的头发。"

丁丁把这根头发包在纸巾里,塞进了自己的口袋:"我们稍后再去查查她,现在咱们得赶紧打扫完,去见科尔内留斯夫人。"

橙色怪盗

十分钟后，孩子们悄悄地离开了沃伦伯伯家。他们找到楼梯间，走下了一层楼。丁丁敲了敲科尔内留斯夫人的门。

门被一个满头白发、穿着一件毛茸茸长袍的妇人打开了，她淡蓝色的眼睛在厚厚的镜片后看起来非常大。

"早上好！"科尔内留斯夫人愉快地说，"我就知道不是只有我喜欢起得像鸟儿一样早。快进来，快进来吧！"

她拄着拐杖，领着他们走进了一间令人感到愉悦的客厅，并说："请坐在沙发上吧，这样我就可以看清你们了。"

孩子们在沙发上坐成一排，科尔内留斯太太坐在他们对面，她凑近身子，仔细打量着他们的脸。

"现在可以告诉我为什么你们三个小孩子要来看望一个我这样的老太太了吧？"

丁丁便告诉了科尔内留斯夫人那幅名画被盗的事。

她说："天哪！我总是错过那些令人激动的时刻。亲爱的，这是什么时候发生的？"

45

露丝说:"昨晚举行街区聚会的时候。"

科尔内留斯夫人激动地拍了拍手,说:"我在我的阳台上看到的那个鬼鬼祟祟的人一定是盗贼!我可是目击证人!"

"嗯,您能不能告诉我们发生了什么?"

科尔内留斯夫人拄着拐杖站了起来:"跟我来。"她走向阳台,并对乔希说:"好孩子,帮我拉开窗帘。"

拉开窗帘后,孩子们发现这个阳台和沃伦伯伯家的一模一样,只是阳台栏杆上多了几个挂着的喂鸟器。

科尔内留斯夫人说:"我喜欢喂鸟,但是我很难看清它们,所以我买了这个东西!"她指向一个馅饼盘大小的圆形放大镜,它被粘在阳台的玻璃门内侧。

丁丁好奇地透过这个放大镜看过去,说:"哇!所有东西都看上去变大了!"

"很有趣吧?"科尔内留斯夫人说,"我昨晚听见了一些奇怪的声音,所以我走过来,透过窗帘偷偷往外看,发现有人正在我的阳台上!"

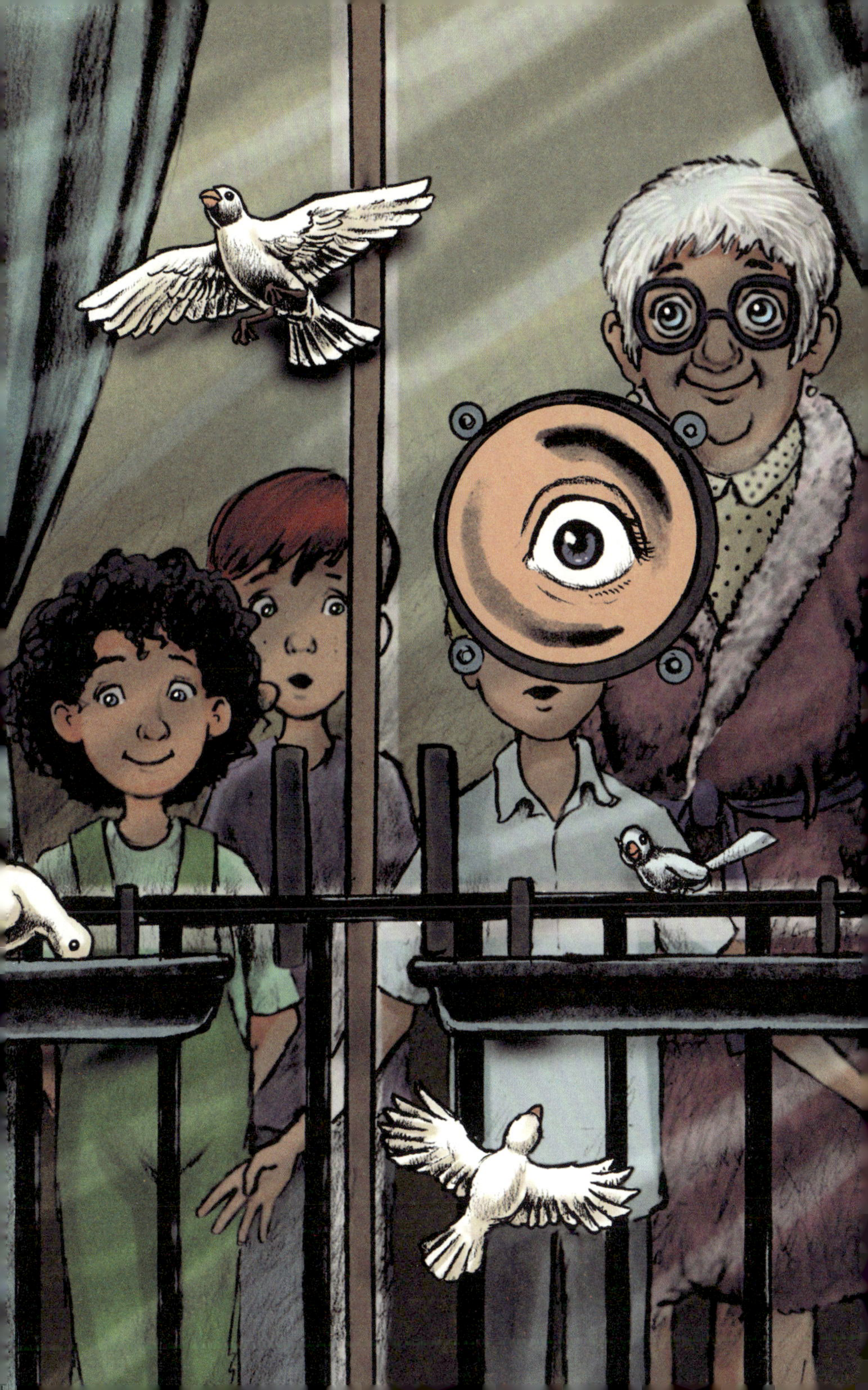

丁丁问:"他长什么样?"

"我还以为你永远不会问这个。"说完,科尔内留斯夫人从睡袍口袋里拿出一张便签纸,并把它递给了丁丁。

纸上用龙飞凤舞的字迹写着几行字:

　　松垮的大衣
　　非常糟糕的仪态
　　布满皱纹的脸庞
　　…………

读到最后几个字的时候,丁丁大吃一惊:

　　橙色的头发

第七章

"你们还觉得这个盗贼是科尔内留斯夫人吗?"丁丁一边问其他两个小伙伴,一边和他们一起走回十楼。

露丝说道:"根据科尔内留斯夫人的描述,布克小姐听上去更像是那个盗贼。"

丁丁笑了:"糟糕的仪态,松垮的衣衫,橙色的头发——这听上去更像乔希啊!"

说完,他打开了他伯伯家的门。

沃伦伯伯说:"你们回来啦。谢谢你们帮忙打扫厨房,这真是一个多么可爱的惊喜啊!准备好吃你们的蓝莓煎饼了吗?"

"我准备好了!"乔希说着,向厨房跑去。

咬了一口煎饼后,丁丁从口袋里拿出叠好的纸巾，他拔出了那根橙色的头发，递给沃伦伯伯看。

"乔希发现这根头发卡在一把椅子上。"他说，"我们认为它是盗贼的。"

沃伦伯伯研究了一下头发，说："这看起来很奇怪。等等，我马上就回来。"

孩子们听到橱柜门开了又关的声音，不一会儿，沃伦伯伯回来了，手里还拿着一个小木箱。

他把煎饼盘移到一边，把盒子放好。然后他揭开盖子，盒子里露出了一个闪闪发光的显微镜。随后，他把显微镜的电源线插入墙上的插座。

"乔希，可以给我一根你的头发吗？"他问道。

"没问题。"乔希猛地拔下一根头发，还做了个鬼脸，然后他把头发递给了沃伦伯伯。

沃伦伯伯把两根头发都放在一个载玻片上，然后把载玻片放在显微镜镜头下。他调整了目镜，并用一只眼睛盯着它。

"嗯，我觉得这是一根真头发。"过了一会儿，沃伦伯伯说道，"但这和你的很不一样，乔希，过来看看，你的头发是右边那根。"

乔希弯下腰看目镜，说："我什么也没看见啊。"

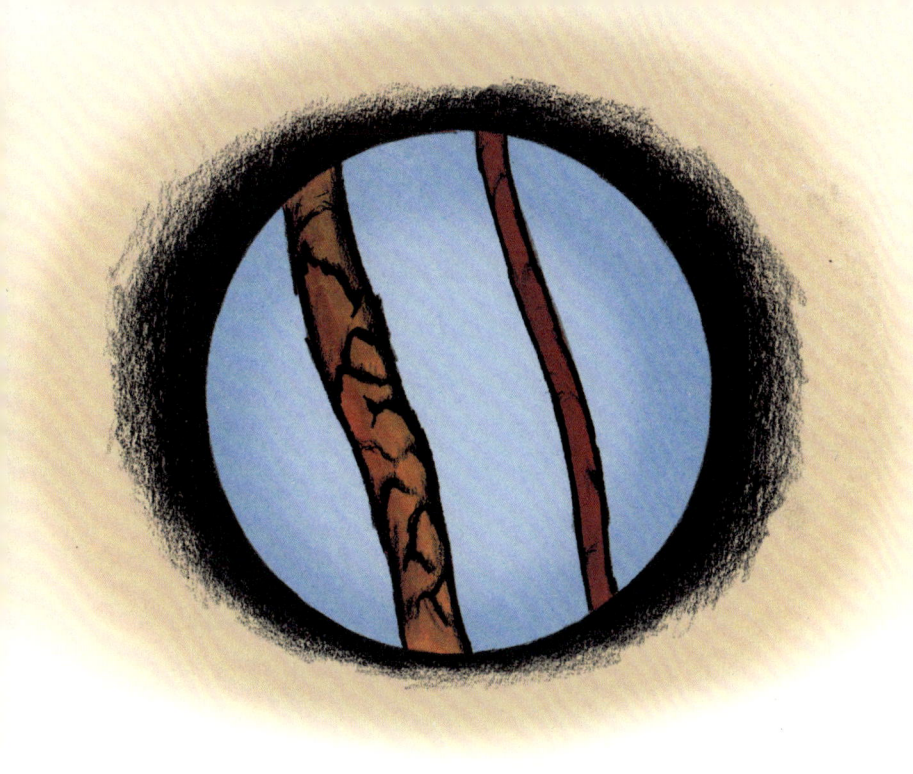

沃伦伯伯说:"闭上一只眼睛试试。"

乔希说:"哇,这下好多了!头发看起来像树干一样!"

接下来是露丝。"这两根头发看起来确实不一样。"她说,"丁丁,快来看看。"

丁丁闭上了一只眼睛,透过目镜向下仔细看了看。显微镜下,右边的头发看上去又细又光滑,然而左边的那根比右边的更粗,颜色也更深一些。

丁丁说:"科尔内留斯夫人告诉我们,她看到一个留着橙色的头发的人在她的阳台上。"

"她真这么说了？"沃伦伯伯说。

露丝点了点头说："她的阳台门上粘着一个小巧的放大镜，这样她就可以看清在喂食器旁吃食的鸟了。"

"我试用过那个放大镜。"丁丁告诉沃伦伯伯，"它能使东西看上去更大更清晰。"他还告诉了沃伦伯伯科尔内留斯夫人对那个出现在她阳台上的人的描述。

"松垮的大衣和糟糕的仪态？好啊，好啊。也许她真的看到了那个盗贼！"沃伦伯伯说，"我最好还是打个电话给科斯特洛警探。"

当他的伯伯在拨打电话时，丁丁示意乔希和露丝跟着他。他们离开了公寓，但丁丁却绕开了电梯。

"我们要去哪里？"乔希问道，"我还想吃点煎饼呢。"

"我们走下去吧。"丁丁说着，并推开楼道口的门，"我不想让任何人看到我们。"

露丝问："看到我们怎么了？"

"我想弄一根布克小姐的头发。"丁丁说,"但我不想让罗杰看到我们,万一他们是同伙呢。"

"所以你现在觉得他们是一伙的啦?"乔希问。

丁丁说:"我不确定,但是我们不能放过任何可能性。"

"哦,天哪。"乔希感叹着,并跳下楼梯。

丁丁和露丝紧紧跟在乔希身后,露丝问丁丁:"你准备怎么弄到她的头发?"

丁丁耸了耸肩,承认道:"我还不知道呢。"

孩子们跑得上气不接下气,终于到了大堂。丁丁在拐角处偷偷观察了一会儿,确定罗杰没有看见他们后,便从后门匆匆溜了出来。

他们没有在大楼后面找到布克小姐。乔希顺着小巷看了一眼,但她也不在。

露丝建议:"我们去前面找找吧。"丁丁和乔希跟着露丝沿着小巷向前走去。他们走到半路时,露丝突然弯下腰,从地上捡起了一样东西。

丁丁和乔希追上来看了看,露丝手上拿着一张宝丽来快照,照片里是一幅镶着框的画。

当丁丁认出那艘漂浮在池塘中的带桨的小船

时，他倒吸了一口凉气，说："这照片拍的就是被偷走的画！"

第八章

照片中,这幅画被立在一张桌子上,还能看见一部分窗户和远处的建筑物。

乔希问:"这张照片怎么会出现在巷子里?"

"我想我知道。"露丝说,"小偷肯定是用这张照片来辨认那幅画的,他得手之后就把照片扔掉了。"

丁丁说:"如果小偷随手把照片扔在这里,那就意味着他很有可能是顺着阳台爬下来的"。

乔希说:"你说的是女字旁的'她'吧。"

露丝摇摇头,问:"但如果布克小姐真这么干了,她为什么要告诉我们她能爬上去?这难道不是在指控她自己吗?"

"也许她提供了一些假情报来迷惑我们呢?"

乔希说，"她确实和我们说过她可以徒手爬楼，还把这张照片扔在小巷里。可事实上，她可能就是拿着钥匙大摇大摆从前门进去的。"

"不管是谁偷了那幅画。"丁丁说，"这个盗贼的指纹肯定留在了这张照片上。"他小心翼翼地把照片塞进衬衫内侧的口袋里，说："我们必须把它交给沃伦伯伯！"

孩子们沿着小巷跑到大楼正门前，周末的车流呼啸而过，几个人匆匆地向地铁站走去，旁边还有一个穿着灰色工作服的男人正在清扫垃圾。

巷子口已经堆了一堆垃圾，当孩子们经过时，乔希不小心踢到了那堆垃圾。

"嘿！小心脚下，小伙子。"拿扫帚的人说。

"对不起。"乔希说着，往旁边挪了挪，用脚把垃圾重新堆好。

然后，他突然跪在地上，从垃圾堆中挑出了一些东西，并对小伙伴们说："嘿，伙计们！快看！"说罢，乔希举起一块橙子皮。

拿着扫帚的清洁工见状忍俊不禁地说："昨晚这里举办了街区聚会，有一个男人把一辆装着一只猩猩和一匹小马的拖车停在了这儿,那只猩猩可真是吃了好多橙子啊!"

丁丁从乔希手里接过果皮,仔细地看了看,发现果皮里夹着一根橙色的长发。

露丝凑过去看了看,说:"这和乔希在厨房里发现的头发一模一样!"

乔希回头看了看小巷,说:"伙计们,爬上阳台的不是布克小姐,而是那只猩猩吧!"

露丝的眼睛都瞪大了:"猩猩确实是攀爬高手!"

乔希补充道:"猩猩还有长长的橙色毛发,也很喜欢吃水果!"

丁丁盯着露丝和乔希说:"你们的意思是那个盗贼是一只猩猩?"

"为什么不是呢?"乔希说,"人们可以训练猩猩做各种各样的事情,为什么不能教它偷一幅画?"

丁丁拍了拍衬衫里放着的照片,说:"如果你猜得没错,它的指纹应该在上面。"

"猩猩有指纹吗?"露丝问道。

丁丁耸耸肩说:"不管是谁给了它照片,都会留下他自己的指纹。"

A to Z 神秘案件

"他的驯兽师!"乔希说。

露丝点点头:"是的,即使是猩猩偷走了这幅画,但真正的贼是教它这么干的人!"

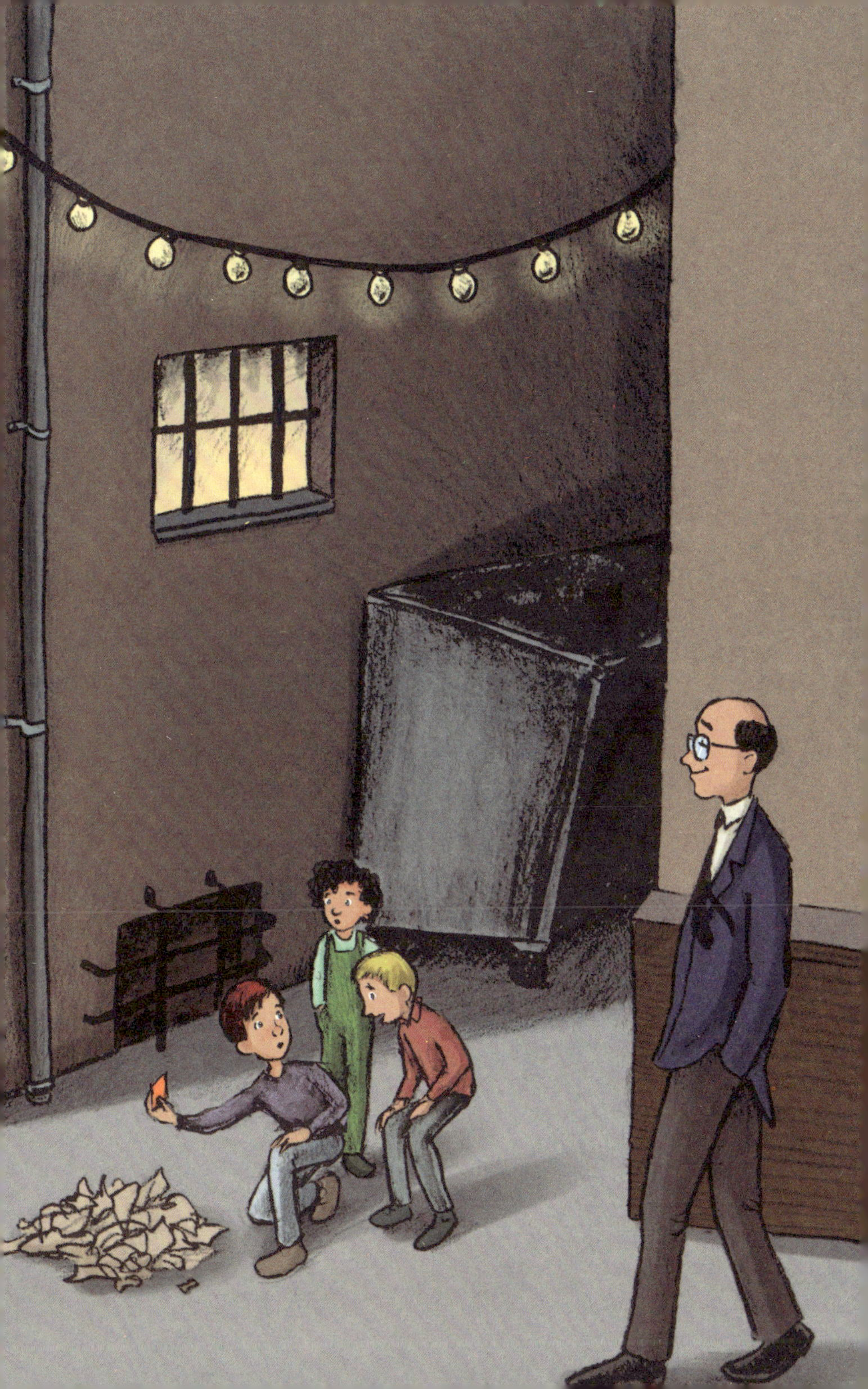

第九章

当丁丁、乔希和露丝跑回家时,沃伦伯伯正闷闷不乐地待在厨房里,对他们说:"福雷斯特·埃文斯刚刚来电话了,说他明天回来!我该怎么向他交代呢?"

丁丁咧嘴笑了:"告诉他我们知道是谁偷了他的画!"

沃伦伯伯手里的咖啡杯差点掉了,他吃惊地说:"你真的知道吗,唐尼?是谁?"

"是猩猩干的!"乔希说。

三个孩子你一言我一语地把他们的推测告诉了沃伦伯伯。

"可是一只猩猩怎么认得出这是珍贵的莫奈真迹呢?"沃伦伯伯问道。

丁丁解开衬衫的扣子，小心翼翼地取出照片放在桌子上，说："我们认为是它的驯兽师教会了它如何辨认这幅画。"

沃伦伯伯仔细端详了这张照片，并说："没错，这是福雷斯特的画。看，这背景是埃菲尔铁塔，这张照片肯定是在巴黎拍的！"

随后，他又摇了摇头，说："我还是觉得难以置信，居然有一只猩猩爬上了我的阳台，吃了我的橙子，还偷走了我朋友的画？这太不可思议了！"

"猩猩非常聪明。"乔希说，"我曾经看过一个关于它们的自然节目，里面有一只猩猩学会了数数，研究人员还教会了另一只猩猩如何打开录像机，并播放录像带！"

沃伦伯伯点了点头，说："我会把这张照片交给科斯特洛警探的。"

露丝问："但是我们怎样才能找到猩猩的主人呢？我们甚至不知道他叫什么。"

"等一下！"丁丁跳起来跑进客厅，拿着昨晚穿的牛仔裤跑了回来。

"我拿了一张他们的传单。"他一边说，一边往裤子口袋里掏。"在这儿呢!"

他把传单摊在厨房的桌子上,只见传单上用大大的字写着:

> 福勒的农场
> 种类颇丰的动物表演
> 承接聚会和学校活动

在这几行字下面是一张昨晚他们见过的男人和女人的照片,他们的姓名被标注在这张照片下面:

> 哈维和金妮·福勒

这张照片旁边是那只骑着小马的猩猩的照片,一旁的说明写着:

> 猩猩奥利,还有小马波莉!

在这张传单的最底下还印着他们的电话号码

和地址。

"他们住在纽约的奥西宁。"沃伦伯伯说,"离这里不远。好样的,唐尼!"

乔希说:"现在我们要做的就是让警探逮捕他们。"

"恐怕还不行。"沃伦伯伯说,"我们没有证据能证明他们训练了动物来偷福雷斯特的画。我们只有很多推论、一张照片和一些可能属于那只猩猩的毛发,但恐怕这些证据并不足以让科斯特洛警探逮捕他们。"

丁丁说:"如果我们能拿到福勒先生或夫人的指纹就好了,这样我们就能将他们的指纹和照片上的指纹进行比对了。"

"这可能是一个突破点。"沃伦伯伯说,"但仍不足以证明就是他们的动物偷走了这幅画。"

"要是我们能拿到一根奥利的毛发呢?"露丝说,"如果它的毛发和我们在厨房里发现的毛发是一样的,那难道不能证明它来过这间公寓吗?"

沃伦伯伯笑了笑,说:"我觉得这样就能够说服科斯特洛警探了,但我们要怎样才能拿到它的毛发呢?"

露丝咧嘴笑着说:"就等您这么问呢。"

第十章

半小时后,沃伦伯伯把电话递给露丝,并说:"祝你好运。"

"不用担心。"乔希说,"露丝可是糊弄盗贼的行家!"

露丝微笑着对着电话说:"您好,请问是哈维·福勒先生吗?我叫露丝·罗斯。明天是我的生日,我父母想请奥利和波莉来演出。我的父亲是福雷斯特·埃文斯,他非常富有!"

两分钟后,她挂断电话,说:"他们会来的!"

丁丁问:"您觉得埃文斯先生会介意我们使用他的房子吗?"

沃伦伯伯笑了:"他肯定非常乐意!我都迫不及待地想告诉他了!"

"我们该怎么去那儿?"乔希问,"我甚至从来没有听说过纽约的拉奇蒙特。"

"离这儿不远,乔希。我会租一辆汽车。现在我得去打几个电话。这可太有趣了!"沃伦伯伯说。

次日清晨,罗杰打电话告诉他们租来的车已经在楼下了。

露丝用沃伦伯伯的贝雷帽和眼镜乔装打扮了一番,丁丁见了说:"这装扮棒极了!福勒先生这下绝不会想到他在街区聚会见过你。"

沃伦伯伯和孩子们下了楼,钻进租来的车里。他开着车带孩子们出了城,一路上他们看到了许多汽车,还穿过了几座桥。最后,丁丁看到一块牌子,上面写着:

拉奇蒙特欢迎您

"我们快到了。"沃伦伯伯说,"福雷斯特有一个美丽的家,还有大片的土地。"

几分钟后,他拐进了一条两旁种满了树木的

车道。车道尽头矗立着一座大大的、用砖砌成的房子,丁丁看到这座房子后面还有一个游泳池和网球场。

"这儿真棒!"乔希说。

"是的,这里很美。"沃伦伯伯说,"但我更喜欢周围住的人多一些,而不是被这些树包围。"

沃伦伯伯停好车后,他们都下了车。两个男人和一个女人从车库里走了出来。

丁丁认出了科斯特洛警探,但他不认识另外两个人。

"这位是我的搭档,丽塔·弗罗斯特警探。"科斯特洛警探向大家介绍道。

"我是特德·帕克博士。"另一个男人向大家做了自我介绍。

"帕克博士是布朗克斯动物园灵长类动物馆的馆长,等抓捕完盗贼后,他将负责照看那些动物。"科斯特洛警探向大家解释了一番。

弗罗斯特警探穿着蓝色的裙子和高跟鞋,她对露丝友好地笑了笑,说:"你准备好扮演千金小姐了吗?"

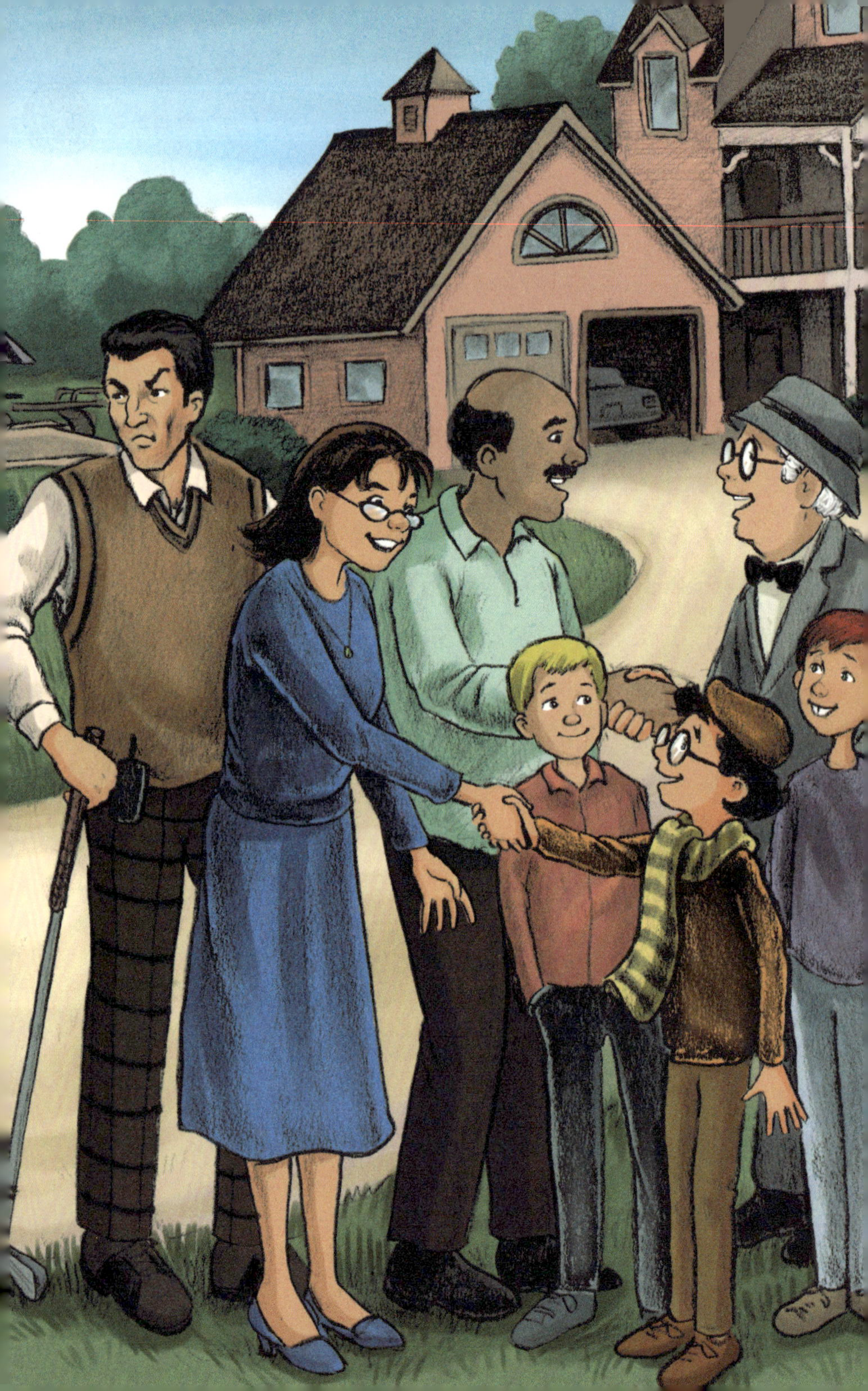

露丝说:"我有一点紧张,万一福勒夫妇认出我了呢?"

"我一点也不担心这个。"弗罗斯特警探说,"如果真如你们所说,那他们甚至不会看你一眼,他们只会满脑子想着怎样闯进这座美丽的房子。"

"好了,我们的计划是这样的。"科斯特洛警探说,"当福勒夫妇的车开进来时,我们的增援车会通知我们。丽塔和我会假扮成埃文斯夫妇,露丝就扮成我们的女儿,也就是今天过生日的主角,其余人都待在车库里,等我说'可以出来了'的指令。还有什么问题吗?"

就在这时,别在科斯特洛警探腰带上的手机响了。他接通电话,听对方说完后便挂断了。

"福勒夫妇的拖车刚刚进入这片区域。"他说,"请大家躲进车库,不要发出任何声音。"

丁丁、乔希、沃伦伯伯和帕克博士走进车库。

"祝你好运。"丁丁轻声对露丝说。当车库门在她面前关上时,露丝向他们竖起了大拇指。

车库里停着两辆亮晶晶的黑色汽车,丁丁就坐在其中一辆车的保险杠上。他能听到拖车驶来的声音,然后他听到车门"砰"的一声关上了,还有一些模糊的交谈声。

乔希把耳朵贴在车库门上,当他听见露丝向"爸爸"撒娇说想拥有一匹自己的小马时,他忍不住咯咯地笑了起来,他轻声说:"她挺乐在其中的嘛!"

丁丁轻推了乔希一下,轻声说:"不许说话!"

乔希失去了平衡,倒在了墙上,撞到一个按钮,车库的门发出"嗡嗡"的声音,缓缓地打开了。

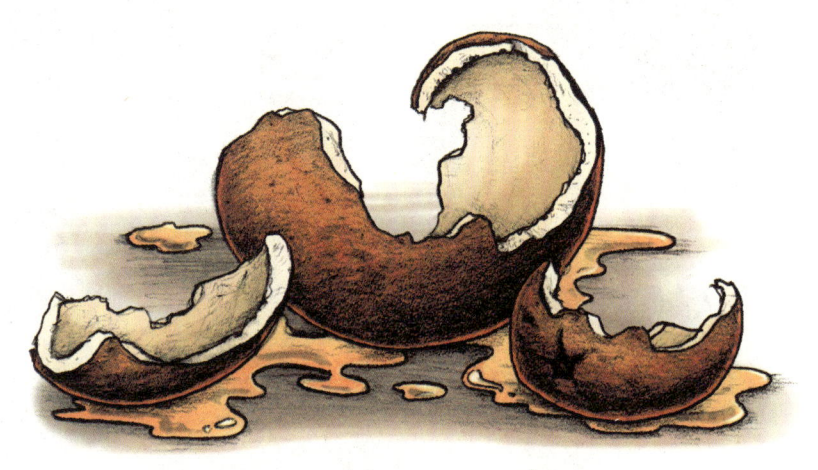

第十一章

当车库外的人都转过身，看着车库里面的人时，丁丁感到自己的脸羞得通红。

拖车停在几码[1]外的地方，透过厚厚的铁网，丁丁看见了奥利和波莉。

"喂，这是怎么回事？"哈维问道。

"嘿，等等。"他的妻子说，"他们是街区聚会上那群人！这是怎么回事，埃文斯先生？"

"我才不是埃文斯先生。"科斯特洛警探说着掏出他的钱包，亮出他的警徽，"我是纽约市警察局的弗兰克·科斯特洛警探。"

说完，科斯特洛警探向帕克博士点了点头，

---

1. 英美制长度单位，1 码 =0.9144 米。——编者

帕克博士就朝着拖车走去。丁丁看到他拿出一把剪刀，从奥利的前肢上剪下几根毛发，又走回了车库。

弗罗斯特警探从她的衣服兜里拿出一个塑料袋，丁丁认出里面装着的是那张宝丽来快照。

她对哈维说："我确信我们能在这张照片上找到你们的指纹，还认得吗？"

哈维低头看了一眼照片，丁丁看到他的喉结上下起伏着。他说："那又怎样？有什么大不了的？有照片怎么了？这种照片我多的是。"

"问题是你不该有这张照片。"科斯特洛警探

说,"你教你的猩猩偷了这张照片里的画。"

哈维自鸣得意地笑了,露出一颗金牙,他说:"我就一个词送给你们,证据,你们有证据吗?"

这时,帕克博士走回人群中,他说:"我们有证据。毛发比对成功了,我刚从奥利身上剪下的毛发和邓肯先生家厨房里发现的一样,并且它们和孩子们在公寓楼前发现的毛发是一样的。"

"谢谢你,帕克博士。"弗罗斯特警探说完看着哈维夫妇,"你们两个因重大盗窃罪被捕。"

"我们什么都没偷,你不能证明我们偷了!"哈维·福勒嚷嚷着,"如果奥利拿了什么愚蠢的画,这跟我有什么关系?"

"放弃吧。"金妮·福勒对丈夫叹了口气,"全都完了。"

她转向弗罗斯特警探,说道:"你说得没错。哈维的堂兄在巴黎的一家保险公司工作,上周,他为一幅莫奈的画办理了保险。当他看到这幅画要运往纽约时,他拍了一张快照,连同画的收件地址一起寄给了我们。"

"金妮,闭嘴!"哈维大喊着,"我们会脱困的，我还有一个堂弟是律师。"

福勒夫人没理她的丈夫，接着说："不管怎么说，当哈维看到邓肯先生住的公寓楼后面的阳台时，他就计划好了训练奥利爬上去偷画，这幅画现在就藏在拖车里。"

科斯特洛警探和弗罗斯特警探给他们戴上手铐，然后大家一起向拖车走去。

这辆拖车有两个隔间，奥利坐在一边，正透过铁网凝视着外面。另一边的波莉正站在那里大嚼干草，它似乎对人类世界正在发生的事情不感兴趣。

"画究竟在哪儿？"弗罗斯特警探问金妮·福勒。

"奥利的笼子底部有个活动底板。"福勒夫人说，"你可以在垫着的稻草下面找到一个把手。"

科斯特洛警探看着乔希："孩子，你愿意爬进去吗？"

乔希深呼吸了一口气："嗯，当然！它不会伤害我的，对吧？"

金妮对乔希笑了笑："尽管去吧，奥利喜欢小孩。"

弗罗斯特警探打开拖车后门，乔希小心翼翼

橙色怪盗

地爬了进去。奥利拖着脚步走了过来,嗅了嗅乔希的头发。

乔希挪开一些稻草,找到了一个又小又圆的把手。他用力一拉,那块活动底板就被掀了起来。

就在这时,一辆出租车停在拖车旁边,一个留着棕色络腮胡的矮个子男人下了车,他说:"沃

伦,这些人都是谁?发生什么事了?"

沃伦伯伯握着福雷斯特·埃文斯的手,说:"欢迎回家,福雷斯特。给我们沏壶茶,我们好好给你说说这整件事!"

橙色怪盗

"他们会怎么处置奥利?它不会坐牢的,对吗?"露丝问道,他们坐在出租车里,沃伦伯伯正开车在回城的路上。

沃伦伯伯摇了摇头:"不会的。帕克博士会把奥利送到婆罗洲去,那里有专门训练猩猩野外生存能力的基地。从现在起,奥利将过上安全、幸福的生活。"

"那波莉呢?"丁丁问。

"它可能有些麻烦。"沃伦伯伯说,"帕克博士一直找不到愿意领养一匹十岁小马的人。"

"我知道谁想要一匹十岁的小马。"露丝说,"我!"

"你?"乔希说,"你要把它养在哪里?"

"我不知道。要是我认识一个家里有谷仓的人就好了!"露丝说着,还用胳膊肘轻轻推了推乔希。

乔希笑着说:"哦,我知道了。好吧,我会问问我的爸爸妈妈,波莉是否可以养在我们家的谷仓里。不过,我的弟弟们也许会想骑它。"

"我的弟弟也会。"露丝说,"我们可以共同拥有波莉,这样我们就都可以骑它了!"

乔希向前俯身拍了拍丁丁的头:"打扫马厩的任务就交给小丁啦!"

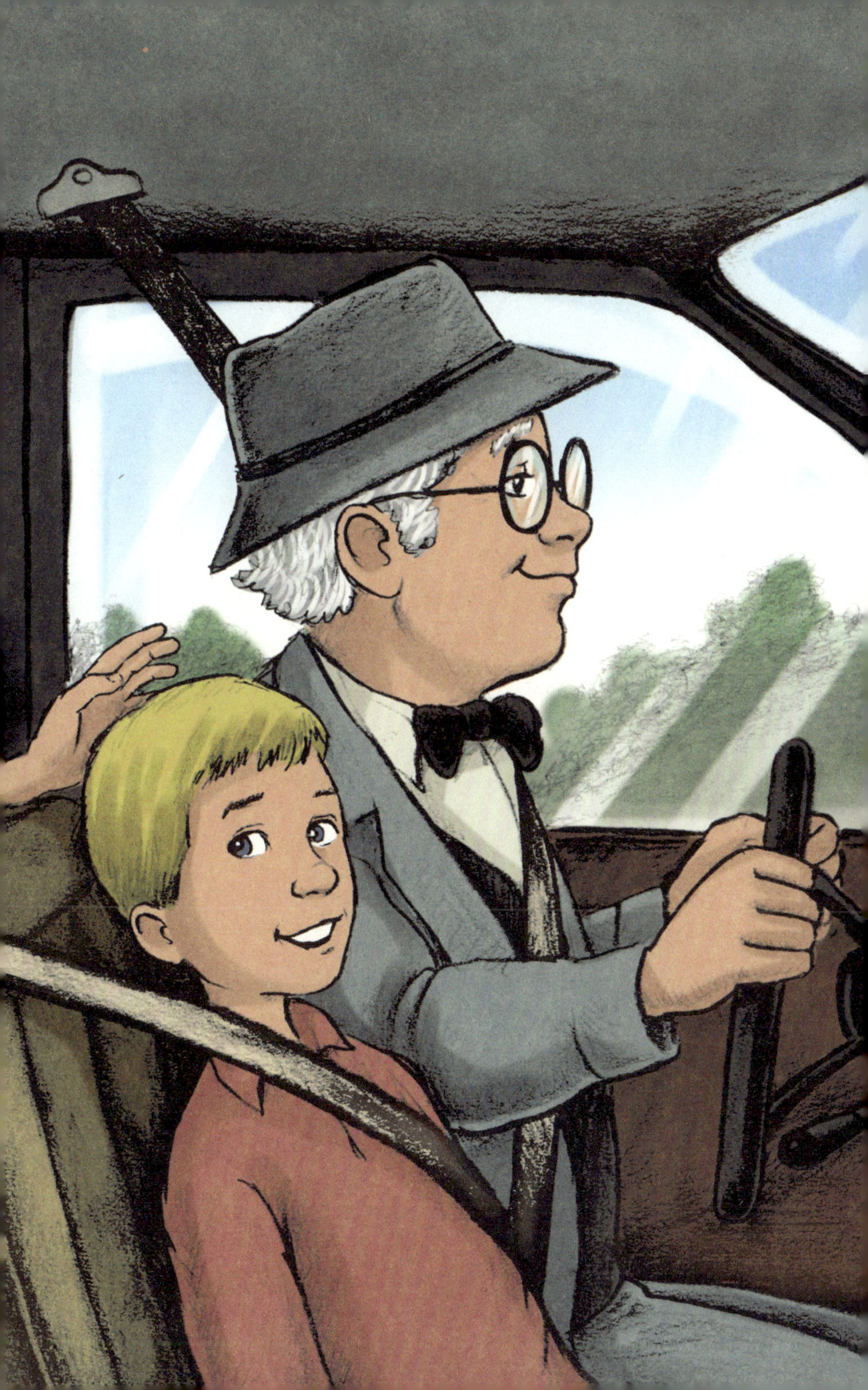

A to Z Mysteries®

The Orange Outlaw

by Ron Roy

illustrated by
John Steven Gurney

MASTER BEDROOM
ENTRY
DINING ROOM
KITCHEN
ORANGES
BATHROOM
BATHROOM
STUDY
LIVING ROOM
GUEST BEDROOM
PAINTING
BALCONY
UNCLE WARREN'S APARTMENT
UNCLE WARREN'S BUILDING
BLOCK PARTY
110th STREET

Welcome to
A to Z Mysteries
on Location at New York City
TO
GREEN LAWN, CT
CT
NY
HUDSON RIVER
OSSINING
NJ
LARCHMONT
NEW YORK CITY
LONG ISLAND
N
W
E
S

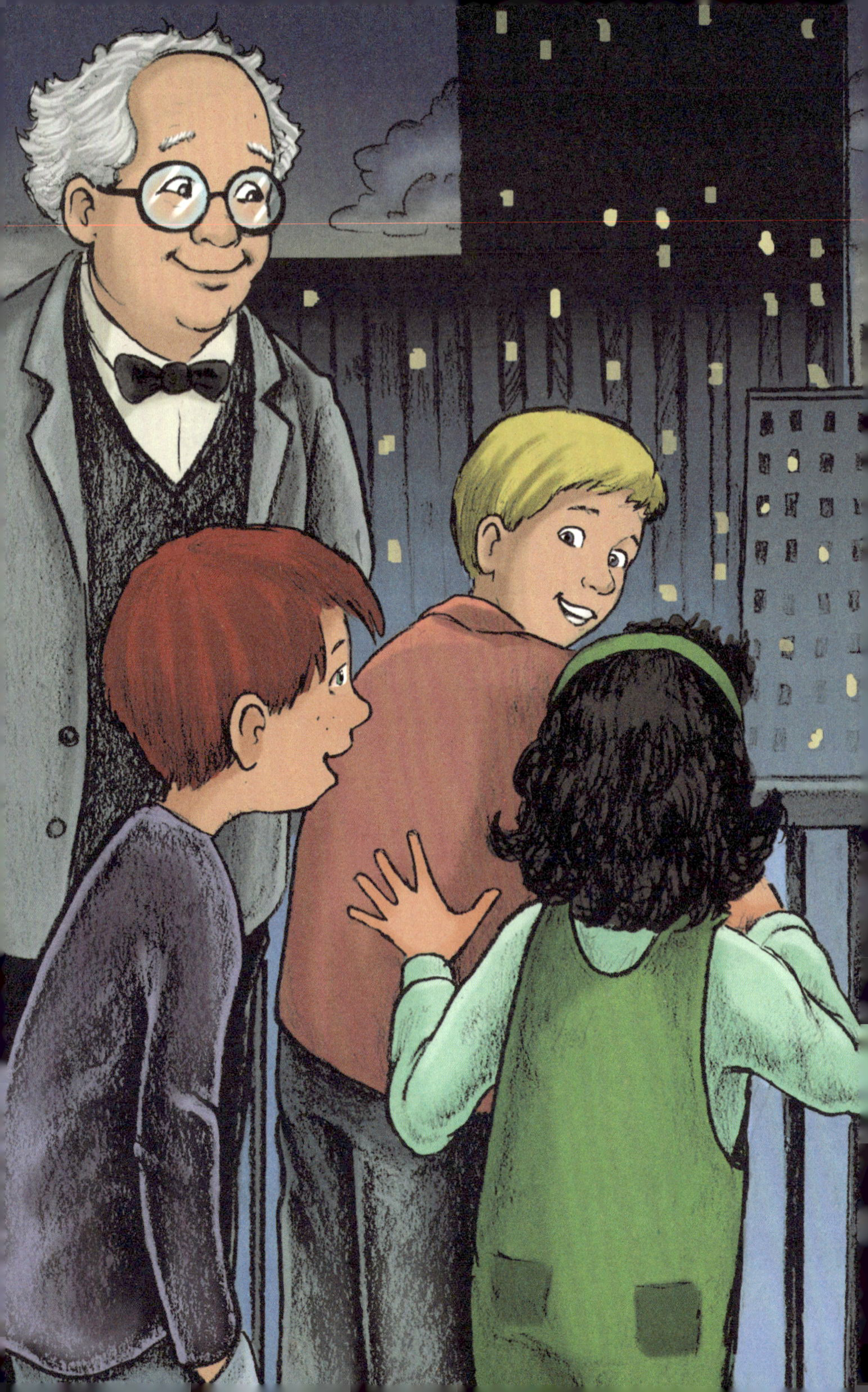

CHAPTER 1

Dink, Josh, and Ruth Rose stood on Uncle Warren's balcony. Nine floors below, the cars, buses, and taxis of New York City zoomed by.

As dusk turned to night, the city's lights began to blink on. People were strolling to restaurants and theaters.

Dink's uncle stepped onto the balcony. "That's a pretty sight, isn't it?" he said.

"It's great," Dink said. "I feel like an eagle up here."

"Thanks for inviting us for the weekend," Josh told him.

"You are entirely welcome, my boy," Uncle Warren said.

"And thanks for inviting us to your block party," Ruth Rose said. "I've never been to one before."

Josh let out a chuckle. "My little brothers have block parties all the time," he said. "They bring their blocks out to the sandbox and throw them at each other."

Uncle Warren laughed. "In New York City, we often have parties where everyone on the block is invited," he explained. "Tonight we plan to raise money for the Central Park Zoo."

"Why does the zoo need money?" asked Ruth Rose.

"Some of the animals need more space," Uncle Warren said.

"Can they make all that money from one party?" Josh asked, gazing down at the street.

"Tonight is just the beginning," Uncle Warren said. "The zoo will be raising money for at least a year."

He looked at his watch. "We'd better get going. But first, I want to show you something."

The kids followed Dink's uncle through the living room to a small study at the back of the apartment. The room held a desk, a chair, and tall shelves crammed with books.

On the desk lay a painting of a rowboat floating on a pond.

"Do you like it?" Uncle Warren asked.

"It's pretty," Ruth Rose said. "I like the flowers on the water."

"Those are lily pads," Uncle Warren said. "This was painted a long time ago by a man named Claude Monet. It's very valuable."

"Is the painting yours?" Dink asked.

"I wish it were, Donny," his uncle said. "My friend

87

A to Z 神秘案件

Forest Evans just bought it vacationing in France. He shipped it to me for safekeeping. He'll collect this beauty when he returns to New York in a couple of days."

Uncle Warren looked at his watch. "It's time to go downstairs," he said. "Help me shut off a few lights."

The kids walked around switching off lights.

"Leave the one over the kitchen table on!" Dink's uncle called.

橙色怪盗

In the kitchen, a hanging light shone down on a wooden bowl filled with oranges. Dink was tempted to take one but decided to wait till later.

They left the apartment and Uncle Warren locked the door. Then they crossed the hall and crowded into the small elevator. Dink pushed the button that said LOBBY.

"What happens to all the cars when you have a block party?" Josh asked as they rode down.

"The police seal off the street," Uncle Warren explained. "You'll see."

A minute later, they left the elevator, crossed the lobby, and walked to the front door.

"Hello, kids," said Roger, the doorman. He looked like royalty in his crisp uniform and pointy mustache. "The block party sure has drawn a lot of people!"

"Are you going?" Ruth Rose asked him.

He shook his head. "Afraid not, missy. I have to stay at the door. But I'll be able to see a lot from here. Have fun! I hear there'll be lots of good stuff to eat."

"Awesome!" Josh said, rubbing his belly.

89

"Still hungry, Josh?" Uncle Warren asked. "Didn't I feed you enough?"

Josh grinned. "That was two hours ago!"

"Josh is like a baby wolf," Ruth Rose said. "He needs to eat ten times a day."

The kids and Uncle Warren walked outside.

It was a warm night in June, and the street was crowded. Music, voices, and food smells filled the air.

"This is so cool, Uncle Warren," Dink said. "We're standing right where cars and buses usually drive!"

"Yes," Uncle Warren said, "and tomorrow morning, they'll be back."

"Evening, Mr. Duncan." a woman behind them said. She was stooped and had a lined face and wild orange hair.

"Hello, Miss Booker," Uncle Warren said. "You haven't met my nephew Donny and his friends, have you? Kids, Miss Booker is the building manager."

The kids each said hello and shook Miss Booker's hand. She was wearing a raincoat even though the sky was clear.

"A pleasure," the woman said. "Enjoy the party."

She turned around and entered the building. Through the glass door, Dink saw her talk to Roger. After a minute, she walked toward the elevator.

"What does a building manager do?" Josh asked.

"Many things," Uncle Warren said. "She fixes leaky faucets, calls electricians, and makes sure the building is kept clean. She'll even deliver packages to my door so Roger doesn't have to leave his station."

"Does she live here, like you?" Ruth Rose asked.

Uncle Warren nodded. "Miss Booker has a small apartment in the basement," he said.

Suddenly, Josh stopped dead in his tracks. "You guys aren't gonna believe this," he said, "but I just saw a flying watermelon!"

CHAPTER 2

Josh led the group over to a guy juggling fruit. Big fruit! A watermelon, a grapefruit, a cantaloupe, and a pineapple circled through the air over the man's head.

"My mother would tell him not to play with his food," Josh whispered.

A boy a little taller than Dink stood in front of the man. "Ready, Dad?" he asked.

When the man nodded, the kid tossed a bunch of bananas into the air.

Everyone watching said, "Ooooooh!" as the bananas joined the rest of the fruit.

Not far from the juggler, the kids noticed a man in a hat and vest leading a pony around a ring. Suddenly,

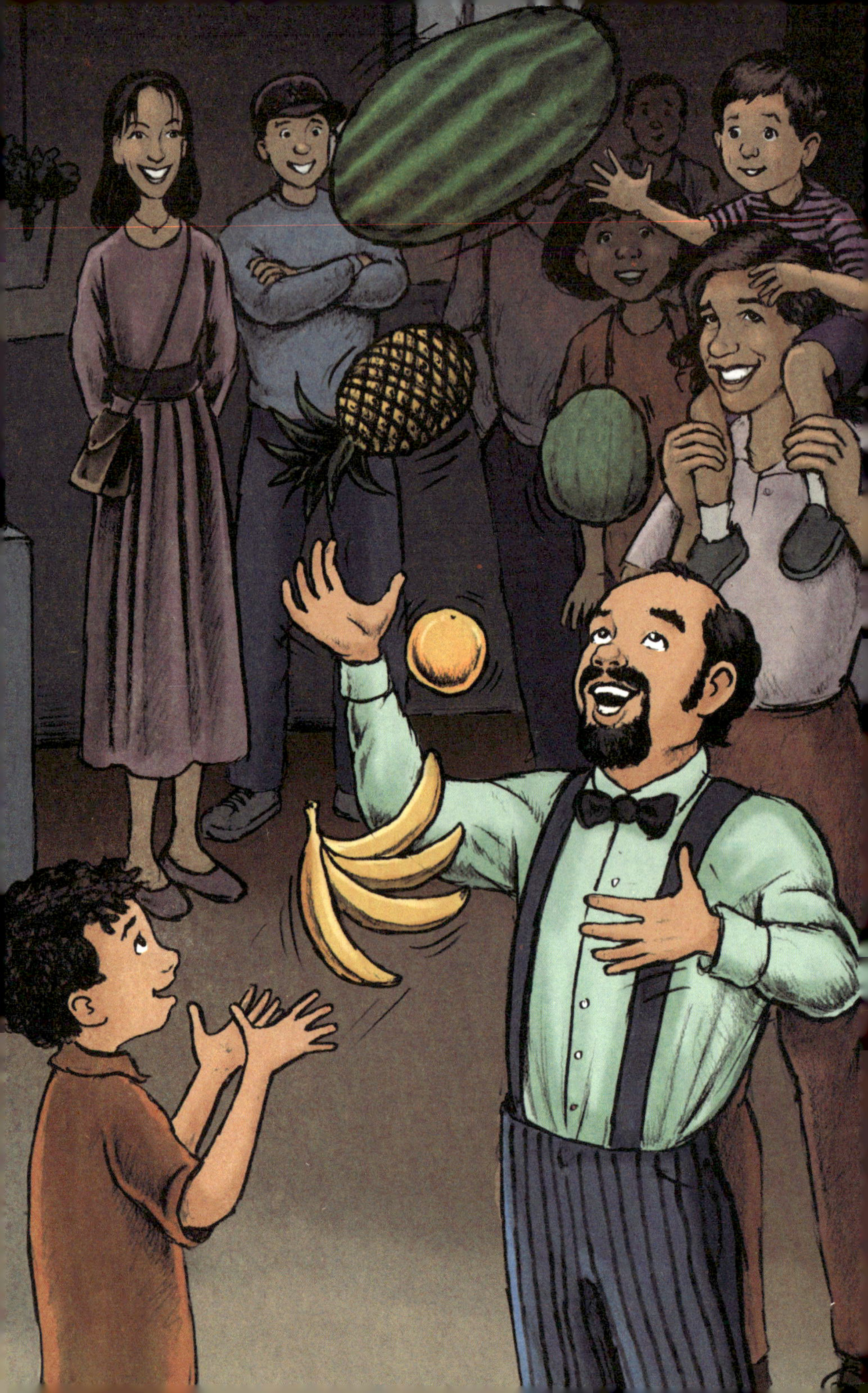

an orangutan dressed as a clown leaped onto the pony. The ape stood on his head as the pony galloped faster and faster.

While everyone cheered, a woman also wearing a hat and vest passed out flyers. Dink took one and stuck it in his pocket.

The man clapped his hands, and the pony jumped

into a trailer with the ape still on its back.

Josh started down the street. "Look at the dummy!" he said.

"Takes one to know one," Dink said, grinning at Josh.

"I think he means the wooden one," Ruth Rose said.

On a small stage sat a man with a wooden doll on his lap. The two were talking to each other.

"I'm hungry!" the dummy said. His hinged mouth opened and closed as he spoke, and his bright eyes moved from side to side.

"Go to sleep," the man answered in a deeper voice.

"Feed me, or I'll report you for dummy abuse!" the dummy said.

"How do they do that?" Josh asked.

The man's voice seemed to be coming out of the dummy's mouth.

The man pulled a cookie from an open bag at his feet. He grinned at the audience and ate it.

"Hey, gimme one of those!" his dummy yelled.

"No."

"Yes!"

"No," the man said. "You've already had dessert."

"Gimme a cookie, or I stop talking," the dummy said.

The audience laughed.

The man sighed and rolled his eyes. "Oh, all right. But just one."

The man reached down and took a second cookie from the bag. He put it in the dummy's mouth. "There, happy now?"

The dummy chewed, swallowed, and burped. The audience loved it. "Thank you," the dummy said to the man.

"You're welcome," the man said. Holding the dummy in his arms, he stood up and bowed.

"Hey, mister. Where'd that cookie go?" Josh called out.

The man smiled at Josh. "Down into his wooden tummy!"

Josh laughed. He turned to Dink, Ruth Rose, and Uncle Warren. "That dummy made me hungry," he said.

"How about some pizza?" Uncle Warren asked. "I

think I noticed a vendor selling slices."

The four walked to the pizza stand and bought slices. They ate them as they enjoyed more of the block party.

When Dink started yawning, his uncle led the group back to the building. Roger was standing just inside the lobby door.

"Did you have a good time?" he asked.

"It was great," Dink said.

"I think the evening will be a big success," Uncle Warren said. "Good night, Roger."

"I sure hope so," Roger said. "Night, Mr. Duncan."

Uncle Warren pushed the button to call the elevator. A minute later, they entered his apartment.

"Why don't you kids get ready for bed, and then we can see what's on TV?" he suggested, heading for his study.

Just as Ruth Rose picked up her backpack, they heard Dink's uncle shout.

The kids ran down the hall and practically bumped into Uncle Warren. His face was white, and he looked sick.

"Uncle Warren, what's the matter?" Dink asked.

"The...the painting," Dink's uncle stammered. "Someone's stolen Forest's painting!"

CHAPTER 3

Dink looked past his uncle into the study. The painting was gone.

"I've got to call the police," Uncle Warren said. He hurried toward the kitchen, leaving the kids standing in the hallway.

"Who could have taken it?" Ruth Rose asked.

"And how?" wondered Josh. "The door was locked."

"Kids, come quickly!" Dink's uncle yelled from the other end of the apartment.

They ran back down the hallway and into the kitchen.

"Look at that!" Uncle Warren said, pointing at the kitchen table.

The tabletop was littered with orange juice and peels. The fruit bowl was overturned. More peels and dribbles of juice covered the floor.

"Yuck, it's all sticky!" Josh said, backing away from a small puddle.

"This is terrible!" Uncle Warren said as he called the police.

"Guys, look!" Ruth Rose was pointing to an orange peel near the balcony.

The kids walked over, and Ruth Rose opened the balcony door. "There's juice on the door handle, too," she said, wiping her hand on her jeans.

They found more orange peels on the balcony.

101

"Guy must've been hungry," Josh observed.

Dink looked down over the balcony railing. "Could this be how the thief got into the apartment?" he asked.

"How?" Josh asked. "On a hang glider? Dink, we're ten stories up, remember?"

Uncle Warren joined them. "A detective will be here soon," he said. Then he noticed the orange peels all over the balcony. "Goodness!"

The kids started to pick up the orange peels.

"Leave them," Uncle Warren said. "The police said not to touch anything."

They walked into the living room and sat down to wait.

"Forest will be devastated," Uncle Warren said. "Thank goodness he had the painting insured! At least he'll get his money back."

Suddenly, Roger's voice came over the small speaker next to the door. "Mr. Duncan, there's a detective here to see you. Shall I send him up?"

Uncle Warren jumped up and ran to the door. Pressing the TALK button on the speaker, he said, "Thank you, Roger." Then he opened the door and walked into the hall.

The kids sat on the sofa staring at the front door. After a few moments, they heard the elevator door open. Dink's uncle said, "Yes, this is the place. I'm Warren Duncan."

Uncle Warren walked back in, followed by a tall man wearing a dark suit and tie.

"Kids, this is Detective Frank Costello," Dink's uncle said.

The man nodded at the kids, then looked around the room. He had black eyes, dark, swept-back hair, and a nose that looked as if it had been broken.

"Where was the painting?" Detective Costello

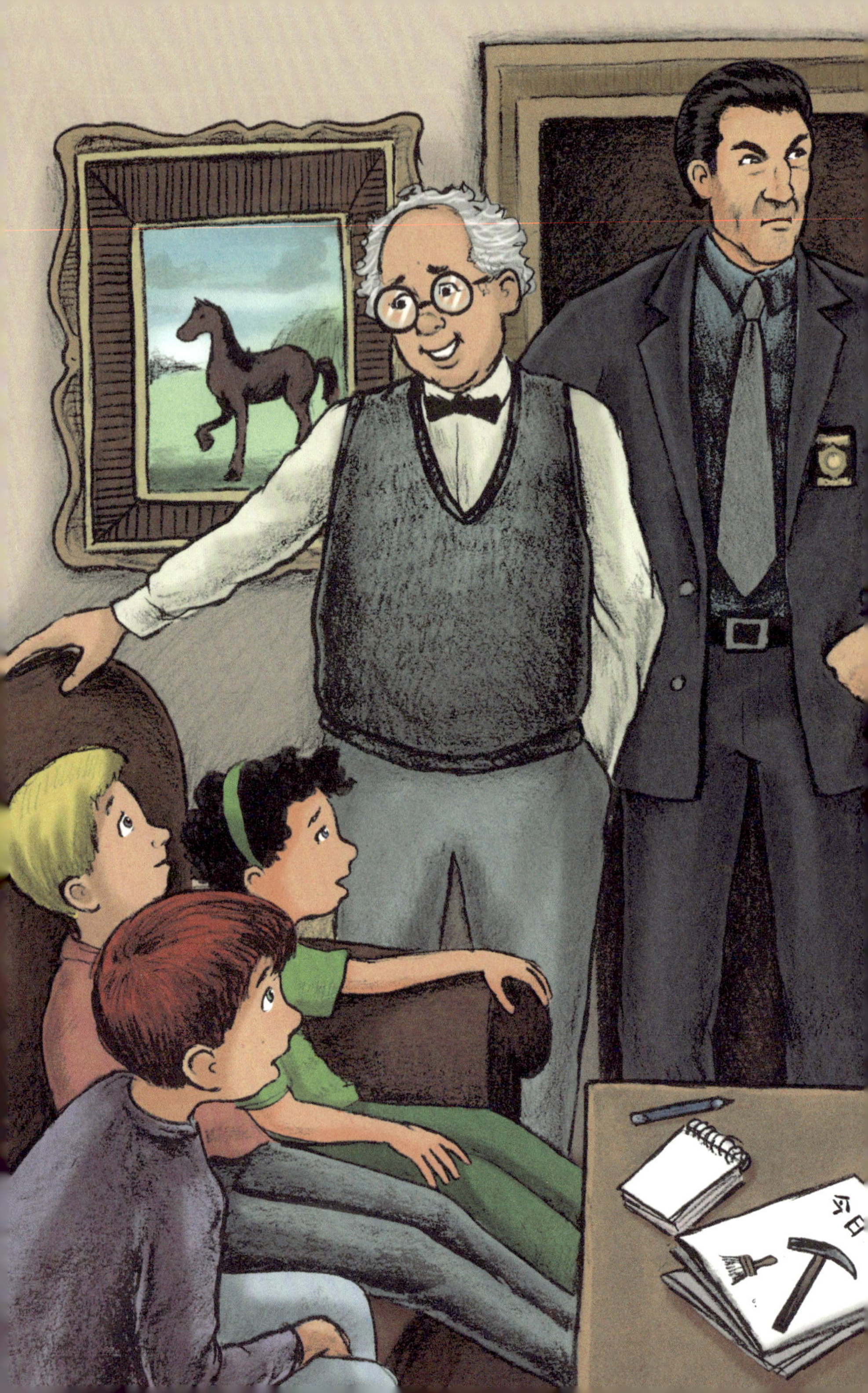

asked.

"Back here," Uncle Warren said, leading him down the hall toward the study.

"Let's go talk to Roger," Ruth Rose said.

"Why?" asked Josh.

"Maybe he saw someone sneaking around," she answered.

"Good idea," Dink said. He grabbed a pad and scribbled a note to his uncle. "Okay, let's go." He and Josh followed Ruth Rose to the elevator.

In the lobby, they found Roger at his desk near the front door. Through the glass, Dink could see that the block party was winding down.

"Going out again?" Roger asked the kids.

Dink shook his head. "Someone stole a valuable painting from my uncle's apartment!" he said.

Roger jumped from his seat. "A theft in our building? I can't believe it!"

"It happened while we were at the block party," Josh said. "The creep ate all the oranges, too!"

"We were wondering if you noticed anyone strange," Ruth Rose put in.

105

Roger shook his head. "I was here the entire time and saw only people who live here," he said. "Absolutely no one else..."

Roger closed his eyes, then opened them slowly. "I just remembered. Mrs. Cornelius on the ninth floor called down about an hour ago. She thought she saw someone on her balcony. I offered to go up and check, but she said not to bother."

"Is her balcony below Dink's uncle's?" Ruth Rose asked.

Roger nodded. "All the balconies on the rear of the building are directly above or below each other."

Ruth Rose looked at Dink and Josh. "Then maybe she saw the thief!"

CHAPTER 4

Dink explained about the orange peels they'd found on his uncle's balcony.

Roger shook his head. "But how would a thief climb the building?" he asked.

"Why don't we go outside and take a look?" Josh suggested. "Maybe we'll find a clue."

"Kids, it's pretty late," Roger said. "Perhaps you should wait till tomorrow..."

"We'll only stay a minute," Dink said.

"Well, okay." Roger directed them to a metal door around the corner from the elevator.

Dink slid back a long bolt and shoved the door open. They walked out into a narrow, well-lit space behind the building. It was completely enclosed except for an alley that led to the street. Next to the building, a Dumpster sat in the shadows.

"I wonder," Ruth Rose said, staring at the Dumpster. "What if the thief climbed on top of that? Could he reach the first balcony?"

Dink stared up. "The first two floors don't have balconies," he observed. "Even standing on the Dumpster, I don't see how the crook could have gotten up or down this way."

"Then he had to go through the front door," Josh said. "But if Roger didn't see him..."

Just then, an angry voice came out of the darkness. "What are you doing back here? This is private property!" "Who... who's there?" Dink asked.

A figure walked out of the shadows. It was Miss Booker. She didn't look happy to see them.

"It's just us," Dink said. "My uncle is Mr. Duncan. We met you at the block party earlier tonight."

The woman stopped a few feet from the kids. Her hands were jammed into her coat pockets. She wore a cap pulled down over her orange hair. "Why are you kids out here?" she asked.

"There was a robbery in my uncle's apartment," Dink said.

Miss Booker nodded. "I know. Roger just told me."

"We thought the crook might have come this way," Ruth Rose said.

"Yeah," Josh said, "except he'd have to have wings."

Miss Booker looked up the side of the building. She touched the bricks with a long finger. "A few years ago, I could've climbed this no problem," she said.

The kids stared at the woman.

Miss Booker smiled. "When I was your age, my father and mother owned a carnival. My brothers did the high wire act. They were known as the Flying Bookers. I was the girl on the trapeze."

"Um, did you happen to see anyone in the alley?" Dink asked.

Miss Booker shook her head. "The alley was blocked off," she said.

"Blocked off? How?" Ruth Rose asked.

"I'll show you." The kids followed Miss Booker down the alley toward the front of the building.

"Right here," Miss Booker said, stopping where

the alley met the street. "There was a trailer parked here during the block party."

"A trailer?" Dink asked, trying to remember.

Just then, Roger opened the front door and leaned out. "Donald, your uncle wants you and your friends to come upstairs," he said.

"Okay, we'll be right in," Dink said. "Good night, Miss Booker. Maybe we'll see you tomorrow."

"Maybe you will," the woman said. Then she turned and walked back down the dark alley.

CHAPTER 5

When the kids stepped out of the elevator, Uncle Warren was waiting in the hallway. "Thank you for leaving me a note, but it's past your bedtime, Donny."

"Is the detective still here?" Dink asked.

"No, he left a few minutes ago," his uncle said. "He checked for fingerprints and took samples of the orange peels and juice."

They walked into the kitchen. The orange peels were gone, but the floor was still sticky. Patches of white fingerprint powder made blotches on the counter and kitchen table. The empty fruit bowl was in the sink.

"Do you know Mrs. Cornelius?" Dink asked his uncle.

Uncle Warren smiled. "A lot of people know Corinne Cornelius," he said. "She was a Broadway actress years ago. She lives in the apartment right below this one. We have tea together all the time. Why do you ask?"

Dink told his uncle what they'd learned from Roger. "Mrs. Cornelius might have seen the thief on her balcony," he said. "Maybe she can tell us what he looks like!"

"Donny, Mrs. Cornelius is quite old," his uncle said. "And I'm afraid her eyesight is failing."

Uncle Warren looked around his kitchen and sighed. "I should clean up, but I'm exhausted. This mess will have to wait till morning," he said. "Now off to bed, kiddos."

"We'll help you tomorrow," Ruth Rose said.

"Thank you, my dear. Sweet dreams, everyone," Uncle Warren said as he padded toward his bedroom.

"I don't know about you guys," Ruth Rose said, "but I couldn't sleep a wink right now."

"Me either," Dink said. The three headed for the living room. Ruth Rose sat next to Dink on the sofa, and Josh plopped down on the carpet.

"I've been thinking," Ruth Rose said. "How many people knew your uncle had a valuable painting in his apartment?"

"Roger might have known about it," Dink said.

Josh sat up. "Of course!" he said. "*Roger's* the crook!"

"But he was at the door all night," Dink said.

"That's what he told us," Ruth Rose said. "He could have been lying. Does Roger have the key to this apartment?"

"Guys, my uncle and Roger are friends," Dink protested. "Plus, he's worked in this building for ages."

"Don't you watch TV?" Josh asked, wiggling his eyebrows up and down. "The butler—I mean, the doorman—did it!"

Dink laughed. "You're crazy. No way Roger snuck up here and stole that painting."

Josh got up and walked into the kitchen. Dink heard the refrigerator door open and close.

"Well, who else knew about it?" Ruth Rose asked.

113

A to Z 神秘案件

"How about Miss Booker?" Josh said when he came back. He was carrying a handful of grapes. "She told us she used to swing on a trapeze. Maybe she climbs buildings now. Plus, she knew we were all out of the apartment during the block party."

Ruth Rose nodded. "She's the building manager, so I'll bet she has keys to all the apartments. She wouldn't have to climb the building!"

"But how would she know my uncle even had the painting?" Dink asked.

"Dink, remember your uncle said one of Miss Booker's jobs is delivering packages?" Ruth Rose said. "Maybe she brought the painting up to your uncle. He might have told her what was inside the wrapping."

"And she might have told Roger," Josh said. "Heck, maybe they did it together. Roger could've been the lookout while she was up here stealing the painting!"

"And tossing orange peels all over the place?" Dink said. "Wouldn't that be kind of dumb?"

"Maybe she did that on purpose," Ruth Rose said. "Leaving orange peels on the balcony would make it look like the crook climbed down the building."

"Yeah," Josh said, "and that would make us think it was someone who didn't have keys."

"Okay, but what about the juice all over the kitchen?" Dink asked. "Why would Miss Booker do that?"

"Easy," Josh said, "she wanted to confuse the cops."

Dink yawned, then stood up and stretched. "Well, whoever it was did a good job confusing me!"

He walked out to the balcony and looked up at the stars. High in the sky, he made out the blinking lights on an airplane. He wondered where the plane was coming from.

Josh and Ruth Rose came and stood next to him.

"I thought of someone else who might have known about the painting," Ruth Rose said.

"Who?" Dink asked.

"Mrs. Cornelius," she answered.

Dink stared at her. "But she's old and can't see well," he said. "My uncle told us that a little while ago."

"He also told us she used to be an actress," Ruth Rose said.

"Besides," Josh added, "you don't need perfect eyesight to steal a painting."

"But if Mrs. Cornelius is the crook, why would she tell Roger she saw someone on her balcony?"

"Maybe she did it to keep anyone from suspecting her," Ruth Rose said.

Dink thought for a moment. "Okay, but how would she get into my uncle's apartment? Or are you going to tell me she swung up on a vine, like Tarzan?"

Josh laughed. "I don't know. Maybe she stole a spare key when she was here having tea," he said. "But I say we go have a talk with Mrs. Cornelius tomorrow morning."

CHAPTER 6

"Josh, wake up."

Dink shook Josh's shoulder, then yanked the covers off him. "Come on, help me clean the kitchen before my uncle gets up."

Josh mumbled something and pulled the covers back over himself.

"He made us breakfast...," Dink said.

Josh shot out of the bed, tripping over his sneakers as he charged into the kitchen.

Ruth Rose was already there, washing the fruit bowl.

"I don't see any food," Josh grumbled.

"No, but you will after we get this mess cleaned up," Dink told him. "Blueberry pancakes are my uncle's specialty."

Josh dropped into a chair. "I've been lied to," he mumbled.

"Come on, Josh," Dink said. "If we work together, we can have this done in ten minutes."

"I'll wash the floor," Ruth Rose said, dragging a mop from a closet.

Dink handed Josh a damp sponge. "While you're sitting there, wipe the chairs and tabletop."

"I thought we were going to talk to Mrs. Cornelius this morning," Josh said, giving the table a fast swipe.

"We are." Dink opened his uncle's address book. "I'm calling her right now."

When Dink had Mrs. Cornelius on the line, he introduced himself and asked if they could visit her for a few minutes. He thanked her and hung up.

"We can go down as soon as we're done cleaning up," he said. "Let's get to work!"

Dink turned the radio on low, and they cleaned to country songs.

"Hey, look what I found!" Josh said. He held up a long orange hair. "It was caught on the back of this chair."

Dink and Ruth Rose walked over and studied the hair. "Looks like one of yours, Josh," Ruth Rose said.

"Is not," Josh said. "My hair is red, not this orange color. And mine's a lot cleaner!"

Ruth Rose took the hair and held it up to the light. "Miss Booker has orange hair," she said.

"We can check her out later," Dink said. He folded the hair inside a paper towel and stuck it in his pocket. "Let's finish up and go see Mrs. Cornelius."

Ten minutes later, the kids quietly left the apartment. They found the stairs and walked down one floor. Dink knocked on Mrs. Cornelius's door.

It was opened by a woman who had white hair and was wearing a fuzzy robe. Behind thick eyeglasses, her pale blue eyes looked huge.

"Good morning!" Mrs. Cornelius chirped. "I see I'm not the only one who likes to get up with the birds. Come in, come in!"

Using a cane, she led them into a cheerful living room. "Please sit on the sofa, where I can see you," she said.

The kids lined up on the sofa. Mrs. Cornelius sat opposite them. She leaned close and studied their faces.

"Now tell me why three children have come to visit an old lady like me," she said.

Dink told Mrs. Cornelius about the stolen painting.

"Goodness!" she said. "I always miss the excitement. When did it happen, dear?"

"Last night, during the block party," Ruth Rose

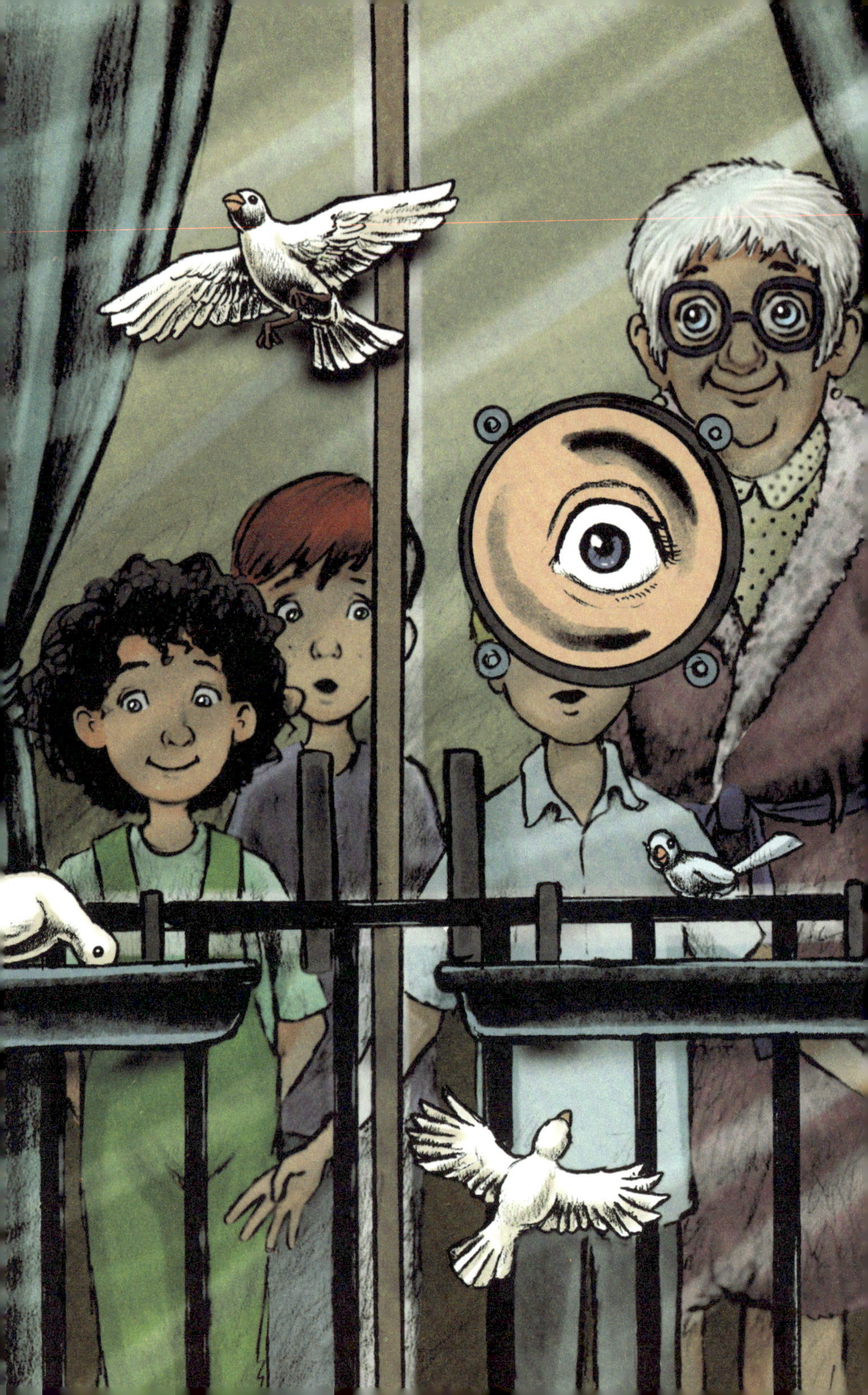

said.

Mrs. Cornelius clapped her hands.

"That prowler I saw on my balcony must have been the thief!" she said. "I'm a witness!"

"Um, we were wondering if you could tell us what happened."

Using her cane for support, Mrs. Cornelius stood up. "Come with me." She walked to her balcony. "Pull those drapes, dear," she said to Josh.

When the drapes were opened, the kids looked out onto the balcony. It was just like Uncle Warren's, except that several bird feeders were attached to the balcony railing.

"I love to feed the birds, but I have trouble seeing them," Mrs. Cornelius said. "That's why I bought this!"

She pointed to a round magnifying glass about the size of a pie plate. It was stuck to the inside of the balcony's glass door.

Dink looked curiously through the magnifying glass. "Wow, everything looks bigger!" he said.

"Isn't it fun?" Mrs. Cornelius said. "I heard a noise

last night, so I walked over and peeked through the drapes. Someone was on the balcony!"

"What did he look like?" Dink asked.

"I thought you'd never ask," Mrs. Cornelius said. She took a pad out of the pocket of her robe and handed it to Dink.

Written in large, spidery letters were the words:

a baggy coat
very poor posture
wrinkled face

Dink gulped when he read the last two words:

orange hair

CHAPTER 7

"Still think the crook is Mrs. Cornelius?" Dink asked as they walked back up to the tenth floor.

"Mrs. Cornelius's description sure does sound like Miss Booker," Ruth Rose admitted.

Dink laughed. "Bad posture, baggy clothes, orange hair—sounds more like Josh!"

He opened the door to his uncle's apartment.

"There you are," Uncle Warren said. "Thank you for cleaning up. What a lovely surprise! Ready for blueberry pancakes?"

"I am!" Josh said, heading for the kitchen.

After taking his first bite of pancake, Dink reached into his pocket for the folded paper towel. He pulled out the orange hair and showed it to his uncle.

"Josh found this stuck to one of the chairs," he said. "We think it came from the crook."

Dink's uncle studied the hair. "This is odd-looking. Wait, I'll be back in a jiffy," he said.

The kids heard cupboard doors opening and closing. A minute later, Dink's uncle was back, carrying a small wooden box.

He moved the pancake platter to one side and set the box in its place. Then he pulled off the lid, revealing a shiny microscope. He plugged the microscope's cord into a wall outlet.

"Josh, may I have one of your hairs?" he asked.

"Sure." Josh grimaced as he yanked out a hair. Then he passed the hair to Uncle Warren.

Dink's uncle laid both hairs on a glass slide, then placed the slide under the microscope lens. He adjusted the scope and put one eye to it.

"Well, I think it's a real hair," Uncle Warren said after a minute. "But it's very different from yours, Josh. Take a look. Your hair is the one on the right."

Josh bent over the scope. "All I see is nothing," he said.

"Try closing one eye," Uncle Warren said.

"Wow, that's better!" Josh said. "The hairs look like tree trunks!"

Ruth Rose was next. "The hairs do look different," she said. "Look, Dink."

Dink closed one eye and peered through the lens. The hair on the right was thin and smooth-looking. The one on the left was fatter and more orange than the other one.

"Mrs. Cornelius told us she saw someone on her balcony with orange hair," Dink said.

"She did?" Uncle Warren said.

Ruth Rose nodded. "She has this neat magnifying glass attached to her balcony door," she said. "So she can watch the birds at her feeders."

"I looked through it," Dink told his uncle. "It makes stuff look bigger and clearer." He told his uncle how Mrs. Cornelius had described the person on her balcony.

"Baggy coat and poor posture? Well, well. Maybe she really did see our thief!" Uncle Warren said. "I'd better call Detective Costello."

While his uncle dialed the phone, Dink motioned for Josh and Ruth Rose to follow him. They left the apartment, but Dink walked past the elevator.

"Where are we going?" Josh asked. "I wanted a few more of those pancakes."

"Let's walk down," Dink said, shoving open the exit door. "I don't want anyone to see us."

"See us what?" Ruth Rose asked.

"I want to get one of Miss Booker's hairs," Dink said. "And I don't want Roger to see us, just in case they're partners."

"So now you think they did it together?" Josh asked.

"I don't know, but we can't take any chances," Dink said.

"Oh, boy," Josh said, skipping down the stairs.

Dink and Ruth Rose followed Josh. "How do you plan to get a hair?" Ruth Rose asked.

Dink shrugged. "I don't know yet," he admitted.

Out of breath, the kids finally reached the lobby. Dink peeked around the corner to make sure Roger wasn't watching; then they hurried out the rear exit.

They didn't see Miss Booker behind the building. Josh took a look down the alley, but she wasn't there either.

"Let's look out front," Ruth Rose suggested.

Dink and Josh followed Ruth Rose down the alley. They were halfway to the front of the building when Ruth Rose bent down and picked something off the ground.

Dink and Josh caught up and looked over her shoulder.

Ruth Rose was holding a Polaroid snapshot. It was a picture of a framed painting.

Dink gasped when he recognized the rowboat floating on a pond.

"It's a picture of the stolen painting!" he said.

CHAPTER 8

In the photograph, the painting stood on a table. Part of a window was also visible, with buildings in the distance.

Josh asked, "What's this doing in the alley?"

"I think I know," Ruth Rose said. "The thief must have used this picture to identify the painting. After he stole it, he threw the picture away."

"If the thief tossed the picture here, that means he probably did climb down the balconies," Dink said.

"You mean *she*," Josh said.

Ruth Rose shook her head. "But if Miss Booker did it," she asked, "why would she tell us she can climb buildings? Wouldn't that just point the finger at her?"

"Maybe she's giving us false clues," Josh said. "She tells us she can climb the building and drops this picture in the alley. But all the time, she probably just went through the front door with her key."

"No matter who stole the painting," Dink said, "the crook's fingerprints should be on this picture." He carefully slipped the snapshot inside his shirt. "We have to show it to my uncle!"

The kids ran down the alley to the front of the building. Weekend traffic whizzed by. A few people hurried toward the subway stop. A man in gray work clothes was sweeping up litter.

A mound of litter stood at the entrance to the alley. As the kids walked past, Josh accidentally kicked the pile.

"Hey, watch your step there, young fella," said the man with the broom.

"Sorry," Josh said, stepping away from the litter. Using his foot, he scraped the stuff back together.

Then he knelt down and picked something out of the debris. "Hey, guys, look!" Josh held up an orange peel.

The man with the broom chuckled. "There was a block party here last night," he said. "A guy had a trailer with an orangutan and a pony parked right here. Man, that orangutan sure ate a lot of oranges!"

Dink took the peel from Josh and looked at it carefully. Caught in the peel was a long orange hair.

Ruth Rose peered over Dink's shoulder. "It's just like the hair Josh found in the kitchen!" she said.

Josh looked back up the alley. "Guys," he said, "Miss Booker didn't climb up those balconies. That orangutan did!"

Ruth Rose's eyes grew wide. "Orangutans are great climbers!" she said.

"And they have long orange hair and eat fruit!" said Josh.

Dink stared at Josh and Ruth Rose. "You mean you think the orangutan is the thief?"

"Why not?" Josh said. "People train orangutans to do all kinds of stuff. Why couldn't one be taught to steal a painting?"

Dink tapped the snapshot inside his shirt. "If you're right, his fingerprints should be on this," he

133

said.

"Do orangutans even have fingerprints?" Ruth Rose asked.

Dink shrugged. "Whoever gave him the picture would have left his fingerprints, too."

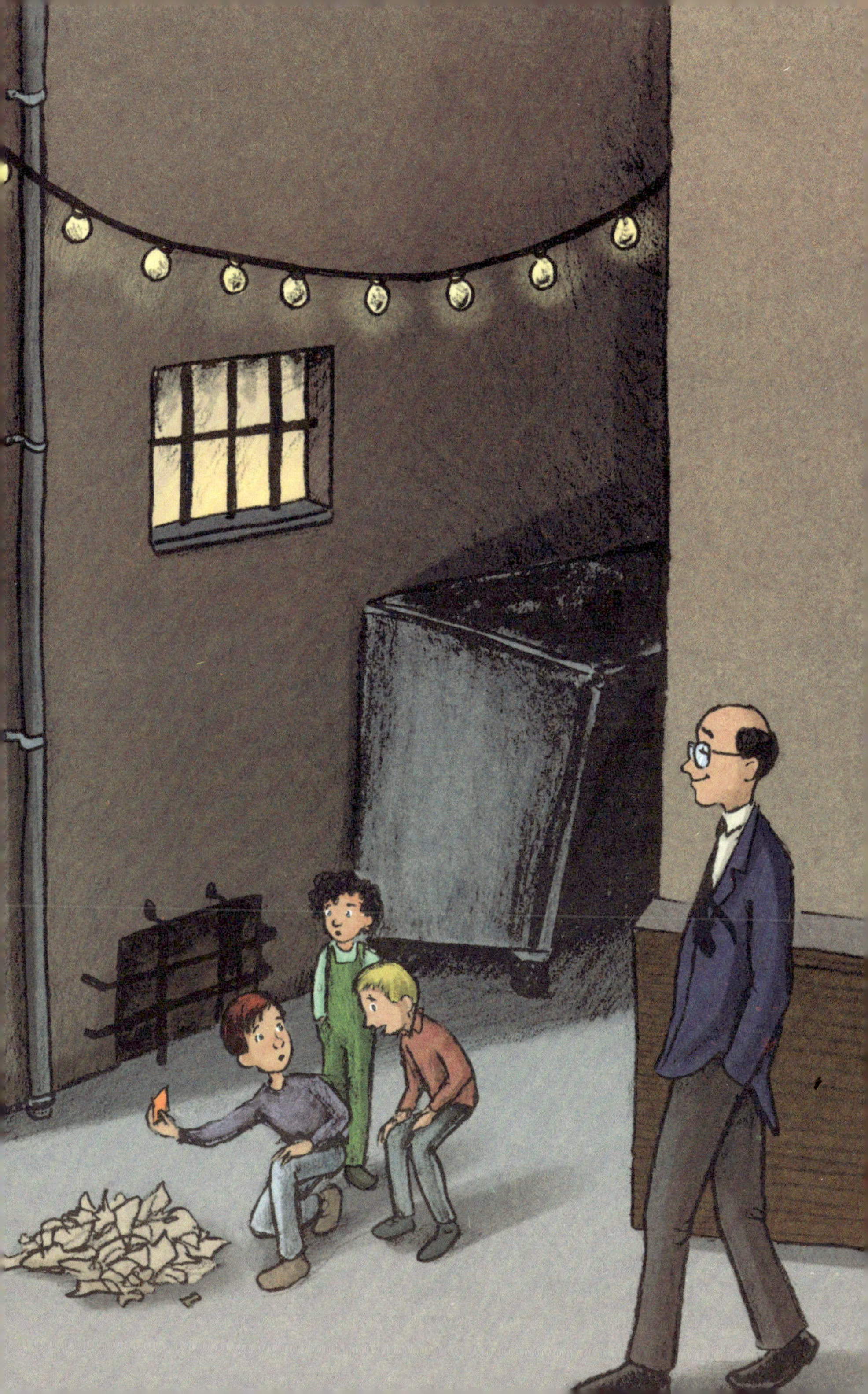

"His trainer!" Josh said.

Ruth Rose nodded. "Yep. The orangutan might have taken the painting, but the real thief is the person who taught him how!"

CHAPTER 9

Uncle Warren was in the kitchen looking glum when Dink, Josh, and Ruth Rose rushed in.

"Forest Evans just called," Uncle Warren said. "He's coming back tomorrow! What will I tell him?"

Dink grinned. "Tell him we know who stole his painting!"

Uncle Warren nearly dropped his coffee cup. "Do you really know, Donny? Who?"

"The orangutan did it!" Josh said.

Interrupting each other, the three kids told Dink's uncle what they thought had happened.

"But how would an ape recognize a valuable Monet?" Uncle Warren asked.

Dink unbuttoned his shirt and carefully placed

the snapshot on the table.

"We think his trainer taught him to recognize the painting," Dink said.

His uncle studied the photograph. "It's Forest's painting, all right," he said. "And look, that's the Eiffel Tower in the background. This picture was taken in Paris!"

Uncle Warren shook his head. "I find this very hard to believe," he said. "An orangutan climbed up to my balcony, ate my oranges, then stole my friend's painting? Incredible!"

"Orangutans are very smart," Josh said. "I saw a nature program about them once. One orangutan learned to count. They taught another one to turn on a VCR and pop in a video!"

Uncle Warren nodded. "I'll give this photo to Detective Costello," he said.

"But how do we find the orangutan's owner?" Ruth Rose asked. "We don't even know his name."

"Wait a minute!" Dink jumped up and ran into the living room. He came back carrying the jeans he'd been wearing the night before.

"I took one of their flyers," he said, digging into the pocket. "Here it is!"

He opened the flyer and spread it on the kitchen table. In large block letters were the words:

FOWLERS' FARM
ANIMAL ACTS OF ALL KINDS
FOR PARTIES AND SCHOOL EVENTS

Below the words was a picture of the man and woman they'd seen the night before. Their names were printed beneath the picture:

HARVEY AND GINNY FOWLER

Beside that picture was another one. In it, the orangutan was riding the pony. The caption said:

OLLIE THE ORANGUTAN
AND POLLY THE PONY!

At the very bottom of the page were a telephone

number and address.

"They live in Ossining, New York," Dink's uncle said. "That's not far from here. Excellent, Donny!"

"Now all we have to do is get that detective to arrest them," Josh said.

"I'm afraid not," Uncle Warren said. "We have no proof that these people trained their animal to steal Forest's painting. We have a lot of theories, a photo, and hairs that might have come from that orangutan. Still, I doubt that's enough for Detective Costello to make an arrest."

"If only we could get Mr. or Mrs. Fowler's fingerprints," Dink said. "Then we could see if they match any of the prints on the snapshot."

"That would be a start," Uncle Warren said, "but still no proof that their animal stole the painting."

"What if we got a hair from Ollie?" Ruth Rose said. "If the hair matched the one we found in the kitchen, wouldn't that prove he was in this apartment?"

Dink's uncle smiled. "I think that would be enough to convince Detective Costello," he said. "But how do we obtain this hair?"

Ruth Rose grinned. "I thought you'd never ask," she said.

CHAPTER 10

Half an hour later, Uncle Warren handed Ruth Rose the telephone. "Good luck," he said.

"Don't worry," Josh said. "She's really good at tricking crooks!"

Ruth Rose smiled into the phone. "Hello, is this Mr. Harvey Fowler? My name is Ruth Rose. My birthday is tomorrow, and my parents want to hire Ollie and Polly. My father is Forest Evans, and he's very rich!"

Two minutes later, she hung up. "They're coming!" she said.

"Do you think Mr. Evans will mind if we use his property?" Dink asked.

His uncle beamed. "He'd love it! I can't wait to tell

him when he returns from Europe."

"How will we get there?" Josh asked. "I've never even heard of Larchmont, New York."

"It's not far, Josh. I'll rent us a car," Uncle Warren said. "Now I have to make a few phone calls. This is going to be such fun!"

Early the next morning, Roger called to let them know the rental car was downstairs.

Ruth Rose was in disguise. She was wearing Uncle Warren's beret and a pair of his glasses.

"You look great!" Dink said. "Mr. Fowler will never remember you from the block party."

Uncle Warren and the kids went downstairs and climbed into the rental car. Dink's uncle drove them out of the city. They saw plenty of traffic and crossed a couple of bridges. Finally, Dink saw a sign that said:

WELCOME TO LARCHMONT

"Almost there," Uncle Warren said. "Forest has a beautiful home and a lot of land."

A few minutes later, he turned into a long driveway

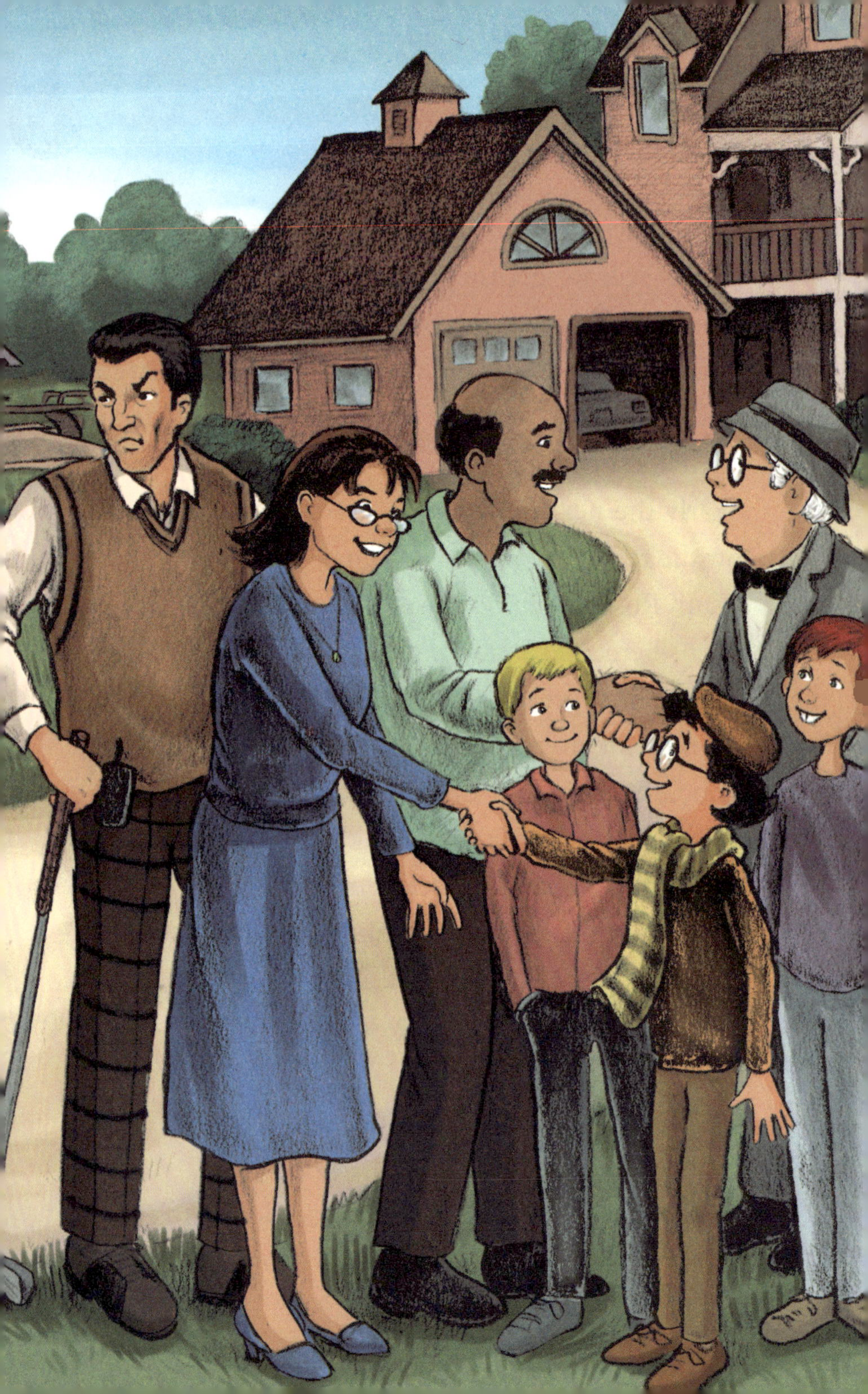

lined with trees. At the end of the driveway stood a large brick house. Behind it, Dink could see a pool and tennis courts.

"Awesome," Josh said.

"Yes, it's lovely out here," Uncle Warren said. "But I'd rather have people around me than trees."

He parked the car, and everyone got out. Two men and a woman walked out of the garage.

Dink recognized Detective Costello but not the other two.

"This is Detective Rita Frost, my partner," Detective Costello said.

"And I'm Dr. Ted Parker," the other man said.

"Dr. Parker is the curator for primates at the Bronx Zoo," Detective Costello explained. "After the arrest, he'll take charge of the animals."

Detective Frost wore a blue dress and heels. She smiled at Ruth Rose. "Are you ready to act like a rich kid?" she asked.

"I'm a little nervous," Ruth Rose said. "What if the Fowlers recognize me?"

"I wouldn't worry about that," the woman said.

"If what you've told us is true, they won't even look at you. He'll be thinking about how to break into this beautiful house."

"Okay, this is the plan," Detective Costello said. "Our backup car will let us know when the Fowlers drive in. Rita and I will pretend to be Mr. and Mrs. Evans. Ruth Rose is our daughter, the one who's having the birthday. Everyone else will stay in the garage until I give the word to come out. Any questions?"

Just then, the cell phone on Detective Costello's belt rang. He answered it, listened, then hung up.

"The Fowlers' trailer just entered the property," he said. "Inside, please, and no talking."

Dink, Josh, Uncle Warren, and Dr.Parker stepped into the garage.

"Good luck," Dink whispered to Ruth Rose.

Ruth Rose gave them a thumbs-up as the garage door came down in front of her.

Two shiny black cars were parked inside the garage. Dink sat on the bumper of one of the cars. He could hear the trailer approaching. Then he heard car doors slamming and some muffled voices.

Josh had his ear to the garage door. He started to giggle when he heard Ruth Rose beg "Daddy" for a pony of her own.

"She gets to have all the fun," he whispered.

Dink gave Josh a nudge. "No talking!" Dink whispered back.

Josh lost his balance and backed into the wall, striking a button. Making a whirring sound, the garage door began to open.

CHAPTER 11

Dink felt himself blushing as everyone outside the garage turned to look at everyone inside.

The trailer stood a few yards away. Through a thick mesh screen, Dink saw Ollie and Polly.

"Say, what's going on here?" Harvey Fowler asked.

"Hey, wait a minute," his wife said. "They were at the block party! What's this all about, Mr. Evans?"

"I'm not Mr. Evans," Detective Costello said. He pulled his wallet out and flipped open his badge. "I'm Detective Frank Costello, New York City Police Department."

Detective Costello nodded at Dr. Parker, who walked over to the trailer. Dink watched him take out a pair of scissors and snip a few hairs from Ollie's arm. Then Dr. Parker went back into the garage.

Detective Frost took a plastic bag from inside her jacket. Through it, Dink recognized the Polaroid picture of the painting.

"I'm sure we'll find your fingerprints all over this photograph," she told Harvey Fowler. "Recognize it?"

Harvey Fowler glanced down at the picture. Dink saw his Adam's apple go up and down. "So? Big deal. What's wrong with having a picture? I've got lots of pictures."

"Trouble is, you have one picture too many," Detective Costello said. "You taught your ape to steal the painting in this photograph."

Harvey Fowler smirked, showing a gold tooth. "I got one word for you: proof. You got any?"

Dr. Parker walked back to the group. "I think so," he said. "The hairs match. The ones I just snipped from Ollie are the same as the one found in Mr. Duncan's kitchen. They're both like the hair the kids found in front of the apartment building."

"Thank you, Dr. Parker," Detective Frost said. She looked at Harvey and Ginny Fowler. "You're both under arrest for grand theft."

"We didn't steal nothing and you can't prove we did!" Harvey Fowler yelled. "I can't help it if Ollie took some dumb painting."

"Give it up," sighed Ginny Fowler to her husband. "It's over."

She turned to Detective Frost. "Everything you said is true. Harvey's cousin works for an insurance company in Paris. Last week, he insured a Monet painting. When he saw that it was being shipped to New York, he took a snapshot and sent it to us. He also sent the address where the painting was going."

"Ginny, be quiet!" Harvey shouted. "We'll get

outta this. I got another cousin who's a lawyer."

Mrs. Fowler ignored her husband. "Anyway, when Harvey saw the balconies on the back of Mr. Duncan's building, he trained Ollie to climb up there," she said. "The painting is hidden in the trailer."

Detectives Costello and Frost handcuffed the Fowlers. Then everyone walked over to the trailer.

It was divided in half. Ollie sat on one side, gazing out through the wire. On the other side, Polly stood munching hay. She didn't seem interested in what was going on in the human world.

"Where is it, exactly?" Detective Frost asked Ginny Fowler.

"There's a false bottom in Ollie's cage," Mrs. Fowler said. "You'll find a handle under the straw."

Detective Costello looked at Josh. "You want to climb in there, kid?"

Josh gulped. "Um, sure. He won't hurt me, will he?"

Ginny Fowler smiled at Josh. "Go ahead. Ollie likes kids."

Detective Frost opened the trailer's rear door and Josh crawled in. Ollie shuffled over and smelled Josh's hair.

Josh moved some of the straw and found a small, round handle. He tugged, and a part of the floor lifted up.

Just then, a taxi pulled up next to the trailer. A short man with a brown beard stepped out. "Warren, who are all these people? What's going on?"

Uncle Warren shook Forest Evans's hand. "Welcome home, Forest. Make us a pot of tea, and we'll tell you the whole story!"

• • •

"What will happen to Ollie?" Ruth Rose asked. They were in the rental car. Dink's uncle was driving them back to the city. "He won't go to jail, will he?"

Uncle Warren shook his head. "Not at all. Dr.

Parker will see that Ollie goes back to Borneo," he said. "There are special camps there where orangutans are taught to live in the wild again. Ollie will have a safe, happy life from now on."

"What about Polly?" Dink asked.

"She could be a problem," Uncle Warren said. "Dr. Parker hasn't been able to find anyone who wants a ten-year-old pony."

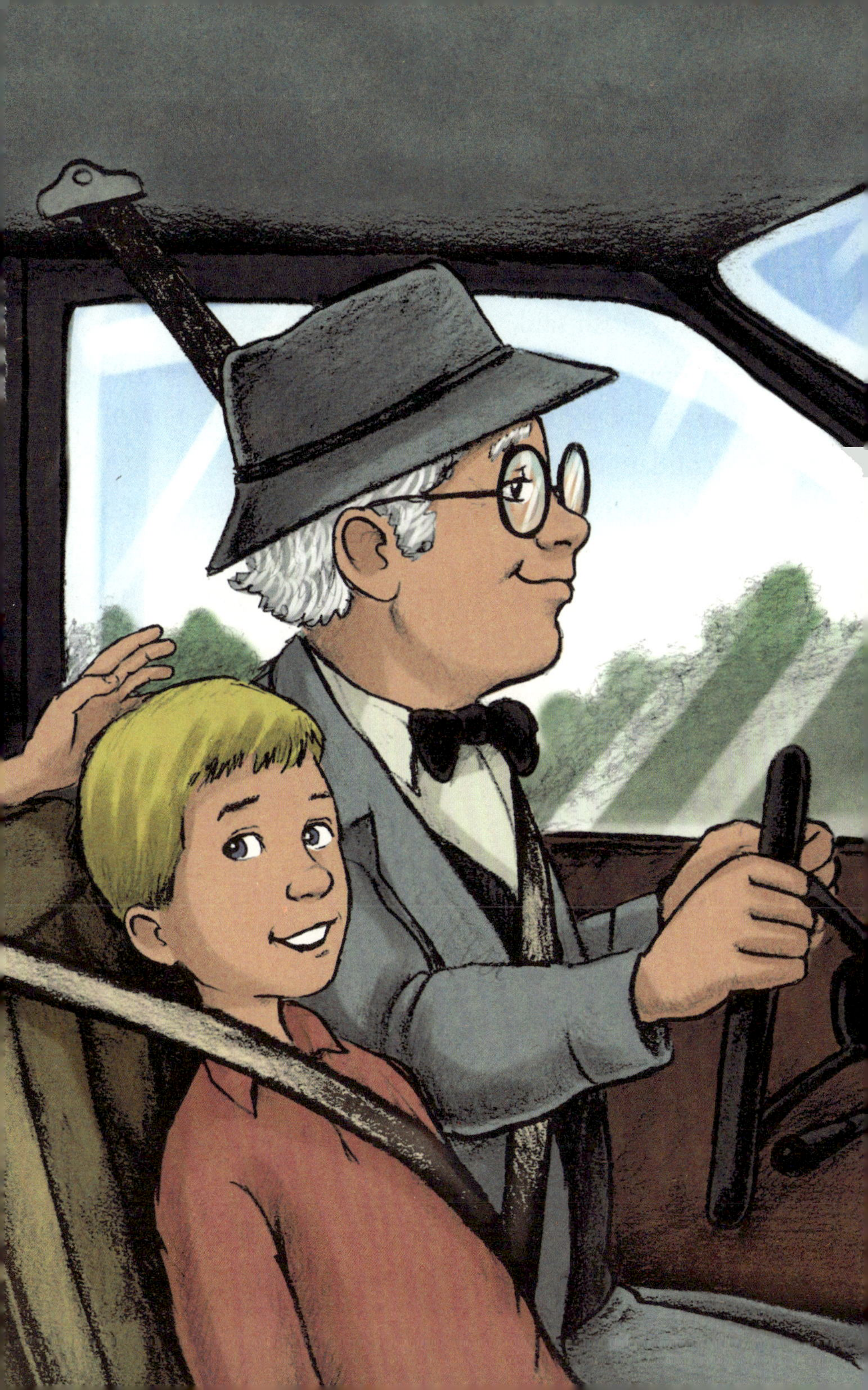

"I know someone who wants a ten-year-old pony," Ruth Rose said. "Me!"

"You?" Josh said. "Where will you keep her?"

"I don't know," Ruth Rose said. She nudged Josh with her elbow. "If only I knew someone with a barn!"

Josh laughed. "Oh, I get it. Okay, I'll ask my folks if Polly can live in our barn. But the twins will want to ride her."

"So will my little brother," Ruth Rose said. "We can all own Polly and we can all ride her!"

Josh leaned forward and patted Dink's head. "And Dinkus can clean out her stall!"

Text copyright © 2001 by Ron Roy
Illustrations copyright © 2001 by John Steven Gurney
All rights reserved under International and Pan-American Copyright Conventions.
Published in the United States by Random House, Inc., New York,
and simultaneously in Canada by Random House of Canada Limited, Toronto.

本书中英双语版由中南博集天卷文化传媒有限公司与企鹅兰登（北京）文化发展有限公司合作出版。

"企鹅"及其相关标识是企鹅兰登已经注册或尚未注册的商标。
未经允许，不得擅用。
封底凡无企鹅防伪标识者均属未经授权之非法版本。

©中南博集天卷文化传媒有限公司。本书版权受法律保护。未经权利人许可，任何人不得以任何方式使用本书包括正文、插图、封面、版式等任何部分内容，违者将受到法律制裁。

著作权合同登记号：字18-2023-258

图书在版编目（CIP）数据

橙色怪盗：汉英对照／（美）罗恩·罗伊著；（美）约翰·史蒂文·格尼绘；史芷溪译. -- 长沙：湖南少年儿童出版社，2024.10. -- （A to Z 神秘案件）.
ISBN 978-7-5562-7818-3

Ⅰ．H319.4

中国国家版本馆CIP数据核字第202435W1Z3号

A TO Z SHENMI ANJIAN CHENGSE GUAIDAO
A to Z 神秘案件　橙色怪盗
［美］罗恩·罗伊 著　［美］约翰·史蒂文·格尼 绘　史芷溪 译

责任编辑：唐 凌　李 炜	策划出品：李 炜　张苗苗　文赛峰
策划编辑：文赛峰	特约编辑：杜天梦
营销编辑：付 佳　杨 朔　周晓茜	封面设计：霍雨佳
版权支持：王媛媛	版式设计：马睿君
插图上色：河北传图文化	内文排版：霍雨佳

出 版 人：刘星保
出　　版：湖南少年儿童出版社
地　　址：湖南省长沙市晚报大道89号
邮　　编：410016
电　　话：0731-82196320
常年法律顾问：湖南崇民律师事务所　柳成柱律师
经　　销：新华书店
开　　本：875 mm × 1230 mm　1/32
字　　数：74千字
版　　次：2024年10月第1版
书　　号：ISBN 978-7-5562-7818-3

印　　刷：三河市中晟雅豪印务有限公司
印　　张：5
印　　次：2024年10月第1次印刷
定　　价：280.00元（全10册）

若有质量问题，请致电质量监督电话：010-59096394　团购电话：010-59320018

A to Z 神秘案件

中英双语

第二辑

The Panda Puzzle
熊猫谜案

[美] 罗恩·罗伊 著
[美] 约翰·史蒂文·格尼 绘　高芸 译

湖南少年儿童出版社
·长沙·

印第安河
劳伦斯出租车公司
沿河路
骑马
小径
租马处
自行车道
树林
林景路
印第安路
消防站
自行车道
大桥路
比尔
自行车店
超市
知更鸟路
乌鸦街
雀鸟巷
歌鸫街
猫头鹰路
野鸡巷
蓝松鸦路
鹌鹑路
健身
中心
森林
自行车道
蓝鸟路
蜂鸟巷
丘鹬路
埃莉餐馆
橡子公寓
橡树街
毛脚
宠物店
中心教堂
自行车道
人民池塘
邮局
社区花园
和鱼塘
绿地储蓄银行
老年公寓
警察局
西绿街
鹅岛
沿河路
老年活动中心
绿地
图书馆
镇公所
主街
儿童动物园
和水族馆
香格里拉
酒店
自行车道

欢迎来到绿地镇
一起解开A to Z神秘案件
北
西
东
南
码头
沿河路
少女岛
租船处
罗思鱼饵店
绿地中学
牧场路
乔希家
鸭子步行道
老鹰巷
绿地小学
丁丁家
露丝家
林梢弯道
牧场路
狐狸小道
银环路
林荫街
鹌鹑路
音乐台
玫瑰园
宜人街
蓟花街
野花路
玫瑰街
中心公园
天鹅池
绿地高中
运动场
体育馆+游泳馆
黄杨木巷
霍华德理发店
角落书店
加油站
清水塘
奇妙温室
狗舍+兽医
东绿街
镇网球场
儿童游泳池
镇游泳池
沿河路
镇棒球场
去往蓝山镇

人物介绍

三人小组的成员，聪明勇敢，喜欢读推理小说，紧急关头总能保持头脑冷静。喜欢在做事之前好好思考！

丁丁

三人小组的成员，活泼机智，喜欢吃好吃的食物，常常有意想不到的点子。

乔希

三人小组的成员，活泼开朗，喜欢从头到脚穿同一种颜色的衣服，总是那个能找到大部分线索的人。

露丝

动物园的饲养员，非常喜欢动物，细心地照料着动物园里的所有动物。因为有熊猫公园的钥匙，被三人组怀疑是绑架熊猫的嫌疑人。

艾琳·纳珀

《熊猫报》的编辑，非常喜欢熊猫，收集了很多关于熊猫的消息。因为剪报纸，被三人组怀疑是绑架熊猫的嫌疑人。

汤姆·斯蒂尔

健身中心的工作人员，他的奶奶投资建造了熊猫公园。因为他也是能够接触熊猫的人，也被三人组怀疑是绑架熊猫的嫌疑人。

菲利普·弗朗西斯

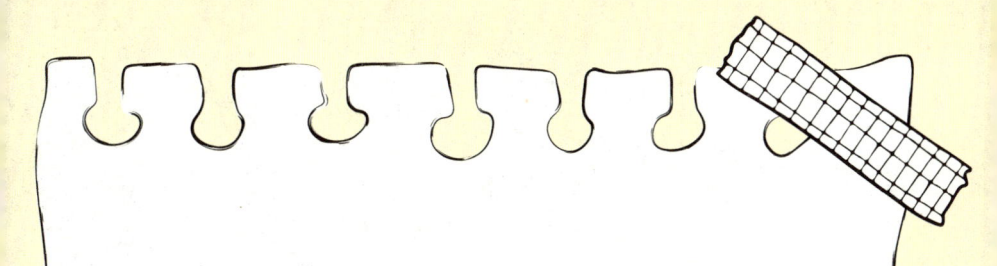

字母 P 代表 peculiar，奇怪的……

台阶尽头的空气中弥漫着灰尘，刺得他们的眼睛很痛。唯一的光线来自上面敞开的活板门。

"小伙伴们，我觉得我们是在一个旧煤窖里。"乔希说，"我爷爷家有一个旧煤窖，就是这样！"

丁丁感觉到眼睛、鼻子和嘴巴里到处都是煤灰，他呛得咳嗽起来。

"看，温妮在那里！"露丝低声喊道。房间的另一头，一双眼睛闪闪发光。

突然，活板门砰的一声关上了，他们立刻陷入一片漆黑之中。接着他们听到了一阵金属碰撞的声音。

"有人把我们锁在里面了！"乔希说，"我什么都看不见！"

"大家不要惊慌，好吗？"露丝说。

"我们原地坐下吧。"丁丁建议道。

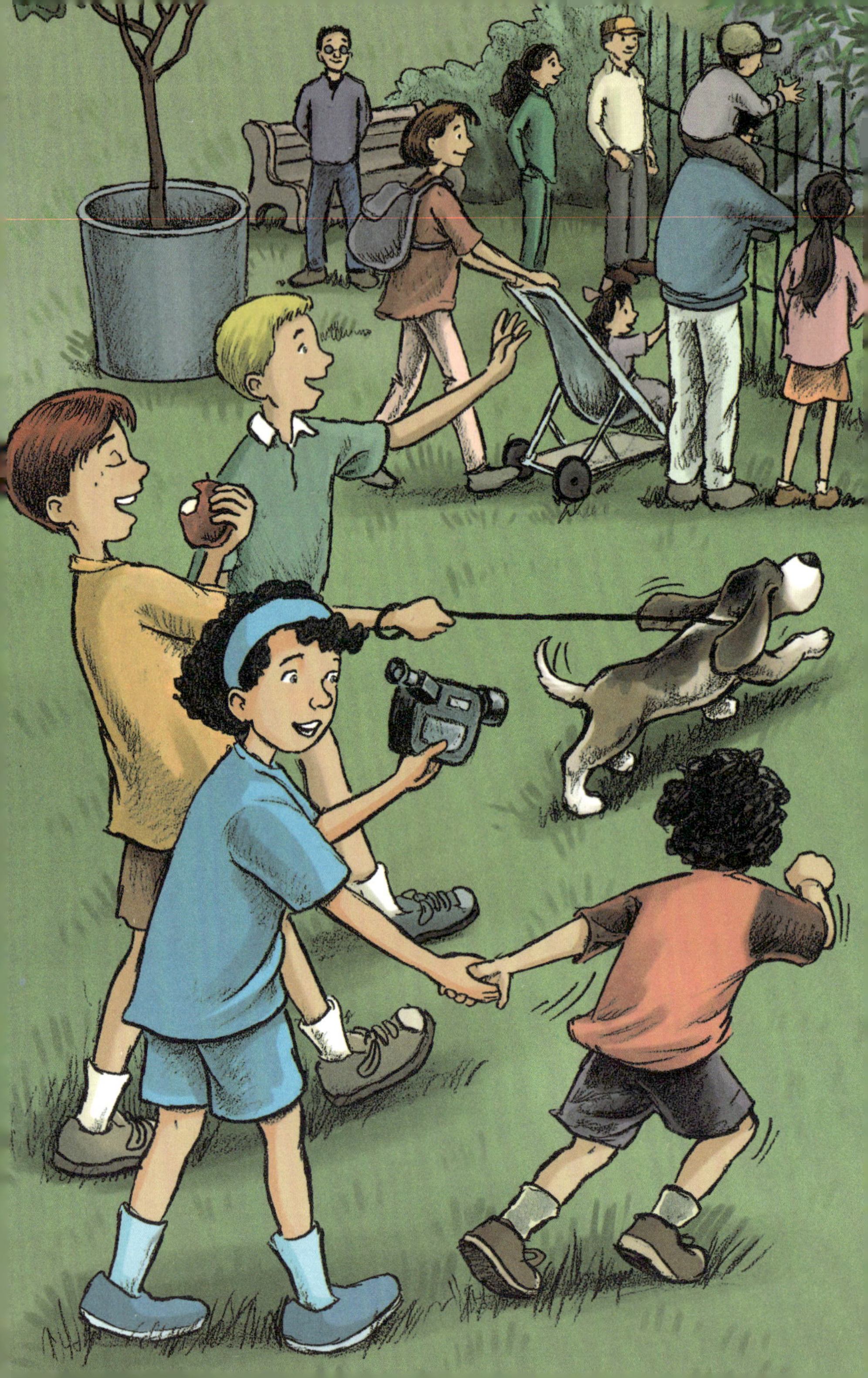

第一章

"真是难以置信,绿地镇有自己的熊猫了。"露丝举起爸爸的摄像机说,"我希望能把它们录下来!"

露丝·罗斯总是喜欢穿一种颜色的衣服。今天,她从头到脚都穿着天蓝色的衣服。

露丝·罗斯带着弟弟纳特,和她的朋友丁丁、乔希一起参观宠物动物园。就在前一天,一只熊猫妈妈带着宝宝来这里安家了!

熊猫馆周围人山人海,四个孩子也在其中。丁丁看到了不少同学,还向法伦警官和他的孙子吉米挥了挥手。

透过熊猫馆四周的细栏杆,孩子们可以看到里面的洞穴和水池。洞穴旁边还种了一些竹子。

丁丁从口袋里掏出一份折叠起来的《熊猫报》。报纸头版报道了熊猫平平和温妮是如何来到绿地镇的,标题是"宠物动物园是熊猫的绝佳去处!"

丁丁说:"我想去问问编辑,我能否写一篇关于熊猫宝宝的报道。"

乔希一边吃苹果,一边拽着狗狗帕尔的牵引绳。"你要是写了报道,我就为你画插图。"他说。

"我可以和熊猫玩吗?"纳特问道。

"不行,纳特。"露丝说,"熊猫只喜欢和其他熊猫一起玩。"

纳特踮起脚尖。"我看不见,"他抱怨道,"前面高个子太多了。"

"那边有一个长椅。"丁丁说,"我们站在椅子上面,就可以看见了。"

孩子们爬上附近的长椅,现在他们可以越过人群看过去了。帕尔深深地舒了口气,扑通一声

躺在草坪上，闭上了眼睛。

游客都站在围栏外面。在另一边，两男一女站在麦克风旁边。

孩子们认出了那位女士。她叫艾琳·纳珀，在宠物动物园工作，负责饲养动物，让它们过得安全舒适。她穿着一件绿色工作服，衬衫口袋上绣着"宠物动物园"的字样。

艾琳旁边那个留着金黄色刺猬头的矮个子男人是汤姆·斯蒂尔——《熊猫报》的编辑。

"打领带的那个人是谁？"乔希问。

乔希问的那个人皮肤黝黑，正在和艾琳窃窃私语。

"那是菲利普·弗朗西斯。"丁丁指着《熊猫报》上的一张照片给乔希看，"他的奶奶给绿地镇捐了一大笔钱，建了这个公园。"

就在这时，菲利普对着麦克风说："大家能听到我说话吗？"

露丝赶忙打开摄像机，对准麦克风。

"大家好，我是菲利普·弗朗西斯。"他说，"众所周知，我奶奶威妮弗雷德·弗朗西斯建造了这个熊猫公园。你们都来看小温妮,我奶奶会很高兴。她把钱捐赠给公益事业,我感到非常荣幸。"

他转向艾琳,说道:"艾琳将会精心照料我们新来的宝贝。"说完,他就把麦克风递给了她。

"谢谢菲利普。"艾琳对着麦克风说,"我只想说,能结识小温妮,我很高兴。它是一个快乐、顽皮的宝宝。"

艾琳把麦克风递给汤姆。"大家好。"这位编辑说,"正如你们所知,《熊猫报》只有一个员工,那就是我。我需要大家的一些帮助,也很乐意刊登有关熊猫的故事、诗歌或照片。"

他笑了笑,又说:"可是我可没办法给你们任何报酬!"

大家都笑了。就在这时,一张黑白相间的脸出现在洞口。

人群顿时安静下来。熊猫妈妈慢慢地走到阳光下,转着头四处看了看,伸着鼻子到处嗅来嗅去。突然,它冲向围栏,撞在金属栏杆上。

汤姆、艾琳和菲利普往后一跳,前面围观的人也纷纷往后退。

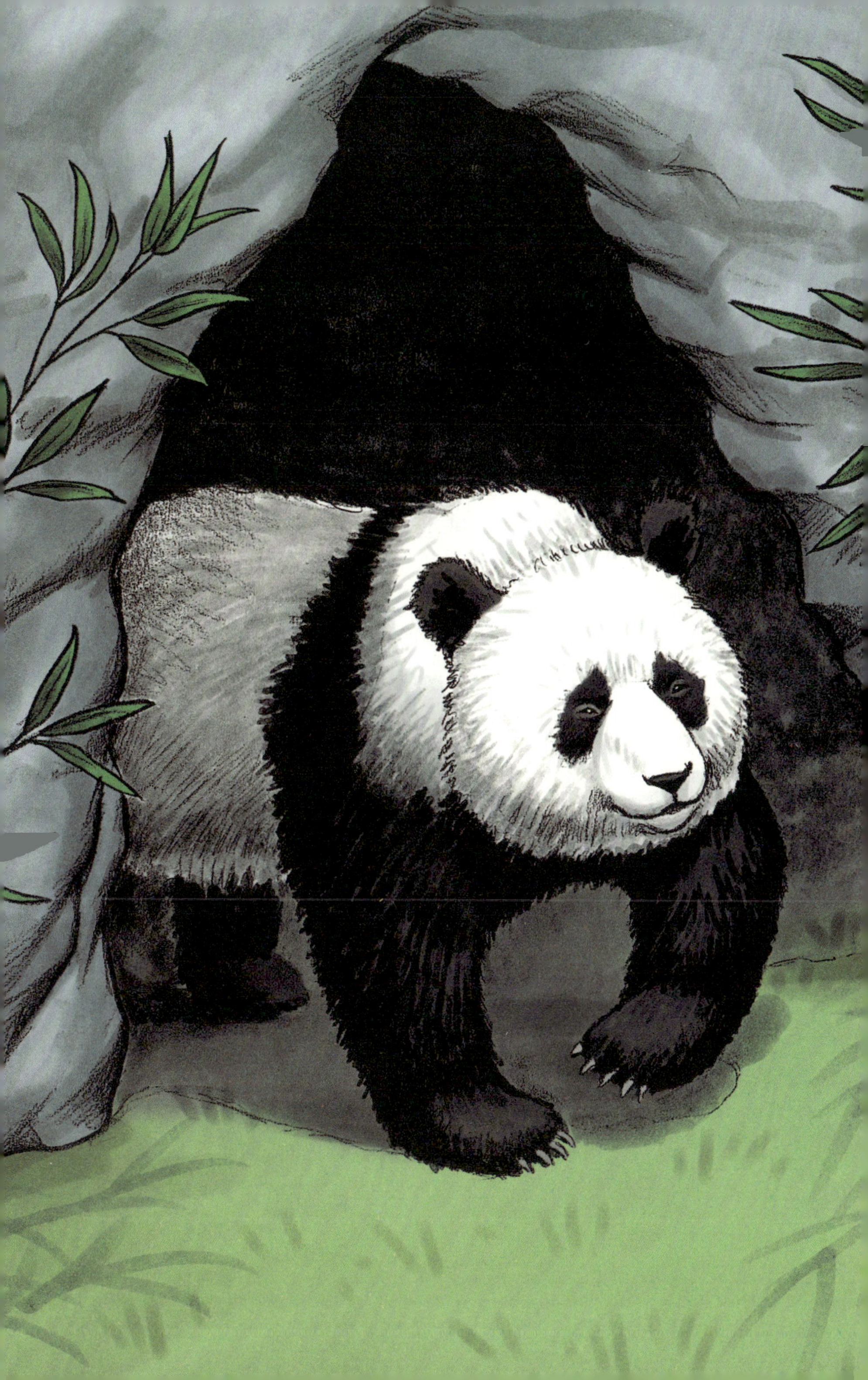

露丝一边拍摄一边问道:"它怎么了?"

平平透过围栏盯着外面看,过了一会儿,才摇摇摆摆地走回洞穴。

一个穿绿色制服的男子匆匆走向艾琳。艾琳把钥匙递给他,他打开了围栏门,小心翼翼地走到洞口,跪下来往里面看。

然后他把手伸进洞里,拽出了一个东西。丁丁觉得,那东西看起来就像一个圆形闹钟,上面还用绳子绑着一张小字条。那个男子重新锁上门,把东西递给了艾琳。她取下字条,默默地看了看上面的内容。

"这太奇怪了!"乔希低声说道,"出什么事了?"

艾琳走到麦克风前,丁丁看到她的手在颤抖。

"这是一封勒索信,"艾琳对着围观的人群说,"温妮被绑架了!"

第二章

"被绑架了!"露丝倒吸了一口冷气。

大家顿时开始议论纷纷。法伦警官跑过去和艾琳交谈。

"温妮在哪里?"纳特问道,"我要看温妮!"

"它这会儿不在。"露丝告诉弟弟。

"它去哪里啦?"这个四岁的孩子不依不饶。

露丝搂着纳特的肩膀,说:"我们也不知道。"

法伦警官走到麦克风前。"大家还是回去吧。"他说,"我们完全有理由相信,温妮是安全的。我们会尽最大努力把它找回来。"

汤姆·斯蒂尔、菲利普·弗朗西斯和艾

琳·纳珀一起离开了熊猫公园。

法伦警官和吉米开始在熊猫馆外围四处走动。人群慢慢散去。

"这是做了一件多么卑鄙的事情啊!"乔希一边说,一边把纳特从长椅上抱下来。

"温妮会怎么样?"露丝问道,"难道它不需要妈妈喂养吗?"

丁丁浏览了一下《熊猫报》上的报道。"报纸上说温妮差不多六个月大了,"他说,"它现在可以自己进食了。"

"走吧,"露丝说,"我们去找法伦警官谈谈。"

孩子们在竹林后面的围栏外追上了警官和他的孙子。帕尔扑通一声趴在地上,把鼻子伸进围栏,不停地嗅着。纳特坐在小狗旁边,轻轻地拍了拍它的头。

"嘿,孩子们,"法伦警官说,"你们有什么发现吗?"

"绑匪索要一百万美元赎金!"吉米脱口而出。

熊猫谜案

"吉米！"爷爷阻止他。

"这是真的吗？"露丝问道。

法伦警官点了点头，说："恐怕是这样的。"他捏着字条的边缘让孩子们看。

乔希大声念道："今晚午夜之前，将一百万美元放在鹅岛的空心树里。别耍花招，否则你们就再也见不到温妮。"

"一百万美元！"露丝喊道，"绿地镇去哪里弄那么多钱？"

"我记得，"法伦警官说，"威妮弗雷德·弗朗西斯留下的钱还剩下一百多万，绑匪一定知道这个情况。"

丁丁仔细地看了看字条，问道："绑匪说的'别耍花招'是什么意思？"

"意思是他来取钱时，我们不能在岛上部署任何警察去抓他，"法伦警官说，"也不能为了追踪，在钞票上动手脚。"

露丝仔细看了看那封勒索信，说："这些字母都是从报纸上剪下来的。"

"是的，"法伦警官说，"也就是说我们无法

17

根据这张字条去找线索。"

突然,帕尔叫了一声。它把爪子伸进围栏,不停地抓挠。

乔希弯腰查看帕尔的举动。"伙伴们,看!"他说。

只见竹丛中藏着一个闪闪发亮的东西。

"是一把刀!"吉米说。

法伦警官跪了下来,说:"的确是。"他挠了挠帕尔的后脑勺,称赞道:"好狗狗!"

法伦警官把一条长长的手臂伸进围栏,捡起了刀。他小心翼翼地把它拿了出来,以免割伤自己。

这把刀的刀刃很薄,软木做的刀柄比较粗。

"看起来像一把鱼刀。"法伦警官说,"这种刀子要是掉进水里,刀柄就会浮起来。"

"爷爷,能把刀给我吗?"吉米问。

熊猫谜案

"恐怕不行，吉米。"法伦警官说，"这是证物。"他从口袋里掏出一块干净的手帕，小心翼翼地把刀包起来。

"嘿，看看这个。"乔希说。他把手伸进围栏，拽出一根竹子，竹子的顶部被整齐地切了下来。

"那儿还有呢，"乔希指着围栏后面说，"有人削了一堆竹子。"

"也许是绑匪想带些竹子给温妮吃。"露丝说。

"至少它不会挨饿。"乔希说。

"这就能解释为什么刀会出现在这里。"法伦警官说，"绑匪怀里抱着不断挣扎的熊猫，可能压根不知道自己把刀弄丢了。"

法伦警官把手伸进口袋，掏出了在平平的洞穴里发现的东西，问道："知道这是什么吗？"

"它看起来像个闹钟。"丁丁说。

"是的，"法伦警官说，"这是一个音量设置得很大的闹钟。我猜绑匪把它扔进了平平的洞穴里，它一响，熊猫就会跑出来。他可能是在温妮从洞穴里出来时抓住了它。"

"如果我们想要它回来，"丁丁说，"绿地镇必须支付一百万美元!"

"你说得对,"法伦警官说,"除非我们先抓到这个坏人。"

"可是我们只有从现在到午夜的这段时间了,"露丝看了看表说,"只有十二小时了!"

第三章

"我肚子饿了。"纳特说,"我们能回家了吗?"

"好吧。"露丝说,"我去给大家做三明治。"

"我得去办公室,检查这些证物上的指纹。"法伦警官说,"不过,除非这家伙很蠢,否则他会戴上手套的。"

他们在警察局分开了。丁丁、乔希、露丝和纳特前往林荫街。

孩子们在露丝家做了午餐。纳特拿着三明治去客厅看恐龙录像片,丁丁、乔希和露丝在厨房的餐桌上吃饭,帕尔趴在乔希脚边打盹。

"快一点了,"丁丁说,"离午夜只剩十一个小时了。"

"那么我们从哪里着手寻找绑匪呢?"乔希问。

"任何人都有可能是绑匪!"丁丁说。

露丝慢慢地嚼着三明治。"不是任何人都有可能。"过了一会儿,她说,"如果那把刀真的是绑匪的,那也许他是个钓鱼爱好者。"

"或者是个女性钓鱼爱好者。"乔希说。

露丝点点头,说:"对。"

"不管是谁,他要么有大门的钥匙,要么能翻越高高的围栏。"乔希说着又伸手去拿三明治,"那么,这会把范围缩小到什么程度呢?"

"还是任何人。"露丝闷闷不乐地说。

纳特在客厅里尖叫起来:"恐龙大战!你们快来看!"

乔希跑到客厅,丁丁和露丝紧随其后。

电视屏幕上,一只暴龙和一只剑龙正在厮打,它们的尾巴来回甩动,暴龙咬着巨牙咆哮。

接着恐龙消失了,场景切换到了博物馆,屏幕上出现了一张男人的脸。"大家好,我是帕莱奥博士。"他说,"下面,我想和大家谈谈刚才的

录像。"

丁丁的脑海里突然闪过一个念头,他说:"露丝,你今天上午在熊猫公园不是录像了吗?为什么不看看你的录像呢?也许我们可以发现一些线索。"

"好主意!"露丝说,"你不介意吧,纳特?"

"我能吃块饼干吗?"纳特笑着问姐姐。

"当然可以。去把饼干盒拿来,我们都吃点,好吗?"

"好!"纳特边说边向厨房跑去。

露丝弹出了恐龙录像带,把摄像机连接到录像机上。

纳特拿着饼干盒回来了,露丝按下了播放键,乔希伸手拿了一块饼干。

屏幕上出现了汤姆、艾琳和弗朗西斯,片刻之后,熊猫平平从洞穴里走了出来。

平平环顾四周,突然它愣住了,然后猛地转过头,向前冲去,一头撞在围栏上。

"它看起来确实很愤怒。"丁丁说。

"要是有人偷了你的宝宝,你也会极其愤怒。"

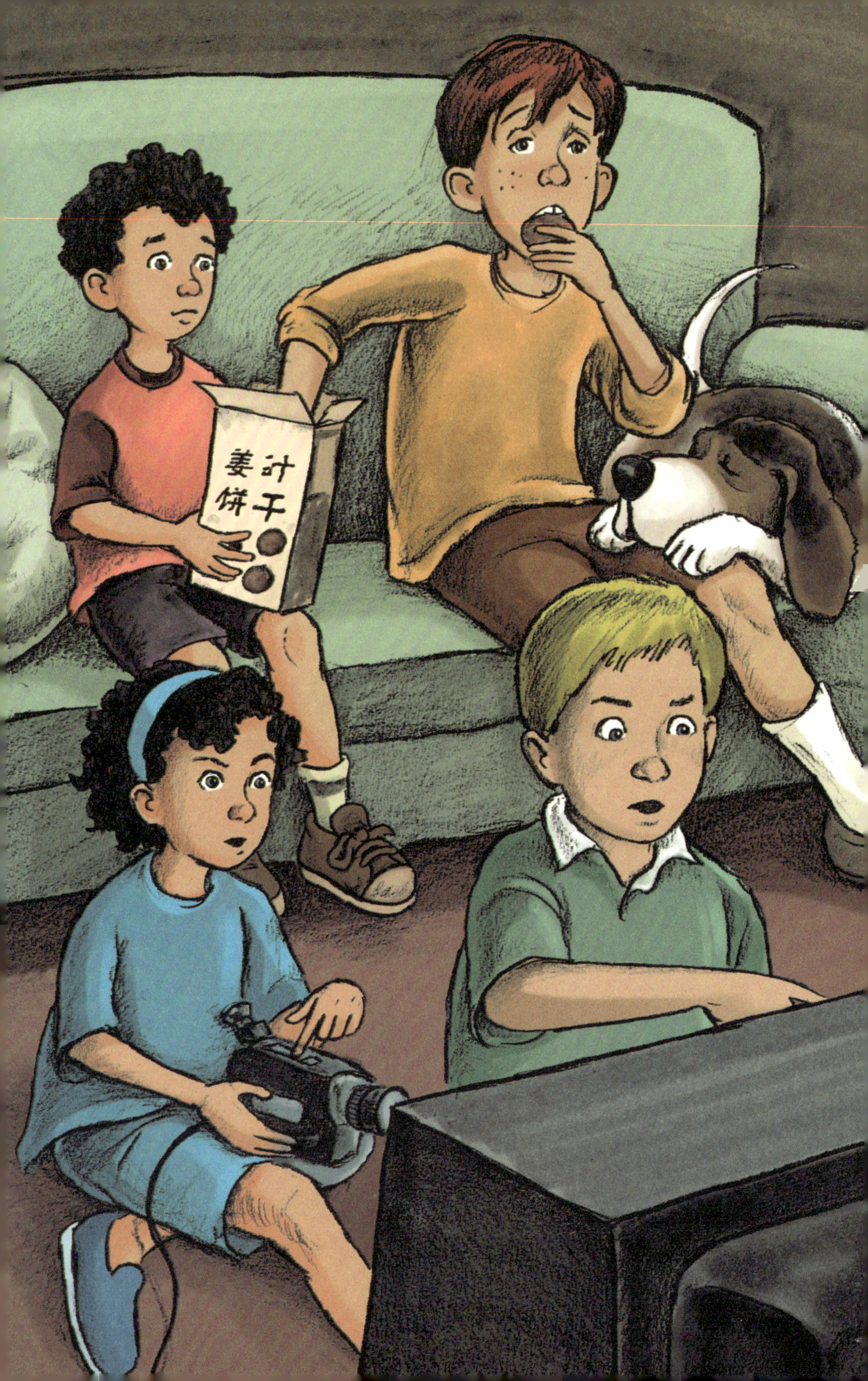
姜汁
饼干

乔希说,"看来它是想攻击围栏外面的什么人。"

"人群中的某个人吗?"露丝问。

"它没有看人群。"丁丁用手在电视屏幕上比画着说,"还记得吗,麦克风在这个位置,是在另一边,也就是它看的这个方向。"

"它在对麦克风发怒?"乔希一边问一边又拿了两块饼干。

"丁丁说得对!"露丝说,"平平看的是站在麦克风前的人。"

丁丁、乔希和露丝盯着电视屏幕。

最后,露丝拔下摄像机的插头,把纳特的恐龙录像带放回了录像机。

"我认为这三个人中有一个人绑架了温妮,"她说,"而且平平知道是谁。"

第四章

"你认为绑架温妮的人就站在麦克风前,对吗?"丁丁问道。

露丝点点头,说:"是的。而且,我认为平平认出了这个人,所以它才猛冲过去!"

"但那家伙可能是在晚上偷走了温妮,"丁丁说,"平平怎么可能看到他呢?"

"也许它没有看到他,"露丝说,"但它可能嗅到了他的气味。"

"对,"乔希说,"大多数动物的嗅觉比人类灵敏得多。"

丁丁盯着电视屏幕,问道:"那么我们怎么知道平平在对谁发怒呢?"

"可惜熊猫不会说话,"乔希说,"否则我们可以直接问它!"

"熊猫不会说话,"露丝说,"但人会说话。我建议,我们去找站在麦克风前的三个人谈谈,就从艾琳开始。"

"你认为是她干的?"丁丁问道。

"我不知道,"露丝说,"但她确实有大门的钥匙。"

"如果她觉察出我们怀疑她,她可能什么都不会说。"乔希说。

露丝指着丁丁的笔记本说:"我们告诉她,我们正在为《熊猫报》写一篇报道。"

"好主意。"丁丁说。

乔希站起来,拍了拍肚皮,说:"我得在四点前回家,照看一小时我的那对双胞胎弟弟。"

露丝拿起饼干盒,里面竟是空的!"乔希,我一块饼干都没吃!"她说。

乔希笑着说:"侦探工作让我都饿了!"

乔希叫醒帕尔,孩子们离开了露丝家。他们

抄近路穿过中心公园的玫瑰园,一只天鹅带着三只小天鹅在湖中嬉戏,帕尔冲着它们叫起来。

经过角落书店时,他们向窗口的帕斯基先生挥手致意。

穿过了一扇爬满金银花藤的木拱门,孩子们来到了宠物动物园。空气中弥漫着一股芳香的气味,一只蜂鸟飞快地飞走了。

艾琳被一群鸭子围着,她不时从制服口袋里掏出小球状的食物喂它们。

"您好,纳珀女士。"露丝说。

"嘿,你们好。"艾琳说,"今天上午你们不是在熊猫公园吗?"

"是啊。我们对绑架事件感到非常难过。"乔希说。

艾琳脸上的笑容消失了。"气得我都不知道该怎么办才好!"她说,"谁会偷走熊猫宝宝呢?"

没人知道该怎么回答这个问题。"好在温妮已经长大,可以吃竹子了。"艾琳说,"如果它还需要母乳喂养的话,我想它都活不下去了。"

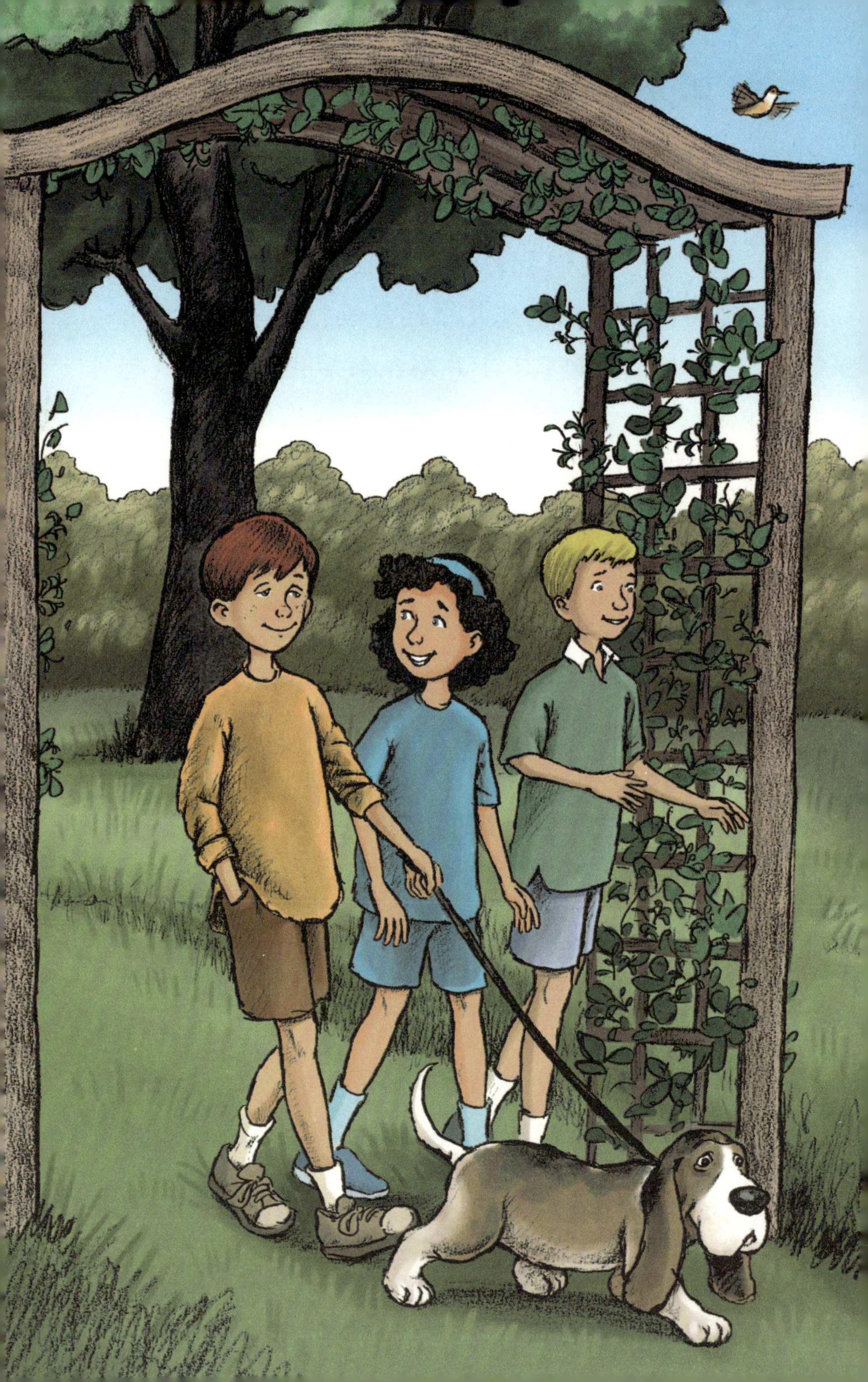

露丝用胳膊肘推了推丁丁。

"嗯,我们打算为《熊猫报》写一篇报道,"丁丁说,"可以问您几个问题吗?"

艾琳打量了丁丁片刻,然后说:"哦,我想可以吧。"

就在这时,帕尔突然叫了起来,吓得鸭子四散奔逃。

"不过,在这之前得让你们的狗狗离我的鸭子远点。"艾琳说。

孩子们跟着艾琳来到背阴的长椅前。她坐下来,伸直了长腿,然后说:"问吧。"

帕尔舒了一口气,趴在地上。艾琳抚摸着它的耳朵。丁丁注意到艾琳的手又大又结实。

大家都在等丁丁提问,但是丁丁的脑海里却突然一片空白。

"平时是谁照顾平平和温妮呢?"露丝赶紧来救场。

"是我。"艾琳说,"我负责喂食,清扫它们活动的区域,以及诸如此类的事情。平平甚至让我抱它的宝宝。"

丁丁做了记录,然后接着问道:"您最后一次见到温妮是什么时候?"

"昨天晚上,"艾琳说,"我去给水池加水,那时大约是八点钟。"

"这么说,是在昨晚八点到今天上午十点之间,有人把它偷走了。"露丝说。

艾琳点点头,丁丁觉得她快要哭了。

丁丁准备好了下一个问题。"有几个人有熊猫馆大门的钥匙?"他问道。

艾琳看着他，过了好一会儿才说："只有我。"她拍了拍挂在腰带上的一串钥匙，继续说："相信我，它从未离开过我的视线。带走温妮的人没有打开过大门。"

一只鸭子摇摇晃晃地走了过来，啄着艾琳的靴子。她把手伸进口袋，又找了几颗小球状的食物，撒在地上。

"我得回去工作了，"说完她就站了起来，低头瞥了一眼丁丁的笔记本。"祝你写作顺利！"

"谢谢。"丁丁说，"顺便问一下，您知道汤姆·斯蒂尔住在哪里吗？"

艾琳摇了摇头，说："不知道，不过你们或许能在他的办公室找到他。"

丁丁一脸茫然地问道："他的办公室？"

"就在老年活动中心，"艾琳怀疑地看了他一眼，"你在为他写报道，竟然不知道他的办公室在哪里，我感到很惊讶。"

第五章

丁丁脑筋转得飞快。"汤姆不知道我们在写报道。"他说,"我们刚刚才决定要写的,希望他能发表。"

"他周末上班?"露丝问。

"我不会感到惊讶,"艾琳说,"尤其是在温妮出事之后。"

孩子们谢过艾琳,离开了宠物动物园。帕尔跟在乔希身后小跑,它的两只长耳朵几乎要贴着地面了。

"你们觉得她是绑匪吗?"丁丁问道。

"我觉得是!"乔希说,"你们看到她的手有多大了吗？她可以绑架一条鳄鱼！"

"可能是她，"露丝说，"她是唯一一个有钥匙的人。"

"我不知道，"丁丁说，"她似乎真的很喜欢动物。"

"也许她更喜欢钱。"乔希皱着眉头说。

他们从后门进入老年活动中心，丁丁看到一块写着"熊猫报"的牌子和一个指向走廊另一头的箭头。

"嗯，我们问他什么问题？"乔希轻声问。帕尔一边跟着他们走，一边在地上嗅来嗅去。

"首先，"丁丁说，"我要问他是否会刊登我的报道。"

"你还没写的那篇报道？"乔希咧嘴笑着问。

"对，就是那篇。"丁丁说。

汤姆办公室的门敞开着，里面传来了柔和的吉他乐曲。他背对着孩子们坐在电脑前，桌子上放着一台小收音机。

丁丁敲了敲门，这位编辑却还在打字，嘴里还随着曲调哼唱着。

熊猫谜案

"进去吧。"露丝一边说,一边走进了房间。

汤姆在椅子上转过身来,说:"你们吓死我了!"然后,他站起身,盯着孩子们看。

他可能只比丁丁高一点点,但那直立的头发和牛仔靴使他又高了三英寸[1]。

他架着一副圆眼镜,两条浓眉都快连在一起了。他的一只手掌心上贴着创可贴。

"打扰了,"丁丁说,"我是丁丁·邓肯。嗯,我在写一篇有关温妮的报道。今天上午,您说过欢迎投稿,所以我……"

汤姆扬起一条浓密的眉毛,看着丁丁,问道:"你是作家?"

丁丁说:"还不是,但我长大后想当作家"。

汤姆低头看了一眼帕尔,问道:"这是谁?"

"它叫帕尔,"乔希说,"它以前的主人是一伙罪犯!"

"嗯。"汤姆又坐了下来。他摘下眼镜,身子往后一靠,双脚放在桌子上。桌子上杂乱地堆放着纸张、剪刀、一瓶胶水、铅笔和一个油乎乎的

---

1. 英美制长度单位,1英寸=2.54厘米。——编者

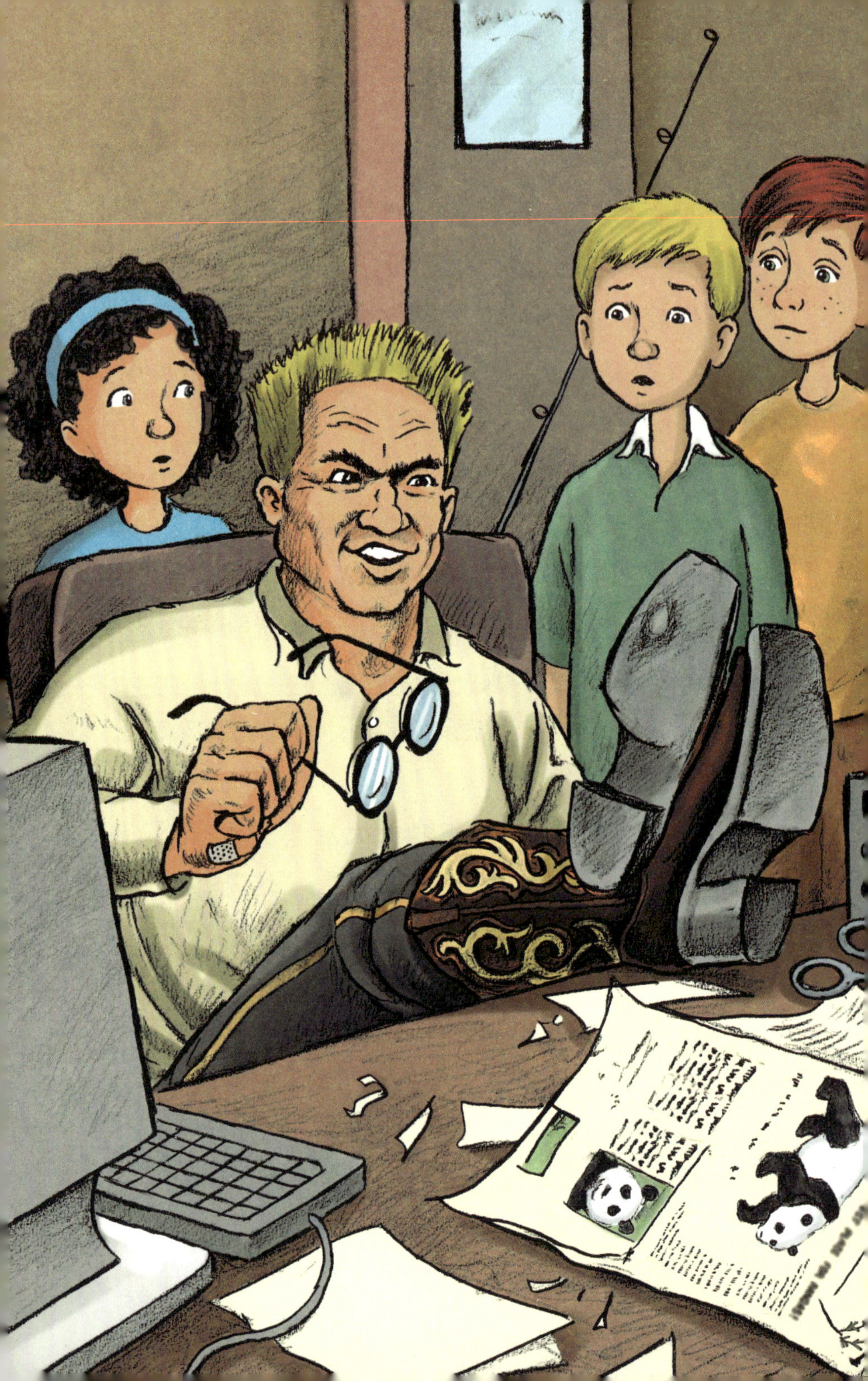

比萨盒。

汤姆举起一份被剪得七零八落的《熊猫报》问道:"你们读过这些文章吗?"

"我们都读过。"露丝回答说。她把自己的那份报纸递给汤姆看。

"我们喜欢熊猫。"乔希说。

汤姆眯起眼睛,盯着自己的鞋尖。房间里只听到时钟的嘀嗒声。"我也喜欢熊猫,"最后,他开口说,"如果我抓到绑架温妮的家伙……"

他擦了擦脸,说:"好吧,写你们的报道吧。如果写得好,我就刊登出来。"

丁丁从口袋里掏出笔记本,说:"我们能问您几个问题吗?"

汤姆叹了口气,看了看手表,说:"我估计还可以抽出几分钟。"

"您知道谁有熊猫馆的钥匙吗?"丁丁问道。

"知道,艾琳有钥匙。"他说,"我想她是唯

一有钥匙的人。"

丁丁点了点头。

"您有没有注意到有怪异的人在熊猫公园附近徘徊？"乔希问道。

汤姆慢慢地摇了摇头，笑着说："只看到像你我这样的普通人。"

"今天上午平平非常生气，您感到惊讶吗？"露丝问道。

"当然，我们都很惊讶。"汤姆说，"菲利普告诉我，他从未见过它如此愤怒。"

"菲利普经常去看熊猫吗？"乔希问道。

汤姆站了起来。"我不知道，"他说，"我得继续工作了。"他伸出左手和大家握手告别。"请原谅我用左手，我右手被纸划破了。"他补充道。

"谢谢，斯蒂尔先生。"丁丁和他握了握手，犹豫了片刻，问道："您知道在哪里可以找到菲利普吗？"

"菲利普在健身中心上班。"汤姆指着主街说。

露丝仔细地看了看汤姆的书桌，问道："斯蒂尔先生，您打算写一篇关于绑架的报道吗？"

熊猫谜案

汤姆朝着乱糟糟的桌子点了点头。"这正是我在做的事情,"他说,"恕我失陪了……"

丁丁答应过几天把报道送来,然后孩子们就离开了。他们匆匆穿过走廊,走出后门,来到阳光下。

"他就是绑匪,"乔希郑重地说,"那个创可贴泄露了他的秘密。被纸划破了,鬼才相信!我敢打赌,肯定是他抓温妮的时候被咬伤了。"

"桌子上有剪刀和胶水,他正在剪报纸。"露丝说,"而那封勒索信上的文字恰好是从报纸上剪下来的!"

"你们看到靠在角落的东西了吗?"乔希问道。

"没有,但你会告诉我们,对吗?"丁丁说。

"钓鱼竿!"乔希说,"记得吗?帕尔在竹子里发现了一把鱼刀。要不我们报警吧!"

"我不能确定。"丁丁说,"这家伙的手受伤了,如果他带着熊猫翻越围栏,应该需要两只手。"

乔希得意地笑着说:"你听说过梯子吗?"

丁丁对他的朋友咧嘴一笑,说:"真的吗?那家伙带着梯子、闹钟、刀和熊猫?也许我们应该找一个杂耍演员!"

第六章

健身中心外面竖着一块牌子,上面写着"禁止宠物入内,禁止光脚,禁止吸烟。"

于是,乔希把帕尔拴在树上,拍了拍它的头,说:"待在这儿,小家伙。"

帕尔舒了口气,扑通一声趴在地上。一双棕色的大眼睛看着乔希、丁丁和露丝走进大楼。

健身中心里面非常宽敞,一侧摆满了健身器材,一排窗户朝向鸫鹩路。

另一侧是一个闪闪发光的游泳池,三个人正在游泳,一名救生员默默地守护着他们。

其他人在使用健身器械锻炼,金属相互撞击

的声音与隐蔽放置的扬声器里传出的摇滚乐交织在一起。

丁丁闻到一股汗液混杂着氯气的味道,不由得皱起了鼻子。

绿色的遮阳篷下有个柜台,正在出售果汁和健康食品。

"我要一杯奶昔!"乔希在音乐声中大喊大叫,"我感觉很虚弱。"

"他们只卖健康奶昔,"露丝告诉他,"是用海藻和豆腐做的。"

"豆腐是什么?"

露丝咯咯地笑了起来。"它是一种白白的,会微微摇晃的东西。"她说,"你不会喜欢的,乔希。"

"菲利普在那里,"丁丁说,"柜台后面。"

菲利普穿着T恤和蓝色短裤,手臂又长又结实。"孩子们,需要帮忙吗?"他问。

"您好,弗朗西斯先生。"丁丁说,"我正在写一篇关于熊猫的报道,我们能采访一下您吗?"

"叫我菲利普吧,"男人微笑着对丁丁说,"你是谁?"

A to Z 神秘案件

"叫他丁丁。"乔希一边说,一边盯着做奶昔的机器。

菲利普察觉到了,问道:"你们渴了吗?我请你们喝杯奶昔如何?"

"好啊!"乔希说,"但是不要加豆腐,或者海藻。"

菲利普笑着说:"那加牛奶、酸奶和草莓怎么样?"

熊猫谜案

"这就对了!"乔希边说边坐在凳子上。

菲利普熟练地将原料倒入搅拌机,搅拌了一分钟,然后将起泡的粉红色混合物倒入三个高脚玻璃杯里。

"我们今天上午也在动物园。"丁丁说。

菲利普把奶昔和吸管放在孩子们面前,说:"我奶奶要是知道了,会伤心欲绝的。"

孩子们开始喝奶昔,乔希用力地吮吸,发出响亮的喷喷声。

丁丁拿起笔问道:"他们为什么叫您菲利普呢?"

"我经常在地垫上锻炼,"菲利普笑了笑说,"我猜想是因为我的后空翻[1]很出名吧。他们为什么叫你丁丁呢?"

乔希笑了起来,结果被奶昔呛到了。

"我的真名是唐纳德·戴维·邓肯,"丁丁告诉他,"我猜是叫丁丁比较顺口吧。"

菲利普看了看丁丁的笔记本,问道:"那你写

---

1. 菲利普的英文名是 Flip,意为"空翻"。——译者

了多少字了？"

"不太多，"丁丁说，"我们正在找了解温妮的人谈话。"

"您奶奶喜欢熊猫吗？"露丝问道，"这就是她留下那么一大笔钱的原因吗？"

菲利普点点头。"奶奶喜欢动物，"他说，"她在世时一直给动物收容所捐款。"

丁丁瞥了一眼笔记本上有关艾琳的记录，问道："您知道谁有熊猫馆的钥匙吗？"

菲利普又点了点头，说："知道，艾琳有一把。但我不知道还有谁有钥匙。"

"您是否看到可疑的人在熊猫公园周围溜达？"乔希问道。

菲利普抬头看着天花板说："也许算不上可疑，不过，《熊猫报》的编辑汤姆似乎经常去那里。"

丁丁用粗体字在笔记本上写下了"汤姆"两个字。

"还有其他问题吗？"菲利普问道，"快到午休时间了。"

孩子们喝完了奶昔。"非常感谢。"丁丁对菲

利普说。

"我很乐意效劳。"菲利普回答说。

就在这时,一个高个子的红发女子向柜台走来。她穿着和菲利普一样的衣服——T恤和蓝色短裤。"对不起,我来晚了。"她对菲利普说,"你现在可以去吃午餐了。"

"没关系,凯特。"他说,"迟到的午餐总比没有午餐好。"

菲利普双手放在柜台上,用手一撑就跳了出来。"祝你们写作顺利。"他一边大步走出门,一边对孩子们说。

孩子们跟着菲利普走了出来,看见他跳上一辆顶架满是灰尘的吉普车。他一边按着喇叭挥手告别,一边把车驶向大桥路。

看着吉普车在主街右拐后,丁丁问道:"嗯,你们是怎么想的?"

"我投他一票。"乔希一边说,一边把拴住帕尔的牵引绳从树上解开。"那家伙一只手绑在背后都能翻越八英尺[1]高的围栏。"

---

1. 英尺:英美制长度单位,1英尺=0.3048米。——编者

露丝笑道:"乔希,十分钟前你还说绑匪是汤姆呢。"

"是啊,"丁丁说,"在那之前,你还确信艾琳是绑匪呢!"

"那你们觉得是谁呢?"乔希问道。

"任何一个人都有可能。"丁丁叹了口气,把笔记本塞进了屁股后面的口袋。

"你们注意到菲利普车上的顶架了吗?"露丝问道,"我不知道那是不是用来固定船只的。"

"我不明白。"乔希说。

"也许菲利普是一个钓鱼爱好者,乔希。"露丝说。"还记得那把刀吗?"

丁丁说:"等一下。"说完,他迅速回到了健身中心。

凯特抬起头,笑着对他说:"来锻炼吗?周末下午三点以后儿童免费。"说完,她从柜台那头递过来三张门票。

"谢谢。"丁丁说完,把门票塞进了口袋。然后双手交叉,放在背后说:"菲利普说过一会儿要去钓鱼,你知道他有船吗?"

"只有一艘旧独木舟,"她说,"不过他今天一天都要上班,没法去钓鱼。"

丁丁感觉脸都红了。"哦,嗯,也许我弄错了。再见!"他飞快地跑了出去。

"他有独木舟。"丁丁告诉小伙伴们。

"瞧瞧!"乔希欢呼道。

"这不能证明什么,"丁丁说,"这三个人都有作案嫌疑。"

"解救温妮的时间不多了,"露丝说,"离午夜只剩八个小时了!"

乔希看了看手表,说:"哎呀!我必须在五分钟内赶到家!"说完就跑了。

第七章

孩子们匆忙赶到乔希家,乔希的爸爸妈妈正在等他。

乔希的妈妈一边上车,一边对他说:"我们大约一个小时后回来。"乔希的爸爸挥了挥手,将车驶出了车道。

布赖恩拽着乔希的胳膊嚷道:"我要骑小马!"

布赖恩的双胞胎弟弟布拉德利拉着乔希的另

一条胳膊,叫道:"不!我想去河里抓乌龟!"

"没有爸爸妈妈的允许,你们俩什么都别想。"乔希说。

"那我们要吃糖果!"布赖恩说。

"不,我们要吃冰激凌!"布拉德利说完,就往家里跑去。

乔希叹了口气,尾随其后。丁丁和露丝笑着跟在乔希后面。进屋后,乔希倒了五杯橙汁。

布赖恩从椅子上跳下来,跑了出去。他很快就回来了,手里拿着一个扁平的纸盒。

"我来帮你!"布拉德利说。

"不,这是我的拼图!"布赖恩大声嚷嚷道,"乔希!"

"你们俩要么一起拼,要么都不要拼。"乔希说,"还有,别用黏糊糊的手拿拼图。"

"这是什么拼图,布拉德利?"露丝问道。

"大飞(灰)熊!"布拉德利一边把拼图倒在桌子上,一边回答。盒子封面上有一只灰熊妈妈和一只灰熊宝宝。

这些拼图比较大,正好适合四岁孩子的小手。两个孩子以前完成过这幅拼图,他们小手飞快地拣着拼图,把它们拼在一起。

几分钟后,拼图还差一块就完成了。可是灰熊宝宝面部的那一块不见了。

"是你拿了!"布赖恩冲布拉德利嚷道。

"我没有,是你拿了!"布拉德利大声回应。

"别吵了。"乔希说。他趴在地板上,往桌子底下看。"这里没有,也许在你们的房间里。"他说。

双胞胎冲出厨房,朝他们的卧室跑去。

二十秒后,他们又跑回了厨房。布拉德利手里拿着那块缺失的拼图,摇摇晃晃地回到椅子上,把它放在恰当的地方。

"在哪里找到的?"乔希问道。

熊猫谜案

"我的床底下。"布拉德利笑着说。

"真希望找到失踪的熊猫也能这么容易。"丁丁说。

露丝坐了起来。"就是这样!"她说,"也许我们应该去找温妮,而不是找绑架它的家伙。"

"但是去哪里找呢?"丁丁问,"它可能被藏在任何一个地方。"

"要是我绑架了一只熊猫,"露丝说,"我会把它藏在哪里?"

乔希从冰箱里拿出一碗苹果,给两个弟弟一人一个,对他们说:"你们可以用苹果核喂小马。"

双胞胎听了之后,立刻从后门冲了出去,争先恐后地跑向谷仓。帕尔摇摇晃晃地跟在他们后面。

丁丁、乔希和露丝也拿着苹果来到户外,坐在屋后的台阶上,看着两个弟弟隔着围栏抚摸着小马波莉。

"熊猫宝宝不像一般的宠物那样容易被驯服,"乔希一边嚼着苹果一边说,"根本不可能把它藏在家里。"

"我敢打赌,温妮一定很想它的妈妈,"露丝说,"它可能会哭个不停,人们会听到它的声音。"

"对,"乔希说,"所以绑匪可能会把它藏在一个很吵闹的地方。"

丁丁看着小马波莉嚼着布赖恩给的苹果核,说:"绑匪得给温妮喂食,所以会把它藏在附近。"

"我知道一个地方,"露丝说,"这个地方又吵又臭,而且离宠物动物园也不远。"

乔希冲露丝咧嘴一笑,说:"我也知道。健身中心,对吧?"

露丝点点头,说:"如果菲利普偷走了温妮,那里绝对是藏匿它的最佳地点。"

"我们要不要回去看看?"丁丁问道。

"但是我们该怎么对付菲利普呢?"乔希问道,"如果他真的是绑匪,我们再去那里,他不会怀疑吗?"

丁丁把手伸进口袋,掏出了那几张门票,说:"孩子们今天免费入场。"

"太好了!"露丝说,"我们既可以去游泳,又可以去窥探!"

第八章

一小时后,孩子们拿着泳衣和毛巾,在健身中心前面会合。

菲利普和凯特在柜台后面值班。健身房里挤满了人,音乐声仍然震耳欲聋。

"又来了?"菲利普问道。

丁丁拿出三张门票放在柜台上,说:"我们来游泳。"

"好主意,"凯特说,"来吧,我告诉你们去哪儿换衣服。"

她领着孩子们向游泳池走去。游泳池里有很多孩子在玩水,几个成年人坐在一旁观看。救生员在游泳池周围巡视,密切关注着游泳的人。

凯特在一排门前停了下来。这一排共有四扇门,其中最外侧的两扇门上分别标着"男"和"女",但中间的两扇门没有做任何标记。

"这里是更衣室。"凯特说,"不许跳水,不许奔跑,注意听丹尼的哨声。第一声哨响时,大家就在原地停止不动。接着,他会连吹两声,这表示孩子们要离开泳池,轮到成人游泳十五分钟。祝你们玩得开心!"

"三分钟后见。"露丝说完,便消失在女更衣室里。

丁丁和乔希走进男更衣室,里面空无一人。四面墙上排列着蓝色的金属储物柜,最里面是淋浴器、洗脸池、厕所和一面落地镜。地上铺着地毯,还有几条长凳,人们换衣服时可以坐一坐。

丁丁走到一个小壁橱前,门上印着"储物间"的字样。他往里面偷偷看了看。

"看到熊猫了吗?"乔希低声问。

丁丁瞥了一眼镜子里的乔希,说:"没有,但我看到一只瘦小的红毛猴。"

储

A to Z 神秘案件

乔希说:"等进了泳池,你就完蛋了。"

孩子们换好泳衣,把衣服放在储物柜里,然后朝游泳池走去。

救生员拦住了他们。"你们好。"他说,"我相信凯特已经向你们解释过规则了,对吧?你们还有大约十分钟的时间,然后就轮到成人游泳了。玩得开心!"

"谢谢,我们会很开心。"丁丁说。

露丝穿着一件青柠绿的泳衣走了出来,孩子们跳进了浅水区。

熊猫谜案

"现在怎么办?"乔希问道,他瞥了一眼柜台后面的菲利普。

丁丁说:"我想知道另外两扇门后面是什么。"

"其中一扇门可能通往保龄球馆,"乔希说,"我认为就在我们脚下的位置。"

"待会儿大人游泳时,也许我们可以去看看。"露丝说,"哨声一响,我们必须从那边上去。"

孩子们一边游泳、戏水,一边等待。乔希试着在水下倒立,结果呛了水,他钻出水面咳嗽起来。

突然哨声响起。

游泳池里所有的人都停止了活动,转身面对救生员。"该成人游泳了!"他喊道,又吹了两下哨子。

孩子们纷纷从水里爬上岸,湿漉漉地到处乱窜。与此同时,大人们纷纷进入游泳池。

更衣室前一片混乱,没有人注意到露丝试着打开那两扇没有标识的门上的把手。其中一扇门锁着,但另一扇门打开了。

"来吧!"露丝一边悄悄地溜了进去,一边低声说道。丁丁和乔希紧随其后。

丁丁关上门,里面一片漆黑。

"我们到底在哪儿?"乔希颤抖着问道。三个孩子身上都湿淋淋地滴着水。

丁丁伸出双臂,摸到了两边光滑的墙壁。又伸出一只光着的脚向前探了探,感觉碰到了木头台阶的边缘。

"我觉得我们可能在楼梯顶端。"他轻声说道。

"我们试着找找灯吧,"乔希说,"我讨厌黑暗。"

"先别急,"露丝说,"我们摸黑下去吧,看看底下有没有灯。"

丁丁说："小心碎片。"

孩子们摸索着走下漆黑的楼梯，来到坚硬冰冷的地面，才停了下来。

"好吧，没有灯我不会再往前走了！"乔希郑重地说，"我觉得自己就像一条居住在洞穴里的盲鱼。"

他们在墙上到处摸索。

"找到了。"露丝说，咔嗒一声，灯亮了。

孩子们站在走廊的尽头。地面是光滑的石头，墙体的下半部分是粗糙的石头，上半部分是看起来较新的油漆板。天花板上乱七八糟，古老的木梁、生锈的管道和蜘蛛网混杂在一起。

"看看这个。"丁丁说，只见在两块石头之间的砂浆上刻着一个日期：1902。"这堵墙是一百多年前建的！"他说。

"而且，现在还令人毛骨悚然。"乔希的牙齿打着战，"这些石头是冰……冰冷的！"

狭窄的走廊里堆满了破损的健身器材、卷起的地垫和巨大的油漆桶。右手边的墙边还放着一排纸箱。

走廊里没有其他的门。

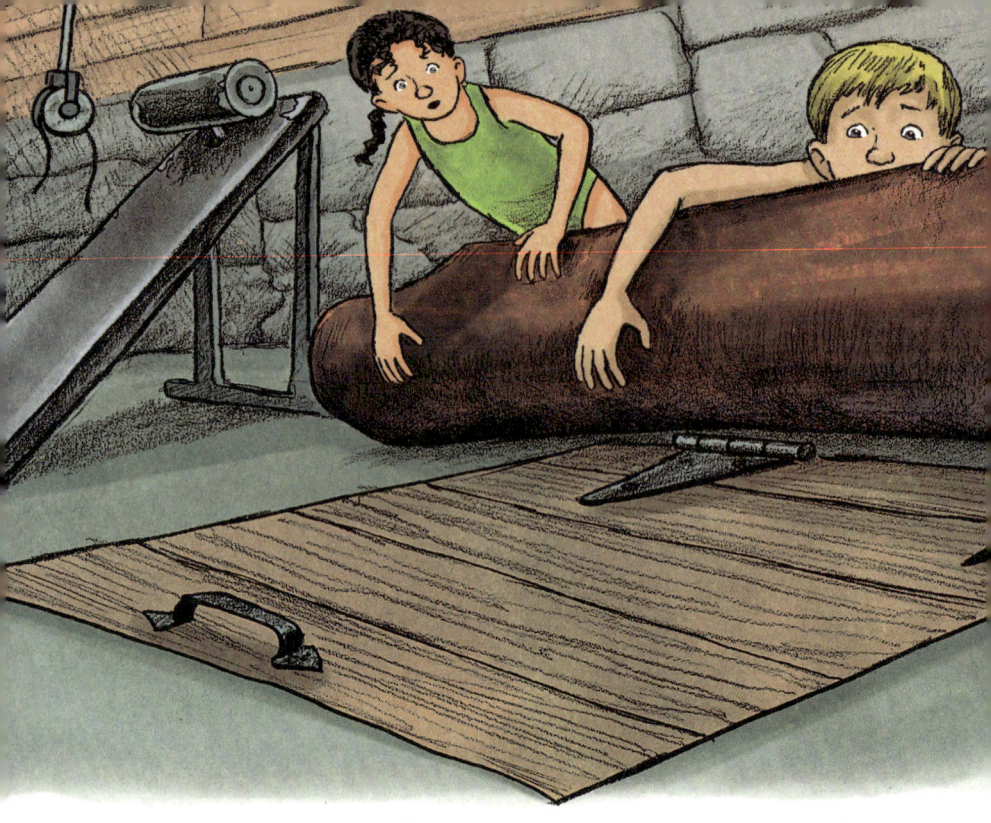

"那是什么声音?"露丝问道,"听起来像打雷。"

丁丁把耳朵贴在左边的墙上,仔细地听了听,说:"我想墙的另一边是保龄球馆。"

孩子们沿着走廊往前走。

"我们依次检查一下这些箱子吧,"露丝说,"温妮很小,藏在哪里都有可能。"

五分钟后,他们检查完毕。大部分箱子都是空的,有几个箱子里面装着白色的填充物。孩子们站在走廊的尽头,思考着下一步该怎么办。那

儿正好有一块地垫,孩子们扑通一声坐在上面。

乔希搓着脚,打了个寒战。

丁丁说:"这么长的走廊却没有一扇门,真是奇怪。"

"也许在健身中心建成之前,这里是一个旧地下室。"露丝说。

"哎哟!"乔希说。

"又怎么啦?"丁丁问道。

"我不知道,但是好痛!"乔希站起身,戳了戳他坐过的垫子。

"帮我把这块垫子抬起来,"他说,"下面有东西。"

孩子们站起来,帮乔希掀起垫子,垫子下面藏着一个活板门的金属把手。

第九章

"我们要打开它吗？"乔希问道。

丁丁没有回答，他抓住把手拉了拉，门很容易就开了，呈现在眼前的是一排向下延伸的石阶。下面黑暗中传来什么东西跑来跑去的声音。

"哎呀，有老鼠！"乔希说，"如果你们认为我要……"

露丝阻止了他："嘘，我还听见了别的声音！"

接着他们都听见了，那是短促的哭泣声。

"是温妮！"露丝说着便跑下了台阶，丁丁和乔希紧跟其后。

台阶尽头的空气中弥漫着灰尘，刺得他们的眼睛很痛。唯一的光线来自上面敞开的活板门。

"小伙伴们，我觉得我们是在一个旧煤窖里。"乔希说，"我爷爷家也有一个旧煤窖，就是这样！"

丁丁感觉到眼睛、鼻子和嘴巴里都是煤灰，他呛得咳嗽起来。

"看，温妮在那里！"露丝低声喊道。房间的另一头，一双眼睛闪闪发光。

突然，活板门砰的一声关上了，他们立刻陷入一片漆黑之中。接着他们听到了一阵金属碰撞的声音。

"有人把我们锁在里面了！"乔希说，"我什么都看不见！"

"大家不要惊慌，好吗？"露丝说。

"我们先在原地坐下吧。"丁丁建议道。

"可是我看不见啊！"乔希抱怨道，"这地方太恶心了！"

丁丁坐了下来，感觉身下有一些煤块，他把它们推到一边。

"我敢打赌,是菲利普把我们锁在里面了。"露丝说,"他一定发现我们的行踪了。"

丁丁听到乔希站了起来,便问道:"你要干吗,乔希?"

"这栋房子很古老,也许锁也很旧。"乔希回答,"或许我可以强行打开它。"

"我来帮你,"丁丁说。他和乔希跌跌撞撞地走上台阶,推搡着活板门,门却纹丝不动。

"哎,这真是个'好主意',乔希。"丁丁说。

他们又摸索着走下台阶,坐在露丝身旁。

"我们怎样才能离开这里呢?"乔希用颤抖的声音问道。

"也许会有窗户,"露丝说,"地下室不是都有窗户的吗?"

"这可不是地下室,"乔希说,"这是过去人家放煤的地方。"

"我敢打赌,除了我们,再也没有人来过这里了。"丁丁说,"这真是个藏温妮的好地方。"

"温妮在哪里呢?"露丝问。

"它可能躲起来了,"丁丁说,"要是我们有

灯就好了。"

"哎呀，如果早知道我们会被困在地下，"乔希说，"我就把手电筒带来了。"

"别担心，"露丝说，"等到了午夜，菲利普拿到了钱就会放我们出去的。"

"嗯，我可不会在这里一直坐到午夜，"乔希说着又站起身来，"我有办法！"

"真的吗？"丁丁问。

"是啊，"乔希光着脚踢开周围的煤块，"我们手拉着手，试着摸到墙，然后就可以摸遍整个房间了。"

"我们摸遍房间要找什么呢？"露丝问道。

"煤槽。"乔希回答。

"放煤的槽？"丁丁问。

"煤槽，丁丁，煤——槽。"乔希说，"爷爷曾经告诉过我，过去人们是如何把煤运进煤窖的。地窖里有一个斜槽，他们就让煤顺着斜槽一直滑到下面。"

"你是说这里会有滑槽之类的装置吗？"露丝问道。

"是啊,而且它能通到外面去!"

于是,孩子们手拉着手,露丝在中间,丁丁和乔希在两边,两边的男孩伸手去摸墙壁。

片刻之后,丁丁被什么东西绊倒了,跪在了一堆煤上。

丁丁用手摸了摸那个东西的形状,说:"我找到一把铲子。"

他扶着铲子想站起来,身体却失去了平衡,摔倒在墙上。

"好吧,"他揉着胳膊说,"我找到了一堵墙。现在怎么办?"

"沿着墙摸,墙上应该有开口,"乔希说,"可能会在高一点的地方。"

三个孩子贴着墙摸索着慢慢往前移动。丁丁用铲子当拐杖,拖着脚,缓慢前行。

丁丁听到黑暗中传来的一阵呜咽声。"没事,温妮,"他说,"我们都是好孩子。"

突然,露丝喊道:"我找到什么东西了!"

"摸上去像什么?"乔希问道。

"就像一个窗框,"她说,"不过没有玻璃——

熊猫谜案

只有一块板子什么的。"

"那一定是煤槽。"乔希说,"有多高呢?"

"在我头顶上方一点点,"露丝说,"不过我能够得着。"

丁丁和乔希摸着墙走到露丝身旁。

"我觉得你找到了煤槽,露丝。"乔希说,"可是我们怎样才能把它打开呢?"

丁丁举起沉重的铁铲,问道:"用这个行吗?"

第十章

丁丁摸了摸盖在煤槽上的木板,说:"木板摸上去感觉很旧。小伙伴们,你们往后退,我用铲子砸开它。"

"你能击中吗?"露丝问,"我甚至都看不见你!"

丁丁又摸了摸煤槽,估计了一下距离。他把铲子举过头顶,用力一挥,但没打中。

"假装你被蒙住了双眼,正在挥棒砸彩罐。"乔希说,"罐子里面装满了糖果、钱币和饼干……"

哐当!

熊猫谜案

丁丁第二次挥铲时击中了什么坚固的东西。既然找准了位置,他每次挥铲都能击中。

"看看它松动了没有。"丁丁气喘吁吁地说。

"等一下,"露丝走上前去摸了摸木板说,"我觉得木板已经破裂了!"

"好吧,你再退回来。"丁丁说。他用尽全力抡起铲子,这一次,木板被砸碎了。

"干得不错!"乔希一边说,一边把碎木板挪开,"哦,真恶心,我碰到黏糊糊的东西了!"

他的话还没说完,一堆湿乎乎的东西就掉了下来,闻起来比煤灰的味道还糟糕。接着,一束阳光透过煤槽照了进来,只见乔希脚边堆满了腐烂的树叶。

"丁丁,你成功了!"露丝喊道,然后开始哈哈大笑。

"怎么啦?"乔希不解地问。

"哈哈,我们的腿和脚全是黑的!看上去像熊猫一样!"

孩子们抬头凝视着阳光照射进来的地方。煤槽是斜的,不难看出煤块是如何滑入地窖的。

A to Z 神秘案件

"我们需要借助一些东西才能攀爬上去。"乔希说。

"我们只有煤块。"露丝说。

"还有那个轻便的铁铲!"丁丁补充道,"如果我们在煤槽的开口下面堆一些煤块会怎么样呢?"

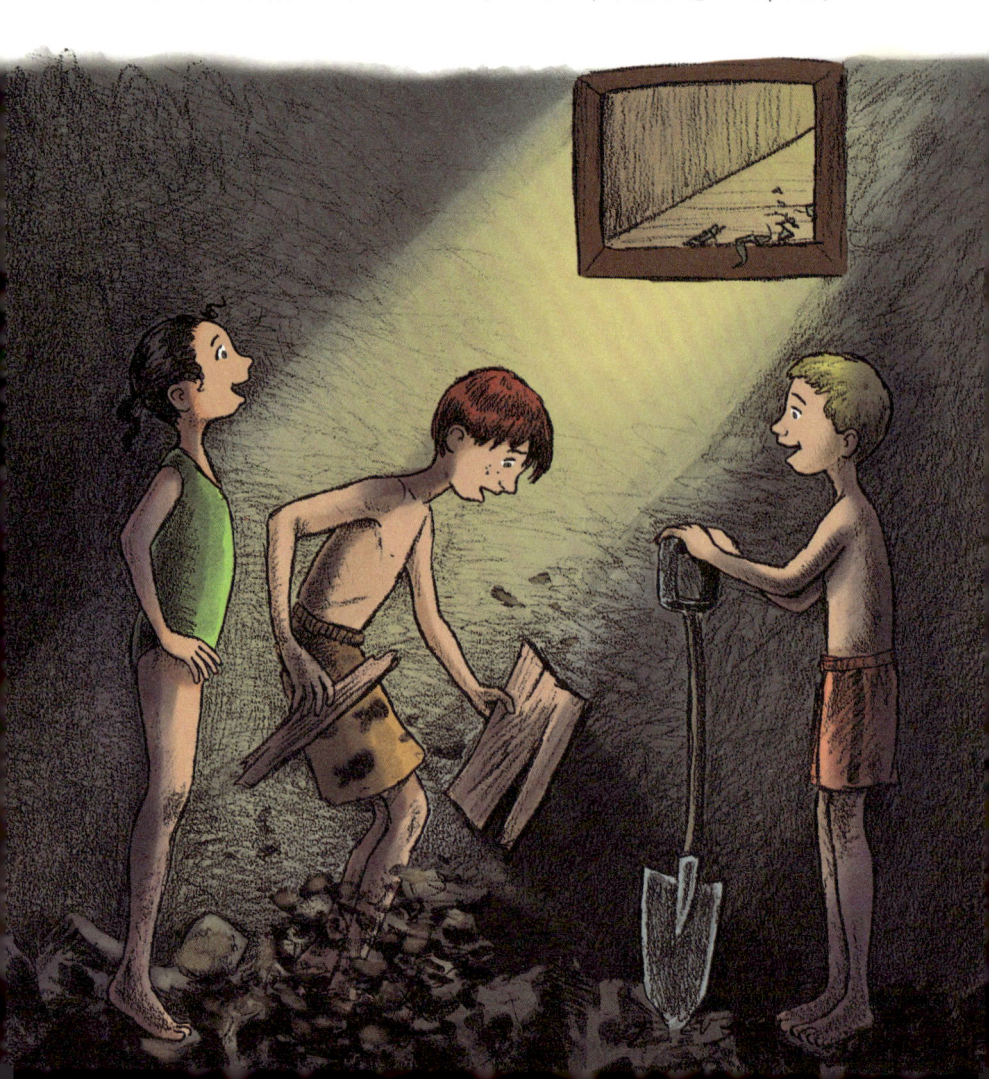

"可是我们怎样才能爬出去呢?"露丝问道,"滑槽很陡,看起来也很滑。"

"我们可以互相往上推。"乔希说,"第一个出去的人可以拉下一个人,里面的人可以把前面的人从下往上推。"

"可是最后一个人怎么办呢?"露丝问道,"谁推他上去?还有,温妮怎么办?"

丁丁说:"我认为,得有人留在这里,其他人去寻求帮助。"

阳光透过煤槽照射下来,孩子们站在那里想办法。

"这样如何?"过了一会儿,乔希说,"露丝,你个子最小,我和丁丁把你推上去,怎么样?你赶快去警察局,我们俩留在这里陪温妮。"

"你确定?"露丝问道,"也许你应该出去,你跑得比我快。"

"不行,我得留下来保护丁丁。"乔希说,"他怕黑。"

"好吧,开始行动吧。"丁丁说,"我们轮流铲煤。"

十分钟之后,露丝就站在了像小山一样的煤堆上。她先把胳膊伸进了煤槽,然后把头和肩膀也伸了进去。"好了,推吧,你们两个!"

丁丁和乔希使劲往上推露丝,直到她只剩脚底还在煤槽外面。"再使把劲!"她声音听起来很低沉,"我够不到那头。"

男孩们用力推着露丝的脚底,她缓缓地爬上煤槽。"好了!"她的声音从远处传来。

丁丁听见她吃力地爬出了洞口。他和乔希抬头望去,看见了她的脸。"尽力找到温妮。"她说完就走了。

丁丁和乔希坐在煤堆上,谁都不想离开那温暖舒适的阳光。

乔希问道:"我们怎样才能找到原本黑白相间,现在却变得浑身乌黑的熊猫呢?"

丁丁说:"我们保持安静,也许就能听到它的声音了。"

于是,他们一动不动地坐在煤堆上,阳光洒落在他们中间,又被闪亮的黑色煤块反射回去。

四周非常安静,丁丁只听得见自己和乔希的

熊猫谜案

呼吸声。但是不管怎么努力,他还是听不见别的声响。

这时,乔希咯咯地笑了起来。

丁丁瞥了他一眼,问道:"有什么好笑的?"

原来,一只漆黑的熊猫宝宝爬到了乔希的腿上,紧紧地依偎着他。

"温妮一定以为你是它妈妈。"丁丁说,"哇!此时此刻多么希望露丝的摄像机在这里啊!"

丁丁和乔希抱着温妮坐在煤堆上,从煤槽射进来的阳光照得他们身上暖洋洋的。

丁丁听到头顶传来了什么声音,便轻声说:"听!"

"好像是有人走路的声音。"乔希一边说,一边把温妮抱得更紧了。

突然,他们听到活板门被打开了,更多的光线射进了房间。

"丁丁?乔希?"是露丝的声音,"我把法伦警官带来了!"

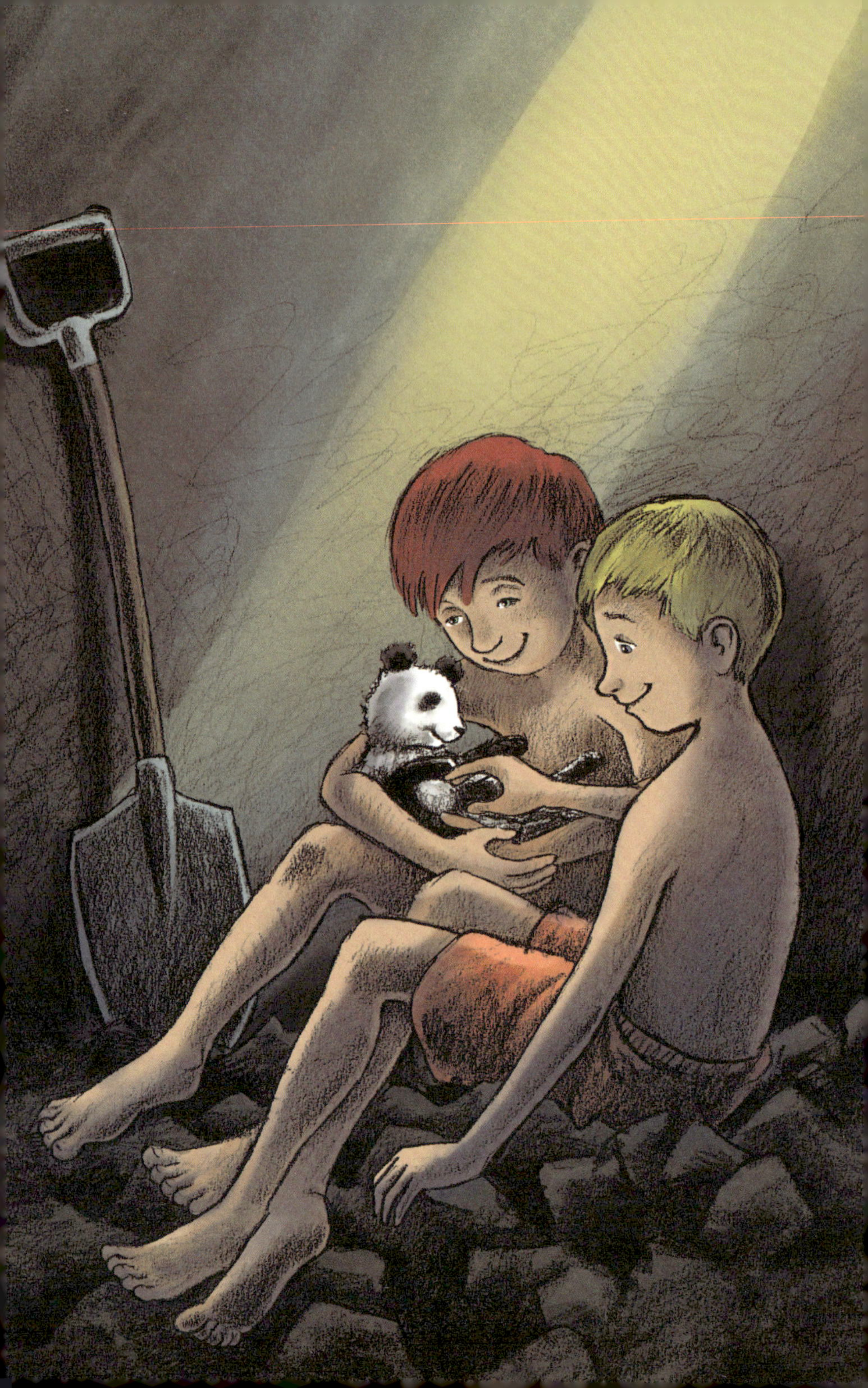

第十一章

那天晚上法伦警官说："要不是你们，菲利普就要逍遥法外了。"

丁丁、乔希和露丝坐在熊猫公园的草坪上。在围栏里面，平平和温妮正在用一根竹子玩拔河游戏。温妮又变成了黑白相间的样子。

丁丁、乔希和露丝也是干干净净的。几个小时前，他们浑身煤灰地回到家里，把他们父母都吓了一跳。

法伦警官继续说道："菲利普本打算在午夜拿到钱后就让你们离开煤窖。"

丁丁问道："所以无法证明他绑架了温妮，也无法证明是他把我们反锁在煤窖里的，对吧？"

法伦警官点了点头，说："没错，没人看见他劫走温妮，也没人看见他锁上活板门。他会把钱藏起来，过个一年半载，再拿出来花。"

"你们真打算将一百万美元放在那棵空心树里吗？"乔希问道。

法伦警官点了点头，说："菲利普知道我们别无选择。"

就在这时，平平打了个哈欠，仰面翻了个身，睡着了。温妮依偎在它身边，嚼着竹子。

丁丁说："可惜菲利普的奶奶威妮弗雷德没能看到这温馨的画面。"

"她给菲利普留了财产吗？"露丝问道。

"留了一些，"法伦警官说，"不过，我猜菲利普认为他应该拥有全部财产。"

"他招供了吗？"乔希问道。

法伦警官点点头，说："你们真应该看看我和露丝走进健身房时他脸上的表情。"

"他以为我还在煤窖里呢。"露丝说，"我看上去一定像个幽灵！"

"他会面临什么惩罚?"丁丁问道。

"他可能会因试图敲诈勒索罪而入狱,"法伦警官说,"此外,他还偷走了温妮,把你们困在煤窖里。"

大家都安静了一会儿。

"有时法官会再给年轻人一次机会,"法伦警官继续说,"尤其是初犯。菲利普似乎对自己的所作所为感到非常懊悔,法官可能会要求他做社区服务来代替一部分刑期。"

"什么是社区服务?"丁丁问道。

"也就是说,菲利普将为绿地镇工作,作为刑罚的一部分。"

"什么样的工作?"乔希问道。

法伦警官笑了。"你们有什么好主意吗?"

"我有,"丁丁说,"他可以免费给孩子们上体操课。"

"他可以在老年中心帮忙,"乔希说,"和老人们一起锻炼。"

"我相信菲利普会乐意的,他也会做得很好。"法伦警官说。

"这样的话,他奶奶也会为他感到骄傲,对吧?"露丝问道。

"我认识他奶奶很多年了,"法伦警官说,"她会为菲利普的行为感到难过。但她总是把人往好的方面想,所以,也一定会给自己的孙子重新做人的机会。"

"这就是人们所说的双赢吧?"乔希问道。

"没错。"法伦警官说,"现在我请大家去埃莉餐馆吃甜筒冰激凌怎么样?"

"这对乔希来说是双倍的幸福啊。"丁丁微笑着对朋友们说。

A to Z Mysteries

The Panda Puzzle

by Ron Roy

illustrated by
John Steven Gurney

INDIAN RIVER
LAWRENCE TAXI
RIVER ROAD
HORSE TRAILS
BIKE PATH
HORSES FOR RENT
WOODS
INDIAN WAY ROAD
WOODVIEW ROAD
FIRE STATION
BIKE PATH
BILL'S BIKES
SUPER MARKET
BRIDGE LANE
ROBIN ROAD
CROW ST
FINCH LA
THRUSH CT
OWL RD
PHEASANT LA
BLUE JAY WAY
WREN DR
FITNESS CENTER
WOODS
BIKE PATH
BLUE BIRD WAY
HUMMINGBIRD LA
WOODCOCK CROSS
ELLIE'S DINER
ACORN APTS
FURRY FEET PET SHOP
OAK STREET
CENTER CHURCH
BIKE PATH
PEOPLE'S POND
POST OFFICE
COMMUNITY GARDEN AND FISH POND
GREEN LAWN $ SAVINGS $ BANK
ELDERLY HOUSING
POLICE STATION
GOOSE ISLAND
WEST GREEN ST
RIVER ROAD
MAIN STREET
GREEN LAWN LIBRARY
SENIOR COMMUNITY CENTER
TOWN HALL
BIKE PATH
CHILDREN'S PETTING ZOO AND AQUARIUM
SHANGRI-LA HOTEL

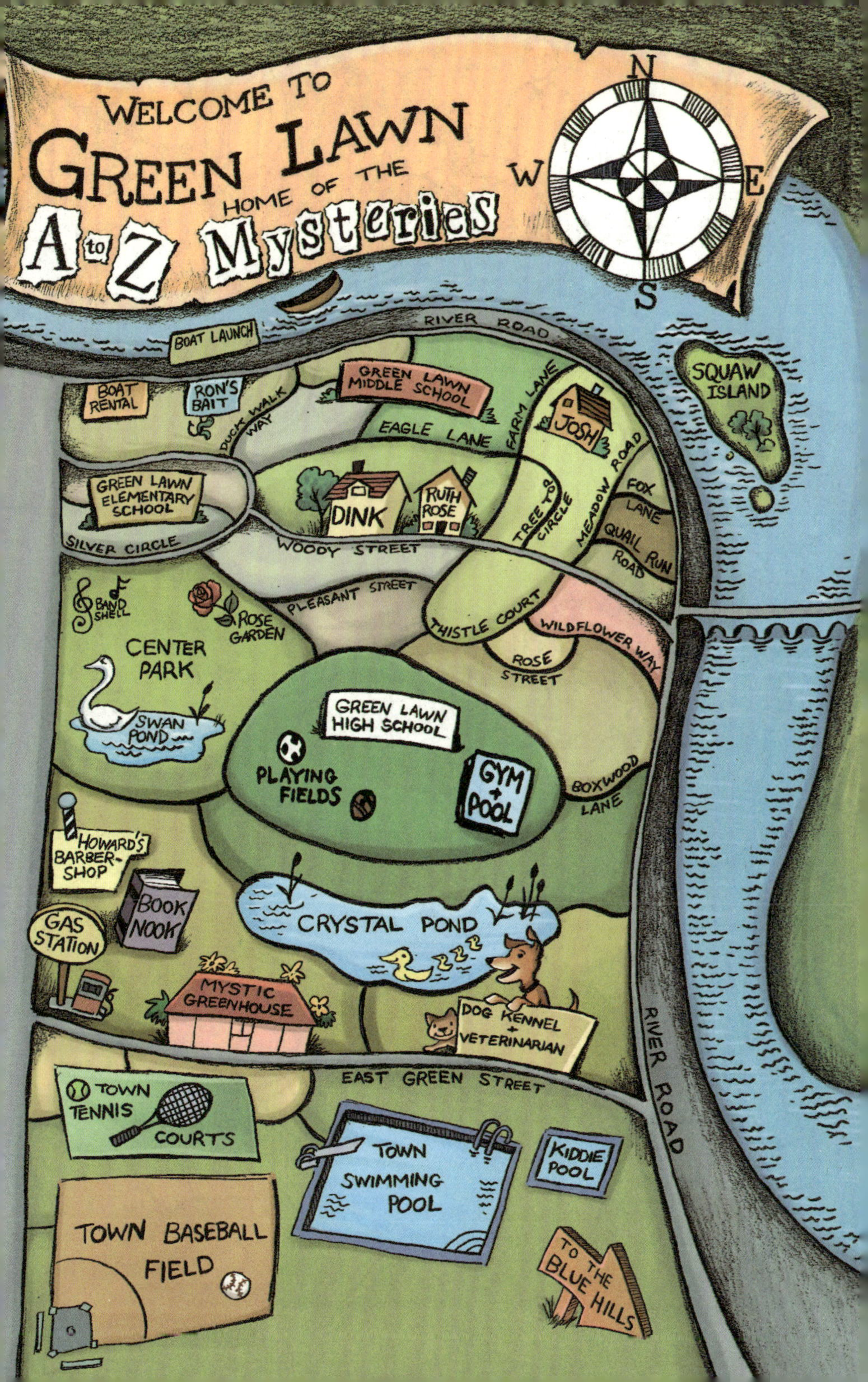

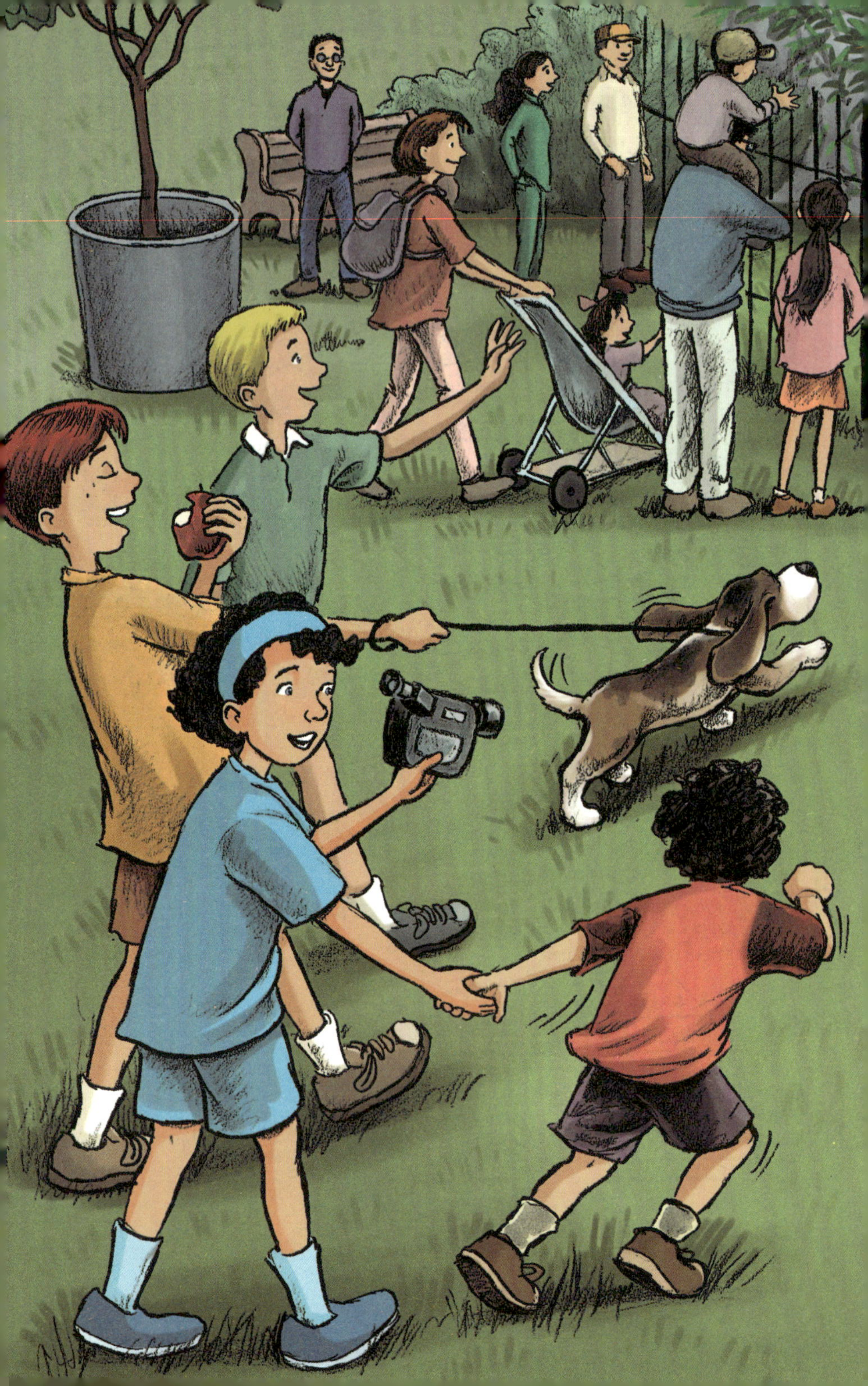

Chapter 1

"I can't believe Green Lawn has its own pandas," Ruth Rose said. She held up her dad's camcorder. "I hope I can get them on videotape!"

Ruth Rose always dressed in one color. Today, she wore sky blue from head to toe.

Ruth Rose, her little brother, Nate, and her friends Dink and Josh were visiting the petting zoo. A mother panda and her baby had arrived just the day before!

All four kids stood in the middle of a crowd near the panda enclosure. Dink recognized a lot of his friends from school. He waved at Officer Fallon and his grandson, Jimmy.

Through the skinny rails of the enclosure fence,

the kids could see a cave and a pool of water. Bamboo grew beside the cave.

From his pocket, Dink pulled out a folded paper. It was an issue of *The Panda Paper*. The front-page story was all about how the pandas, Ping and Winnie, had come to Green Lawn. The headline was PETTING ZOO PERFECT PLACE FOR PANDAS!

"I'm going to ask the editor if I can write a story about the baby panda," Dink said.

Josh was chomping on an apple and holding Pal's leash. "If you do, I'll draw its picture for you," he said.

"Can I play with the panda?" asked Nate.

"Sorry, Natie," Ruth Rose said. "Pandas only like to play with other pandas."

Nate was on tiptoes. "I can't see," he complained. "There's too many big people."

"There's a bench over there," Dink said. "We can see better if we stand on it."

The four kids climbed onto a nearby bench. Now they could see over the crowd. Pal flopped on the lawn with a big sigh and closed his eyes.

The crowd stood just outside the fence. Off to one

side, standing near a microphone, were two men and a woman.

The kids recognized the woman. Her name was Irene Napper, and she worked at the petting zoo. She fed the animals and made sure they were safe and comfortable. She was wearing a green uniform with the words PETTING ZOO stitched onto her shirt pocket.

Next to Irene was a short man with spiky yellow hair. That was Tom Steele, the editor of *The Panda Paper*.

"Who's the guy wearing the necktie?" Josh asked.

The man Josh had asked about was very tan. He was whispering something to Irene Napper.

"That's Flip Frances," Dink said. He showed Josh a picture in *The Panda Paper*. "His grandmother gave the money to Green Lawn to build this park."

Just then, Flip Frances spoke into the microphone. "Can you all hear me?" he asked.

Ruth Rose turned on the camcorder and aimed it toward the microphone.

"Hi, everyone, I'm Flip Frances," he said. "As

many of you know, it was my grandmother, Winifred Frances, who made Panda Park possible. Granny Win would be happy that you all came to meet little Winnie. And I'm pleased that her money went to such a good cause."

He turned to Irene Napper. "Irene is taking good care of our new arrivals," he said, handing her the microphone.

"Thanks, Flip," Irene said into the mike. "I just want to say that I've loved getting to know little Winnie. She's a happy, playful baby."

Irene passed the mike to Tom Steele. "Hello, everyone," the editor said. "As you know, *The Panda Paper* has a very small staff—me! I could use some help. I'd love to print your stories, poems, or pictures about pandas."

Tom Steele grinned. "But I can't pay you anything!"

Everyone in the crowd laughed.

Just then, a black-and-white face appeared inside the cave's entrance.

The crowd quieted. Slowly, the mother panda moved into the sunlight. Her head swiveled around

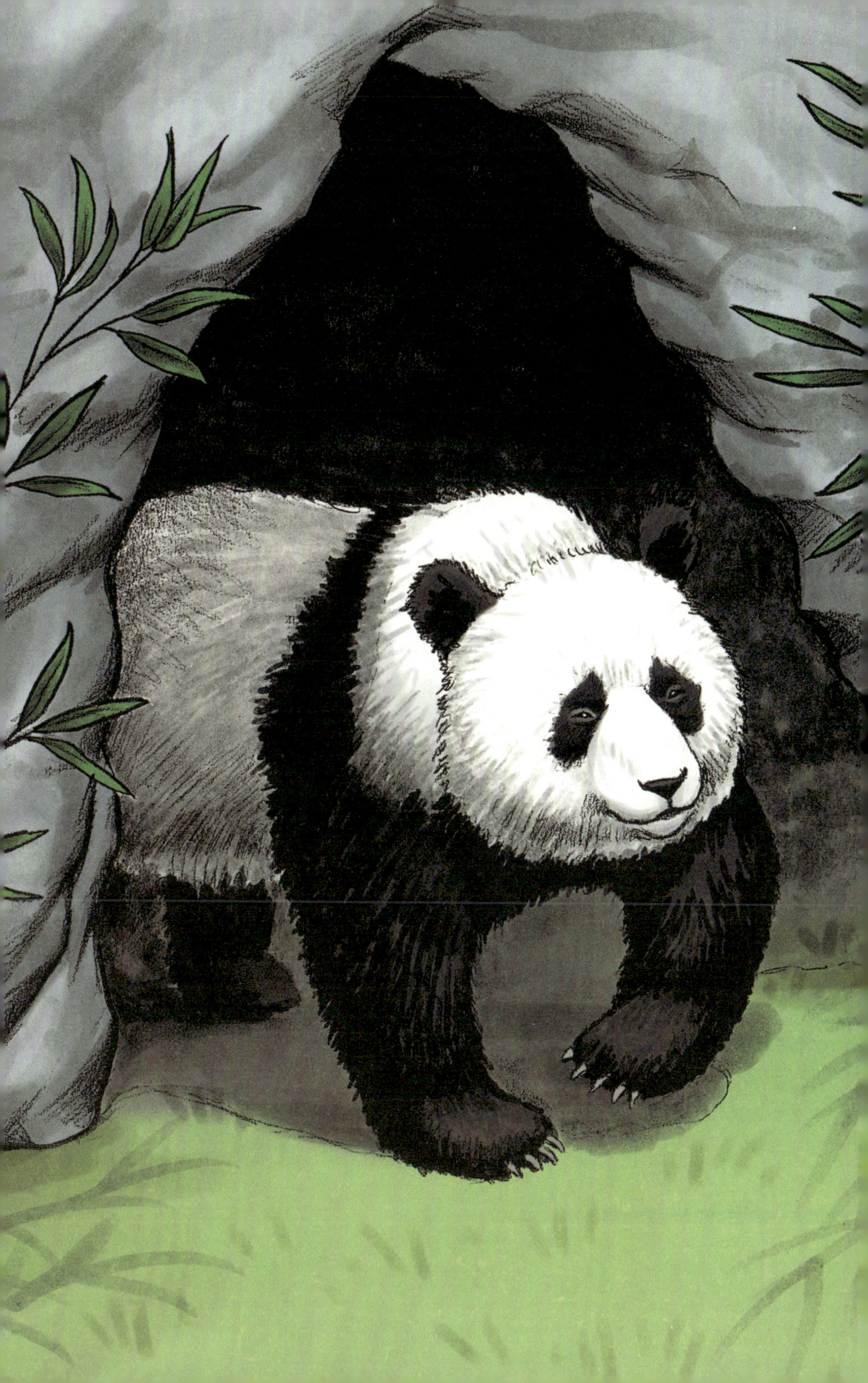

and she lifted her nose into the air. Suddenly she charged the fence and threw her body against the metal rails.

Tom Steele, Irene Napper, and Flip Frances leaped back. People at the front of the crowd jumped back, too.

"What's wrong with her?" Ruth Rose asked, catching it all on videotape.

Ping stared through the bars of the fence. After a minute, she waddled back into her cave.

A man in a green uniform hurried over to Irene Napper. Irene handed him her keys, and the man unlocked the fence gate. Carefully, he crossed over to the cave, knelt down, and looked inside.

Then he reached in and pulled something out. To Dink, it looked like a round alarm clock. A small piece of paper was tied around it with a string. The man relocked the gate and handed the object to Irene. She removed the paper and silently read what was written on it.

"This is so weird!" Josh whispered. "What's going on?"

熊猫谜案

Irene stepped back to the microphone. Dink noticed her hand was shaking.

"This is a ransom note," Irene told the crowd. "Winnie has been kid- napped!"

Chapter 2

"KIDNAPPED!" Ruth Rose gasped.

Everyone in the crowd began talking at once. Officer Fallon ran to talk to Irene.

"Where's Winnie?' Nate asked. "I want to see Winnie!"

"Winnie has gone away for a little while," Ruth Rose told her little brother.

"Where?" the four-year-old insisted.

Ruth Rose put her arm around Nate's shoulders. "We don't know yet,"she said.

Officer Fallon stepped up to the microphone. "Folks, you might as well go home," he said. "We have every reason to believe that Winnie is safe. We'll do our best to get her back."

Tom Steele, Flip Frances, and Irene Napper left Panda Park together.

Officer Fallon and Jimmy began walking around the outside of the panda enclosure.

The crowd slowly wandered away.

"What a lousy thing to do!" Josh said, helping Nate down from the bench.

"What's going to happen to Winnie?" Ruth Rose asked. "Doesn't she need her mother to feed her?"

Dink glanced at the story in *The Panda Paper*. "It says Winnie's almost six months old," he said. "She's eating by herself now."

"Come on," said Ruth Rose. "Let's go talk to Officer Fallon."

The kids caught up with the police chief and his grandson outside the fence behind the bamboo forest. Pal flopped on his belly and stuck his nose through the fence rails. Nate sat next to him and patted the dog's head.

"Hey, kids," Officer Fallon said. "Some situation,

eh?"

"The kidnappers want a million bucks for Winnie!" Jimmy Fallon blurted out.

"Jimmy!" his grandfather said.

"Is it true?" Ruth Rose asked.

Officer Fallon nodded. "I'm afraid that's what this says," he said. Holding the note by its edges, he let the kids inspect it.

Josh read the note aloud:

"Leave one million dollars in the hollow tree on Goose Island by midnight tonight. No tricks, or you'll never see Winnie again."

"A MILLION DOLLARS!" Ruth Rose cried. "Where would Green Lawn get all that money?"

"As I recall," Officer Fallon said, "there's still over a million left from the money Winifred Frances left. The kidnapper must know that."

Dink examined the note. "What does the kidnapper mean by 'tricks'?" he asked.

"He means we shouldn't put any police officers on the island to catch him when he comes for the money," Officer Fallon said. "Or tamper with the bills

熊猫谜案

so we can trace them."

Ruth Rose studied the ransom note. "These letters were cut out of a news- paper," she said.

"Yes," Officer Fallon said. "Which means we can't trace the note."

Suddenly Pal let out a woof. He stuck a paw through the fence and began scratching.

Josh bent down to see what Pal was doing. "Guys, look!" he said.

Partly hidden among the bamboo stalks was something shiny.

"It's a knife!" Jimmy Fallon said.

Officer Fallon got down on his knees. "It sure is," he said. He scratched Pal behind the ears. "Good dog!"

Officer Fallon stuck a long arm through the fence and picked up the knife. He brought it out, being careful not to cut himself.

The knife had a thin blade and a fat handle made of cork.

"Looks like a fishing knife," Officer Fallon said. "If the knife gets dropped in the water, the handle will float."

"Can I have it, Grandpa?" Jimmy asked.

"Afraid not, Jimmy," Officer Fallon said. "This is evidence." He drew a clean handkerchief from his pocket and carefully wrapped the knife.

"Hey, look at this," Josh said. He reached through the fence and pulled back a stalk of bamboo. The top had been sliced neatly off.

"There's more," Josh said, pointing through the fence. "Someone cut a bunch of this stuff."

"Maybe the kidnapper took some bamboo to feed Winnie," Ruth Rose said.

"At least she won't be hungry," Josh said.

"That explains the knife," Officer Fallon said. "With a struggling panda in his arms, the kidnapper probably never knew he dropped it."

Officer Fallon reached into his pocket. He pulled out the object that had been found in Ping's cave. "Know what this is?" he asked.

"It looks like an alarm clock," Dink said.

"It is," Officer Fallon said. "It's an alarm clock with the volume set on loud. I'm guessing the kidnapper tossed it into Ping's cave, knowing the pandas would run out when the thing went off. He probably grabbed Winnie as she came out of the cave."

"And if we want her back," Dink said, "Green Lawn has to pay a million dollars!"

"You're right," Officer Fallon said, "unless we find the bad guy first."

"But we only have till midnight," Ruth Rose said. She looked at her watch. "That's only twelve hours from now!"

Chapter 3

"I'm hungry," Nate announced. "Can we go home?"

"Okay," said Ruth Rose. "I'll make us some sandwiches."

"And I've got to get to my office and check these things for fingerprints," Officer Fallon said. "But unless this guy was stupid, he'd have worn gloves."

They separated at the police station. Dink, Josh, Ruth Rose, and Nate headed for Woody Street.

At Ruth Rose's house, the kids made lunch. Nate took his sandwich to the living room to watch a dinosaur video.

Dink, Josh, and Ruth Rose ate theirs at the kitchen

table. Pal snoozed at Josh's feet.

"It's almost one o'clock," Dink said. "Eleven hours till midnight."

"So where do we start looking for a panda kidnapper?" asked Josh.

"It could be anyone!" Dink said.

Ruth Rose chewed slowly. "Not anyone," she said after a minute. "If that knife really was the kidnapper's, maybe he's a fisherman."

"Or a fisherwoman," said Josh.

Ruth Rose nodded. "Good point."

"Whoever it was either has a key to the gate or can climb over tall fences," Josh went on. He reached for another sandwich. "So who does that narrow it down to?"

"Anyone," Ruth Rose said glumly.

Nate screeched from the living room. "Dinosaur fight! Come see, you guys!"

Josh ran to the living room, with Dink and Ruth Rose following.

On the TV screen, a Tyrannosaurus and a Stegosaurus were circling each other. Their tails lashed back and forth.

The Tyrannosaurus roared and snapped his enormous teeth.

Then the dinosaurs were gone, and the scene switched to a museum. A man's face appeared on the screen. "Hello, I'm Dr. Paleo," he said, "and I'd like to talk to you about what you just saw in this video."

An idea popped into Dink's head. "Ruth Rose, didn't you tape what happened at Panda Park this morning? Why don't we watch your video? Maybe we'll see some clues."

"Good idea," Ruth Rose said. "Do you mind, Natie?"

"Can I have a cookie?" Nate asked, grinning at his sister.

"Sure. Bring the box in here so we can all have some, okay?"

"O-kay!" Nate said, racing toward the kitchen.

Ruth Rose ejected the dinosaur video, then plugged the camcorder into the VCR.

Nate came back with the cookie box. Josh reached for one as Ruth Rose hit the Play button.

The kids watched as Tom Steele, Irene Napper,

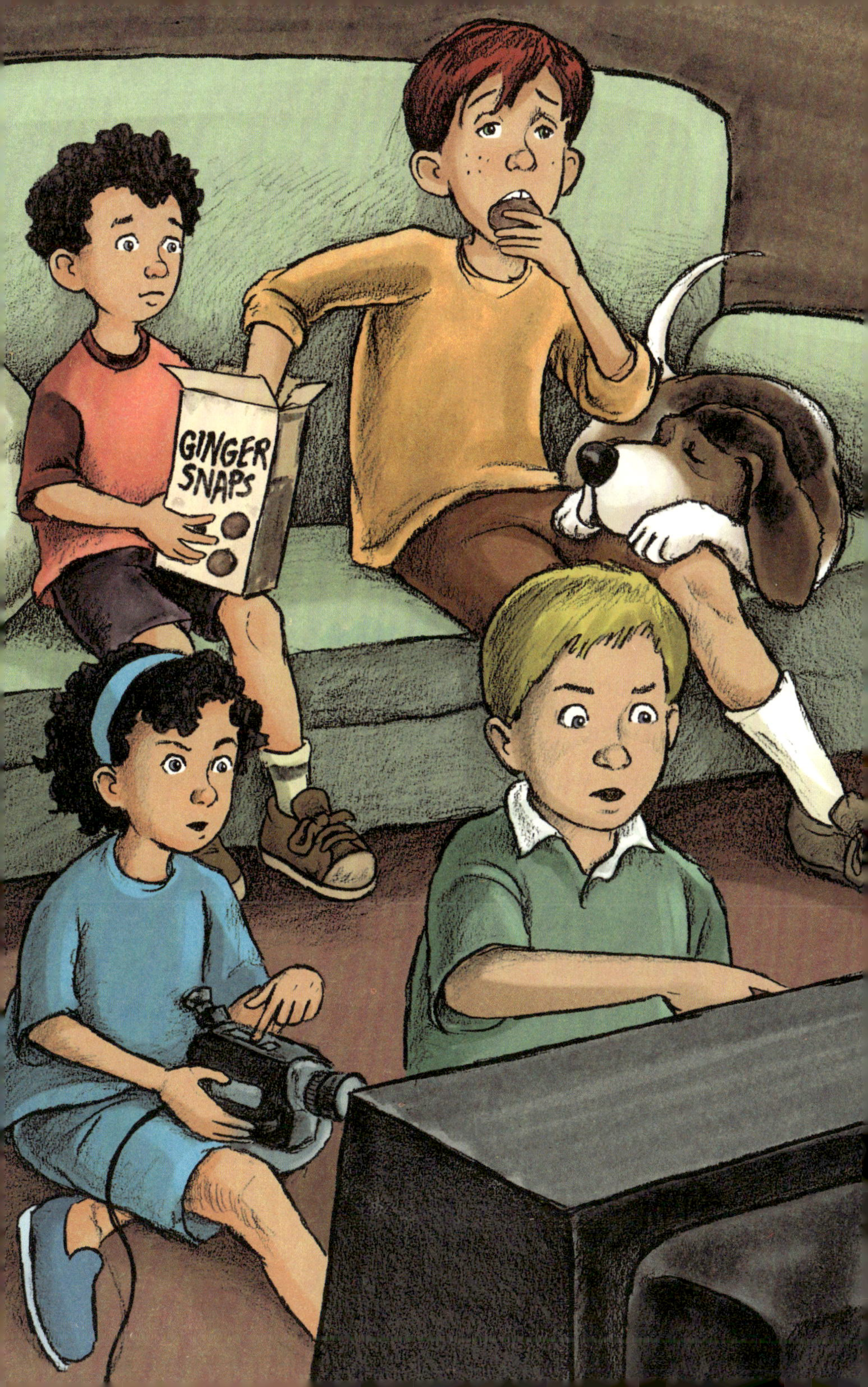
GINGER
SNAPS

and Flip Frances came on the screen. Seconds later, Ping emerged from her cave.

Ping looked around, froze, then turned her head sharply. Suddenly she rushed forward and began throwing herself against the fence.

"She sure looks angry," Dink said.

"You'd be mad, too, if someone stole your baby," Josh said. "It looks like she's trying to attack someone outside the fence."

"Someone in the crowd?" Ruth Rose asked.

"She's not looking at the crowd," Dink said. He put his finger on the TV screen. "Remember, the microphone was there, off to the side. That's where she's looking."

"She's mad at the microphone?" Josh asked, grabbing two more cookies.

"Dink's right!" Ruth Rose said. "Ping is looking at the people standing at the microphone."

Dink, Josh, and Ruth Rose stared at the TV screen.

Finally, Ruth Rose unplugged the camcorder and put Nate's dinosaur tape back into the VCR.

熊猫谜案

"I think one of those three people kidnapped Winnie," she said, "and Ping knows which one."

Chapter 4

"You think Winnie's kidnapper was standing right there at the micro-phone?" Dink asked.

Ruth Rose nodded. "Yes, and I think Ping recognized him or her. That's why she charged the fence!"

"But the guy probably stole Winnie at night," Dink said, "so how could Ping have seen him?"

"Maybe she didn't see him," Ruth Rose said, "but she might have smelled him."

"Right," Josh said. "Most animals can smell a lot better than humans."

Dink stared at the TV screen. "So how do we figure out who Ping was growling at?" he asked.

104

"Too bad pandas can't talk," Josh said. "We could just ask her!"

"Pandas can't talk," Ruth Rose said, "but people can. I say we interview the three people who were standing at the microphone, starting with Irene Napper."

"You think she did it?" Dink asked.

"I don't know," Ruth Rose said. "But she does have a key to the gate."

"If she thinks we suspect her, she might clam up," Josh said.

Ruth Rose pointed at Dink's notebook. "We'll tell her we're writing a story for *The Panda Paper*."

"Good idea," Dink said.

Josh stood up and patted his stomach. "I have to be home by four to watch the twins for an hour," he said.

Ruth Rose grabbed the cookie box. It was empty! "Joshua, I didn't get a single cookie!" she said.

Josh grinned. "Detective work makes me hungry!"

Josh woke up Pal, and the kids left Ruth Rose's house.

105

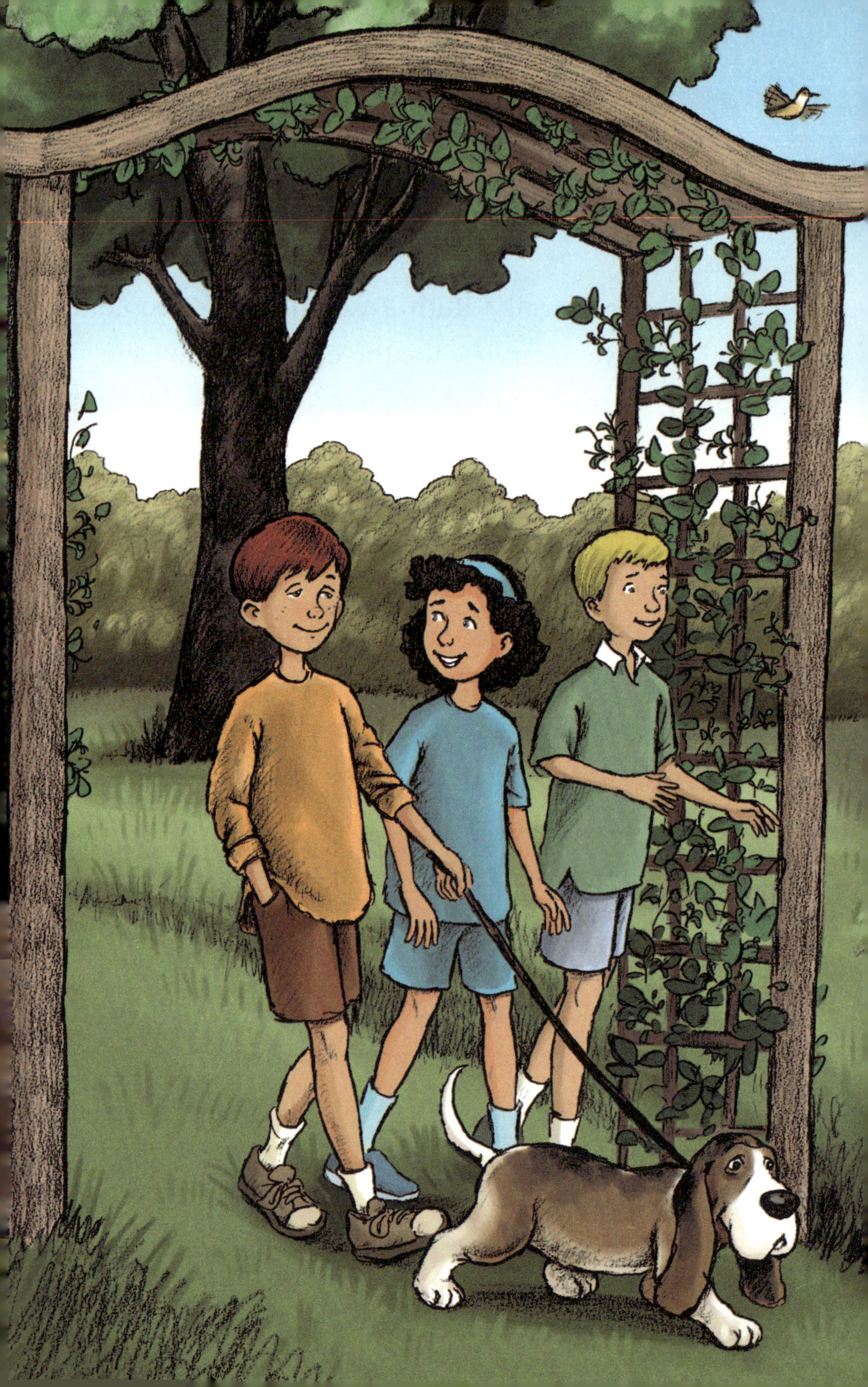

熊猫谜案

They took a shortcut through the rose garden in Center Park. Pal barked at a swan being trailed by three cygnets.

They passed the Book Nook and waved at Mr. Paskey in his window.

At the petting zoo, they passed under a wooden arch. A honeysuckle vine climbed the arch, filling the air with a sweet smell. A hummingbird darted away.

They found Irene Napper surrounded by ducks. She was feeding them pellets that she pulled from one of her uniform pockets.

"Hi, Ms. Napper," Ruth Rose said.

"Well, hi," Irene said. "Say, weren't you kids at Panda Park this morning?"

"Yeah. We're sorry about the kidnapping," Josh said.

Irene's smile disappeared. "I'm so angry I don't know what to do!" she said. "Who would steal a baby panda?"

No one knew what to say. "Good thing Winnie's old enough to eat bamboo," Irene said. "If she still needed her mother's milk, I don't think she'd make it."

Ruth Rose nudged Dink.

"Um, we're writing a story for *The Panda Paper*," Dink said. "Could we ask you some questions?"

The woman looked at Dink for a moment. "Yeah, I guess," she said finally.

Just then, Pal barked, and the ducks scattered.

"But first let's move your dog away from my ducks," Irene said.

The kids followed Irene to a shady bench. She sat and stretched out her long legs.

"Shoot," Irene said.

Pal sighed and dropped to the ground. Irene

108

started stroking his ears. Dink noticed that Irene's hands were large and strong-looking.

Everyone was waiting for Dink to ask a question. But Dink's mind was suddenly blank.

"Who takes care of Ping and Winnie?" Ruth Rose asked, coming to Dink's rescue.

"I do," Irene said. "I feed them, clean out their area, all that stuff. Ping even let me hold her baby."

Dink wrote down what Irene said. Then he asked, "When did you last see Winnie?"

"Last night," Irene said, "when I added fresh water to their pool. That was about eight o'clock."

"So someone snatched her between then and ten o'clock this morning," Ruth Rose said.

Irene nodded. Dink thought she might cry.

Dink had his next question all ready. "How many people have keys to the gate?" he asked.

Irene looked at him. "Only me," she said finally. She patted a key ring hanging from her belt. "And trust me, this was never out of my sight. Whoever took Winnie didn't unlock that gate."

A duck waddled over and pecked at Irene's boot.

109

She reached into her pocket, found a few more pellets, and flung them to the ground.

"I've got to get back to work," she said, standing up. She glanced down at Dink's notebook. "Good luck with your story!"

"Thanks," Dink said. "By the way, do you know where Tom Steele lives?"

Irene shook her head. "No, but you'll probably find him in his office."

Dink looked blank. "His office?"

"It's in the senior community center," Irene said. She gave him a suspicious look. "I'm surprised you don't know that, since you're writing a story for him."

Chapter 5

Dink had to think fast. "Tom Steele doesn't know we're doing a story," he said. "We just decided to write it a little while ago. We're hoping he'll publish it."

"Does he work on Sundays?" Ruth Rose asked.

"I wouldn't be surprised," Irene said. "Especially after what happened to Winnie."

The kids thanked Irene and headed out of the petting zoo. Pal trotted behind Josh with his long ears nearly touching the ground.

"Think she's the kidnapper?" Dink asked.

"I do!" said Josh. "Did you see the size of her hands? She could kidnap a crocodile!"

"It could be her," Ruth Rose said. "She's the only one with a key."

"I don't know," Dink said. "She really seems to like animals."

"Maybe she likes money better," Josh said, wiggling his eyebrows.

They entered the senior community center through a rear door. Dink spotted a sign saying THE PANDA PAPER and an arrow pointing down a hallway.

"Um, what do we ask this guy?" Josh whispered. Pal sniffed the floors as they walked.

"For one thing," Dink said, "I'll ask him if he'll put my story in his paper."

"The one you haven't written yet?" Josh asked with a grin.

"Yeah, that one," said Dink.

Soft guitar music greeted them at an open door. Tom Steele was sitting at a computer with his back to the kids. A small radio sat on the desk.

Dink knocked on the doorjamb. The editor went on typing. He was humming along with the tune.

"Come on," Ruth Rose said, and she walked into

the room.

Tom Steele whirled around in his chair. "You scared me!" he said. He stood up and stared at the kids.

He was probably only a little taller than Dink, but his spiky hair and cowboy boots added another three inches.

He wore round glasses under thick eyebrows that met in the middle. One of his hands had a Band-Aid across the palm.

"Sorry," Dink said. "I'm Dink Duncan and, um, I'm writing a story about Winnie. This morning, you said you wanted stories, so I—"

Tom raised one hairy eyebrow at Dink. "You're a writer?"

"Not yet, but I want to be when I grow up," Dink said.

Tom glanced down at Pal. "Who's this?"

"His name's Pal," Josh said. "He used to belong to crooks!"

"Hmph," Tom said, sitting back down. He removed his glasses, leaned back, and plunked his boots on

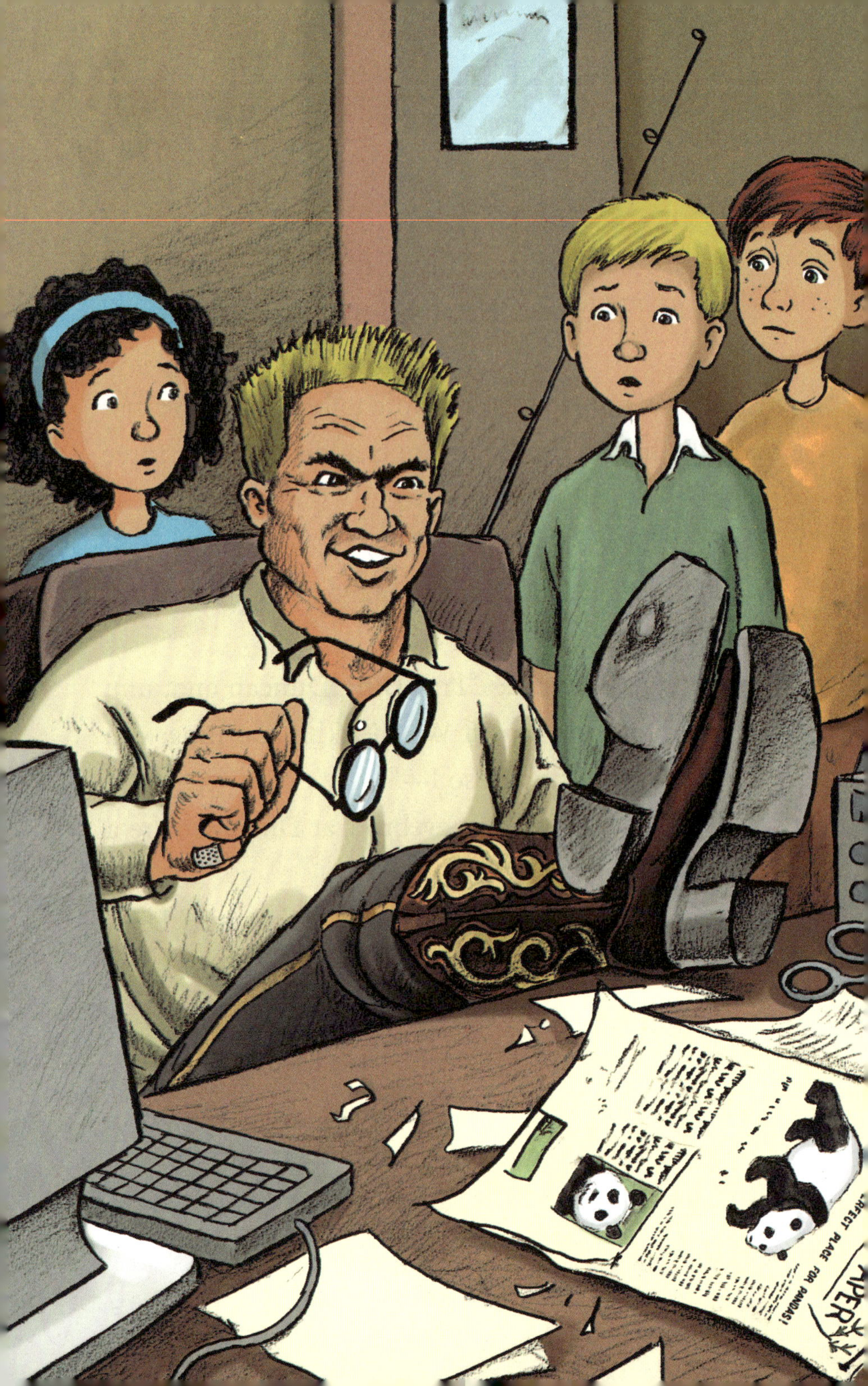
RFECT PLACE FOR PANDAS!
APER

the top of his desk. The desk was littered with papers, scissors, a bottle of glue, pencils, and an oily pizza box.

Tom held up an issue of *The Panda Paper*. There were holes in the paper where sections had been cut out.

"Have you been reading any of these?" he asked.

"We read them all," Ruth Rose said. She showed Tom her own copy.

"We like pandas," Josh said.

Tom squinted his eyes. He stared at the tips of his boots. The only noise in the room was the ticking of a clock. "I like pandas, too," he said finally. "If I get my hands on whoever kidnapped Winnie . . ."

He rubbed his face. "Okay, write your story. If it's good, I'll print it."

"Could we ask a few questions?" Dink pulled his notebook from a pocket.

Tom sighed and glanced at his watch. "I guess I

can spare a few more minutes," he said.

"Do you know anyone who has a key to the panda enclosure?" Dink asked.

"Yeah, Irene Napper does," he said. "I think she's the only one."

Dink nodded.

"Have you ever noticed anyone weird hanging around Panda Park?" Josh asked.

Tom shook his head slowly. "Just normal-looking people like you and me," he said, grinning.

"Were you surprised when Ping got upset this morning?" Ruth Rose asked.

"Sure, we all were," Tom said. "Flip told me he'd never seen her so angry."

"Does Flip Frances visit the pandas a lot?" Josh asked.

Tom stood up. "I have no idea," he said, "and I have to get back to work." He stuck out his left hand to shake. "Excuse the wrong hand. I got a bad paper cut on the other one."

"Thanks, Mr. Steele," Dink said, shaking the hand. He hesitated, then added, "Do you know where we can find Flip Frances?"

"Flip works at the fitness center," Tom said, pointing toward Main Street.

Ruth Rose took a close look at the top of Tom's desk. "Are you going to write a story about the kidnapping, Mr. Steele?" she asked.

The man nodded toward the mess on his desk. "That's what I'm doing right now," he said. "So if you'll excuse me..."

Dink promised to bring his story by in a couple of days, and the kids left. They hurried back down the hall, out the back door, and into the sunshine.

"He's the one," Josh announced. "That Band-Aid gave it away. Paper cut, my aunt Fanny! I bet Winnie bit his hand when he grabbed her."

"He had scissors and glue on his desk, and he was cutting out newspaper clippings," Ruth Rose said. "The ransom note had letters cut out of newspapers!"

"And did you guys see what was leaning in the corner?" Josh asked.

"No, but you're going to tell us, right?" Dink said.

"A fishing pole!" Josh said. "And that was a fishing knife Pal found in the bamboo. I say we call the cops!"

"I don't know," Dink said. "This guy has a hurt hand. And he'd need both hands if he was climbing a fence carrying a panda."

Josh smirked. "Ever heard of ladders?"

Dink grinned at his friend. "What, the guy carries a ladder, an alarm clock, a knife, and a panda? Maybe we should be looking for a juggler!"

Chapter 6

A sign outside the fitness center said NO PETS, NO BARE FEET, NO SMOKING.

Josh tied Pal to a tree, patted his head, and said, "Stay, boy."

Pal sighed and flopped down. His big brown eyes watched Josh, Dink, and Ruth Rose enter the building.

The fitness center was one enormous room. One end was filled with exercise equipment. A bank of windows looked out at Wren Drive.

A shimmery pool took up the other end of the room. A lifeguard watched three swimmers doing laps.

Other people were using the weights and machines.

The clang of metal hitting metal fought with the rock music blaring from hidden speakers.

Dink wrinkled his nose. He smelled a combination of sweat and chlorine.

A green awning was stretched over a counter where juice and health foods were being sold.

"I need a milkshake!" Josh said, shouting above the music. "I feel weak."

"They sell health shakes," Ruth Rose informed him. "They make 'em from seaweed and tofu."

"What's tofu?"

Ruth Rose giggled. "It's white and wiggly," she said. "You'd hate it, Josh."

"There's Flip," Dink said, "behind the counter."

Flip Frances was wearing a T-shirt and blue shorts. He had long, muscular arms. "Can I help you kids?" he asked.

"Hi, Mr. Frances," Dink said. "I'm writing a story about the pandas. Could we interview you?"

"Call me Flip," the man said, smiling at Dink. "Who're you?"

"Call him Dink," Josh said, eyeing the shake machine.

Flip noticed and asked, "You guys thirsty? How about a shake on me?"

"Sure!" Josh said. "But no tofu, please. Or seaweed."

Flip Frances laughed. "How about milk, yogurt, and strawberries?"

"Now you're talking!" Josh said, hoisting himself onto a stool.

Flip expertly tossed ingredients into a blender. He switched it on for a minute, then poured the frothy pink concoction into three tall glasses.

"We were there this morning," Dink said.

Flip slid the shakes and a jar of straws in front of the kids. "My granny Win would be broken-hearted if she knew," he said.

The kids began drinking. Josh made loud slurping noises through his straw.

Dink picked up his pencil. "Why do they call you Flip?" he asked.

"I work out a lot on the floor mats," Flip said. He grinned. "I guess I'm famous for my back flips. Why do they call you Dink?

Josh started to laugh and choked on his shake.

"My real name is Donald David Duncan," Dink told him. "I guess Dink is easier."

Flip looked at Dink's notebook. "So how much have you written?" he asked.

"Not much," Dink said. "We're talking to people who know Winnie."

"Did your grandmother like pandas?" Ruth Rose asked. "Is that why she left all that money?"

Flip nodded. "Granny Win loved animals," he said. "She used to donate money to animal shelters all

熊猫谜案

the time."

Dink glanced at his notes about Irene Napper. "Do you know who has keys to the panda enclosure?" he asked.

Flip nodded. "Yup. Irene has one. I don't know who else."

"Have you seen anybody strange hanging around Panda Park?" Josh asked.

Flip looked up at the ceiling. "Not strange, maybe, but that guy who writes *The Panda Paper* seems to be there a lot. Tom Steele."

In his notebook, Dink wrote TOM STEELE in dark letters.

"Anything else?" Flip asked. "It's almost my lunch break."

The kids finished their shakes. "Thanks a lot," Dink told Flip.

"Glad to do it," he answered.

Just then, a tall redheaded woman approached the counter. She was dressed like Flip, in a T-shirt and blue shorts. "Sorry I'm late," she said to Flip. "You can take off for lunch now."

123

"No problem, Kate," he said. "Late lunch is better than no lunch."

Flip placed both hands on the counter and vaulted over. "Good luck with your story," he said to the kids as he strode out the door.

Dink, Josh, and Ruth Rose followed Flip out. They saw him leap into a dusty jeep with a rack on top. He tooted and waved as he pulled onto Bridge Lane.

"Well, what do you think?" Dink asked, watching the jeep turn right on Main Street.

"He gets my vote," Josh said, untying Pal's leash from the tree. "That guy could climb an eight-foot fence with one arm tied behind his back."

Ruth Rose laughed. "Joshua, ten minutes ago you said the kidnapper was Tom Steele."

"Yeah," Dink said, "and before that, you were sure it was Irene Napper!"

"So who do you think it is?" Josh asked.

"It could be any of them," Dink said with a sigh. He shoved his notebook into his back pocket.

"Did you guys notice that rack on Flip's jeep?" Ruth Rose asked. "I wonder if that's for a boat."

"I don't get it," Josh said.

"Maybe Flip is a fisherman, Josh," Ruth Rose said. "Remember the knife?"

"Wait a sec," Dink said. He zipped back inside the fitness center.

Kate looked up and smiled at him. "Come to work out? Kids get in free after three o'clock on Sundays." She slid three passes across the counter.

"Thanks," Dink said, slipping the passes into a pocket. Then he crossed his fingers behind his back. "Flip said something about going fishing later. Do you know if he has a boat?"

"Just an old canoe," she said. "But he can't go fishing. He's working all day."

Dink felt himself blush. "Oh, um, maybe I made a mistake. See ya!" He darted back outside.

"Canoe," he said.

"See!" Josh crowed.

"That doesn't prove anything," Dink said. "All three of the people we talked to could have done it."

"And time is running out for Winnie," Ruth Rose said. "Eight hours till midnight!"

Josh looked at his watch. "Yikes!" he said, starting to run. "I have to be home in five minutes!"

Chapter 7

The kids hurried to Josh's house. His parents were waiting.

"We'll be back in about an hour," Josh's mom told him as she climbed into the family car. Josh's dad waved and pulled out of their driveway.

"I wanna ride the pony!" Brian yelled, tugging at Josh's arm.

"No! I wanna catch turtles in the river!" Brian's twin

brother, Bradley, bellowed, yanking the other arm.

"You can't do either one without Mom and Dad's permission," Josh said.

"Then we get candy!" Brian said.

"No, we get ice cream!" Bradley argued, bolting for the house.

Josh sighed and followed his brothers. Dink and Ruth Rose laughed, trailing after Josh. Inside, Josh poured five glasses of orange juice.

Brian jumped off his chair and ran from the room. He was back in a flash with a flat cardboard box.

"Let me help!" Bradley said.

"No, it's my puzzle!" Brian yelled. "Josh!"

"You guys do the puzzle together or not at all," Josh said, "and don't get your sticky little fingers all over the pieces."

"What's the puzzle, Bradley?" Ruth Rose asked.

"Gwizzly bears!" Bradley answered, dumping the pieces onto the table. The picture on the box top showed a mama grizzly bear and her cub.

The puzzle pieces were large, just right for four-year-old fingers. Brian and Bradley had done this puzzle before. Their hands flew over the pieces, jamming them into place.

A few minutes later, the puzzle was complete, except for one piece. The baby grizzly bear's face was missing.

"You took it!" Brian yelled at Bradley.

"Did not. You did!" Bradley yelled right back.

"Don't argue, guys," Josh said. He dropped down to the floor and looked under the table. "Not here. Maybe it's in your room."

The twins flew out of the kitchen and thundered toward their bedroom.

Twenty seconds later, they charged back into the kitchen. Bradley held the missing piece in his little hand. He lurched back onto his chair and fitted the piece into place.

熊猫谜案

"Where'd you find it?" Josh asked.

"Under my bed," Bradley said, grinning.

"I wish finding a missing panda bear was that easy," Dink said.

Ruth Rose sat up. "That's it!" she said. "Maybe we should be looking for Winnie, not the guy who took her."

"But where?" Dink asked. "He could've stuck her anywhere."

"If I kidnapped a panda bear," Ruth Rose said, "where would I hide it?"

Josh took a bowl of apples out of the refrigerator and gave one to Brian and one to Bradley. "You can feed the cores to the pony," he told them.

The twins shot out the back door, racing each other to the barn. Pal waddled after them.

Dink, Josh, and Ruth Rose took their apples outside. They sat on the back steps and watched the twins pet Polly through the corral rails.

"Baby panda bears aren't house-broken like regular pets," Josh said, munching his apple. "You couldn't really hide one in your house."

129

"And I bet Winnie misses her mom," Ruth Rose said. "She'd probably cry a lot. People would hear her."

"Right," said Josh. "So the kidnapper probably hid her where it's already noisy."

Dink watched Polly the pony chomp Brian's apple core. "The kidnapper has to feed Winnie, so he'd keep her nearby."

"I know a place," Ruth Rose said. "It's noisy and smelly, and not far away from the petting zoo."

Josh grinned at Ruth Rose. "I do, too. The fitness center, right?"

Ruth Rose nodded. "If Flip stole Winnie, that would be a perfect place to hide her."

"Should we go back and have a look?" Dink asked.

"But what do we do about Flip?" Josh asked. "If he really is the kidnapper, won't he be suspicious when we show up again?"

Dink reached into his pocket and brought out the passes. "Kids get in free today," he said.

"Excellent!" Ruth Rose said. "We can go over for a swim and a snoop!"

Chapter 8

The kids met in front of the fitness center an hour later. They were carrying their bathing suits and towels.

Flip and Kate were behind the counter. The gym was crowded, and the music was still blasting.

"Back again?" Flip asked.

Dink laid the three passes on the counter. "We came for a swim," he said.

"Great idea," said Kate. "Come on, I'll show you where to change."

She led the kids toward the pool. There were a lot of other kids splashing around. A few grown-ups sat on the side, watching. The lifeguard prowled around

A to Z 神秘案件

the pool, keeping a sharp eye on the swimmers.

Kate stopped in front of a row of four doors. Two of them were labeled MEN and WOMEN. But the two doors in the middle were unmarked.

"Here are the changing rooms," Kate said. "No diving, no running, and listen for Danny's whistle. If he blows it once, everyone freeze. Then he'll blow it again twice. That means kids get out of the pool for fifteen minutes while the adults swim. Have a good time!"

"See you in three minutes," Ruth Rose said, and disappeared into the girls' changing room.

Dink and Josh went into theirs and found themselves alone. Blue metal lockers lined the four walls. At the far end were showers, sinks, toilets, and a floor-to-ceiling mirror. The floor was carpeted, and there were benches to sit on.

Dink walked over to a small closet with STORAGE stenciled on the door. He peeked inside.

"See any pandas?" Josh whispered.

Dink glanced at Josh in the mirror. "No, but I see a skinny redheaded monkey."

"You are so dunked when I get you in the pool,"

Josh said.

The boys changed, stashed their clothes in two lockers, and headed for the pool.

The lifeguard stopped them. "Hi, guys," he said. "I'm sure Kate explained the rules, right? You've got about ten minutes before adult swim. Have fun!"

"Thanks, we will," Dink said.

Ruth Rose came out wearing a lime green bathing suit. The kids jumped into the water at the shallow end.

"Now what?" Josh asked, glancing toward Flip behind the counter.

"I wonder what's behind those two other doors," Dink said.

"One might lead to the bowling alley," Josh said. "I think it's right below us."

"Maybe we can check them out during adult swim," Ruth Rose said.

"When the whistle blows, make sure you climb out on that side."

While they waited, the kids swam and splashed each other. Josh tried standing on his head underwater. He came up coughing.

133

ST

熊猫谜案

Suddenly the whistle blew.

Everyone in the pool turned and faced the lifeguard. "Adult swim!" he yelled, and blew the whistle twice more.

There was a wet stampede as the kids clambered out of the water. At the same time, the adults tried to climb into the pool.

Most of the confusion was right in front of the changing rooms. No one noticed as Ruth Rose tried the handles on the unmarked doors. One was locked, but the other one opened.

"Come on!" Ruth Rose whispered as she slipped through. Dink and Josh were right behind her.

When Dink pulled the door closed, it was pitch-black.

"Where the heck are we?" Josh asked, shivering. All three kids were dripping pool water.

Dink put his arms out and touched smooth walls on each side. He inched one bare foot forward and felt the edge of a wooden step.

"I think we might be at the top of a staircase," he whispered.

A to Z 神秘案件

"Let's try to find a light," Josh said. "I hate the dark."

"Not yet," Ruth Rose said. "Let's feel our way down and see if there's a light at the bottom."

"Watch out for slivers," Dink said.

The kids made their way down the dark stairs. They reached a hard, cold floor and stopped.

"Okay, I'm not going any farther without light!" Josh announced. "I feel like one of those blind fish that live in a cave."

They felt around on the walls.

熊猫谜案

"Got it," Ruth Rose said. There was a click, and the lights came on.

The kids were standing at one end of a corridor. The floor was smooth stone. The bottom half of the walls was rougher stone, with newer-looking painted boards on the top. The ceiling was a mess of ancient wooden beams, rusty pipes, and spider webs.

"Check this out," Dink said. Scratched into the mortar between two stones was a date: 1902. "This wall was built a hundred years ago!"

"And it's still creepsville," Josh said through chattering teeth. "These stones are c-cold!"

The narrow corridor was filled with broken gym equipment, rolled-up floor mats, and large paint containers. A row of cardboard boxes lined the right-hand wall.

There were no other doors in the corridor.

"What's that noise?" Ruth Rose asked. "It sounds like thunder."

Dink leaned his head against the wall on his left. "I think the bowling alley is on the other side," he said.

The kids began walking along the hallway.

"Let's look in every box," Ruth Rose said. "Winnie's small, so she could be hidden anywhere."

Five minutes later, they'd run out of boxes. Most had been empty, but a few held white packing peanuts. The kids stood at the end of the corridor and thought about what to do next. A floor mat had been left there. The kids flopped down on it.

Josh rubbed his bare feet and shivered.

"It's weird that they'd have this long hall with no doors," Dink said.

"Maybe it was an old basement before the fitness

center got built," Ruth Rose said.

"Ouch!" Josh said.

"Now what?" Dink asked.

"I don't know, but it hurts!" Josh got up and poked the mat where he'd been sitting.

"Help me lift this thing," he said. "There's something under it."

The kids got up and helped Josh lift the mat. Hidden underneath was the metal handle of a trapdoor.

Chapter 9

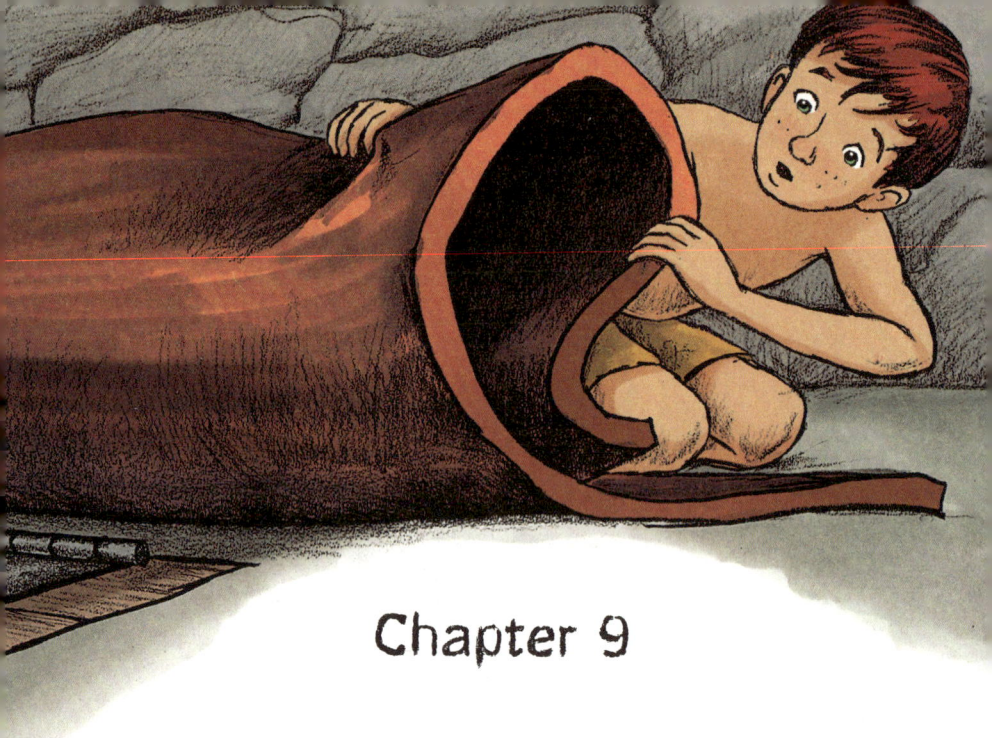

"Should we open it?" Josh asked.

Without answering, Dink grabbed the handle and pulled. The door came up easily. Beneath it were stone stairs leading down. They heard something skittering about in the darkness below.

"Yuck, rats!" Josh said. "If you think I'm going—"

"Shhh, I heard something else!" Ruth Rose said.

Then they all heard it. It was a squeaking, crying noise.

"That's Winnie!" Ruth Rose said. She ran down the stairs. Dink and Josh were right behind her.

The air at the bottom of the steps was filled with

熊猫谜案

some kind of dust. It stung their eyes. The only light came through the open trapdoor.

"Guys, I think we're in an old coal cellar," Josh said. "My grandfather has one, and it's just like this!"

Dink could feel the coal dust in his eyes and nose and on his lips. He began to cough.

"Look, there's Winnie!" Ruth Rose whispered. Across the room glowed a pair of eyes.

Suddenly the trapdoor slammed shut. Instantly they were in total darkness. Then they heard the sound of metal on metal.

"Someone locked us in!" Josh said. "I can't see anything!"

"Let's not panic, okay?" Ruth Rose said.

"Let's just sit down where we are," Dink suggested.

"But I can't see!" Josh complained. "This place is disgusting!"

Dink sat down. Underneath him, he felt a few lumps of coal. He brushed them aside.

"I'll bet Flip locked us in," Ruth Rose said. "He must have figured out where we went."

Dink heard Josh standing up. "What're you doing,

A to Z 神秘案件

Josh?"

"This building is old, so maybe the lock is, too," Josh said. "I might be able to force it."

"I'll help you," Dink said. He and Josh stumbled up the steps and shoved against the trapdoor. It didn't move.

"Well, it was a good idea, Josh," Dink said.

They found their way back down the steps and sat next to Ruth Rose.

"How are we supposed to get out of here?" Josh asked in a shaky voice.

"Maybe there's a window," Ruth Rose said. "Don't basements have windows?"

"But it's not a basement," Josh said. "It's just a room where they kept the coal in the old days."

"I bet no one ever comes down here anymore," Dink said. "It was a good place to hide Winnie."

"Where is she, I wonder?" Ruth Rose said.

"She's probably hiding," Dink said. "If only we had a light."

"Gee, if I'd known I was gonna be trapped underground," Josh said, "I'd have brought my flashlight."

"Don't worry," Ruth Rose said. "Flip will let us out

after he collects his money at midnight."

"Well, I'm not sitting here till midnight," Josh said, standing up again. "I have a plan!"

"You do?" Dink said.

"Yeah," Josh said, sliding lumps of coal out of the way with his bare feet. "Let's hold hands and try to find the walls. Then we can feel around the whole room."

"What're we feeling for?" Ruth Rose asked.

"The coal chute," Josh said.

"The coal shoot?" Dink said. "Like in a gun?"

"The coal chute, Dinkus. C-H-U-T-E," Josh said. "My grandfather told me how coal used to get delivered. They slid it down a chute right into the basement."

"So you're saying there's one of those slide things here somewhere?" Ruth Rose asked.

"Yeah, and it'll lead to the outside!"

The kids held hands, with Ruth Rose in the middle. Dink and Josh reached out and groped for the walls.

Seconds later, Dink tripped over something. He landed on his knees in a pile of coal.

"I found a shovel," Dink said, running a hand over the metal shape.

He used the shovel to help him stand. He lost his balance and fell against a wall.

"Okay," he said, rubbing his elbow. "I found a wall. Now what?"

"Feel along for some kind of opening," Josh said. "It might be kind of high up."

All three kids moved along the wall, feeling their way. Dink used the shovel like a cane as he shuffled along.

Once Dink heard a whimper. "It's okay, Winnie," he said into the darkness. "We're the good guys."

Suddenly Ruth Rose shouted, "I FOUND SOMETHING!"

"What's it feel like?" Josh asked.

"Like a window frame," she said. "But there's no glass—there's a piece of board or something where the glass should be."

"That must be the chute," Josh said. "How high up is it?"

"A little above my head," Ruth Rose said. "But I can reach it."

Dink and Josh felt their way along the wall until they were standing next to Ruth Rose.

"I think you found it, Ruth Rose," Josh said. "But how do we get it open?"

Dink lifted the heavy metal shovel. "Will this do?" he asked.

Chapter 10

Dink felt the wood that covered the chute. "It feels old," he said. "Back away, you guys. I'll smack it with the shovel."

"How will you hit anything?" Ruth Rose asked. "I can't even see you!"

Dink felt the chute again, judging its distance. He raised the shovel over his head, swung, and missed.

"Pretend you're blindfolded and you're swinging at a pinata," Josh said. "It's filled with candy, money, cookies..."

THWACK!

Dink's second swing struck something solid. Now

that he had the right location, he was able to hit it every time he swung.

"See if it's loose," Dink said, out of breath.

"Wait a minute," Ruth Rose said. She stepped forward and felt for the wood. "I think you cracked it!"

"Okay, get back again," Dink said. He swung the shovel with all his might. This time, the wood shattered.

"You got it!" Josh said, pulling broken wood away. "Oh, gross, there's something slimy on me!"

As he spoke, a pile of wet stuff fell into the room. It smelled worse than the coal dust. A beam of sunlight fell through the chute. At Josh's feet was a pile of rotted leaves.

"You did it, Dink!" Ruth Rose cried. Then she started to laugh.

"What?" Josh asked.

"Our legs and feet are black! We look like pandas!"

The kids stared up at the sunlight. The chute was slanted. It was easy to see how coal would come sliding down into the cellar.

"We need something to climb on," Josh said.

"All we have is the coal," Ruth Rose said.

147

"And my handy-dandy coal shovel!" Dink added. "What if we make a pile right under the opening?"

"But how do we climb out?" Ruth Rose asked. "The chute is steep and looks slippery."

"We can boost each other up," Josh said. "The first one out can pull up the next one. The ones on the inside

熊猫谜案

can push."

"But how about the last person?" Ruth Rose asked. "Who boosts him up? And what about Winnie?"

"I guess somebody has to stay here while the others get help," Dink said.

The kids stood and thought, with the sunlight streaming down through the chute.

"How's this?" Josh said after a minute. "Ruth Rose, you're the smallest. What if Dink and I boost you through the chute? We can stay here with Winnie while you run to the police station."

"Are you sure?" Ruth Rose asked. "Maybe you should go. You're a faster runner."

"Nah, I have to stay to protect Dink," Josh said. "He's afraid of the dark."

"Okay, let's get to work," Dink said. "We'll take turns shoveling."

Ten minutes later, Ruth Rose stood on a small mountain of coal. She stuck her arms into the chute, then her head and shoulders. "Okay, push, you guys!"

Dink and Josh pushed Ruth Rose until only the bottoms of her feet were sticking out of the chute.

"More!" she said, her voice sounding hollow. "I can't reach the other end."

As the boys pushed the bottoms of her feet, Ruth Rose inched up the chute. "Okay!" came her faraway voice.

Dink could hear her scrambling to pull herself out. When he and Josh looked up the chute, they saw her face at the other end. "Try to find Winnie," she said. Then she was gone.

Dink and Josh sat on the coal they'd piled up. Neither wanted to leave the comforting shaft of sunlight.

"How do we find a black-and-white panda who's now all black?" Josh asked.

"Maybe if we're real quiet, we'll hear her," Dink said.

They sat totally still on their hill of coal. The sunlight fell between them, bouncing off the shiny black chunks.

Dink heard his own breathing and Josh's. But try as he might, he couldn't hear anything else.

Then Josh giggled.

"What's funny?" Dink asked, glancing over at Josh.

A coal-black baby panda had crawled onto Josh's lap. It was snuggling up against him.

熊猫谜案

"Winnie must think you're her mama," Dink said. "Boy, do I wish I had Ruth Rose's camcorder now!"

Dink and Josh sat and cuddled with Winnie. The sunlight coming through the chute warmed them up.

Dink heard something over his head. "Listen," he whispered.

"Sounds like someone walking," Josh said, holding Winnie tighter.

Suddenly they heard the trapdoor opening and more light fell into the room.

"Dink? Josh?" It was Ruth Rose's voice. "I brought Officer Fallon!"

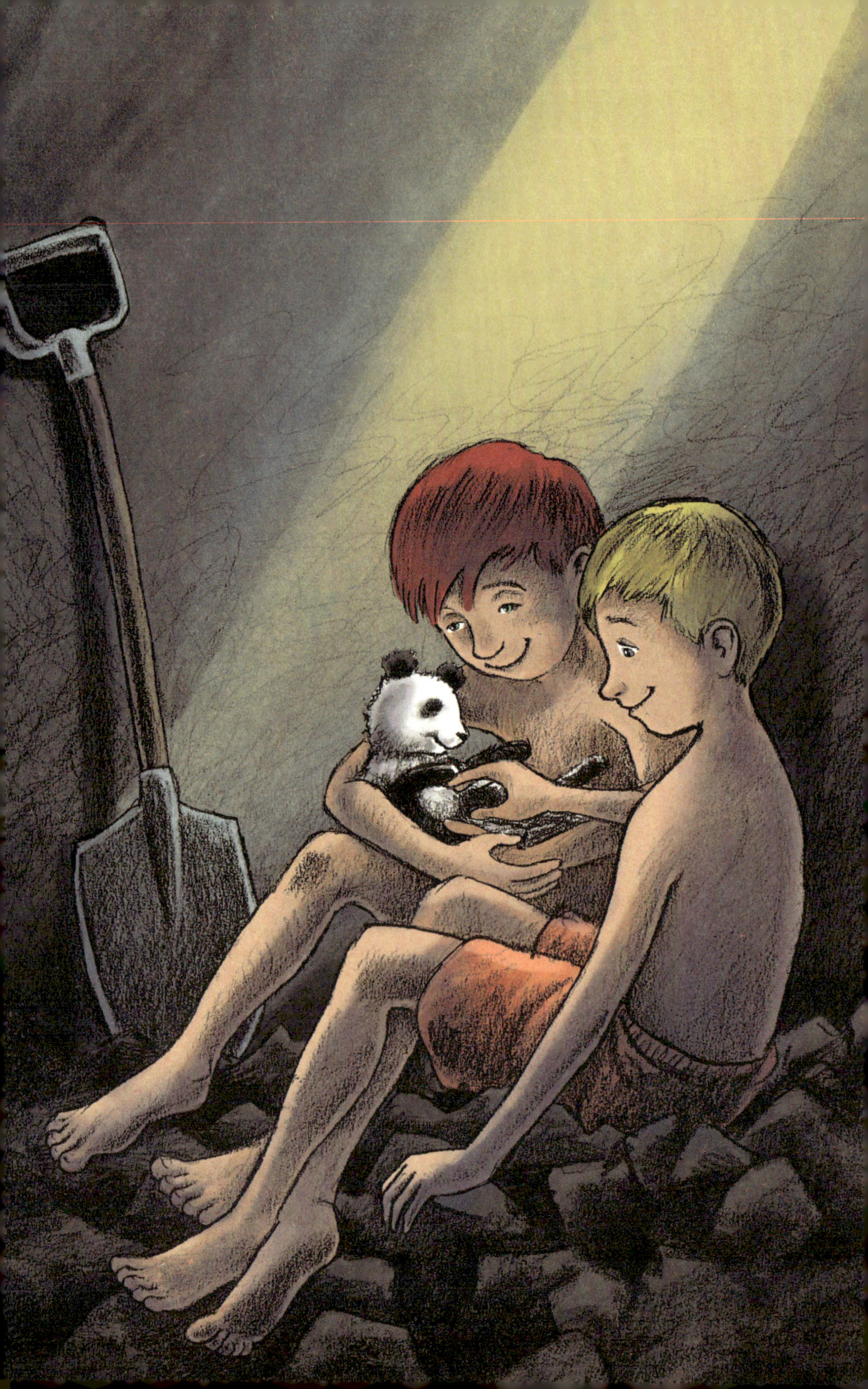

Chapter 11

"If it hadn't been for you kids, Flip would have gotten away with it," Officer Fallon said later that evening.

Dink, Josh, and Ruth Rose were sitting on the lawn at Panda Park. Inside the fence, Ping and Winnie were playing tug-of-war with a stalk of bamboo. Winnie's fur was once again black-and-white.

Dink, Josh, and Ruth Rose were clean, too. A few hours ago, they had surprised their families by showing up completely covered with coal dust.

"He'd have picked up the money at midnight, then let you kids out of the coal cellar," Officer Fallon continued.

"So no one could have proved that he took Winnie

or locked us in, right?" Dink asked.

Officer Fallon nodded. "That's right," he said. "No one saw him take Winnie or lock that trapdoor. He'd have hidden the money somewhere. In a year or so, he might have begun spending it."

"Were you really going to leave a million bucks in that hollow tree?" asked Josh.

Officer Fallon nodded. "Flip knew we had no choice," he said.

Just then, Ping yawned, rolled over on her back, and went to sleep. Winnie cuddled next to her and chewed the bamboo stalk.

"Too bad Win Frances isn't here to see this," Dink said.

"Did she leave Flip any money?" Ruth Rose asked.

"Some," Officer Fallon said. "But I guess Flip thought he was entitled to all of it."

"Did he confess?" Josh asked.

Officer Fallon nodded. "You should have seen his face when I walked into that gym with Ruth Rose."

"He thought I was still in the coal cellar," Ruth Rose said. "I must have looked like a ghost!"

154

"What will happen to him?" Dink asked.

"He'll probably go to jail for attempting to extort money," Officer Fallon said. "Plus, he stole Winnie and trapped you kids in the coal cellar."

Everyone was quiet for a moment.

"Sometimes a judge will give a young person a second chance," Officer Fallon went on, "especially if it's his first crime. Flip seems very sorry for what he did. The judge might ask him to do community service in place of some of his jail time."

"What's community service?" Dink asked.

"That means that Flip would do work for Green Lawn as part of his sentence."

"What kind of work?" Josh asked.

Officer Fallon smiled. "Got any good ideas?"

"I do," Dink said. "He could give free gymnastics lessons to kids."

"And he could help out in the senior center," Josh said. "He could do exercises with the old people."

"I'm sure Flip would be willing. He'd be good at it, too," Officer Fallon said.

"And his grandmother would be proud of him,

right?" Ruth Rose asked.

"I knew Win Frances for many years," Officer Fallon said. "She'd be sad about what Flip tried to do. But she was a woman who always gave people the benefit of the doubt. Win would give her grandson a second chance, too."

"So is this what they mean by a Win-Win

situation?" Josh asked.

"Exactly," Officer Fallon said. "Now how about I treat us to ice cream cones at Ellie's?"

"That's a Josh-Josh situation," Dink said, smiling at his friends.

Text copyright © 2002 by Ron Roy
Illustrations copyright © 2002 by John Steven Gurney
All rights reserved under International and Pan-American Copyright Conventions.
Published in the United States by Random House, Inc., New York,
and simultaneously in Canada by Random House of Canada Limited, Toronto.

本书中英双语版由中南博集天卷文化传媒有限公司与企鹅兰登（北京）文化发展有限公司合作出版。

"企鹅"及其相关标识是企鹅兰登已经注册或尚未注册的商标。
未经允许，不得擅用。
封底凡无企鹅防伪标识者均属未经授权之非法版本。

©中南博集天卷文化传媒有限公司。本书版权受法律保护。未经权利人许可，任何人不得以任何方式使用本书包括正文、插图、封面、版式等任何部分内容，违者将受到法律制裁。

著作权合同登记号：字18-2023-258

图书在版编目（CIP）数据

熊猫谜案 ：汉英对照 /（美）罗恩・罗伊著 ；（美）约翰・史蒂文・格尼绘 ；高芸译. -- 长沙 ：湖南少年儿童出版社, 2024.10. -- （A to Z神秘案件）.
ISBN 978-7-5562-7818-3
Ⅰ．H319.4
中国国家版本馆CIP数据核字第20244J501M号

A TO Z SHENMI ANJIAN XIONGMAO MI'AN
A to Z神秘案件 熊猫谜案

［美］罗恩・罗伊 著　　［美］约翰・史蒂文・格尼 绘　　高芸 译

责任编辑：唐 凌　李 炜	策划出品：李 炜　张苗苗　文赛峰
策划编辑：文赛峰	特约编辑：杜天梦
营销编辑：付 佳　杨 朔　周晓茜	封面设计：霍雨佳
版权支持：王媛媛	版式设计：马睿君
插图上色：河北传图文化	内文排版：李 洁

出 版 人：刘星保
出　　 版：湖南少年儿童出版社
地　　 址：湖南省长沙市晚报大道89号
邮　　 编：410016
电　　 话：0731-82196320
常年法律顾问：湖南崇民律师事务所　柳成柱律师
经　　 销：新华书店
开　　 本：875 mm×1230 mm　1/32　　印　　刷：三河市中晟雅豪印务有限公司
字　　 数：85千字　　　　　　　　　　　印　　张：5
版　　 次：2024年10月第1版　　　　　　印　　次：2024年10月第1次印刷
书　　 号：ISBN 978-7-5562-7818-3　　　定　　价：280.00元（全10册）

若有质量问题，请致电质量监督电话：010-59096394　团购电话：010-59320018

A to Z 神秘案件 中英双语 第二辑

The Quicksand Question
流沙之谜

[美] 罗恩·罗伊 著
[美] 约翰·史蒂文·格尼 绘　曹幼南 译

湖南少年儿童出版社　小博集
·长沙·

印第安河
劳伦斯出租车公司
沿河路
骑马
小径
自行车道
租马处
树林
林景路
印第安路
消防站
自行车道
大桥路
比尔
自行车店
超市
知更鸟路
乌鸦街
雀鸟巷
歌鸫街
猫头鹰路
野鸡巷
蓝松鸦路
鹪鹩路
健身
中心
森林
自行车道
蓝鸟路
蜂鸟巷
丘鹬路
埃莉餐馆
橡子公寓
毛脚
宠物店
橡树街
自行车道
中心教堂
人民池塘
邮局
社区花园
和鱼塘
绿地储蓄银行
老年公寓
警察局
西绿街
鹅岛
沿河路
老年活动中心
绿地
图书馆
镇公所
主街
儿童动物园
和水族馆
香格里拉
酒店
自行车道

欢迎来到绿地镇
一起解开A to Z神秘案件
北
西
东
南
沿河路
码头
租船处
罗恩鱼饵店
鸭子步行道
绿地中学
老鹰巷
农场路
乔希家
少女岛
绿地小学
丁丁家
露丝家
林梢弯道
牧场路
狐狸小道
银环路
林荫街
鹌鹑路
音乐台
玫瑰园
宜人街
蓟花街
野花路
玫瑰街
中心公园
天鹅池
绿地高中
运动场
体育馆
游泳馆
黄杨木巷
霍华德理发店
角落书店
加油站
清水塘
奇妙温室
狗舍+兽医
东绿街
镇网球场
儿童游泳池
镇游泳池
沿河路
镇棒球场
去往蓝山镇

人物介绍

三人小组的成员，聪明勇敢，喜欢读推理小说，紧急关头总能保持头脑冷静。喜欢在做事之前好好思考！

丁丁

三人小组的成员，活泼机智，喜欢吃好吃的食物，常常有意想不到的点子。

乔希

三人小组的成员，活泼开朗，喜欢从头到脚穿同一种颜色的衣服，总是那个能找到大部分线索的人。

露丝

绿地镇的警长，经常在关键时刻出现，帮助三人小组。

法伦警官

绿地超市的经理，带孩子们去参观了超市的车间，告诉他们关于货物托盘的信息。

德里克·罗布

消防站的消防员，盗窃案前夜牧场着火，赶到火灾现场救火。

杰克

字母 Q 代表 quicksand，意思是流沙……

突然，乔希停下了脚步。他转过身来，满脸惊慌地叫道："我的脚陷进去了！"

丁丁看到，乔希的身子开始下沉，水已经没到了乔希的膝盖！

"我的脚拔不出来了！"乔希大叫，"可能是流沙！"

"别急！"丁丁说。他扑上前去，一把抓住了乔希的胳膊。

丁丁马上感觉到沙子在没过他的脚面、脚踝，逐渐没过他的膝盖。他也陷进去了！

"别动！"丁丁大叫，"往后躺下。"

丁丁自己躺到水里做了个示范。他面朝上漂了起来。虽然他的腿还陷在沙子里，但身体已经不再往下沉了。

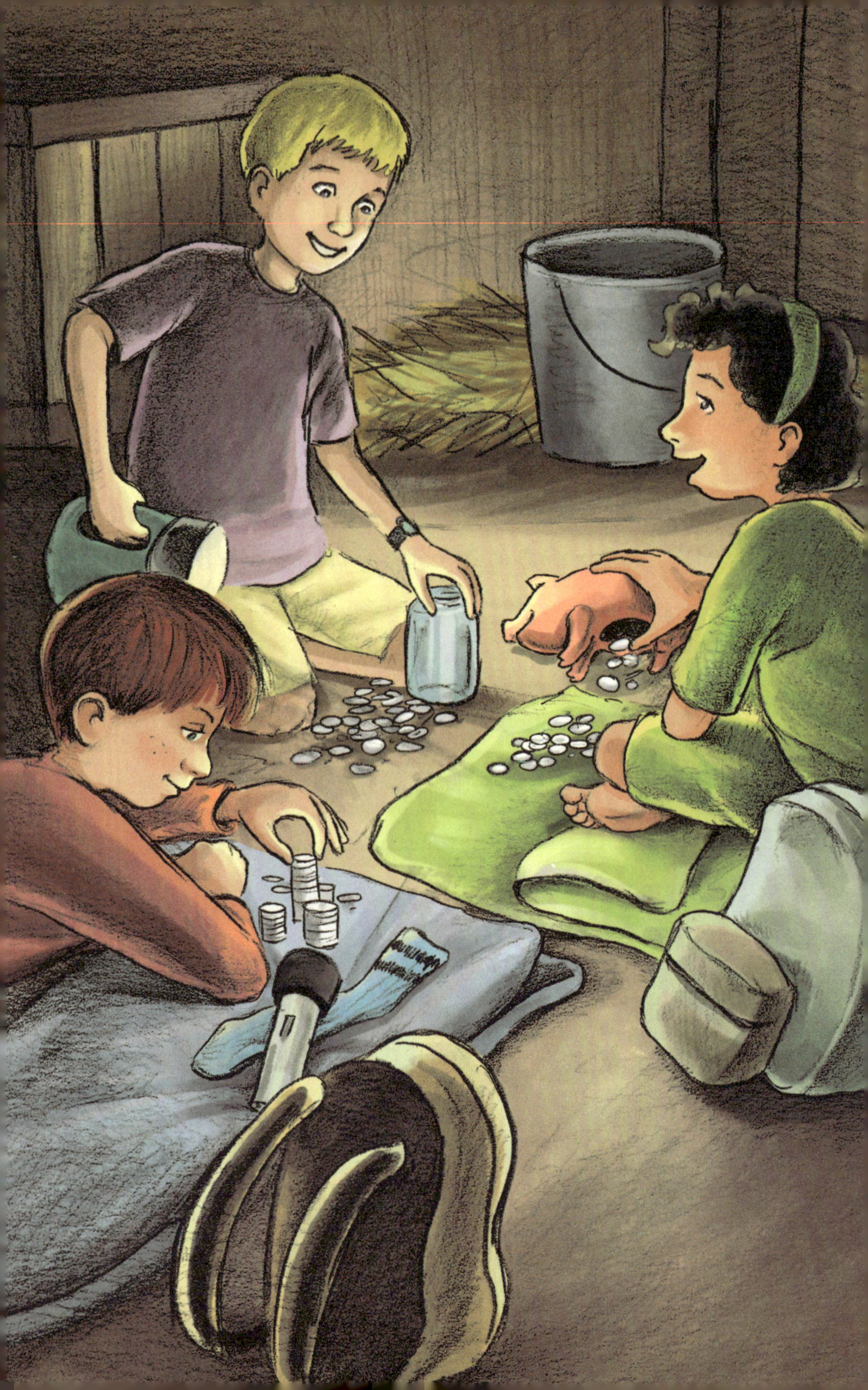

第 一 章

　　这是一个周六的晚上。丁丁、乔希和露丝在乔希家的谷仓里过夜。

　　丁丁把一罐硬币倒在他的睡袋上。"我简直不敢相信，鸭子储蓄箱快要满了。"他说。

　　"我知道。"露丝说着，也将她的小猪存钱罐里的钱全部倒了出来，"我们已经存钱存了整整一年了！"

　　"你们俩先别说话。"乔希说着，把五美分、十美分、二十五美分的硬币整齐码放在睡袋上，"你们要是说话，我就数不清了！"

　　"鸭子储蓄箱"是一个大型塑料存钱罐，形

状像鸭子，被放置在主街上的消防站内。它有四英尺[1]高，由透明塑料制成。镇上的所有人都会往里面投钱，这些钱将专门用于为鸭子们建造一座特殊的桥。

多年来，鸭妈妈们都要穿过沿河路，才能去大桥路附近的树林里筑巢。孵化出小鸭子后，鸭妈妈又要领着鸭宝宝们穿过沿河路回到河里。

问题是鸭宝宝们个头太小了，不易让人看见，因此，许多司机差一点发生交通事故。最后，镇里召开了一次会议，来决定该怎么办。

有个人建议雇保安护送鸭子们过马路。

一个差点把车开进河里的人，想要把鸭子们圈起来，关进笼子里。

另一个人提议在沿河路下挖一条隧道。

丁丁学校的一个女孩，想出了一个绝佳的主意。"我的爷爷奶奶住在佛罗里达州，他们在院子里也养了鸭子。"她解释道，"那些鸭子需要穿过一条繁忙的街道，因此我爷爷建造了一座小

---

1. 英尺：英美制长度单位，1英尺=0.3048米。——编者

流沙之谜

桥。我奶奶在桥面上撒了玉米,让鸭子们知道这座桥是专门为它们建造的。现在,鸭子们每次过街时都会从这座桥上经过。"

所有人都很喜欢这个主意。

高中的工艺课老师普兰克先生举起了手。"这座桥可以由我班上的学生们来设计。"他说,"等我们攒够了钱,我再帮着他们一起把桥建起来。"

现在储蓄箱快要满了。周一上午,绿地储蓄银行的行长菲斯凯尔先生会把储蓄箱里的钱清点出来。下周学校一放学,普兰克先生和高中生们就会开始建桥了。

乔希数完了自己的钱。"九美元十美分。"他说着,揉了揉自己的肚子,"数钱数饿了!"他抓起自己的背包,掏出一盒巧克力豆曲奇饼干。他还带了苹果、胡萝卜和狗粮饼干。

小马波莉卧在马厩里的一堆干草上睡觉,乔希的小狗帕尔蜷缩在它的身边。

外面,六月的蟋蟀在谷仓后的田野里嚯嚯地叫着。

A to Z 神秘案件

"我存了十美元二十二美分。"丁丁说,"你呢,露丝?"

"十四美元三十美分。"露丝回答,"你们觉得鸭子储蓄箱里有多少钱?"

露丝喜欢穿同一种颜色的衣服。今天,她全套服装和她的睡袋是同一种颜色:橙绿色。她穿着这种颜色的短裤和T恤衫。

"里面有很多钱。"乔希说,"已经满到了鸭子的脖颈处。我们还要放进去三十多美元!"

他打开饼干盒,自己拿了两块饼干,将剩下的递给露丝。

流沙之谜

"我们应该为这座桥想个名字。"他说,"'摇摆通道'怎么样?"他踢掉鞋子,钻进了睡袋。

丁丁关掉手电筒,说:"'鸭子过道'怎么样?"

"'动物大穿越'呢?"露丝说。

"这个我喜欢。"丁丁说着,打了个哈欠。

乔希也关上了他的手电筒,哼了一声说:"'动物大穿越',露丝?天哪,为什么不叫'兔子桥'?"

黑漆漆的谷仓中响起了露丝的笑声。"叫'动物大穿越'是因为其他动物也可能会从桥上经过。"她说,"兔子、乌龟、浣熊……"

"还有野牛。"乔希补充道。

几分钟后,孩子们进入了梦乡。波莉在马厩里发出轻轻的嘶鸣声,帕尔在干草堆上打着呼噜。

过了很久,有什么动静把丁丁吵醒了。他在睡袋里坐了起来。黑暗中,他旁边的乔希和露丝就像两团黑乎乎的东西。

接着,丁丁听到了波莉跺蹄子的声音。当他

13

的眼睛适应黑暗之后,他看见白色的小马站了起来,帕尔也醒了。

丁丁爬出睡袋,朝着小马和小狗走去。他抚摸着波莉温热的鼻子,轻声问道:"怎么啦,波莉?"

波莉打了个响鼻,抖了抖鬃毛。丁丁蹲下身子,挠了挠帕尔的耳后。"我猜你只是做了个噩梦。"他喃喃道。

丁丁用手电筒照了一下自己的手表,现在是凌晨一点。他睡意全无,于是推开谷仓的门,走到了外面。

夜晚温暖而寂静。蟋蟀也沉入了梦乡。乔希家除了后门上的一盏小灯亮着,其他地方一片漆黑。

丁丁深吸了一口气,空气中弥漫着刚刚修剪过的草坪的味道。他赤着脚,踩在松软的草地上,感到很清凉。他打了个哈欠,伸了个懒腰,绕着谷仓散起步来。

谷仓后面是一片宽阔的牧场。牧场边缘就是沿河路,路的另一边是印第安河。在阳光明媚的

流沙之谜

日子里，你可以看到河面上波光粼粼。但现在，牧场、道路和河水全都隐藏在黑暗里。

正当丁丁要返回谷仓时，他注意到远处有两个光点。

汽车前灯，他想。牧场上怎么会有汽车？

随后光点消失了。丁丁自嘲地笑了笑。汽车当然不在牧场上，而是在沿河路上。

丁丁悄悄溜回谷仓，爬进自己的睡袋，然后闭上了眼睛。

突然，波莉开始嘶鸣，帕尔也开始汪汪叫。

"怎么啦？"乔希昏昏沉沉地问。他打开手电筒，照向波莉。

"快看它！"露丝说。

波莉害怕得眼珠转来转去，用后腿撑起了身子，前腿踢向马厩。帕尔吠叫着跑向乔希。"有什么东西让它们感到很不安。"丁丁说，"它们不久前就把我吵醒了。"

然后三个孩子就闻到了气味。

"烟！"乔希大叫道，奋力挣脱出了睡袋。

孩子们跑到外面，想看看是不是有什么东西

燃烧起来了。但夜色寂静，到处漆黑一片。

丁丁走到谷仓后面。"你们快来这里！"他大声喊道。

乔希和露丝匆匆绕过屋角。丁丁指着河水的方向。一团橙色的火光在夜色中摇曳闪烁。

"牧场着火了！"乔希叫道。

第二章

绿地镇的消防车五分钟内就到了火场。丁丁、露丝、乔希,以及乔希的家人,他们站在谷仓旁,看着消防员们将火扑灭。

"我要去看消防车!"乔希的弟弟布拉德利在他爸爸的怀里扭动着身子央求道。

"不行。"他爸爸说,"而且火已经被扑灭了,你该去睡觉了。"

"不,我不想睡觉!"布拉德利的双胞胎兄弟布赖恩抗议道,"现在是玩耍时间!"

乔希的爸爸忍不住笑了。

丁丁看了一眼手表,时间大概是凌晨一点

半。他能看见牧场那边消防车的灯光，但消防员的声音他听不清楚。

几分钟后，他们看见消防车开走了。消防车尾灯很快就消失在沿河路上。"好了，结束了。"乔希的妈妈牵着布赖恩的手说，"所有人都回去睡觉。"

"你们三个，再回去睡一觉。"乔希的爸爸说着，抱起布拉德利朝屋内走去。

"好的，爸爸。"乔希说。他们三个和帕尔慢腾腾地走进了谷仓。帕尔再次趴到波莉旁边的草堆里，他们三个则爬回了各自的睡袋。

丁丁突然坐了起来。"嘿，伙伴们，我刚刚想到，我可能看到了放火的人！"他说。

"你这话是什么意思？"乔希问。

"我们闻到烟味之前，波莉吵醒了我。"丁丁解释道，"于是我出去看了看，看到了远处河边有汽车前灯的灯光！"

"也许是有人在露营。"露丝说着，打了个哈欠，"我们早上可以去查看一下。"

流沙之谜

已经是早上了,丁丁心想。他也像露丝一样打了个哈欠,又躺了下去。他正要睡着时,听到黑暗中传来沙沙声。

他僵住了,脑海中想象着有什么夜间生物正朝他爬过来,想要爬进他的睡袋。

接着,他听到了咀嚼声,还闻到了饼干的味道。

"乔希!"丁丁说,"你差点害我心脏病发作!"

"对不起。"乔希一边吞咽着饼干,一边说,"我有点饿了!"

当孩子们醒来时,阳光透过谷仓布满灰尘的窗户照射了进来。小鸟们在歌唱,孩子们从睡袋里钻出来,穿上了各自的运动鞋。

"我们去着火的地方看一看吧。"乔希说。他的衣服皱巴巴的,头发也乱糟糟的。

帕尔用它那双褐色的大眼睛注视着乔希。

"好吧,你也去。"他说着,将帕尔的皮带扣到它的颈圈上。露丝给波莉喂了一根胡萝卜,然后他们就离开了谷仓。

孩子们步行穿过牧场，阳光透过树木间的缝隙照射下来。高高的小草上结满了露水，很快就打湿了他们的运动鞋和双腿。

"快看！"露丝叫道。他们的正前方是一堆湿漉漉的、被熏黑了的木头，空气中弥漫着一股烟味和潮湿的灰烬气味。

这里的地面更加潮湿，消防水管溅出的水在地上形成了水坑。丁丁注意到，周围的草都被踩踏了，地上一片泥泞，留下了深深的脚印。

"为什么会有人在这里点火呢？"乔希环顾四周，问道。他们所站的位置靠近沿河路。路的另一边，有一小段河岸延伸到印第安河。

"也许他们是在烤棉花糖。"露丝说。她找了一根长棍子，开始在烧焦的木头和灰烬中间翻找起来。

"在深夜？"乔希问，"谁会在深夜吃棉花糖？"

丁丁笑了出来："你啊，饼干怪兽先生。"

乔希也笑了。

"这是什么？"露丝问。

她捡起一块木板，把它擦干净。这块木板

流沙之谜

大约有六英寸[1]长,三英寸宽,两端都已经被烧焦了,只剩中间部分没有被烧到。木板上用黑色的墨印着几个字母:ET CO。"ET CO是什么意思?"乔希问。

"CO可能是'康涅狄格州(Connecticut)'这个单词最前面的两个字母。"露丝说。

"或者是'科罗拉多州(Colorado)'。"丁丁补充道。

"我在想,有人放火是不是就是为了烧掉这个。"露丝一边说,一边仔细看着这块窄窄的木板。

"要是能知道有多少个字母被烧掉了的话,就好办了。"丁丁说,"ET CO可能是好几个单词的一部分,比如,'宠物梳子(pet comb)'或'湿外套(wet coat)'。"

"或者是'甜棉花糖'(sweet cotton candy)。"乔希补充道。

---

1. 英寸:英美制长度单位,1英寸=2.54厘米。——编者

"CO也可能是'公司（corporation）'的缩写。"露丝说着，将木板塞进了裤子的后口袋里。

"我觉得是指'吃饼干（get cookies）'！"乔希叫道，转身开始跑起来，"最后一个跑回谷仓的人没有饼干吃！"

第三章

乔希第一个冲进谷仓,丁丁和露丝紧随其后。

乔希立刻扑向饼干盒。他打开盒子,倒吸了一口凉气。"快报警!"他大声叫道,"我被人抢劫了!"

丁丁笑着看向他的朋友说:"他们抢走了什么,你的脑子吗?"

"比那还更严重。"乔希盯着空空的饼干盒说,"他们抢了我的饼干!"

"天哪,我的小猪存钱罐不见了!"露丝说,"我就把它放在了我的睡袋上。"

丁丁把手伸进自己的睡袋的开口,四处摸索

起来。"我装钱的罐子也不见了!"他说。

乔希拉开自己的睡袋。"现在我是真的生气了!"他说,"我装钱的袜子也不见了!"

乔希看向他的两个朋友。"我们不在的时候,有人偷偷溜进了这里。"他说。

"饼干也许是被浣熊拿走的。"露丝说着,环顾了一下谷仓。

"我从书上看到过,乌鸦有时会偷亮晶晶的硬币。"丁丁说。

乔希突然露出了笑容。"不,不是浣熊或乌鸦。"他扬着眉毛说,"我想是两只小猴子!"

"双胞胎!"丁丁和露丝同时叫道。

三个孩子冲出谷仓,跑过院子。乔希冲进厨房,大声叫道:"不许动!"

布赖恩和布拉德利正跪在厨房的椅子上,玩着桌子上的一堆硬币。操作台上放着乔希的蓝色袜子、丁丁的花生酱罐子和露丝的小猪存钱罐。"乔希!"布拉德利大声叫道,"快看我们在谷仓里找到了什么!"

"海盗的宝藏!"布赖恩叫道。

流沙之谜

"错了,是我们的宝藏。"乔希朝着他的两个弟弟怒吼。

布拉德利做了个鬼脸,说:"但是,这是我们发现的,那里没人!"

"这些钱有特定的用途,"丁丁对双胞胎说,"是我们为鸭子们存的。"

"鸭子们为什么会需要钱呢?"布赖恩问。

露丝向他们解释,这些钱将用于建造一座桥,这样,鸭妈妈和鸭宝宝们就能安全地过马路了。

"好吧。"双胞胎异口同声地说。

"还有,我的饼干呢?"乔希挥着手中的饼干盒问,"还给我!"

两个小男孩爆发出一阵咯咯的笑声。

"还不了——它们进了我们的肚子!"布赖恩得意扬扬地说。

五个孩子吃过早餐,乔希让布拉德利和布赖恩去叫醒父母。

乔希和露丝打扫卫生,丁丁把所有的硬币都放进饼干盒里。之后,乔希伸手去牵帕尔的皮带,但帕尔已经自己叼着皮带坐到了门口。

"真是聪明的狗狗。"乔希说着,将皮带扣到了帕尔的颈圈上。丁丁则吃力地抱起重重的饼干盒。

帕尔和孩子们沿着老鹰巷走到银环路,然后穿过主街,到达了消防站。他们看见,法伦警官正从停在消防站前的巡逻警车上下来。

"早上好,孩子们!"警官说,"你们起得可真早。"他弯下腰,摸了摸帕尔柔软的耳朵。

丁丁举起饼干盒说:"我们来投钱!"

流沙之谜

法伦警官笑了。他伸手从车里拿出一罐硬币,说:"我也是。"

"您听说昨晚的火灾了吗?"露丝问。

"听说了。"法伦警官回答,"是场小火灾,我猜消防员轻轻松松就把火扑灭了。现在的问题是,谁放的火?"

"我看见那附近有汽车前灯的灯光,"丁丁向警官报告,"但那是在起火之前。"

"起火前多久?"法伦警官问。

丁丁回忆了一下,说:"不知道,可能十分钟左右。"

法伦警官把他装硬币的罐子放在车顶,然后掏出笔记本翻开,在上面记了几行字。

"这个算是线索吗?"露丝问。她从口袋里拿出那块被烧了一半的木板。

"这是在哪里找到的,露丝?"他问。

"我们今天早上去了火灾现场。"露丝告诉他,"这东西是在灰烬堆里找到的。"

法伦警官仔细看了看那四个字母。"CO通常是'公司(company)'的简写,"他说,"但在

27

O 后面应该还有个小圆点。"

"那个小圆点也许已经被烧掉了?"露丝说。

法伦警官在笔记本上把这一点记录了下来。"探案工作做得不错。"他表扬露丝。

乔希的眼睛一亮。"也许这块木板是从装蛇的笼子上拆下来的,"他说,"写的是'不要抚摸眼镜蛇(Don't pet cobra)'。"

所有人都哈哈大笑。

"好了,我们去把钱投进去吧,这样就能拯救那些鸭子了。"法伦警官说着,将他的笔记本塞进口袋,拿起他的存钱罐。

他们一起走进消防站。某处传来收音机的声

流沙之谜

音,后面墙上的时钟显示时间是上午九点。

绿地镇的消防车停在水泥地上,旁边有一辆更小型的卡车,车门上写着"救援"两个字。

后面的墙上有三扇门。靠另一面墙立着灰色的金属储物柜,储物柜下方放着一排橡胶靴。帕尔走了过去,嗅了嗅其中一只靴子。

"喂!"法伦警官叫道,"有人吗?"

其中一扇门开了,一个穿着深蓝色制服的男人走了出来。"是谁呀?"他问。

"法伦警官和他的几个朋友。"警官说着,晃了晃手里的硬币罐,硬币哗啦作响,"我们是来投钱的。"

丁丁也举起饼干盒。"这越来越重了!"他说。

"太好了!"那个男人说,"到后面来。"

孩子们和法伦警官跟着那个男人来到消防站的后面。男人走向另一扇门,将门推开后让到一旁。"就在里面。"他说。

透过这扇门,丁丁只看见一块地毯、一台电视机和几把看起来很舒服的椅子。

"储蓄箱在哪儿?"乔希问,同时打量着那个男人的周围。

"就立在角落里,它一直在那儿。"男人说着,转身看向屋内。

鸭子储蓄箱并没有在角落里。

房间里根本没有鸭子储蓄箱的踪影。

第四章

"简直不可置信!"男人惊呼道,"储蓄箱昨晚还在,我自己还往里面投钱了!"

"是不是有人把它搬到消防站的其他地方了?"法伦警官问。

男人摇摇头说:"我们把它放在电视休息室,是因为这样能提醒每个人都投硬币进去。另外,那东西几乎有一吨重!"

法伦警官把他的硬币罐交给乔希,拿出了笔记本。"昨晚你去牧场那边灭火了吗?"他问。

男人摇摇头说:"没有,去的应该是杰克和伦尼。"

法伦警官在笔记本上记了下来，问："我在哪里能找到他们呢？"

这个消防员笑了笑。"他们还在另一个房间里小睡，"他说，"应该快要起来了。"

"他们醒来后，请让他们给我打电话。"法伦警官说着，将笔记本放回口袋。

"没问题。"男人回答。

法伦警官和孩子们走到外面。帕尔正趴在警车边上，将头搁在它的大前爪上。

"我想起了一件事。"丁丁说，"昨晚放火的那个人之所以放火，可能是因为他想把这里的人引出去。"

"我也这么认为。"法伦警官说，"放火可能只是想转移人的注意力。"

"对！"乔希说，"这样他们就能趁这里没人时偷偷溜进来，把储蓄箱偷走。"

"谁会做这么卑鄙的事呢？"露丝问。

"喜欢钱而又讨厌鸭子的人！"乔希说。

"会不会与我昨晚看见的那辆汽车有关？"丁丁说，"我在起火前看见了亮着的前灯。"

流沙之谜

"很有可能。"法伦警官说。

一位老人牵着一条拴着皮带的小狗经过。老人又高又瘦,一头白发;小狗又矮又胖,浑身白毛。帕尔呜呜地叫着,来回摇动尾巴。

老人由着他的小狗摇摇摆摆地走到帕尔身边。"你们好,"老人说,"这是伦道夫。你们的这条巴塞特短腿猎犬友好吗?"

乔希点点头说:"帕尔喜欢每一个人!"

帕尔嗅了嗅小狗,舔了舔小狗的脸。伦道夫翻滚在地上,整个身子扭来扭去。

"这里出了什么事吗?"老人好奇地看着法伦警官问。

"只是在调查一桩可能发生了的盗窃案。"法伦警官说。

老人扬了扬他那浓密的白色眉毛。"会不会与我昨晚看见的那个疯狂司机有关?"他问。

法伦警官又拿出笔记本翻开。"请告诉我您看见了什么。"他说。

"过了凌晨一点钟不久,我被消防车的声音吵醒了。"老人说,"于是我牵着伦道夫出门呼吸

33

新鲜空气。我们走到印第安路与主街的交叉路口时,一辆吉普车沿着主街从我们身边快速驶过!"老人用两只手比了个一英尺宽的距离,"差这么点就撞到伦道夫了!"

法伦警官开始在自己的笔记本上写东西。"您是……?"

"撒迪厄斯·波克特,"老人回答,"住在印第安路10号。"

"您看清那辆吉普车的车牌号了吗,波克特先生?"

"哎呀,没有!"老人说,"那辆车的速度太快了。"

"您注意到司机的模样了吗?"法伦警官又问。

波克特先生摇摇头说:"不好意思,我的视力不太好。吉普车里有两个人,但我不记得司机长什么样子了。"

法伦警官合上笔记本,打算收起来。"不管怎样,还是要感谢您,波克特先生。您说的对我们很有帮助。"

"但是我记得坐在副驾驶座的那个人。"波克

流沙之谜

特先生又说。

"是吗?"法伦警官又打开了笔记本。

波克特先生笑着说:"是的,因为他的模样太奇怪了。坐在副驾驶座的人看起来就像一只巨大的鸭子!"

第五章

丁丁、乔希和露丝相互交换了一个眼神。

法伦警官盯着波克特先生说:"那个人看起来像只鸭子?能否详细说明一下,波克特先生?"

波克特先生笑着说:"我看见了反光的头和鸭嘴。现在想来,那个人一定是剃了个光头,长着一只大鼻子。"

法伦警官向波克特先生道了谢,记下了他的电话号码。老人牵着小狗继续散步去了。

"开吉普车的那个人一定就是盗贼!"乔希脱口而出,"鸭子储蓄箱就在副驾驶座上。"

"波克特先生看见吉普车时,那个司机可能

流沙之谜

已经偷了储蓄箱,正在逃跑!"露丝补充道。

法伦警官走向警车。"我会发布消息,让人留意一辆载着一只'鸭子'的吉普车。"他说。

"您介意帮我们保管一下这些钱吗?"丁丁问。他走到警车边,把饼干盒递给法伦警官。

"这个是您的罐子,还给您。"乔希把硬币罐还给了法伦警官。

"没问题。"法伦警官说着,把两个装钱的容器放在座位上,"别担心,我们会把鸭子桥建造起来的。"

他钻进车里,沿着主街驶去。

"那个盗贼现在可能消失得无影无踪了。"丁丁说。他朝着主街与沿河路的交叉路口走去。

"这真让人生气!"露丝说,"全镇居民存了一整年的钱没了,现在我们又要重新开始存!"

孩子们穿过沿河路,坐到了河岸的草地上。帕尔对着一群在杂草中觅食的鸭子汪汪地叫着,鸭子们迅速朝着河的对岸游去。

"也许法伦警官能找到他。"丁丁说。

"我不知道该怎么找。"乔希说,"那辆吉普车现在可能已经在几百英里[1]外了。"

"没事,我们还有这个。"露丝说着,举起了印有字母ET CO的那块木板,"这些字母一定有什么含义!"

乔希捡起一块石头,掷向河里。孩子们看着石头沉入满是沙子的河底。

"有什么想法吗?"丁丁问。

"有,我们去埃莉餐馆吧。"乔希说,"一杯奶昔总是能让我思维敏捷。"

"乔希,我们必须集中精力去找被偷的钱。"露丝说,"想一想那些鸭宝宝吧!"

"好吧,但我们还没想出计划。"乔希说。

丁丁看了看手表。"我们为什么不去看一看昨晚值班的消防员是不是起床了呢?"他提议。

"好主意。"露丝说,"也许他们把火扑灭之后,在回来的路上看见了那辆吉普车。"

孩子们跟在帕尔后面,走回了消防站。一个

---

1. 英里:英美制长度单位,1英里=1.609千米。——编者

高个子男人正用一块布擦着救援卡车。卡车的引擎盖上放着一杯咖啡。

"早上好。"他打着哈欠，跟孩子们打了个招呼。

"早上好。"丁丁说,"请问您是值夜班的消防员吗?"

"您有没有听说发生了盗窃案?"没等消防员回答丁丁的问题,乔希就抢着问。

男人点点头。"我叫杰克。"他说,"有人偷走了鸭子储蓄箱,我真的感到很难过。"

他端起咖啡,坐到了车子的前保险杠上。"我和伦尼去了牧场灭火。到了之后发现火势很小,可能只是露营者留下的火种引发了火灾。"

"法伦警官认为是盗贼放的火。"乔希说。

"我们觉得,他们放火的目的是引你们离开消防站。"丁丁说,"我昨晚在起火点附近看见了亮着的车前灯。"

"一位遛狗的老人看见一辆吉普车在主街上开得飞快。"露丝补充说,"他看到了吉普车里的鸭子储蓄箱!"

杰克惊得张大了嘴巴:"真的吗?"

"请问您在沿河路上有没有碰到一辆吉普车呢?"乔希问。

杰克摇摇头说:"我们在往返的路上都没有看

见任何车辆。"

"您有没有看见有什么人在这附近转悠呢?"露丝问。

杰克俯下身,轻轻揉了揉帕尔的耳朵。"昨晚没有,但几天前,有人在这附近转悠。他借用了我们这里的洗手间,然后就离开了。"

"他看见鸭子储蓄箱了吗?"丁丁问。

"可能看见了。那东西很难不被看见。"杰克说。

"您还记得他长什么样吗?"乔希问。

杰克耸了耸肩。"大高个,和我一样高,但应该比我重。"他说,"哦,他长着一对招风耳,看起来就像在头上粘了两朵大蘑菇。"

第六章

孩子们向杰克道了谢,然后离开了。

"那个人可能就是盗贼!"露丝说。

"我也这么认为。"丁丁说,"那个盗贼一定得是大高个,这样他才能搬得动那个装满硬币的鸭子储蓄箱。"

"现在我可以去喝杯奶昔了吗?"乔希问,"求你们了,我饿了!"

"但你得答应我们,喝奶昔时不发出让人难堪的喷喷声。"丁丁说。

帕尔拽着皮带走在前面,拉着他们来到埃莉餐馆。他们坐到了一个靠窗的卡座里。帕尔趴

流沙之谜

到桌子底下,把头搁到了乔希的脚上。

"嘿,孩子们。"埃莉和他们打招呼。她给帕尔端来了一碗水,拍了拍它的头。

然后,她掏出点单用的本子,说:"来点什么?我们今天的特价菜是鼻涕虫炖菜和蜘蛛意面。"

"好吃。"露丝说,"但乔希只要一杯奶昔就行了。"她从后口袋里掏出印着 ET CO 的木板,放到了桌子上。

"那是什么?"埃莉问。

"是线索。"露丝说,"你听说鸭子储蓄箱的事了吗?它昨晚被偷了。"

"接着说!"埃莉说,她坐到了丁丁的身旁,"告诉我详细情况!"

孩子们对埃莉说了火灾、快速行驶的吉普车的事,以及他们从消防站的杰克那里得知的消息。

"这是从余烬里捡到的。"露丝摸着那块木板说,"我们一直想弄清楚 ET CO 的意思。"

埃莉拿起木板,仔细查看着字母。突然,她露出了微笑,将木板还给露丝。"好吧,这部分

43

谜团我能解决。跟我到后面来吧。"她说。

"在这儿待着别动。"乔希对帕尔说。然后，孩子们跟着埃莉走到柜台后面，穿过厨房，走出后门。

埃莉朝着放在地上的一个小型木头台子走去。台面由窄窄的木板制成，这些木板又被钉在了较厚的木板上。

"我之前见过这种东西。"乔希说，"我爸爸曾订购过一批砖块，砖块运来的时候就是放在这种木头台子上。"

"它被称为货物托盘。"埃莉说。

"快看！"露丝说。她指着印有文字的托盘，上面的文字是：东方货物托盘公司[1]。

露丝拿着那块被烧掉一半的木板凑近托盘上的文字。黑色的字迹完全一样。

"这种托盘是哪里制造的？"丁丁问。

"我不知道。"埃莉说，"这个托盘是从超市

---

1. 英语原文为"EASTERN PALLET COMPANY"，包含有"ETCO"字母组合。——译者

拿的，我想用这些木板在花园四周做一个栅栏。"

"任何人都能拿吗？"露丝问。

埃莉耸了耸肩，说："我猜是这样的。我是向超市经理要的，他叫德里克·罗布。你们还要喝奶昔吗？"

"要！"乔希说。他带头返回了餐馆内。

孩子们点完单，又坐回了卡座。

露丝靠近丁丁和乔希，说："我敢打赌，那个盗贼就是用超市的货物托盘来生的火！"

"要是这样的话，德里克·罗布可能会记得他！"丁丁说。

"那我们去问一问吧。"露丝提议。

"拜托，我们能不能先喝完奶昔？"乔希问。

第七章

孩子们喝完奶昔,离开埃莉餐馆,沿着主街往回走,前往绿地超市。

乔希将帕尔的皮带系到了自行车停放架上。"我们马上回来。"他对狗狗说。

丁丁、乔希和露丝走进超市,来到果蔬区。堆得有如金字塔的橙子和苹果在灯光下闪着诱人的光芒。

他们站在堆积如山的西瓜旁边,环顾四周。购物的顾客很多,许多超市员工在四下忙碌。所有的超市员工都穿着白衬衫、黑裤子,系着绿围裙。

丁丁走到一个留着棕色卷发的女人身边。她正在将一袋袋葡萄陈列好。她围裙上别着的名牌上写着:嘿!我是朱迪。

丁丁问她经理办公室在哪里。

"往里走,"朱迪指着后面说,"生鲜肉类区左边的红门。"

孩子们沿她所指的方向找到了那扇门。丁丁敲了敲门。

"请进!"一个低沉有力的声音响起。

露丝打开门,他们走了进去。办公室里堆满了文件柜、一箱箱破损了的罐头食品,还有一张放着文件的木桌子。

桌子后面坐着一个穿着衬衫、打着领带的男人。男人满面笑容,桌子上的名牌上印着:德里克·罗布。

"嘿!"男人说,"有什么需要我帮忙的吗,孩子们?"

"昨晚有人在我家谷仓后面的牧场放火。"乔希说,"我们觉得,放火的人是用你们这家超市的货物托盘来生火的。"

德里克·罗布

露丝让罗布先生看了看那块被烧过的木板。

罗布先生仔细查看了字母 ET CO。"没错,看上去一样。"他说,"我们的许多商品运来时都是码放在这种托盘上的。"

"几天前,您有把托盘给过一个高个子男人吗?"丁丁问。

罗布先生笑了。"通常谁想要托盘,都可以去拿。"他说,"来吧,我领你们去看一看。"

罗布先生领着孩子们走出了办公室。他们经过一面长长的墙,墙上挂满了员工的照片。丁丁认出了朱迪,那个给他指路的女人。

49

"走这扇门。"罗布先生说着,推开一对宽大的弹簧门,"小心那些叉车!"

孩子们发现,他们来到了一个巨大的房间,这里到处都是工人和箱子,充斥着噪声。男男女女忙着拆开板条箱,把货物装上手推车。

"看。"乔希说。一辆黄色的叉车停在了一堆箱子旁边,箱子码放在一个托盘上。司机拉动控制杆,降下叉车的两只货叉。叉车向前移动,将货叉插进托盘下方。司机再次拉动控制杆,货叉将箱子连同托盘一起从地板上抬了起来。

叉车立刻开始往后退,不断发出嘀嘀的警报声。孩子们和罗布先生往后退了几步,看着叉车载着托盘驶向房间的另一头。

"太酷了!"乔希赞叹道,"我希望我也能拥有一辆这样的车。"

罗布先生轻声笑着说:"这些叉车很贵的,孩子。现在跟我来。"他领着孩子们来到一个又高又宽,有点像车库入口的地方。

"如果你们顺着那些台阶走下去,"罗布先生伸手指着说,"会看到码放在地上的托盘。人们

流沙之谜

随时都可以来拿，拿回去拆了做柴火什么的。"

"所以，任何人都可以随时来拿，对吗？"丁丁问。

"没错。"罗布先生说，"半夜来都可以。"

第八章

"好吧,至少我们弄清楚了盗贼是从哪里拿的木板。"露丝说。

孩子们走出超市,站在超市与消防站之间的空地上。

"那家伙用吉普车载着鸭子储蓄箱去了哪里呢?"乔希问,"波克特先生说他经过了主街,但我们不知道他去了哪个方向。"

"不对,我们知道。"露丝说。

乔希看着她说:"露丝,那家伙既可能往北去了,也可能往南走了。"

露丝摇了摇头。"他不可能往南走。"她说,

流沙之谜

"波克特先生告诉我们,他是在印第安路的拐角遇到吉普车的。如果当时吉普车是从消防站开出来的,那它一定是在往北开。"

"她说得对。"丁丁说,"往北是沿河路方向。"

乔希看向那个方向,说:"到了沿河路,他可能右转驶往蓝山镇,或左转驶往哈特福德市。"

"我们去找波克特先生谈一谈吧。"露丝提议,"他可能还记得吉普车拐往了哪个方向。"

"我们去哪里找他?"丁丁问。

"他住在印第安路10号。"露丝说。

乔希笑了起来,摇着头问:"你怎么连这也能记住啊?"

露丝只是笑了笑。

孩子们将帕尔的皮带从自行车停放架上解了下来,然后从消防站后面抄近路前往印第安路。

印第安路10号是一栋砌着灰色瓦片的小房子,前面围着白色的栅栏。院子里长着一丛丛蔷薇,枝条垂在栅栏上。一条石板小路从栅栏门通往门廊,波克特先生正坐在门廊下的摇椅上,伦道夫趴在他的膝上。

"你们好，又见面了。"老人打招呼道。

"嘿，"丁丁站在栅栏门边说，"关于您昨晚看见的吉普车，我们有几个问题。我们可以和您谈谈吗？"

"当然可以。"波克特先生说，"进来吧！小心那些蔷薇，上面的刺很容易扎伤胳膊和腿！"

丁丁打开栅栏门，孩子们走了进去。

"你们进来后，可以把门关上吗？"波克特先生大声说，"伦道夫总觉得，它能独自出去探索外面的世界！"

露丝对着波克特先生笑了笑，关上了栅栏门，并确保门闩插好了。

孩子们小心翼翼地走过蔷薇丛，走上门廊，来到波克特先生的跟前。帕尔抬头看着伦道夫，不断摇着尾巴。

"好吧，伦道夫，你可以见一见你的朋友。"波克特先生说。他把他的狗放到了帕尔身边的地上。

然后，他站起身来，把长椅上的报纸拿了起来，对孩子们说："请坐。"

等孩子们在长椅上并排坐下，波克特先生又

流沙之谜

坐回摇椅上。

　　椅子旁边的矮茶几上放着一副眼镜。波克特先生戴上眼镜，微笑着看向孩子们。"现在，请告诉我发生了什么事。"他说，"为什么你们对那辆吉普车这么感兴趣？"

　　孩子们和波克特先生说了募捐、发生火灾和鸭子储蓄箱被盗的事。

　　"您看到的副驾驶座上坐着的并不是乘客，"丁丁说，"而是鸭子储蓄箱。"

　　"啊，我真是老糊涂了。"波克特先生说，"我当时就觉得很奇怪，月光照在他的脸上怎么会反光呢？原来只是一只塑料鸭子！"

　　"嗯，您知不知道那辆车到了沿河路后朝哪个方向拐了？"丁丁问，"它开转向灯了吗？"

　　波克特先生摇摇头说："没有，它根本没开灯，这也是为什么直到车差点碾到我的脚趾，我才看到它！"

　　波克特先生朝他们倾了倾身体。"你们想听听我的意见吗？那个司机根本就没打算在沿河路上拐弯。"他说，"我认为那辆吉普车是直接朝着

河里开的!"

丁丁倒吸了一口凉气。"直接朝着河里开?"他问。

老人点点头说:"没错,除非那辆吉普车会飞。"

"这也就解释了为什么消防车里的人在路上没有遇到吉普车。"丁丁说。

"我想为你们的鸭子桥捐款。"波克特先生说。他从口袋里掏出一只皮质小荷包,从中取出四个二十五美分的硬币,探身递给乔希。"我一

流沙之谜

直很喜欢鸭子。"

"非常感谢，先生。"乔希接过钱说，"我们要是找到了储蓄箱，我会帮您投进去的。"

孩子们和帕尔离开了波克特先生和他的小狗。他们走到印第安路与主街的交叉路口，然后左转，朝着河的方向走去。

沿河路与河水之间有一块草地。有些地方的草已经被压平了，朝着河面的方向倒去。

孩子们走近了些，发现有两条并行的平坦压痕。

乔希弯腰看向被碾压的草地。"这压痕看上去就是轮胎印。"他说，"波克特先生没说错！"

丁丁、乔希和露丝坐下来，看向河面。帕尔将两条前腿迈进河水里，开始喝起水来。乔希牵着皮带，防止帕尔继续往河中间走。

"吉普车能直接从河里开到对岸吗？"露丝问。

"当然可以。"乔希回答，"我在电视上看到过，有人开着吉普车从比这还深的水里通过。"

"我们应该去对岸看一看，那里是否也有轮胎印。"丁丁说。

乔希皱起眉头说:"但我们怎么——"

"快看。"丁丁打断了他,指着一条顺流而下的平底小船。划船的男人身材高大,与小船很不般配,就好像是一个成年人坐在儿童自行车上。男人划得很慢,一边划一边不断看向两边的河水。

小船放慢了速度,然后停了下来。男人将一只桨从桨架上取了下来,朝着水里戳去。他在船的两边各戳了好几下。

之后,男人又把桨装回桨架,将长长的胳膊伸入水里。突然他停下了动作,然后笑了起来。

男人往脸上和头上泼了一些河水,像一只弄湿了身体的狗,不断摇晃着自己的头。随后他抓起两只桨,向对岸划去。

到了对岸后,他下了船,拖着船往前走。男人和船全都消失在了树林里。

"你们看到那个人的身材有多高大了吗?"丁丁问。

"不仅如此。"乔希说,"你们注意到他的耳朵了吗?像蘑菇!"

第九章

"那他就是盗贼!"露丝说。

"他在找什么呢?"丁丁问。

"也许储蓄箱在吉普车过河时掉了下来。"露丝说。

"那个鸭子储蓄箱很大。"乔希说,"难道箱子掉进水里,就看不见了吗?"

"嗯,他一定是找到了什么东西。"露丝说。

"我要去看看那东西是什么。"乔希说。他把帕尔的皮带系到一棵树上,然后脱下鞋子,蹚入河水中。

"等等我!"丁丁说着,迅速脱掉自己的运

动鞋。

"我也去!"露丝也踢掉自己的鞋。

他们的脚踩进温暖的浅水里。丁丁能感觉到脚趾间的细沙,水很清澈,他可以看到河底的小鹅卵石。

"这里开始变得泥泞了。"乔希在丁丁前面几码[1]远的地方说。

突然,乔希停下了脚步。他转过身来,满脸惊慌地叫道:"我的脚陷进去了!"

丁丁看到,乔希的身子开始下沉,水已经没到了乔希的膝盖!

"我的脚拔不出来了!"乔希大叫,"可能是流沙!"

"别急!"丁丁说。他扑上前去,一把抓住了乔希的胳膊。

丁丁马上感觉到沙子在没过他的脚面、脚踝,逐渐没过他的膝盖。他也陷进去了!

"露丝!"丁丁大喊,"别过来!"

---

1. 码:英美制长度单位,1 码 =0.9144 米。——编者

流沙之谜

"我去喊人来帮忙!"露丝大声叫道。然后她转过身,蹚着水花回到岸边。

丁丁看着她爬上河岸,赤着脚快速穿过沿河路。帕尔用力拉扯着皮带,不断吠叫。

乔希挣脱了丁丁的手,挣扎着想要回去岸边。但他越挣扎,就越往下沉。

"别动!"丁丁大叫,"往后躺下。"

丁丁自己躺到水里做了个示范。他面朝上漂了起来。虽然他的腿还陷在沙子里,但身体已经不再往下沉了。

"照着做——很有用!"他对乔希喊道。

丁丁听到哗啦一声,乔希也躺进了水里。丁丁能听见自己怦怦的心跳声。为了让自己冷静下来,他闭上了眼睛,放任身体漂在水面上。

突然,帕尔更加疯狂地吠叫起来。丁丁转过头,看见杰克和另一个男人拿着梯子朝河边跑过来。露丝紧跟在他们身后。

到了河边,他们把梯子扔进了水里。

"别乱动!"杰克对着丁丁和乔希大喊,"你们保持现有姿势。我和伦尼会马上把你们拉上来。"

两个消防员将水里的梯子推向丁丁。梯子靠近时，丁丁一把抓住梯子最末端的横档。

"抓紧了，孩子！"杰克叫道。

消防员用力拉着梯子。丁丁能感觉到自己的腿被强大的吸力吸着，仿佛流沙不想放他走似的。

但是杰克和伦尼的力气比流沙的大。丁丁的双腿很快就从泥沙中拔了出来。丁丁的脚终于碰触到了坚实的河底，他蹚着水花快速上了岸。

消防员立刻又把梯子用力推回河里。杰克蹚进水中，推着梯子前进，直到乔希抓住了最后一个横档。杰克和伦尼左右手交替不断拉着梯子，像拉鱼一样把乔希从水里拉了出来。丁丁和乔

希并排坐着,喘着粗气。他们两个浑身湿漉漉的,满脸通红。帕尔舔着乔希的脸,在他那沾满泥沙的双腿之间跳过来跳过去。"再也别这么做了!"露丝说。

"别担心。"乔希说,"我连洗澡都不会再用浴缸了!"

所有人都哈哈大笑起来。

"顺便介绍一下,"杰克说着,拍了拍另一个消防员的背,"这是伦尼。"

伦尼朝着孩子们微笑。"很高兴认识你们。"他说。

"能够认识您，我们更高兴。"丁丁说，站起身来和伦尼握手。

"你们几个孩子去河里做什么？"伦尼问。

"那辆吉普车就在河里！"乔希说。

"这是真的吗？"丁丁问，"乔希，我们还不知道——"

"它就在河里。"乔希说着，穿上了他的鞋子，"我躺在水面上时，有什么尖尖的东西刺到了我的腿。我伸手去摸，摸到了吉普车的天线！那一定就是船上那个人找到的东西！"

"我们必须去找法伦警官。"露丝说。

"不用了。"杰克一边说，一边把手举了起来，"我在消防站已经给他打了电话，你们听。"

他们听到越来越近的警笛声。不到半分钟，一辆巡逻警车就呼啸而至，在河边停了下来。法伦警官从车里跳了出来，匆忙中差点滑入河里。

"你们几个孩子都没事吧？"他一边说，一边着急地逐一打量起他们来。

"我们没事。"丁丁说，"乔希发现了盗贼的吉普车！"

流沙之谜

"是吗?在哪里?"

乔希指着河水说:"那里,埋在流沙里。"

"我从来都不知道康涅狄格州还有流沙。"露丝说。

"有水和沙的地方,就可能有流沙。"伦尼说,"我曾是海豹突击队队员,我见过很多次流沙。"

"但这条河我们蹚水走过很多次,"乔希说,"我从来也没有陷进去过。"

"只是偶然会遇到。"伦尼解释说,"事实上,这里完全可能出现流沙。河流浅,水流缓慢,河底有很多沙子。"

"但是你们怎么知道要来这里找呢?"法伦警官问孩子们。

"我们去见了波克特先生。"丁丁解释说,"他告诉我们,那辆吉普车好像直接往前开了,并没有在沿河路拐弯。于是我们来了这里,发现了轮胎印。"

"后来,我们看见了一个划船的人。"乔希接着说,"他在水里寻找什么东西。当他找到后,他就离开了。"

"于是乔希决定来一次泥沙浴。"露丝笑着说。

三个大男人和三个孩子望向河面。碧蓝的天空,波光粼粼的河水,金黄色的沙子,一切看上去那么宁静祥和。

"如果吉普车真的在河里,"法伦警官说,"那鸭子储蓄箱可能也在那里。"

"我们要怎么把它弄出来呢?"露丝问。

法伦警官挠了挠下巴说:"这个问题问得好。"

"我想我有办法了。"伦尼说。

第十章

所有人都看向伦尼。

"流沙就是由沙子和水混在一起,形成的类似粥一样的东西。"他解释说,"流沙下面是一层坚硬的黏土或岩石。流沙会一直位于硬层上方,因为它无法排出去。"

"可是硬层在下面多深的地方呢?"法伦警官问道。

"找出答案的唯一办法是到那里去看看。"伦尼说,"如果这几个孩子在沙子里发现的是突出来的天线,那么吉普车一定就埋在沙子表层。"

"所以,我们要钩住车子,把它拉出来。对

吧，伦尼？"杰克问。

"没错，要是我能找到保险杠的话。"伦尼说，"我下水去看看情况。你回消防站去把卡车开来。"

二十分钟后，一切准备就绪。杰克开着救援卡车回到河岸。地上放着一根长长的缆绳，缆绳的一头系着一个大钩子，另一头接进了卡车后部的绞盘。

伦尼拿着缆绳一头的钩子，站在河边。

"好了。"杰克朝着伦尼喊道，"去挂上钩子吧！"

伦尼拽着缆绳和钩子，在河水中半漂半游地前行。丁丁、乔希和露丝蹲在树下看着。帕尔的头靠在乔希的膝盖上。

法伦警官坐在警车里，正对着车载电话说话。一小群人站在沿河路边上看热闹。

"我真心希望鸭子储蓄箱还在吉普车里。"丁丁说。

"希望伦尼不会陷进流沙里。"乔希补充道。

"好了，我想我到了吉普车尾部的上方。"伦

流沙之谜

尼喊道。他深吸一口气,一头扎进了水里。

一分钟过去了,每一个人都瞪大眼睛,注视着伦尼消失的地方。丁丁看了一眼手表。

"他一定是陷在流沙里了!"乔希叫道。

"别慌。"杰克说,"他要是遇到麻烦,我们会拉着缆绳把他拽上来的。"但是杰克也露出了焦急之色。

突然,水面上泛起了水花。伦尼像钓鱼线上的软木一样冒了出来。他吐出嘴里的异物,抖掉

手臂和肩膀上的泥沙。

"怎么下去了这么久?"杰克朝着他的搭档喊道。

"那辆吉普车下沉的角度不好。"伦尼大声回答,"很倒霉,保险杠的位置比我想象的要低。"

"你把钩子挂上去了吗?"杰克问。

伦尼笑着说:"当然。把它拉上来,杰克!"

杰克快步上了卡车,操纵控制杆。缆绳开始慢慢地卷入绞盘。随着缆绳收紧,绞盘开始受力,发出像指甲刮在黑板上的尖锐的声音。所有人都盯着河面。

一辆黄色吉普车的尾部突然露出了水面。

"它在那儿!"露丝叫道。

法伦警官站到了孩子们的身后。"好吧,真是没想到。"他嘀咕道。

吉普车被拉出流沙时,在场的人都听到了吮吸声。吉普车一点一点地向着河岸移动,看上去就像一个黄色水怪。水和沙子从金属外壳和玻璃上倾泻而下。

吉普车的后轮胎终于着了地。湿漉漉的驾驶

流沙之谜

座上满是泥沙,上面放着鸭子储蓄箱。由于箱内渗入了沙子和水,透过透明的塑料箱壁,人们几乎看不清里面的硬币。

"连着里面的水和淤泥,这个储蓄箱一定有一吨重。"伦尼说,"我是肯定举不起来。"

"我们把吉普车拖回消防站吧。"杰克提议,他爬进救援卡车的驾驶座,"我们将使用起重机把储蓄箱吊起来,然后把钱倒出来晾干。"

"我想看一看仪表盘上的杂物箱里有什么东西。"法伦警官说。

伦尼点点头,打开了吉普车的门,里面的泥水冲到了地上。随着泥水一起冲出来的,还有湿漉漉的旧汉堡包装纸、一件T恤衫和一条绿色的烂毛巾。

"好了,"伦尼说,"拖走吧。"

救援卡车拖着吉普车向消防站缓缓驶去,吉普车还在不断往外渗水。法伦警官开着警车跟在后面。热闹看完了,人们也开始散去。

"我们跟着去吧,看他们把钱从储蓄箱里倒出来。"丁丁说。

"我们能先去吃午餐吗?"乔希一边问,一边解开系在树上的帕尔的皮带,"我发誓,我都饿瘦了。"

"好吧,我们可以去我家吃午餐。"露丝说,"我可不想让乔希饿瘦了。"

帕尔闻了闻从吉普车里随着泥水冲出来的湿汉堡包装纸。

"看,我的狗都饿了。"乔希打趣道。

"等一下,伙伴们。"露丝说。她用鞋尖踢了踢那条湿毛巾。

只不过这不是一条毛巾,而是一条绿围裙,上面别着的名牌在阳光下闪闪发亮。

名牌上印着:嘿!我是马丁。

第十一章

孩子们站在那里低头看着名牌。

"我以前见过这样的围裙和名牌,"丁丁说,"在超市里!"

"马丁一定在那里工作!"乔希说,"我们去逮捕他!"

"我们不能逮捕任何人。"露丝说,"我们必须去告诉法伦警官!"

露丝捡起围裙,拧干水分。然后,孩子们跑上长着草的斜坡,穿过沿河路。帕尔跟在乔希的身边,和他们一起奔跑。

在消防站的车道上,他们看见了杰克、伦尼

和其他几个消防员。吉普车停着的地方有一摊河水。

"您见到法伦警官了吗?"丁丁问其中一个消防员。

"他刚走。"那人说着,指了指吉普车上打开着的杂物箱,"他拿到了一些文件,然后离开了。"

"他是不是去了警察局?"露丝问。

那个消防员耸了耸肩,说:"他没说。"

丁丁看向乔希和露丝。"我们现在该怎么办?"他问。

"如果马丁就是盗贼,我们必须去告诉法伦警官。"露丝说。

"但是可能已经太晚了。"乔希说,"如果马丁就在隔壁超市工作,他可能已经看见了被拖到这里的吉普车。"

乔希快速扫了一眼超市,说:"他现在可能正看着我们呢!"

丁丁考虑了片刻。"我们不久前刚看见马丁在小船上,所以也许他今天没来超市上班。"他

流沙之谜

说，"他可能还不知道我们找到了吉普车。"

露丝仍然拿着那条湿围裙，看向草坪对面的超市。"走吧。"她说，"如果马丁今天没来上班，也许我们能在他住的地方找到他。如果他上班了，我们就去告诉法伦警官。"

他们穿过消防站和超市之间的草坪。乔希将帕尔系在自行车停放架上，然后三个孩子匆匆走进了超市。

"睁大眼睛，寻找长着蘑菇耳朵的大高个。"乔希低声说。

但是超市里挤满了周日购物的人。几十个系着绿色围裙的员工忙碌地走来走去。很多男性员工都很高大。

"我们要怎么找他？"露丝问，"马丁可能在超市的任何角落！"

"我有个主意。"丁丁说，"我们之前在这儿时，我看见了许多员工的照片。我们去看一看吧。"

乔希和露丝跟着丁丁往超市后面走。他们穿过宠物食品区的过道，在乳品区右转，最后在挂着照片的墙跟前停了下来。

"在那里。"丁丁指着照片说。那个他们看见的划船的人,在最下面一排的照片里。他是唯一一个有一对巨大耳朵的人。

"马丁·弗利斯。"丁丁念出了照片下的姓名。

"我们要怎么办?"乔希问。

露丝举起那条围裙。"我们得弄清楚,他此刻在不在这里。"她说,"我们先去看看罗布先生在不在办公室吧。"

超市经理的办公室离照片墙只有几码远,门是开着的,丁丁能听到罗布先生的声音。

"他办公室里有人。"丁丁低声对乔希和露丝说。他们站在门外等着。

"马丁,我不明白。"罗布先生说,"昨天你还为能在这里工作而高兴,今天你却要辞职。"

"对不起。"一个低沉的声音回应,"我想离开镇子。我的……我的祖母生病住院了,所以我今天就得离开了,我还需要把工资领了。"

乔希凑近偷偷往里看,然后回头看向丁丁和露丝,他的双眼瞪得大大的。"马丁·弗利斯!"

他低声说。

"我们该怎么办?"露丝问。

"由我们来接手。"有人轻声说。这一次,声音来自露丝的身后。

是法伦警官和基恩警官。"这是吉普车里的东西吗?"法伦警官指着那条湿围裙问。

露丝点点头。

法伦警官拿起围裙,走进了罗布先生的办公室。基恩警官跟他在身后,把门关上了。

丁丁、乔希和露丝靠门更近了些,听着里面的动静。

"马丁·弗利斯,你因盗窃罪被捕了。"他们听到法伦警官说。

A to Z 神秘案件

一个小时后,孩子们坐在法伦警官的办公室里。马丁·弗利斯被关了起来。

"你们是怎么知道要去哪里找他的?"丁丁问法伦警官。

"吉普车的登记证在杂物箱里。"法伦警官说,"上面有他的姓名和地址。我一个电话就知道了他在超市工作。"

"他为什么没有像我一样陷进流沙里呢?"乔希问。

法伦警官耸了耸肩,说:"最有可能的情况是,吉普车陷下去时,他意识到自己陷入了某个泥潭。他一定是跳了过去,或者是游到了能立住脚的地方。"

"消防员们打开储蓄箱了吗?"露丝问。

法伦警官站起身,打开抽屉,拿出了孩子们的饼干盒和他自己的硬币罐。"我们为什么不去看看呢?"他问。

三周后,鸭子桥完工了。高中的孩子们将工作完成得棒极了。这座桥是木制的,看上去和普

流沙之谜

通的桥没什么两样,只是桥面比大多数桥要窄。桥头钉了一块小标牌,上面写着:欢迎鸭子们。

桥的一端建在河岸上,以优美的弧度横跨沿河路。汽车能从桥的下方通过,鸭子们安全了。

绿地镇决定在大桥完工后的第二天举行盛大的开幕式。丁丁、乔希和露丝打包了一些野餐用的午餐食物,带着帕尔、乔希的两个弟弟,还有露丝的小弟弟纳特,前往新建好的鸭子桥。

法伦警官和他的孙子吉米也来了,杰克和伦尼也现身了。丁丁还看到了波克特先生和他的小狗伦道夫。

纳特、布赖恩和布拉德利守着桥头,不让帕尔上桥,露丝打开了一块毯子。她找了一处平坦的地方铺毯子。

"你能快点吗,露丝?"乔希说,"三明治的味道让我馋得受不了。"

"你也可以过来帮忙呀,乔希。"丁丁说。他从露丝手里抓起毯子的一头,帮着她把毯子铺开。然后他打开野餐篮。

帕尔和三个年幼的孩子看到三明治、饼干和

欢迎
鸭子们

西瓜,朝着他们跑了过来。

在孩子们吃午餐时,第一个提议建桥的女孩在桥面上撒上了碎玉米。所有人都翘首以待。

一些年幼的孩子开始跑来跑去,玩起了捉迷藏。人们开始聊起天来。有人打开了收音机,两个带着飞盘的大孩子来回扔着飞盘玩了起来。

"这里太吵了。"乔希嘟哝道,"就像在开派对似的。只有疯了的鸭子才可能上那座桥。"

慢慢地,其他人都不想等了,回家去了。

流沙之谜

"鸭子们在哪里呢?"纳特问露丝。

"也许这里安静一些后,我们就能看见了。"她低声说。

"好吧,我们真的要安静!"布赖恩说,"安静,布拉德利!"

"我又没说话!"布拉德利争辩道,"你安静点!"

乔希将两个弟弟拉到自己身边。"如果你们想看鸭子,你们就必须和帕尔一样保持安静。"

他低声说。

帕尔趴在毯子上睡着了。纳特、布赖恩和布拉德利扑倒在它的两侧,像小狗一样紧挨着它。

"好样的。"露丝对乔希说。

"你们觉得鸭子们真的会来吗?"丁丁低声问。

"最好能来,"乔希嘟哝道,"我为了它们差点被淹死!"

六个孩子等了一下午。几个小的孩子都睡着了,丁丁、乔希和露丝玩起了大富翁游戏,帕尔在双胞胎的中间安静地打着呼噜。

乔希正要落子到丁丁的旅馆上时,露丝突然低声说:"快看!"

一只鸭子站在弧形桥的最高处。它转头四下张望,仿佛在看有没有没危险。确认没有危险之后,它轻声嘎嘎叫了起来。五只小黄鸭摇摇摆摆地向它走去。

丁丁俯下身,叫醒纳特、布赖恩和布拉德利。他们像雕像一样坐在那儿,看着鸭子们从沿河路上方安全地通过。

A to Z Mysteries®

The Quicksand Question

by Ron Roy

illustrated by
John Steven Gurney

INDIAN RIVER
LAWRENCE TAXI
RIVER ROAD
HORSE TRAILS
BIKE PATH
HORSES FOR RENT
WOODS
INDIAN WAY ROAD
WOODVIEW ROAD
BIKE PATH
FIRE STATION
BILL'S BIKES
SUPER MARKET
BRIDGE LANE
ROBIN ROAD
CROW ST
FINCH LA
THRUSH CT
OWL RD
PHEASANT LA
BLUE JAY WAY
WREN DR
FITNESS CENTER
WOODS
BIKE PATH
BLUE BIRD WAY
HUMMINGBIRD LA
WOODCOCK CROSS
ELLIE'S DINER
ACORN APTS
FURRY FEET PET SHOP
CENTER CHURCH
BIKE PATH
OAK STREET
PEOPLE'S POND
POST OFFICE
COMMUNITY GARDEN AND FISH POND
GREEN LAWN $ SAVINGS $ BANK
GOOSE ISLAND
RIVER ROAD
POLICE STATION
ELDERLY HOUSING
WEST GREEN ST
MAIN STREET
SENIOR COMMUNITY CENTER
GREEN LAWN LIBRARY
TOWN HALL
BIKE PATH
CHILDREN'S PETTING ZOO AND AQUARIUM
SHANGRI-LA HOTEL

WELCOME TO
GREEN LAWN
HOME OF THE
A to Z Mysteries
N
E
S
W
RIVER ROAD
BOAT LAUNCH
BOAT RENTAL
RON'S BAIT
DUCK WALK WAY
GREEN LAWN MIDDLE SCHOOL
EAGLE LANE
FARM LANE
JOSH
SQUAW ISLAND
GREEN LAWN ELEMENTARY SCHOOL
DINK
RUTH ROSE
TREE TOP CIRCLE
MEADOW ROAD
FOX LANE
QUAIL RUN ROAD
SILVER CIRCLE
WOODY STREET
PLEASANT STREET
THISTLE COURT
WILDFLOWER WAY
ROSE STREET
BAND SHELL
ROSE GARDEN
CENTER PARK
SWAN POND
GREEN LAWN HIGH SCHOOL
PLAYING FIELDS
GYM + POOL
BOXWOOD LANE
HOWARD'S BARBER-SHOP
BOOK NOOK
GAS STATION
CRYSTAL POND
MYSTIC GREENHOUSE
DOG KENNEL + VETERINARIAN
RIVER ROAD
EAST GREEN STREET
TOWN TENNIS COURTS
TOWN SWIMMING POOL
KIDDIE POOL
TOWN BASEBALL FIELD
TO THE BLUE HILLS

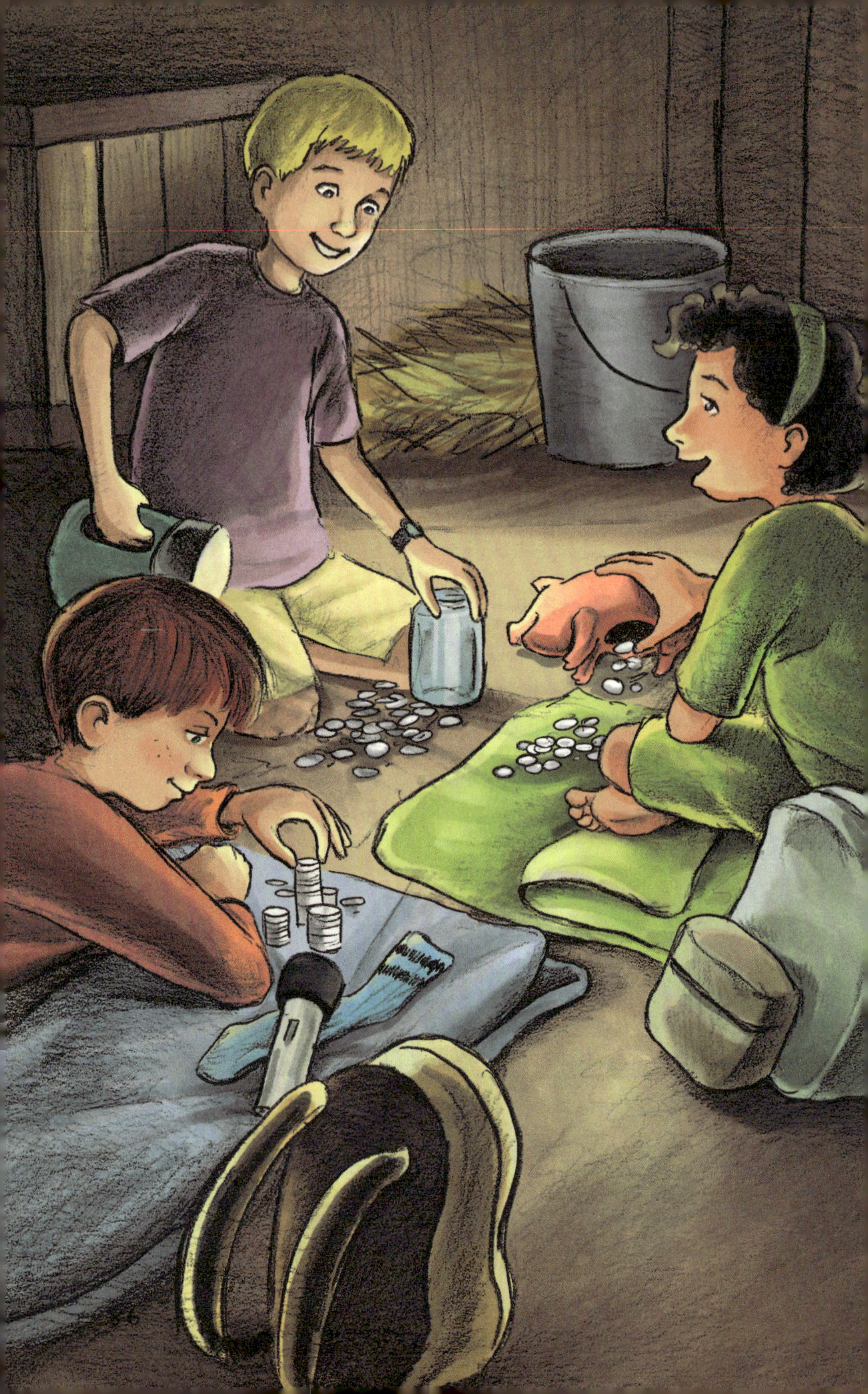

Chapter 1

It was Saturday night. Dink, Josh, and Ruth Rose were having a sleep-over in Josh's barn.

Dink tipped a jarful of coins onto his sleeping bag. "I can't believe the duck bank is nearly full," he said.

"I know," Ruth Rose said, emptying her piggy bank. "We've been saving for a whole year!"

"Quiet, you two," Josh said, stacking nickels, dimes, and quarters on his sleeping bag. "I can't count if you're talking!"

The "duck bank" was a large plastic bank, shaped like a duck, that stood in the fire station on Main Street. It was four feet tall and made of clear plastic. Everyone in town had been dropping money into it.

They were going to use the money to pay for a special bridge just for ducks.

For years, mother ducks had been crossing River Road to build nests in the woods near Bridge Lane. After their ducklings were born, the mother ducks would lead their ducklings back across the road to the river.

The problem was, the little ducks were hard to see. Many drivers had almost had accidents. Finally, the town held a meeting to decide what to do.

One person suggested hiring a duck crossing guard.

A man who had almost driven off the road wanted the ducks rounded up and put in cages.

Another person suggested digging a tunnel under River Road.

But a girl from Dink's school had the best idea. "My grandparents feed ducks in their yard in Florida," she'd explained. "The ducks have to cross a busy street, so my grandfather built a little bridge. My grandmother sprinkled corn on the bridge to let the ducks know it was for them. Now the ducks use the bridge all the time."

Everyone loved the idea.

Mr. Plank, the shop teacher at the high school, raised his hand. "The kids in my class can design the bridge," he said. "When we've collected enough money, I'll help them build it."

Now the bank was nearly full. On Monday morning the money would be counted by Mr. Fiskell, the president of the Green Lawn Savings Bank. As soon as school let out next week, Mr. Plank and the high school kids would start building the bridge.

Josh finished counting his money. "Nine dollars and ten cents," he said. He rubbed his stomach. "Money makes me hungry!" He grabbed his backpack and pulled out a tin of chocolate chip cookies. He also had some apples, carrots, and dog biscuits.

In her stall, Polly the pony lay sleeping on a pile of hay. Josh's dog, Pal, was curled up next to her.

Outside, June crickets were chirping in the field behind the barn.

"I've got ten dollars and twenty-two cents," Dink said. "What about you, Ruth Rose?"

"Fourteen dollars and thirty cents," Ruth Rose said. "How much do you suppose is in the duck bank?"

Ruth Rose liked to wear all one color. Tonight her outfit matched her sleeping bag: she wore lime green shorts and T-shirt.

"A lot," Josh said. "It's up to the duck's neck. And the three of us are putting in over thirty dollars!"

He opened the tin of cookies, took two for himself, and passed the rest to Ruth Rose.

"We should think of a name for the bridge," he said. "How about Waddle Way?" He kicked off his sneakers and slipped into his sleeping bag.

Dink switched off his flashlight. "What about calling it Duck Drive?"

"How about Critter Crossing?" Ruth Rose said.

流沙之谜

"I like that," Dink said, yawning.

Josh shut off his flashlight. He snorted. "Critter Crossing, Ruth Rose? Gee, why not call it Bunny Bridge?"

Ruth Rose laughed in the dark barn. "Critter Crossing is good because other animals might use the bridge," she said. "Bunnies, turtles, raccoons..."

"Buffalo," Josh added.

After a few minutes, the kids drifted off to sleep. Polly whinnied softly in her stall. Pal snored on his pile of hay.

Much later, something woke Dink. He sat up in his sleeping bag. Next to him, Josh and Ruth Rose were only lumps in the darkness.

Then Dink heard Polly stamp her hooves. When his eyes adjusted, he could see that the white pony was standing. Pal was awake, too.

Dink crawled out of his sleeping bag and walked over to the animals. He stroked Polly's warm nose. "What is it, girl?" he whispered.

Polly snorted and shook her mane. Dink knelt and scratched Pal behind his ears. "Bet you just had a bad dream," he murmured.

Using his flashlight, Dink checked his watch. It

was one o'clock, and he was wide awake. He pushed the barn door open and walked outside.

The night was warm and quiet. Even the crickets were asleep. Josh's house was dark except for a small light over the back door.

Dink took a deep breath. The air smelled like the lawn had just been mowed. The springy grass felt cool under his bare feet. He yawned, stretched, and walked around the barn.

Behind the barn was a broad meadow. Next to the meadow was River Road, and on the other side of that was Indian River. On a sunny day, you could see the light glinting off the river. But now the meadow, the road, and the river were covered in darkness.

Dink was about to go back inside when he noticed two dots of light in the distance.

Car headlights, he thought. What's a car doing in the meadow?

Then the lights disappeared. Dink smiled at himself. Of course the car wasn't in the meadow—it was on River Road.

Dink slipped back into the barn, crawled into his

sleeping bag, and closed his eyes.

Suddenly Polly started to whinny and Pal began barking.

"What's going on?" Josh asked groggily. He switched on his flashlight and turned the beam on Polly.

"Look at her!" Ruth Rose said.

Polly's eyes were rolling in fright. She rose on her hind legs and kicked at her stall. Pal barked and ran over to Josh. "Something's been bugging them," Dink said. "They woke me up a little while ago."

Then all three kids smelled it.

"Smoke!" Josh yelled, kicking his way out of his sleeping bag.

The kids ran outside, expecting to see something burning. But the night was peaceful and dark.

Then Dink walked behind the barn. "Guys, over here!" he shouted.

Josh and Ruth Rose hurried around the corner. Dink pointed toward the river. A small orange blaze flickered in the night.

"There's a fire in the meadow!" Josh said.

Chapter 2

It took Green Lawn's fire truck only five minutes to get to the fire. Dink and Ruth Rose stood next to the barn. They watched with Josh and his family as the firefighters put out the blaze.

"I wanna go see the fire truck!" Josh's brother Bradley announced, wiggling in his father's arms.

"Afraid not," his dad said. "Besides, the fire's out, and you're going to bed."

"No, I wanna stay up!" Bradley's twin, Brian, complained. "It's time to play!"

Josh's dad just laughed.

Dink looked at his watch. It was about one-thirty. Across the meadow, he could see the fire truck's lights.

流沙之谜

The firefighters' voices sounded muffled.

A few minutes later, they saw the fire engine leaving. Soon the taillights disappeared on River Road. "Okay, the excitement's over," Josh's mother said, taking Brian's hand. "Back to bed, everyone."

"You three get some sleep," Josh's dad said as he carried Bradley toward the house.

"Okay, Dad," Josh said. The kids and Pal straggled into the barn. Pal flopped into the hay pile next to Polly again, and the kids climbed into their sleeping bags.

Suddenly Dink popped up. "Hey, guys, I just realized something. I may have seen who set the fire!" he said.

"What're you talking about?" Josh asked.

"Polly woke me up before we smelled the fire," Dink explained. "I went out to look around and saw headlights over by the river!"

"Maybe someone was camping," Ruth Rose said. She yawned. "We can check in the morning."

It's already morning, Dink thought, copying Ruth Rose's yawn. He lay back down. As he was falling asleep, he heard a scratchy sound in the dark.

He froze, imagining some night creature crawling over—or into—his sleeping bag.

Then he heard munching, and he smelled cookies.

"Josh!" Dink said. "You almost gave me a heart attack!"

"Sorry," Josh said, swallowing. "I was hungry!"

When the kids woke up, sunlight was streaming through the dusty barn window. Birds chirped. The kids kicked out of their sleeping bags and stepped into their sneakers.

"Let's go see that fire," Josh said. His clothes were wrinkled and his hair stood in spikes.

Pal gazed up at Josh with big brown eyes.

"Okay, you can come, too," he said, snapping Pal's leash onto his collar. Ruth Rose fed Polly a carrot, and then they left the barn.

The sun peeked through the trees as the kids hiked across the meadow. The tall grass was heavy with dew. Their sneakers and legs were soon soaked.

"Look!" Ruth Rose said. Straight ahead was a soggy pile of blackened wood. The air stunk of smoke and wet ashes.

流沙之谜

The ground was even wetter here. There were still puddles from the firefighters' hoses. Dink noticed deep footprints in the mushy, trampled grass.

"Why would somebody light a fire here?" Josh asked, looking around. They were standing near the edge of River Road. On the other side of the road, a short bank dropped off to Indian River.

"Maybe they were roasting marshmallows," Ruth Rose said. She found a long stick and began poking the mess of charred wood and ash.

"In the middle of the night?" Josh asked. "Who eats then?"

Dink laughed. "You do, Mr. Cookie Monster."

Josh grinned.

"What's this?" Ruth Rose asked.

She picked up a hunk of wood and wiped it clean. It was about six inches long and three inches wide. Both ends were charred, but the middle hadn't been burned. Stamped into the board with black ink were the letters ET CO. "What's ET CO?" Josh asked.

"CO could be the first two letters of Connecticut," Ruth Rose said.

"Or Colorado," Dink added.

"I wonder if someone started the fire just to get rid of this," Ruth Rose said, examining the narrow piece of wood.

"It would be nice to know how many letters got burned off," Dink said. "ET CO could be part of lots of words, like pet comb or wet coat."

"Or sweet cotton candy," Josh added.

"The CO could be short for corporation," Ruth Rose suggested, shoving the wood into her back pocket.

"I think it stands for get cookies!" Josh yelled. He started to run. "Last one back to the barn doesn't get any!"

Chapter 3

Josh burst through the barn doors first. Dink and Ruth Rose barreled in right behind him.

Josh immediately pounced on the cookie tin. He opened it, then gasped. "Call the cops!" he yelled. "I've been robbed!"

Dink grinned at his friend. "What'd they take, your brain?"

"Worse," Josh said, peering into the empty cookie tin. "They took my cookies!"

"Hey, my piggy bank is missing!" Ruth Rose said. "I left it right on my sleeping bag."

Dink poked his hand into the opening of his sleeping bag. He felt around. "My money jar isn't here, either!" he said.

Josh pulled open his sleeping bag. "Now I'm really mad!" he said. "My money sock is gone!"

Josh looked at his friends. "Someone snuck in here while we were gone," he said.

"Raccoons might have taken the cookies," Ruth Rose said, glancing around the barn.

"And I read that crows sometimes steal shiny coins," Dink offered.

Suddenly Josh grinned. "No, it wasn't raccoons or crows," he said, wiggling his eyebrows. "I think it was two little monkeys!"

"The twins!" shouted Dink and Ruth Rose at the same time.

The three kids charged out of the barn and raced across the yard. Josh stormed through the kitchen door and yelled, "Freeze!"

Brian and Bradley were kneeling on kitchen chairs, playing with a pile of coins on the table. On the counter were Josh's blue sock, Dink's peanut butter jar, and Ruth Rose's piggy bank. "Josh!" cried Bradley. "Look what we found in the barn!"

"It's pirate treasure!" yelled Brian.

"No, it's not. It's our treasure," Josh growled at his little brothers.

Bradley made a face. "But we found it. Nobody was there!"

"This is special money," Dink told the twins. "We saved it for the ducks."

"Why do ducks need money?" asked Brian.

Ruth Rose explained how the money would be used to build a bridge so mommy ducks and baby ducks could cross the road safely.

"Okay," the twins said together.

"Now, what about my cookies?" Josh asked, waving the cookie tin. "Give 'em back!"

The two little boys erupted in giggles.

"We can't—they're in our stomachs!" Brian crowed.

The five kids ate breakfast, and then Josh told Bradley and Brian to go wake up their parents.

Dink scooped all their coins into the cookie tin while Josh and Ruth Rose cleaned up. Then Josh reached for Pal's leash. But Pal was already sitting by the door with his leash in his mouth.

"Smart doggie," Josh said as he clipped the leash to Pal's collar. Dink lugged the heavy cookie tin.

Pal and the kids took Eagle Lane to Silver Circle, then crossed Main Street to the fire station. They saw Officer Fallon getting out of his cruiser in front of the station.

"'Morning, kids," the police chief said. "You're up early." He bent down and stroked Pal's soft ears.

Dink held up the cookie tin. "We came to make a deposit!"

流沙之谜

Officer Fallon grinned. He reached into his cruiser and pulled out a jar of coins. "Me too."

"Did you hear about the fire last night?" Ruth Rose asked.

"Yes, I did," Officer Fallon said. "It was small, and I guess the fire department put it out easily. The question is, who started it?"

"I saw a car's headlights near there," Dink reported. "But that was before the fire."

"How long before?" Officer Fallon asked.

Dink thought back. "I don't know, maybe ten minutes or so."

Officer Fallon set his coin jar on the roof of his cruiser. Then he pulled out his pad, flipped it open, and made a few notes.

"Could this be a clue?" Ruth Rose asked. She pulled the partly burned wood from her pocket.

"Where'd you find that, Ruth Rose?" he asked.

"We went to the scene of the fire this morning," she told him. "This was in the ashes."

Officer Fallon examined the four letters. "CO is usually short for company," he said, "but there should

103

be a period after the O."

"Maybe the period got burned off?" Ruth Rose said.

Officer Fallon made a note on his pad. "Good detective work," he said to Ruth Rose.

Josh's eyes lit up. "Maybe the wood was from a snake's cage," he said. "Don't pet cobra."

They all laughed.

"Well, let's add our money so we can save those ducks," Officer Fallon said, slipping his notebook into a pocket and reaching for his money jar.

They walked into the fire station together. Somewhere

a radio played softly. A clock on the rear wall said nine o'clock.

The Green Lawn fire engine was parked on the concrete floor. Next to it was a smaller truck with RESCUE written on both doors.

On the back wall were three doors. Gray metal lockers stood along another wall. Below the lockers was a row of rubber boots. Pal walked over and sniffed a boot.

"Hello!" Officer Fallon called out. "Anybody home?"

One of the doors opened. A man wearing a dark blue uniform stepped out. "Who's there?" he said.

"Officer Fallon and some friends," the police chief said, rattling his jarful of coins. "We brought more money."

Dink held up the cookie tin. "This is getting heavy!" he said.

"Great!" the man said. "Come on back here."

The kids and Officer Fallon joined the man at the rear of the firehouse. The man walked over to another of the doors. He shoved it open and stepped aside. "Right in here," he said.

Through the door, Dink could see a rug, a TV set, and several comfortable-looking chairs.

"Where's the bank?" Josh asked, peering around the man.

"Standing in the corner, right where it's always been," the man said, turning to look into the room.

Except that the duck bank wasn't standing in the corner.

The duck bank wasn't anywhere in the room.

Chapter 4

"I can't believe it!" the man said. "That bank was here last night. I know because I put money in it!"

"Would anyone have moved it to a different spot in the firehouse?" Officer Fallon asked.

The man shook his head. "We kept it here in the TV lounge so everyone would be reminded to drop coins in. Plus, the thing weighs a ton!"

Officer Fallon handed Josh his jar of coins and took out a notebook. "Did you put out that meadow fire last night?" he asked.

The man shook his head. "Nope, that would've been Jake and Lenny."

Officer Fallon wrote in his notebook. "Where would I

find them?"

The firefighter smiled. "Still snoozing in the other room," he said. "They should be getting up any time now."

"Have them give me a call after they're awake," Officer Fallon said, slipping his notebook into a pocket.

"No problem," the man answered.

Officer Fallon and the kids walked outside. Pal lay next to the cruiser with his head on his big front paws.

"I just thought of something," Dink said. "Maybe whoever lit that fire last night did it to get the men out of the firehouse."

"I had the same thought," Officer Fallon said. "The fire could have been a diversion."

"Yeah!" Josh said. "So they could sneak in here when no one was around and steal the bank!"

"Who would do such a lousy thing?" Ruth Rose said.

"Someone who loves money and hates ducks!" Josh said.

"Could it have been the car I saw last night?" Dink

said. "I saw those headlights right before the fire."

"Very possibly," Officer Fallon said.

An elderly man walked past with a dog on a leash. The man was tall and thin. The dog was short and round. They both had white hair. Pal whined and wagged his tail back and forth.

The man let his little dog waddle over to Pal. "Hello," the man said. "This is Randolph. Is your basset friendly?"

Josh nodded. "Pal likes everyone!"

Pal sniffed the little dog, then licked his face. Randolph rolled over and wiggled his whole body.

"Any trouble here?" the man asked, looking curiously at Officer Fallon.

"Just investigating a possible theft," Officer Fallon said.

The man raised his bushy white eyebrows. "Would it have anything to do with that crazy driver I saw last night?" he asked.

Officer Fallon took out his notebook again and flipped it open. "Please tell me what you saw," he said.

"A fire engine woke me some time after one o'clock," the man said. "So I took Randolph outside for some fresh air. We were at the corner of Indian Way Road when a jeep came tearing past us up Main Street!" The man held his hands a foot apart. "Missed Randolph by that much!"

Officer Fallon began writing in his notebook. "You are Mr....?"

"Thaddeus Pocket," the man said. "Number 10 Indian Way Road."

"Were you able to read the jeep's license plate, Mr. Pocket?"

"Mercy, no!" the man said. "It was speeding much too fast."

"Did you happen to notice the driver?" Officer Fallon asked.

Mr. Pocket shook his head. "I'm sorry, my eyesight isn't wonderful anymore. There were two men in the jeep, but I don't remember the driver."

Officer Fallon closed his notebook and began to put it away. "Thanks anyway, Mr. Pocket. You've been very helpful—"

"But I do remember the man sitting beside the driver," Mr. Pocket went on.

流沙之谜

"You do?" Officer Fallon opened his notebook again.

Mr. Pocket grinned. "Yes, but only because he was so odd-looking. The man in the passenger seat looked just like a giant duck!"

Chapter 5

Dink, Josh, and Ruth Rose exchanged glances.

Officer Fallon was still looking at Mr. Pocket. "The man looked like a duck? Can you explain, Mr. Pocket?"

Mr. Pocket smiled. "I noticed a shiny head and a duck's beak. Now I realize the man must have had a shaved head and a large nose."

Officer Fallon thanked Mr. Pocket and wrote down his phone number. The man and his dog continued their walk.

"That guy driving the jeep must have been the thief!" Josh blurted out. "The duck bank was in the passenger seat!"

流沙之谜

"When Mr. Pocket saw the jeep, the driver had probably just stolen the bank and was making his getaway!" Ruth Rose added.

Officer Fallon walked over to his cruiser. "I'll get word out to watch for a jeep carrying a duck," he said.

"Would you mind holding on to our money?" Dink asked. He stepped over to the cruiser and handed Officer Fallon the cookie tin.

"And here's yours back." Josh returned Officer Fallon's jar.

"Will do," Officer Fallon said, setting both containers on the seat. "Don't worry, we'll get our duck bridge built yet."

He climbed into the car and pulled away down Main Street.

"That crook could be anywhere by now," Dink said. He started walking toward the corner of Main and River Road.

"It makes me so mad!" Ruth Rose said. "The town has been saving up for a year, and now we have to start all over again!"

The kids crossed River Road and sat in the grass

113

above the riverbank. Pal woofed at a family of ducks feeding in the weeds. The ducks paddled quickly away toward the other side.

"Maybe Officer Fallon will find him," Dink said.

"I don't know how," Josh said. "That jeep could be hundreds of miles away by now."

"Well, we still have this," Ruth Rose said, holding up the chunk of wood stamped with ET CO. "These letters must mean something!"

Josh picked up a stone and tossed it into the river. The kids watched the stone sink to the sandy bottom.

"Any ideas?" Dink asked.

"Yeah, let's go to Ellie's," Josh said. "A milkshake always helps me think better."

"Josh, we have to focus on finding that money," Ruth Rose said. "Think of those baby ducks!"

"Okay, but we don't have a plan," Josh said.

Dink checked his watch. "Why don't we see if the firemen who were on duty last night are up yet?" he suggested.

"Good idea," Ruth Rose said. "Maybe they saw the jeep when they were coming back from the fire."

With Pal leading, the kids walked back into the fire station. A tall man was wiping the rescue truck with a cloth. A mug of coffee rested on the truck's hood.

"'Morning," he said, yawning.

115

"Good morning," Dink said. "Are you one of the night firemen?"

"Did you hear about the robbery?" Josh asked before the man could answer Dink's question.

The man nodded. "My name's Jake," he said. "I'm really bummed that someone stole that duck money."

He picked up his coffee and sat on the truck's front bumper. "Lenny and I were gone, putting out a fire in the meadow. It turned out to be small, probably left burning by some campers."

"Officer Fallon thinks the crooks set it," Josh said.

"We figure they did it to get you to leave the firehouse," Dink said. "I saw some headlights near where the fire was set last night."

"And a man walking his dog saw a jeep speeding up Main Street," Ruth Rose added. "He saw the duck bank in the jeep!"

Jake's mouth fell open. "Really?"

"By any chance, did you pass a jeep on River Road?" Josh asked.

Jake shook his head. "Didn't see any vehicles, going or coming back."

流沙之谜

"Did you see anyone hanging around here?" Ruth Rose asked.

Jake leaned down and gave Pal's ears a gentle rub. "Not last night, but a few days ago some guy was poking around in here. He used our bathroom, then left."

"Did he see the duck bank?" Dink asked.

"Probably. The thing's pretty hard to miss," Jake said.

"Do you remember what he looked like?" Josh asked.

Jake shrugged. "Big guy, as tall as me but heavier," he said. "Oh, and his ears really stuck out. Looked like he had two overgrown mushrooms glued to his head."

Chapter 6

The kids thanked Jake and left.

"That guy could have been the robber!" Ruth Rose said.

"I think so, too," Dink said. "The thief would have to be big to carry that duck filled with coins."

"Now can I get a milkshake?" Josh asked. "Please? I'm starving!"

"If you promise not to slurp and embarrass us," Dink said.

With Pal tugging on his leash, they walked to Ellie's Diner. They sat in a booth by the windows. Pal crawled under the table and rested his head on Josh's feet.

流沙之谜

"Hi, kids," Ellie said. She brought Pal a bowl of water and patted him on the head.

Then she pulled out her pad. "What'll it be? Our specials are slug stew and spider spaghetti."

"Yum," Ruth Rose said, "but Josh simply has to have a milkshake." She pulled the ET CO wood from her back pocket and laid it on the table.

"What's that?" asked Ellie.

"It's a clue," Ruth Rose said. "Did you hear about the duck bank? It got stolen last night!"

"Go on!" Ellie said. She sat next to Dink. "Tell me everything!"

The kids told Ellie about the fire, the speeding jeep, and what they'd learned from Jake at the firehouse.

"This came from the fire," Ruth Rose said, touching the chunk of wood. "We've been trying to figure out what ET CO stands for."

Ellie picked up the wood and examined the letters. Suddenly she smiled and handed it back to Ruth Rose. "Well, that part of the mystery I can solve. Come on out back," she said.

"Stay," Josh told Pal. Then the kids followed Ellie

119

behind the counter, through the kitchen, and out the back door.

Ellie walked over to a small wooden platform lying on the ground. It was made of narrow boards that had been nailed across thicker ones.

"I've seen those before," Josh said. "When my dad ordered a bunch of bricks, they came loaded on one of these things."

"It's called a pallet," Ellie said.

"Look!" Ruth Rose said. She pointed to words stamped into the pallet boards: EASTERN PALLET COMPANY.

Ruth Rose held her partly burned piece of wood next to the words. The black printing was identical.

"Where do they make these things?" Dink asked.

"Beats me," Ellie said. "This one came from the supermarket. I'm using the wood to build a fence around my garden."

"Could anyone get one?" Ruth Rose asked.

Ellie shrugged. "I guess. I talked to the store manager, a guy named Derek Robb. So do you still want milkshakes?"

"Yes!" Josh said. He led the way back into the

diner.

The kids gave Ellie their orders, then slid back into the booth.

Ruth Rose leaned toward Dink and Josh. "I'll bet

the crook used pallets from the supermarket to start the fire!" she said.

"If he did, maybe Derek Robb remembers him!" Dink said.

"So let's go ask," Ruth Rose suggested.

"Can we please drink our milkshakes first?" Josh asked.

Chapter 7

After the kids had finished their milkshakes, they left Ellie's and walked back up Main Street to Green Lawn's supermarket.

Josh tied Pal's leash to a bike rack. "We'll be right back," he told his dog.

Inside, Dink, Josh, and Ruth Rose walked through the fruit and vegetable section. Tall pyramids of oranges and apples gleamed under the lights.

They stood next to a mountain of watermelons and glanced around the store. A lot of people were shopping, and a lot of workers were scurrying about. All the store employees wore dark pants, green aprons, and white shirts.

Dink walked over to a woman with curly brown hair. She was arranging bags of grapes into a display. A name tag pinned to her apron said HI! I'M JUDY.

Dink asked her where the manager's office was.

"Go to the rear of the store," Judy said, pointing. "It's the red door just left of the meat department."

The kids followed her directions, and Dink knocked on the door.

"Come in!" a voice boomed.

Ruth Rose opened the door and the kids walked in. The office was cluttered with filing cabinets, boxes of damaged canned goods, and a wooden desk covered with papers.

Behind the desk sat a smiling man in a shirt and tie. DEREK ROBB was printed on a nameplate on his desk.

"Hi there," the man said. "How can I help you kids?"

"Someone set a fire in the meadow behind my barn last night," Josh said. "We think whoever set it used pallets from this store."

Ruth Rose showed Mr. Robb the chunk of burned

wood.

Mr. Robb examined the letters ET CO. "Yep, looks the same," he said. "A lot of our merchandise comes stacked on these things."

"Did you give any pallets to a tall man a couple of days ago?" Dink asked.

Mr. Robb smiled. "People who want pallets usually just take them," he said. "Come on, I'll show you."

Mr. Robb led the kids out of his office. They passed a long wall covered with framed photographs of employees. Dink recognized Judy, the woman who'd given him directions.

"Right through here," Mr. Robb said, pushing through a wide pair of swinging doors. "Watch out for the forklifts!"

The kids found themselves in a giant room filled with workers, boxes, and noise. Men and women were unpacking crates and loading stuff on carts.

"Look," Josh said. A yellow forklift stopped near a bunch of boxes stacked on a pallet. The driver pulled a lever, and the forklift's two arms lowered. The truck moved forward, and the arms slid under the pallet. The driver moved the lever again, and the arms raised the pallet of boxes off the floor.

Suddenly the forklift began to back up, beeping. The kids and Mr. Robb stepped back as the forklift carried the pallet to the other end of the room.

"Cool!" Josh said. "I wish I had one of those things."

Mr. Robb chuckled. "They're pretty expensive, kiddo. Now follow me." He led the kids to a tall, wide opening like a garage door.

"If you go down those steps," Mr. Robb said, pointing, "you'll see a stack of pallets on the ground. Folks stop by and take them all the time. They break 'em up for firewood, whatever."

"So anyone could just come and take one," Dink said, "at any time?"

"That's right," said Mr. Robb. "Even in the middle of the night."

Chapter 8

"Well, at least we know where the thief got the wood for the fire," Ruth Rose said.

The kids were outside again, standing between the supermarket and the fire station.

"So where did the guy take the duck bank in his jeep?" Josh asked. "Mr. Pocket said he was on Main Street, but we don't know which direction he was going."

"Yes, we do," Ruth Rose said.

Josh looked at her. "Ruth Rose, the guy could have been heading north or south."

Ruth Rose shook her head. "He couldn't have been heading south," she said. "Mr. Pocket told us the jeep passed him on the corner of Indian Way Road. If it was coming from the fire station, the jeep had to be going north."

"She's right," Dink said. "And north is toward River Road."

Josh looked in that direction. "So when he got to River Road, he either turned right toward Blue Hills, or left toward Hartford."

"Let's go talk to Mr. Pocket," Ruth Rose suggested. "He might remember which way the jeep turned."

"Where do we find him?" Dink asked.

"He lives at number 10 Indian Way Road," Ruth Rose said.

Josh laughed and shook his head. "How can you remember stuff like that?" he asked.

Ruth Rose just smiled.

The kids collected Pal from the bike rack, and then they cut behind the fire station to Indian Way Road.

Number 10 was a small gray-shingled house behind a white fence. Rosebushes filled the yard and drooped over the fence. A stone path led from the gate to the porch, where Mr. Pocket was sitting in a rocking chair. Randolph was on his lap.

"Well, hello again," the elderly man called out.

"Hi," Dink said, standing at the gate. "We had some questions about the jeep you saw last night. Could we talk to you?"

"Of course," Mr. Pocket said. "Come on in! Mind the roses—those thorns love arms and legs!"

Dink opened the gate and the kids stepped through.

"Would you mind closing it behind you?" Mr. Pocket called. "Randolph thinks he can go exploring without me!"

Ruth Rose smiled at Mr. Pocket. She pulled the gate shut and made sure the latch snapped into place.

The kids walked carefully past the rosebushes and joined Mr. Pocket on his porch. Pal looked up at Randolph and wagged his tail.

"Okay, Randolph, you can visit your friend," Mr. Pocket said. He set his dog on the porch near Pal.

Then he stood and removed a bunch of newspapers from a long bench. "Please sit," he told the kids.

The kids lined up on the bench and Mr. Pocket

dropped back into his chair.

A pair of eyeglasses lay on a low table next to the chair. Mr. Pocket put on his glasses and smiled at the kids. "Now, please tell me what's going on," he said. "Why all the interest in this jeep?"

The kids told Mr. Pocket about the money being collected, the fire, and the theft of the duck bank.

"That wasn't a passenger you saw in the seat next to the driver," Dink said. "It was the duck bank."

"Well, I'll be pickled!" Mr. Pocket said. "I remember thinking it was strange how the moon reflected off his face. And all the time, it was a plastic duck!"

"Um, you wouldn't happen to know which way he turned on River Road?" Dink said. "Did he have a blinker on?"

Mr. Pocket shook his head. "Nope. Didn't have any lights on at all. That's why I didn't see him till he almost ran over my toes!"

Mr. Pocket leaned forward. "And if you want my opinion, the driver never meant to turn on River Road," he said. "I truly believe he aimed his jeep straight for the river!"

Dink gulped. "Right into the water?" he said.

The old man nodded. "Yep. Unless that jeep knew how to fly."

"That would explain why the guys in the fire truck didn't pass the jeep," Dink said.

"I'd like to make a donation for your duck bridge," Mr. Pocket said. He fished a small leather pouch from his pocket and took out four quarters. He leaned over and handed them to Josh. "Always liked ducks."

"Thanks a lot, sir," Josh said as he accepted the money. "If we find the bank, I'll put it in for you."

流沙之谜

The kids and Pal left Mr. Pocket sitting on his porch with his dog. They walked to the corner of Main, then turned left and headed for the river.

Between the edge of River Road and the water, there was a patch of weeds. Some of them were crushed flat, lying toward the river.

When the kids were close enough, they realized that there were actually two flattened strips, side by side.

Josh bent over the smashed grass. "They sure look like tire tracks to me," he said. "Mr. Pocket was right!"

Dink, Josh, and Ruth Rose sat and looked out over the river. Pal put his front feet in the river and began lapping up water. Josh held the leash so Pal couldn't go out any farther.

"Could the jeep drive right across the river?" Ruth Rose asked.

"Sure," Josh said. "On TV I've seen guys in jeeps plow right through water deeper than this."

"We should go look on the other side for more tracks," Dink said.

Josh frowned. "But how do we—"

"Look," Dink interrupted, pointing to a flat-bottomed rowboat coming down the river. The man rowing the boat seemed too big for it, like a grown-up sitting on a kid's bike. The man rowed slowly, peering over the sides into the water as he moved.

The boat slowed, then stopped. The man removes one of oars from the oarlock. He began poking the oar into the water. He did it several times, on both sides of the boat.

Then the man set the oar back into the oarlock. He stretched a long arm into the water. He paused a moment, then suddenly laughed.

The man splashed some water onto his face and head. He shook his hair like a wet dog, grabbed both oars, and began rowing for the opposite shore.

When he reached land, he got out and dragged the boat behind him. The man and the boat disappeared into the trees.

"Did you see how big that guy was?" Dink asked.

"Not only that," Josh said. "Did you notice his ears? Mushrooms!"

Chapter 9

"That was the thief!" Ruth Rose said.

"But what was he looking for?" Dink asked.

"Maybe the bank fell out of the jeep when it was crossing," Ruth Rose suggested.

"That duck is pretty big," Josh said. "Wouldn't he be able to see it just lying in the water?"

"Well, he found something," Ruth Rose said.

"And I'm going to find out what," Josh said. He looped Pal's leash around a tree, pulled off his sneakers, and started wading into the river.

"Wait for me!" Dink said, yanking off his own sneakers.

"I'm coming, too!" said Ruth Rose, kicking off her

sandals.

They pushed their feet through the warm, shallow water. Dink could feel the fine sand between his toes. The water was so clear he could see the tiny pebbles on the bottom.

"It's getting kind of muddy," Josh said, a few yards ahead of Dink.

Suddenly Josh stopped. He turned around with panic on his face. "I'm stuck!" he cried.

As Dink watched, Josh started to sink. The water was up to his knees!

"I can't pull my feet out!" Josh yelled. "I think it's quicksand!"

"Wait a minute!" Dink said. He lunged ahead and grabbed Josh's arm.

Then Dink felt the sand closing over his own feet and his ankles, climbing steadily to his knees. He was stuck, too!

"Ruth Rose!" Dink shouted. "Don't come any closer!"

"I'll run for help!" Ruth Rose yelled. She turned and splashed back to shore.

流沙之谜

Dink watched her climb the bank and race across River Road in her bare feet. Pal was straining on his leash and barking.

Josh pulled out of Dink's grasp, struggling to walk back toward the edge. But the more he struggled, the deeper he sank.

"Don't move!" Dink yelled. "Get on your back."

To demonstrate, Dink fell backward into the water. He floated on his back, facing up. His legs were still stuck, but at least he wasn't sinking.

"Do it—it works!" he called to Josh.

Dink heard a splash as Josh fell over into the water. He could hear his own heart pounding in his ears. Trying to calm himself, he closed his eyes and let his body float.

Suddenly Pal began to bark even more wildly. Turning his head, Dink saw Jake and another man running toward the river carrying a ladder. Ruth Rose was right behind them.

At the river's edge, the men flopped the ladder into the water.

"Don't move!" Jake yelled out to Dink and Josh.

137

"Just stay the way you are. Lenny and I will have you out in a jiffy."

The firefighters shoved the ladder out into the water toward Dink. When it was near enough, he grabbed the last rung.

"Hold on, kid!" Jake yelled.

The men pulled the ladder. Dink could feel suction on his legs, as if the quicksand didn't want to let him go.

But Jake and Lenny were stronger than the quicksand. Suddenly Dink's legs oozed free of the muck. When Dink's feet touched solid river bottom, he splashed ashore.

Immediately, the men thrust the ladder back out over the river. Jake waded in and pushed the ladder until Josh could grab a rung. Pulling the ladder hand over hand, he and Lenny hauled Josh out of the river like a fish. Dink and Josh sat side by side, catching their breath. They were both sopping wet and red-faced. Pal lapped Josh's face and jumped all over his muddy legs. "Don't ever do that again!" Ruth Rose said.

"Don't worry," Josh said. "I'm never even taking a bath again!"

流沙之谜

Everyone burst out laughing.

"By the way," Jake said, slapping the other man on the back, "this is Lenny."

Lenny smiled at the kids. "Glad to meet you," he said.

"Not as glad as we are," Dink said, standing up to shake Lenny's hand.

"What were you kids doing out there?" Lenny asked.

"That's where the jeep is!" Josh said.

"It is?" Dink asked. "Josh, we don't know—"

"It's there," Josh said, pulling on his sneakers. "When I was lying in the water, something sharp stuck me in the leg. I reached down and felt the jeep's antenna! That must be what that guy in the boat found!"

"We have to go get Officer Fallon," Ruth Rose said.

"No need to," Jake said, holding a hand in the air. "I called him from the station. Listen."

They heard a siren coming closer. Twenty seconds later, a cruiser roared up to the river and stopped. Officer Fallon jumped out and practically slid into the river in his haste.

139

"You kids all right?" he said, looking from one face to the other.

"We're fine," Dink said. "And Josh found the crook's jeep!"

"You did? Where?"

Josh pointed out into the water. "Out there, buried in quicksand."

"I never even knew there was quicksand in Connecticut," Ruth Rose said.

"Quicksand can be anywhere there's water and sand," Lenny said. "I was a Navy SEAL, and I saw plenty of the stuff."

"But we've waded in the river lots of times," Josh

said. "I never got stuck before."

"Sometimes you find it only in small pockets," Lenny explained. "In fact, right here is a perfect spot for it. Lots of sand under shallow, slow-moving water."

"But how did you know to look here?" Officer Fallon asked the kids.

"We went to see Mr. Pocket," Dink explained. "He told us it seemed like the jeep went straight instead of turning on River Road. So we came here and found tire tracks."

"Then we saw a guy in a boat," Josh added. "He was looking for something in the water. He found it,

141

then took off."

"That's when Josh decided to take a mud bath," Ruth Rose said with a grin.

The three men and three kids looked out over the river. The blue sky, sparkling water, and golden sand looked so peaceful.

"If you're right about the jeep," Officer Fallon said, "the duck bank is probably down there, too."

"But how can we get it out?" Ruth Rose asked.

Officer Fallon scratched his chin. "That's a good question," he said.

"I think I have the answer," Lenny said.

Chapter 10

Everyone looked at Lenny.

"Quicksand is just a kind of soup made of sand and water," he explained. "Beneath the quicksand there's a layer of hard clay or rock. The quicksand lies on top of that hard stuff because it can't drain out."

"But how far down is the hard layer?" Officer Fallon asked.

"The only way to find out is to get out there in the stuff," Lenny said. "But if these kids found the antenna sticking up, the jeep must be just beneath the surface of sand."

"So we'll get a hook on that baby and pull it out, right, Lenny?" Jake asked.

A to Z 神秘案件

"Yeah, if I can find the bumper," Lenny said. "I'll go out there and see what's what. You go back to the firehouse and get the truck."

Twenty minutes later, everything was in place. Jake had backed the rescue truck to the riverbank. A long cable with a big hook on one end lay on the ground. The other end snaked into the winch on the back of the truck.

Standing at the water's edge, Lenny held the hook end of the cable.

"Okay," Jake called to Lenny. "Go fishing!"

Dragging the cable and hook, Lenny half floated, half swam out into the river. Dink, Josh, and Ruth Rose hunkered down under a tree and watched. Pal's head was resting on Josh's knees.

Officer Fallon sat in his cruiser, talking into his car phone.

A small crowd of people stood watching on the edge of River Road.

"I sure hope the duck bank is still in the jeep," Dink said.

"And I hope Lenny doesn't get stuck in the quicksand,"

Josh added.

"Okay, I think I'm right over the rear of the jeep," Lenny yelled. He took a deep breath and plunged under the water.

A minute passed. Everyone stared at the spot where Lenny had disappeared. Dink glanced at his watch.

"The quicksand must have him!" Josh yelled.

"Let's not panic," Jake said. "If he gets in trouble, we'll haul him out by the cable." But Jake looked worried.

Suddenly the surface of the water erupted. Lenny popped up like a cork on a fishing line. He began spitting and shaking mud from his arms and shoulders.

"What took you so long?" Jake yelled to his partner.

"The jeep sank at an angle," Lenny called back. "So unfortunately, the bumper is lower down than I thought."

"Did you get the hook on it?" Jake asked.

Lenny grinned. "Of course I did! Pull her in, Jake!"

Jake ran to the truck and threw a lever, and the cable began to inch backward into the winch. As the cable tightened, the winch strained, making a noise like fingernails on a chalkboard. Everybody stared at the river.

Out in the water, the back end of a yellow jeep suddenly broke the surface.

"There it is!" Ruth Rose cried.

Officer Fallon had come to stand behind the kids. "Well, I'll be darned," he muttered.

They all heard a sucking sound as the quicksand gave up the jeep. Inch by inch, the jeep oozed toward the riverbank like some yellow sea monster. Water and sand cascaded off the metal and glass.

Finally, the jeep's rear tires came to rest against the riverbank. In the passenger seat, wet and muddy, sat the duck bank. The coins were barely visible through the clear plastic because of the sand and water that had seeped in.

"This bank must weigh a ton with all that water and muck inside," Lenny said. "I know I can't lift it."

"Let's haul the jeep back to the firehouse," Jake suggested. He climbed into the driver's seat of the rescue truck. "We'll use the hoist to lift the bank, then empty out the money and let it dry."

"And I'd like to see what's in that glove compartment," Officer Fallon said.

Lenny nodded. He opened the jeep's doors, letting muddy water flood out onto the ground. With it came a soggy mixture of old hamburger wrappers, a T-shirt, and a ragged green towel.

"Okay," Lenny said. "Take 'er away."

The rescue truck slowly pulled the jeep toward the firehouse. Water was still oozing out. Officer Fallon followed in his cruiser. With the excitement over, people began to wander away.

"Let's go watch them empty out the bank," Dink said.

"Could we get some lunch first?" Josh asked as he untied Pal's leash from the tree. "I swear I'm losing weight here."

"Okay, we can go to my house and eat," Ruth Rose said. "I wouldn't want Josh to get any skinnier."

Pal was sniffing the wet hamburger wrappers that had just poured out of the jeep.

"See, even my dog is hungry," Josh teased.

"Wait a minute, guys," Ruth Rose said. Using the toe of her sandal, she kicked at the wet towel.

Only it wasn't a towel. It was a green apron. And flashing in the sun was a name tag, pinned to the material.

Three words were printed on the name tag: HI! I'M MARTIN.

Chapter 11

The kids stood looking down at the name tag.

"I've seen an apron and name tag like this before," Dink said. "In the supermarket!"

"Martin must work there!" Josh said. "Let's go arrest him!"

"We can't arrest anybody," Ruth Rose said. "We have to tell Officer Fallon!"

Ruth Rose scooped up the apron and wrung out the water. Then the kids raced up the grassy slope and across River Road. Pal loped alongside Josh.

On the firehouse driveway, they saw Jake, Lenny, and a couple of other firefighters. The jeep was standing in a puddle of river water.

"Have you seen Officer Fallon?" Dink asked one of the firefighters.

"You just missed him," the man said, pointing to the jeep's open glove compartment. "He grabbed some papers and left."

"Do you know if he went to the police station?" Ruth Rose asked.

The firefighter shrugged. "He didn't say."

Dink looked at Josh and Ruth Rose. "What should we do?" he asked.

"If Martin is the crook, we need to let Officer Fallon know," Ruth Rose said.

"But it might be too late," Josh said. "If Martin works next door, he might have seen the jeep being dragged over here."

Josh quickly glanced toward the supermarket. "He could be watching us right now!"

Dink thought for a minute. "We saw Martin in a rowboat a while ago, so maybe he isn't working at the market today," he said. "He might not know we found the jeep."

Ruth Rose was still holding the damp apron. She

looked across the lawn toward the supermarket. "Come on," she said. "If Martin isn't working today, maybe we can find out where he lives. And even if he is working, we'll tell Officer Fallon."

They crossed the lawn that separated the fire station from the supermarket. Josh left Pal tied to the bike rack again, and the kids hurried inside.

"Keep your eyes peeled for a big guy with mushroom ears," Josh whispered.

But the store was packed with Sunday shoppers. Dozens of workers in green aprons scurried around. Many of the male employees were pretty big.

"How will we ever find him?" Ruth Rose asked. "Martin could be anywhere!"

"I have an idea," Dink said. "When we were here before, I saw a bunch of pictures of employees. Let's check 'em out."

Josh and Ruth Rose followed Dink toward the back of the store. They cut through the pet food aisle, took a right at the dairy department, and stopped in front of the wall of photographs.

"There he is," Dink said, pointing. The man they'd

seen in the rowboat was in the bottom row of pictures. He was the only one with huge ears.

"Martin Fleece," Dink said, reading the name under the picture.

"What should we do?" Josh asked.

Ruth Rose held up the apron. "We have to find out if he's here," she said. "Let's see if Mr. Robb is in his office."

The store manager's office was only a few yards from the wall of pictures. The door was open, and Dink could hear Mr. Robb's voice.

"Someone's in there with him," Dink whispered to Josh and Ruth Rose. They stood just outside the door.

"Marty, I just don't understand," Mr. Robb was saying. "Yesterday you were happy to work here, and today you want to quit."

"I'm sorry," a deep voice responded. "But I have to go out of town. My . . . my grandmother is in the hospital, so I have to leave today. And I'll need my paycheck, too."

Josh peeked around the corner. When he looked back at Dink and Ruth Rose, his eyes were huge.

"Martin Fleece!" he whispered.

"What can we do?" Ruth Rose asked.

"Let us take it from here," a quiet voice said, this time from behind Ruth Rose.

It was Officer Fallon with Officer Keene. "Did this come from the jeep?" Officer Fallon asked, pointing at the wet apron.

Ruth Rose nodded.

He took the apron and walked into Mr. Robb's office. Officer Keene followed and closed the door.

Dink, Josh, and Ruth Rose stepped closer and listened.

"Martin Fleece, you are under arrest for theft," they heard Officer Fallon say.

One hour later, the kids were sitting in Officer Fallon's office. Martin Fleece was in jail.

"How did you know where to find him?" Dink asked Officer Fallon.

"The jeep's registration was in the glove compartment," Officer Fallon said. "His name and address were on it. One phone call told me he worked in the supermarket."

"How come he didn't get caught in the quicksand like I did?" Josh asked.

Officer Fallon shrugged. "Most likely, when the jeep got stuck, he realized he was in some kind of deep mud. He must have leapt clear, or swum till he could walk out of the river."

"Did the firefighters open the bank yet?" Ruth Rose asked.

Officer Fallon stood up. He opened his drawer and took out the cookie tin and his jar of money. "Why don't we go find out?" he asked.

Three weeks later, the duck bridge was completed. The high school kids had done a great job. The bridge was wooden and looked like a regular bridge, only it was much narrower than most. A small sign said DUCKS WELCOME.

One end of the bridge was on the riverbank, and it curved gracefully over River Road. Cars would be able to pass under it, and the ducks would be safe.

The town decided to have a grand opening the day after the bridge was finished. Dink, Josh, and Ruth Rose packed a picnic lunch. With Pal, the twins, and Ruth Rose's brother, Nate, they headed to the new duck bridge.

Officer Fallon was there with his grandson, Jimmy. Jake and Lenny both showed up, and Dink noticed Mr. Pocket and Randolph.

While Nate, Brian, and Bradley kept Pal off the bridge, Ruth Rose unfolded a blanket. She looked for a flat place to spread it.

"Can you hurry it up, Ruth Rose?" Josh said. "Those sandwiches are calling me!"

"You could help out, Josh," Dink said. He grabbed one end of the blanket from Ruth Rose and helped her spread it. Then he opened the picnic basket.

Pal and the three little kids came running when they

saw the sandwiches, cookies, and watermelon slices.

As the kids ate their lunch, the girl who had first suggested the bridge sprinkled cracked corn all along it. Everybody waited.

Some little kids began running around, playing tag. People started to chat with each other. Someone turned on a radio, and two big kids with a Frisbee tossed it back and forth.

"Too much noise," Josh muttered. "It's like a party. A duck would have to be crazy to cross that bridge."

Gradually, everyone else got tired of waiting and went home.

"Where are the ducks?" Nate asked Ruth Rose.

"Maybe now that it's quieter, we'll see them," she whispered.

"Okay, we'll be real quiet!" Brian said. "Be quiet, Bradley!"

"I'm not talking!" Bradley argued. "You be quiet!"

Josh pulled his two brothers close to him. "If you want to see the ducks, you have to be as quiet as Pal,"

he whispered.

Pal was lying on the blanket, sound asleep. Nate, Brian, and Bradley flopped down on both sides of the dog. They cuddled up to him like puppies.

"Good move," Ruth Rose told Josh.

"Think the ducks will really come?" Dink whispered.

"They'd better," Josh mumbled. "After I nearly drowned for them!"

The six kids waited all afternoon. The little ones fell asleep. Dink, Josh, and Ruth Rose played Monopoly. Pal snored peacefully between the twins.

Josh was just about to land on Dink's hotel when Ruth Rose whispered, "Look!"

A duck stood at the very top of the curved bridge. She turned her head in all directions, as if looking for danger. Seeing none, she quacked quietly. Five little yellow ducks waddled up to her.

Dink leaned over and woke Nate, Brian, and Bradley. Then they all sat like statues and watched the ducks cross safely over River Road.

Text copyright © 2002 by Ron Roy
Illustrations copyright © 2002 by John Steven Gurney
All rights reserved under International and Pan-American Copyright Conventions.
Published in the United States by Random House Children's Books,
a division of Random House, Inc., New York,
and simultaneously in Canada by Random House of Canada Limited, Toronto.

本书中英双语版由中南博集天卷文化传媒有限公司与企鹅兰登（北京）文化发展有限公司合作出版。

"企鹅"及其相关标识是企鹅兰登已经注册或尚未注册的商标。
未经允许，不得擅用。
封底凡无企鹅防伪标识者均属未经授权之非法版本。

©中南博集天卷文化传媒有限公司。本书版权受法律保护。未经权利人许可，任何人不得以任何方式使用本书包括正文、插图、封面、版式等任何部分内容，违者将受到法律制裁。

著作权合同登记号：字18-2023-258

图书在版编目（CIP）数据

流沙之谜：汉英对照/（美）罗恩·罗伊著；（美）约翰·史蒂文·格尼绘；曹幼南译. -- 长沙：湖南少年儿童出版社，2024.10. --（A to Z神秘案件）.
ISBN 978-7-5562-7818-3

Ⅰ. H319.4

中国国家版本馆CIP数据核字第20243Y7Q51号

A TO Z SHENMI ANJIAN LIUSHA ZHI MI

A to Z神秘案件 流沙之谜

[美]罗恩·罗伊 著　[美]约翰·史蒂文·格尼 绘　曹幼南 译

责任编辑：唐凌 李炜	策划出品：李炜 张苗苗 文赛峰
策划编辑：文赛峰	特约编辑：张晓璐
营销编辑：付佳 杨朔 周晓茜	封面设计：霍雨佳
版权支持：王媛媛	版式设计：马睿君
插图上色：河北传图文化	内文排版：李洁

出 版 人：刘星保
出　　版：湖南少年儿童出版社
地　　址：湖南省长沙市晚报大道89号
邮　　编：410016
电　　话：0731-82196320
常年法律顾问：湖南崇民律师事务所 柳成柱律师
经　　销：新华书店
开　　本：875 mm×1230 mm　1/32　　印　　刷：三河市中晟雅豪印务有限公司
字　　数：87千字　　　　　　　　　　　印　　张：5
版　　次：2024年10月第1版　　　　　　 印　　次：2024年10月第1次印刷
书　　号：ISBN 978-7-5562-7818-3　　　 定　　价：280.00元（全10册）

若有质量问题，请致电质量监督电话：010-59096394　团购电话：010-59320018

A to Z 神秘案件

中英双语

第二辑

THE RUNAWAY RACEHORSE

逃跑的赛马

[美] 罗恩·罗伊 著
[美] 约翰·史蒂文·格尼 绘　高琼 译

湖南少年儿童出版社
·长沙·

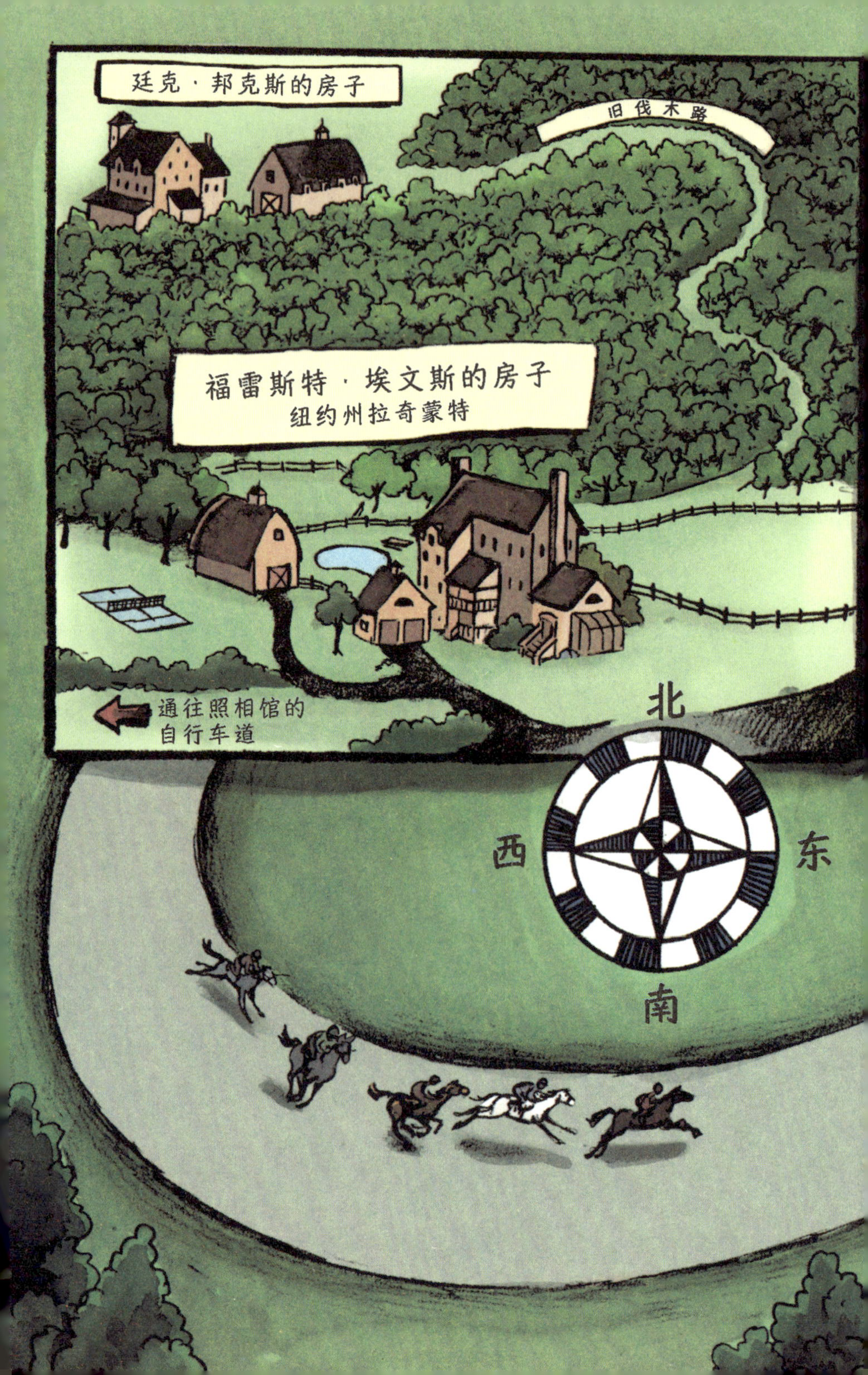

廷克·邦克斯的房子
旧伐木路
福雷斯特·埃文斯的房子
纽约州拉奇蒙特
通往照相馆的
自行车道
北
西
东
南

欢迎来到纽约州拉奇蒙特
纽约州萨拉托加温泉市
一起解开 A to Z 神秘案件

萨拉托加温泉市
佛蒙特州
新罕布什尔州
马萨诸塞州
绿地镇
康涅狄格州
纽约州
拉奇蒙特

俱乐部
正面看台
马棚

萨拉托加
赛马场
纽约州萨拉托加温泉市

起跑门栅

人物介绍

三人小组的成员，聪明勇敢，喜欢读推理小说，紧急关头总能保持头脑冷静。喜欢在做事之前好好思考！

丁丁

三人小组的成员，活泼机智，喜欢吃好吃的食物，常常有意想不到的点子。

乔希

三人小组的成员，活泼开朗，喜欢从头到脚穿同一种颜色的衣服，总是那个能找到大部分线索的人。

露丝

居住在纽约州的拉奇蒙特，丁丁的伯伯，和自己的朋友福雷斯特一起买了一匹名叫"旋风"的赛马。

沃伦伯伯

居住在纽约州的拉奇蒙特，是沃伦伯伯的朋友，邀请孩子们来观看赛马比赛。

福雷斯特·埃文斯

是一名骑师，负责照顾"旋风"的日常饮食，训练它参加赛马比赛。

莎妮·菲尔茨

福雷斯特的邻居，将赛马"旋风"卖给了福雷斯特，留下了一匹名叫"饼干"的母马。

廷克·邦克斯

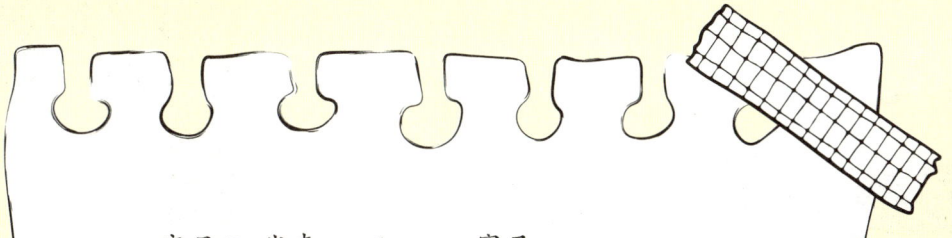

字母 R 代表 racehorse，赛马……

"我想要给它拍张照片。"露丝说。于是孩子们朝领奖处走去。他们扭动身子从人群中挤了过去，来到舞者身旁。

只见舞者的胸部和腿部汗淋淋的，绑在脚踝上的白布带脏兮兮的。它的骑师也是全身脏兮兮的，但他还是面带微笑，让人们拍照。

"伙伴们，靠近一点，"露丝说，"我想给你们和舞者拍张照片。"

丁丁和乔希走过去，站在舞者前面。那匹马用头轻轻地顶了顶乔希的背，弄得他咯咯直笑。

骑师摇了摇缰绳，舞者就把头放在了丁丁的肩膀和乔希的肩膀中间。

露丝拍下了照片。这时，只听见她的照相机发出了嗡嗡声，提醒她胶卷用完了。

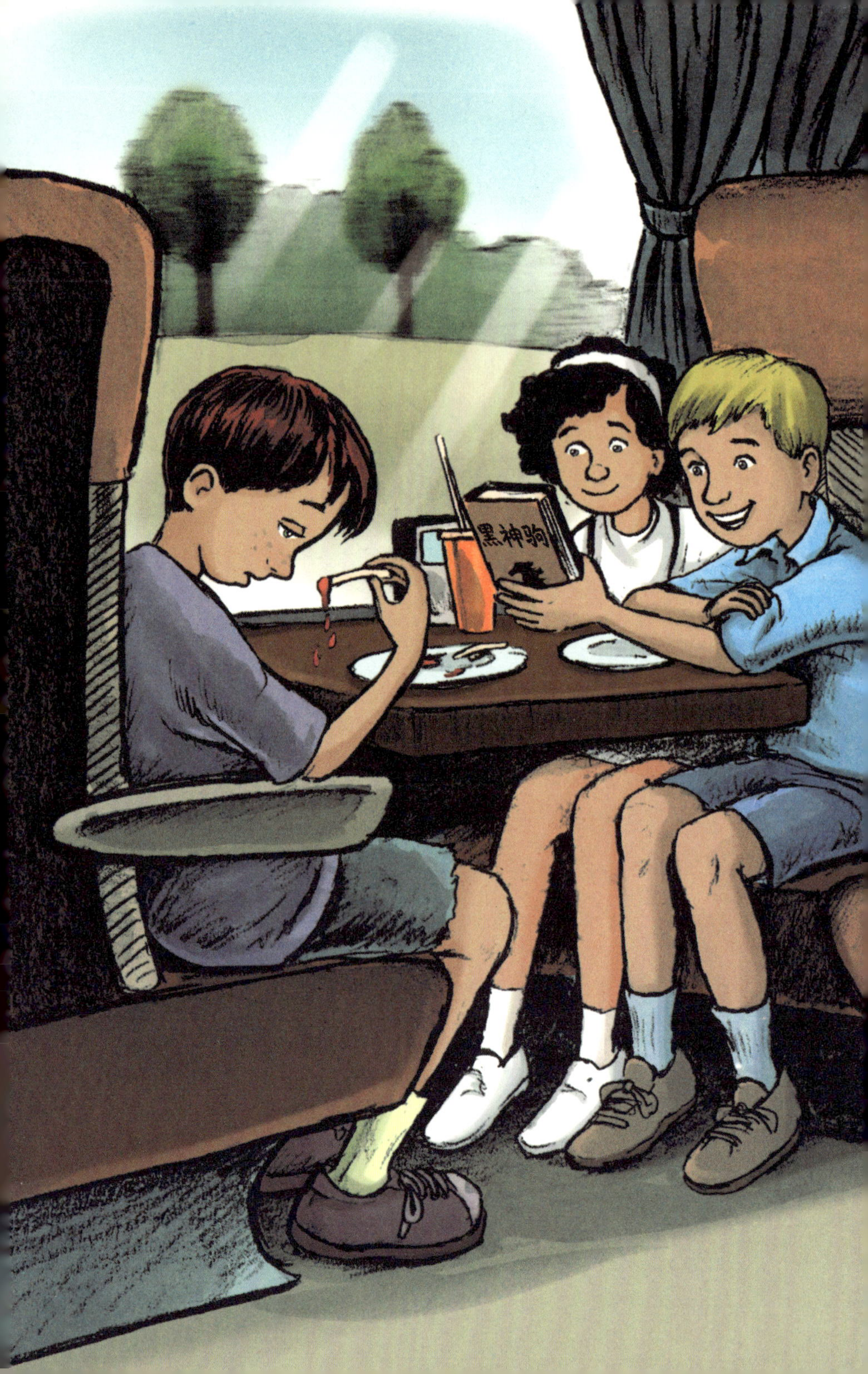
黑神驹

第 一 章

乔希拿起一根薯条,蘸上番茄酱,在盘子上写下自己姓名的首字母。接着,他咬了一口那根薯条,一滴番茄酱滴落在他的T恤衫上。

"真倒霉,这可是我最喜欢的T恤衫呢!"乔希说。

丁丁放下手中的书本,朝他这位长着一脸雀斑、一头红发的朋友咧嘴笑了。"这下好了,成了你先前最喜欢的T恤衫了。"他说。

乔希、丁丁和露丝正乘坐火车前往纽约州的拉奇蒙特,去看望他们的朋友福雷斯特·埃文斯。福雷斯特和丁丁的伯伯沃伦一起买了一匹赛马。孩子们受邀去观看这匹名为"旋风"的赛马在萨拉托加温泉市的一场赛马比赛。

乔希拿起一张餐巾纸，擦拭那块红色的污渍，结果越擦越脏。

"乔希在用手指画画呢。"露丝对丁丁说。

"有朝一日我会成为一名著名的番茄酱画家。"乔希一边说，一边凝视着车窗外面，"咱们什么时候到那儿啊？"

"再过几分钟就到了。"露丝一边说，一边查看她的火车时刻表。

"我迫不及待想要见到旋风了，"丁丁说，"我以前从来没有见过真正的赛马呢。现在我满脑子想的都是马，所以我正在阅读这个呢。"

只见他举起自己手中的书本。这本书是沃尔特·法利撰写的《黑神驹》。书的封面上是一匹漂亮的黑色骏马，马儿长着一双狂野的眼睛和一身飘逸的鬃毛。

丁丁·邓肯真正的名字是唐纳德，中间名是戴维。不过，他当初开口学说话时，想要说自己的全名"唐纳德·戴维·邓肯"，说出来的

却是"丁丁"。从那以后,丁丁就成了他的小名。

"快看我带的是什么。"露丝一边说,一边从双肩包里拿出一本书。书的封面上是一个骑马的女孩,书名是《学骑马》。

"乔希,你带了与马有关的书吗?"丁丁问道。

乔希咧嘴笑着说:"没有呢。到时候我想要知道什么,问你们两个就行了,你们会告诉我的。"接着,他往自己的双肩包里扔了几块方糖。

"你肚子还饿吗?"丁丁打趣地问道。

"这是给旋风准备的。"乔希说。

就在这时,列车乘务员进入餐车,走了过来。"下一站就是拉奇蒙特。"他告诉孩子们。

"噢,等一等!"露丝一边说,一边把手伸进自己的双肩包翻找,随即拿出了她新买的照相机。

露丝喜欢全身上下同一种颜色的装扮。今天,她身上的所有穿戴,从头上的束发带到脚上的运动鞋,全都是白色的。就连她的照相机也是白色的!

"请您帮我们拍张照好吗?"她向列车乘务员请求说。

A to Z 神秘案件

"非常乐意。"列车乘务员说。他接过照相机,将镜头对准孩子们:"说'茄子'!"

"茄子!"孩子们异口同声地说。

随后列车乘务员把照相机还给露丝。"祝你们今天玩得开心。"他说。

火车开始慢慢减速,最后停了下来。丁丁、

逃跑的赛马

乔希和露丝抓起各自的双肩包，走到车厢尽头。列车乘务员放下一段脚踏梯，孩子们下了火车来到站台上。

这时，丁丁听到有人叫自己的名字。他看见自己的伯伯沃伦和福雷斯特·埃文斯正朝他们走过来。丁丁的伯伯个子矮矮的，身材胖胖的，戴着一副眼镜。福雷斯特·埃文斯的棕色胡子修剪得整整齐齐，他上身穿着T恤衫，下身穿着牛仔裤。

"哎呀，是温克、高希和图思·托斯[1]啊！"福雷斯特向他们打招呼说。

孩子们之前见过福雷斯特，那时他的画作在沃伦伯伯的公寓里被人偷走了。

"嘿，埃文斯先生！"他们异口同声地回应。

"请叫我福雷斯特，好吗？"他说。

丁丁拥抱了他的伯伯。

"火车之旅一路上怎么样？"沃伦伯伯问道。

---

1. 温克、高希和图思·托斯，分别指丁丁、乔希和露丝，此处福雷斯特没能记清楚孩子们的确切名字，只是凭记忆打招呼，所以有出入。——译者

"好极了!"乔希回答说,"火车上的汉堡太好吃了!"

福雷斯特领着大家来到一辆黑色汽车前,然后打开了车子的后门。孩子们背着双肩包上了车。沃伦伯伯坐在前排,在福雷斯特的旁边。大家在各自的座位上安顿好之后,福雷斯特发动汽车,驶出了停车场。

"您有多少匹马?"乔希问道。

"只有旋风这一匹马。"福雷斯特回答说。

"赛马比赛的时候,是您骑在它背上吗?"露丝接着问道。

福雷斯特哈哈大笑起来:"骑马的人不是我,

我体重太沉了。职业骑师们个子小、体重轻。我雇了一位名叫莎妮的女士来当旋风的骑师。"

"真了不起!"乔希激动地叫起来,"我从来没见过女骑师呢。"接着他又补充了一句,"我也从来没见过男骑师。"

福雷斯特在一排小商店附近放慢了行驶速度,手指轻轻一弹打开了转向灯。丁克、乔希和露丝认出了这条长长的、绿树成荫的车道。他们以前和丁丁的伯伯一起来过一次。

过了一会儿,福雷斯特把汽车停在了车库里。只见一条石子路一直延伸到一栋大砖房前面。房子后面是一座石砌的马棚,马棚的一边是网球场,另一边是游泳池。

"我们到了。"福雷斯特说。

孩子们背着双肩包,从汽车后座下了车。

"我们什么时候可以见到旋风呢?"乔希一边问,一边朝马棚的方向望去。

"就现在!"福雷斯特回答说。

沃伦伯伯朝房子走去,孩子们则跟在福雷斯特后面朝马棚走去。

乔希把手伸进口袋翻找，然后拿出了一块方糖。"我给旋风带了这个。"他说。

"这个主意不错，乔希，"福雷斯特说，"不过旋风不喜欢吃糖。它是我见过的唯一不喜欢吃糖的马呢！"

乔希把方糖放回口袋里。这时，孩子们走进了凉爽、昏暗的马棚。丁丁深深地吸了一口气。"这里的味道真好闻。"他说。

"我也这样觉得。"福雷斯特说着，也深深地吸了一口气，"没有什么东西闻起来比得上干草和马的香味。"

"可别忘了还有巧克力。"乔希补充说道。

大家都哈哈大笑起来，福雷斯特带路，朝着马棚后门旁边的一个马隔间走去。马棚的后门敞开着，阳光倾泻进来。只见马棚后面有一大片砾石地，上面停放着一辆卡车。

马隔间的门也是敞开着的，不过里面并没有马。

"真奇怪。"福雷斯特一边说，一边把马隔间的门关上。他思忖了片刻，随即笑了笑。

逃跑的赛马

"我敢肯定,是莎妮带着旋风出去训练了。"他说,"他们应该很快就会回来。我们走吧,你们先去屋子里安顿下来。"

他领着丁丁、乔希和露丝走出马隔间,来到屋子里。他们经过一个小房间,只见房间的地板上放着靴子,挂钩上挂着夹克衫。

"这是一间湿物存放室。"福雷斯特一边介绍,一边解开自己的鞋带,把靴子脱下来。

他领着孩子们穿过另一扇门来到了厨房。厨房的墙壁是黄色的,操作台和地板上铺着蓝色的瓷砖。

福雷斯特指着一条低矮的长凳说:"你们现在可以把自己的双肩包放在那儿。"

于是孩子们把他们的双肩包放在了长凳上。丁丁瞥了一眼用磁铁吸附在冰箱门上的剪报。剪报上是一匹黑马的照片,黑马的额头上有一块菱形的白斑。剪报的标题是:无可匹敌的本地赛马。

"这就是旋风吗?"丁丁问道。

"就是它。"福雷斯特回答说。

"真漂亮。"露丝接着说。

"它真正的样子比照片上还要更漂亮。"福雷斯特一边说，一边指着冰箱，"你们几个孩子喜欢吃水果吗？"

"我们什么都喜欢吃呢！"乔希说。

福雷斯特在桌子上放上葡萄和草莓。孩子们坐了下来，开始吃水果。

突然，厨房的门猛地打开了。一位小个子女士跑进了厨房，只见她上身穿着法兰绒衬衫，下身穿着牛仔裤，脚上穿着马靴。

"嘿，莎妮，"福雷斯特说，"跟丁丁、乔希和露丝打个招呼吧。他们来这里是要观看你和旋风

明天的赛马比赛呢。"

"它不见了！"莎妮气喘吁吁地说。

"谁不见了？"

"旋风不见了！"她说，"我刚到这儿，打算带它出去。我朝它的马厩里看了一眼，发现里面空空如也！"

第二章

福雷斯特惊讶地抬起头来。突然,他脸上的表情又放松了下来。

"别担心。我敢肯定,旋风又去看它妈妈了。"福雷斯特说,"我来给邦克斯先生打个电话问问吧。"

"邦克斯先生是谁呀?"露丝问道。

"廷克·邦克斯是我家隔壁牧场的主人,"福雷斯特说,"他本来想饲养赛马,但是他运气一直不大好,于是他把自己的马匹全都卖掉了。就这样,我和沃伦才买到了旋风。邦克斯先生只留下了旋风的妈妈,一匹漂亮的老母马,名叫饼干。"

"旋风是怎么去看它妈妈的呢?"丁丁问道。

莎妮皱了皱眉头。"这个淘气鬼会从马隔间里跑出来,抄近路穿过树林,去找它妈妈。"她说。

"我很好奇,这次它是什么时候跑出去的呢?"福雷斯特说,"今天早上沃伦过来的时候,它还在。我们还一起进马隔间看了它呢。"

"这么说,它可能跑出去一整天了!"莎妮说。

福雷斯特缓缓地点了点头,说:"没错,事实可能就是这样,莎妮。不过大家别担心。上一次它跑了出去,后来我发现它安然无恙,正跟它妈妈待在一起嚼干草呢。"

福雷斯特伸手拿起电话,拨通了电话号码。他先是倾听了一会儿,随即挂断了电话。

"邦克斯先生家的电话占线。"他一边说,一边看着孩子们,"你们要是吃好了,就坐上我的卡车一起去那里一趟,怎么样?"

"那我去给旋风的马厩里放一些新鲜稻草吧。"莎妮说。她出了门,朝马棚的方向走去。

福雷斯特把水果放回冰箱,孩子们跟在他身后走出了厨房。

他领着孩子们来到马棚后面的砾石停车场。只见福雷斯特的皮卡车上装满了一捆捆的干草。

"你们谁想要坐在后面的货斗里,跟干草捆待在一起啊?"福雷斯特问道。

"我去!"乔希说。

"我也去,"露丝说,"要不然,乔希会害怕的。"

"你们一定要抓牢了,"福雷斯特说,"我们会穿过树林,走那条旧伐木路,那里的路面颠簸不平。"

露丝和乔希爬上卡车的货斗,坐在干草捆上。丁丁爬进驾驶室,坐在福雷斯特旁边。

福雷斯特发动卡车,驶进了树林。丁丁的身子在座位上颠来颠去,因为轮胎在凹凸不平的路上颠簸着。低矮的树枝拂过驾驶室的顶部。

丁丁扭过头,透过后车窗往外看。只见乔希和露丝在哈哈大笑,同时用手抓着卡车的侧板。

几分钟过后,他们驶出了树林。丁丁看到,前面有一个马棚和一所房子。福雷斯特把车开进停车道,停在另一辆卡车后面。

逃跑的赛马

附近的一棵树上拴着一条狗。见到他们,这条狗跳了起来,开始叫唤。

"安静,巴斯特,"福雷斯特朝车窗外说道,"要乖乖的。"

这时,一个男人从马棚后面走了过来。只见他身穿工作衫和牛仔裤,皮带上有一个大大的银色搭扣。沾满泥巴的长筒胶靴几乎到了他的膝盖。

"躺下,巴斯特。"男人说。巴斯特停止叫

唤，扑通一声趴倒在地上。

"下午好，廷克。"福雷斯特打招呼说。

廷克·邦克斯走了过来，身子靠在车门上。只见他长着一张瘦削的脸，一双锐利的蓝眼睛，还有一对浓密的眉毛。

"你好，福雷斯特，"他说，"我卖给你的那匹马一如既往奔跑如风吧？"

福雷斯特点点头，笑了笑。"到目前为止，每一场比赛他都赢了。"他说。

"能赢是好事。"邦克斯先生说，他朝着远处看了几秒钟，"不过令我感到庆幸的是，我现在已经不再从事赛马这个行当了。养马有太多的事情要做啦。"

他朝驾驶室里面瞥了一眼，说："今天是什么风把你给吹来了？"

"我担心旋风又不见了。"福雷斯特告诉邦克斯先生，"它会不会是来看它妈妈了呢？"

邦克斯先生扬了扬眉毛。"据我所知，它没有来这里，"他一边说，一边朝马棚那边望去，"咱们过去看看好了。"

逃跑的赛马

孩子们跟着邦克斯先生和福雷斯特走进一个大马棚。就在他们进去的时候,丁丁听到了一声马的嘶鸣。"我们听见你的声音了,饼干。"邦克斯先生说。

马棚里面凉爽而昏暗。阳光透过高高的窗户照进来,空气中飘浮着灰尘。阁楼上放着一排排干草捆。地板打扫得干干净净。

丁丁朝好几个马隔间里面瞧了瞧。每一个马隔间都打扫得干干净净,每一个马隔间都空空如也。

邦克斯先生在一个马隔间前面停下了脚步,只见这个马隔间的顶门板敞开着。一匹黑眼睛的浅棕色马站在那儿等着,它的额头上有一小块白斑。

"这就是旋风的妈妈。"福雷斯特告诉孩子们。他用手轻轻地拍了拍马的鼻子。

"今天看到你儿子了吗,老太太?"邦克斯先生问他的这匹马。

饼干好像能听懂似的,左右摇晃着它的大脑袋。

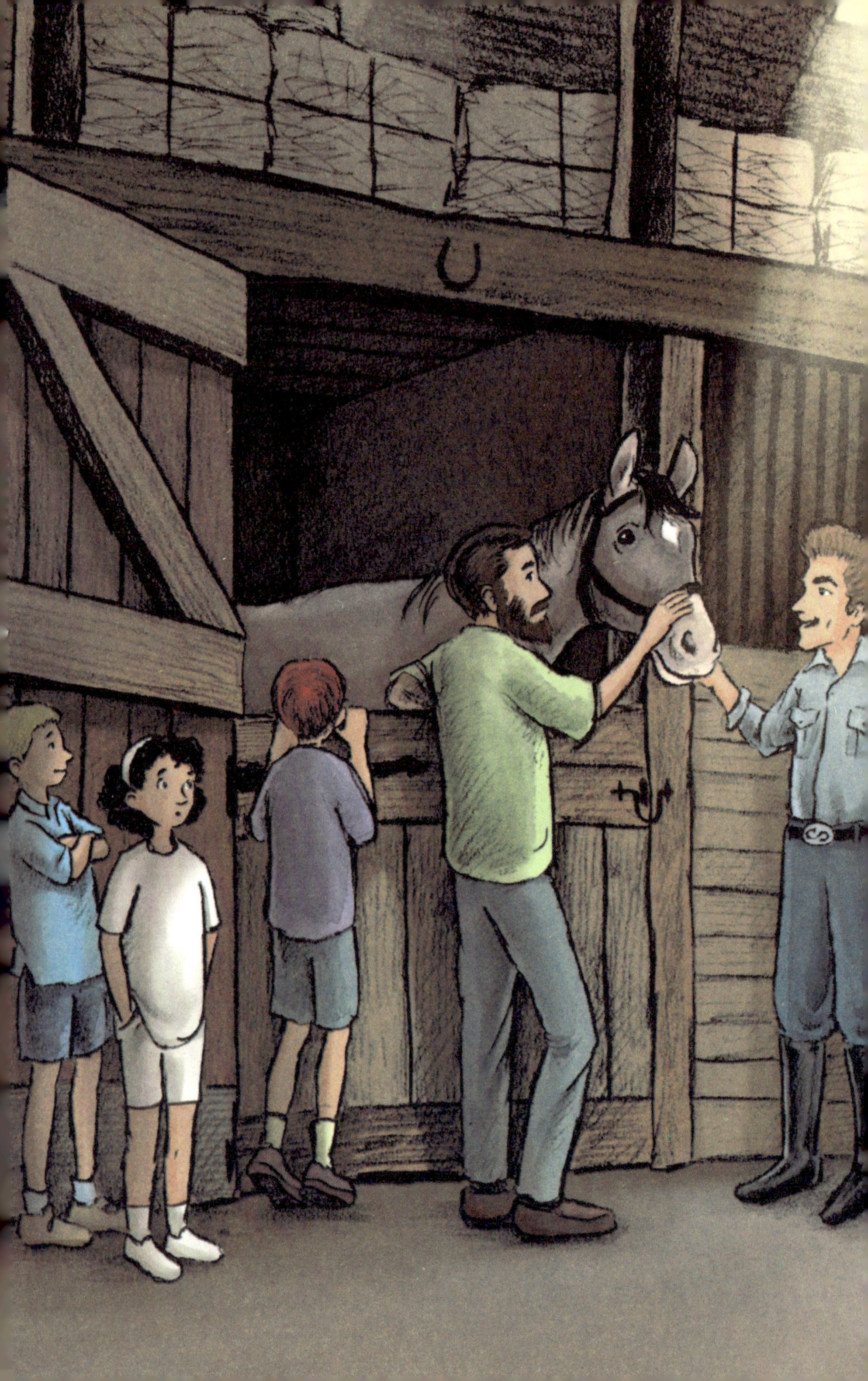

"我还以为它一定在这里呢。"福雷斯特说。他瞥了一眼那几个空空的马隔间。

"恐怕我浪费了你的时间。"福雷斯特对邦克斯先生说,"快点,孩子们。该打电话报警了。"

第三章

廷克·邦克斯一脸严肃地说:"要是旋风来这里了,我会告诉你的。"

"非常感谢。"福雷斯特说,"明天它要去参加萨拉托加的比赛呢。"

"真的吗?"邦克斯先生说,"祝你好运。"

他们一起离开了马棚。天色越来越暗了。福雷斯特驾驶着卡车穿过树林时,丁丁听到了打雷的声音。树枝开始被风吹得来回摇晃。

福雷斯特把车开得更快了。"我最好在下雨之前赶回家,以免乔希和露丝淋到雨!"他说。

福雷斯特刚在自家的马棚后面把卡车停好,

雨点就开始飞溅在风挡玻璃上。"咱们快跑吧!"他说着就从驾驶室里跳了下来。

大雨倾盆而下,丁丁、乔希和露丝尖叫着奔跑起来。不过几秒钟的时间,他们就已经全身湿透了。

进了屋,福雷斯特给孩子们递上了毛巾。他们把各自的头发和脸擦干了。

"我去打电话报警,这会儿你们安顿好准备睡觉吧。"他说,"露丝,你睡在那间蓝色卧室。两个男孩子,门厅对面的卧室里有双层床。"

于是,孩子们抓起双肩包,朝着福雷斯特家的后面走去。露丝在一个贴着蓝色墙纸的卧室外面停下了脚步。

"一会儿见。"她说完就走进了自己的卧室。

丁丁和乔希也进了他们的卧室,换上了干燥的T恤衫。

过了一会儿,露丝敲了敲门,走了进来。她湿漉漉的头发看上去比平时更卷曲了。

"旋风可能会发生什么事呢?"她问丁丁和乔希。

丁丁望向卧室的窗户外面。透过雨幕,他看到了马棚。不过,他看不到马棚的后门。

"我想,可能有人把它偷走了。"丁丁说。

"把它偷走了?!"乔希说,"就在光天化日之下?"

丁丁用手一指。"人从屋子里看不见马棚的后门,"他说,"而且任何人都可以从那里进进出出。"

露丝透过淌着雨水的窗户向外看。"要怎样才能把马偷走呢?"她问,"需要拖车吗?"

"或者小偷自己可以骑着马离开呢。"乔希说。

"等雨停了,咱们去马棚后面找找有没有什么蛛丝马迹吧。"露丝说。

"说不定警察有好消息带给福雷斯特呢。"丁丁说。

孩子们朝厨房走去。

只见福雷斯特也正透过窗户凝视着外面的雨。他耸着双肩,焦虑地用手指轻轻敲着操作台。

沃伦伯伯坐在桌子旁边,喝着一杯茶。

"您打电话报警了吗？"丁丁问。

福雷斯特转过身来，点了点头。"我报过警了。他们告诉我，没有人给他们打过电话说见到一匹走失的马，"他说，"我开始担心了。"

"您有想过或许是有人把它偷走了吗？"丁丁问。

福雷斯特看着他，眨了眨眼睛，说："旋风被人偷走？我觉得有这种可能。"

"福雷斯特，你有没有什么邻居也在养马呢？"沃伦伯伯问道。

"有几个，怎么了？"

"因为旋风很可能不是唯一失踪的马，"沃伦伯伯说，"也许你应该给附近的人都打个电话。"

"好主意。我会打电话的。"福雷斯特说。

"等雨停了，我们一起帮您找旋风。"露丝说。

福雷斯特点了点头。"那太好了。现在我该去打电话了。"他说着就离开了厨房。

孩子们跟沃伦伯伯一起喝牛奶、吃饼干，看着雨水顺着窗户往下流。

过了几分钟，福雷斯特返回来了。"我给两

个养马的朋友打了电话,"他说,"他们的马没有失踪,但他们说会帮我留意旋风的。"

雨还在下,他们玩起了拼字游戏。没轮到福雷斯特玩的时候,他就抽空跑去给更多的邻居打电话。

雨终于停了,乌云散去,天放晴了。丁丁往窗户外望去,只见阳光在树木和灌木丛上闪烁。

"我去买些晚餐吃的东西吧。"沃伦伯伯说。他从挂钩上取下一串车钥匙,离开了屋子。

"好吧,孩子们,咱们一起去找马吧。"福雷斯特说。

他和孩子们穿上运动鞋,走出厨房,来到了院子里。他们的脚踩在湿漉漉的草地上,发出咯吱咯吱的声音。

他们来到马棚后面。福雷斯特朝树林走去,一边吹着口哨,一边大声呼喊:"旋风!"

丁丁、乔希和露丝在潮湿的地面上寻找轮胎留下的痕迹或者脚印。

"什么也没有,"乔希嘟囔着说,"就算真的留下了什么线索,也被雨水冲洗掉了。"

突然，孩子们听到从马棚里传来一声轻轻的嘶鸣。

丁丁朝福雷斯特大声地呼喊，福雷斯特跑了过来。

"是旋风吗？"福雷斯特问。他们一起跑进了马棚。

只见旋风的马隔间外面站着一匹全身湿透、浑身是泥的马。

"你跑到哪儿去了，伙计？"福雷斯特问自己的马。

旋风摇摇头，雨水和泥巴从它的鬃毛上飞溅出来。它重重地跺着前蹄，注视着面前的人群。

福雷斯特走过去，抓住旋风的笼头。笼头上也同样满是泥巴。

福雷斯特哈哈大笑，摇了摇头。"看来你是在一个大泥坑里打了个滚，"他说，"孩子们，你们知道该怎样给马洗澡吗？"

"知道，"乔希说，"我的小马一直是我们帮它洗澡的呢。"

福雷斯特指了指一根冲水软管和几个水桶，

还有几块海绵。接着他递给露丝一瓶绿色的肥皂液。"小心马腿,别被它踢了。"他说。

福雷斯特把一根皮带扣在旋风的笼头上,把皮带的另一端挂在一根柱子上。"先把泥巴洗掉,然后用肥皂液把它好好地洗干净。"

就在这时,他们听到屋子里传来电话铃声。

"我去接吧，"福雷斯特说，"等你们把旋风擦干了，把它牵回马隔间里去。"说完，他急匆匆回屋里去了。

丁丁装满了一桶水，接着把冲水软管对准旋风。马儿站着一动不动，泥水从它身子两侧倾泻而下。

露丝往水桶里倒了一些肥皂液，桶里的水变成了绿色。肥皂水的味道闻起来就像新割的青草的味道。

孩子们把三块大海绵浸入肥皂水里，接着开始给旋风洗澡，一人负责擦洗一个身体部位。旋风的眼珠子骨碌碌地转，打量着三个孩子。

"嘿，你们快看这里。"乔希说。他指着旋风身子的一侧。只见上面有一个椭圆形的印记，形状像鸡蛋，大小跟他的一只手差不多，印记里面还有几道波浪线。

"乔希，你又在用手指画画吗？"露丝打趣道。

"不是我画的！"乔希说，"这个印记原本就已经在这儿了。"

三个孩子仔细地观察着那个印记。

A to Z 神秘案件

"看上去像是有人用什么东西给它盖了个戳！"乔希说。

第四章

"可能是旋风在泥巴里打滚的时候弄上的，"丁丁说，"可能是滚到了石头上或者木头上。"

"没错，很可能是这样。"乔希说。他用沾满肥皂水的海绵在那个奇怪的印记上擦了擦，印记立刻消失不见了。

丁丁又把冲水软管对着旋风，把肥皂泡沫冲洗掉。

露丝发现墙上挂着几条毛巾，于是他们把毛巾拿来给旋风擦身体。

擦干的旋风，变得油光水滑。露丝从柱子上把旋风的皮带解下来，准备把它送回马隔间。

"来吧,伙计。"她说。

旋风朝着露丝骨碌碌地转着眼珠子。它紧绷着腿,就是不肯向前走。

"干得漂亮,孩子们!"福雷斯特一边说,一边走进马棚,"它看上去完全换了一个样!"

"它不肯回马隔间。"露丝说。

"我来试试吧。"福雷斯特说着,从露丝手中接过皮带,开始抚摸旋风的脖子,还伏在旋风的一只耳朵边低声地说着什么。不一会儿,旋风走进了自己的马隔间,把鼻子伸进燕麦桶里,开始吃起东西来。

福雷斯特为旋风关上了马隔间的门。"它在外面经历了暴风雨,回到家又看到这么多的陌生人,很可能受到了一点惊吓。"他说。

就在这时,莎妮骑着一辆山地自行车从马棚后门进来了。只见她跳下车,把自行车靠在墙上,穿着沾满泥巴的高筒靴大步走过来。"真是个调皮鬼。"她一边说,一边把手伸进马隔间的门去抚摸旋风的鼻子。

旋风骨碌碌地转着眼珠子,仰起头,退回到

角落里。

"放松点,伙计。"莎妮小声地说,又看向福雷斯特,"它好像怕我呢。"

"它对我也一样。"露丝说。

五个人看着马,马也看着他们。

"说不定它身体不舒服。"丁丁说。

"在外面吃了什么脏东西吧?"乔希问。

"有可能。"福雷斯特说。"不过,它看上去没什么不对劲的地方。而且,刚刚它还吃了燕麦呢。"

莎妮仔细地打量着旋风:"真希望明天比赛的时候它能跑得飞快。"

"萨拉托加离这儿有多远?"丁丁问。

"几个小时,就在奥尔巴尼附近。"莎妮告诉他。她又看着福雷斯特说:"我六点钟过来把旋风装上拖车。这样,它在比赛之前就有足够的时间休息放松了。"

"好的,"福雷斯特说,"现在去看看沃伦给我们买了些什么当晚餐吧。"

福雷斯特看着自己的马说:"不要再玩失踪把

戏了,伙计。"

莎妮拉上马隔间上面的门板,并检查了门闩,确保门已经闩好了。

"明天萨拉托加见。"她说。孩子们看着她跨上她的山地自行车,骑着车子出了门。她穿着沾满泥巴的胶质高筒靴蹬着车,样子有点滑稽。

沃伦伯伯带着吃的回来了。很快他们就吃上了丰盛的大餐。晚餐过后,他们继续把拼字游戏玩完了。

九点钟的时候,福雷斯特站起身来,打着哈

欠。"明天还得忙上一整天呢,"他说,"我准备去睡了。"

"我也是。"沃伦伯伯说,"明天早上见。"他拍了拍丁丁的头,离开了房间。

两个男孩子沿着门厅蹑手蹑脚地走进他们的卧室。就在丁丁和乔希爬上床的时候,他们听到了敲门声。

露丝打开了门。"达菲鸭睡衣不错嘛,乔希。"她说着大踏步走进房间,手里拿着一本书。

"嘎嘎。"乔希学着鸭子的声音叫了两声。

露丝坐在丁丁的床尾,把书放在大腿上。"我想读点东西给你们听听。"她说。

"噢,太好了!"乔希说,"我们可以一边听,一边喝牛奶、吃饼干吗?"

露丝把书举了起来。"这本书是教你如何骑马的,"她说,"不过里面有一个章节是关于骑师的。"

她打开书,开始朗读:"骑师必须赢得马的信任。一个好的骑师通过定期喂马、定期帮马清洗身体来赢得马的信任。大多数马会逐渐喜欢上它们的骑师,跟骑师成为朋友。"

露丝抬起头来:"听到这段话,你们有什么想法吗?"

"比如说?"乔希问道。

"好吧,莎妮在场时,你们注意到旋风的表现了吗?"露丝问道。

"它看上去的确对她不太友好。"丁丁说。

"没错,她一进门,旋风就往后退。"乔希说。

"是的,"露丝说,"我觉得旋风害怕莎妮!"

第五章

丁丁感觉到有一只手拍了拍他的肩膀,于是他从熟睡中醒了过来。他床边的灯亮了。只见被子上放着《黑神驹》这本书,书还是打开的。

睡眼惺忪的他看到了伯伯的脸庞。

"早上好,唐尼[1],"沃伦伯伯小声地说,"该起床了。"

"嘿,沃伦伯伯。"丁丁说。

"你们两个男孩子得抓紧时间,"沃伦伯伯说,"福雷斯特想要一吃完早餐就上路呢。"他朝

---

1. 唐尼:丁丁真正的名字"唐纳德"的昵称。——译者

丁丁笑了笑,离开了房间。

丁丁把自己的枕头朝乔希的床上扔了过去,然后走进卫生间。乔希嘟囔了几句,不过很快他们都穿好了衣服,朝厨房走去。

福雷斯特和露丝正坐在桌子旁喝燕麦粥。沃伦伯伯从炉子上端起装燕麦粥的锅,给丁丁和乔希每人盛了一碗。

"昨天晚上大家都睡得好吗?"福雷斯特问道。

"我睡得很香。"露丝一边说,一边舀了一些红糖在自己的燕麦粥上。今天她的着装颜色为紫色:紫色束发带、紫色上衣、紫色打底裤,还有紫色运动鞋。

"我也是。"丁丁接话说,"美中不足的是,乔希打了一整晚的呼噜。"

大家快速吃完早餐,离开屋子,挤进福雷斯特的卡车。丁丁、乔希和露丝坐在后排座位上。他们每个人都带了书,乔希把枕头也带来了。

福雷斯特把卡车驶出自家的停车道,开车穿过拉奇蒙特。转了好几个弯之后,他驶上了一条宽阔的公路。丁丁看见一块牌子,上面写着:奥

逃跑的赛马

尔巴尼，一百二十英里[1]。

几个小时过后，他们到达了萨拉托加温泉市。福雷斯特把卡车开进一个停车场。

大家全都下了卡车，舒展着身体。在高高的树底下，丁丁看到一个长长的绿色马棚。马棚附近有男有女，他们有的在梳理马毛，有的在给马喂食，有的在对马进行训练。放眼望去，到处都是马！

露丝拍了一些马的照片，还拍了一张马棚的照片——阳光照耀下的一个绿色的木制马棚。

"咱们去找莎妮吧，"福雷斯特提议，"她在E号马棚，21号马隔间。"

于是他们穿过树林，沿着一条宽阔的道路向前走。道路两边矗立着马棚。每个马棚的一侧都用油漆写着一个大大的字母。

砾石人行道上挤满了人。一些人在遛马，另一些人只是在观看。

1.英里：英美制长度单位，1英里＝1.609千米。——编者

"E号马棚在那儿呢。"乔希说着,朝前面冲去。

福雷斯特、沃伦伯伯,还有孩子们在21号马隔间找到了莎妮。只见她一只脚踩在一捆干草上,正在用一块布擦拭着她的马靴。地板上放着一罐黑色鞋油。

"嘿,莎妮。"福雷斯特跟她打招呼。

莎妮穿着白色的马裤，上身穿着一件绿色的真丝赛马衫，赛马衫的两个袖子上有黄色的条纹。她的左手臂上绑着一根布带，上面缝着数字"21"。她的头发盘了起来，头上戴着一顶安全帽，帽子上面蒙着一层黄色真丝。椭圆形的护目镜搁在安全帽的帽舌上。

莎妮放下擦鞋布，笑着跟大家打招呼："嘿，

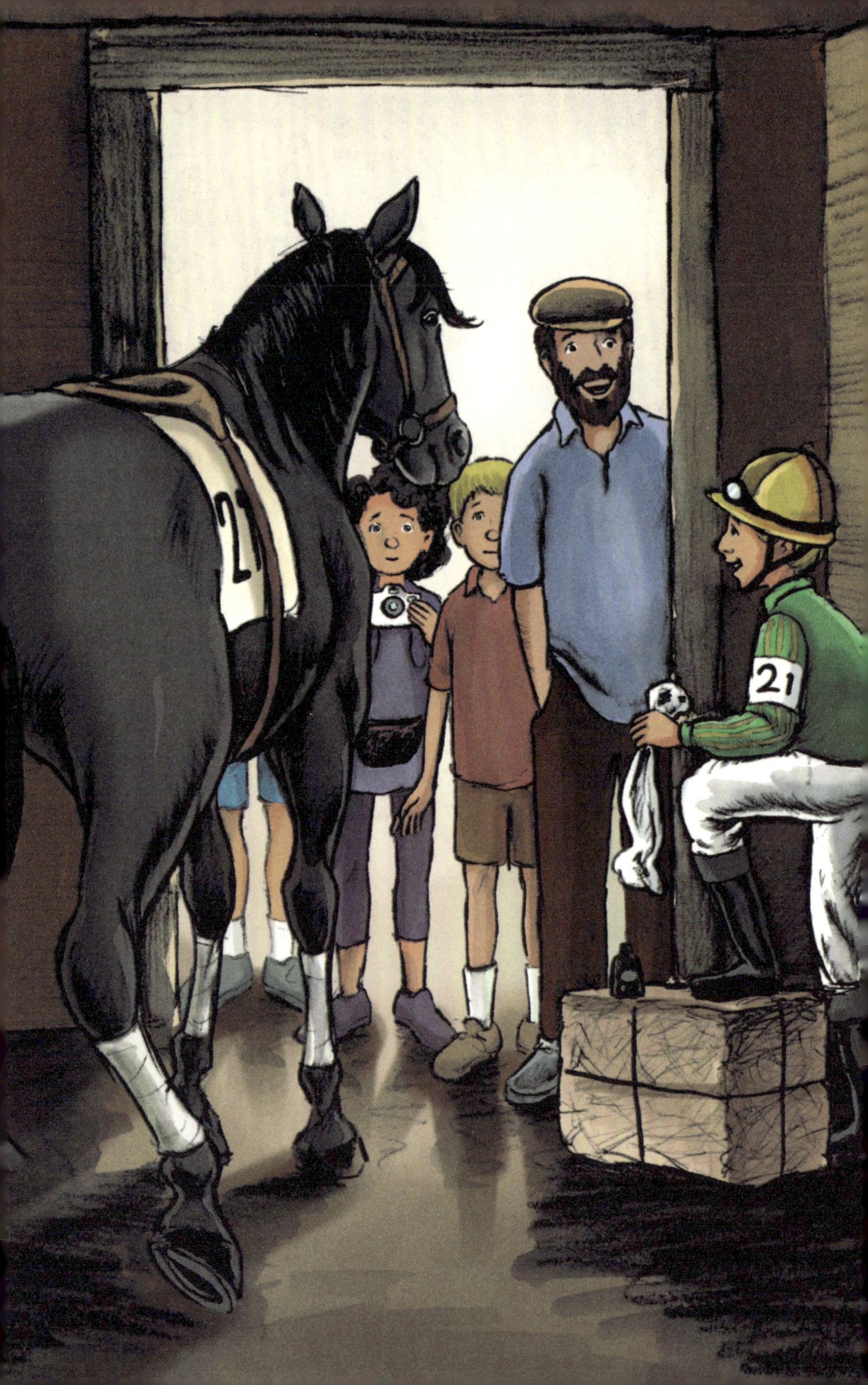
21

逃跑的赛马

大家好。"

"没什么问题吧?"福雷斯特问道。

"今天早上它不想进拖车。"莎妮说,"而且,我们到达这里之后,它无论如何不想让我给它做赛前准备。"

"早上好,旋风,"福雷斯特跟自己的马打招呼,"你为什么要为难莎妮呢,伙计?"

大家都往马隔间里面瞧。只见旋风站在一个角落里,打量着刚进来的这群人。

"它看上去棒极了,莎妮。"福雷斯特说,"干得不错。"

莎妮已经把旋风的皮毛刷得油光锃亮。在近乎黑色的皮毛的映衬下,她绑在马的脚踝上的白色布带看上去白得像雪一样。

"你为什么要戴护目镜呢?"露丝问莎妮。

"为了保护我的眼睛。"莎妮说,"比赛的时候,跑在我前面的马会扬起尘土。如果你看过我在雨中赛马就知道了,全身上下都是泥土呢!"

"比赛什么时候开始?"丁丁问道。

"我们在第二组,"莎妮回答道,"两点钟

比赛。"

"到时候我们大家都会为你呐喊助威。"沃伦伯伯说。

"我能给你和旋风拍张照片吗?"露丝问莎妮。

"当然可以。"莎妮说。她走进马隔间,一只手抓着旋风的笼头。旋风转动眼珠看着她,然后把头用力往后仰。

露丝说得没错,丁丁心里这样想着,旋风一点都不喜欢莎妮。

露丝按下了照相机的快门。

第六章

"好了,各位,到咱们的座位上去吧。"福雷斯特说道。

要走到福雷斯特的私人包厢,他们得爬三段楼梯。正面看台上挤满了人。赛场上播放着音乐,每个人似乎都很开心。

观看赛马的包厢里有一排座位,座位上方有一个小顶棚。两边是其他的私人包厢。从包厢正前方可以清楚地看到起跑门栅以及椭圆形的赛马道。

"赛马路程是多少?"乔希问道。

"绕赛马道两圈。"福雷斯特回答说。

只见一个座位上放着一沓赛马名单。福雷斯特把赛马名单分发给大家。"旋风的名字在第二页。"他说。

孩子们快速地翻阅名单，找到了旋风的名字。莎妮作为旋风的骑师，也在名单上。

"这也太令人兴奋了吧！"露丝说。她把照相机放在了自己的椅子下面。

一位身穿白色夹克的服务员过来让他们点午餐。他们简单地点了一些食物：五个芝士汉堡和五杯柠檬汁。

"赛马结束的地点在哪里？"乔希问道。

"在终点线呀。"沃伦伯伯说，"就在那儿，起跑门栅后面。"

服务员端来了他们点的食物。就在吃午餐的时候，他们看见一群马和骑师来到了赛马道上。有些马欢腾跳跃、昂首阔步。骑师们都穿着颜色鲜艳的赛马服，戴着莎妮那样的护目镜。

参赛马匹中有白马、灰马、黑马，还有好几匹颜色深浅不一的棕色马。其中有一匹是金色的帕洛米诺马。

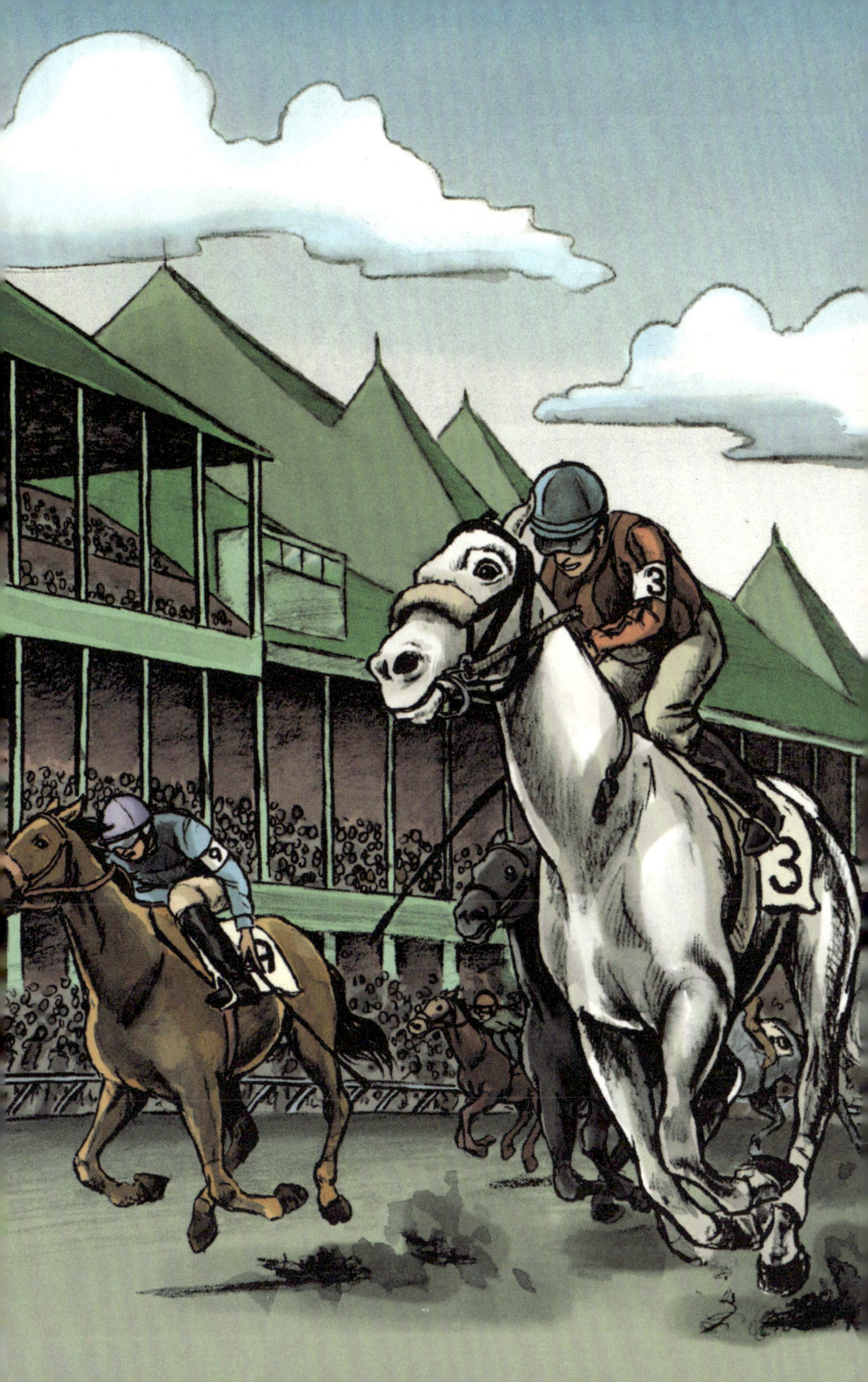

在马主人们的包厢下面，人们沿着赛马道围栏站成一排。看到赛马出现在起跑门栅处的那一刻，人群开始欢呼。

突然，喇叭里传来一位男士的声音。"女士们，先生们，下午好！"他大声喊道，"第一组的比赛马上就要开始了！"在他喊出赛马和骑师的名字时，骑师策马来到起跑门栅处。

接下来，随着一声响亮的铃声响起，几匹赛马冲向赛马道。只见骑师们站在马镫上，头深深地往下弯，贴近马脖子。

观赛的人群呐喊着，欢呼着。即便在一片嘈杂声中，孩子们也能听到马蹄在赛马道上发出的嘚嘚声。每一匹马的身后都飞扬起一团团尘土。

逃跑的赛马

"目前领先的是快乐玛丽!"广播员激动地大声播报,"星爆落后一个身位!蔓越莓酱位于第三!"

随即,比赛结束了。一匹白马率先飞快地冲过了终点线。

"快乐玛丽领先半个身位,赢得了第一名!"

广播员大声宣布。

孩子们看着骑师骑着快乐玛丽神气地昂首奔向领奖处。一位身穿连衣裙、头戴宽边帽的女士递给骑师一个奖杯。一位身穿西装的男士满脸笑容，特意摆了一个姿势来照相。"那个人是马的主人。"福雷斯特告诉孩子们。

"接下来就是咱们的比赛了吧？"丁丁看着赛马名单问。

"没错，几分钟之后就开始了。"福雷斯特回答说，用手指着赛马道，"参赛的马已经出来了。"

三个孩子站起身来。

"哪匹马是旋风？"露丝已经把照相机准备好了，"好多匹黑马的前额上都有白色印记呢。"

福雷斯特在她身后指给她看。"那匹白马的前面就是旋风。"他说，"看见莎妮的黄色帽子了吗？此外，你可以看到旋风的马鞍座毯上有一个大大的数字'21'。"

赛马和骑师们来到起跑门栅处。只听广播员大声宣布："21号旋风，骑师为莎妮·菲尔茨！"丁丁、乔希和露丝欢呼起来。露丝拍下了一张照

片。福雷斯特把两根手指放进嘴里吹了个口哨。

这时,喇叭里传来广播员的声音:"现在第二组的比赛即将开始!十二匹骏马参赛!"

随着起跑的铃声响起,比赛开始了。观赛的人群开始大声喊叫,不过并没有盖过广播员的声音。

"场面多么壮观啊,各位!花裤子领先,击掌紧随其后!外圈的漂亮气球追上来了!快看,舞者正悄悄接近漂亮气球!舞者超过了击掌。现在领先的是舞者!"

丁丁、乔希和露丝全都站起身来。他们欢呼

雀跃:"加油,旋风!"

可是旋风远远地落在了后面。当所有的赛马冲向终点线的时候,21号旋风跑在倒数第二位。

比赛结束之时,旋风落得更靠后了。它跑了最后一名。

孩子们失望地坐了下来。福雷斯特则呆呆地注视着赛马道。

"发生什么事了?"沃伦伯伯问。

福雷斯特摇了摇头。"旋风从来没有跑得如此糟糕过,"他说,"这不对劲!"

第七章

"唉，它尽力了。"沃伦伯伯拍着福雷斯特的肩膀说。

"我知道我不能指望旋风每场比赛都能赢，"福雷斯特承认，"可是它从来都没有跑得这么糟糕过！"

"我们能过去看看它吗？"丁丁问道。

"当然可以。"福雷斯特说着看了一下自己的手表，"十五分钟之后回到这里跟我们会合，好吗？"

孩子们从正面看台的台阶上走下来，朝马棚跑去。他们走进E号马棚，从一匹匹赛马身旁经过。这些赛马从马隔间里好奇地打量着他们。

"旋风在那儿。"乔希用手指着说。只见旋风浑身是汗,被拴在21号马隔间外面。莎妮正在用毛巾给它擦身子。

这时,莎妮抬起头来对孩子们点了点头。

"你们没赢,我感到很难过。"露丝说。

"谁都不会比我更难过。"莎妮喃喃地说。她的赛马服脏兮兮的,安全帽已经摘下来了,头发披散下来,湿漉漉、乱蓬蓬的。她脸上除了原来戴护目镜的地方是干净的,其他地方全是汗渍和赛马道上的尘垢。原本锃亮的黑色靴子现在已经被尘土染成了棕色。

莎妮跪下来,开始给旋风解开腿上绑着的布带。布带上也满是污渍。

莎妮一边收拾,一边不住地摇头。"赛跑的时候,旋风好像变成了另外一匹马。"她说。

她起身离开去找垃圾箱扔脏布带,留下旋风拴在马厩里。

"说不定旋风只是太累了呢。"丁丁说。

"有可能。"露丝同意丁丁的猜测,"不过,骑师可以让赛马放慢速度。"

逃跑的赛马

乔希看着露丝说:"你觉得是莎妮故意让旋风输掉比赛的吗?"

露丝耸耸肩说:"我不知道。"

莎妮回来后把旋风解开了。她不得不用力拉着旋风走上斜坡。在她牵着旋风走进拖车时,它骨碌碌地转动着眼珠子。

莎妮关上了拖车门,并插上门闩。接下来,她一句话也没有说,爬进驾驶室,把车开走了。

"旋风和莎妮之间肯定发生了什么奇怪的事情。"露丝说。

"说不定旋风只是今天运气不好罢了。"丁丁说。

露丝看了看自己的手表。

"我们该回去了。"她说。

于是孩子们朝看台方向走去。就在这时,丁丁注意到有一小群人正围着一匹黑马和它的骑师。"是赢了比赛的那匹赛马。"他说。

"没错,那匹马叫舞者。"乔希补充说。

"我想要给它拍张照片。"露丝说。于是孩子们朝领奖处走去。他们扭动身子从人群中挤了过

A to Z 神秘案件

去，来到舞者身旁。

只见舞者的胸部和腿部汗涔涔的，绑在脚踝上的白布带脏兮兮的。它的骑师也是全身脏兮兮的，但他还是面带微笑，让人们拍照。

这时，一位头戴牛仔帽，面戴墨镜的男士走上前来，握了握骑师的手。"表现得真棒，安迪。"他说。

"小菜一碟，比先生。"骑师回答他说。

"伙伴们，靠近一点，"露丝说，"我想给你们和舞者拍张照片。"

丁丁和乔希走过去，站在舞者前面。那匹马

用头轻轻地顶了顶乔希的背,弄得他咯咯直笑。

骑师摇了摇缰绳,舞者就把头放在了丁丁的肩膀和乔希的肩膀中间。

露丝拍下了照片。这时,只听见她的照相机发出了嗡嗡声,提醒她胶卷用完了。

丁丁看了看自己的手表:"快点,伙伴们。他们正在等着我们呢。"

孩子们匆忙离开,找到了看台上的福雷斯特和沃伦伯伯。

"旋风看上去状态怎么样?"福雷斯特问道。

"很疲倦的样子。"乔希说,"莎妮把它装上拖车,然后就开车走了。"

"我想我们也该走了。"福雷斯特说。于是他们朝停车场走去。

福雷斯特和沃伦伯伯走在前面,后面跟着丁丁、乔希和露丝。

露丝举起她的照相机。"我迫不及待要把胶卷冲洗出来,"她低声说道,"我觉得最后那张照片是一条重要线索!"

第八章

"旋风说不定是生病了呢。"回去的路上,沃伦伯伯说出了自己的想法。

福雷斯特点了点头。"我会打电话给兽医,请他过来一趟。"他说。

孩子们坐在后排座位上。乔希靠着自己的枕头睡着了,嘴巴张着。露丝在他身旁读自己带的那本《学骑马》。

丁丁则把书放在他的膝盖上,注视着车窗外面,看着一路的风景一闪而过。听着汽车轮胎的嗡嗡声,他昏昏欲睡。于是他闭上了眼睛。

醒来时,丁丁听见了伯伯的说话声:"快到家

了，孩子们。"

丁丁睁开眼睛，眨巴了几下，朝车窗外望去。他认出了福雷斯特家停车道前面的商店。

"那里有一家照相馆。"露丝说，"可以停一下车吗，福雷斯特？"

"当然可以。"福雷斯特说着就把车停在了那家小商店前面。只见橱窗上有一条颜色鲜艳的标语：照片洗印，一小时可取！

露丝从车上跳下来，跑进了商店。一分钟过后她回来了。"我又买了一卷胶卷。"她说。

这时，乔希坐直了身子，环顾四周。"我们这是在哪儿？"他问道。

丁丁用手指戳了戳乔希T恤衫的背面："乔希，你的衣领有一块黑色的污渍。"

乔希把后面的衣领扯到前面，并把衣领抻了抻。"真讨厌！"他说，"这是在哪里弄脏的？"

"说不定是昨天从旋风身上蹭到的泥巴。"丁丁提示说。

"丁丁，"乔希说，"咱们给旋风洗过澡后，我换过T恤衫了。"

"在萨拉托加的时候,你会不会靠在了没有干的油漆或者别的什么东西上呢?"露丝问道。

乔希想了想。"我不这么认为,"他说,"如果是那样的话,我的衣领上就不只是这一处污渍了。"他耸了耸肩。

福雷斯特把车拐进了停车道,不一会儿,他们就到家了。

"我要去换掉我的T恤衫。"大家全都下车之后,乔希说。

"不!我们还是先去看看莎妮和旋风回来了没有吧。"露丝说。她看了丁丁和乔希一眼。

"好的。"福雷斯特说,"我去打电话,看看

能否联系上兽医。"

沃伦伯伯从车上拿走了乔希的枕头和孩子们的书。丁丁、乔希和露丝朝马棚走去。马隔间里空荡荡的,没有看见莎妮的人影。

"好了,出什么事了?"乔希问露丝。孩子们在干草捆上坐了下来。

"还记得我给你们两个和舞者拍的那张照片吗?"露丝问道,"听我说,我觉得那张照片里还有别人。那个人就是邦克斯先生!"

两个男孩子看上去一脸茫然。

"那个戴着墨镜和牛仔帽的男人就是邦克斯先生!"露丝说道。

"你确定吗?"丁丁追问道,"我原本以为那个家伙是舞者的主人呢。"

"我觉得我认出了他昨天系的皮带上的大搭扣。"露丝说,"我拍下了一张照片,这样咱们就能确定这一点了。"

"好吧,如果是邦克斯先生,那他为什么不告诉福雷斯特他也要去萨拉托加呢?"丁丁不解地问道。

"这也正是我想要知道的。"露丝说,"他之前为什么要说自己不再从事赛马这一行当了呢?"

"也许舞者的主人不是邦克斯先生。"乔希说,"他可能跟我们一样,到那儿去只是为了近距离地看看获胜的马罢了。"

"可是他和那位骑师互相认识。"露丝说。

丁丁点了点头。"如果在萨拉托加的那个人的确是邦克斯先生的话,"他说,"那么他一定在隐瞒什么!"

第九章

就在这时,沃伦伯伯走进了马棚。只见他脚上穿着一双平底人字拖鞋,身上穿着一套泳衣,手里拿着一条毛巾。

"来一起游泳吗?"他问孩子们。

"当然。"丁丁回答道。孩子们跟着沃伦伯伯朝屋子走去。

"游完泳后,咱们一起去取照片吧。"露丝小声地说。

孩子们换好泳衣跳入游泳池,加入福雷斯特和沃伦伯伯的行列。他们用一个塑料球玩起了抢球游戏。

"还是没有莎妮和旋风的影子,"福雷斯特说着,朝马棚的方向点了点头,"真希望他们在路上没遇上什么麻烦。"

"我们打算去取照片,"露丝说,"等我们返回来的时候,说不定莎妮已经在这儿了呢。"

"公路边上有一条安全的自行车道,"福雷斯特说,"祝你们一路愉快。"

孩子们擦干身子,穿上衣服,然后穿过草坪。

"我很好奇,是什么事情让莎妮耽搁了这么久还没回来呢?"孩子们走在停车道上的时候,丁丁不禁问道。

"可能是她停下车吃东西了吧。"乔希摸着自己的肚子说。

几分钟后,他们走进了照相馆。乔希一眼就看见了一个放着糖果的货架,于是买了一包玛氏巧克力豆。

露丝的胶卷已经冲洗好了。她向店员付了钱,然后他们动身返回福雷斯特家,到家之后就可以私下悄悄地看照片了。

乔希撕开巧克力豆的包装袋,一粒一粒地大

逃跑的赛马

口咀嚼起来。

　　回到福雷斯特家，孩子们径直朝马棚走去。莎妮和旋风还是没有回来。

　　露丝打开装照片的小袋子，把照片拿出来。有一些照片是给她的猫咪拍的，然后是列车乘务员帮他们拍的那张。

剩下的照片拍的是在萨拉托加看到的马和马棚。其中有一张拍的是赛马道上的一匹马,不过照片模糊不清。接下来的那张是莎妮和旋风在E号马棚。

最后一张是在领奖处拍的。照片中是丁丁和乔希,还有位于两人中间的舞者的头。戴牛仔帽的男人站在背景里。他系着一条皮带,皮带上面有个大大的银色搭扣。

"的确是邦克斯先生。"丁丁说。

孩子们仔细研究起这张照片。露丝把照片拿得离眼睛更近了一些。

"伙伴们,你们看出舞者的前额上有什么异样之处了吗?"她问道。

"看上去闪闪发亮呢。"丁丁仔细看着照片说。

"还有,它的前额比脸上其他地方的颜色更深。"乔希说。

"从远处看绝对注意不到。"露丝说。

"什么东西让它看起来是这个样子的呢?"丁丁问道。

"深色的东西,比如鞋油。"乔希说。

"等等,"露丝说,"乔希,看看你T恤衫上的污渍!"

乔希俯下身子,以便让丁丁和露丝能够看到他的衣领。

"看上去像是鞋油。"丁丁说。

"没错!"乔希说,"我想起来了!露丝,你拍这张照片的时候,我感觉到舞者在我的背上蹭了一下。"

"所以说,这块污渍是舞者蹭上去的了!"露丝说。

"可是,为什么有人想在马的前额上涂鞋油呢?"丁丁不解地问道。

"这个我不知道,不过我倒是知道谁会这么干。"露丝说,"就在比赛之前,莎妮用黑色鞋油擦过她的靴子!"

"可是,莎妮和舞者毫不相干啊。"乔希指出这一点。

露丝一张张地翻看着照片,直到找到莎妮和旋风在E号马棚里拍的那张。她对着照片看了一会儿,然后把它放在丁丁、乔希和舞者的那张合影旁边。

"哇，"乔希惊讶地说，"这两匹马看上去就像一对双胞胎！"

丁丁拿起莎妮在 E 号马棚的那张照片："唯一不同的是，这匹马的前额上有一个白色印记。"

"鞋油可以遮盖掉舞者前额上的白色印记。"露丝说。

"可是,莎妮或者邦克斯先生,或者不管什么人,为什么要把舞者前额上的白色印记遮盖掉呢?这有什么关系呢?"乔希问。

丁丁陷入了沉思。突然,他记起莎妮在比赛之后说当时她觉得自己骑的是另外一匹马。"这就对了!"丁丁说着,打了个响指。

"什么对了?"乔希问。

"伙伴们,假如之前咱们清洗的那匹马不是旋风呢?"丁丁说。

"你说这话是什么意思?"乔希问。

"我的意思是,假如有人把旋风偷走,然后送回了另外一匹马做它的替身呢?"

听到这话,乔希和露丝只是盯着丁丁看。

"好吧,这样就能解释为什么它的表现这么奇怪了。"露丝最后说道。

"还有它为什么输掉了比赛。"乔希补充说。

"还可以解释鞋油的事。"丁丁接话说。

"啊?"乔希惊讶地说。

"嗯。"丁丁说,"为什么有人要偷一匹像旋风那样跑得那么快的赛马呢?"

"为了赢得比赛!"露丝说。

"没错。"丁丁说,"假如的确有人把旋风偷走了,并让它参加比赛,那么这个人一定会想法子对旋风进行伪装。"

"比如用鞋油遮盖住它前额上的印记!"乔希说。

"这么看来,这就是邦克斯先生出现在那里的原因了。"露丝说,"一定是他把旋风偷走,并让它假扮舞者参加比赛的。"

"而且我敢打赌,莎妮在替他做事。"乔希说,"换马对她来说是一件轻而易举的事。"

"还有,我们看见她有鞋油。"丁丁说。

"我想去问莎妮几个问题。"露丝说。

"莎妮现在在哪儿呢?"乔希问。

"问得好。"露丝环顾了一下空荡荡的马棚,叹了口气。

"就算她的确把赛马换掉了,我们又怎么能证明她在比赛中骑的不是旋风呢?"丁丁问。

"我知道一个办法。"乔希说着,把手伸进口袋里,拿出一块方糖,"福雷斯特说过,旋风不

喜欢吃糖。等莎妮回来了,我把这个给旋风——不管它叫什么名字吧。假如它把糖吃了,我们就知道它不是旋风了!"

第十章

"你真是个天才!"露丝说。

"我知道。"乔希说。

丁丁瞥了一眼空荡荡的马棚:"现在我们要做的就是等莎妮回来。"

露丝把照片塞回小袋子里。"嗯,我嘛,依我看,不用等她了。"她说,"快点,咱们再去调查一下邦克斯先生的地盘吧。"

"到了那里之后,我们要怎么做呢?"孩子们快步走上福雷斯特家的停车道时,乔希问道。

"寻找旋风。"露丝说,"你带的那些方糖还有吗?"

逃跑的赛马

乔希拍了拍自己的口袋:"有。"

孩子们从福雷斯特家的马棚后面抄近路,朝旧伐木路走去。

几分钟过后,他们就来到了邦克斯先生的房子和马棚。

"我没看见那条狗呢。"乔希低声说。

"我也没看见邦克斯先生的卡车。"丁丁说。

"咱们去马棚里看看吧。"露丝说。孩子们溜进了马棚。马棚里静悄悄的,光线昏暗,只有从布满灰尘的窗户里透进来的一点光亮。

"饼干不见了!"丁丁说着,在饼干空荡荡的马隔间前停下了脚步,"它去哪里了呢?"

突然,他们听到了一声马的嘶鸣,好像是在回答丁丁的问话。"快过来。"丁丁说着,朝外面走去。

马棚后面是一片开阔地,一条小路从高高的杂草中间穿过。孩子们沿着这条小路进入一片树林。走到树林的另一边时,孩子们停下脚步,睁大了眼睛。他们面前是一块空地,再往前是一座长长的棚屋。一辆用来装马的拖车在这座低矮的建筑后面半掩半现。

孩子们推开棚屋的大门往里面瞧。丁丁闻到了刺鼻的粪肥味，皱起了鼻子。

棚屋的一半用木栅栏围了起来。只见饼干站在栅栏后面，一动不动地盯着刚进来的几个人。

紧挨着饼干的另一个马隔间里还有一匹马，它身上套着笼头。这匹深色的马看起来跟旋风长得很像，只是它光亮的前额上没有一块菱形的白斑。

"这就是那匹获胜的赛马。"乔希低声说。

"这是旋风吗？"丁丁轻声问。

这时，乔希剥开一块方糖，朝栅栏走去，并伸手递过去。深色的马凑过来用鼻子闻了闻，随即哼了一声，摇了摇头。

"它不要糖！"乔希激动地大声喊起来。他伸出手，小心翼翼地摸了摸赛马的前额。当他把手拿开时，手指上沾上了一些黑色的东西。

丁丁从墙上取下一条挂在钉子上的毛巾，一只手抓住赛马的笼头，另一只手替它擦拭前额。

擦掉了更多黑色的东西之后，马的前额上露

出一部分菱形的白斑。

丁丁感觉后背起了一层鸡皮疙瘩。"莎妮的确把马给换了！"他说。

"这就是旋风。"露丝说。她打开装照片的小袋子，找到莎妮和赛马在E号马棚的那张照片，并把它举到真正的旋风旁边。"福雷斯特家的那匹马跟它长得一模一样。"

"我们必须去把这件事告诉福雷斯特！"乔希说。

"告诉他什么？"只听见一个声音问道。

孩子们转过身去，看见邦克斯先生和巴斯特站在棚屋门口。邦克斯先生依旧穿着他在领奖处时穿的那身衣服，包括那个银色的皮带搭扣。"坐下来，狗狗。"邦克斯先生对巴斯特说。狗狗在主人身边坐了下来，从喉咙深处发出了一声低沉的咆哮。

"这么说，你们已经发现了。"邦克斯说，朝丁丁手里的毛巾点了点头，"甚至发现了我的鞋油花招。"

他的鞋油花招？丁丁心里思忖着。突然，丁

丁恍然大悟。原来给旋风涂鞋油的那个人不是莎妮！而是邦克斯先生！此外，他们之前清洗的那匹马身上的污泥印记是邦克斯先生的皮带搭扣留下的！偷走旋风的人不是莎妮。她也以为自己在比赛中骑的马是旋风。整件事情是邦克斯先生自己一个人干的！

丁丁朝着光线昏暗的棚屋四周瞥了一眼，寻找其他的出口。可是窗户全都关上了，而且窗户太高了。

"现在，你们只要把这些照片交给我就行了。"邦克斯先生说着伸出了一只手。这个男人笑了，不过不是昨天他脸上浮现出来的那种友好的微笑。

丁丁从露丝手上拿过照片，递给了邦克斯先生。

"我们不需要这些照片了。"丁丁说，"我们知道这就是旋风，而且我们知道，是你从埃文斯先生那里把它偷走的。"

邦克斯先生哈哈大笑起来。"旋风？我不知道你在说什么。"他说，"这匹马是我买来的。它

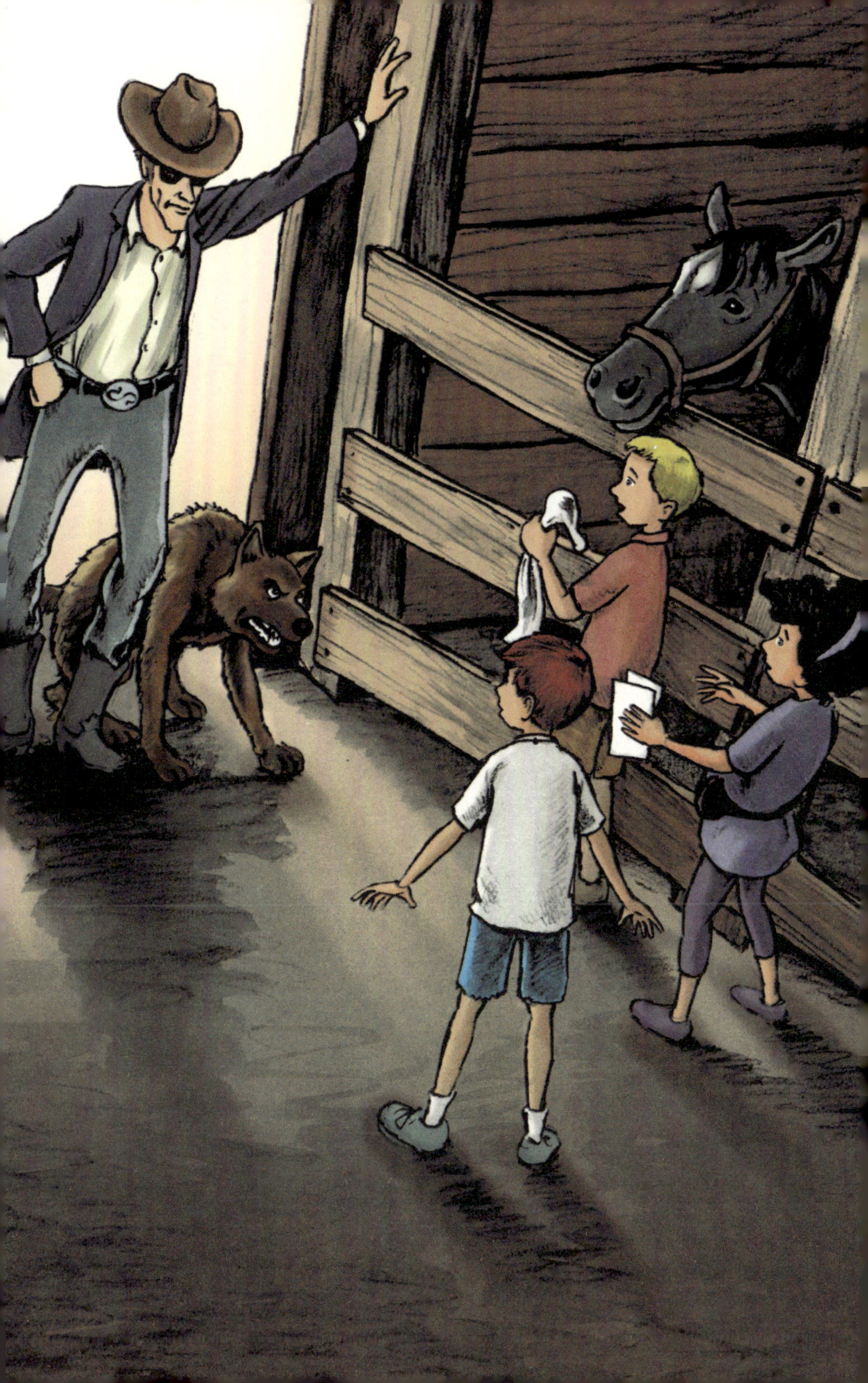

碰巧长得像旋风，我有什么办法呢？它碰巧跑起来像风一样快，我又有什么办法呢？"

他把照片塞进自己的衬衫里，说："谁也无法证明这匹马是我从福雷斯特那里偷来的。"

"我们不需要证明什么，廷克，"一个声音说道，"有所有这些证人就够了。"

福雷斯特、沃伦伯伯和莎妮一起走进了棚屋。

一个小时过后，大家围坐在福雷斯特的野餐桌前吃着汉堡。

"你们是怎么知道我们在那儿的？"丁丁问道。

"你们刚要离开时，我正好回来了。"莎妮说，"看见你们脸上坚定的表情，我决定把事情告诉福雷斯特。"

"我们及时赶到了棚屋，听到了你们谈话的所有内容。"福雷斯特说，"邦克斯先生就要坐牢了。"

"邦克斯先生真的以为自己可以瞒天过海吗？"露丝问道。

福雷斯特点了点头。"嗯，他很幸运，找到了一匹跟旋风长得一模一样的赛马，就连额头上

逃跑的赛马

菱形的白斑都一模一样。"他说,"我被他骗了,不过莎妮注意到了一个不同之处。"

"旋风的态度通常很友好。"莎妮说,"那匹

长得跟旋风一模一样的马表现得好像不认识我一样,当时我就起疑心了。从萨拉托加返回的路上,我中途在兽医那里停了车。兽医给那匹马抽了血,结果证明我骑的那匹马不是旋风。"

"那匹马叫舞者。"福雷斯特说,"邦克斯先生把两匹马的名字也互相交换了。原来把马卖给邦克斯的那个女主人对她的马不太好,这就是为什么那匹马害怕莎妮,因为莎妮的声音让它想起了虐待过它的主人。"

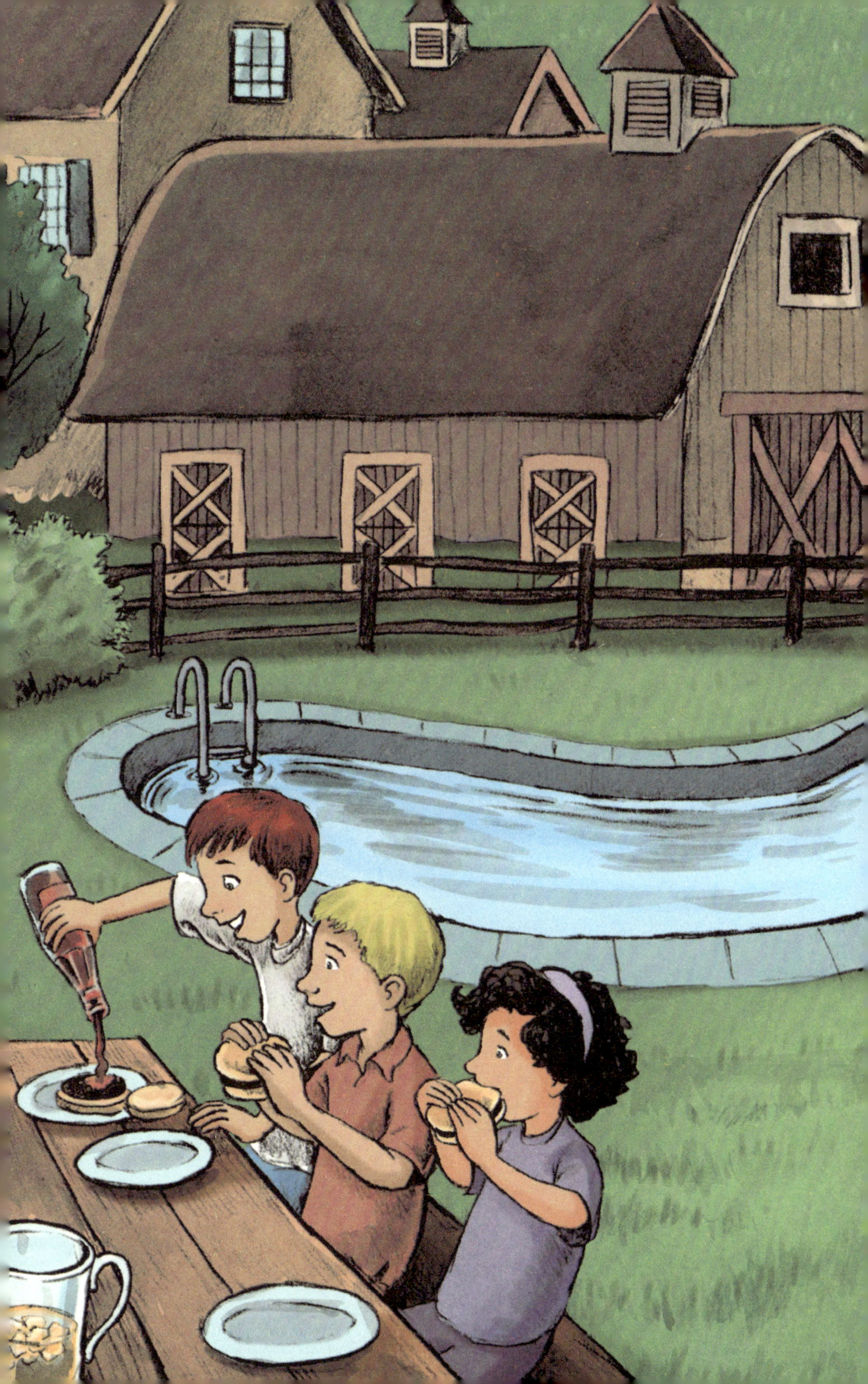

"等邦克斯先生进了监狱，舞者和饼干该怎么办呢？"露丝担心地问道。

福雷斯特眨了眨眼睛。"我已经安排好了，我要把它们买下来。"他说，"从现在开始，旋风就不用为了去看它妈妈而逃跑了。"

"太棒了！"乔希说。他拿起自己的汉堡咬了一大口。就在这时，一滴番茄酱喷了出来，溅落在他干净的白色T恤衫上。

A to Z Mysteries®

The Runaway Racehorse

by Ron Roy

illustrated by
John Steven Gurney

TINKER BUNKS'S HOUSE
THE OLD LOGGING ROAD
FOREST EVANS'S HOUSE
LARCHMONT, NY
BIKE PATH TO PHOTO FINISH
N
W
E
S

A to Z Mysteries
ON LOCATION IN
LARCHMONT, NY +
SARATOGA SPRINGS, NY
SARATOGA SPRINGS
VT
NH
MA
GREEN LAWN
CT
NY
LARCHMONT
CLUBHOUSE
GRANDSTAND
STABLES
ADMISSION
SARATOGA
RACETRACK
SARATOGA SPRINGS, NY

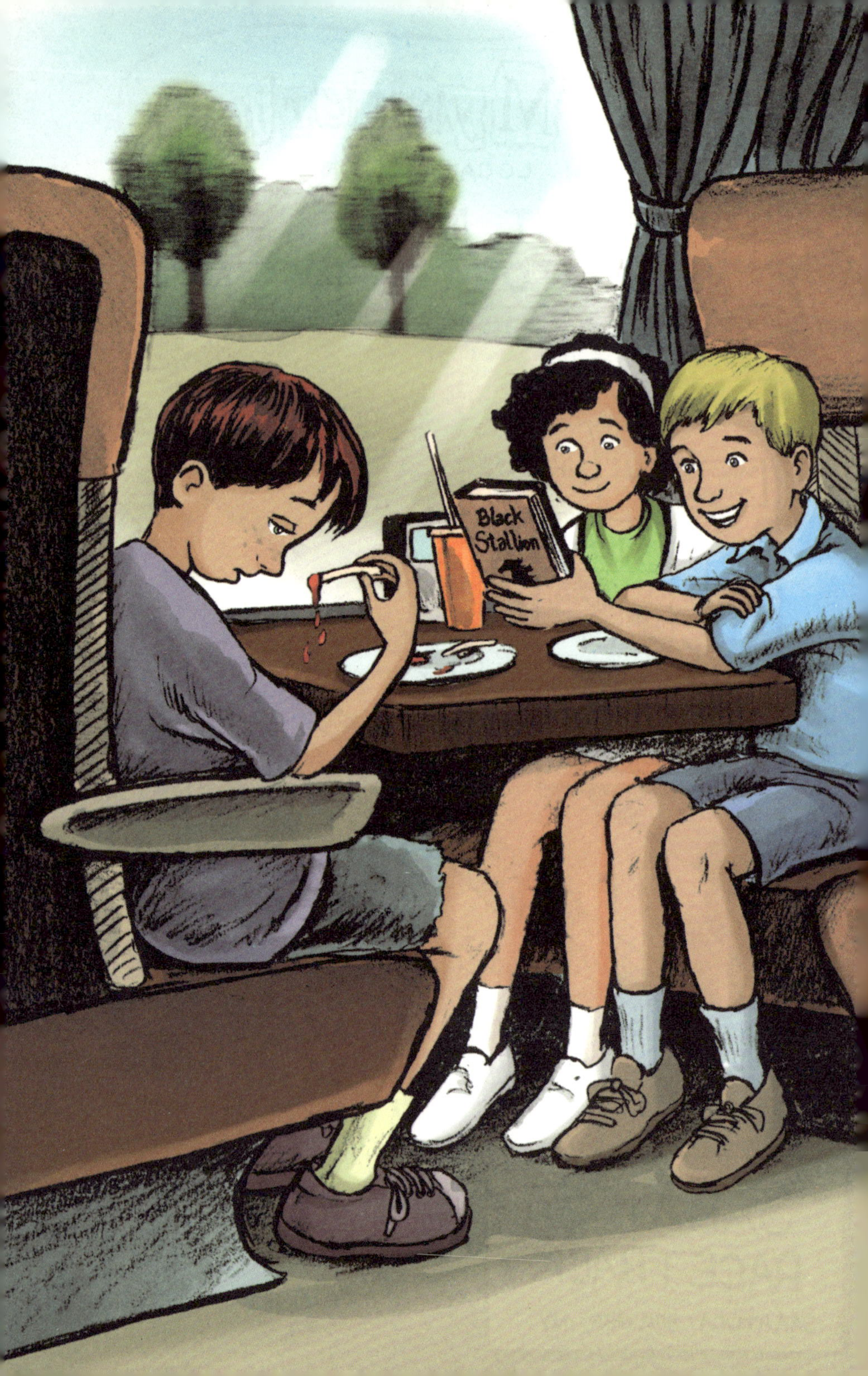
Black Stallion

Chapter 1

Josh picked up a French fry, dipped it in ketchup, and drew his initials on his plate. When he ate the French fry, a glob of ketchup plopped onto his shirt.

"Rats, this is my favorite T-shirt!" Josh said.

Dink put down his book and grinned at his freckle-faced, red-headed friend. "Was your favorite shirt," he said.

Josh, Dink, and Ruth Rose were taking a train to Larchmont, New York, to visit their friend Forest Evans. Forest and Dink's uncle Warren had bought a racehorse together. The kids were invited to watch the horse, Whirlaway, run in a race in Saratoga Springs.

Josh picked up a napkin and wiped at the red

stain. He only made it worse.

"Josh is finger-painting," Ruth Rose said to Dink.

"Someday I'll be a famous ketchup artist," Josh said. He gazed out the window. "When do we get there?"

"In a few minutes," Ruth Rose said, checking her train schedule.

"I can't wait to see Whirlaway," Dink said. "I've never met a real racehorse before. All I can think about is horses! That's why I'm reading this."

He held up his book. It was *The Black Stallion* by Walter Farley. The cover showed a beautiful black horse with wild eyes and a flowing mane.

Dink Duncan's real first name was Donald, and his middle name was David. But when he first started to talk and tried to say "Donald David Duncan," it came out as "Dink." Dink had been his nickname ever since.

"Look what I brought," Ruth Rose said, pulling a book from her backpack. The cover showed a girl on a horse. The book's title was *Learning to Ride*.

"Josh, did you bring a horse book?" Dink asked.

Josh grinned. "Nope. I figured you guys will tell

me anything I need to know." He dropped a few sugar cubes into his backpack.

"Still hungry?" Dink teased.

"They're for Whirlaway," Josh said.

Just then the conductor walked through the dining car. "Larchmont is next," he told the kids.

"Oh, wait!" Ruth Rose said, digging in her backpack. She brought out her new camera.

Ruth Rose liked to dress all in one color. Today everything was white, from her headband down to her sneakers. Even her camera was white!

"Would you please take our picture?" she asked the conductor.

"My pleasure," said the man. He took the camera and focused it on the kids. "Say 'cheese'!"

"Cheese!" they all said.

The conductor handed Ruth Rose her camera. "Have a great day," he said.

The train slowed, then stopped. Dink, Josh, and Ruth Rose grabbed their backpacks and walked to the end of the car. The conductor lowered a set of stairs, and the kids climbed down to the platform.

Dink heard someone call his name. He saw his uncle Warren and Forest Evans walking toward them. Dink's uncle was short and round and wore glasses. Forest Evans had a trimmed brown beard and wore jeans and a T-shirt.

逃跑的赛马

"Why, it's Wink, Gosh, and Tooth Toes!" Forest said.

The kids had met Forest when his painting had gotten stolen from Uncle Warren's apartment.

"Hi, Mr. Evans!" they all said.

"Please call me Forest, okay?" he asked.

Dink hugged his uncle.

"How was the train ride?" Uncle Warren asked.

"Great!" Josh said. "The hamburgers were awesome!"

Forest led them to a black car and opened a rear door. The kids piled in with their backpacks. Uncle Warren sat next to Forest up front. Forest started the car and pulled out of the parking lot.

"How many horses do you have?" Josh asked.

"Just Whirlaway," Forest said.

"Do you ride him in races?" Ruth Rose asked.

Forest laughed. "No, I'm too heavy. Professional jockeys are small and light. I hired a woman named Sunny to be Whirlaway's jockey."

"Awesome!" Josh said. "I've never met a girl jockey before." Then he added, "I've never met a boy jockey, either."

Forest slowed down near a group of small shops and flipped on his turn signal. Dink, Josh, and Ruth Rose recognized the long, tree-lined driveway. They had been here once before with Dink's uncle.

A minute later, Forest stopped at his garage. At the end of a stone path stood a large brick house. Out back a stone barn nestled between a tennis court and a swimming pool.

"Here we are," Forest said.

The kids climbed out of the backseat with their backpacks.

"When can we meet Whirlaway?" Josh asked, looking

toward the barn.

"Right now!" Forest said.

Uncle Warren headed to the house while the kids followed Forest toward the barn.

Josh dug in his pocket and pulled out a sugar cube. "I brought this for Whirlaway," he said.

"That was a nice idea, Josh," Forest said. "But Whirlaway doesn't like sugar. He's the only horse I've seen who doesn't!"

Josh stuck the cube back in his pocket as the kids entered the cool, dim barn. Dink took a deep breath. "It smells nice in here," he said.

"I agree," Forest said. He also took a deep breath. "There's nothing like the sweet smell of hay and horse."

"Don't forget chocolate," Josh added.

They all laughed as Forest led the way to a stall near the barn's rear doors. The doors were open and sunlight poured in. Out back was a truck parked on a wide area of gravel.

The stall door was also open, but there was no horse inside.

"That's funny," Forest said, closing the stall door. He thought for a moment, then smiled.

"I'll bet Sunny took Whirlaway out for exercise," he said. "They should be back soon. Let's go get you guys settled in the house."

He led Dink, Josh, and Ruth Rose back outside and into the house. They passed through a small room with boots on the floor and jackets hanging on pegs.

"This is the mudroom," Forest said, untying and kicking off his boots.

He took the kids through another door into the kitchen. The room was yellow with blue tiles on the counter and floor.

Forest pointed to a low bench. "You can leave your backpacks there for now," he said.

The kids stood their packs on the bench. Dink glanced at a newspaper clipping stuck to the refrigerator door with a magnet. There was a picture of a dark horse with a diamond-shaped blaze on his forehead. The headline read LOCAL HORSE BEATS ALL.

"Is that Whirlaway?" Dink asked.

"That's him," Forest said.

"He's real pretty," Ruth Rose said.

"He's even prettier in person," Forest said, opening the fridge. "You kids like fruit?"

"We like everything!" Josh said.

Forest set grapes and strawberries on the table. The kids sat down and began to snack.

Suddenly the door burst open. A small woman in jeans, riding boots, and a flannel shirt rushed into the kitchen.

"Hi, Sunny," Forest said. "Say hello to Dink, Josh, and Ruth Rose. They're here to watch you and Whirlaway race tomorrow."

"He's gone!" Sunny said, trying to catch her breath.

"Who's gone?"

"Whirlaway!" she said. "I just got here to take him out. When I looked in his stall, it was empty!"

Chapter 2

Forest looked up in surprise. Then suddenly, his face relaxed.

"Don't worry, I'll bet Whirlaway went to visit his mother again," Forest said. "I'll call Mr. Bunks."

"Who's Mr. Bunks?" Ruth Rose asked.

"Tinker Bunks owns the ranch next to my property," Forest said. "He tried to raise horses for racing. He never had much luck, so he sold off his stock. That's how Warren and I got Whirlaway. Mr. Bunks kept Whirlaway's mother, a nice old mare named Biscuit."

"How does Whirlaway visit his mother?" Dink

asked.

Sunny frowned. "The rascal gets out of his stall and cuts through the woods," she said.

"I wonder when he got out this time," Forest said. "He was here this morning when Warren got here. We went in and visited him."

"So he could have been gone all day!" Sunny said.

Forest nodded slowly. "Yes, it's possible, Sunny. But let's not worry. Last time he ran away, I found him safe and sound, munching hay with his mother."

Forest reached for the phone and dialed. He listened, then hung up.

"Mr. Bunks's line is busy," he said. He looked at the kids. "If you're finished, why don't we jump in my truck and take a ride over there?"

"I'll throw down some fresh straw in Whirlaway's stall," Sunny said. She headed out the door toward the barn.

Forest put the fruit back in the fridge and the kids followed him out the kitchen door.

He led them to the gravel parking area behind the barn. Forest's pickup truck was filled with bales of hay.

"Who wants to ride in the back with the hay?" Forest asked.

"I do!" Josh said.

"I will, too," Ruth Rose said. "Otherwise, Josh will be scared."

"Just make sure you hang on," Forest said. "We're taking the old logging road through the woods and it's pretty bumpy."

Ruth Rose and Josh scrambled into the truck's bed and sat on hay bales. Dink climbed into the cab next to Forest.

Forest started the truck and drove into the trees. Dink bounced in his seat as the tires rolled over bumps in the road. Low branches brushed the top of the cab.

Dink turned around to look through the rear window. Josh and Ruth Rose were laughing and holding on to the sides of the truck.

A few minutes later, they came out of the woods. Up ahead Dink saw a barn and a house. Forest pulled into the driveway and stopped behind another truck.

A dog was tied to a nearby tree. He leaped up and

started barking.

"Calm down, Buster," Forest said out his window. "Be a good dog."

A man came from behind the barn. He was wearing a work shirt, jeans, and a leather belt with a big silver buckle. Muddy rubber boots came up nearly to his knees.

"Lie down, Buster," the man said. Buster stopped barking and flopped down on the ground.

"Afternoon, Tinker," Forest said.

Tinker Bunks walked over and leaned on the door. He had a thin face, sharp blue eyes, and thick brows.

"Good day to you, Forest," he said. "That horse I sold you still running like the wind?"

Forest nodded and smiled. "He's won every race so far," he said.

"Winnin' is good," Mr. Bunks said. He looked off into the distance for a few seconds. "But I'm glad the racing business is behind me now. A lot of work, horses."

He peered into the cab. "So what brings you here today?"

"I'm afraid Whirlaway has disappeared again," Forest told Mr. Bunks. "Any chance he's come to visit his mother?"

Mr. Bunks arched his eyebrows. "Not so far as I know," he said, glancing toward the barn. "Let's go have a look."

The kids followed Mr. Bunks and Forest into a large barn. As they entered, Dink heard a horse whinny. "We hear you, Biscuit," Mr. Bunks said.

The barn was cool and dim. Dust hung in the air

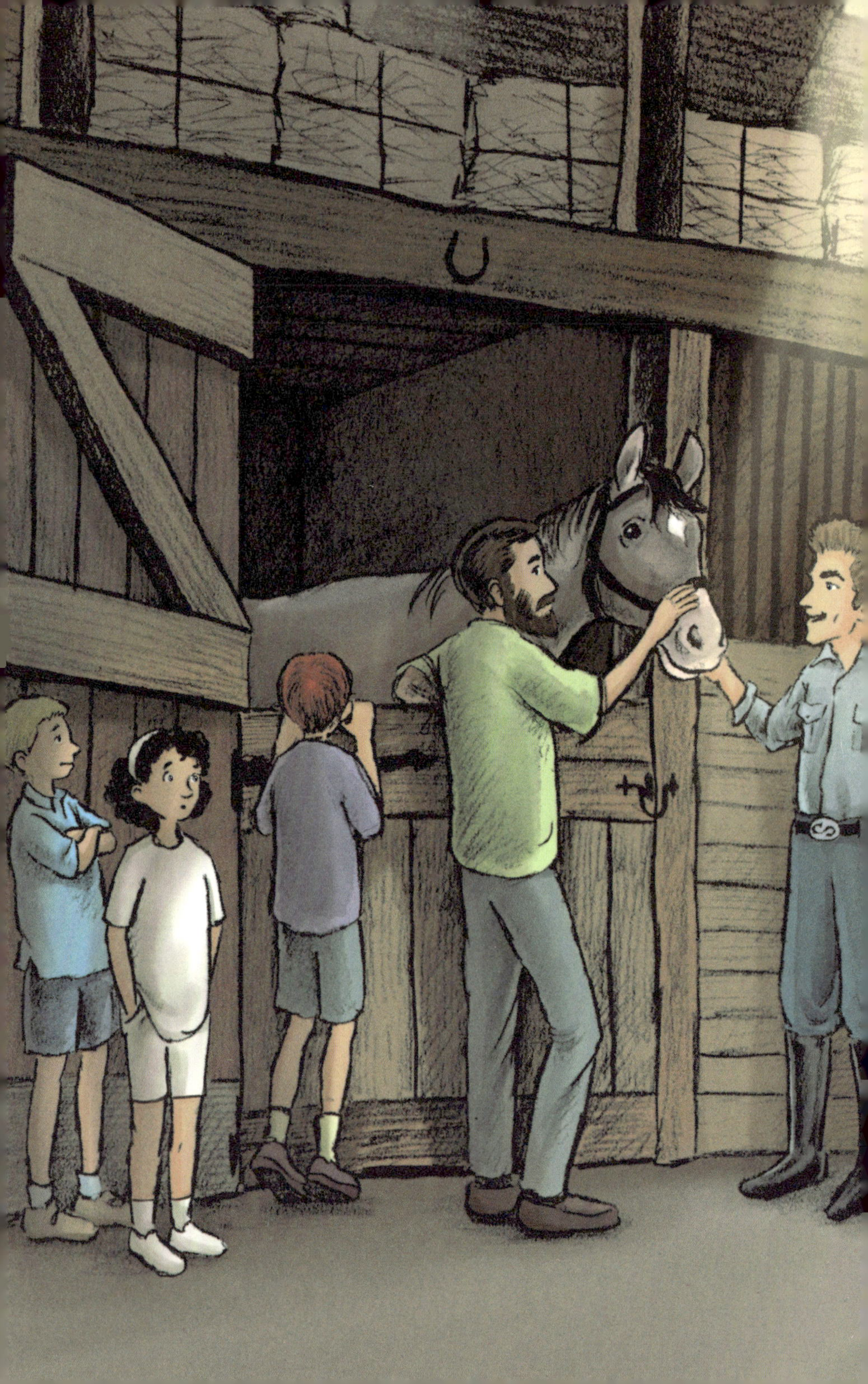

where sunlight came through high windows. A loft held rows of hay bales. The floor was swept clean.

Dink peeked into several stalls. Each was clean and empty.

Mr. Bunks stopped at a stall with its top door open. A pale brown horse with dark eyes stood there waiting. She had a small white mark on her forehead.

"This is Whirlaway's mom," Forest told the kids. He patted Biscuit on her nose.

"Have you seen your son today, old girl?" Mr. Bunks asked his horse.

As if she understood, Biscuit shook her large head from side to side.

"I thought for sure he'd be here," Forest said. He peered into a few of the empty stalls.

"I'm afraid I've wasted your time," Forest told Mr. Bunks. "Come on, kids. It's time to call the police."

Chapter 3

Tinker Bunks looked serious. "If he shows up, I'll give you a shout."

"I'd appreciate that," Forest said. "He's running at Saratoga tomorrow."

"Is he now!" Mr. Bunks said. "I wish you luck."

They all left the barn. The sky had grown darker. As Forest drove through the woods, Dink heard thunder. Wind began to whip tree branches back and forth.

Forest drove faster. "I'd better get us home before Josh and Ruth Rose have a shower!" he said.

Forest parked behind his barn just as raindrops

began to splatter the windshield. "Let's run for it!" he said, leaping from the cab.

Dink, Josh, and Ruth Rose ran, squealing, as the clouds opened up. In seconds they were soaking wet.

Inside the house, Forest handed them towels. They dried their hair and faces.

"Why don't you settle in while I call the police," he said. "Ruth Rose, you're in the blue bedroom. Guys, you're bunking right across the hall."

The kids grabbed their backpacks and headed toward the back of Forest's house. Ruth Rose stopped outside a bedroom with blue wallpaper.

"See you guys in a minute," she said, and disappeared inside.

Dink and Josh walked into their room and changed into dry shirts.

A minute later, Ruth Rose knocked and came in. Her wet hair was even curlier than usual.

"What could have happened to Whirlaway?" she asked Dink and Josh.

Dink looked out the bedroom window. Through the rain, he could see the barn. But he couldn't see the barn's rear doors.

"You know, someone could have stolen him," Dink said.

"Stolen him!" Josh said. "In broad daylight?"

Dink pointed. "You can't see the back doors of the barn from the house," he said. "Anyone could go in and out that way."

Ruth Rose peered through the streaming window. "How would you steal a horse?" she asked. "Would you need a trailer?"

"Or the thief could just ride him away," Josh said.

"Let's go look behind the barn for clues when the rain stops," Ruth Rose said.

"Maybe the police had some good news for Forest," Dink said.

They headed for the kitchen.

Forest was also staring out the window into the rain. His shoulders were hunched, and he was nervously tapping his fingers on the counter.

Uncle Warren was sitting at the table, drinking a mug of tea.

"Did you call the police?" Dink asked.

Forest turned away from the window and nodded. "Yes. They told me no one's called in about a stray horse," he said. "I'm getting worried."

"Do you think someone might have stolen him?" Dink asked.

Forest looked at him and blinked a few times. "Stolen Whirlaway? I suppose it's possible."

"Forest, have you any neighbors who own horses?" Uncle Warren asked.

"A few, why?"

"Because Whirlaway may not be the only missing horse," Uncle Warren said. "Perhaps you should call around."

"Good idea. I will," Forest said.

"We'll help you look for him when the rain stops," Ruth Rose said.

Forest nodded. "That'll be great. Now I'd better get on the phone," he said as he left the kitchen.

The kids drank milk and ate cookies with Uncle Warren. They watched the rain streak down the windows.

Forest came back a few minutes later. "I called

逃跑的赛马

two friends who own horses," he said. "None are missing, but my friends said they'd keep an eye out for Whirlaway."

The rain continued. They played Scrabble. When it wasn't his turn, Forest kept jumping up to call more neighbors.

Finally the rain stopped and the clouds cleared. When Dink looked out the window, sunlight sparkled off trees and bushes.

"I'll go pick up some food for dinner," Uncle Warren said. He took a set of car keys from a hook and left the house.

"Okay, kids, let's go look for my horse," Forest said.

He and the kids put on sneakers and headed through the kitchen door to the yard. The wet grass squished under their feet.

They walked behind the barn. Forest headed toward the woods, whistling and yelling, "Whirlaway!"

Dink, Josh, and Ruth Rose checked the wet ground for tire tracks or footprints.

"Nothing," Josh muttered. "Even if there were

clues, the rain washed them away."

Suddenly the kids heard a soft whinny from inside the barn.

Dink yelled for Forest, who came running.

"Whirlaway?" Forest said. They all ran into the barn.

Standing outside Whirlaway's stall was a wet, muddy horse.

"Where have you been, boy?" Forest asked his horse.

Whirlaway shook his head. Water and mud flew off his mane. He stomped his front foot and gazed at the humans.

Forest walked over and grasped Whirlaway's halter. It, too, was muddy.

Forest laughed and shook his head. "Looks like you've been rolling in a big mud puddle," he said. "Kids, do you know how to wash a horse?"

"Yes," Josh said. "We wash my pony all the time."

Forest pointed to a hose and some buckets and sponges. He handed Ruth Rose a container of green soap. "Just be careful of his feet," he said.

Forest snapped a leather lead onto Whirlaway's halter, then hooked the other end to a post. "Rinse the mud off first, then soap him down good."

Just then they heard a phone ringing from the house. "I'd better get that," Forest said. "When Whirlaway is dry, just put him back in his stall." He hurried back to the house.

Dink filled a bucket with water, then turned the hose on Whirlaway. The horse stood still as muddy water cascaded off his sides.

Ruth Rose poured some soap into the bucket, making the water turn green. The suds smelled like freshly cut grass.

The kids soaked three big sponges in the soapy water. They each began washing a different part of the horse. Whirlaway rolled his eyes and tried to watch all three kids.

"Hey, look at this," Josh said. He pointed to the horse's side. There was a mark in the mud. It was egg-shaped, about as big as his hand. Inside the oval was some kind of wiggly shape.

"Josh, have you been finger-painting again?" Ruth Rose teased.

"I didn't do that!" Josh said. "It was already there."

The three kids looked closely at the imprint.

"It almost looks like someone stamped him with something!" Josh said.

Chapter 4

"Whirlaway could have gotten that when he was rolling in the mud," Dink said. "He probably rolled over a rock or piece of wood."

"Yeah, probably," Josh said. He wiped his soapy sponge over the strange sign and it disappeared.

Dink trained the hose on Whirlaway again to rinse off the soap.

Ruth Rose found some towels hanging on the wall, and they rubbed Whirlaway's coat.

When he was dry and shining, Ruth Rose unhooked Whirlaway's lead from the post to put him in his stall. "Come on, boy," she said.

Whirlaway rolled his eyes at Ruth Rose. He stiffened his legs and refused to walk.

"Good job, kids!" Forest said as he walked into the barn. "He looks like a new horse!"

"He won't go in his stall," Ruth Rose said.

"Let me try," Forest said. He took the lead from Ruth Rose and began stroking Whirlaway's neck. He spoke softly in the horse's ear. After a minute, Whirlaway walked into his stall. He stuck his nose into the oats bucket and began eating.

Forest closed the stall door behind Whirlaway. "He was probably a little spooked from being out during the storm and coming home to all these strangers," he said.

Just then Sunny rode through the barn's rear doors on a mountain bike. She hopped off, leaned the bike against a wall, and strode over in tall, muddy boots. "There's the bad boy," she said, reaching over the stall door to pet his nose.

Whirlaway rolled his eyes, threw his head up, and backed into a corner.

"Easy, boy," Sunny murmured. She looked at Forest.

"He seems scared of me."

"He did the same thing with me," Ruth Rose said.

The five humans watched the horse, who was also watching them.

"Maybe he doesn't feel good," Dink suggested.

"Could he have eaten something bad while he was gone?" Josh asked.

"It's possible," Forest said. "But he looks fine. And he just ate some oats."

Sunny studied the horse. "I hope he runs okay tomorrow."

"How far away is Saratoga?" Dink asked.

"A few hours. It's near Albany," Sunny told him. She looked at Forest. "I'll come over at six and load Whirlaway into the trailer. I'll be there in plenty of time for him to relax before his race."

"Good," Forest said. "Now let's go see what Warren bought for our supper."

Forest looked at his horse. "No more disappearing tricks, fella," he said.

Sunny pulled the stall's top door shut and checked that the latch was in place.

"See you tomorrow in Saratoga," she said. The kids watched her straddle her mountain bike and ride out the door. She looked funny pedaling a bike in muddy rubber boots.

Uncle Warren was back with groceries. Soon they were all eating a hearty meal. After supper, they finished the Scrabble game.

At nine o'clock Forest stood up and yawned. "Long day tomorrow," he said. "I'm ready to turn in."

"Sounds good to me, too," said Uncle Warren. "See you all in the morning." He patted Dink on the head and left the room.

The kids padded down the hall to their rooms. As Dink and Josh were crawling into their beds, they heard a knock.

Ruth Rose opened the door. "Nice Daffy Duck jammies, Josh," she said, marching into the room with her book.

"Quack-quack," Josh said.

Ruth Rose sat on the end of Dink's bed with the book on her lap. "I want to read you guys something," she said.

"Oh, goody," Josh said. "Can we have milk and cookies, too?"

Ruth Rose held up her book. "This is really about learning to ride your own horse," she said. "But there's a chapter about jockeys."

She opened the book and began reading: "Jockeys must earn the horse's trust. A good jockey does this by feeding and grooming the horse regularly. Most horses learn to like their jockeys and become friends."

Ruth Rose looked up from the page. "Does anything strike you about that?" she asked.

逃跑的赛马

"Like what?" said Josh.

"Well, did you notice how Whirlaway acted around Sunny?" Ruth Rose said.

"He sure didn't seem very friendly to her," said Dink.

"Yeah, he backed away as soon as she came in," said Josh.

"Exactly," Ruth Rose said. "I think Whirlaway's afraid of Sunny!"

Chapter 5

A hand on his shoulder woke Dink from a sound sleep. The light next to his bed was on. *The Black Stallion* lay on the bedcovers, still opened.

Through sleepy eyes, he looked into his uncle's face.

"Morning, Donny," Uncle Warren said quietly. "Time to get up."

"Hi, Uncle Warren," Dink said.

"You boys have to hop to it," Uncle Warren said. "Forest wants to get on the road right after breakfast." He smiled at Dink and left the room.

Dink tossed his pillow over at Josh's bed, then

逃跑的赛马

walked into the bathroom. Josh grumbled, but soon they were both dressed and headed for the kitchen.

Forest and Ruth Rose were sitting at the table eating oatmeal. Uncle Warren took a pot off the stove and filled bowls for Dink and Josh.

"Everyone sleep all right?" Forest asked.

"I did," Ruth Rose said. She spooned some brown sugar over her cereal. Today her color was purple: purple leggings, purple blouse, purple headband, purple sneakers.

"Me too," Dink said. "Except for Josh's snoring all night."

They ate quickly, then left the house and piled into Forest's car. Dink, Josh, and Ruth Rose sat in the backseat. They each had their books, and Josh had brought his pillow.

Forest turned out of his driveway and drove through Larchmont. After making a few turns, he was on a wide highway. Dink saw a sign that said ALBANY, 120 MILES.

A few hours later, they arrived in Saratoga Springs.

Forest pulled his car into a parking lot.

They all climbed out of the car and stretched their legs. Under tall trees, Dink saw long green barns. Near the barns, men and women were grooming horses, feeding horses, exercising horses. There were horses everywhere!

Ruth Rose took pictures of horses and one of a barn with the sun shining on the green wood.

"Let's go find Sunny," Forest suggested. "She'll be in barn E. Stall number twenty-one."

They cut through some trees, following a wide path. Barns stood on both sides of the path. Each barn had a large letter painted on one side.

The gravel walkway was crowded with people. Some were walking horses; others were just looking.

"There's barn E," Josh said, sprinting ahead.

Forest, Uncle Warren, and the kids found Sunny outside stall 21. She had one foot on a bale of hay and was buffing her riding boot with a cloth. A can of black boot polish sat on the floor.

"Hi, Sunny," Forest said.

Sunny wore white riding pants. Her silk racing shirt was green with yellow stripes on the arms. Circling her left arm was a cloth band with the number 21 stitched on. Her hair was tucked up under a hard hat covered in yellow silk. Oval-shaped goggles rested on the hat's visor.

Sunny dropped the cloth and smiled. "Hi, everyone," she said.

"Any problems?" Forest asked.

"He didn't want to walk into the trailer this morning," Sunny said. "And he definitely didn't like me getting him ready once we got here."

"Good morning, Whirlaway," Forest said to his horse. "Why are you giving Sunny a hard time, eh, boy?"

Everyone peered into the stall. Whirlaway was standing in a corner with his eyes on the newcomers.

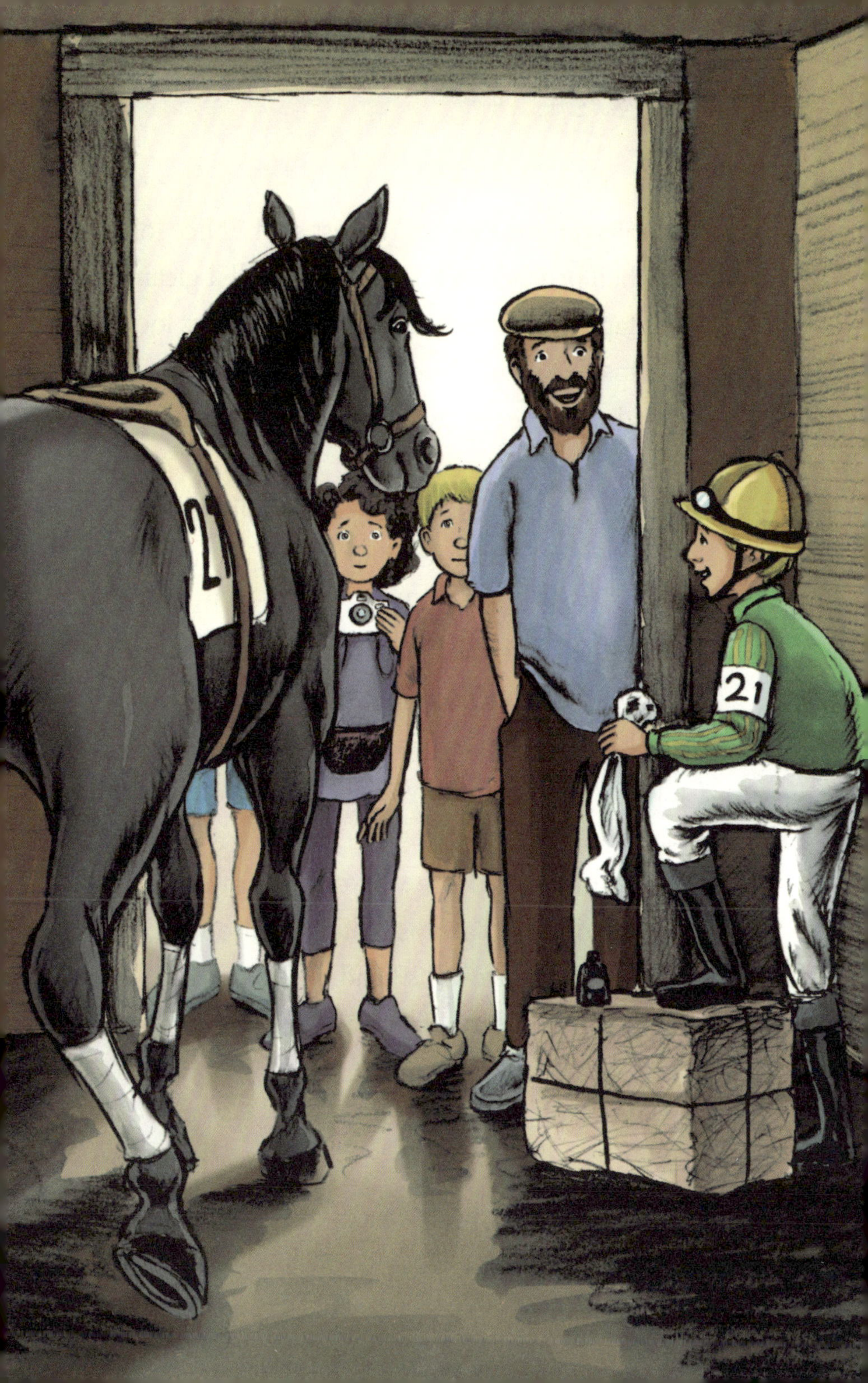
21

"He looks terrific, Sunny," Forest said. "Nice job."

Sunny had brushed Whirlaway's coat till it gleamed. The white tape she'd wrapped around his ankles looked snowy against his nearly black coat.

"Why do you wear goggles?" Ruth Rose asked Sunny.

"To protect my eyes," Sunny said. "During races, the horses in front of me kick up dirt. You should see me when I race in the rain. Totally covered in mud!"

"What time is the race?" Dink asked.

"We're in the second one," Sunny said. "Two o'clock."

"We'll be cheering you on," Uncle Warren said.

"Can I take a picture of you and Whirlaway?" Ruth Rose asked.

"Sure," Sunny said. She walked into the stall and put her hand on Whirlaway's halter. Whirlaway rolled his eyes at her and threw his head back.

Ruth Rose is right, thought Dink. Whirlaway doesn't like Sunny at all.

Ruth Rose snapped a picture.

Chapter 6

"Okay, gang, let's go grab our seats," Forest said.

To get to Forest's private box, they had to climb up three flights of stairs. Throngs of people filled the grandstand. Music was playing, and everyone seemed to be having a good time.

The viewing box had a row of seats under a little roof. On both sides were other private boxes. Straight ahead was a perfect view of the starting gate and oval racetrack.

"How long is the race?" Josh asked.

"Twice around the track," Forest said.

A stack of race programs was on one seat. Forest

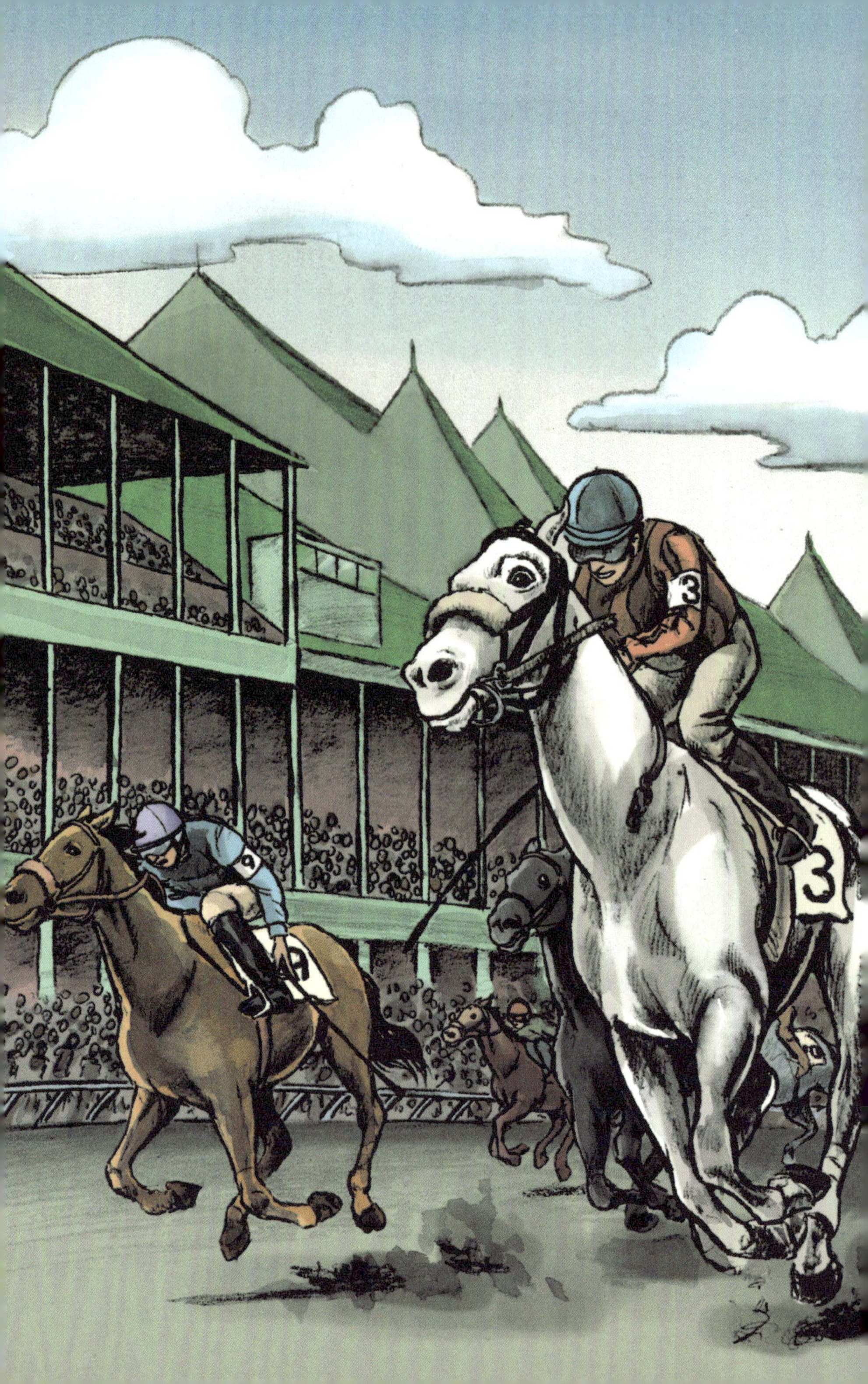

3
9
3

handed them out. "Whirlaway's on page two," he said.

The kids quickly checked and found Whirlaway's name. Sunny was listed as Whirlaway's jockey.

"This is so exciting!" Ruth Rose said. She set her camera on the floor under her chair.

A waiter wearing a white jacket came and took their lunch order. They made it simple for him: five cheeseburgers, five lemonades.

"Where do the horses end up?" Josh asked.

"At the finish line," Uncle Warren said, "down there behind the starting gate."

The waiter brought their food. As they ate, they watched a group of horses and their riders come out onto the track. Some of the horses were bucking and prancing. The jockeys were outfitted in bright colors. Each rider wore goggles like Sunny's.

The horses were white, gray, black, and several shades of brown. One was a golden palomino.

Down below the owners' boxes, people were lined up along the track fence. They began cheering when they saw the horses at the starting gate.

Suddenly a man's voice came over the speakers.

"GOOD AFTERNOON, LADIES AND GENTLEMEN!" he cried. "THE FIRST RACE IS ABOUT TO BEGIN!" While he called out the names of the horses and jockeys, the riders moved their horses up to the starting gate.

Then a loud bell sounded, and the horses burst onto the track. The jockeys stood in the stirrups, their heads bent low over the horses' necks.

The crowd shouted and cheered. Even above the noise, the kids could hear the thunder of the horses' hooves on the track. Clumps of dirt flew into the air behind each horse.

"AND IT'S MERRY MARY IN THE LEAD!" the announcer exclaimed. "STARBURST IS A LENGTH

BEHIND! CRANBERRY SAUCE IS THIRD!"

Then it was over. A white horse had rocketed across the finish line first.

"AND IT'S MERRY MARY BY HALF A LENGTH!" yelled the announcer.

As the kids watched, the jockey pranced Merry Mary to the winner's circle. A woman wearing a dress and a wide hat presented the jockey with a trophy. A man in a suit beamed and posed for a picture. "That's the horse's owner," Forest informed the kids.

"Is our race next?" Dink asked, checking his program.

"Yes, in just a few minutes," Forest said. He pointed to the track. "The horses are coming out already."

The three kids stood up.

"Which one is Whirlaway?" Ruth Rose said, getting her camera ready. "There are a lot of dark horses with white marks on their foreheads."

Forest pointed over her shoulder. "In front of the white horse," he said. "See Sunny's yellow hat? And you can see the big twenty-one on Whirlaway's saddle blanket."

The horses and riders approached the starting gate. When the announcer shouted, "NUMBER TWENTY-ONE IS WHIRLAWAY, RIDDEN BY SUNNY FIELDS!" Dink, Josh, and Ruth Rose cheered. Ruth Rose snapped a picture. Forest put two fingers in his mouth and whistled.

Then the announcer's voice boomed over the loudspeakers. "NOW THE SECOND RACE! AN

EVEN DOZEN BEAUTIES OUT THERE!"

And then the starting bell sounded, and the race was on. The crowd began yelling, but didn't drown out the announcer's voice.

"WHAT A SIGHT, FOLKS! FANCY PANTS IS OUT FRONT. HIGH FIVE IS NEXT! HERE COMES PRETTY BALLOON ON THE OUTSIDE! AND LOOK AT THIS. DANCER IS SNEAKING UP ON PRETTY BALLOON. HE'S PASSING HIGH FIVE. DANCER IS IN THE LEAD!"

Dink, Josh, and Ruth Rose were on their feet. They jumped and yelled, "Come on, Whirlaway!"

But Whirlaway was nowhere near the front. Number

21 was second to last as the horses barreled toward the finish line.

By the time the race was over, Whirlaway had fallen back even more. He came in dead last.

The kids sat down, disappointed. Forest stared at the racetrack.

"What happened?" Uncle Warren said.

Forest shook his head. "Whirlaway has never run so badly," he said. "There's something wrong!"

Chapter 7

"Well, he tried," Uncle Warren said, laying his hand on Forest's shoulder.

"I know I can't expect Whirlaway to win every race," Forest agreed. "But he's never run this poorly!"

"Can we go see him?" Dink asked.

"Sure," Forest said, checking his watch. "Meet us back here in about fifteen minutes, okay?"

The kids clambered down the grandstand steps and ran toward the barns. They entered barn E and walked past curious horses peering from stalls.

"There's Whirlaway," Josh said, pointing. The horse, slick with sweat, was tied outside stall 21. Sunny was wiping him down with towels.

Sunny looked up and nodded at the kids.

"I'm sorry you didn't win," Ruth Rose said.

"Not as sorry as I am," Sunny muttered. Her outfit was filthy. She had removed her helmet, and her hair hung down, damp and straggly. Where her goggles had been, her face was clean. The rest was smeared with sweat and track grime. Her once shiny black boots were now brown with dust.

Sunny knelt down and began unwinding the tape from Whirlaway's legs. The tape was grimy.

Sunny shook her head as she worked. "Whirlaway was running like a different horse," she said.

She walked away to find a trash can for the soiled tapes, leaving Whirlaway tied to his stall.

"Maybe Whirlaway was just tired," Dink said.

"Maybe," Ruth Rose agreed. "But jockeys can make horses go slower."

Josh looked at Ruth Rose. "You think Sunny made Whirlaway lose the race?"

Ruth Rose shrugged. "I don't know."

Sunny came back and untied Whirlaway. She

had to tug him up the ramp. He rolled his eyes as she walked him into the trailer.

Sunny closed and latched the trailer door. Without saying a word, she climbed into the cab and drove away.

"Something weird is definitely going on between Whirlaway and Sunny," Ruth Rose said.

"Whirlaway might just be having a bad day," Dink said.

Ruth Rose looked at her watch.

"We'd better get back," she said.

They started walking toward the viewing stands. Dink noticed a small group of people gathered around a dark horse and its rider. "There's the winner," he said.

"Yeah, Dancer," said Josh.

"I want to get a picture," Ruth Rose said. The kids walked to the winner's circle. They wiggled through the crowd until they were standing next to Dancer.

Dancer's chest and legs were sweaty. The white tape that covered his ankles was dirty. The jockey was dirty, too. He smiled as people took pictures.

A man wearing a cowboy hat and dark glasses

reached up and shook the jockey's hand. "Well done, Andy," he said.

"Piece of cake, Mr. Bee," the jockey answered.

"Guys, move closer," Ruth Rose said. "I want to get a picture of you and Dancer."

Dink and Josh stepped over and stood in front of Dancer. Josh giggled when the horse butted him gently in the back.

The jockey flicked the reins, and Dancer put his head between Dink's and Josh's shoulders.

Ruth Rose snapped the picture. Her camera made a whirring noise, letting her know that the roll of film had run out.

Dink looked at his watch. "Come on, guys. They're waiting for us."

They hurried away and found Forest and Uncle Warren in the viewing box.

"How does Whirlaway look?" Forest asked.

"Tired," Josh said. "Sunny loaded him and they took off."

"I guess we'd better leave, too," Forest said. They headed for the parking lot.

Dink, Josh, and Ruth Rose walked behind Forest and Uncle Warren.

Ruth Rose held up her camera. "I can't wait to get my film developed," she whispered. "I think that last picture is a big clue!"

Chapter 8

"Maybe Whirlaway is sick," Uncle Warren suggested on the way back.

Forest nodded. "I'll call the vet and get him to come over," he said.

The kids sat in back. Josh slept against his pillow with his mouth open. Next to him, Ruth Rose read *Learning to Ride*.

Dink's book was on his lap. He gazed out the window, watching the scenery flash by. The hum of the car's tires made him feel sleepy. His eyes closed.

The next thing Dink heard was his uncle's voice saying, "Almost home, kids."

Dink opened his eyes, blinked, and looked out the window. He recognized the shops just before Forest's driveway.

"There's a photo place," Ruth Rose said. "Can we stop, Forest?"

"Sure thing," Forest said. He pulled up in front of the small shop. A cheerful sign in the window said PHOTO FINISH. ONE HOUR!

Ruth Rose hopped out and ran inside. She was back a minute later. "I got more film," she said.

Josh sat up and looked around. "Where are we?" he asked.

Dink poked his finger at the back of Josh's shirt. "Josh, there's a black smear on your collar."

Josh twisted his shirt around and stretched out the collar. "Yuck!" he said. "Where did that come from?"

"Maybe it's mud from Whirlaway yesterday," Dink suggested.

"Dink," Josh said, "I changed my shirt after we washed him."

"Could you have leaned against wet paint or something at Saratoga?" Ruth Rose asked.

147

Josh thought for a second. "I don't think so," he said, "and if I had, there'd be more than just a mark on my collar." He shrugged.

Forest made the turn into his driveway, and a minute later they were home.

"I've got to change my shirt," Josh said when they had all climbed out of the car.

"No! Let's go see if Sunny and Whirlaway are back yet," Ruth Rose said. She gave Dink and Josh a look.

"Great," Forest said. "I'll see if I can get the vet on the phone."

Uncle Warren took Josh's pillow and the books.

Dink, Josh, and Ruth Rose headed for the barn. The stall was empty, and Sunny was nowhere to be seen.

"Okay, what's up?" Josh asked Ruth Rose. They sat on hay bales.

"You know that picture I took of you guys with Dancer?" Ruth Rose asked. "Well, I think someone else was in it. Mr. Bunks!"

Both boys looked blank.

"The man in the sunglasses and cowboy hat was Mr. Bunks!" Ruth Rose said.

"Are you sure?" Dink asked. "I thought that guy was the horse's owner."

"I think I recognized his big belt buckle from yesterday," Ruth Rose said. "I took a picture so we could be sure."

"Well, if it was him, why didn't Mr. Bunks tell Forest that he was going to be at Saratoga, too?" Dink asked.

"That's what I want to know," Ruth Rose said. "And why did he say he was out of the racing business?"

"Maybe Mr. Bunks doesn't own Dancer," Josh said. "He might have been there like us, just to see the winner up close."

"But he and the jockey knew each other," Ruth Rose said.

Dink nodded. "If that was Mr. Bunks at Saratoga," he said, "he is definitely hiding something!"

Chapter 9

Just then Uncle Warren walked into the barn. He was wearing flip-flops and a bathing suit and carrying a towel.

"Coming for a swim?" he asked.

"Sure," Dink said. The kids followed Uncle Warren toward the house.

"After we swim, let's go get my film," Ruth Rose said quietly.

The kids changed and joined Forest and Uncle Warren in the pool. They played keep-away with a plastic ball.

"Still no sign of Sunny and Whirlaway," Forest

said, nodding toward the barn. "I sure hope they didn't have any trouble on the road."

"We're going to get my film," Ruth Rose said. "Maybe she'll be here when we get back."

"There's a safe bike path on the side of the road," Forest said. "Have a nice walk."

The kids dried off, pulled on their clothes, and headed across the lawn.

"I wonder what's taking Sunny so long to get back here?" Dink asked as they hiked down the driveway.

"She could have stopped for food," Josh said. He rubbed his belly.

A few minutes later, they walked into Photo Finish. Josh immediately spied a rack of candy, so he bought a bag of M&M's.

Ruth Rose's film was ready. She paid the clerk, and they started walking back to Forest's, where they could look at the pictures in private.

Josh ripped open his candy and began munching, one piece at a time.

When they got back to Forest's, the kids headed straight to the barn. Sunny and Whirlaway had still not returned.

Ruth Rose opened the packet of pictures and took them out. There were a few of her cat, then the one taken by the train conductor.

The next pictures were of horses and the barn at Saratoga. Then there was one of the horses on the track, but it was blurry. Next was Sunny with Whirlaway in barn E.

The last picture was taken at the winner's circle. It showed Dink and Josh with Dancer's head between them. The man in the cowboy hat was standing in the background. He was wearing a leather belt with a big silver buckle.

"It's Mr. Bunks, all right," Dink said.

The kids studied the picture. Ruth Rose brought it closer to her eyes.

"Guys, do you see anything weird about Dancer's forehead?" she asked.

"It looks shiny," Dink said, peering closely.

"And darker than the rest of his face," Josh observed.

"From a distance, you'd never notice," Ruth Rose said.

"What could make it look like that?" asked Dink.

"Something dark, like shoe polish," Josh said.

"Wait a minute," Ruth Rose said. "Josh, let's see that mark on your shirt."

Josh leaned in so Dink and Ruth Rose could inspect his collar.

"It looks like shoe polish," said Dink.

"Yes!" Josh said. "Now I remember! Ruth Rose, when you took our picture, I felt Dancer nudge me in the back."

"So Dancer made that mark!" Ruth Rose said.

"But why would anyone want to put shoe polish on a horse?" Dink asked.

"I don't know, but I know who could have done it," Ruth Rose said. "Sunny was polishing her boots with black polish right before the race!"

"But Sunny doesn't have anything to do with Dancer," Josh pointed out.

Ruth Rose shuffled through the pictures until she found the one of Sunny and Whirlaway in barn E. She looked at it for a second, then placed it next to the one of Dink and Josh with Dancer.

"Wow," Josh said. "The horses look like twins!"

Dink picked up the picture of Sunny in barn E. "Except this one has a white mark on his forehead."

"The shoe polish could be covering up a white mark on Dancer's forehead," Ruth Rose said.

"But why would Sunny, or Mr. Bunks, or anybody want to cover up a white mark on Dancer's forehead?

Why would it matter?" Josh asked.

Dink thought about that. Then he remembered Sunny's comment after the race, about how she felt like she was riding a different horse. "That's it!" Dink said, snapping his fingers.

"What's what?" Josh asked.

"Guys, what if the horse we washed wasn't Whirlaway?"

逃跑的赛马

Dink asked.

"What do you mean?" asked Josh.

"I mean, what if someone stole Whirlaway, then brought back a different horse to replace him?"

Josh and Ruth Rose just stared at Dink.

"Well, that would explain why he acted so strange," Ruth Rose finally said.

"And why he blew the race," Josh said.

"It would also explain the shoe polish," said Dink.

"Huh?" said Josh.

"Well," Dink said, "why would someone want to steal a fast racehorse like Whirlaway?"

"To win races!" Ruth Rose said.

"Right," said Dink. "And if someone did steal Whirlaway and enter him in a race, he'd be sure to disguise him somehow."

"Like covering up the mark on his forehead with shoe polish!" said Josh.

"So that's why Mr. Bunks was there," Ruth Rose said. "He must have stolen Whirlaway and entered him in the race as Dancer."

"And I'll bet Sunny's working for him," Josh said.

"It would have been easy for her to switch the horses."

"Plus, we saw her with shoe polish," Dink said.

"I'd like to ask Sunny a few questions," Ruth Rose said.

"Where is Sunny?" Josh asked.

"Good question," said Ruth Rose, looking around the empty barn. She sighed.

"And if she did switch horses, how can we prove the horse she rode in the race wasn't Whirlaway?" Dink asked.

"I know a way," Josh said. He reached into his pocket and pulled out a sugar cube. "Forest said Whirlaway doesn't like sugar. When Sunny gets back, I'll offer this to Whirlaway—or whoever it is. If he eats the sugar, we'll know it's not Whirlaway!"

Chapter 10

"You're a genius!" Ruth Rose said.

"I know," Josh said.

Dink glanced around the empty barn. "Now all we have to do is wait for Sunny."

Ruth Rose stuffed the pictures back into the packet. "Well, I, for one, am not waiting around," she said. "Come on, let's go check out Mr. Bunks's place again."

"What are we gonna do when we get there?" Josh asked as they hurried up Forest's driveway.

"Look for Whirlaway," Ruth Rose said. "Do you still have those sugar cubes?"

Josh patted his pocket. "Yep."

The kids cut behind Forest's barn and headed for the logging road.

A few minutes later, they reached Mr. Bunks's house and barn.

"I don't see that dog anywhere," Josh whispered.

"And I don't see Mr. Bunks's truck," Dink said.

"Let's check out the barn," Ruth Rose said. The kids slipped into the barn. It was quiet and dim, with a little light coming through the dusty windows.

"Biscuit's gone!" Dink said, stopping in front of her empty stall. "Where is she?"

As if in answer, they heard a horse whinny. "Come on," Dink said, heading outside.

Behind the barn was an open field with a path leading through the tall weeds. The kids followed the trail and entered a stand of trees. As they reached the far side of the trees, the kids stopped and stared. They were in a clearing in front of a long shed. A horse trailer was partially hidden behind the low building.

The kids pulled open the wide shed door and peeked inside. Dink wrinkled his nose at the sharp manure smell.

Half of the shed was fenced off with boards. Behind the fence was Biscuit, staring at the newcomers.

In a separate stall next to Biscuit's was another horse, wearing a halter. The dark horse looked just like Whirlaway, except that there was no white diamond on this horse's shiny forehead.

"It's the horse who won," Josh breathed.

"Is it Whirlaway?" Dink whispered.

Josh unwrapped a sugar cube, walked over to the fence, and held out his hand. The dark horse stepped closer for a sniff. Then he snorted and shook his head.

"He won't take it!" Josh exclaimed. He reached out and carefully touched the horse's forehead. When he brought his hand away, his fingers were smeared with something black.

Dink took a towel from a nail on the wall. Holding the horse's halter with one hand, he wiped his forehead.

More black came off, revealing part of a white diamond shape.

Dink felt goose bumps crawl up his back. "Sunny did switch horses!" he said.

"This is Whirlaway," Ruth Rose said. She opened

her envelope of pictures. She found the one of Sunny and the horse in barn E and held it up next to the real Whirlaway. "The horse back at Forest's place is his double!" she said.

"We have to tell Forest!" Josh said.

"Tell him what?" a voice said.

The kids whirled around. In the shed doorway stood Mr. Bunks and Buster. Mr. Bunks was still wearing the clothes he'd worn in the winner's circle, including the silver belt buckle. "Sit, dog," Mr. Bunks said to Buster. The dog sat at his master's side. A low growl came from deep in his throat.

"So you figured it out," Mr. Bunks said. He nodded at the towel in Dink's hand. "Even my boot polish trick."

His boot polish trick? Dink thought. Suddenly Dink realized the truth. Sunny had not been the one to put the boot polish on Whirlaway! It was Mr. Bunks! And it had been Bunks's belt buckle that made the mark in the mud on the horse they washed! It wasn't Sunny who had stolen Whirlaway. She thought she was riding Whirlaway in the race. Mr. Bunks had done it alone!

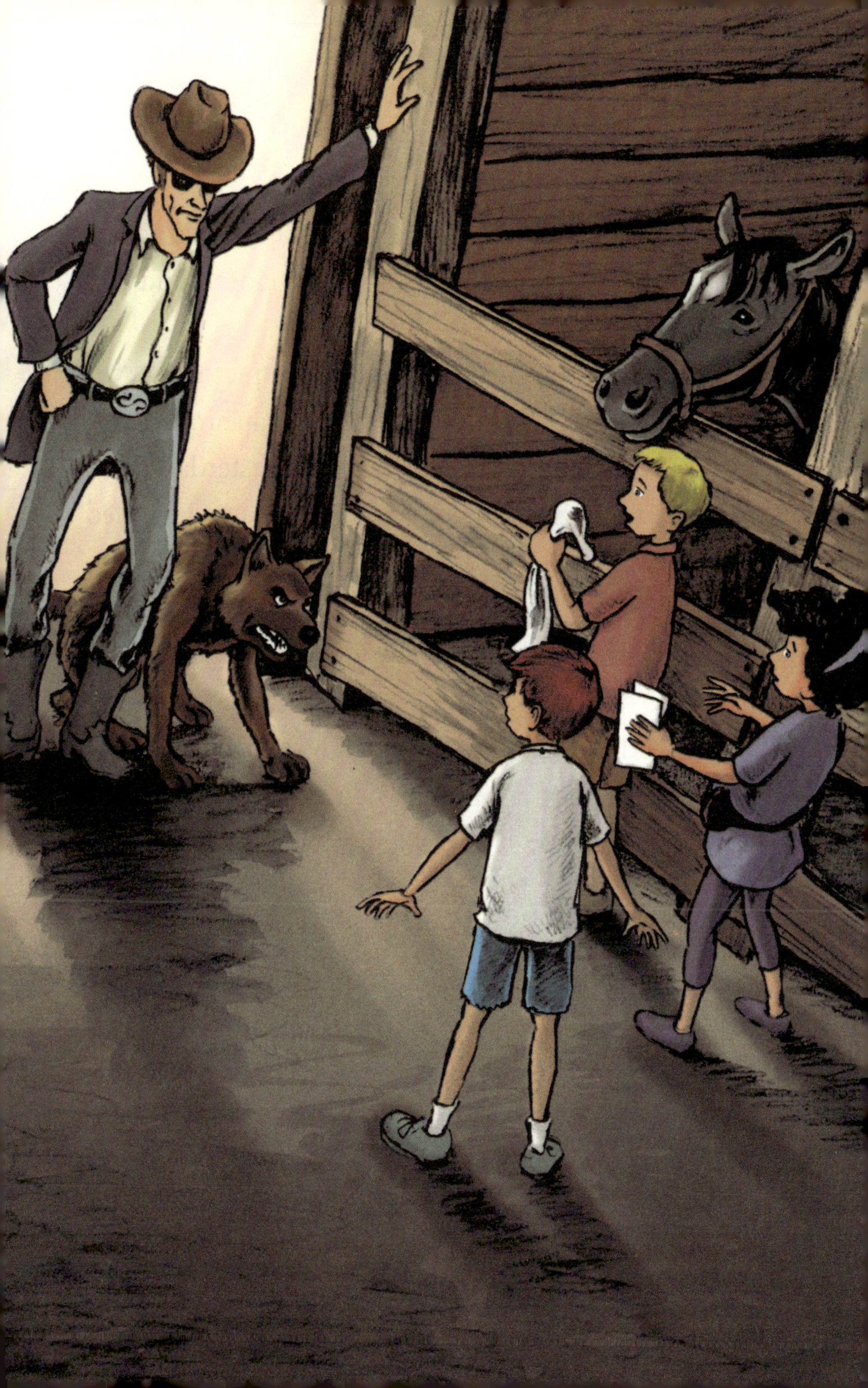

A to Z 神秘案件

Dink glanced around the dim shed, looking for another way out. The windows were closed and too high up.

"Now, if you'll just pass me those pictures," Mr. Bunks said, holding out a hand. The man smiled, but it wasn't the friendly smile he'd shown yesterday.

Dink took the photos from Ruth Rose and handed them to Mr. Bunks.

"We don't need the pictures," Dink said. "We know this is Whirlaway and we know you stole him from Mr. Evans."

Mr. Bunks laughed. "Whirlaway? I don't know what you're talking about," he said. "I bought this horse. Can I help it if he just happens to look like Whirlaway? Can I help it if he just happens to run like the wind?"

He slipped the photos inside his shirt. "No one will ever prove I stole this horse from Forest."

"We won't have to prove anything, Tinker," a voice said. "Not with all these witnesses."

Forest, Uncle Warren, and Sunny walked into the shed.

An hour later, everyone sat around Forest's picnic table eating burgers.

"How did you guys know where we were?" Dink asked.

"I was coming back just as you were leaving," Sunny said. "You had such determined looks on your faces, I decided to tell Forest."

"And we reached the shed in time to hear everything," Forest said. "Mr. Bunks is going to jail."

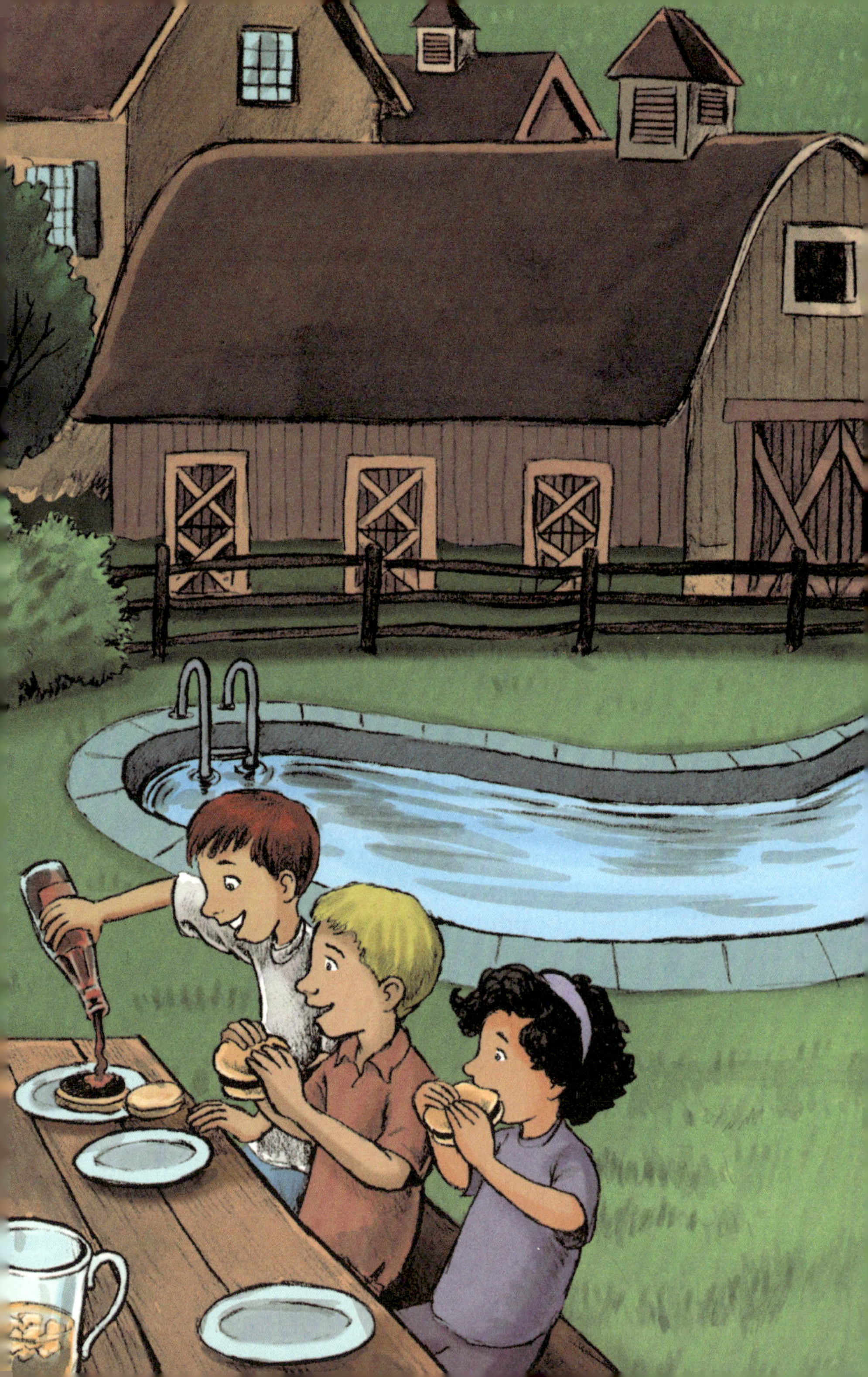

"Did Mr. Bunks actually think he could get away with this?" Ruth Rose said.

Forest nodded. "Well, he was lucky to find Whirlaway's double. Even the white face diamonds are the same," he said. "I was fooled, but Sunny noticed a difference."

"Whirlaway is usually so friendly," Sunny said. "I got suspicious when the look-alike acted like he didn't know me. On the way home from Saratoga, I stopped at the vet's. He took a blood sample that'll prove the horse I rode isn't Whirlaway."

"That horse is called Dancer," Forest said. "Bunks switched names, too. Turns out the woman he bought Dancer from didn't treat her horse very well. That's why he was afraid of Sunny. Her voice reminded him of his abusive owner."

"What will happen to Dancer and Biscuit when Mr. Bunks goes to jail?" Ruth Rose asked.

Forest winked. "I've arranged to buy them," he said. "From now on, Whirlaway won't have to run away to visit his mother."

"Awesome!" Josh said. He picked up his hamburger and took a big bite. As he did, a glob of ketchup

逃跑的赛马

squirted out and landed on his clean white T-shirt.

Text copyright © 2002 by Ron Roy
Illustrations copyright © 2002 by John Steven Gurney
All rights reserved under International and Pan-American Copyright Conventions.
Published in the United States by Random House Children's Books,
a division of Random House, Inc., New York,
and simultaneously in Canada by Random House of Canada Limited, Toronto.

本书中英双语版由中南博集天卷文化传媒有限公司与企鹅兰登（北京）文化发展有限公司合作出版。

"企鹅"及其相关标识是企鹅兰登已经注册或尚未注册的商标。
未经允许，不得擅用。
封底凡无企鹅防伪标识者均属未经授权之非法版本。

©中南博集天卷文化传媒有限公司。本书版权受法律保护。未经版权利人许可，任何人不得以任何方式使用本书包括正文、插图、封面、版式等任何部分内容，违者将受到法律制裁。

著作权合同登记号：字18-2023-258

图书在版编目（CIP）数据

逃跑的赛马 ：汉英对照 /（美）罗恩·罗伊著 ；
（美）约翰·史蒂文·格尼绘 ；高琼译. -- 长沙 ：湖南少年儿童出版社，2024.10. --（A to Z神秘案件）.
ISBN 978-7-5562-7818-3

Ⅰ. H319.4

中国国家版本馆CIP数据核字第2024VP8893号

A TO Z SHENMI ANJIAN TAOPAO DE SAIMA

A to Z神秘案件 逃跑的赛马

[美] 罗恩·罗伊 著　　[美] 约翰·史蒂文·格尼 绘　　高琼 译

责任编辑：唐凌　李炜	策划出品：李炜　张苗苗　文赛峰
策划编辑：文赛峰	特约编辑：张晓璐
营销编辑：付佳　杨朔　周晓茜	封面设计：霍雨佳
版权支持：王媛媛	版式设计：马睿君
插图上色：河北传图文化	内文排版：李洁

出 版 人：刘星保
出　　版：湖南少年儿童出版社
地　　址：湖南省长沙市晚报大道89号
邮　　编：410016
电　　话：0731-82196320
常年法律顾问：湖南崇民律师事务所　柳成柱律师
经　　销：新华书店
开　　本：875 mm×1230 mm　1/32
字　　数：94千字
版　　次：2024年10月第1版
书　　号：ISBN 978-7-5562-7818-3
印　　刷：三河市中晟雅豪印务有限公司
印　　张：5.375
印　　次：2024年10月第1次印刷
定　　价：280.00元（全10册）

若有质量问题，请致电质量监督电话：010-59096394　团购电话：010-59320018

A to Z 神秘案件

中英双语

第二辑

The School Skeleton
学校里的人体骨骼

COME HOME, MR. BONES

WE MISS YOU!

[美] 罗恩·罗伊 著
[美] 约翰·史蒂文·格尼 绘　王芬芬 译

湖南少年儿童出版社
HUNAN JUVENILE & CHILDREN'S PUBLISHING HOUSE
小博集 BOOKY KIDS
·长沙·

地图

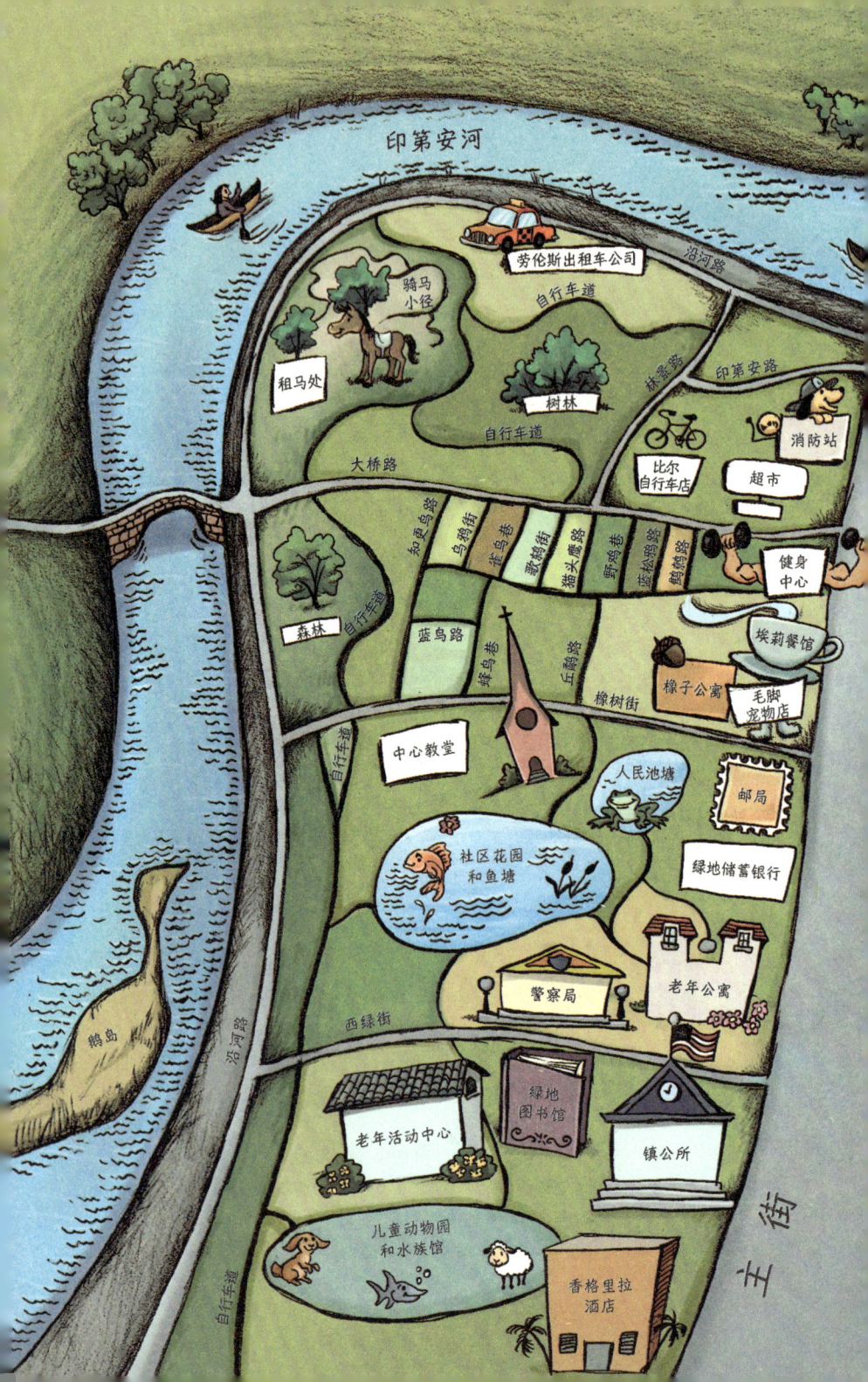

- 印第安河
- 劳伦斯出租车公司
- 沿河路
- 骑马小径
- 自行车道
- 租马处
- 树林
- 林荫路
- 印第安路
- 消防站
- 比尔自行车店
- 超市
- 大桥路
- 自行车道
- 知更鸟路
- 乌鸦巷
- 鹩哥街
- 猫头鹰路
- 野鸡巷
- 蓝松鸦路
- 鹌鹑路
- 健身中心
- 森林
- 自行车道
- 蓝鸟路
- 蜂鸟巷
- 丘鹬路
- 橡树街
- 埃莉餐馆
- 橡子公寓
- 毛脚宠物店
- 中心教堂
- 人民池塘
- 邮局
- 社区花园和鱼塘
- 绿地储蓄银行
- 老年公寓
- 警察局
- 鹅岛
- 沿河路
- 西绿街
- 老年活动中心
- 绿地图书馆
- 镇公所
- 自行车道
- 儿童动物园和水族馆
- 香格里拉酒店
- 主街

欢迎来到绿地镇
一起解开A to Z神秘案件
北
西
东
南
沿河路
码头
少女岛
租船处
罗思鱼饵店
绿地中学
牧场路
乔希家
鸭子步行道
老鹰巷
绿地小学
丁丁家
露丝家
林梢弯道
牧场路
狐狸小道
银环路
林荫街
鹌鹑路
音乐台
玫瑰园
宜人街
蓟花街
野花路
玫瑰街
中心公园
天鹅池
绿地高中
运动场
体育馆+游泳馆
黄杨木巷
霍华德理发店
角落书店
加油站
清水塘
奇妙温室
狗舍+兽医
东绿街
沿河路
镇网球场
儿童游泳池
镇游泳池
镇棒球场
去往蓝山镇

人物介绍

三人小组的成员，聪明勇敢，喜欢读推理小说，紧急关头总能保持头脑冷静。喜欢在做事之前好好思考！

丁丁

三人小组的成员，活泼机智，喜欢吃好吃的食物，常常有意想不到的点子。

乔希

三人小组的成员，活泼开朗，喜欢从头到脚穿同一种颜色的衣服，总是那个能找到大部分线索的人。

露丝

肖特基小姐

学校医务室的护士，喜欢开玩笑。认真细心，同时也非常关心孩子们。

尼特先生

学校的门卫，白发，高个子，经常出现在学校各处干活，曾被三人组怀疑是偷走骷髅的人。

迪奥达托先生

一年级的老师，高个子，配合孩子们调查骷髅被盗事件。

校长,非常有童心,关爱学生,希望尽自己所能,给孩子们的童年增加一些乐趣。

狄龙先生

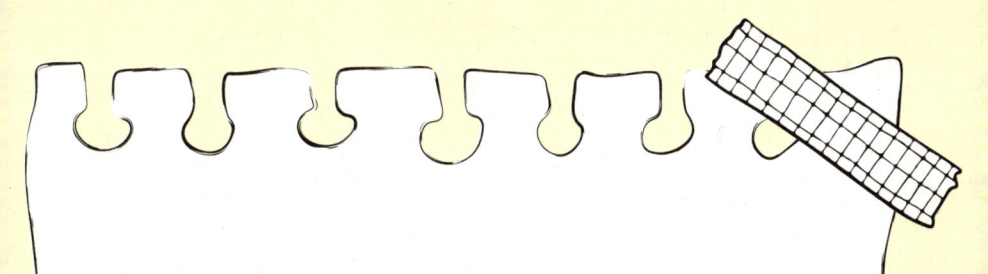

字母 S 代表 shock，震惊……

丁丁盯着空空的角落。他记得学校的骷髅一直放在那里。肖特基小姐会拿着骷髅到每个教室，给孩子们讲解吃蔬菜喝牛奶如何强壮骨骼。

节假日，她经常给骷髅先生穿上节日盛装。

丁丁看到现在角落里只有一条红围巾挂在钩子上。"它不在那儿。"丁丁说。

肖特基小姐转身。"可别跟我这个学校护士开玩笑哟！"她笑着对丁丁说。

"我没开玩笑。"丁丁指着空空的角落说，"您看。"

肖特基小姐一看，惊讶地张大了嘴巴。"完了，我有的忙了。"她说，"它不见了！"

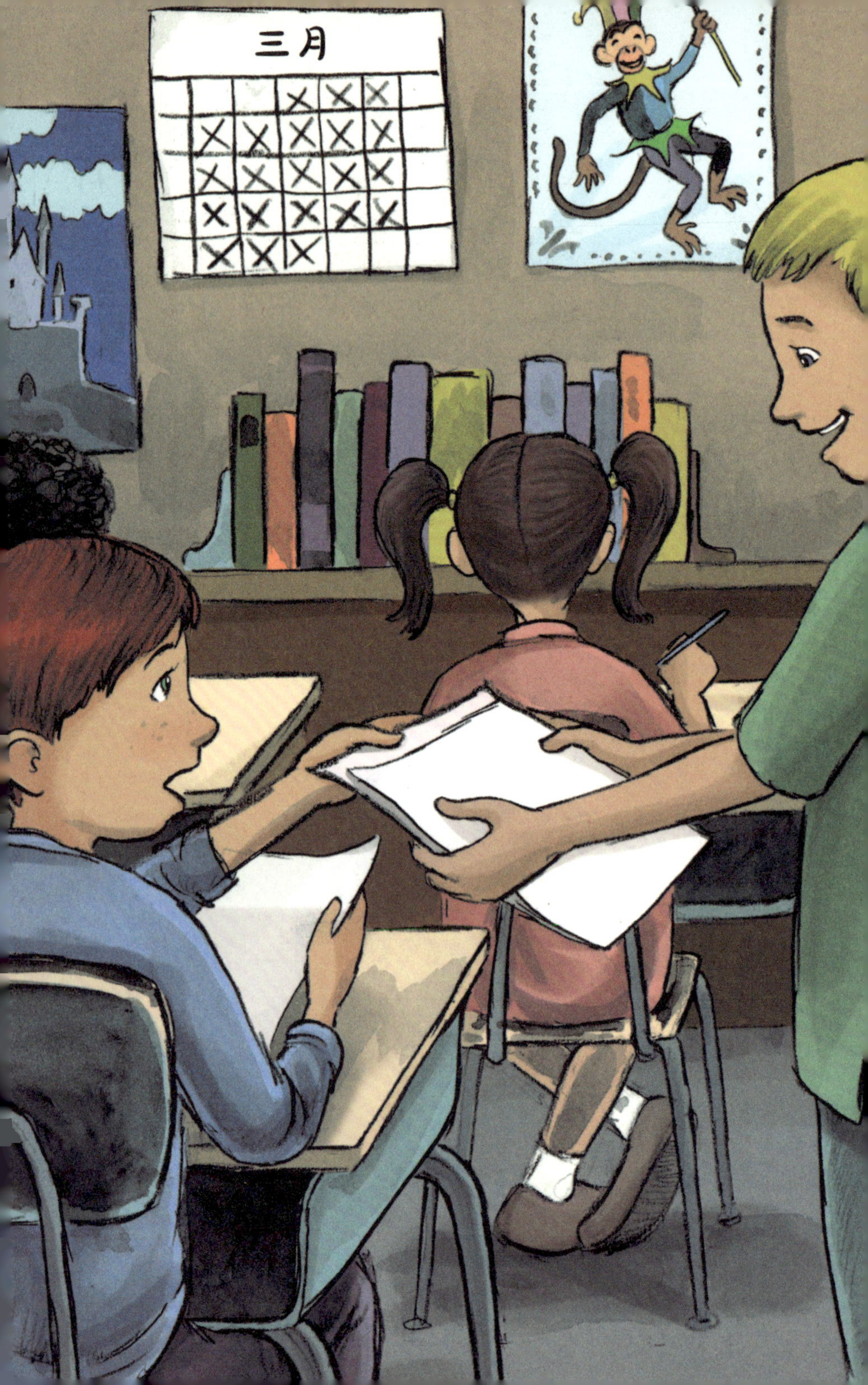
三月

第一章

"丁丁,你可以把数学试卷发给同学们吗?"伊格尔夫人问。

"噢,天哪,数学考试。"乔希嘀咕。

伊格尔夫人笑了。"是的,乔希。每周一上午十点,我们都要进行一场数学考试。"她说,"好了,我希望你们认真答题,积极思考,奋笔疾书!"

孩子们在课桌里找笔。随即一些人在削笔刀旁排队。

丁丁喜欢他的老师和教室。教室里一眼望去有很多书,墙上贴着明亮的海报,还有从窗外倾泻进来的阳光。伊格尔夫人将一块地垫和几个大靠枕放在了图书角,那是这间教室里丁丁最爱的地方。

丁丁的全名是唐纳德·戴维·邓肯。刚学说话时,他只会说"丁丁"两个字,所以这就成了他的小名。

他走到放试卷的架子旁,拿了一沓试卷,发给其他三年级的同学。

丁丁走到朋友乔希的课桌旁时,乔希窃笑着低声说:

老师的宠物,老师的宠物,
丁丁生病了,要去看兽医。

乔希·平托又高又瘦。他喜欢让他的红色头发垂在长满雀斑的前额。

丁丁对乔希眨了眨眼,然后把一张试卷放在他的课桌上。

"我可以拿两张吗?"乔希问,从丁丁抱着的试卷中抽了一张。

学校里的人体骨骼

"哎哟!"丁丁大叫一声,盯着手指。他的手指被割了一道小口子,正在流血。

"怎么了?"伊格尔夫人一边朝丁丁走来,一边问。

"我被试卷割到了。"丁丁答。

"那一定很痛,"伊格尔夫人说,递给他一张餐巾纸,"最好去医务室,贴个创可贴。"

丁丁用餐巾纸压着伤口,朝门口走去。经过露丝的课桌时,她咧着嘴朝他笑。"赶紧回来考试哟!"她打趣道。

露丝·罗斯·哈撒韦住在林荫街丁丁家隔壁。她的黑色头发富有弹性,蓝色眼睛机灵敏捷。她总是从头到脚穿一个颜色,今天她选择的衣服的颜色是淡黄色。

"马上就回来。"丁丁说。他出了教室,往医务室走。白发、高个子的尼特先生是学校的门卫,他正在扫地。他的皮带上挂着一个金属的钥匙扣,扫地时钥匙碰撞发出叮当的声音。他朝丁丁挥了挥手。

丁丁给他看伤口。

"噢，那一定很痛。"尼特先生说。

丁丁经过了一排储物柜和公告栏。他的伤口刺痛，于是把餐巾纸压得更紧了些。

经过校长办公室时，校长秘书沃特斯夫人正坐在办公桌前。透过她身后的另一扇门，丁丁看到校长狄龙先生正在打电话。

沃特斯夫人对丁丁微笑。"你是来见狄龙先生的吗？"她问。

丁丁站在门口，举起受伤的手指。"我被纸割伤了。"他说。

沃特斯夫人摇头。"那一定很痛。"她说。

丁丁点头，赶紧走到隔壁的医务室。丁丁进去时，肖特基小姐正在看日历。

"竟然就快到三月底了，你信吗？"她问丁丁，"离暑假还有八十二天！"

丁丁举着手指。"哦，我被纸割伤了。"他说。

"噢，那一定很痛，"肖特基小姐说，"我得替你截肢。"丁丁惊讶地张大嘴巴，肖特基小姐哈哈大笑。丁丁也笑了。

"去后面，我用来'折磨'人的东西都在那

学校里的人体骨骼

儿。"护士说。她带着丁丁穿过医务室后面的门。

肖特基小姐指着房间中央的一张检查台。"请坐上去。"她说着,走到一个白色的壁橱前。

丁丁坐在检查台上,环顾四周。他闻到一股香味,还看见一扇关闭着的门,旁边的桌子上有一瓶花。

肖特基小姐回头说:"我这里有蝙蝠侠创可贴、神奇女侠创可贴和兔宝宝创可贴。你选一个,孩子。"

"请给我蝙蝠侠创可贴。"丁丁说。他盯着一

个角落，那里有一个钩子，之前一直挂着学校的骷髅。

"肖特基小姐，骷髅先生在哪儿？"

护士背对着丁丁。"它一直在角落里挂着啊。"

丁丁盯着空空的角落。他记得学校的骷髅一直放在那里。肖特基小姐会拿着骷髅到每个教室，给孩子们讲解吃蔬菜喝牛奶如何强壮骨骼。节假日，她经常给骷髅先生穿上节日盛装。

丁丁看到现在角落里只有一条红围巾挂在钩子上。"它不在那儿。"丁丁说。

肖特基小姐转身。"可别跟我这个学校护士开玩笑哟！"她笑着对丁丁说。

"我没开玩笑。"丁丁指着空空的角落说，"您看。"

肖特基小姐一看，惊讶地张大了嘴巴。"完了，我有的忙了。"她说，"它不见了！"

"也许有人借走了吧。"丁丁说。

"什么时候借的呢？"她说，"我七点三十分进来时，骷髅先生还在。我之所以知道，是因为我把围巾挂在了它上面。有人偷走了骷髅，麻烦

学校里的人体骨骼

大了!"

肖特基小姐直摇头。"先不管了,看下你的伤口。"她边说边拿掉餐巾纸。

大约五秒钟后,她清理完丁丁的手指,贴了一张创可贴。"赶紧回教室,我去告诉校长骷髅先生不见了。"肖特基小姐说。她抓起丁丁的手,塞了两块包装着的巧克力到他手里。

"谢谢。"他说。

"不用谢,"她答,"如果你告诉别人是我给你的巧克力,我可不会承认哟!"

她拍了拍丁丁的肩膀,和他一起走到过道。丁丁回教室的路上,一边欣赏着创可贴,一边吃掉了一块巧克力。

他进教室时,伊格尔夫人正背对着他。每个孩子都低着头在写试卷。

回座位经过露丝的课桌时,丁丁把另一块巧克力放在她桌上。"嘿,我呢?"乔希尖声说。

丁丁咧嘴一笑,坐到座位上。

第二章

"对不起,我把你割伤了。"上午休息时,乔希对丁丁说。三月的风还很凉,吹得丁丁双眼湿润。天空漂浮着灰色的云朵,一些雪堆还未融化。

"没事。"丁丁说。一个足球滚到脚边,他踢回给一群小孩。

"还痛吗?"露丝问。她的帽子和围巾跟身上其他的黄色服饰非常搭配。

"不痛。"丁丁答道。他想起了肖特基小姐办公室的事。"你们知道吗?骷髅先生不见了!"

"骷髅?"乔希说。

学校里的人体骨骼

丁丁点头。"我去贴创可贴时,发现骷髅不见了,"他说,"肖特基小姐都不知道它失踪了。"

"被人偷了吧?"露丝说。她打开丁丁给她的巧克力。

"干吗要偷一个骷髅?"乔希说,他盯着露丝手里的巧克力。"分我一点好吗?"他问。

露丝把巧克力掰成两半,给了乔希一块。

丁丁耸肩。"肖特基小姐最后看见骷髅是早上七点三十分。"他说。

这时他们听见口哨声。大家排成一队,进了教室。

伊格尔夫人正等在门口。"一会儿去体育馆,"她对全班同学说,"狄龙先生要宣告事情。"

在老师们的带领下,三、四、五年级的学生排着队来到体育馆。幼儿园和一、二年级的学生已经一排排地坐在地上了。狄龙先生站在篮球筐下面。

大孩子们也坐好后,狄龙先生面带微笑。"上午好,孩子们!"他说,"我要宣告一个不好的消息,"他接着说,"今天早些时候,学校的骷髅从医务室不翼而飞了。"

大家窃窃私语。一个声音低沉的五年级男孩说:"谁偷了骷髅?僵尸吗?"他的伙伴们哈哈大笑,老师给他使了个眼色。

"谁有骷髅失踪的消息?"狄龙先生接着说,"请举手。"

没人举手。

"好吧,我们似乎碰到了一个真正的谜团。"狄龙先生说。他对坐在地上看着他的几百个孩子微笑。"我需要你们帮忙解开谜团,所以我打算给予奖励,找到骷髅先生的班级将获得哈特福特新水族馆的免费门票。"

"噢吔!"很多孩子激动地大喊。

露丝转向丁丁和乔西。"我一直叫爸爸妈妈带我去呢!"她说。

"我也是。"丁丁说,"水族馆里有一条白鲸宝宝!"

"现在解散。"狄龙先生说,"祝你们今天过得愉快并有好运气,能解开骷髅失踪的谜团!"

孩子们起身,在各自的老师身边集合,离开

学校里的人体骨骼

体育馆。丁丁听见周围的同学们都在议论失踪的骷髅。一个小男孩低声说:"也许骷髅复活走掉了!"

"如果弄清楚谁需要骷髅,"丁丁说,"就知道谁拿走了。"

丁丁、乔希和露丝跟随伊格尔夫人回教室时,一路想着这件事。

经过正在擦玻璃的尼特先生。他微笑地朝他们招手。

"可能是他拿走了,"乔希低声说,"那个钥匙圈上很可能有学校所有房间的钥匙。"

"乔希,尼特先生拿走骷髅干吗?"露丝问。

"她说得对,"丁丁说,"照你这么说,音乐老师阿丽亚小姐或美术老师洛夫先生都有嫌疑。"

"好吧,反正有人拿了。"乔希说。

露丝摇头。"不一定就是大人吧?"她说,"也可能是五年级的人偷走了骷髅先生。记得吗?有一次他们从一年级教室里拿走了纸板鲸鱼,将它挂在了旗杆上。"

"是的,太酷了。"乔希说。

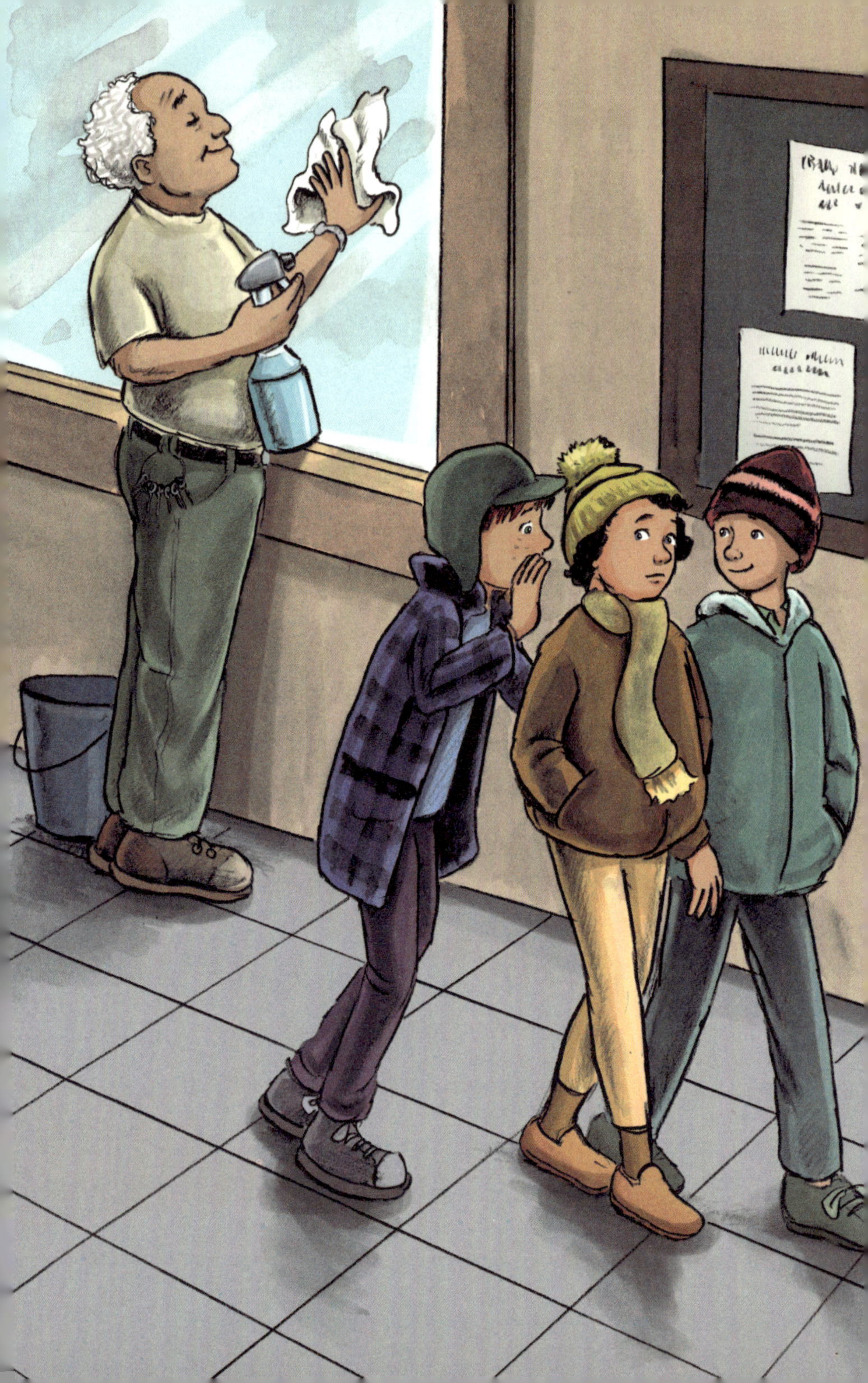

学校里的人体骨骼

回到教室,伊格尔夫人要孩子们拿出作文本。"快到午餐时间了,不如我们写一个故事吧?"她说。

"写什么呢?"博比问。

伊格尔夫人俏皮地微笑。"写失踪的学校骷髅!"她说。

第三章

"你的故事题目是什么?"两人站在储物柜旁,乔希问丁丁。下午三点,正是大家放学回家的时间。

丁丁边穿夹克衫边咧嘴笑。"题目是《乔希偷学校骷髅,将永被监禁》。"丁丁说。

"哈哈哈。"乔希回应。

"我的故事叫《骷髅的咒语》,"露丝说,"骷髅先生给所有红头发的男孩子施咒语。"

"你俩真是诙谐有趣。"三人朝出口走时,乔希说。肖特基小姐从办公室探出头,大声叫丁

学校里的人体骨骼

丁:"你的手指怎么样了?"

"好了,谢谢。"丁丁边转动手指边回答。

"那就好,进来,我给你两张创可贴带回家。"

"你还是个小宝宝呢。"三人挤进肖特基小姐的办公室时,乔希轻声说。

"他就是忌妒你的蝙蝠侠创可贴。"露丝说。

"呵呵,"乔希说,"蝙蝠侠都过时了,现在蜘蛛侠才是学校里最火的。"

孩子们跟着肖特基小姐来到后面的房间。丁丁拿创可贴时,乔希和露丝察看了平时挂骷髅先生的角落。

"看,灰尘里有个鞋印!"露丝说。

肖特基小姐和丁丁过去看。

"看起来像运动鞋的,"丁丁说,"看见锯齿形纹路了吗?"

"这是左脚。"乔希认出来了。

"这是成人的尺寸。"露丝说。

"可能是小偷把骷髅先生从钩子上取下来时,留下了这个鞋印。"丁丁说。

"有可能——反正不是我的鞋印。"肖特基小

姐抬起左脚说。她的白色护士鞋更短，鞋底的纹路也不一样。

"今天早上有老师来过这儿吗？"露丝问肖特基小姐。

学校里的人体骨骼

"据我所知没有。"护士答,"到这儿后,我去了教师休息室泡咖啡。八点回到这儿,但我压根没有注意看骷髅先生。"

"所以拿走骷髅先生的人是在七点三十到八点之间动手的,对吧?"乔希问。

肖特基小姐摇头。"不对。整个上午我进进出出,去了一、二年级的教室。十点丁丁来包扎伤口,在这之前任何人都有可能偷走骷髅先生。"

这时传来一声轻柔的敲门声。"抱歉打扰,请问我现在可以打扫这个房间吗?"有人说。

是拿着扫把的尼特先生。

"你好,汤姆,快进来。"肖特基小姐说。

"我先把这个鞋印画下来,您再扫地好吗?"乔希问尼特先生。

"当然可以,我先扫前面的办公室。"尼特先生说。

"我们应该量一下长度。"露丝说。

肖特基小姐给了乔希一张纸和一支笔,给了露丝一把尺子。

乔希很快就画好了鞋印。

25

A to Z 神秘案件

"务必把锯齿形纹路画下来。"丁丁说,他站在乔希身后看。

露丝量好了鞋印。"正好十一英寸[1]长。"她说。乔希在画好的鞋印旁写上十一英寸。

"只要找到穿这个鞋码的人,"乔希说,"就能找到骷髅先生,赢得水族馆门票了。"

"但是很多老师都穿运动鞋,"露丝说,"怎么找到这个人呢?"

"我知道可以问谁,"丁丁说,"问沃特斯夫人。所有老师取邮件都要经过她的办公桌,也许她会注意老师们穿的鞋。"

"赶紧去,再晚她就回家了。"露丝说。

肖特基小姐打开文件柜旁的小门。"从这儿去校长办公室更近。"她说。

孩子们穿过小门,沃特斯夫人果然还在办公桌旁。她盯着自己敞开的钱包。

"你们好啊,孩子们,"她一边说,一边合上钱包放进抽屉,"你们怎么还在这儿?"

---

1. 英寸:英美制长度单位。1英寸=2.54厘米。11英寸约为28厘米。——编者

学校里的人体骨骼

"我们想找到骷髅先生。"露丝说。

"我们在原来挂骷髅先生的位置的地板上找到一个鞋印,"丁丁说,"是运动鞋的。"

"我们认为是偷走骷髅先生的人留下的鞋印。"乔希说,"如果能找到这个小偷,我们班就能赢得门票!"

"只有一个鞋印吗?可能你们得找一条腿的小偷。"沃特斯夫人眨巴着眼睛说。

乔希咯咯地笑,把画了鞋印的纸放在办公桌上。"您知道谁穿这种鞋吗?"他问。

这时小门又开了。系着红围巾的肖特基小姐探出脑袋。

"大家再见!"肖特基小姐说,"孩子们,享受你们寻找骷髅的经历吧。"

"再见,克莱尔。"沃特斯夫人说。

门关上了。

沃特斯夫人仔细看了看乔希画的鞋印,摇了摇头。"我平常只留意老师们穿的衣服,"她说,"从来没有看过他们的鞋底。"

她用手指摸着锯齿形纹路。"这种图案看着

27

眼熟，我觉得一定在哪儿见过。"

她笑着说："回家的路上我再想想。"

沃特斯夫人瞥了一眼时间，起身。"我得走了，"她说着，朝壁橱走去。但她拉壁橱门时，门却纹丝不动。

于是她又回到办公桌前，从抽屉里拿出钱包和毛衣。"我先是丢了爽身粉，"她说，"现在又丢了脑子！"

这时狄龙先生站在他的办公室门口。"你们好啊，孩子们。还在这儿？"

丁丁告诉狄龙先生，他们在肖特基小姐的检查室发现了鞋印，并给他看画下来的鞋印。

"我们认为小偷穿的是这种运动鞋。"露丝说。

"如此看来，可以把我排除在外了。"狄龙先生说。他抬起一只脚，给孩子们看他那锃亮的流苏乐福鞋[1]，鞋底光滑。

"我也一样。"沃特斯夫人说。她抬起一只小小的高跟鞋。"那个鞋印有我的脚两倍长！"

1.乐福鞋：俗称"船鞋"，是一种低帮的、可以一脚蹬的浅口便鞋。——编者

第四章

孩子们步行回家，乔希看着自己画的左鞋印，问道："我们怎么找到穿这种运动鞋的人呢？"

"也可能是个女人。"露丝说。

乔希转身，咧着嘴笑。"会不会是伊格尔夫人？"他说，"也许是她偷了骷髅先生。"

露丝哈哈大笑。"不可能，她的脚看起来和我妈妈的一样小，"她说，"我妈妈穿六码的鞋。"

"去我家，咱们把学校所有的成年人列个名单，"丁丁建议，"就能想出办法检查他们的鞋子了。"

"为何不去你家吃点东西呢?"乔希问,"吃点火鸡三明治和上面有香草冰激凌的苹果派如何?"

"要不要来点豚鼠的食物?"丁丁说。

丁丁在厨房里找到了一盘饼干和妈妈留下的一张字条,上面写着她外出买东西了。孩子们拿着饼干和乔希的画来到丁丁房间。

丁丁给了露丝一张便笺。

露丝写的时候,丁丁在爸爸的壁橱里找到一双运动鞋。鞋底的一个小圈里面印着"十码"。然后他拿尺子量了量运动鞋,鞋刚好是十一英寸长,和他们在肖特基小姐办公室发现的鞋印一样长。

"伙伴们,我觉得偷骷髅的人穿十码的鞋。"他说。

"那很多男老师都穿这个码的鞋啊。"乔希说。

露丝把名单给他们看。"我列了十三个人。"她说。

"算上狄龙先生和尼特先生了吗?"丁丁问。

露丝点头。"算上了。在学校工作的所有成年人都算上了。"

学校里的人体骨骼

"我们可以画掉五个名字,"乔希说,"伊格尔夫人、沃特斯夫人和肖特基小姐都是小脚。狄龙先生今天穿的乐福鞋。"

"还有一个是谁呢?"丁丁问。

"门卫尼特先生啊。"乔希说。

"为什么把他画掉?"露丝问,"他可是穿的运动鞋。"

乔希笑了。"但他穿的运动鞋是我见过的最大的,起码十三码!"

露丝在乔希刚提到的五个人名前画上了×。

丁丁看着剩下的八个名字。"四个女性和四个男性,"他说道,同时扔了一块饼干到豚鼠的笼子里,"你们认为偷骷髅的人是其中一个吗?"

"有一个办法,"乔希说,"拿他们的鞋子跟我画的鞋印做对比。"

"去哪儿拿他们的鞋子呢?"丁丁问。

"直接说我们找到了鞋印,然后问是否可以量他们的脚长,看他们的鞋底。"

"有一个问题,"露丝说,"假如某位老师真的拿走了骷髅,他不会同意咱们量他的脚!"

31

"那这位老师就有嫌疑啊。"乔希说。

"但如果两位老师不同意呢?"丁丁问,"我们还是无法知道是谁偷的。"

"但至少把范围缩小到了两个人,"露丝说,"然后我们再继续想办法。"

"最好快点做决定,"乔希说,"学校的每个孩子都想赢得水族馆的门票。"

"但只有我们发现了鞋印,"露丝说,"具有领先优势。"

"领先不了多久,"乔希说,"肖特基小姐和尼特先生也看见了鞋印。况且我把画下的鞋印拿给沃特斯夫人和狄龙先生看了。过不了多久,全校都会知道的。"

"好吧,那就明天跟这八位老师说。"丁丁说。

"我们可以在他们的邮箱里放一封信。"露丝建议。

"好主意!"丁丁说。他坐在电脑前面,乔希和露丝给他出主意。下面是信件内容:

尊敬的_____：

　　我们有骷髅失踪案的线索。请问今天能和您聊一聊吗？请选择同意_____或不同意_____，并将回信放到伊格尔夫人的邮箱里。

　　谢谢！

签名：_____

丁丁·邓肯

乔希·平托

露丝·罗斯·哈撒韦

　　丁丁复印了八份。根据露丝列的名单，孩子们给这八位老师各准备了一封信。

　　"这方法肯定有用，"写完信后，丁丁说，

"明天上午请沃特斯夫人把这些信放进老师们的邮箱里。"

"到了下午,咱们班就可以得到水族馆的门票了。"乔希咧着嘴对朋友们笑着说。

"乔希,别高兴得太早。"露丝说。

"为什么?如果我们找到了符合那个鞋印的鞋,就能找到拿走骷髅先生的人了,这样不就赢得了门票吗?"

露丝摇头。"不对。我们要找到骷髅先生,才能赢得门票。"她说,"我们四处去量人们的脚长时,其他孩子可能已经找到骷髅先生了!"

第五章

第二天早上,三人在学校门口集合,此时第一辆校车还未到校。教师停车区只有两三辆车。

"希望沃特斯夫人今天不会来得太晚,"走进学校时,乔希说,"必须在老师们进校前把这些信放进邮箱里。"

他们加快脚步,沿着安静的过道来到校长办公室。沃特斯夫人正在脱外套。

"狄龙先生还没来呢。"孩子们进来时,她说。

"我们是来找您的。"丁丁说。

"哦，那好啊！"沃特斯夫人说，翻动着手里的日历。"天哪，三月份怎么就过完了啊！好了，孩子们，需要我帮忙吗？"

丁丁、乔希和露丝说明来意。

"你们真的认为是某位老师拿走了骷髅？"她问道。

"不确定，"丁丁答，"但那个鞋印看起来像成年人的。您可以帮忙把这些信放到那几位老师的邮箱里吗？"

他把打印出来的八封信递给沃特斯夫人。她看完笑了。

"我当然愿意，"她说，"祝你们好运，找到骷髅先生。解开这个谜团，狄龙先生会很开心的！"

沃特斯夫人起身，走到教师们的邮箱旁边，把八封信投进不同的邮箱。

孩子们向她道谢告别。这时上课铃响起，学生们从前门冲进来。

他们三人走进教室，看见伊格尔夫人在讲台上。"哎呀，哎呀，看看这几位积极分子！"她说。

学校里的人体骨骼

三个孩子再次解释,他们发现了一个鞋印,并且写好了八封信,计划好了如何找出偷骷髅的人。他们还把乔希画的鞋印给伊格尔夫人看了。

"你们打算问每一位老师是否愿意让你们测量脚长吗?"伊格尔夫人笑着问。

"是的,因为那个鞋印是我们发现的唯一线索。"露丝说。

"希望我们班赢得门票。"乔希说。

伊格尔夫人笑了。"好的,只要八位老师同意,你们三个等会儿就可以离开教室。"她说。

早上的时间过得很慢。丁丁不停地看时钟,乔希不停地叹气,在课桌前坐立不安。

终于,上数学课时,一位五年级学生来到教室,递给伊格尔夫人一沓纸。

她翻看这沓纸,把丁丁叫到讲台。"这些是回信,"她轻声说,"八位老师都回复同意。现在去吧,祝你们好运!"

丁丁、乔希和露丝安静地出了教室。他们带了八张画纸、一把尺子、乔希画的鞋印和露丝列的教师名单。

"伙伴们，我刚刚想到了一个问题，"露丝在走廊上说，"昨天留下鞋印的人，今天可能换了一双鞋。"

"说得对，"丁丁说，"凡是这个鞋码的人，我们都要问一下今天和昨天是否穿的同一双鞋。"

他们沿着走廊走。一间教室门口，有人挂了一块牌。上面写着：回家吧，骷髅先生。我们想你了！这行字间还画了一个骷髅。

戴骷髅面具的三个女孩在走廊上跑来跑去。"骷髅先生，你在哪儿？"一个女孩说。另外两个女孩哈哈大笑。

五年级的教室外面，一个纸骷髅从天花板上垂下来。

"整个学校都在找丢失的骷髅，"乔希低声说，"我们必须最先找到！"

"咱们最好快点，"露丝说，"也许其他人还不知道现场留下的鞋印。"

名单上第一位是学前班老师阿卢比基小姐。他们先给她看了乔希画的鞋印，再询问了她能否描一下她的左脚。

学校里的人体骨骼

"当然可以，"阿卢比基小姐笑着说，"但我告诉你们，那个鞋印比我的鞋大很多。"

乔希在纸上描下老师鞋的轮廓，孩子们咯咯地笑。然后乔希把纸拿到过道上跟自己画的鞋印对比。

"肯定不是她，"他说，"阿卢比基小姐的鞋才七英寸长。"

露丝在名单上阿卢比基小姐的名字前画了一个大大的×。并在名字旁边写上：太小。

他们来到隔壁教室，看了一眼一年级的迪奥达托先生。这位高个子老师正在黑板上写：谁偷了学校的骷髅？

丁丁敲门，迪奥达托先生抬起头。"同学们，有访客来了。"他笑着说。

乔希在纸上描迪奥达托先生的运动鞋时，教室里的学生都围过来看。

丁丁、乔希和露丝向迪奥达托先生道谢后便走了。乔希在过道上对比着两个鞋印。迪奥达托先生的运动鞋至少有十三英寸长。鞋底的纹路是小方格，不是锯齿形。

A to Z 神秘案件

"画掉他的名字。"丁丁说。露丝在迪奥达托先生的名字前画上 ×，并写上：太大。

学校里的人体骨骼

"还有六个人要查验。"乔希说,他盯着露丝的名单,"假如这六个人都不是,我们该怎么办呢?"

"肯定是这个名单上的某个人,"丁丁说,"陌生人怎么会潜入学校,带走骷髅呢?"

孩子们挨个把老师们的鞋描到纸上,量尺寸,再与乔希画的鞋印对比。露丝挨个画掉这些老师的名字。

只剩下一位老师还未查验,露丝的名单现在是这样的:

× 幼儿园——阿卢比基小姐——太小

× 一年级——迪奥达托先生——太大

× 二年级——科伦佩特小姐——太小

× 三年级——伊格尔夫人——太小

× 四年级——夸特罗先生——星期一未到校

× 五年级——戈尔登夫人——太小

× 校长——狄龙先生——星期一穿的乐福鞋

× 秘书——沃特斯夫人——太小

× 护士——肖特基小姐——太小

× 美术老师——洛夫先生——太大

×音乐老师——阿丽亚小姐——太小

×门卫——尼特先生——实在太大

体育老师——帕尔默先生

"这些老师都不可能踩出那个鞋印。"露丝说。

"最后一个名字是谁?"丁丁问。

"体育老师帕尔默先生。"她答。

乔希食指中指交叉,祈求好运。"也许就是他!"他说。

他们发现帕尔默先生正坐在办公桌前,孩子们进来时,他微笑着。

"我看了你们的信。"他说。

"谢谢您同意见我们,"丁丁说,"请问能量一下您的鞋子吗?"

帕尔默先生笑了。"当然可以。但我保证昨天上午没有偷骷髅。因为那时我在医院急诊室。"

他站起来伸出左脚。他的左脚打了石膏。"昨天上车时,我踩到冰摔了一跤。"他说。

他指着角落的一副拐杖。"我连午餐都拿不了,更别提骷髅了!"

第六章

"希望您的脚尽快康复。"丁丁说。

"谢谢,希望你们找到骷髅。"帕尔默先生说道。

孩子们出了办公室,朝自己的教室走。

"我们一定有什么地方弄错了,"乔希说,"这些人中一定有一个是罪犯。"

"罪犯?"丁丁说。

乔希笑了。"是啊,就是偷骷髅的人。"

"如果不是这份名单上的人,那会是谁呢?"露丝问,"那个鞋印不可能是变魔法变出

来的啊。"

"我在想这个鞋印会不会是用来糊弄人的。"丁丁说。

"什么意思?"乔希问。

"我曾看过一个故事,讲的是几个小孩造出假的熊脚印糊弄父母,"丁丁说,"他们把几双直筒袜卷起来,缠在一个旧耙子上。然后围着自家房子，在雪地里造出'熊'脚印。"

"但是偷骷髅的人为何要留下一个假鞋印呢？"露丝问。

丁丁耸肩。"到底为什么要偷走学校的骷髅呢？"

"哼，这个小偷太坏了，"乔希咕哝着，"跟一群单纯的小孩耍花招，真不是好人！"

丁丁和露丝哈哈大笑。快到教室时，他们还在咯咯地笑。

"等一下，我把这张画放起来。"乔希说。

"停！"乔希朝储物柜走时，露丝大声喊，"别动！"

"怎么了？"乔希倒抽了一口气，一只手捂着胸口，"我差点被你吓出心脏病！"

"看，你差点就踩到了！"露丝指着地上的一圈白色粉末。圆圈中间有一个鞋印。

这个鞋印看着有点眼熟。

露丝一把从乔希手中拿过他画的鞋印，蹲在新鞋印旁边。"伙伴们，对比一下。"她说。

丁丁和乔希弯腰仔细看。这是一个有锯齿形纹路的左脚鞋印。露丝把乔希画的鞋印放在地上，两个鞋印看起来一模一样。

"噢，天哪！"乔希激动地说，"骷髅盗贼在这儿！"

这时伊格尔夫人从教室门探出脑袋。"怎么了？"她问。

露丝指着地上的鞋印。"伊格尔夫人您看。"

"小偷回来了！"乔希说。

"他径直走向了你的储物柜，"丁丁接着说，满脸坏笑，"僵尸就在你后面哟！"

"不可能！"乔希争辩，"看，鞋印在你和我的储物柜之间呢。"

"也许他偷了你俩中一个人柜子里的东西呢。"露丝说。

学校里的人体骨骼

伊格尔夫人蹲下,用食指沾了一点白色粉末,放在鼻子边闻。"嗯,"她说,"闻起来像爽身粉。男孩子们,你们怎么不打开储物柜呢?"

"你先打开。"乔希对丁丁说。

"好啊,"丁丁说,"谁叫你是一个胆小鬼呢。"

"我不是。"

"你是。"

"好了,孩子们。"伊格尔夫人说。

丁丁拉开储物柜的门。他的夹克衫挂在钩子上。层板上的书摆放得井然有序。午餐袋放在书上面。

"没有少东西,"丁丁说,"轮到你了,乔希。"

"好嘞,"乔希说着,拉开储物柜门上的锁。他的夹克衫挂在钩子上。书本堆在层板上。书上面放着棕色的午餐袋。

但是午餐袋前面有一个白色纸团。

"这是什么?"乔希问,"不是我放在这儿的。"

丁丁前倾身子,小声说:"也许是小偷留下的字条!"

"哦,太好了。"乔希抓起纸团说,"嘿,里面有东西!"

乔希打开纸团时,一个金属物件掉到地上。

但是丁丁、乔希、露丝和老师都盯着乔希手里的纸。

纸上画着一个笑脸骷髅。骷髅前额中间还写了一个大大的"2"。

伊格尔夫人弯腰捡起掉在地上的东西。"这真是奇怪啊。"她手里拿着一把闪闪发亮的钥匙,说道。

第七章

丁丁、乔希、露丝和伊格尔夫人回到教室。

"现在又有一个谜团要解决,"伊格尔夫人对全班说,"乔希、丁丁和露丝,你们何不告诉同学们你们在做的事?"

三个孩子告诉大家,他们先是发现了一个鞋印,并给大家看了乔希描的鞋印。接着他们又描了老师们的鞋子轮廓并测量长度,试图找出是谁留下的鞋印。

乔希的画、露丝的名单和八只鞋子轮廓图都放在伊格尔夫人的讲台上。还有乔希储物柜里发

现的骷髅画以及钥匙。

"还有一件事,"伊格尔夫人说,"有人在乔希储物柜旁的地上撒了粉末,留下了另一个鞋印。"

她看着孩子们。"你们有什么看法?"

博比举手。"我认为是偷走骷髅的人把钥匙放在乔希储物柜里的。"他说。

"但是为什么呢?"露丝问,"我们又不知道这把钥匙是开什么锁的。"

伊格尔夫人拿起钥匙,走到教室门口。她把钥匙插进锁孔,试着锁门。

"不配套。"她说。她又用钥匙试了讲台抽屉。"也不配套。"

"我们可以用这把钥匙把学校里所有的锁都试一下。"弗兰基提议。

伊格尔夫人点头。"弗兰基,你的想法不错,但是学校里的门和桌子加起来有几十把锁呢。"

"这把钥匙会不会是开手提箱或者保险箱的呢?"丁丁问。

伊格尔夫人笑着对丁丁说:"好建议。"

"也许是某人家里的钥匙呢。"汤米说。

"你们的想法都很好,"伊格尔夫人说,"但是走遍绿地镇,去试每一把锁,这是不现实的。"

"我想不明白的是,为什么要这样做,"丁丁说,"明知道我们会发现,为什么还留下鞋印和钥匙呢?"

乔希举手。"还有,为什么小偷要把这些放到我的储物柜里?"他问。

"他也许不是故意的,"露丝说,"储物柜上没有写名字。小偷或许随手选了一个三年级的储物柜。"

"说得对,"伊格尔夫人说,"班上任何人都可能发现这个钥匙!"

大家面面相觑、窃窃私语。

伊格尔夫人把讲台上的所有证据堆放在一

起，连同钥匙，递给乔希。"现在我们要上课了。"她说。

丁丁、乔希和露丝放学回家时，风刮得更大了，天气更冷了。
"去我家吧，"露丝说，"我来做热巧克力。"
"有淡奶油吗？"乔希问。
"只有棉花糖。"露丝说。
"是又大又厚的棉花糖吗？"
"不是，乔希，又小又碎的棉花糖。"露丝答。
"我喜欢大的棉花糖。"乔希嘟囔着。

几分钟后，露丝打开家门，让他们进去。妈妈留了一张字条，说带弟弟纳特去看牙医了。

厨房里，露丝的猫咪泰格正躺在桌子上，沐浴在一缕阳光中。露丝赶走泰格，然后用微波炉做热巧克力。

丁丁和乔希坐在餐桌旁。乔希把钥匙和骷髅画放在泰格待过的有阳光的地方。

"我认为漏掉了什么没考虑到，"丁丁低头看着钥匙和画说，"小偷偷走了骷髅，留下一个鞋

学校里的人体骨骼

印。然后放了一把钥匙在你的储物柜里,还在地上撒了粉末,留下另一个鞋印。这是想给我们透露信息,但是什么信息呢?"

露丝拿来三个杯子和一袋棉花糖放在桌子上。

他们都把棉花糖扔进热巧克力里面。

"我想起一件事,"她说,"沃特斯夫人不是说她丢了爽身粉吗?"

"但我储物柜旁边的鞋印不是她留下的。"乔希说。

"我知道,"露丝说,"可能是有人偷了她的爽身粉,用来留下那个鞋印。也许小偷想让大家怀疑是沃特斯夫人拿走了骷髅。"

孩子们喝着热巧克力,思考着。

"这个人只有是能进入沃特斯夫人办公室的人,才能从桌子里拿走爽身粉。"丁丁最后说。

"比如狄龙先生!"露丝说。

"对,但是那两个鞋印都不是他的,"乔希说,"记得吗?他穿的是底部没有纹路的乐福鞋。"

"而且狄龙先生为何要偷东西,再嫁祸给秘书呢?"丁丁问,"这没道理啊!"

53

"我在想是否学校还有其他我们不知道的东西被偷了呢？"露丝说。

"嗯，那只有沃特斯夫人知道了，"丁丁说，"我们明天再跟她聊一聊。"

乔希拿起那张包钥匙的骷髅画。"你们觉得骷髅上写的'2'是什么意思？"他问，"学校没有两个骷髅，对吧？"

"高中和初中可能也有，"露丝说，"他们的骷髅也被偷了吗？"

"没有吧，不然早就听说了。"丁丁说。

"我不想住在一个僵尸四处偷骷髅的镇上。"乔希嘟囔着。

"无论如何，这把钥匙肯定有什么含义。"丁丁说。他把钥匙放在画里的骷髅嘴巴旁边。"快告诉我们，骷髅先生！"

"等等！"露丝大叫。她往上移动钥匙，移到离"2"几英寸远的地方。"这表示什么？"

乔希扔了一个棉花糖到杯子里。"表示'钥匙头'，"他说，"'钥匙脸'？'钥匙骨骼'？"

露丝摇头。她指着钥匙。"钥匙，"她说。

学校里的人体骨骼

接着她指着骷髅上的数字。"2。"然后指着骷髅的身子。"骷髅,"她说,"我认为这里的意思是'找到骷髅的钥匙[1]'!"

---

1. 骷髅的钥匙:英语中 2(two)的发音同 to,所以钥匙、2 和骷髅就可以组成一句话"找到骷髅的钥匙(key to skeleton)"。——编者

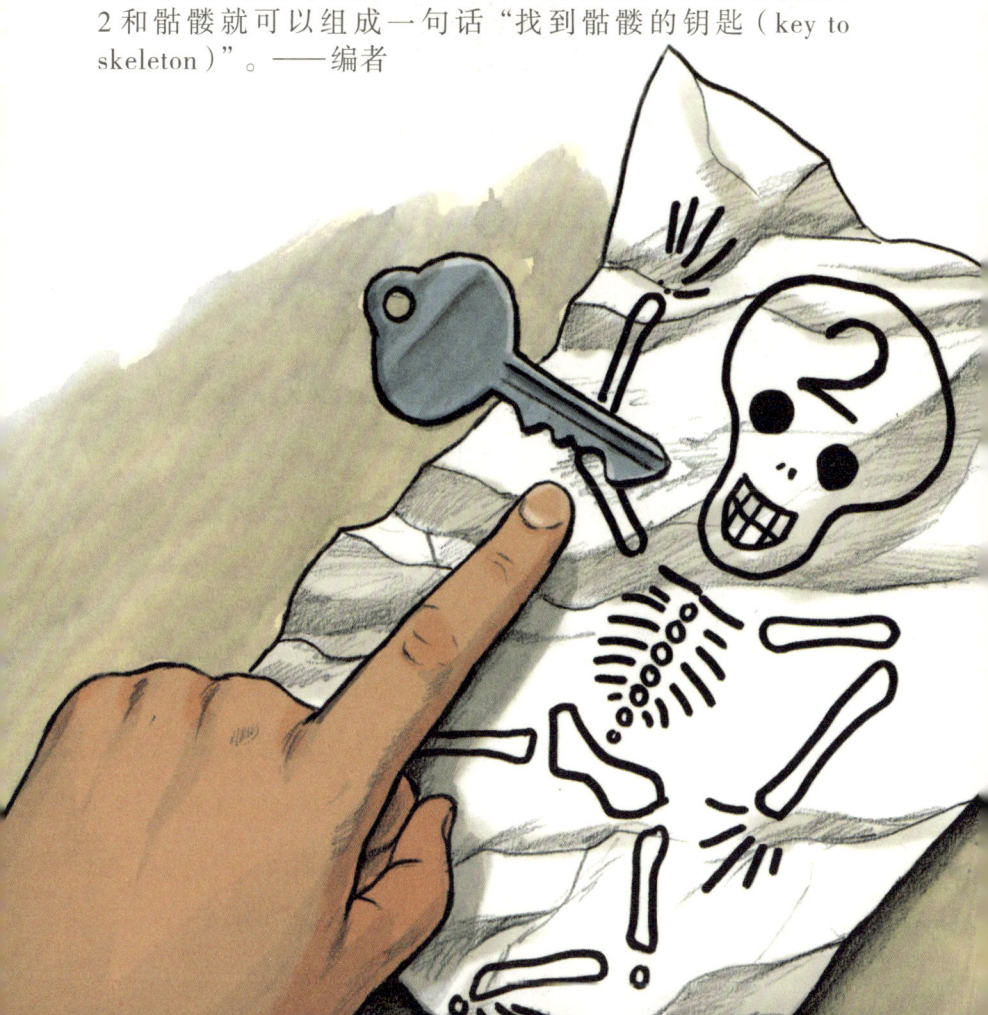

第八章

"我认为这是想告诉我们,这把钥匙可以打开藏骷髅的地方。"露丝接着说。

"但是在哪里呢?"乔希问,"这把钥匙甚至可能打开加利福尼亚的某把锁。"

"骷髅可能还在学校里面,"丁丁说,"大白天的谁能把它带出教学楼呢?"

"但大白天的谁又能把它藏在校园里面呢?"露丝问,"一定会被人发现的。"

"除非是肖特基小姐做的,"乔希说,"她总是拿着骷髅先生去各个班级。"

学校里的人体骨骼

丁丁摇头。"相信我,看见骷髅丢了的时候,她非常惊讶。"

"而且那个鞋印也不是她的。"露丝说。

孩子们盯着桌上的画和钥匙。

"为什么给我们一把钥匙?"乔希问。他吃得满嘴都是巧克力。"莫非这家伙想被抓住?"

"似乎他想让我们找到骷髅。"露丝说。

"好吧,至少还没有人找到骷髅,"丁丁说,"我们还有机会为班级赢得门票。"

露丝拿起钥匙,放在眼前看。"真奇怪。这把钥匙看起来是崭新的。"她说。

"你怎么知道?"丁丁问。

"上面没有划痕,"露丝说,"而且亮闪闪的。"她从口袋里掏出家里的钥匙,"看,我家的钥匙有很多小划痕,都是插在锁孔里磨出来的。但乔希的钥匙看起来像新配的。"

"那怎么找出这把钥匙是开什么锁的?"乔希问,他喝完了最后一点热巧克力。

"可以问尼特先生,"丁丁建议,"他有教学楼的所有钥匙。"

A to Z 神秘案件

"等等,是不是他把钥匙放进乔希的储物柜的?"露丝问。

"那意味着是他拿走了骷髅,"丁丁说,"但他的鞋很大,记得吗?"

"除非他的鞋印是假的,"乔希说,"就像那些弄出熊脚印的孩子一样。"

丁丁用骷髅画包好钥匙,递给乔希。"明天把这个给他看,"他说,"别弄丢了。钥匙可是最有用的线索!"

学校里的人体骨骼

第二天早上，飘着一些雪花，丁丁、乔希和露丝急匆匆地进了校园。

"从没听说过四月一号还下雪的。"乔希嘀咕着，他戴了一顶能罩住耳朵的绿色帽子。

尼特先生在教学楼的地下室有一间小办公室。孩子们在那儿找到了他，他坐在工作台前的凳子上，正在打开一个装订机。

"早上好，尼特先生。"丁丁说。

白发的尼特转身微笑。"早上好啊，孩子们。你们怎么来这儿了？逃学吗？"

乔希从口袋里掏出包好的钥匙。打开那幅画，拿出钥匙给尼特先生看。"您见过这样的钥匙吗？"他问。

尼特先生接过钥匙，将它放在工作台上的灯光下看。他仔细查看了钥匙的两面，然后摇头。"没见过。但我可以告诉你们这把钥匙是配的。在五金店用原配钥匙配的。"

"露丝，被你说对了！"乔希惊呼，"你真聪明。"

露丝笑而不言。

59

尼特先生从腰间取下钥匙圈，放在工作台上。他翻动钥匙，拿了几把跟乔希的对比。"看，原配钥匙上面有生产公司的名字。比如这把是耶鲁钥匙。"

他轻拍了一下乔希的钥匙。"但你的钥匙没有厂商,是配的。哪儿来的钥匙?"他问,把钥匙还给乔希。

"在我的储物柜里……"

这时一位五年级的学生咚咚咚地下楼梯来到地下室。他比丁丁高,有着深褐色的头发、调皮的黑眼睛。

"哦,你好啊,克里,"尼特先生说,"有什么事?"

"我在储物柜里发现了这个,不知您能否告诉我是开什么锁的。"克里说。他递给尼特先生一把亮闪闪的钥匙。

大家都盯着克里的钥匙。

"你还发现了一幅骷髅画吗?"露丝问。

克里点头。"是的,画纸包着钥匙。"

"另外你储物柜外面是不是还有一个鞋印?"丁丁问,"印在粉末上?"

克里疑惑地看着丁丁。"对啊。你怎么知道?"

"因为我的储物柜旁边也有,"乔希说,"我还在储物柜里发现了用这个包着的钥匙。"说完他把骷髅画给克里看。

克里把手伸进口袋,掏出一张皱巴巴的纸。两个男孩把画展平,放在尼特先生的工作台上。两幅画和两把钥匙一模一样。

"哎呀,你们认为这跟肖特基小姐消失的骷髅有关系吗?"尼特先生问。

"肯定有关系,"克里指着数字"2","我们班上的同学一下就弄明白了。钥匙和画的意思是'找到骷髅的钥匙'。我们要找到骷髅,获得新水族馆的门票!"

又有人咚咚咚地下楼。这次是两个二年级的女孩。她们手拉着手,看见四个高年级的孩子在这儿,有点不好意思。

"苏珊和简,对吧?"尼特先生笑着对两个小

学校里的人体骨骼

朋友说。

女孩们点头。苏珊轻轻推了一下简,简张开手。"科伦佩特小姐想问,您是否知道这把钥匙是开什么锁的。"她腼腆地说。

钥匙和克里及乔希手里的一样。

"你们肯定也是在储物柜里发现的钥匙,对吧?"尼特先生说。

简点头。"还有一张滑稽的骷髅画,额头上写了数字'2'!"

第九章

绿地小学没有食堂。所有学生都从家里带午餐。

丁丁、乔希和露丝拿出午餐袋,坐在有阳光的秋千上吃。很多孩子都出来吃午餐。

"金枪鱼的,"乔希闻着他的三明治说,"你们带了什么?"

露丝看了一眼塑料袋里面。"熏肠和芝士的。"她说。

丁丁的三明治是鸡蛋沙拉的。"谁想交换?"他问。

学校里的人体骨骼

"我要鸡蛋的。"露丝说。

"我要熏肠和芝士的。"乔希说。

"好,"丁丁说,"我要金枪鱼的。"

三个孩子交换了三明治,开始吃起来。

"学校里每个班级都有一个学生发现了一把钥匙和一幅画。"丁丁吞了一口三明治,说道。

"所以有六把钥匙、六幅画和六个鞋印。"乔希塞了满嘴的三明治说。

露丝摇头。"现在每个班都想赶在其他班前面,找到肖特基小姐的骷髅。"她叹气,"那大约有一百个学生呢!"

两个小男孩经过,找位子吃午餐。一个男孩拿着骷髅画。

"连幼儿园小朋友都参与进来了!"乔希大声说,用脚扬起一些沙子,"不公平。"

"我刚想到,"露丝说,"狄龙先生办公室有一扇门连着医务室。他可以趁肖特基小姐不在时,溜进去拿走骷髅。"

"对他而言,分分钟的事。"乔希说。

"伙伴们,我记得我们早就下了定论,狄龙先

65

生不是小偷,"丁丁说,"他当天没有穿运动鞋。"

"但是他可以轻而易举地拿走沃特斯夫人的爽身粉,"露丝提醒丁丁,"爽身粉、连着医务室的门……所有这些都指向狄龙先生。"

"但是校长为何要偷学校的骷髅呢?"丁丁反问,"他可是会奖励找到骷髅的人啊!"

乔希卷好自己的午餐袋。"我们再去见见沃特斯夫人。也许她想起了在哪儿见过锯齿形纹路的运动鞋鞋底。"

三个孩子冲进教学楼,直奔校长办公室。

"把午餐的东西先放下吧,"丁丁说,在储物柜前停下。他们打开储物柜门,把午餐袋放进去。

他们看见沃特斯夫人坐在办公桌前,前面摆了一杯茶。

孩子们进来时,她抬起头。"学校里真是邪门了,"她说,"一开始肖特基小姐的骷髅不见了,然后我的东西丢了。我的壁橱钥匙找了两天都没找到!接下来还会出什么事呢?"

"您找不到钥匙?"乔希问,手已经伸进了

学校里的人体骨骼

口袋。

"是的。我想把钱包和外套放进壁橱,但找不到钥匙。"沃特斯夫人说。

乔希拿出包着钥匙的骷髅画,拆开画,把钥匙放在沃特斯夫人的桌上。"是这把吗?"

沃特斯夫人拿起钥匙,仔细查看。"不是,不是我丢的钥匙。"

"是不是用您那把钥匙配的呢?"丁丁问。

"有可能。"沃特斯夫人看着丁丁,"为什么有人拿走我的钥匙去配一把呢?你在哪儿找到的钥匙,乔希?"

"在我的储物柜里,"他说,"和这个放在一起。"他给沃特斯夫人看骷髅画。

"一把钥匙和一幅骷髅画?"她说,"这是什么意思?"

"我们认为这把钥匙跟丢失的骷髅有关系,"露丝说,"所以骷髅可能在您的壁橱里!"

"我的壁橱!谁干的?"

沃特斯夫人起身,走到壁橱前面。丁丁、乔希和露丝跟着她。

A to Z 神秘案件

　　沃特斯夫人把钥匙插入锁孔，转动。壁橱门慢慢开了。

　　衣帽钩上挂着的正是学校的骷髅。骷髅先生正咧着嘴大笑。

　　"是骷髅先生！"露丝激动地尖叫。

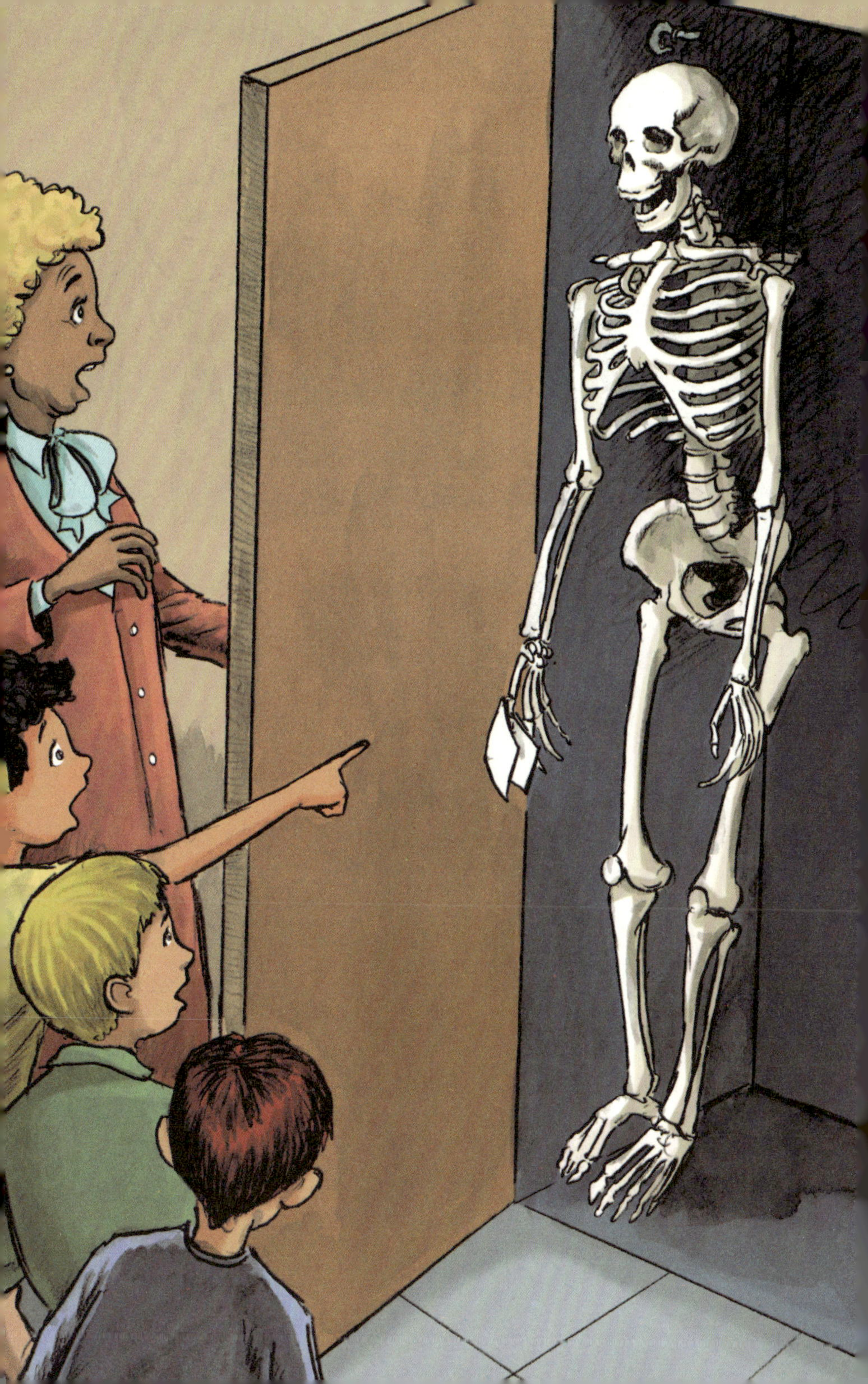

第十章

狄龙先生从办公室快步走出来。"怎么了?"

沃特斯夫人还没来得及回答,肖特基小姐冲进了这间小办公室。

"是谁在尖叫?有人受伤吗?"肖特基小姐大声问,先看了看三个孩子,"你们没事吧?"

"没事,您的朋友在这儿,肖特基小姐。"沃特斯夫人把壁橱门完全打开。

"啊,天哪!"肖特基小姐惊讶地说,"这是什么?"

她取下粘在骷髅手上的一张折叠的纸,大声

念道:"愚人节快乐!"

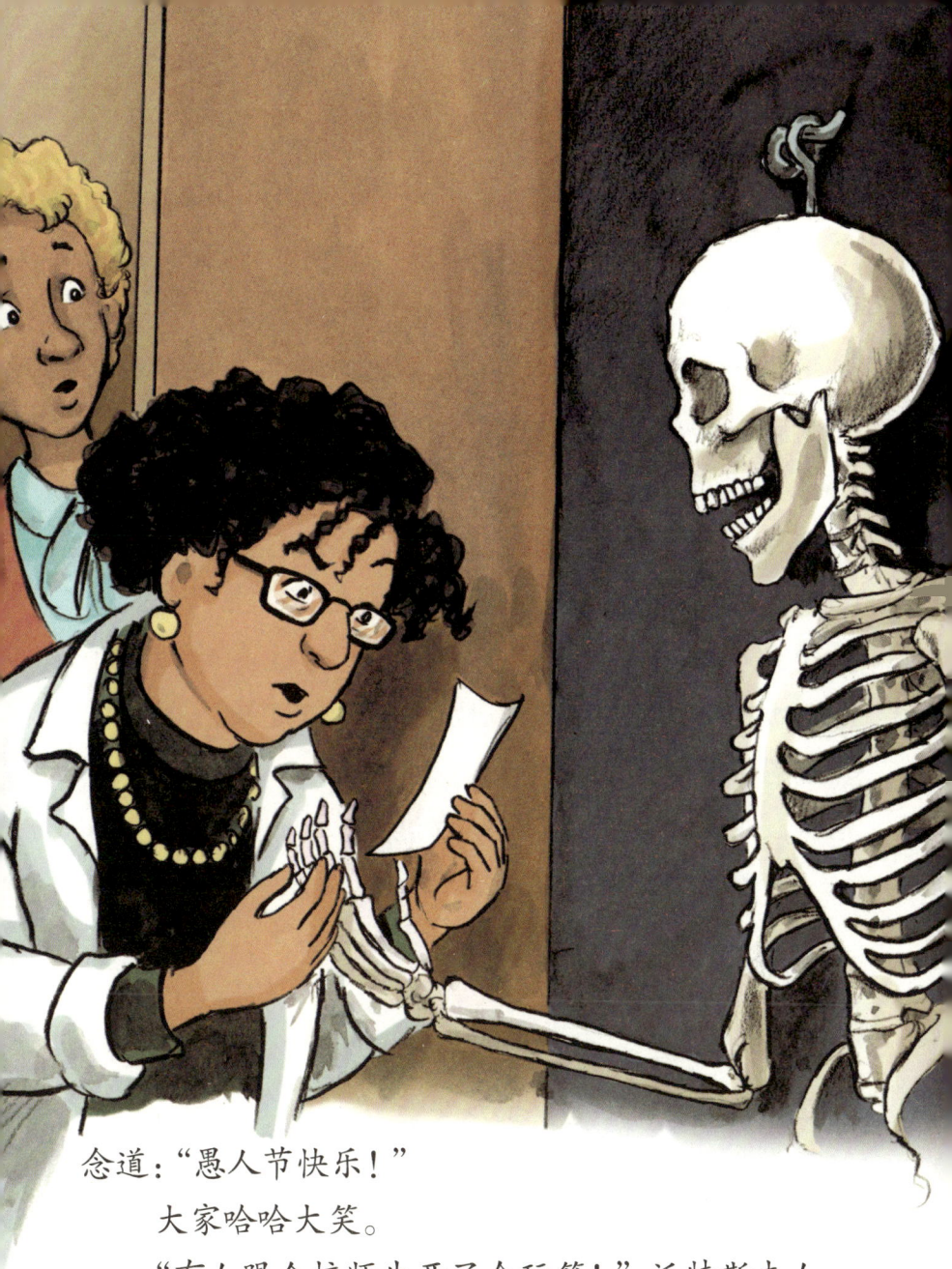

大家哈哈大笑。

"有人跟全校师生开了个玩笑!"沃特斯夫人说道。

A to Z 神秘案件

"好了,骷髅先生物归原主了。"肖特基小姐说,把骷髅从钩子上取下来。

"说声再见吧。"她挥舞着骷髅的手说,然后拿着骷髅回她办公室。

沃特斯夫人走到办公桌前,看着日历。"今天还真是愚人节,"她说,"我竟然完全忘记了。"

她拿着外套走到壁橱,挂在钩子上,然后弯腰从壁橱底部捡起什么东西。转过身时,她手里拿着一双运动鞋。她把鞋子翻过来,让大家看鞋底。

"锯齿形纹路!"乔希说。

"这就是那双人人谈论的运动鞋吗?"狄龙先生说,"怎么跑到你的壁橱里面去了,沃特斯夫人?"

沃特斯夫人盯着她的老板好一会儿,然后摇头。"我也不知道,狄龙先生。"

"呃,打扰一下,我知道是怎么回事。"丁丁说道。

狄龙先生看着丁丁。他的眼镜片上闪着光。"你真的知道?告诉我们,丁丁。"

学校里的人体骨骼

丁丁的脸唰的一下红了。"好,有人决定在全校开一个愚人节玩笑,所以拿走了肖特基小姐的骷髅,藏在沃特斯夫人的壁橱里。"

丁丁看着沃特斯夫人。"他还拿走了您的钥匙,所以您开不了壁橱门。"

"但这个人为什么要把运动鞋藏起来?"狄龙先生问。

"因为他留下了一个鞋印,"乔希说,"后来他计划制造更多鞋印。"

"他就借用沃特斯夫人的爽身粉来制造鞋印。"露丝说,朝丁丁和乔希笑。

"他拿走了钥匙,配了六把。"丁丁接着说。他还画了六幅骷髅画,把画和钥匙放在六个不同的储物柜里,一个年级放了一份。

狄龙先生摇头。"太令人惊讶了!他为什么要这么做呢?"

"我认为他想让所有孩子都去寻找骷髅。"丁丁说。

"我听糊涂了,"狄龙先生说。他坐在沃特斯夫人椅子上,"怎么可能会有一个陌生人进入学校，做了这么多事，还没被发现呢？"

丁丁看了一眼乔希和露丝，只见两人都点了点头。

"我们认为此人是在这儿工作的，先生。"丁丁说。

"某位老师吗？"狄龙先生说，"是谁？为什么这么做？"

丁丁、乔希和露丝看着狄龙先生。他们一直盯着看，校长都脸红了。

"噢，天哪！"沃特斯夫人惊讶地大声说，"是您，对吗？"

"我被抓住了。"狄龙先生说，咧着嘴笑。

"但是您想被抓住，"露丝说，"所以您才留下那些鞋印和钥匙，还有骷髅画。"

狄龙先生点头。"对，我想被抓住，因为我喜欢愚人节。我在你们这个年龄，总是盼着这一天，一直恶作剧！"

"我也是！"沃特斯夫人说，"我姐姐总是在她的毛衣抽屉中发现青蛙。"

"现在没有人开玩笑或恶作剧了，"狄龙先生

接着说,"每年的愚人节都悄无声息溜走了,没人关注。"

"所以我决定今年愚人节要有所不同。每个人都会记住今年的愚人节。"

狄龙先生脱下乐福鞋,穿上锯齿形底纹的运动鞋。"想念这双鞋了,"他说,"我每天早上都穿这双鞋来学校,然后换上乐福鞋。"

丁丁笑了。"我们四处去测量老师们的鞋长,结果这双鞋一直在壁橱里面。"

校长也笑了。"坦白地说,我很开心。周一我去肖特基小姐办公室的水池洗手。时间很早,没人在那儿。然后我看见了双肩搭着她围巾的骷髅,那时突然有了这个念头。"

校长双眼闪烁。"我抓起骷髅,从连接两间办公室的门里返回,把它藏在沃特斯夫人的壁橱里。她的钥匙插在锁上没有拔下,所以我就锁上柜门,拿走了钥匙。"

"然后您就换了鞋,对吗?"乔希问。

狄龙先生点头。"我开始不知道留下了一个鞋印。后来听你们说了,我就决定留下更多鞋印，所以才借用沃特斯夫人的爽身粉。"

"现在请还给我。"她说。

大家再次哄堂大笑。

狄龙先生笑着说："你们三个是最先找到骷髅先生的，可以用对讲机宣布。"

"宣布什么？"丁丁问。

"哎呀，当然是宣布旅游啊！我已经租好了车，带全校同学去水族馆。"狄龙先生说。

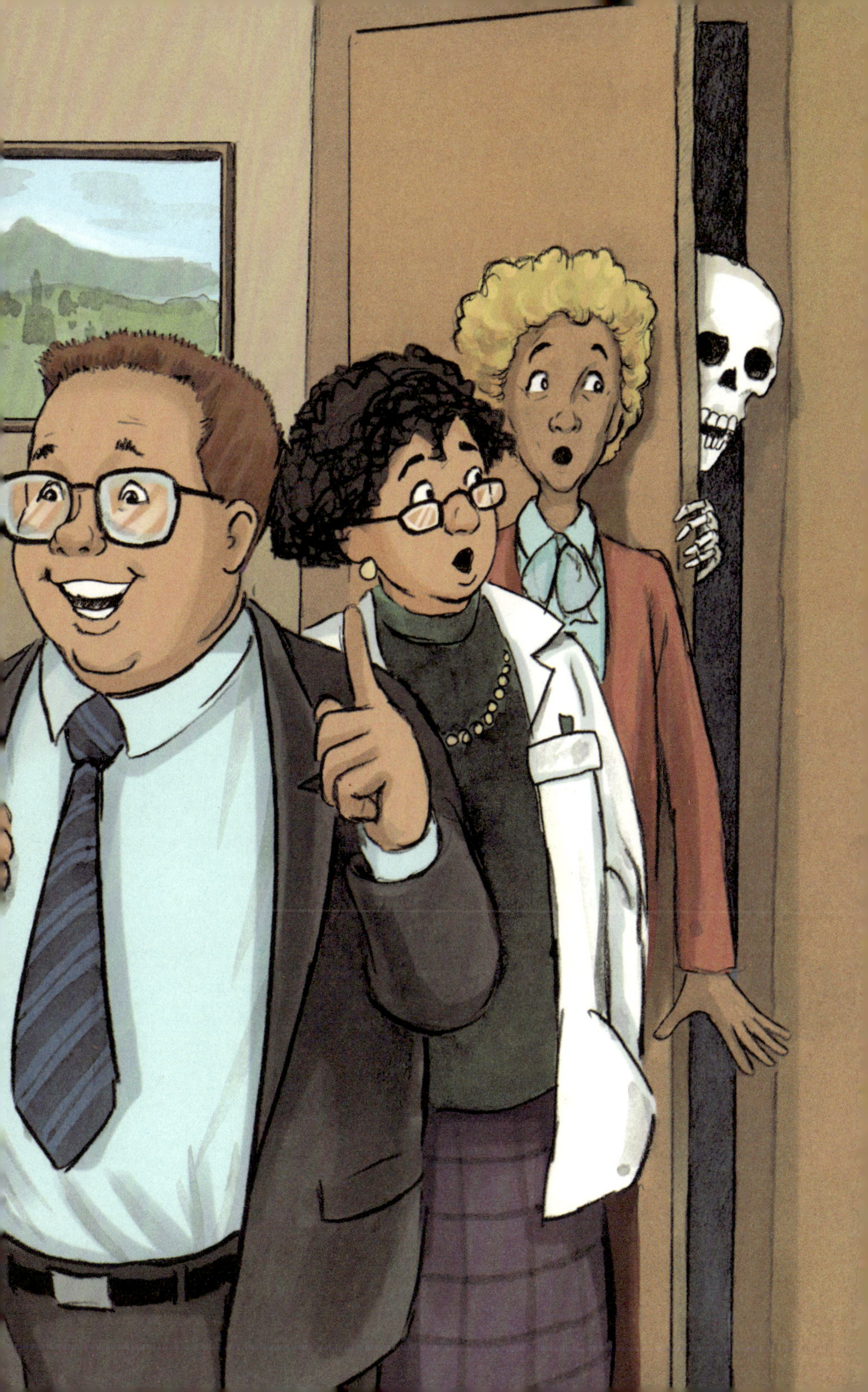

"每个人都去吗?"露丝问。

"每个人都参与了寻找骷髅先生,所以人人都有奖励。"狄龙先生说。

突然骷髅先生的脑袋从连接门后探出。

"我也有奖励吗?"骷髅先生问。

A to Z Mysteries®

The School Skeleton

by Ron Roy

illustrated by
John Steven Gurney

INDIAN RIVER
LAWRENCE TAXI
RIVER ROAD
HORSE TRAILS
BIKE PATH
HORSES FOR RENT
WOODS
WOODVIEW ROAD
INDIAN WAY ROAD
FIRE STATION
BIKE PATH
BILL'S BIKES
SUPER MARKET
BRIDGE LANE
ROBIN ROAD
CROW ST
FINCH LA
THRUSH CT
OWL RD
PHEASANT LA
BLUE JAY WAY
WREN DR
FITNESS CENTER
WOODS
BIKE PATH
BLUE BIRD WAY
HUMMINGBIRD LA
WOODCOCK CROSS
ELLIE'S DINER
ACORN APTS
FURRY FEET PET SHOP
BIKE PATH
CENTER CHURCH
OAK STREET
PEOPLE'S POND
POST OFFICE
COMMUNITY GARDEN AND FISH POND
GREEN LAWN SAVINGS BANK
GOOSE ISLAND
RIVER ROAD
POLICE STATION
ELDERLY HOUSING
WEST GREEN ST
MAIN STREET
SENIOR COMMUNITY CENTER
GREEN LAWN LIBRARY
TOWN HALL
BIKE PATH
CHILDREN'S PETTING ZOO AND AQUARIUM
SHANGRI-LA HOTEL

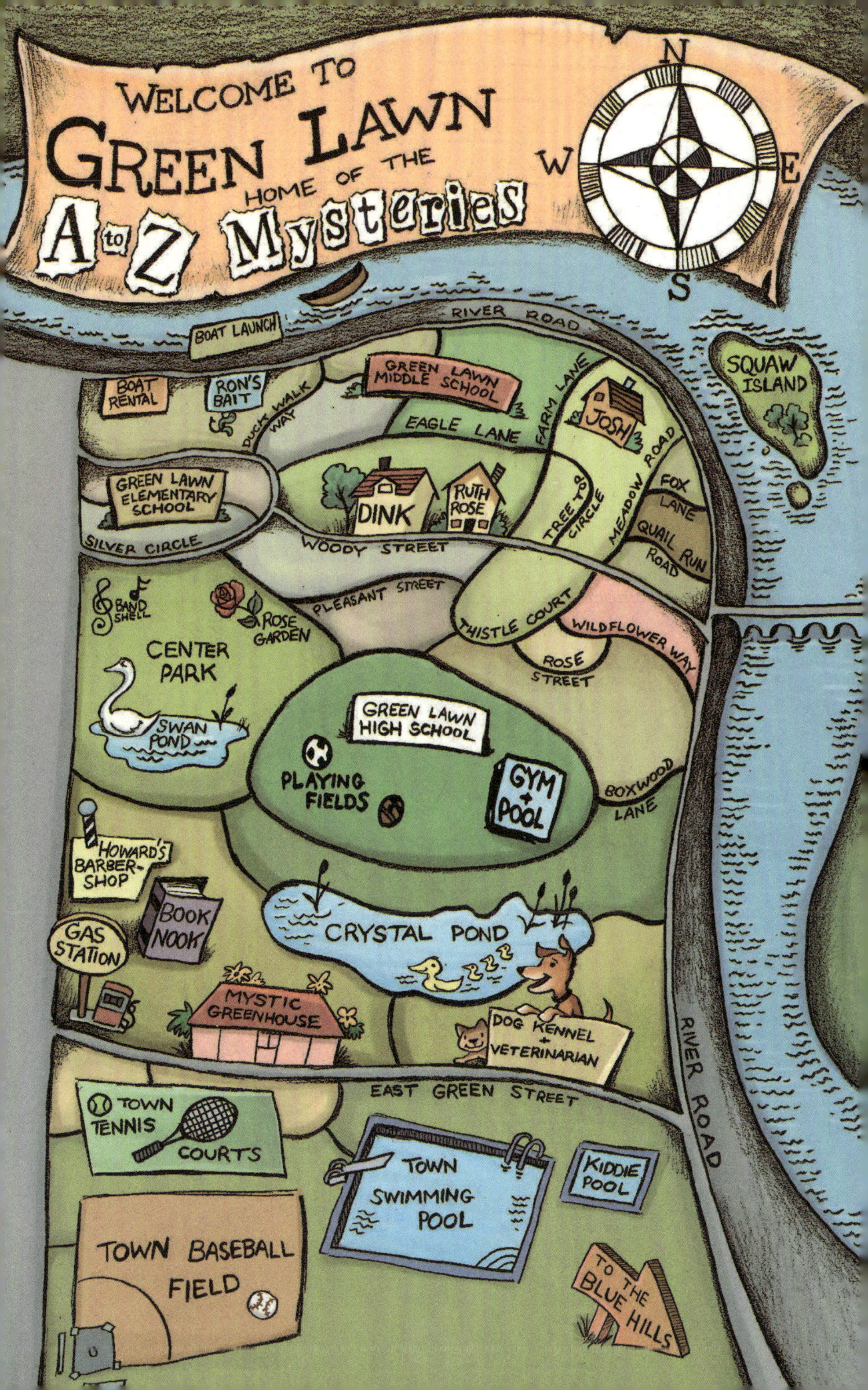

MARCH

Chapter 1

"Dink, would you mind passing out math paper to everyone?" Mrs. Eagle asked.

"Oh, no, a math quiz," Josh groaned.

Mrs. Eagle smiled. "Yes, Josh. We have one every Monday at ten o'clock," she said. "Now, I'd like to see bright eyes, quick minds, and sharp pencils!"

Kids fumbled inside their desks for pencils. Then some of them formed a line at the pencil sharpener.

Dink liked his teacher and his room. Everywhere he looked he saw books, cheerful posters on the walls, and sunlight coming through the windows. Mrs. Eagle had brought in a rug and some big pillows for the reading corner. That was Dink's favorite spot in the room.

Dink's full name was Donald David Duncan. But when he first learned to talk, all he could say was "Dink!" Now that was his permanent nickname.

He walked to the paper shelf, grabbed a stack, and began handing it out to the other third graders.

When Dink got to his friend Josh's desk, Josh grinned and whispered,

Teacher's pet, teacher's pet.
When Dink gets sick, he goes to the vet.

Josh Pinto was tall and thin. He had red hair that liked to fall over his freckled forehead.

Dink crossed his eyes at Josh. Then he slid a piece of paper onto his desk.

"Can I have two?" Josh asked, pulling another sheet from Dink's stack.

"Ouch!" Dink yelped, looking at his finger. There was a thin cut, and it was beginning to bleed.

"What's the matter?" Mrs. Eagle asked, walking over to Dink.

"I got a paper cut," Dink said.

"I'll bet that hurts," Mrs. Eagle said, handing him a tissue. "You'd better go to the nurse's office and get a Band-Aid."

Dink pressed the tissue against his cut and headed for the door. When he passed Ruth Rose's desk, she grinned at him. "Hurry back for the quiz!" she teased.

Ruth Rose Hathaway lived next door to Dink on Woody Street. She had bouncy black hair and quick blue eyes. She always dressed in one color, from head to toe. Today's color was daffodil yellow.

"I'll be back," Dink said. He left the room and headed toward the nurse's office. Mr. Neater, the tall, white-haired school janitor, was sweeping the floor. He wore a metal key ring on his belt. The keys jangled when he pushed the broom. He waved at Dink.

Dink showed him his cut.

"Ooh, bet that hurts," Mr. Neater said.

Dink walked past a long line of lockers and bulletin boards. His paper cut was stinging, so he squeezed the tissue tighter.

When he passed the principal's office, the secretary, Mrs. Waters, was sitting at her desk. Behind her, through another door, Dink saw the principal, Mr. Dillon, talking on the telephone.

Mrs. Waters smiled at Dink. "Are you here to see Mr. Dillon?" she asked.

Dink stopped at the doorway and held up his finger. "Paper cut," he said.

Mrs. Waters shook her head. "Bet that hurts," she said.

Dink nodded and hurried next door to the nurse's office. Miss Shotsky was staring at her calendar when Dink walked in.

"Can you believe it's almost the end of March?" she asked Dink. "Eighty-two days till summer vacation!"

Dink held up his finger. "Um, I got a paper cut," he said.

"Ooh, I'll bet that hurts," Miss Shotsky said. "I'll have to amputate." Dink's mouth fell open, and Miss Shotsky burst out laughing. Then Dink laughed, too.

"Come on in the back, where I keep all my torture stuff," the nurse said. She led Dink through a doorway behind her desk.

Miss Shotsky pointed to the examining table in

学校里的人体骨骼

the middle of the room. "Hop up there, please," she said as she walked over to a white cabinet.

Dink sat on the table and looked around the room. Something smelled nice. Then he noticed a vase of flowers on a table next to a closed door.

Over her shoulder Miss Shotsky said, "I have Batman Band-Aids, Wonder Woman Band-Aids, and bunny rabbit Band-Aids. Your choice, kiddo."

"Batman, please," Dink said. He stared at the corner of the room where the school skeleton usually hung from a hook.

"Miss Shotsky, where's Mr. Bones?"

The nurse had her back to Dink. "Hanging in the corner, where he always is."

Dink stared at the empty corner. The school skeleton had been there as long as Dink could remember. Miss Shotsky would bring it to each classroom when she told the kids how eating vegetables and drinking milk made strong bones. At holiday time, she always dressed Mr. Bones in costumes.

The only thing Dink saw in the corner was a red scarf hanging on a hook.

"He's not there," Dink said.

Miss Shotsky turned around. "Don't play tricks on the school nurse," she said, grinning at Dink.

"I'm not," Dink said, pointing at the vacant corner. "Look."

Miss Shotsky looked. Her mouth dropped open. "Well, I'll be hog-tied," she said. "He is gone!"

"Maybe someone borrowed him," Dink said.

"I don't know when," she said. "Mr. Bones was right there when I came in at seven-thirty. I know because I put my scarf on him. No, someone swiped

学校里的人体骨骼

my skeleton!"

Miss Shotsky shook her head. "Anyway, let's look at your boo-boo," she said, removing the tissue.

In about five seconds, she had cleaned Dink's finger and wrapped a Batman Band-Aid around it. "Now scoot back to class so I can tell Mr. Dillon about Mr. Bones," Miss Shotsky said. She grabbed Dink's hand and dropped two wrapped chocolates into his palm.

"Thanks a lot," he said.

"You're welcome," she said. "And if you tell anyone the nurse gave you candy, I'll deny it!"

She patted Dink's shoulder and walked him to the hallway. Admiring his Band-Aid, Dink ate one of the chocolates on his way back to class.

Mrs. Eagle had her back to Dink when he walked into his classroom. Every kid's head was bent over the math quiz.

On the way to his seat, Dink dropped the other candy onto Ruth Rose's desk. "Hey, what about me?" Josh squeaked.

Dink grinned and slipped into his seat.

Chapter 2

"Sorry I gave you a paper cut," Josh told Dink at morning recess. The cool March wind made Dink's eyes water. Gray clouds blew across the sky, and a few mounds of snow still hadn't melted.

"No problem," Dink said. A soccer ball rolled against his feet, and Dink kicked it toward a bunch of kids.

"Does it still hurt?" Ruth Rose asked. Her hat and scarf matched the rest of her yellow outfit.

"Nope," Dink said. Then he remembered what had happened in Miss Shotsky's office. "But guess what?

学校里的人体骨骼

Mr. Bones has disappeared!"

"The skeleton?" Josh said.

Dink nodded. "I noticed it was missing when I got my Band-Aid," he said. "Miss Shotsky didn't even know it was gone."

"I wonder if someone stole it," Ruth Rose said. She unwrapped the chocolate Dink had given her.

"Why would anyone steal a skeleton?" Josh said, eyeing the candy in Ruth Rose's hand. "Share?" he asked.

Ruth Rose broke the candy in half and passed a chunk to Josh.

Dink shrugged. "The last time Miss Shotsky saw it was around seven-thirty this morning," he said.

Just then they heard a whistle blow. Everyone lined up and entered the building. Mrs. Eagle was waiting inside the door. "We're going to the gym for a few minutes," she told her class. "Mr. Dillon has an announcement to make."

Led by their teachers, the third, fourth, and fifth graders trooped into the gym. The kindergarteners and first and second graders were already sitting in

91

rows on the floor. Mr. Dillon was standing under the basketball hoop.

When the bigger kids were also seated, Mr. Dillon smiled. "Good morning, kids!" he said. "I have some sad news to report," he went on. "Earlier today, the school skeleton disappeared out of the nurse's office."

Everyone started to talk. A fifth-grade boy with a deep voice said, "Who'd steal a skeleton? A zombie?" His buddies laughed, and his teacher gave him a look.

"If anyone has any information about the missing skeleton," Mr. Dillon went on, "please raise your hand."

No one raised a hand.

"Well, it seems we have a genuine mystery on our hands," Mr. Dillon said. He smiled at the hundred kids who sat watching him. "And I need your help solving it. So I've decided to offer a reward. The classroom that finds Mr. Bones will get free tickets to the new aquarium in Hartford."

"Ooh!" a lot of kids cried.

Ruth Rose turned to Dink and Josh. "I've been asking my parents to take me," she said.

学校里的人体骨骼

"Me too," Dink said. "They've got a baby beluga whale!"

"Now you're excused," Mr. Dillon said. "Have a nice day, and best of luck solving the case of the missing skeleton!"

The kids stood up, gathered around their teachers, and left the gym. All around him Dink heard kids talking about the missing school skeleton. He heard one little boy whisper, "Maybe it came alive and walked away!"

"Maybe if we figured out why anyone would want a skeleton," Dink said, "we could figure out who took it."

Dink, Josh, and Ruth Rose thought about this as they followed Mrs. Eagle back to their classroom.

They passed Mr. Neater, cleaning a window. He smiled and waved.

"Maybe he took it," Josh whispered. "That key ring probably has keys to all the rooms in the school."

"Josh, why would Mr. Neater want a skeleton?" Ruth Rose asked.

"She's right," Dink said. "You might as well accuse

93

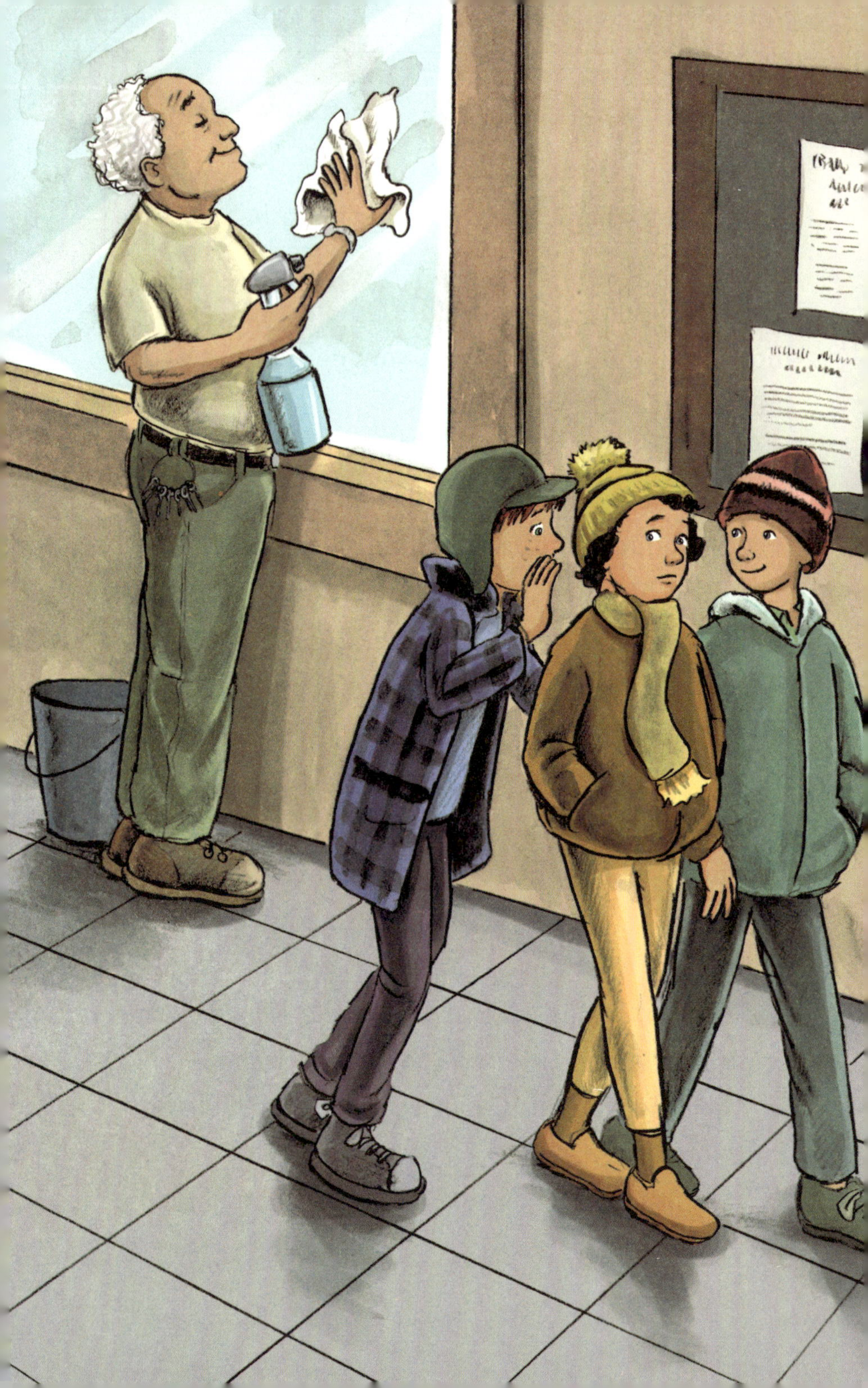

学校里的人体骨骼

Miss Aria, the music teacher, or Mr. Love, the art teacher."

"Well, someone took it," Josh said.

Ruth Rose was shaking her head. "But why does it have to be an adult?" she asked. "Maybe the fifth graders stole Mr. Bones. Remember when they took that papier-mâché whale from the first-grade room and hung it from the flagpole?"

"Yeah, that was so cool," Josh said.

Back in their room, Mrs. Eagle told the kids to take out their writing journals. "Since we have only a little time left before lunch, why don't we spend it writing a story?" she said.

"What about?" Bobby asked.

Mrs. Eagle smiled slyly. "About a vanishing school skeleton!" she said.

Chapter 3

"What did you call your story?" Josh asked Dink at their lockers. It was three o'clock, and everyone was going home.

Dink grinned as he put on his jacket. "It's called 'Josh Stole the School Skeleton and Should Go to Jail Forever,'" Dink said.

"Ha-ha," Josh said.

"Mine's called 'The Skeleton's Curse,'" Ruth Rose said. "Mr. Bones puts a curse on all boys with red hair."

"You guys are a riot," Josh said as the kids walked

学校里的人体骨骼

toward the exit. Miss Shotsky poked her head out of her office and called to Dink, "How's that finger?"

"Fine, thanks," Dink said, wiggling it at her.

"Well, come on in and let me give you a couple of Band-Aids to take home."

"What a baby," Josh whispered as the three kids piled into Miss Shotsky's office.

"He's just jealous of your Batman Band-Aid," Ruth Rose said.

"Yeah, right," Josh said. "Batman is out. Spider-Man rules the school!"

The kids followed Miss Shotsky into the back room. While Dink got more Band-Aids, Josh and Ruth Rose examined the corner where Mr. Bones usually hung.

"Look, there's a footprint in the dust!" Ruth Rose said.

Miss Shotsky and Dink walked over to look.

"It looks like a sneaker," Dink said. "See the zigzag tread?

"It's the left foot," Josh pointed out. "An adult's size," Ruth Rose said.

97

"Maybe the thief made this footprint when he lifted Mr. Bones off the hook," Dink said.

"Could be—it sure isn't my footprint," Miss Shotsky said, holding her left foot up. Her white nurse's shoe was shorter, and the tread on the bottom was different.

"Were any teachers in here this morning?" Ruth Rose asked Miss Shotsky.

"Not that I know of," the nurse answered. "After I got here, I went to the teachers' lounge to make coffee. I came back at eight o'clock, but I didn't even look at Mr. Bones."

"So whoever took Mr. Bones had to do it between seven-thirty and eight, right?" asked Josh.

Miss Shotsky shook her head. "Nope. I was in and out of here all morning, visiting the first- and second-grade rooms. Anyone could have taken Mr. Bones any time before ten o'clock, when Dink came in with his paper cut."

Just then there was a soft knock on the examining room door. "Excuse me, but could I sweep this room now?" someone said.

It was Mr. Neater with his broom.

"Hi, Tom, come on in," Miss Shotsky said.

"Could I make a drawing of this footprint before you sweep?" Josh asked Mr. Neater.

"Sure, I'll start in the front office," Mr. Neater said.

"And we should measure it," Ruth Rose said.

Miss Shotsky gave Josh a paper and pencil. She handed Ruth Rose a ruler.

Josh made a quick sketch of the print.

"Be sure to get that zigzag pattern," Dink said, peering over Josh's shoulder.

Ruth Rose measured the footprint. "It's exactly eleven inches long," she said. Josh wrote ELEVEN INCHES next to the drawing.

"So all we have to do is find out who wears this kind of shoe," Josh said, "and we find Mr. Bones and win the tickets to the aquarium."

"But a lot of the teachers wear sneakers," Ruth Rose said. "How do we find the right one?"

"I know who we can ask," Dink said. "Mrs. Waters. All the teachers walk past her desk to get their mail. Maybe she notices the shoes they wear."

"Let's hurry before she goes home," Ruth Rose said.

Miss Shotsky opened a small door next to her filing cabinet. "Here's a shortcut to the principal's office," she said.

Sure enough, when the kids walked through the door, there was Mrs. Waters at her desk. She was staring into her open purse.

"Hi, kids," she said, closing her purse and putting it in a drawer. "Still here?"

"We're trying to find the skeleton," Ruth Rose said.

"We found a footprint on the floor where Mr. Bones hangs," Dink said. "It's a sneaker."

"We think the guy who stole the skeleton made the print," Josh said. "If we find him, our room wins the tickets!"

"Just one footprint? Maybe you should be looking for a one-legged thief," Mrs. Waters said with a twinkle in her eye.

Josh giggled and placed his drawing on her desk. "Do you know anyone who wears this kind of sneaker?" he asked.

Just then the small door opened again. Miss Shotsky peeked in, wearing her red scarf.

"Good night, all," Miss Shotsky said. "Happy skeleton hunting, kids."

"Good night, Claire," said Mrs. Waters.

The door closed.

Mrs. Waters studied Josh's drawing, then shook her head. "I usually notice what the teachers are wearing," she said. "But I never see the bottoms of their feet."

She traced the zigzag tread with her finger. "Although this pattern does seem familiar. I feel sure I've seen it somewhere."

She smiled. "Knowing me, I'll think of it halfway home."

Mrs. Waters glanced at the clock and stood up. "Time for me to leave," she said, heading toward her coat closet. But when she tried to open the door, it wouldn't budge.

Mrs. Waters walked back to her desk and pulled her purse and a sweater from a drawer. "First I lose my powder," she said. "Now I think I'm losing my head!"

Just then Mr. Dillon appeared in the doorway to his office. "Hey, kids. Still here?"

Dink told Mr. Dillon about the footprint in Miss Shotsky's examining room. Josh showed him his drawing.

"We think the thief was wearing sneakers like this," Ruth Rose said.

"Well, that leaves me out," Mr. Dillon said. He raised one foot and showed the kids the smooth sole of his shiny tassel loafer.

"Me too," Mrs. Waters said. She pointed a small high-heeled shoe at them. "That footprint is twice as big as my feet!"

Chapter 4

As the kids walked home, Josh studied his drawing of the left footprint. "How can we find the guy who wears this sneaker?" he asked.

"It could be a woman," Ruth Rose said.

Josh turned and grinned. "What about Mrs. Eagle?" he said. "Maybe she stole Mr. Bones."

Ruth Rose laughed. "No, her feet look as small as my mom's," she said. "My mom wears size six."

"Let's go to my house and make a list of all the grown-ups at the school," Dink suggested. "Then we can figure out how to check their shoes."

"Why don't we go to your house and make a snack?" Josh asked. "How about a turkey sandwich and apple pie with vanilla ice cream on top?"

"How about guinea-pig food?" Dink said.

In his kitchen, Dink found a plate of cookies and a note from his mom, saying she was shopping. The kids walked up to Dink's room with the cookies and Josh's drawing.

Dink handed Ruth Rose a pad.

While she wrote, Dink went to his dad's closet and found a pair of his sneakers. On the bottom he found a circle with SIZE TEN stamped inside. Then he got a ruler and measured the sneaker. It was eleven inches long, the same as the footprint they had found in Miss Shotsky's office.

"Guys, I think the skeleton snatcher wears a size ten," he said.

"I'll bet a lot of the male teachers wear that size," Josh said.

Ruth Rose showed them her list. "I got thirteen people," she said.

"Did you count Mr. Dillon and Mr.Neater?" Dink

asked.

Ruth Rose nodded. "Yup. All the adults who work at the school."

"We can cross off five names," Josh said. "Mrs. Eagle, Mrs. Waters, and Miss Shotsky all have smaller feet. And Mr. Dillon was wearing loafers today."

"Who's the fifth?" Dink asked.

"The custodian, Mr. Neater," Josh said.

"Why cross him off?" Ruth Rose asked. "He wears sneakers."

Josh laughed. "But they're the biggest sneakers I've ever seen. I think he wears about size thirteen!"

Ruth Rose put an X in front of the names of the five people Josh had mentioned.

Dink looked at the eight remaining names. "Four women and four men," he said, dropping a hunk of cookie into his guinea pig's cage. "Do you think one of them took the skeleton?"

"One way to find out," Josh said. "Check their shoes against my drawing."

"How do we do that?" Dink asked.

"Just tell them about the footprint we found, then

ask them if we can measure their feet and check the treads of their sneakers."

"There's one problem," Ruth Rose said. "If one of the teachers did take the skeleton, he won't let us measure his feet!"

"Then we'll know he's the guilty one," Josh said.

"But what if two teachers say no?" Dink asked. "Then we still wouldn't know which one did it."

"But at least we'd have narrowed it down to two," Ruth Rose said. "Then we could figure out what to do next."

"We'd better decide," Josh said. "Every kid at school wants to win those aquarium tickets."

"But we're the only ones who know about the footprint," Ruth Rose said. "We've got a head start."

"Not for long," Josh said. "Miss Shotsky and Mr. Neater saw the footprint, too. And I showed the drawing to Mrs. Waters and Mr. Dillon. Pretty soon the whole school will know."

"Okay, let's talk to those eight teachers tomorrow," Dink said.

"We could put notes in their mailboxes," Ruth

Rose suggested.

"Great idea!" Dink said. He sat at his computer, and Josh and Ruth Rose gave him suggestions. This is what they came up with:

DEAR _____,
WE HAVE A CLUE TO THE MYSTERY OF THE MISSING SKELETON. MAY WE TALK TO YOU TODAY? PLEASE CHECK YES _____ OR NO _____ AND PUT THIS IN MRS. EAGLE'S MAILBOX.
THANK YOU!

SIGNED,_____
DINK DUNCAN, JOSH PINTO, AND RUTH ROSE HATHAWAY

Dink printed eight copies. Using Ruth Rose's list

学校里的人体骨骼

of names, the kids addressed a letter to each.

"That should do it," Dink said when they were finished. "We'll ask Mrs. Waters to put them in the mailboxes tomorrow morning."

"And by afternoon, our class will have tickets to the aquarium," Josh said, grinning at his friends.

"Don't get your hopes up yet, Josh," Ruth Rose said.

"Why not? If we find the right shoe, we find the person who took Mr. Bones, right? So we win the tickets, right?"

Ruth Rose shook her head. "Wrong. We have to find the skeleton to win the tickets," she said. "While we're running around measuring people's feet, some other kid might find Mr. Bones!"

Chapter 5

The next morning they met in front of the school before the first bus showed up. There were only a couple of cars in the teachers' parking lot.

"I hope Mrs. Waters isn't late today," Josh said as they entered the school. "We need to get these notes in the mailboxes before the teachers get here."

They hurried along the silent hallway to the principal's office. Mrs. Waters was just taking off her coat.

"Mr. Dillon isn't in yet," she said when the kids walked in.

学校里的人体骨骼

"We came to see you," Dink said.

"Well, isn't that nice!" the secretary said, flipping a page on her calendar. "Goodness, where did March go already? Now, how can I help you kids?"

Dink, Josh, and Ruth Rose explained their idea.

"You honestly think one of our teachers took that skeleton?" she asked.

"We don't know," Dink said. "But the footprint looks like an adult's. Would you mind putting these in the right mailboxes?"

He handed Mrs. Waters the eight notes they'd printed. She read one and smiled.

"Of course I will," she said. "And I wish you luck finding Mr. Bones. I know Mr. Dillon will be happy to have this mystery solved!"

Mrs. Waters stood up, walked to the teachers' mailboxes, and placed the notes in eight different slots.

The kids thanked her and left. Just then the bell rang, and students began rushing through the front door.

They walked to their room and found Mrs. Eagle

111

at her desk. "My, my, look who's eager to get started!" she said.

Once more, the kids explained about the footprint, the eight notes, and their plan for finding the person who took the school skeleton. They showed her Josh's drawing of the footprint.

"And you plan to ask each teacher if you can measure his or her feet?" Mrs. Eagle asked, grinning.

"That footprint is our only clue," Ruth Rose said.

"We want our class to win the tickets," Josh said.

Mrs. Eagle smiled. "All right, if the teachers agree, you three may leave the room later," she said.

The morning seemed to last forever. Dink kept glancing at the clock, and Josh kept sighing and fidgeting at his desk.

Finally, during math, a fifth grader came into the room and handed Mrs. Eagle a stack of papers.

She looked through the stack, then called Dink up to her desk. "Here are your responses," she whispered. "All eight have checked YES. You might as well go now, and good luck!"

Dink, Josh, and Ruth Rose quietly left the room.

学校里的人体骨骼

They brought with them eight sheets of drawing paper, a ruler, Josh's footprint sketch, and Ruth Rose's list of teachers' names.

"Guys, I just thought of something," Ruth Rose said in the hallway. "Whoever made that footprint yesterday might be wearing different shoes today."

"You're right," Dink said. "So anyone whose shoe is about the right size, we'll ask if they wore the same shoes yesterday."

They started walking down the hall. On one classroom door, someone had hung a sign. It said: COME HOME, MR. BONES. WE MISS YOU! There was a drawing of a skeleton under the words.

Three girls wearing skeleton masks scampered down the hallway. "Mr. Bones, where are you?" one of the girls said. The other two laughed at their friend.

Outside the fifth-grade room, a paper skeleton hung from the ceiling.

"The whole school is looking for the skeleton," Josh muttered. "We have to find it first!"

"Then we'd better get going," Ruth Rose said. "Maybe no one else knows about the footprint yet."

113

First on her list was Miss Alubicki, the kindergarten teacher. They showed her Josh's drawing and asked if she would let them trace her left foot.

"Of course," Miss Alubicki said, smiling. "But I can already tell you, that foot is a lot bigger than mine."

The little kids giggled as Josh traced around her foot on a piece of paper. Outside in the hall, Josh compared it with his drawing.

"It's definitely not her," he said. "Miss Alubicki's foot is only seven inches long."

Ruth Rose drew a big X in front of Miss Alubicki's name on her list. After the name she wrote: TOO SMALL.

They went next door and peeked into Mr. Diodato's first-grade class. The tall teacher was writing at the chalkboard: WHO STOLE THE SCHOOL SKELETON?

Dink knocked, and Mr. Diodato looked up. "We have visitors, class," he said, grinning.

While Josh traced Mr. D.'s sneaker onto a sheet of paper, the first graders gathered around.

Dink, Josh, and Ruth Rose thanked Mr. D. and

学校里的人体骨骼

left. In the hall, Josh measured what he had traced onto the paper. Mr. Diodato's sneaker was almost thirteen inches long. The bottom tread had little squares, not zigzags.

"Cross him off, too," Dink said. Ruth Rose put an X by Mr. Diodato's name and wrote: TOO BIG.

"Six more names to go," Josh said, glancing at Ruth Rose's list. "What if it's none of them?"

"It must be someone on this list," Dink said. "How could a stranger sneak into the school and walk out with a skeleton?"

One by one, the kids traced teachers' shoes onto paper and measured them. They compared the tracings with Josh's drawing. One by one, Ruth Rose put X's next to the names.

With only one more name to go, Ruth Rose's list looked like this:

× KINDERGARTEN—MISS ALUBICKI—TOO SMALL
× FIRST GRADE—MR. DIODATO—TOO BIG
× SECOND GRADE—MISS CRUMPET—TOO SMALL
× THIRD GRADE—MRS. EAGLE—TOO SMALL
× FOURTH GRADE—MR. QUATRO—ABSENT MONDAY
× FIFTH GRADE—MRS. GOLDEN—TOO SMALL

× PRINCIPAL—MR. DILLON—WAS WEARING LOAFERS MONDAY

× SECRETARY—MRS. WATERS—TOO SMALL

× NURSE—MISS SHOTSKY—TOO SMALL

× ART TEACHER—MR. LOVE—TOO BIG

× MUSIC TEACHER—MISS ARIA—TOO SMALL

× JANITOR—MR. NEATER—WAY TOO BIG

GYM TEACHER—MR. PALMER

"Not one of these people could have made that footprint," Ruth Rose said.

"Who's the last name?" Dink asked.

"Mr. Palmer, the gym teacher," she answered.

Josh crossed his fingers. "Maybe he's the one!" he said.

They found Mr. Palmer sitting behind his desk. He smiled when the kids walked into his office.

"I read your note," he said.

"Thanks for seeing us," Dink said. "May we measure your shoes?"

Mr. Palmer grinned. "Sure. But I guarantee I didn't steal that skeleton yesterday morning. I was in the emergency room at the hospital."

He stood up and held out his left foot. There was a white cast on it. "I slipped on some ice getting into my car yesterday," he said.

He pointed to a pair of crutches leaning in a corner. "I can hardly carry my lunch, let alone a skeleton!"

Chapter 6

"I hope your foot gets better fast," Dink said.

"Thanks, and I hope you find the skeleton," Mr. Palmer said.

The kids left and walked toward their room.

"We must've figured something wrong," Josh said. "One of these people has to be the perp."

"The perp?" Dink said.

Josh grinned. "Yeah, you know, the guy that did it."

"So if it wasn't anyone on this list, who was it?" Ruth Rose asked. "That footprint didn't get there by magic."

"I wonder if it could be a trick footprint," Dink said.

"What do you mean?" Josh asked.

"I read a story once about some kids who made fake bear tracks to fool their parents," Dink said. "They taped some rolled-up socks onto an old rake. Then they stamped 'bear' tracks in the snow all around their house."

"But why would the skeleton snatcher leave a fake footprint?" Ruth Rose asked.

Dink shrugged. "Why would anyone steal the school skeleton in the first place?"

"Well, whoever did it is pretty mean," Josh grumbled. "Playing tricks on innocent kids isn't nice!"

Dink and Ruth Rose burst out laughing. They were still giggling as they got close to their room.

"Wait a sec, I want to put this drawing away," Josh said.

"STOP!" Ruth Rose shouted as Josh stepped up to his locker. "DON'T MOVE!"

"What!" Josh gasped, smacking his chest with one hand. "You almost gave me a heart attack!"

"Look what you almost stepped on!" Ruth Rose pointed to a circle of white powder on the floor. In the center of the circle was a footprint.

It was a very familiar footprint.

Ruth Rose grabbed Josh's footprint sketch from his hand and knelt next to the new print. "Check it out, guys," she said.

Dink and Josh bent down for a closer look. It was a left footprint with a zigzag pattern. When Ruth Rose placed Josh's drawing on the floor, the two footprints were identical.

"Oh my gosh!" Josh cried. "The skeleton snatcher was here!"

Just then Mrs. Eagle popped her head through the door. "What's going on?" she asked.

Ruth Rose pointed at the footprint. "Look, Mrs. Eagle."

"He's back!" Josh said.

"And he came right to your locker," Dink added, grinning. "The zombie is after you!"

"No way!" Josh argued. "See, the footprint is halfway between my locker and yours."

"Maybe he stole something from one of your lockers," Ruth Rose said.

Mrs. Eagle knelt and put her finger in the white stuff. Then she lifted her finger to her nose. "Hmm," she said. "This smells like talcum powder. Why don't you boys open your lockers?"

"You go first," Josh told Dink.

"Okay," Dink said. "Since you're such a scaredy-cat."

"Am not."

"Are too."

"Boys," Mrs. Eagle said.

Dink pulled open his locker door. His jacket hung on a hook. On the shelf, his books were neatly arranged. His lunch bag sat on top of his books.

"Nothing's missing," Dink said. "Now you, Josh."

"No problem," Josh said, flipping up the latch on his locker door. His jacket hung on the hook. His books were stacked on the shelf. His brown-bag lunch was perched on the books.

But in front of the lunch bag was a twisted

piece of white paper.

"What's that?" Josh asked. "I didn't put that there."

Dink leaned close and whispered, "Maybe it's a note from the snatcher!"

"Yeah, right," Josh said, grabbing the paper twist. "Hey, there's something inside!"

When Josh untwisted the paper, a metal object fell onto the floor.

But Dink, Josh, Ruth Rose, and their teacher were all staring at the paper in Josh's hand.

It was a drawing of a smiling skeleton. Someone had sketched a big "2" in the center of its forehead.

Mrs. Eagle bent down and picked up what had fallen. "How odd," she said, showing the kids a shiny key.

Chapter 7

Dink, Josh, Ruth Rose, and their teacher walked back into the classroom.

"Now we have another mystery to solve," Mrs. Eagle told the class. "Josh, why don't you and Dink and Ruth Rose tell the class what you've been up to?"

The three kids told their classmates about the first footprint and showed them Josh's drawing. Then they explained how they had traced and measured each teacher's shoe to try and find the one who had left the footprint.

Josh's drawing, Ruth Rose's list, and the eight shoe

outlines were on Mrs. Eagle's desk. Also on the desk were the drawing of the skeleton and the key that Josh had found in his locker.

"One more thing," Mrs. Eagle said. "Someone sprinkled powder on the floor near Josh's locker, then made another footprint."

She looked at the class. "Any ideas?"

Bobby raised his hand. "I think the same person who took the skeleton put the key in Josh's locker," he said.

"But why?" asked Ruth Rose. "We don't know what the key goes to."

Mrs. Eagle took the key and walked over to the classroom door. She slipped the key into the keyhole and tried to lock the door.

学校里的人体骨骼

"It doesn't work in this one," she said. Then she tried the key in her desk lock. "Nor this one."

"We could try all the locks in the school," Frankie suggested.

Mrs. Eagle nodded. "Good idea, Frankie, but there are dozens of doors and desks."

"Could the key go to a suitcase or a safety-deposit box?" Dink asked.

Mrs. Eagle smiled at Dink. "Good thinking."

"Maybe it's the key to someone's house," Tommy said.

"These are all good ideas," Mrs. Eagle said. "But it's not practical to go around Green Lawn trying the key in every keyhole."

"What I can't figure out is why he's doing this," Dink said. "Why leave footprints and a key that he knew we'd find?"

Josh raised his hand. "And why did the guy pick my locker to leave it in?" he asked.

"Maybe he didn't," Ruth Rose said. "The lockers don't have our names on them. The guy might have just picked any third-grade locker."

127

"You're right," Mrs. Eagle said. "Maybe the key was meant to be found by anyone in this room!"

Everyone looked at each other and started whispering.

Mrs. Eagle made a pile of all the evidence on her desk and handed it to Josh along with the key. "But now we have to get back to work," she said.

It was windier and colder as Dink, Josh, and Ruth Rose walked home after school.

"Let's go to my house," Ruth Rose said. "I'll make hot chocolate."

"With whipped cream?" Josh asked.

"Marshmallows," Ruth Rose said.

"The big, fat ones?"

"No, Josh, the little, bitty ones," Ruth Rose answered.

"I like the big ones," Josh mumbled.

A few minutes later, Ruth Rose let them in with her key. She found a note from her mom, saying she'd taken Ruth Rose's little brother, Nate, to the dentist.

In the kitchen, Ruth Rose's cat, Tiger, was lying on

the table in a patch of sun. Ruth Rose shooed Tiger away, then made hot chocolate in the microwave.

Dink and Josh sat at the table. Josh laid the key and the drawing of the skeleton on the sunny spot vacated by Tiger.

"I think we're missing something," Dink said, looking down at the key and the drawing. "The guy steals a skeleton and leaves a footprint. Then he plants a key in your locker and leaves another shoe print in powder that he sprinkled on the floor. He's trying to tell us something, but what?"

Ruth Rose brought three mugs and a bag of marshmallows to the table.

They all floated marshmallows on their hot chocolate.

"I just remembered something," she said. "Didn't Mrs. Waters tell us she was missing her powder?"

"But she didn't make that footprint outside my locker," Josh said.

"I know," Ruth Rose said. "But someone could have stolen her powder to use it to make that footprint. Maybe the thief wants everyone to suspect

Mrs. Waters of taking the skeleton."

The kids sipped their hot chocolate and thought about that.

"It would have to be someone who can get into her desk to get the powder," Dink said finally.

"Like Mr. Dillon!" Ruth Rose said.

"Yeah, but the footprints aren't his, either," Josh said. "Remember he was wearing those loafers with no tread on the bottom."

"And why would Mr. Dillon steal something and blame it on his secretary?" Dink asked. "It doesn't make sense!"

"I wonder if anything else has been stolen from the school that we don't know about," Ruth Rose said.

"Well, if anyone would know, it's Mrs. Waters," Dink said. "We could talk to her again tomorrow."

Josh picked up the skeleton picture that had been wrapped around the key. "What do you guys think this '2' on the skull means?" he asked. "The school doesn't have two skeletons, does it?"

"The high school and the middle school might have their own," Ruth Rose said. "Did anyone steal

学校里的人体骨骼

their skeletons?"

"I doubt it, or we'd have heard something," Dink said.

"I don't want to live in a town where some zombie goes around stealing skeletons," Josh grumbled.

"Anyway, this key must mean something," Dink

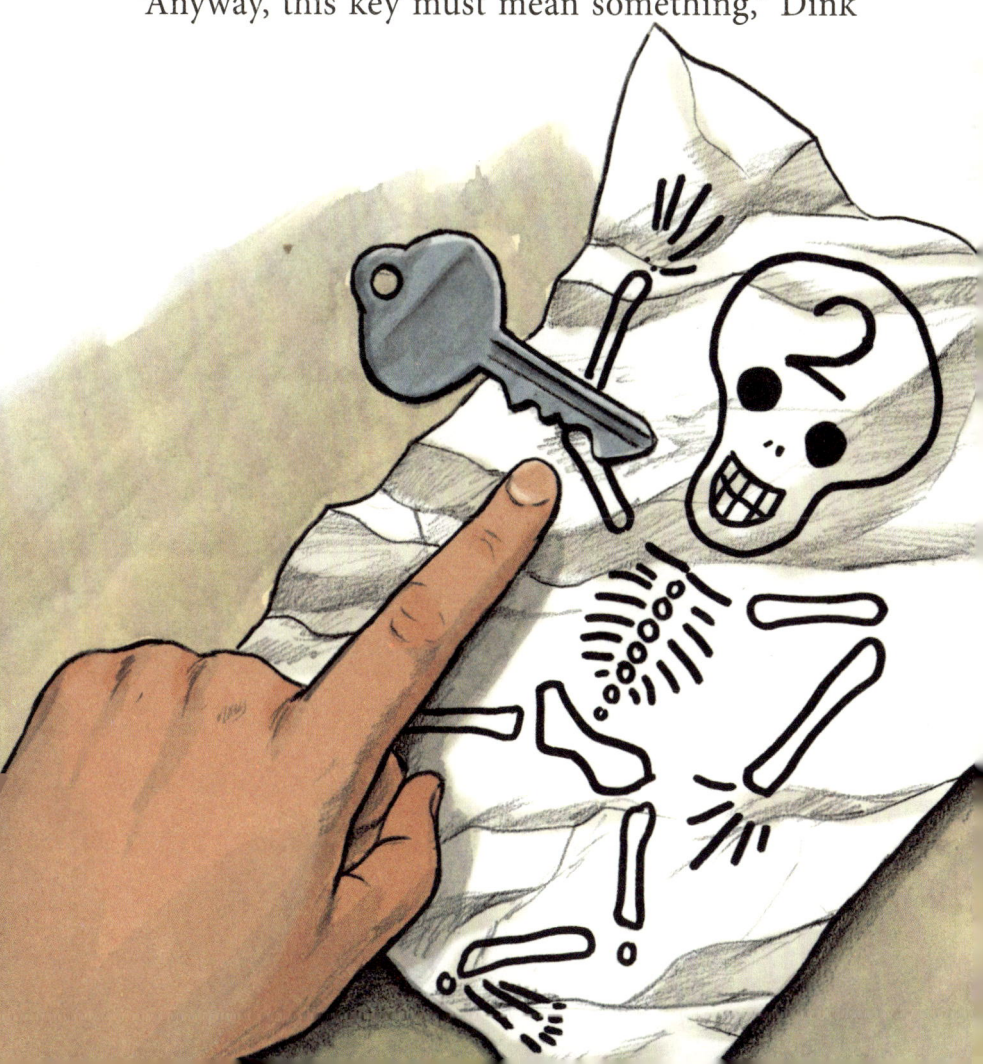

said. He placed the key next to the skull's mouth. "Talk to us, Mr. Bones!"

"Wait a minute!" Ruth Rose cried. She moved the key up a few inches, next to the big "2." "What does that say?"

Josh dropped a marshmallow into his mug. "It says 'key-head,'" he said. "'Key-face'? 'Key-bones'?"

Ruth Rose shook her head. She pointed at the key. "Key," she said. Then she pointed at the number on the skull. "Two," she continued. Then she pointed to the skeleton's body. "Skeleton," she said. "I think it says 'key to skeleton'!"

Chapter 8

"I think he's trying to tell us that this key unlocks wherever Mr. Bones is hidden," Ruth Rose continued.

"But where?" Josh asked. "The key could go to a lock in California."

"The skeleton is probably still in the school," Dink said. "How could anyone carry it out of the building in broad daylight?"

"But how could anyone hide it inside the school in broad daylight, either?" Ruth Rose asked. "Somebody would have been bound to notice."

"Unless Miss Shotsky did it," Josh said. "She

carries Mr. Bones to classes all the time."

Dink shook his head. "Trust me, she was surprised when she saw the skeleton was missing."

"And that wasn't her footprint," Ruth Rose said.

The kids stared at the drawing and the key.

"Why give us the key?" asked Josh. He had a chocolate mustache. "Does this guy want to get caught?"

"It's almost like he wants us to find Mr. Bones," Ruth Rose said.

"Well, at least no other kid has found the skeleton yet," Dink said. "We can still win aquarium tickets for our class."

Ruth Rose picked up the key and held it close to her eyes. "That's strange. This key looks brand-new," she said.

"How can you tell?" Dink asked.

"There are no scratches on it," Ruth Rose said. "And it's very shiny." She dug her house key out of her pocket. "See, my key has a lot of tiny marks from where it rubs against the inside of the door lock. But Josh's key looks like it was just made."

"So how do we find out what it opens?" Josh asked, slurping the last of his hot chocolate.

"We could ask Mr. Neater," Dink suggested. "He has keys to everything in the building."

"Wait, could he have put the key in Josh's locker?" Ruth Rose asked.

"That would mean he took the skeleton," Dink said. "But his shoes are way too big, remember?"

"Unless he faked the footprints," Josh said, "like

those kids who made the bear tracks."

Dink wrapped the key in the skeleton drawing

and handed it to Josh. "Let's show him this tomorrow," he said. "And don't lose it. The key is our best clue!"

A few snowflakes fell as Dink, Josh, and Ruth Rose hurried into the school building the next morning.

"Whoever heard of snow on the first of April," Josh muttered. He was wearing a green hat pulled down over his ears.

Mr. Neater had a small office in the school basement. The kids found him there, sitting on a stool in front of a workbench. He was trying to unjam a stapler.

"Good morning, Mr. Neater," Dink said.

The white-haired man turned and smiled. "Hey,

kids. What brings you down here? Playing hooky?"

Josh pulled the wrapped key from his pocket. He removed the drawing and showed the key to Mr. Neater. "Have you ever seen a key like this?" he asked.

Mr. Neater held the key under the light over his workbench. He examined both sides before he shook his head. "Nope, don't think so. But I can tell you it's a copy. This key was made from another, probably in some hardware store."

"You were right!" Josh marveled. "How come you're so smart, Ruth Rose?"

Ruth Rose just smiled.

Mr. Neater unclipped the key ring from his belt and plunked it down on the workbench. He fanned the keys and compared a few with the one Josh had given him. "See, an original key has the name of the company that makes it. Like this one is a Yale key."

He tapped Josh's key. "But yours has no name—it was copied from another key. Where'd you get it?" he asked, handing the key back to Josh.

"It was in my locker with . . ."

学校里的人体骨骼

Just then a fifth grader came clomping down the basement stairs. He was taller than Dink and had dark brown hair and dark, mischievous eyes.

"Well, hi, Cory," Mr. Neater said. "What's up?"

"I found this in my locker and wondered if you could tell me what it goes to," Cory said. He handed Mr. Neater a shiny key.

Everyone stared at Cory's key.

"Did you find a drawing of a skeleton with the key?" Ruth Rose asked.

Cory nodded. "Yup, all twisted around the key."

"And was there a footprint outside your locker?" Dink asked. "In powder?"

Cory looked suspiciously at Dink. "Yeah. How'd you know?"

"Because there was one near my locker, too," Josh said. "And I found a key in my locker, with this wrapped around it." He showed Cory his picture.

Cory dug into his pocket and drew out a twisted paper. Both boys laid the drawings flat on Mr. Neater's bench. The pictures—like the keys—were identical.

"Say, do you suppose this has anything to do with

139

Miss Shotsky's skeleton disappearing?" Mr. Neater asked.

"Sure it does," Cory said. He pointed to the number "2." "The kids in my class figured it out easy. The key and the picture mean 'key to the skeleton.' We're gonna find the skeleton and get free tickets to the new aquarium!"

More footsteps clunked down the basement stairs. This time it was two second-grade girls. They were holding hands and looked embarrassed to see four older kids there.

"Susan and Jane, right?" Mr. Neater said, smiling at the two little kids.

The girls nodded. Susan nudged Jane, who opened her hand. "Miss Crumpet wanted to know if you know what this key fits," she said shyly.

The key was the same as the two that Cory and Josh held.

"Bet you found this key in your locker, right?" Mr. Neater said.

Jane nodded. "And a silly picture of a skeleton with a '2' on his head!"

Chapter 9

Green Lawn Elementary didn't have a cafeteria. All the kids brought their lunches from home.

Dink, Josh, and Ruth Rose took their bags outside and sat on the swings in the sun. A lot of other kids came out to eat, too.

"Tuna fish," Josh said, smelling his sandwich. "What've you guys got?"

Ruth Rose peeked inside her plastic bag. "Baloney and cheese," she said.

Dink's sandwich turned out to be egg salad. "Who wants to trade?" he asked.

"I'll take the egg," Ruth Rose said.

"I want the baloney and cheese," Josh said.

"Good," Dink said. "I wanted the tuna."

The kids swapped sandwiches and began eating.

"A kid from each class in the school found a key and a drawing," Dink said after he'd swallowed his first bite.

"So there are six keys and six drawings and six footprints," Josh said around a mouthful of sandwich.

Ruth Rose shook her head. "Now every class is trying to find Miss Shotsky's skeleton before anyone else does." She sighed. "That's about a hundred kids!"

Two small boys walked past, looking for a place to eat their lunches. One of the boys carried a drawing of a skeleton.

"Even the little kindergartners!" Josh wailed, kicking some sand. "It's not fair."

"I just thought of something," Ruth Rose said. "There's a door that connects Mr. Dillon's office to the nurse's office. He could have snuck in when Miss Shotsky wasn't there and taken the skeleton."

"It would take him only a couple of minutes," Josh

143

said.

"Guys, I thought we already decided the snatcher couldn't be Mr. Dillon," Dink said. "He wasn't wearing sneakers."

"But he could easily have taken Mrs. Waters's powder," Ruth Rose reminded him. "The powder, the door to the nurse's office . . . everything else points to Mr. Dillon."

"But why would the school principal steal the school skeleton?" Dink asked. "He's the one offering the reward for finding Mr. Bones!"

Josh balled up his lunch bag. "Let's go see Mrs. Waters again. Maybe she's remembered where she saw that zigzag sneaker sole."

The kids hurried into the school and headed for the principal's office.

"Let's leave our lunch stuff," Dink said, stopping at his locker. They opened their locker doors and put their lunch bags inside.

They found Mrs. Waters sitting at her desk with a cup of tea in front of her.

She looked up when the kids walked in. "This

school has gone wacky," she said. "First Miss Shotsky's skeleton disappears. Then I start losing things. I've been searching for my closet key for two days! Whatever will be next!"

"You're missing a key?" Josh asked, already digging in his pocket.

"Yes. I haven't been able to put my purse and coat in the closet," Mrs. Waters said.

Josh found the skeleton drawing wrapped around the key. He removed the paper and put the key on Mrs. Waters's desk. "Is this it?"

Mrs. Waters picked up the key and examined it. "No, this isn't the one I lost."

"Could it be a copy of your key?" Dink asked.

"I suppose." Mrs. Waters looked at Dink. "Why would anyone take my key and make a copy? Where did you find it, Josh?"

"In my locker," he said. "Along with this." He showed Mrs. Waters the picture of the skeleton.

"A key and a skeleton?" she said. "What does it mean?"

"We think the key leads to the skeleton," Ruth

145

Rose said. "So it might be in your closet!"

"My closet! Who would do such a thing?"

Mrs. Waters stood up and marched over to her coat closet. Dink, Josh, and Ruth Rose followed her.

Mrs. Waters inserted the key into the lock and turned it. The door slowly swung open.

Hanging from Mrs. Waters's coat hook was the school skeleton. Mr. Bones had a big grin on his face.

"IT'S MR.BONES!"Ruth Rose screamed.

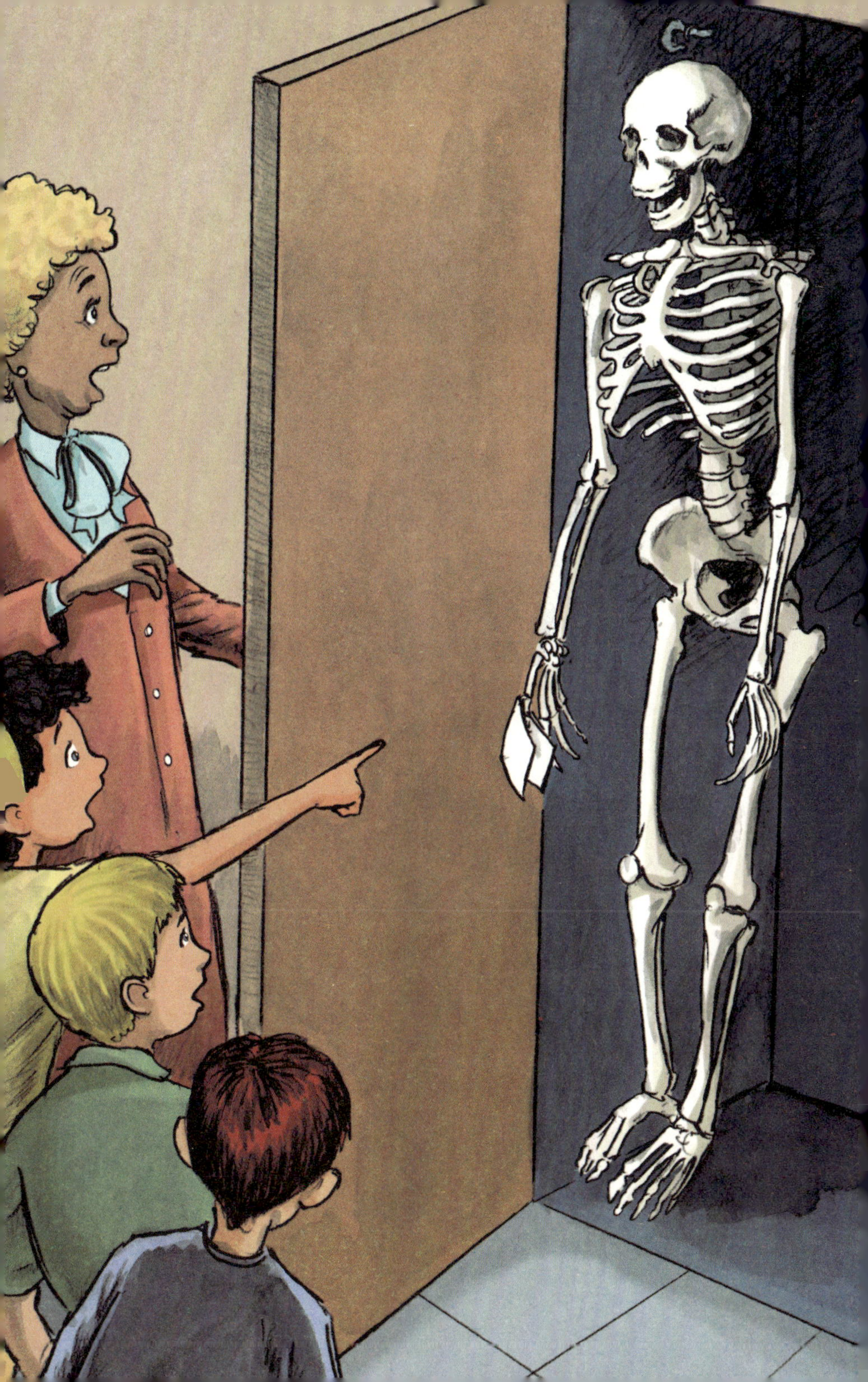

Chapter 10

Mr. Dillon came flying out of his office. "What's the matter?"

Before Mrs. Waters could answer, Miss Shotsky burst into the little room.

"Who screamed? Anyone hurt?" Miss Shotsky cried, looking first at the three kids. "Are you kids all right?"

"Yes, and here's your friend, Miss Shotsky." Mrs. Waters pulled the closet door all the way open.

"Well, for heaven's sake!" Miss Shotsky exclaimed. "And what's this?"

She removed a folded paper that had been taped to the skeleton's hand. She read it out loud: "APRIL FOOLS!"

They all burst out laughing.

"Someone has been playing a trick on the whole school!" Mrs. Waters said.

"Well, Mr. Bones is going back where he belongs," Miss Shotsky said. She lifted the school skeleton off the hook.

"Say bye-bye," she said, waving the skeleton's hand. Then she carried it into her office.

Mrs. Waters went to her desk. She looked at her calendar. "Today is April Fools' Day," she said. "It totally slipped my mind."

She carried her coat to the closet. She placed it on the hook, then bent down and picked something up off the closet floor. When she turned around, she was holding a pair of sneakers. She turned them over so everyone could see the bottoms.

"Zigzag treads!" Josh said.

"Are those the sneakers that everyone's been talking about?" Mr. Dillon said. "How did they get in your coat closet, Mrs. Waters?"

Mrs. Waters stared at her boss for a moment, then shook her head. "I have no idea, Mr. Dillon."

"Um, excuse me, I think I know," Dink said.

Mr. Dillon looked at Dink. The lights glinted off his eyeglasses. "You do? Tell us, Dink."

Dink blushed. "Well, someone decided to play an April Fools' Day joke on the whole school. So he took Miss Shotsky's skeleton and hid it in Mrs. Waters's closet."

Dink looked at Mrs. Waters. "He took your key so you wouldn't be able to open the door."

"But why would this person hide his sneakers?" Mr. Dillon asked.

"Because he left a footprint," Josh said. "And he planned to make more footprints later."

"And he borrowed Mrs. Waters's powder to do it with," Ruth Rose said, grinning at Dink and Josh.

"He took the key somewhere and had six copies made," Dink went on. "He drew six skeletons and left them and the keys in six different lockers, one for each classroom."

Mr. Dillon shook his head. "Amazing! Why would he do such a thing?"

"I think he wanted all the kids to search for the skeleton," Dink said.

"I'm confused," Mr. Dillon said. He sat in Mrs. Waters's chair. "How could some stranger come into the school and do all this without being seen?"

Dink glanced at Josh and Ruth Rose. They both nodded.

"We think it was someone who works here, sir," Dink said.

"One of the teachers?" Mr. Dillon said. "But who? And why?"

Dink, Josh, and Ruth Rose looked at Mr. Dillon. They kept staring until the principal blushed.

"Oh my goodness!" Mrs. Waters cried. "It was you, wasn't it?"

"Caught," Mr. Dillon said, grinning.

"But you wanted to get caught," Ruth Rose said. "That's why you left footprints and keys and notes."

Mr. Dillon nodded. "Yes, I wanted to get caught. You see, I love April Fools' Day. When I was your age, I couldn't wait for this day. I played pranks all the time!"

"I did, too!" Mrs. Waters said. "My sister was always finding frogs in her sweater drawer."

学校里的人体骨骼

"No one plays tricks or pranks anymore," Mr. Dillon went on. "Each year April first just slips by, unnoticed.

"So I decided that this year would be different. This year, everyone would remember April Fools' Day."

Mr. Dillon kicked off his loafers and pulled on the zigzag sneakers. "I've missed these," he said. "I wear them to school every morning, then change to my loafers."

Dink laughed. "We went around measuring teachers' feet, and all the time those sneakers were in the closet."

The principal grinned. "I have to admit, I had a lot of fun. On Monday I went in to wash my hands at Miss Shotsky's sink. It was early; no one was here. Then I saw the skeleton with her scarf draped around its shoulders, and that's when I got the idea."

His eyes twinkled. "I grabbed the skeleton, came back through our connecting door, and hid it in Mrs. Waters's closet. She leaves the key in the lock, so I just locked the door and kept the key."

"Then you changed your shoes, right?" Josh asked.

Mr. Dillon nodded. "I didn't realize I'd left a footprint. But when you told me that later, I decided to leave more footprints, and that's when I borrowed Mrs. Waters's powder."

"And I expect it back, please," she said.

Everyone laughed again.

Mr. Dillon smiled. "Since you three kids were

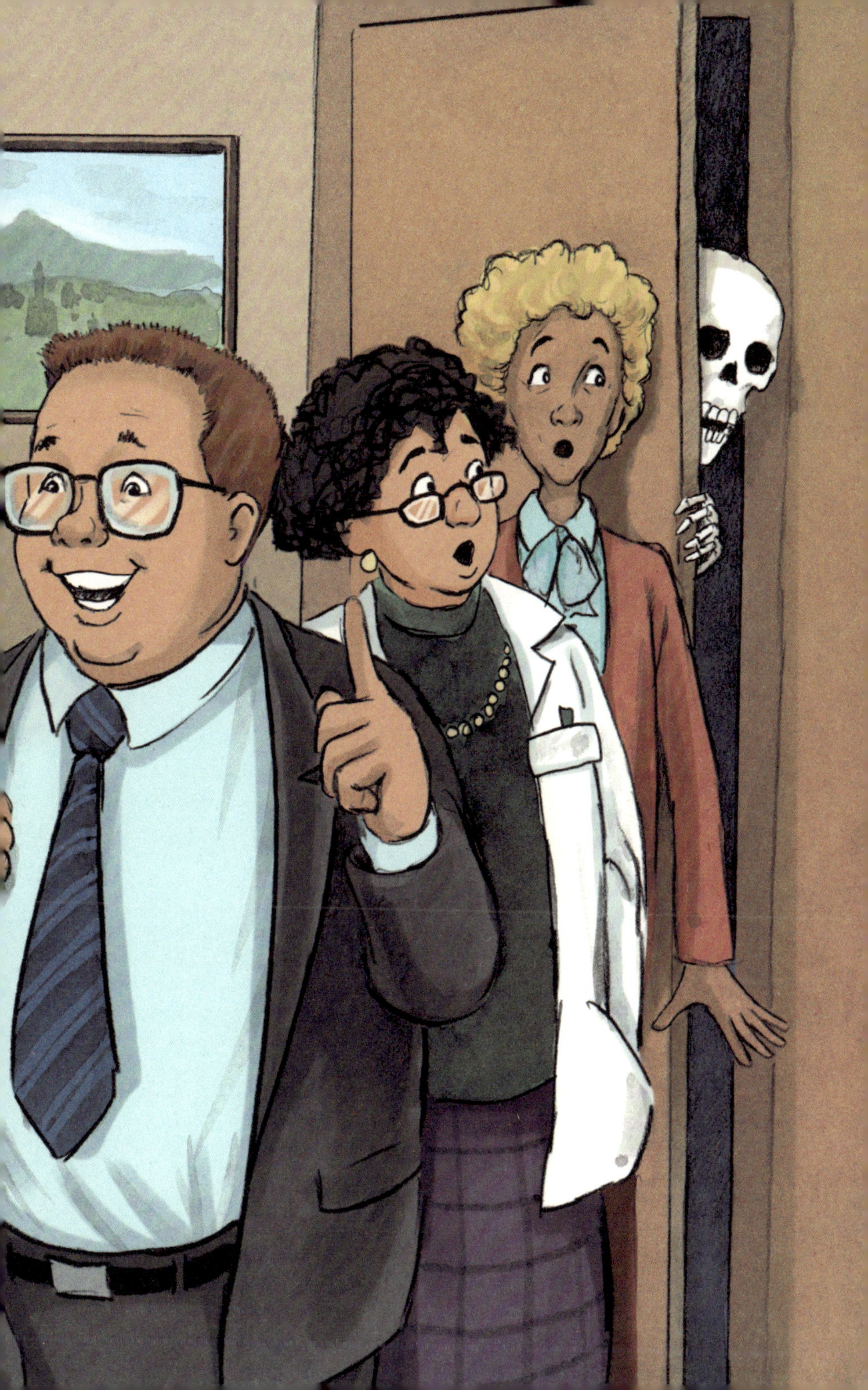

the first to find Mr. Bones, you get to make the announcement over the intercom."

"What announcement?" Dink asked.

"Why, about the trip, of course! I've hired buses to take the entire school to the aquarium," Mr. Dillon said.

"Everyone is going?" asked Ruth Rose.

"Everyone searched for Mr. Bones, so everyone gets the prize," said Mr. Dillon.

Suddenly Mr. Bones's head popped through the connecting door.

"Even me?" the skeleton asked.

Text copyright © 2003 by Ron Roy
Illustrations copyright © 2003 by John Steven Gurney
All rights reserved under International and Pan-American Copyright Conventions. Published in the United States by Random House Children's Books, a division of Random House, Inc., New York, and simultaneously in Canada by Random House of Canada Limited, Toronto.

本书中英双语版由中南博集天卷文化传媒有限公司与企鹅兰登（北京）文化发展有限公司合作出版。

"企鹅"及其相关标识是企鹅兰登已经注册或尚未注册的商标。
未经允许，不得擅用。
封底凡无企鹅防伪标识者均属未经授权之非法版本。

©中南博集天卷文化传媒有限公司。本书版权受法律保护。未经权利人许可，任何人不得以任何方式使用本书包括正文、插图、封面、版式等任何部分内容，违者将受到法律制裁。

著作权合同登记号：字18-2023-258

图书在版编目（CIP）数据

学校里的人体骨骼：汉英对照 /（美）罗恩·罗伊著；（美）约翰·史蒂文·格尼绘；王芬芬译. -- 长沙：湖南少年儿童出版社，2024.10. --（A to Z神秘案件）.
ISBN 978-7-5562-7818-3

Ⅰ．H319.4

中国国家版本馆CIP数据核字第2024EX2625号

A TO Z SHENMI ANJIAN XUEXIAO LI DE RENTI GUGE

A to Z神秘案件 学校里的人体骨骼

[美] 罗恩·罗伊 著　　[美] 约翰·史蒂文·格尼 绘　　王芬芬 译

责任编辑：唐 凌　李 炜	策划出品：李 炜　张苗苗　文赛峰
策划编辑：文赛峰	特约编辑：杜天梦
营销编辑：付 佳　杨 朔　周晓茜	封面设计：霍雨佳
版权支持：王媛媛	版式设计：马睿君
插图上色：河北传图文化	内文排版：李 洁

出 版 人：刘星保
出　　 版：湖南少年儿童出版社
地　　 址：湖南省长沙市晚报大道89号
邮　　 编：410016
电　　 话：0731-82196320
常年法律顾问：湖南崇民律师事务所　柳成柱律师
经　　 销：新华书店
开　　 本：875 mm×1230 mm　1/32
字　　 数：83千字
版　　 次：2024年10月第1版
书　　 号：ISBN 978-7-5562-7818-3
印　　 刷：三河市中晟雅豪印务有限公司
印　　 张：5
印　　 次：2024年10月第1次印刷
定　　 价：280.00元（全10册）

若有质量问题，请致电质量监督电话：010-59096394　团购电话：010-59320018

A to Z 神秘案件 中英双语
第二辑

THE
TALKING
T. REX

会说话的
霸王龙

[美] 罗恩·罗伊 著
[美] 约翰·史蒂文·格尼 绘 周丽娟 译

湖南少年儿童出版社 小博集
·长沙·

印第安河
劳伦斯出租车公司
沿河路
骑马
小径
自行车道
租马处
树林
林景路
印第安路
自行车道
大桥路
比尔
自行车店
消防站
超市
知更鸟路
乌鸦街
雀鸟巷
歌鹤街
猫头鹰路
野鸡巷
蓝松鸦路
鹌鹑路
健身
中心
森林
自行车道
蓝鸟路
蜂鸟巷
丘鹬路
埃莉餐馆
橡子公寓
橡树街
毛脚
宠物店
自行车道
中心教堂
人民池塘
邮局
社区花园
和鱼塘
绿地储蓄银行
老年公寓
警察局
西绿街
鹅岛
沿河路
绿地
图书馆
老年活动中心
镇公所
主街
儿童动物园
和水族馆
香格里拉
酒店
自行车道

欢迎来到绿地镇
一起解开A to Z神秘案件
北
西
东
南
沿河路
码头
少女岛
绿地中学
租船处
罗思鱼饵店
鸭子步行道
老鹰巷
农场路
乔希家
绿地小学
丁丁家
露丝家
林梢弯道
牧场路
狐狸小道
银环路
林荫街
鹌鹑路
音乐台
玫瑰园
宜人街
蓟花街
野花路
玫瑰街
中心公园
天鹅池
绿地高中
运动场
体育馆+游泳馆
黄杨木巷
霍华德理发店
角落书店
加油站
清水塘
奇妙温室
狗舍+兽医
东绿街
镇网球场
镇游泳池
儿童游泳池
沿河路
镇棒球场
去往蓝山镇

人物介绍

三人小组的成员,聪明勇敢,喜欢读推理小说,紧急关头总能保持头脑冷静。喜欢在做事之前好好思考!

丁丁

三人小组的成员,活泼机智,喜欢吃好吃的食物,常常有意想不到的点子。

乔希

三人小组的成员,活泼开朗,喜欢从头到脚穿同一种颜色的衣服,总是那个能找到大部分线索的人。

露丝

丁丁、乔希和露丝的朋友，他带了一个惊喜来到绿地镇。

尤德·惠特

尤德的朋友。

迪安·怀特费瑟

尤德雇的帮手。

斯库普·雷克

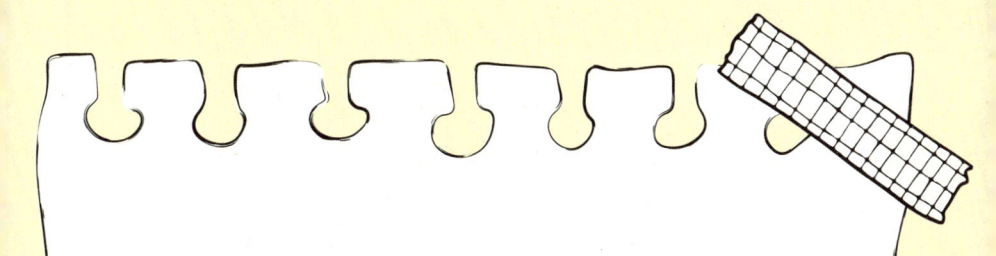

字母T代表T. Rex，霸王龙……

尤德从口袋里掏出一个塑料袋。"如果你们到四周转一转，捡些纸片，那就是帮了大忙。"他说。

当尤德向卡车走去时，丁丁、乔希和露丝便分散开来，开始捡垃圾。

丁丁俯身去捡一张皱巴巴的传单，这时，他听到一声大叫。他抬头看了看，那叫声是从蒂龙附近传来的。只见尤德、迪安和斯库普聚集在那扇打开的门前。

即使在一百英尺以外，丁丁也能听到尤德的大叫："我不相信！"

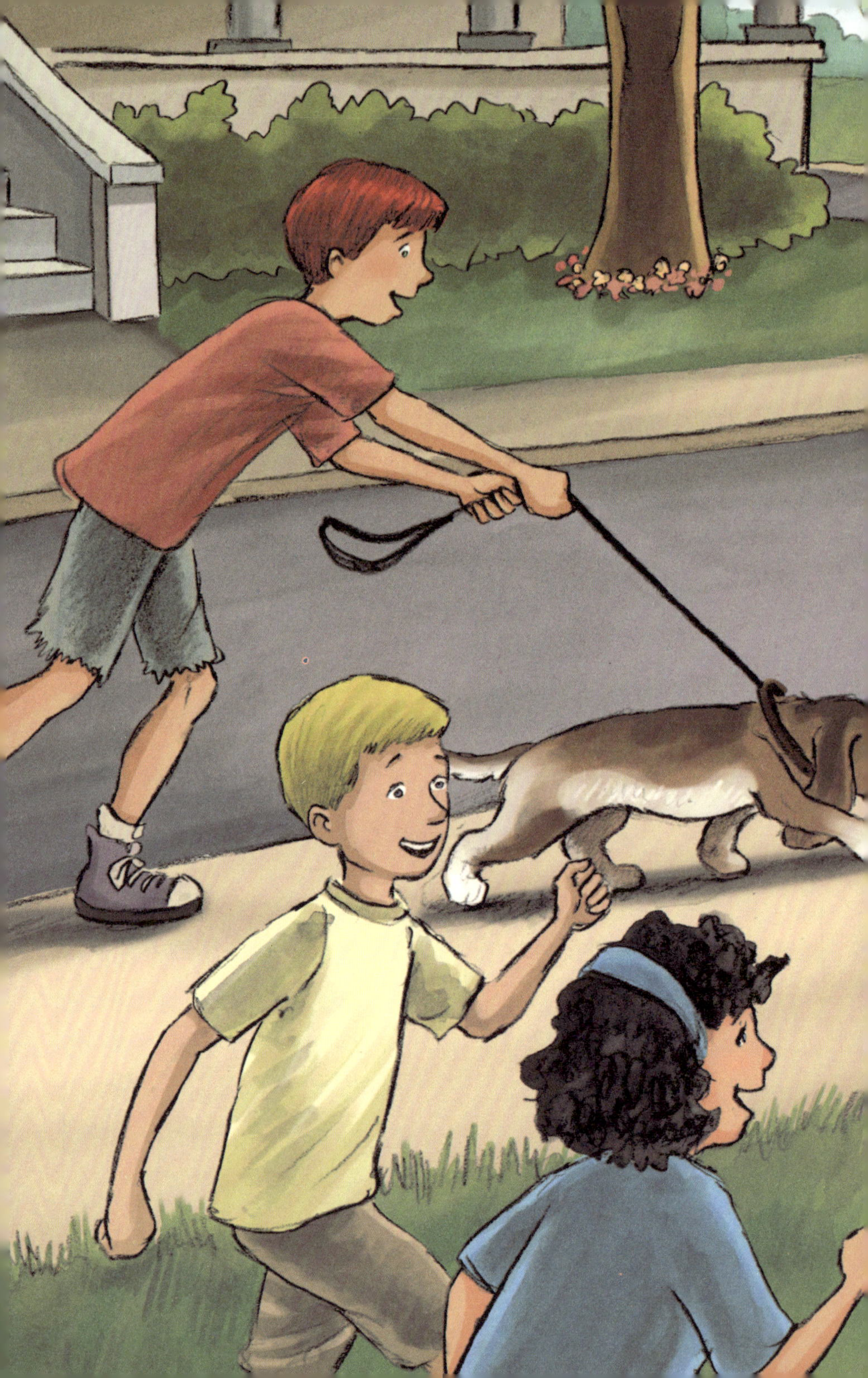

第一章

丁丁、乔希和露丝急匆匆地向高中走去。这天是7月3日,因而他们都穿着短裤和T恤衫。乔希的狗狗帕尔,系着牵引绳,一直在前面领路。它一路上不是嗅嗅这个就是嗅嗅那个,耷拉下来的耳朵都快拖到地面上了。

"我迫不及待地想再见到尤德。"丁丁说。丁丁的全名叫唐纳德·戴维·邓肯,但大部分人都叫他丁丁。

三个孩子是在参观尤德父母在蒙大拿州的度假农场时认识尤德的。乔希在那儿发现了一个大大的金块,他把金块给了尤德,以便帮尤德交大

A to Z 神秘案件

学学费。现在,尤德要来绿地镇见他们了。

"我想知道他在明信片上说的大惊喜是什么。"露丝说。露丝喜欢穿一身同种颜色的衣服。今天她从束发带到运动鞋都是深蓝色的。这种颜色和她那双锐利的蓝眼睛很是相配。

"快把明信片读给我们听听。"乔希对丁丁说。

丁丁从口袋里掏出一张明信片。他们在宜人街停下脚步,丁丁读起明信片来:

丁丁、乔希、露丝:

    你们好!我将于7月3日带一个大惊喜来到绿地镇。请于当天中午到高中操场与我见面吧。到时见!

你们的朋友,
尤德

"也许大惊喜是一个大比萨呢。"乔希说。

"你倒是想得美。"露丝说。

"看,那是波克特先生。"丁丁说着,转身朝中心公园走去。他们的朋友撒迪厄斯·波克特正

会说话的霸王龙

站在镇上的玫瑰园里。他戴着工作手套,手里拿着一把铲子。他的小狗伦道夫正盯着天鹅池里的一群鸭子看。

乔希扔下牵引绳,帕尔便跑过去和那只毛茸茸的小狗打招呼。

"您好,波克特先生!"露丝说。

"嘿,你们好,孩子们。"头发花白的老人说:"你们都为明天晚上的烟花表演做好准备了吗?我看到工人们正在游泳池附近布置场地。"

"我们都会去的,"乔希说,"您和伦道夫会去吗?""我会去,"波克特先生说,"但老伦道夫更喜欢待在家里。它不喜欢听巨大的声响。"

"帕尔也会待在家里,"乔希说,"它甚至连生日蜡烛都不喜欢!"

波克特先生开始挖一株看上去已经枯死了的玫瑰,那株玫瑰上既没有花朵也没有叶子。一辆手推车里放着一株健康的玫瑰,这株玫瑰上长满了绿油油的叶子。

"想不想帮我种这株新玫瑰?"波克特先生问孩子们。

11

丁丁看了看自己的手表,说:"好啊,但是之后我们要去高中见一个朋友。他的名字叫尤德·惠特。他正在上学,将来准备成为一个教师。"

"他带了一个大惊喜从蒙大拿州赶过来!"露丝说。

"这花不了多长时间。"波克特先生说。他一边移除原有的玫瑰,一边分派起任务来。

露丝往坑里撒一把肥料。

丁丁往坑里铲一些松散的土。

乔希用花园里的水管往坑里灌满水。

"今晚老天爷可能会给我们下点雨。"波克特先生一边说,一边抬头看了看天上的云。他从手推车里提起那株新玫瑰,把它放进坑里,并确保它直直的。

"这样看上去好极了,"波克特先生说,"你们三个真是超级棒的园丁。丁丁,如果你愿意把手推车放回棚屋里,我就来填埋剩下的土。"

丁丁把铲子递给波克特先生,把手推车推到花园棚屋前。只见棚屋的门用一个旧螺丝刀别

会说话的霸王龙

着。丁丁打开门,把手推车推了进去。

拥挤的小棚屋里几乎没有地方摆放小推车。架子上堆满了盆子、罐子、一袋袋肥料、水桶、园艺书籍以及丁丁父母也有的那些工具。干净的砖铺地板上摆放着一些耙子、铲子、园艺桩和一卷卷水管。

丁丁把手推车斜放在棚屋后部的一堆空麻布袋上。他重新用螺丝刀把门别好,然后离开。

正当丁丁走到其他人身边时,一辆红色小汽车从主街驶出,向高中方向驶去。一股蒸汽从汽车引擎盖下冒了出来。

"那是你们的朋友吗?"波克特先生问,"但愿他不是一路开着这样的车从蒙大拿州过来的!"

"我们要走了,"丁丁说,"想见见尤德吗,波克特先生?"

"现在不行,"波克特先生说,"我和伦道夫需要吃午餐,还需要小睡一会儿。谢谢你们帮忙。"

孩子们带上帕尔,朝那辆红色的小汽车跑去。车子停了下来,一个高个子年轻人从车里

13

走了下来。那人长着一头黑色鬈发，肩膀很宽。他穿着一件T恤衫，一条半截牛仔裤和一双红色高帮运动鞋。

"那不是尤德。"当他们走近那人时，丁丁说。

第二章

那人转过身来,挥了挥手。"嘿,你们一定是丁丁、乔希和露丝吧。我是斯库普·雷克。我和尤德还有他的朋友迪安一起工作。他们马上就到。"

斯库普掀开汽车引擎盖,更多的蒸汽从里面冒了出来。他从前排座位上提来一壶水,然后拧开散热器的盖子。突然他大叫一声,接着把手指放进嘴里。

"你们觉得我现在应该得到教训了吧!"斯库普边说边摇头。他从口袋里掏出一个创可贴,撕掉贴膜,用绿色的创可贴包住手指。

就在这时，一辆长长的平板卡车停在了斯库普的车旁。一块棕色的防水布罩着平板卡车车身，遮住了一个又大又鼓的东西，整个东西都是用绳索绑住的。驾驶室的门打开了，一个又高又瘦的人跳到了地面上。他穿着牛仔裤、短袖衬衫，戴着一顶牛仔帽。"你们好。"那人说着，笑容满面地看着丁丁、乔希和露丝。

"你好，尤德！"孩子们异口同声地说。

一个男人从卡车的副驾驶座那边跳了出来。他个子矮小，却精瘦结实，黑色的头发扎成一个马尾。他穿着工作靴、宽松短裤和一件扯掉了袖子的法兰绒衬衫。

"伙计们，我想让你们认识一下我的室友，也是我最好的朋友，迪安·怀特费瑟。"尤德说。"迪安，这是丁丁，乔希和露丝。"

迪安绕过卡车向孩子们走来。他长着一双黑色的眼睛，露出了友好的笑容。他的衬衫口袋里装满了笔，走路时，腰带上挂着的一串钥匙叮当作响。

孩子们和迪安握了握手。随后尤德和迪安逗着帕尔玩起来，帕尔则给了他们两人大大的湿吻。

"好啦,我们开始干活怎么样?"迪安说着,瞥了一眼天空,"我打赌,到半夜会下雨。"他开始解绳索。

斯库普钻回自己的小车。"我来的时候经过了酒店,"他说,"我去看看我们的房间。"他把车开走,这回引擎盖下只冒出一点点蒸汽。

"要我们帮忙吗?"露丝问。

迪安对她笑了笑,说:"我最喜欢听这样的话了。"

"我们解开绳索时,你们可以把绳索卷起来,"尤德说,"只要把它们放在地上就好了。"

乔希告诉帕尔好好待着,然后孩子们都过来帮忙。过了一会儿,绳索全部解开了。尤德和迪安把防水布猛地拉到了地上。

当丁丁看到是什么东西这么鼓的时候,他往后跳了一下。他正直直地盯着一只霸王龙的头呢!

"来看看霸王龙蒂龙吧,"尤德笑着说,"等组装好后,它看上去会更棒的。"

丁丁倒吸了一口气。"你们从哪儿弄来的?"他问。

会说话的霸王龙

"我们买来的。"尤德说。

乔希咧嘴笑了。"从恐龙玩具店里买来的吧?"他打趣道。

"不是,是从制作它的人那里买的,"迪安说,"那个人打算开一个恐龙主题公园,但后来他失去了兴趣。他在报纸上打了个广告,我们看到广告,就买下了蒂龙和这辆卡车。"

"嗯,你为什么需要一只恐龙?"露丝问。

"为了筹集资金,"尤德说,"迪安和我想教孩子们了解曾经生存在蒙大拿州的恐龙的知识。我们已经决定在度假农场后面的一块土地上建一个小型博物馆。"

"到时候蒂龙将成为引人注目的明星。"迪安补充说。

"我们第一次见到蒂龙时,它就像你们现在所见到的一样,全都零散地放在那个人的仓库里。我设计了一个电脑程序,让蒂龙能够移动并且说话。我们带着它周游全国,筹集捐款。"

"斯库普也是老师吗?"丁丁问。

"不是,我们在怀俄明州遇见了斯库普。他

当时正在找工作,因此我们雇了他。"尤德说,"他负责订酒店房间,为我们在校外举办活动获取许可,制作传单之类的事情。等博物馆建好后,他还想在那儿工作呢。"

迪安爬上卡车车身,说:"我们把这家伙组装起来吧,尤德。"

"你们怎么组装它呢?"丁丁问。

"很简单,就像用立体零件拼装模型一样。"迪安说着,指了指卡车车身上的一个盒子,里面装着大号的螺母、螺栓,还有电缆。

"蒂龙是用什么做的?"露丝问,"它很重吗?"

"不是很重。"尤德说。他从迪安手里接过霸王龙的尾巴,然后轻轻地把尾巴放在地上。

"制作蒂龙的材料主要是玻璃纤维和橡胶。它的骨头是铝做的。它的牙齿、脚指甲和眼睛是塑料做的。"

孩子们轻轻碰了碰一个六英寸[1]长的牙齿。

1.英寸:英美制长度单位。1英寸=0.0254米。——编者

会说话的霸王龙

"它看上去很逼真!"乔希说。

"当心,这些边缘有的很锋利。"迪安说。他咧嘴一笑,晃了晃手指,那手指上缠着一个绿色的创可贴。

这时,斯库普的红色小汽车疾驰而来,大家都看了过去。斯库普停好车,手里拿着一沓纸从车里钻了出来。

"孩子们,你们愿不愿意帮忙呢?"他问,"你们能不能拿着这些传单在镇上发一发?"

斯库普把传单递给露丝。她看了看最上面的一张。只见一张霸王龙照片的下面写着这样几行文字:

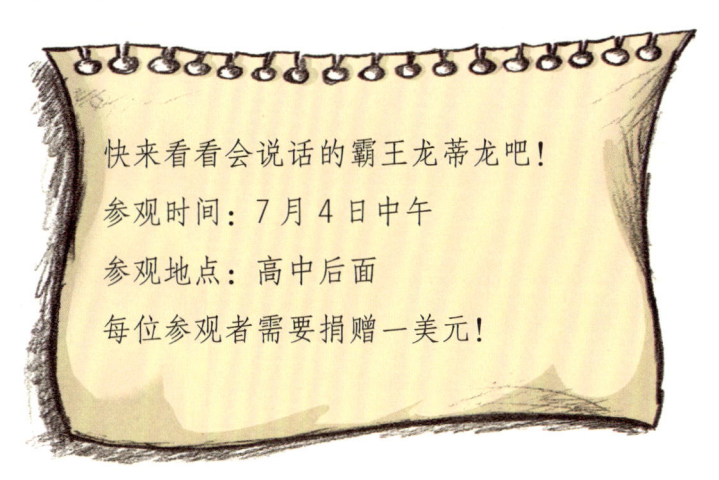

快来看看会说话的霸王龙蒂龙吧!
参观时间:7月4日中午
参观地点:高中后面
每位参观者需要捐赠一美元!

"当然，你们三个人是免费看的。"尤德从露丝肩膀后面看过来说。

"太酷了！"乔希说。

"我们应该把传单发给谁呢？"丁丁问。

"任何人，每个人，"斯库普说，"商店里的人啊，朋友们啊，任何喜欢恐龙的人。"

露丝把那沓传单分成三小份。他们每人拿一份。

"你们能看着帕尔吗？"乔希问。

"没问题。"斯库普说。

孩子们拿着传单朝主街走去。

一个小时后，孩子们回来了。"明天全镇的人都会来看蒂龙的！"丁丁说。

"太棒了！你们现在觉得它怎么样？"尤德指了指蒂龙问。

蒂龙站立着，用厚实的后腿和尾巴保持平衡。它的身体和尾巴展开后比一辆校车还长，而且它差不多和丁丁家的房子一样高。它的后足和帕尔一样长。此时，帕尔正在嗅它的一个巨大的

塑料脚指甲。

"这也……这也……"丁丁想不出合适的词。

尤德和迪安哈哈大笑起来。

"蒂龙还不是真实尺寸，"迪安说，"成年霸王龙会更大些。来吧，我给你们看看这家伙肚子里有什么。"

他解开一串钥匙，将其中一把钥匙插进蒂龙身体一侧的一个小孔里。当迪安转动钥匙时，一个小金属环弹了出来。迪安拉了拉金属环，随即一扇带有铰链的门打开了。

"太棒了！"乔希说，"这真是深藏不露啊！"

迪安从门内拿起一个橡胶楔子，用它把门撑住。接着，他从门外伸手进去，将一个带铰链的折叠楼梯拉了下来。"瞧一瞧吧。"他说。

孩子们跪在楼梯上，往恐龙肚子里仔细瞧。只见恐龙肚子的内壁由多条铝棒支撑着。一排钩子上挂着一些工具、一圈圈绳索和电线。恐龙肚子里没有窗户，很闷热。

地板上有个地方铺着一块地毯，一台笔记本电脑放在地毯中央的一张小桌子上。一束灰色的

A to Z 神秘案件

电脑线弯弯曲曲地穿过地板,其中有几根电脑线延伸到恐龙的胸部,然后在颈和头的地方消失不见了。

"电脑操控一切,"迪安说,"只要点击鼠标,我就能让蒂龙的尾巴、嘴和前腿动起来。"

迪安从孩子们身边挤过去,走进蒂龙的肚子。"我在蒂龙的头部放了一个扩音器。"迪安解

释道,他给大家看了一个小麦克风,"我对着这个说话,听起来就像是蒂龙在说话。"

"你现在能让它说话吗?"乔希问。

"那得等到明天,"迪安说,"从今天早上五点开始,我们一直在赶路,我实在是精疲力竭了。我得睡上差不多十个小时呢!"

迪安和孩子们从蒂龙肚子里钻了出来,然后迪安把那扇门关上。

"你们都住在香格里拉吗?"露丝问。

"尤德和斯库普是,"迪安说,"我准备睡在这儿。"迪安从卡车里拖出一个睡袋,然后把睡袋扔到地上。

"你为什么睡在外面?"丁丁问。

迪安咧嘴一笑。"他们两个打呼噜。"他说着,指了指斯库普和尤德,"而且,我喜欢睡在星空下。还有就是,我要看守蒂龙。第二天早晨,我会去酒店,到他们那里洗澡。"

"在哪里能买到好吃的汉堡包,"斯库普问孩子们,"以及明天的早餐?"

"埃莉餐馆!"三个孩子异口同声地说。

露丝朝主街指了指。"餐馆在宠物店和健身中心之间。"她说。

"谢谢你们帮忙,明天见。"尤德说。

三人钻进那辆红色小汽车,接着斯库普开着车向主街驶去。一阵轰隆隆的雷声在孩子们头顶上方响起,孩子们赶紧朝家里跑。

第三章

晚上，雷声把丁丁吵醒。他舒舒服服地躺在床上，隔窗看着暴风雨。一道雷电闪过，他想起了蒂龙，它还站在外面的黑暗和雨水中。

第二天，丁丁八点半左右来到高中。他抬头凝视蒂龙。这只恐龙在蓝天下显得又高又安静。它嘴巴闭着，眼睛凝望远方。暴风雨过后，草地依旧湿漉漉的。雾气升腾起来，随即又在太阳底下蒸发不见了。

尤德、迪安和斯库普都不见人影。丁丁走到卡车边，往车窗里看去。只见迪安的睡袋还铺在座位上。

一会儿后,露丝带着她的弟弟纳特来了。她穿了一身橙色,从束发带到袜子再到运动鞋都是橙色的。当纳特看到蒂龙时,他惊讶地张大嘴巴。他走到蒂龙的一只后腿前,摸了摸。"这摸起来像是一个橡胶恐龙玩具。"他说。

乔希和他的两个弟弟——布赖恩和布拉德利迈着轻快的步伐穿过操场向这边跑来。帕尔扯着狗链子一路向前跑。

这对双胞胎停住脚步。"这是一只坦克龙!"布赖恩叫了起来。

"不,不是!"布拉德利争辩起来,"这是一只火车龙!"

乔希笑了起来:"伙计们,这是一只霸王龙。"

"它不是真恐龙,对吧,乔希?"布拉德利问。

乔希松开帕尔的狗链子。"不是,"他说,"它只是一个会动的大玩偶。"

斯库普把他的红色小汽车停靠在蒂龙旁边。他跳出车子,向孩子们走来。

"早上好,"斯库普说,"昨晚有暴风雨,对吧?雷声差点把我们从床上震下来。"

会说话的霸王龙

斯库普坐在地上,穿着一双凉鞋。他那双湿漉漉的运动鞋被他绑在一起,挂在汽车天线上。

迪安和尤德穿过中心公园向这边走来。

"嘿,孩子们。"尤德说。"斯库普,你错过了一顿美味的早餐。那个埃莉做的华夫饼太好吃了!"

斯库普点了点头。"我似乎睡不醒。"他说。

尤德看着纳特、布赖恩和布拉德利说:"你们喜欢恐龙吗?"

三个孩子眉开眼笑,点了点头。

"我最喜欢霸王龙了!"纳特说。镇上的人开始陆续抵达,他们站在蒂龙周围,看得目瞪口呆。丁丁朝角落书店里的帕斯基先生挥手打招呼,他还看见了香格里拉酒店的主人斯皮韦茨夫妇。

丁丁看见自己的妈妈、乔希的妈妈和露丝的妈妈一同出现。乔希的妈妈提了一个野餐篮。

"伙计们,去和妈妈坐一起,好吗?"乔希问两个双胞胎。

"我们能带帕尔走吗?"布赖恩问。

乔希把狗链子递给布赖恩。"可以,但不要让它跑掉了。等妈妈离开的时候带它回家,好吗?"

"为什么所有事都让布赖恩做?"布拉德利抱怨道。

乔希叹了口气:"你们俩可以一起牵狗,好吗?"

纳特、布赖恩和布拉德利带着帕尔向他们的妈妈走去。

"这真是太好了。"尤德看着逐渐增多的人群说。"迪安,要不然你去给蒂龙做准备,我和斯库普来收钱,怎么样?"

当孩子们挑选地方坐下的时候,丁丁见到更多镇上他认识的人。奥利里家的一群孩子出现了,丁丁跟他们挥手打招呼。一些人带了椅子或毯子过来坐。高中操场上挤满了人。

尤德和斯库普穿过人群,从每个人那里收取一美元。当手里塞满钱时,他们向卡车走去,把钱锁进驾驶室里。就这样,他们每人各跑了两三趟。

会说话的霸王龙

"他们一定赚了很多钱，"乔希说，"我打赌，这儿有两百人！"

尤德拿着一个无线麦克风爬上卡车车身。"各位，谢谢光临！"他对着人群说。

等大家安静下来，尤德接着解释他们为什么筹钱。"我们的博物馆将于明年夏天建成，我希望你们当中的一些人能前去参观。"他说。

尤德把麦克风对准恐龙，说："现在我希望你们所有人来认识一下我的朋友蒂龙。蒂龙，向这些好心人介绍一下你自己好吗？"

没有任何事情发生。蒂龙站在那里，安安静静，一动不动，一句话也没说。

"我猜蒂龙今天早上有点害羞。"尤德说，接着，他用更大的声音说，"蒂龙，你能跟我们这儿的所有朋友打个招呼吗？要是你听得见我说话，就摇摇尾巴吧。"

这引起了一些笑声，但蒂龙依旧一动不动。

观众里的一些孩子开始坐不住了。一个坐在丁丁身后的男孩低声嘀咕："不知道我们的钱还能不能要回来。"

后来，突然，蒂龙的尾巴向右摆动一下，再向左摆动一下。它的小小前臂上下挥舞起来。蒂龙张开嘴巴，用低沉的声音说："嘿！"

"嘿，蒂龙！"人们也大声回应它。

"你们当中有多少人知道我是哪个种类的恐龙？"蒂龙问。丁丁听出了蒂龙嘴里发出的声音是迪安的。

每个孩子和大人都举起手。"霸王龙！"纳特大声喊道。

"没错，我是一只霸王龙。"蒂龙说。

"那么，今天早上，你们当中有多少人记得要吃一顿丰盛的早餐呢？"

大部分人都举了手。

"嗯。"蒂龙点了点巨大的头，说，"大概七千万年前，我可是吃其他恐龙当早餐的呢！"

大家都哈哈大笑起来。

尤德跳下卡车，和丁丁、乔希还有露丝坐到一起。

"迪安擅长和观众交流，对不对？"尤德说。

"你会发誓说蒂龙真的在说话。"丁丁说。

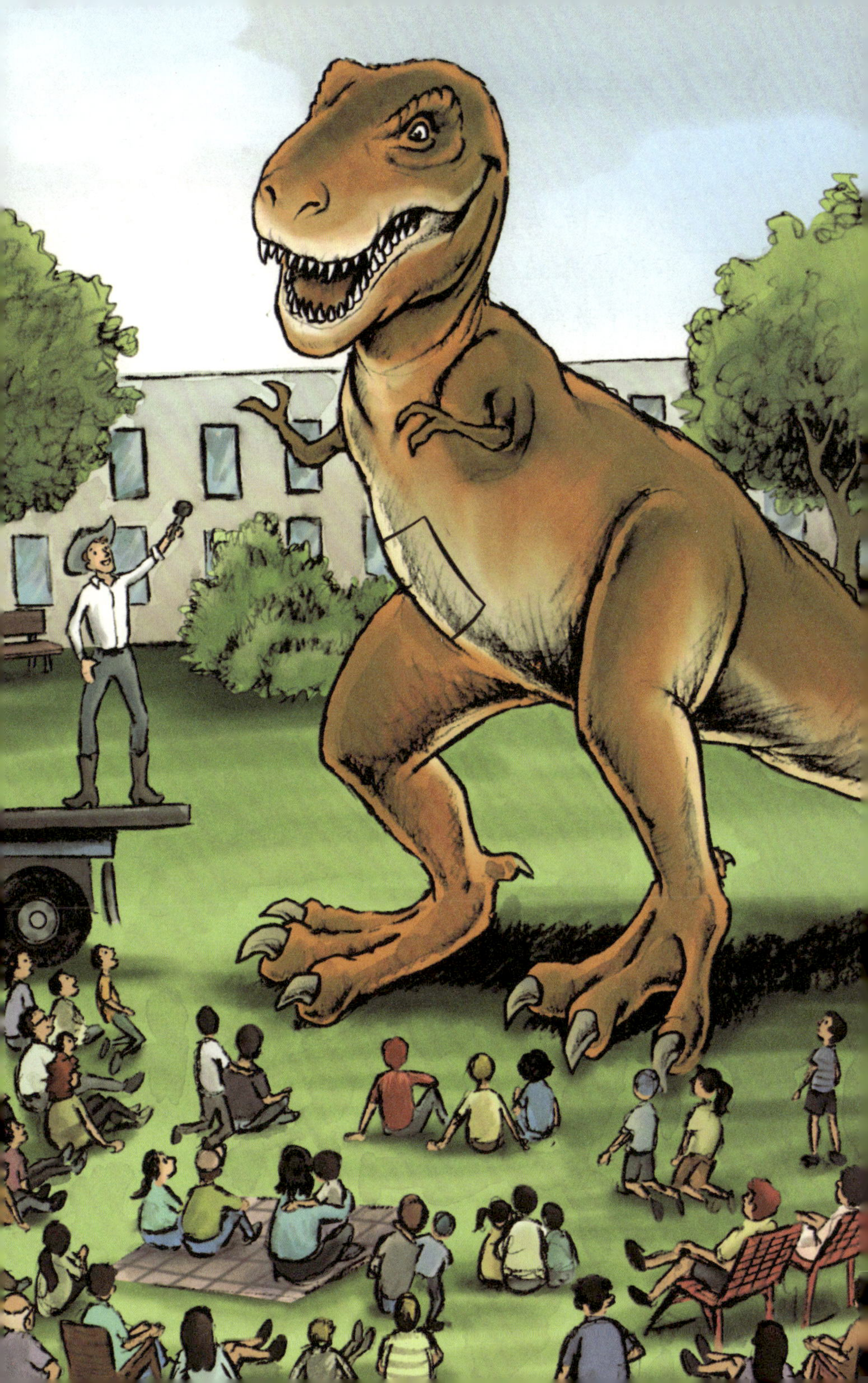

尤德点点头，说："是啊，迪安是个机械天才。不过，开始的时候他吓了我一跳。我还以为电脑出了故障呢。"

蒂龙向观众讲述了曾经出现在北美洲的恐龙的知识。它讲了它们吃什么，怎么保护自己以及怎么抚养后代。

这场表演持续了大约半个小时。"我希望你们都去图书馆，了解更多关于恐龙的知识。"蒂龙一边说，一边挥起小胳膊和大家告别，"明年夏天来蒙大拿州看我吧！"

当人们开始离开时，许多孩子大声喊道："再见，蒂龙！"

"这真是太酷了！"乔希对尤德说，"到目前为止，你们已经去过多少学校了？"

尤德挠了挠头："啊，我都不太清楚，大概五十个吧。斯库普把这些都记下来了。我想我们回蒙大拿州前，他还安排了二十多所学校的活动。"

迪安从蒂龙肚子里钻出来，走到孩子们和尤德坐的地方。

会说话的霸王龙

"太棒了,"尤德对迪安说,"但是刚开始的时候发生什么事了?"

迪安耸了耸肩。"我无法让笔记本电脑启动,"他说,"一根电缆松了。"

"好啦,至少你修好了它。"尤德边说边站起来。"天越来越热了,我想吃点冰激凌。不然打扫完卫生以后,我们在埃莉餐馆见面吧?蒂龙请客!"

"你可是让乔希高兴了。"露丝说,"我们能做点什么吗?"

尤德从口袋里掏出一个塑料袋。"如果你们到四周转一转,捡些纸片,那就是帮了大忙。"他说。

当尤德向卡车走去时,丁丁、乔希和露丝便分散开来,开始捡垃圾。

丁丁俯身去捡一张皱巴巴的传单,这时,他听到一声大叫。他抬头看了看,叫声是从蒂龙附近传来的,尤德、迪安和斯库普聚集在那扇打开的门前。

即使在一百英尺[1]以外,丁丁也能听到尤德的大叫:"我不相信!"

---

1. 英尺:英美制长度单位。1 英尺 = 0.3048 米。——编者

第四章

丁乔、乔希和露丝朝着蒂龙跑去。"发生什么事了？"丁丁问。

"我们的钱被偷了——这就是发生的事！"斯库普说。

"是你们今天刚筹集到的钱吗？"乔希问。

尤德摇了摇头。"不是，今天的钱还在。"他举着两沓厚厚的绑着橡皮筋的钞票，"我准备把今天的钱和其他钱放在一起，但是那些钱不见了。"

迪安指了指蒂龙肚子里的地板，地板上的桌子、椅子和地毯都被移动过。摆放桌子和椅子的

A to Z 神秘案件

会说话的霸王龙

地方，地板上被凿了一个方形的洞。一个铰链门打开了，露出一个隔间，隔间里面空无一物。

"我把它打造成一个藏东西的地方，"迪安说，"我们把钱装进一个行李袋，放在这里。自从离开蒙大拿州，我们就一直把钱放在这里。"

"里面有多少钱？"乔希问。

尤德脸色变白。"迄今为止我们赚到的所有钱，"他用颤抖的声音说，"差不多五千美元。"

六双眼睛盯着空荡荡的隔间。

"我不明白什么人能在什么时候进入这里。"斯库普说。

尤德闭上眼睛想了一会儿。"昨天我们把蒂龙组装好后，我就把行李袋放到了这里。"他说。

"因此有人在昨天下午和今天早上这段时间把钱偷走了，"迪安说，"但这不可能发生在昨天晚上，因为我就睡在这儿。"

"我要去找法伦警官！"露丝说，"他是警察局长。"

"他现在又能做什么呢？"尤德问，"钱早就不见了。"

39

"法伦警官抓过很多小偷。"丁丁说。

乔希低头瞥了一眼地面,因为出了太阳,地面现在干了。"他也许能在附近找到某些线索。"

"他们叫警察来是对的,尤德,"迪安说,"我们必须尽一切努力把钱找回来。"

"我马上就回来!"露丝说着,一溜烟跑了。

"好吧,没人能偷走这笔钱。"尤德说。他解开衬衫,把钱塞进衬衫里面。

丁丁感觉乔希在捏他的胳膊。丁丁看向乔希时,乔希摇头示意丁丁和他一同离开。

丁丁跟着乔希离开了他们三个人。

"我很不愿意这么说,"乔希低声说,"但我认为他们中间有一个人偷了那些钱。"他朝尤德、迪安和斯库普抬了抬下巴。

"他们为什么要这样做?"丁丁问,"尤德和迪安确实想建博物馆,而斯库普将会在那儿工作。他们不会偷他们自己的钱,乔希。"

"可是还有谁有那扇门的钥匙或者知道蒂龙肚子里那个藏东西的地方呢?"乔希坚持说。

丁丁摇了摇头。他踢了一颗小石子一脚,

说:"谁也无法让我相信尤德会做这样的坏事。"

就在这时,露丝和法伦警官穿过中心公园急匆匆地赶过来了。丁丁和乔希朝恐龙这边走回来。

法伦警官介绍了自己,接着从衬衣口袋里掏出笔记本和笔。"露丝把发生的事情告诉了我。"他一边说一边看着他们三个人,"请问能告诉我你们的名字吗?"

他写下每个人的姓名。"斯库普?"他问,"这是个绰号吗?"

斯库普咧嘴一笑。"是的,以前我是我们大学校报的编辑。我得这个绰号是因为我总是第一个拿到独家新闻。我的真名叫迈克尔·雷克。"

法伦警官把这个记了下来。"能带我看看你们最后一次见到这笔钱的地方吗?"

迪安指着门内空无一物的隔间说:"钱一直放在里面,除了我们在路上开车的时候,那时候我们就把钱放在卡车里,放在我们身边。"

"昨天下午,我把行李袋放进那个隔间,"尤德说,"那是我最后一次见到它。"

"把你们的钱存进银行不是更安全吗?"法伦警官问。

"我们以为把钱放在恐龙肚子里很安全,"尤德说,"除了我们没有人知道那个隐藏的隔间。而我计划把钱带回去存进我在蒙大拿州的银行账户。"

"那个隔间上锁了吗?"警察局长边问边做笔记。

尤德摇了摇头。"没有,但是我们一直将外面这扇门锁着。"

法伦警官检查了钥匙孔。他取下橡胶楔子,把门顺着铰链前后摇动。"谁有这扇门的钥匙?"

"我有一把。"迪安说着,拍了拍他的钥匙串。

尤德也举起他的钥匙串。"仅有的另一把钥匙。"他说。

法伦警官又在笔记本上记了下来。"那么,昨天下午,惠特先生把钱放进了那个隔间。"法伦警官说,"接着今天早上,表演结束后,怀特费瑟先生来找钱,发现钱不见了,是这样吗?"

"其实不是,"迪安说,"是我做的表演,但

会说话的霸王龙

是是尤德发现钱不见的。"

"钱有可能是昨天晚上被偷的吗？"法伦警官说，"你们睡在哪儿？"

"我和斯库普睡在酒店里，"尤德说，"我们把钱留在隔间里。我们一直这么做。迪安睡在外面。他喜欢看守蒂龙。"

法伦警官看起来很是不解。"谁是蒂龙？"他问。

"那是我们对恐龙的称呼。"斯库普解释说。

法伦警官瞥了迪安一眼。"你晚上一直睡在外面吗？"他问，"即使是下雨的时候？"

迪安笑了笑，说："不是，雨开始下的时候，我就把睡袋搬进卡车里了。"

法伦警官又在笔记本上做了记录，接着他转身面对着尤德说："有没有可能有人溜进你的房间，趁你睡觉的时候拿走了你的钥匙？"

尤德摇了摇头，说："房门是锁着的。"

法伦警官看着迪安。"你的钥匙呢，怀特费瑟先生？"他问，"你睡在外面的时候，你的钥匙放在哪里？"

43

迪安举起他的钥匙串。"别在我的腰带上，跟我一起在我的睡袋里。"

法伦警官把门打开，看着电脑。"谁操作它（蒂龙）？"

"我，"迪安说，"还有我的电脑。"

"所以据你所知，那个行李袋今天早上还藏在地板下面。"法伦警官说。

"没错。"迪安说。

法伦警官仔细观察了蒂龙内部。"那么你就一直坐在电脑旁边，那笔钱的上面，对吧，怀特费瑟先生？"

迪安点了点头。"但是我想那时钱已经被偷了，"他说，"表演结束后，当尤德移开桌子、拉开地毯时，行李袋就不见了。"

法伦警官插上橡胶楔子，让那扇门微微敞开。他看着他们三人，说："先生们，我们穿过街道去我的办公室吧。我希望你们想想昨天你们来这儿以后发生的所有事情。我想要你们把一切都写下来——即使是最微小的细节，无论看起来有多么不重要。"

会说话的霸王龙

"这要花多长时间?"斯库普问,"我们还有很多其他学校要去。明天应该到纽黑文去。"

"那我们最好赶紧行动。"法伦警官说。

第五章

丁丁、乔希和露丝看着尤德、迪安、斯库普跟着法伦警官向警察局走去。头顶上,蒂龙睁着大大的塑料眼睛凝视前方。

"这下可好,"丁丁嘟囔着,"尤德来看我们,可他的钱却被偷了。"

"我就是不明白小偷是怎么偷钱的,"露丝说,"昨天下午我们都在这儿,而且昨天晚上迪安看守蒂龙。再说,表演的时候迪安还被锁在蒂龙肚子里。"

"所以也许迪安就是小偷,"乔希说,"他可以在昨天晚上甚至今天表演的时候把钱拿走。那

会说话的霸王龙

扇门关上以后,没人看得见他的所作所为。"

"但是我们知道他做了什么,"丁丁说,"他一直在操控电脑。否则,蒂龙不会移动或者说话。"

"那就对了,"乔希说,"蒂龙在刚开始的几分钟里没有动,记得吗?也许就在那时迪安偷了行李袋。"

丁丁摇了摇头。"我不相信迪安会偷他最好的朋友的东西。"他说。

就在这时,基恩警官开着巡逻车停了下来。他捧着一卷黄色警戒带和几根木桩,从车里钻了出来。"嘿,孩子们,"他说,"有点兴奋,是吗?"

他把警戒带和木桩放在地上,走到蒂龙前面。橡胶楔子还在原来的地方,他用橡胶楔子把门撑得更开。基恩警官向门内瞥了一眼,说道:"哟,你们都可以在里面烤馅饼了。"

基恩警官开始把木桩插进蒂龙周围的地上。接着,他将标示犯罪现场的警戒带围在木桩上,绕着恐龙围成一个大圈。

"我们去埃莉餐馆行吗?"乔希说,"我的脑子需要我喝点东西。"

孩子们动身穿过中心公园。

"你真的觉得迪安是小偷吗?"露丝问乔希。

"是的,"乔希说,"他有钥匙,而且还知道钱藏在什么地方。"

"斯库普呢?"露丝问,"他会不会从迪安或尤德那里借走钥匙?"

"如果他借走钥匙,他们会跟法伦警官说的。"乔希回答。

"也许小偷另有其人,"丁丁说,"一个会开锁的陌生人。"

"但是迪安一直睡在恐龙外面,"露丝说,"小偷怎么能越过他?"

"所以我才觉得是迪安。"乔希说着,拉开了埃莉餐馆的门。

孩子们迅速坐进一个靠窗的隔间,只见一张蒂龙展览的传单贴在窗玻璃上。

埃莉挥了挥手,然后走了过来。

"嘿,孩子们。你们怎么没去看恐龙表演?"

会说话的霸王龙

她问。

"表演结束了。"乔希说,"不过有人偷了他们的钱!"

埃莉迅速坐到乔希身边。"谁偷了谁的钱?"她惊讶地睁大眼睛问。

露丝跟她讲了藏在恐龙肚子里的钱的事。

"这些可怜的家伙,"埃莉说着站了起来,"今天早晨他们进来吃早餐的时候还都很兴奋呢。"

"法伦警官正在调查这个案子。"露丝说。

"很好!"埃莉说。"乔希,你的舌头都快掉出来了。喝点新鲜柠檬汁怎么样?"她问。

孩子们同意了,接着埃莉端来三个高脚杯。

乔希对着吸管吸了一大口,说:"那么,你们都同意迪安是小偷了?"

丁丁搅动他的柠檬汁。"我不同意。迪安不会蠢到在昨天晚上他看守蒂龙的时候去偷钱,"他说,"这会使矛头直接指向他。"

乔希摇了摇头,说:"他也可能在表演的时候拿走行李袋。"

"怎么拿?"露丝问。

"很简单,"乔希说,"他把自己锁在蒂龙肚子里。他移动桌子和地毯,抓起行李袋,然后把地毯和桌子摆回去。这只要一分钟。"

"接下来呢?"丁丁问,"他把行李袋放在哪儿?"

丁丁和露丝盯着乔希，等他回答。

乔希对他们眨了眨眼。他吸了一小口柠檬汁。"好吧，事情是这样的，"他说，"迪安对我们说过他在恐龙肚子里做了那个小隔间，对吧？那么，如果他还做了另外一个只有他自己知道的隔间呢？那里就是他藏钱的地方！"

丁丁从自己的玻璃杯子上方看着乔希。"你觉得钱还在蒂龙肚子里？"

"为什么不在？"乔希问，"这很巧妙。没人会想到去那儿找钱。"

露丝眯起眼睛看着乔希，说："像你这样鬼点子多的人除外。"

"我说我们去搜一搜霸王龙老伙计——蒂龙吧，"乔希说着，喝完他的柠檬汁，"如果我说得没错，迪安一找到机会就会去取那个行李袋。"

"尽管我不愿意承认，但乔希说得有道理，"露丝说，"去蒂龙肚子里找找也不会有什么损失。"

孩子们把钱放在桌子上，向埃莉挥手告别，动身返回高中。

一会儿后,孩子们就在被黄色犯罪现场警戒带围住的蒂龙旁边看着它。基恩警官已经走了。

"谁也不该越过警戒带。"丁丁说。

"我们可以说我们没看到警戒带。"乔希建议。

"没错,"丁丁说,"现在是大白天,我们看不见明黄色的警戒带。"

"但是如果是晚上呢?"露丝说着,看了看丁丁,"我们今天晚上可以来。"

丁丁摇了摇头。"算了吧,伙计们。今晚我们要和我们的父母去看烟花。"

乔希伸出一只胳膊搂住丁丁的肩膀。"好极了,"乔希说,"当他们抬头仰望天空的时候,我们可以溜之大吉。"

丁丁最后同意了。"但我是为了尤德才这么做的。"他说。

孩子们听到一声狗叫,接着看到波克特先生和伦道夫正在检查花园里的玫瑰丛。孩子们走过去打招呼。

"您听说偷钱的事了吗?"露丝问。

"听说了,我真为那些年轻人感到难过。"波

克特先生说,"有什么消息吗?"

丁丁摇了摇头。

"但是今天晚上可能会有突破。"乔希说着,用手肘轻轻推了推丁丁。

"我们的玫瑰丛看起来很漂亮,"波克特先生说,"但我必须处理掉这株枯死的玫瑰。丁丁,想不想去帮我把手推车推来?"

丁丁向棚屋跑去。手推车就在他上次放置的那个地方,斜靠在麻布袋上。丁丁离开时,注意到地板砖上有泥巴脚印。

丁丁把手推车推给了波克特先生。

"谢谢。"波克特先生边说边把枯死的玫瑰放进手推车里,"我要把这个扔进学校的大垃圾箱里。"波克特先生离开了,伦道夫跟在手推车一旁飞快地奔跑。

"快看,那是尤德和斯库普!"乔希说着,指着恐龙的方向。

他们两人站在警戒带外面。尤德正在说话,并用一只手指了指着蒂龙身侧的门。斯库普则在摇着脑袋回答他。

孩子们离他们太远,听不到他们说了什么。过了一会儿,他们两人钻进斯库普的小汽车,开车走了。

迪安没和他们在一起。

"法伦警官一定把迪安当成嫌疑人扣留了。"丁丁说着,突然觉得肚子里甜甜的柠檬汁发酸。

第六章

孩子们回家的时候,谈论起偷钱的事情。

乔希停下脚步。一双绿色的眼睛闪现出狡黠的光芒。"我知道了,"他低声说,"我知道是谁偷了钱。"

"谁?"丁丁说。

"是蒂龙!"乔希说,"当大家都睡着的时候,它走到银行,存了一笔恐龙存款。"丁丁推了乔希一把,露丝也对乔希翻了个白眼。

分开之前,他们约好先碰面,然后一同去看烟花。"把你们的睡袋放在我家,"丁丁说,"我父母说看完烟花后我们可以睡在外面。"

"还要穿黑色的衣服。"乔希说。

八点半的时候,乔希、露丝还有他们的家人在丁丁家碰面。丁丁、乔希和露丝将他们的睡袋堆放在野餐桌上。大人们携带了毯子、一袋袋爆米花和防虫喷雾剂。纳特、布赖恩和布拉德利都带了他们最喜欢的毛绒动物玩具。

三家人步行到主街后向左拐,走到霍利加油站后再向左拐。从那儿沿着东绿街再走一小段路就到了游泳池,也就是放烟花的地方。

"你们三个为什么都穿着一身黑色的衣服?"露丝的爸爸问,"看起来像忍者。"

"我们希望蚊子在黑暗中看不见我们。"露丝说着,瞥了一眼丁丁。

丁丁、乔希和露丝走在前面,把其他人撇在了后面。

"说得好。"乔希确定没人听得见的时候说。

过了一会儿,他们都抵达了镇游泳池。这儿已经聚集了几百人。游泳池、网球场和棒球场附近的草坪上铺满了毯子,摆满了椅子。

消防车就停在附近,以备不时之需。

会说话的霸王龙

"我看见了尤德、斯库普和迪安。"乔希说。他们三人坐在那儿,斜倚着棒球场周围的围栏。"我们去和他们坐一起吧。"

"我们不能去,"露丝说,"如果我们去了,过一会儿他们会看见我们溜走。"

"好吧,我们至少过去打个招呼吧。"丁丁说。

"好啊,我们可以看看迪安会不会露出愧疚之色。"乔希发表了自己的意见。

孩子们在毯子和椅子之间穿梭。尤德第一个发现了他们,并站起身来。

"你们好!"尤德挥了挥手说,"想和我们坐一起吗?"斯库普和迪安也打了招呼,但没站起身来。

"不行,"乔希说,"我们必须待在父母身边。"

"法伦警官是个好人,"尤德说,"我真希望他能找到我们的钱。我们明天就要拆卸蒂龙,然后离开。"

"你们要去哪儿?"露丝问。

"先去纽黑文,然后去好多其他城镇。"斯库普说,"我们还要赚更多的钱。"

迪安没有加入谈话。他那双黑色的眼睛直直地盯着前方。

"晚上好。"一个声音传来,是林克莱特先生在说话,他是香格里拉酒店的经理。他坐在几英尺之外的一张草坪椅上,大家都跟他打了招呼。

"但愿你们那个房间很舒服。"林克莱特先生对尤德和斯库普说。

"房间非常舒服。"尤德回答。

就在这时,一道蓝色光圈在他们头顶点亮了天空。"啊!"成百上千的人叫了起来。

"开始了!"露丝说,"我们最好去找我们的父母。"

"明天一起去埃莉餐厅吃早餐怎么样?"尤德问,"我不想和你们不辞而别。"

"好啊,"丁丁说,"什么时候?"

"我们会很早起来将蒂龙装上卡车,"他说,"所以,九点钟怎么样?"

"我们会到那儿。"丁丁说。孩子们向他们的家人走去。他们在网球场附近找了个地方,在那

里他们还可以盯着围栏边上的三个人。

"伙计们，你们听到尤德的话了吗？"露丝说，"他们明天就要把蒂龙拆掉！"

"所以如果迪安把钱藏在那儿，他必须在拆掉蒂龙之前把钱拿走。"乔希说。

"或者是别的任何人。"丁丁补充说。

"相信我，是迪安，"乔希继续说，"你们注意到他刚才的样子了吗？他只是坐着，没跟任何人说一句话。依我看，这就叫'做贼心虚'。"

志愿消防员已经围着放烟花的地方设置了低矮的路障。警察在沿河路摆放了绕行标志，不让车辆开进来。穿白色T恤衫的消防队员穿过人群，分发着小小的美国国旗。

烟花在孩子们头顶绽放，他们看了好几分钟。只见天空的颜色从一片漆黑变成红色、白色和蓝色。人群又是鼓掌，又是吹口哨，又是大声喊叫。

"等下一个巨大烟花爆炸时，我们就溜之大吉吧。"乔希小声说。

片刻后，天空中绽开了一朵巨大的黄色花朵。当大家抬头仰望天空的时候，丁丁、乔希和露丝在黑暗中悄悄溜走了。

他们飞快地穿过东绿街，向高中的草坪跑去。

一轮浑圆的明月照在恐龙身上，恐龙投下的阴影遮住了半个操场。在孩子们身后，天空依旧被烟花照亮。一阵微风吹过操场，黄色警戒带被风吹在木桩上，哗啦作响。

"现到该怎么办？"丁丁问，"我真的不喜欢待在这儿，伙计们。"

"我也不喜欢，"露丝说，"但是要是行李袋还在蒂龙肚子里，我们今晚就必须找到它！"

第七章

"就这么办吧,"乔希说,"这会耗费我们五分钟时间。如果找不到钱,我们就回去看烟花吧。"

孩子们从黄色警戒带下面爬过去。他们藏在蒂龙黑色的影子里。那个橡胶楔子把门撑开一英寸宽。乔希取下橡胶楔子,把门打开。

"我看不见任何东西!"丁丁说,"在黑暗中我们怎么找呢?"

"等等。"露丝说。她从口袋里掏出一个小手电筒。她把手电筒打开,让光线经过折叠楼梯照进蒂龙的肚子里。

桌子和地毯仍然移在一旁。隔间的盖子向上打开，隔间里面仍旧空无一物。接着，露丝关掉了手电筒。

丁丁把折叠楼梯拉下来，然后他们往上爬进蒂龙的肚子里。等乔希轻轻把门关上时，丁丁把折叠楼梯收回去。

这下，他们仿佛置身于一个黑漆漆且闷热些的洞穴里。

"这里真是热死了！"乔希抱怨的声音从黑暗中传来。

丁丁双膝跪地，用一只胳膊靠着小桌子。先前放行李袋的隔间就在他前面，但他却看不见。

"我们快点搞定吧，"丁丁说，"我想在家人发现之前返回放烟花的地方。"

露丝打开手电筒，在这个狭小的空间里照了一圈。"好啦，乔希，给我们看看那个隐秘的藏东西的地方吧。"她说。

"那个地方不会一眼就瞧得出，"乔希说，"找找那些没人能想到的地方吧。"

乔希跪在地上转过身子，面对着恐龙的两条

会说话的霸王龙

后腿。这两条腿用大号螺栓和身体其他部位固定在一起。"我打赌这些腿里是空的。"乔希说。

乔希摸了摸四周,果然,他能把一只手臂伸进一条腿里。"下面什么都没有。"他说。

丁丁检查了另一条腿,但是里面也没有藏任何东西。

"看看它上面的头怎么样?"露丝问。她的手电筒的光线沿着电缆往上照到恐龙的胸部和颈部。

最上面只有一个黑洞显示那就是头部位置。

"我们找找吧。"丁丁说。他站起身来,想要把手伸到蒂龙头部的洞里。

"我不够高。"

"等一下。"乔希说。他把笔记本电脑从桌子上搬起来,放到地板上,然后把桌子挪到丁丁面前。

丁丁爬到桌子上,再次伸手。这次,他的手臂伸进了蒂龙头里,他用手在里面四处摸。"我摸到的都是从电脑上接过来的电线,"丁丁说,"但是我的手臂不够长,够不着上面。"

63

"里面容纳得下我吗?"露丝问。

"有可能,"丁丁说,"头部是空心的。"

乔希咯咯笑了起来,说:"就像你的头一样。"

"让我爬上去,"露丝说,"我站在桌子上,然后你们推我一把。"

露丝和丁丁换了一下位置。乔希把手电筒含在嘴里,和丁丁一同把露丝举到蒂龙的喉咙处。露丝在恐龙的头里消失不见了,只有她的脚还露在外面,接着她的脚也不见了,然后他们看见她脸朝下看着他们。

"上面什么也没有,除了一个连着那些电线的小扩音器,"露丝说,"还有一堆牙齿。"

乔希用手电筒照了照恐龙内壁。"我找不到其他任何还能藏一堆钱的地方。"他说。

"那我们该怎么办?"丁丁问。

"首先,给这里透点气。"乔希说。他把手电筒递给丁丁,然后伸手去开门。

丁丁关掉手电筒。"别把门开得太大,"他说,"我可不想因为闯进一头恐龙的肚子而被抓起来!"

会说话的霸王龙

乔希推了推门，门没有动。"帮帮我，丁丁。门卡住了。"

两个男孩用肩膀斜抵着门，用力推。

"一定是我们关门的时候，门锁住了，"乔希说，"我忘记用那个橡胶做的东西把门撑住！"

丁丁打开手电筒，把光朝上对着露丝。"如果我把这个递给你，你能让它从恐龙嘴巴里射出光吗？"他问，"如果你高声喊叫，或许有人听得见。"

露丝摇了摇头，说："恐龙嘴巴是闭上的。"

"我们得试着想点办法，"丁丁说着，挥舞着手电筒，"我可不想整个晚上都待在这里！"

"有了，"乔希说，"我想我知道怎么启动迪安的电脑了。如果我能让蒂龙的嘴巴张开，我们就能通过麦克风和扩音器呼喊求救。"

"在烟花的响声中，没人能听见我们的呼喊，"露丝说，"但你让我想到了另一个主意，乔希。如果你能打开蒂龙的嘴巴，也许我能从那里爬出去！"

"露丝，蒂龙的头离地面太远了。"丁丁说。

丁丁看着乔希，说："这里有什么东西能让我们做成爬出去用的梯子吗？"

突然，乔希从丁丁手里一把抓过手电筒。他用手电筒照了一下恐龙的内壁，直到光线落到那排钩子上。"我想这样。"乔希说。

"怎样呢？"丁丁说。

乔希伸手抓起一圈绳索。"用这个，"他说，"我们可以用绳索把露丝放到蒂龙嘴巴外面的地上！"

丁丁抬头看着露丝。"你觉得你行吗？"丁丁问。

露丝点了点头。"蒂龙的嘴巴非常大。"她说。

"就像乔希的嘴巴一样。"丁丁说着，对他的朋友咧嘴笑了起来。

"非常好笑。"乔希说。他把手电筒递给丁丁，然后坐在笔记本电脑前面。他把电脑打开，然后敲击一些按键。

电脑屏幕上出现了几个图标。其中一个图标标注着"蒂龙"。乔希将图标点开，然后出现一个窗口，窗口显示出一系列选项。其中一个选项

是"嘴巴"。

"对啦,"乔希说,"准备好,露丝!"

乔希点击"嘴巴"选项。片刻之后,丁丁听到一阵摩擦声。

"成功了!"露丝大声喊道,"蒂龙的嘴巴张开了!"

第八章

丁丁把手电筒放在地板上,然后将绳索的一头绑在折叠楼梯上。乔希将绳索的另一头扎成个绳圈,绳圈大到足以让露丝钻进去。乔希站在桌子上,把绳圈递给露丝。

"你确定要这样做吗?"丁丁问。

"这很简单,"露丝说,"我经常沿着绳梯从我堂哥的树屋上向下爬。"

"我们会拉住绳子,直到你准备好往下降,"乔希说完,又补充道:"当心那些牙齿!"

"好的,给我一分钟时间。"露丝的脸消失不见了,松散的绳索也被她拉走了一部分。"好

会说话的霸王龙

啦！"她高声喊，"把我慢慢放下去吧。"

男孩们感觉到绳索因为露丝的重量而紧绷起来。他们让绳索从手指间慢慢滑动。丁丁感觉到摩擦使他的手掌灼热起来。

后来绳索彻底松了下来。

"她下去了吗？"乔希问。

他们俩都听到有人在大力敲击带龙身体一侧的门。"我马上就回来！"露丝高声喊道。

丁丁和乔希坐下来，斜倚着一侧弧形内壁。露丝的手电筒发出的光线越来越暗淡，因此丁丁把手电筒关掉了。

"要是这里有个空调就好了。"过了一会儿，乔希说道。他用自己的T恤衫擦掉脸上的汗水。

"为什么不说你希望待在一个装满食物的冰箱里呢？"丁丁说。

乔希咧嘴笑了起来，说："或者有个微波炉和一块比萨也好啊。不过，有个大电风扇我就能心满意足了。"

两个男孩坐在黑暗中。丁丁感觉到汗水流进了他的眼睛里。

"我快被烤熟了。"乔希呻吟着说。

"别像个小孩子似的。"丁丁说,"想想待在一只真正的霸王龙的肚子里会是什么样子!"

乔希在黑暗中咯咯笑了起来。"恐龙吃小孩吗?"他问。

"不吃,乔希,因为那时候还没有人类。"丁丁说,"还有,如果霸王龙尝了你一口,它会把你吐出来的。"

乔希戳了戳丁丁的肋骨。

丁丁也对着他戳了回去。

正当乔希像摔跤一样抱住丁丁脖子的时候,他们听到外面有砰砰的声音。

乔希倒吸了一口气,说:"你猜是不是迪安来取钱了?"

丁丁爬到门边,把耳朵贴在门上。门打开了,他差点掉到了尤德身上。尤德身后站着法伦警官和露丝。

"你们的确陷入了困境,"法伦警官说着,用他的手电筒照了照丁丁的眼睛,"还好我在放烟花的地方找到了尤德。"

尤德放下楼梯,这样丁丁和乔希就能爬下来,回到地面上。

"谢谢,"乔希说,"我们在里面都要融化了!"

"我猜你们没有找到钱。"尤德说,"露丝告诉了我们你们在做什么。"

丁丁摇了摇头,说:"对不起。"

"恐怕那个偷行李袋的人早就带着钱消失不见了。"法伦警官说。

尤德点了点头。"这件事一定发生在昨天晚上我们睡觉之后。"他说,"我只是不明白它是怎么发生的。"

法伦警官用手电筒在地上照了照,说:"昨天晚上下了雨,所以即使小偷留下了脚印,也会被冲刷掉。"

脚印,丁丁想。"我在花园棚屋里看到过湿湿的脚印,"丁丁在黑暗中指着玫瑰园的方向,"我当时是去拿波克特先生的手推车。"

"这意味着下雨之后,有人进到那儿,"露丝说,"而且那时是半夜!"

"也许,那些脚印就是小偷留下的。"法伦警官说,他将一只手搭在丁丁肩膀上说,"带我去看看。"

丁丁带着大家穿过漆黑的草坪。"就是这儿。"他们来到花园棚屋时,他说。

"请你们待在外面。"法伦警官对乔希、露丝和尤德说。他的手电筒的光照到了螺丝刀上。法伦警官取下螺丝刀,把门打开。他用手电筒在地板上照了照,只见干了的泥脚印从门口延伸到棚屋后部。

"帮我拿着,"法伦警官说着,把手电筒递给了丁丁,"站在门口,这样我就有光照着。"

法伦警官走了进去,跪下来检查脚印。接着,他又从棚屋这头走到那头,对任何足以藏人的大物件的里面、下面和后面进行检查。

在棚屋后部,他移动手推车,用鞋尖踢了踢那堆麻布袋,然后扯出其中几个麻布袋放在地板上。

丁丁看见他弯着腰,从剩下的麻布袋下面掏出一个东西来。

"尤德,你能进来一下吗?"法伦警官大声喊道。

尤德把头探进门内。

"这是你们正在找的东西吗?"

法伦警官提着一个深棕色的行李袋。行李袋鼓鼓的,里面好像塞满了东西。行李袋一侧有一条长长的拉链。

尤德笑容满面,说道:"您找到它了!"

法伦警官把袋子从棚屋里拎了出来,放在地上。在手电筒光线的照射下,他拉开拉链,袋子里装满了用橡皮筋绑着的几千元美钞。

法伦警官抬头看着尤德,问道:"这是你们的钱吗?"

尤德点了点头,说:"希望钱都在这儿。"

"那是什么?"丁丁问。他指了指一个淡绿色的东西,那东西粘在帆布行李袋的一侧。

"那是一个创可贴。"露丝说。

"不要碰。"法伦警官提醒道。他从口袋里掏出一个小塑料袋,用笔尖把创可贴拨进袋子里,然后将袋子密封好。

"我想知道这个东西是谁的。"他用手电筒照着塑料袋子。

"昨天斯库普贴了一个那样的创可贴,"露丝说,"他被汽车散热器烫伤了手指。"

"我看见迪安的手指上也贴了一个。"乔希说。

"我们都用创可贴。"尤德说。他把手伸进他的牛仔裤口袋里,掏出来一个绿色的创可贴。

法伦警官把尤德这个平整的创可贴放在袋子里那个用过的创可贴旁边。这两个创可贴一模一样。

第九章

"你们三个人都用这种创可贴吗？"法伦警官问尤德。

尤德点了点头。"装卸蒂龙的时候，会经常弄伤手指，"他说，"所以我买了一盒创可贴，我们都装一些在口袋里备用。"

法伦警官看了看行李袋，说："谁最后动过这个袋子？"

"我是唯一一个把钱放进袋子里的人，"尤德说，"我一定是贴了创可贴，后来我把行李袋塞进隔间的时候，创可贴从我手指上脱落了。"

"创可贴也可能是小偷偷行李袋的时候从手

指上脱落的,"法伦警官说,"不论这小偷是谁。"他仔细看了尤德一眼。

尤德思考了片刻,说:"我知道这看起来很像是我们三个人当中的一个偷了这些钱,"他说,"但是我肯定没偷,而且我也不相信迪安和斯库普会这么做。"

"小偷会不会另有其人呢?"丁丁问。

"但会是谁呢?"法伦警官说,"尤德,你告诉过我只有你和迪安有进入恐龙内部的钥匙。"

"没错,"尤德说,"但迪安是我最好的朋友。"

法伦警官把小塑料袋和笔塞进口袋。"斯库普·雷克和迪安·怀特费瑟两个人,谁更有机会拿到那个行李袋?"他问尤德。

尤德看着自己的双脚。"我想是迪安,"他含含糊糊地说,"他昨晚睡在蒂龙旁边。"

法伦警官把手搭在尤德肩膀上。"我想让你去我的办公室等我,我去把迪安找过来,"他说,"你觉得他还在看烟花的地方吗?"

"我想是的。"尤德说。

"同时,我会把这些钱放进我们的保险

柜,"法伦警官继续说,"过一会儿我会去警察局找你。"

尤德看上去很尴尬,他转身朝主街走去,没过多久就消失在黑暗中。

法伦警官看着丁丁、乔希和露丝。"你们的父母可能正在找你们,"他说,"我带你们回去,好吗?"

丁丁、乔希和露丝跟着法伦警官来到他的巡逻车旁,坐到后排座位上。法伦警官载着他们朝主街驶去。

五颜六色的烟花依旧点亮着镇游泳池上方的天空。法伦法官将车停在网球场和棒球场之间。

孩子们看着他朝棒球场围栏走去,接着他们去寻找自己的父母。

"原来你们在这儿!"丁丁的妈妈说,"我们还以为你们被外星人拐走了呢!"丁丁看着自己的手表,意识到他们已经离开了将近半个小时。

孩子们坐在能看见法伦警官的地方。法伦警官朝迪安走去,他们两人站着说了一会儿话。接着,法伦警官带着迪安走向他的巡逻车。巡逻车

77

驶入主街，随后消失不见了。

"我真不敢相信尤德的朋友会偷他的钱。"露丝说。

乔希躺在草地上，说："我现在在想蒂龙以后会怎么样。"

"我想尤德和斯库普会雇个人来代替迪安。"丁丁说。

"斯库普在哪儿？"露丝问。

"他不是和迪安一起在围栏边吗？"丁丁问。

"不，"乔希说，"只有迪安在那儿。也许斯库普返回酒店了。他说昨晚因为暴风雨，他没睡好觉。"

丁丁想起了昨天晚上，暴风雨在窗外肆虐。他想象着迪安在雨中醒来，冲进卡车的情景，脑海中浮现出棚屋地板上那些泥脚印，还有那天早上，斯库普挂在汽车天线上的湿漉漉的运动鞋。

"伙计们，我想我们都错怪迪安了！"丁丁突然说，"我想是斯库普偷了那些钱，而且是他把钱藏在了花园棚屋里！"

"但是他没有钥匙。"乔希说。

会说话的霸王龙

"我想斯库普知道,雨一旦开始下,迪安就不会睡在外面。迪安搬到卡车驾驶室里避雨,就在那时,斯库普进入了蒂龙的肚子。"

"怎么进入的呢?斯库普没有钥匙。"乔希再次说。

"斯库普一定用了什么办法,趁尤德睡着的时候拿到了他的钥匙,"丁丁说,"斯库普偷走了行李袋,把它藏在棚屋里,然后再跑回酒店。他一定是打算之后再返回棚屋,取走那笔钱。"

露丝的呼吸急促起来。"也许斯库普现在就在那儿!"她说,"他可以像我们一样,悄悄溜走!"

"来吧!"丁丁说。孩子们飞速跑过奇妙温室,从角落书店后面抄近路,朝玫瑰园奔去。他们气喘吁吁地蹲在离棚屋十码[1]远的玫瑰丛后面,只见一道亮光在敞开的门内闪烁着。

---

1. 码:英美制长度单位,1 码 = 0.9144 米。——编者

"有人在里面！"乔希生气地低声说。

三个孩子蹑手蹑脚地靠近，直到他们可以看到棚屋里面。他们看见一个黑头发的人跪在一堆麻布袋前。当那个人站起身来，他们知道他就是斯库普·雷克。

"我们该怎么办？"露丝低声说。

"螺丝刀在这儿，"乔希说，"我去把他锁在里面！"

"不！"丁丁说，"我们去找法伦警官吧！"

乔希摇了摇头，说："没时间了！斯库普找不到钱，就会溜走！"说着，他立马穿过玫瑰丛，向棚屋爬去。"哎哟！"他叫了一声。

"怎么了？"露丝低声说。

"该死的刺！"乔希低声回答。

斯库普突然冲出棚屋，他把手电筒对准乔希。还没等其他人反应过来，斯库普一把抓住了乔希的胳膊。

"好吧，孩子们，你们把钱怎么着了？"他问。

"你放开他！"露丝一边喊，一边和丁丁一起冲到乔希身边。

会说话的霸王龙

"是的,放开他。"一个低沉的声音说。法伦警官和迪安从棚屋后面走了出来。

第十章

一个小时过后,在丁丁家的后院,孩子们躺在各自的睡袋里。他们凝望着天上的星星。

"北斗七星!"乔希说着,坐了起来。

"我想我看见火星了!"丁丁说。

"那儿有一颗流星。快许个愿吧!"露丝说,"我希望自己能成为第一个女总统!"

"我希望露丝成为总统,然后让我负责她的餐后甜点。"乔希说。

丁丁和露丝坐起来哈哈大笑。

"我希望尤德和迪安把蒂龙留在绿地镇。"丁丁说。

"好啊，"乔希说，"那真是太好了。我们可以让它走遍整个镇子。"

"人们会为了乘坐蒂龙付钱。"露丝补充说，"我们可以把钱寄给尤德和迪安，让他们建博物馆。"

三个孩子叹了口气，又躺回睡袋里了。

"我还是想不明白斯库普是怎么拿到尤德的钥匙的。"露丝说。

"哦，这很简单，"乔希说，"我早就想明白了。"

丁丁忽然坐了起来，气鼓鼓地看着他的朋友说："那你打算告诉我们吗？"

乔希故意叹了口气说："昨天斯库普听到迪安说晚上会下雨。他知道迪安可能会搬到什么地方去避雨。我想就是在那个时候，斯库普下定决心去偷钱。他一直等到尤德睡熟，再拿走他的钥匙。"

"但是斯库普是怎么进入尤德的房间的呢？"丁丁问。

"他不需要进入，"乔希说，"他们睡在同一个房间里。"

"约书亚[1],你是怎么知道的?"露丝问。

乔希咧嘴一笑,说:"还记得林克莱特先生在放烟花的地方跟我们打招呼吗?我听到他问尤德和斯库普他们那个房间怎么样——他说的是'那个房间'而不是'那些房间'。"

"还好法伦警官出现在了棚屋里,"丁丁说,"他是怎么知道斯库普会去那儿的?"

"可能是迪安说服了他,"乔希说,"一定是迪安想到,小偷能得到钥匙的唯一途径就是晚上从尤德那里拿,而迪安也知道尤德和斯库普住同一个房间。"

"唉,虽然我不愿意承认,"丁丁说,"但你真的非常聪明。"

"我知道,"乔希说,"不过,还是谢谢啦。"

"不客气。"丁丁说。

"也许等我当上总统后,应该让你负责联邦

---

1. 乔希的全名叫约书亚·平托。——编者

调查局。"露丝说。

　　乔希打了个哈欠说："算了吧。我宁愿负责食物。"

　　三个孩子在黑暗中笑了起来。随后，伴着头顶闪烁的繁星，他们慢慢进入了梦乡。

A to Z Mysteries®

The Talking T. Rex

by Ron Roy

illustrated by
John Steven Gurney

INDIAN RIVER
LAWRENCE TAXI
RIVER ROAD
HORSE TRAILS
HORSES FOR RENT
BIKE PATH
WOODS
BIKE PATH
WOODVIEW ROAD
INDIAN WAY ROAD
FIRE STATION
BILL'S BIKES
SUPER MARKET
BRIDGE LANE
ROBIN ROAD
CROW ST
FINCH LA
THRUSH CT
OWL RD
PHEASANT LA
BLUE JAY WAY
WREN DR
FITNESS CENTER
WOODS
BIKE PATH
BLUE BIRD WAY
HUMMINGBIRD LA
WOODCOCK CROSS
ELLIE'S DINER
ACORN APTS
FURRY FEET PET SHOP
CENTER CHURCH
BIKE PATH
OAK STREET
PEOPLE'S POND
POST OFFICE
COMMUNITY GARDEN AND FISH POND
GREEN LAWN $ SAVINGS $ BANK
ELDERLY HOUSING
POLICE STATION
WEST GREEN ST
RIVER ROAD
GOOSE ISLAND
MAIN STREET
SENIOR COMMUNITY CENTER
GREEN LAWN LIBRARY
TOWN HALL
BIKE PATH
CHILDREN'S PETTING ZOO AND AQUARIUM
SHANGRI-LA HOTEL

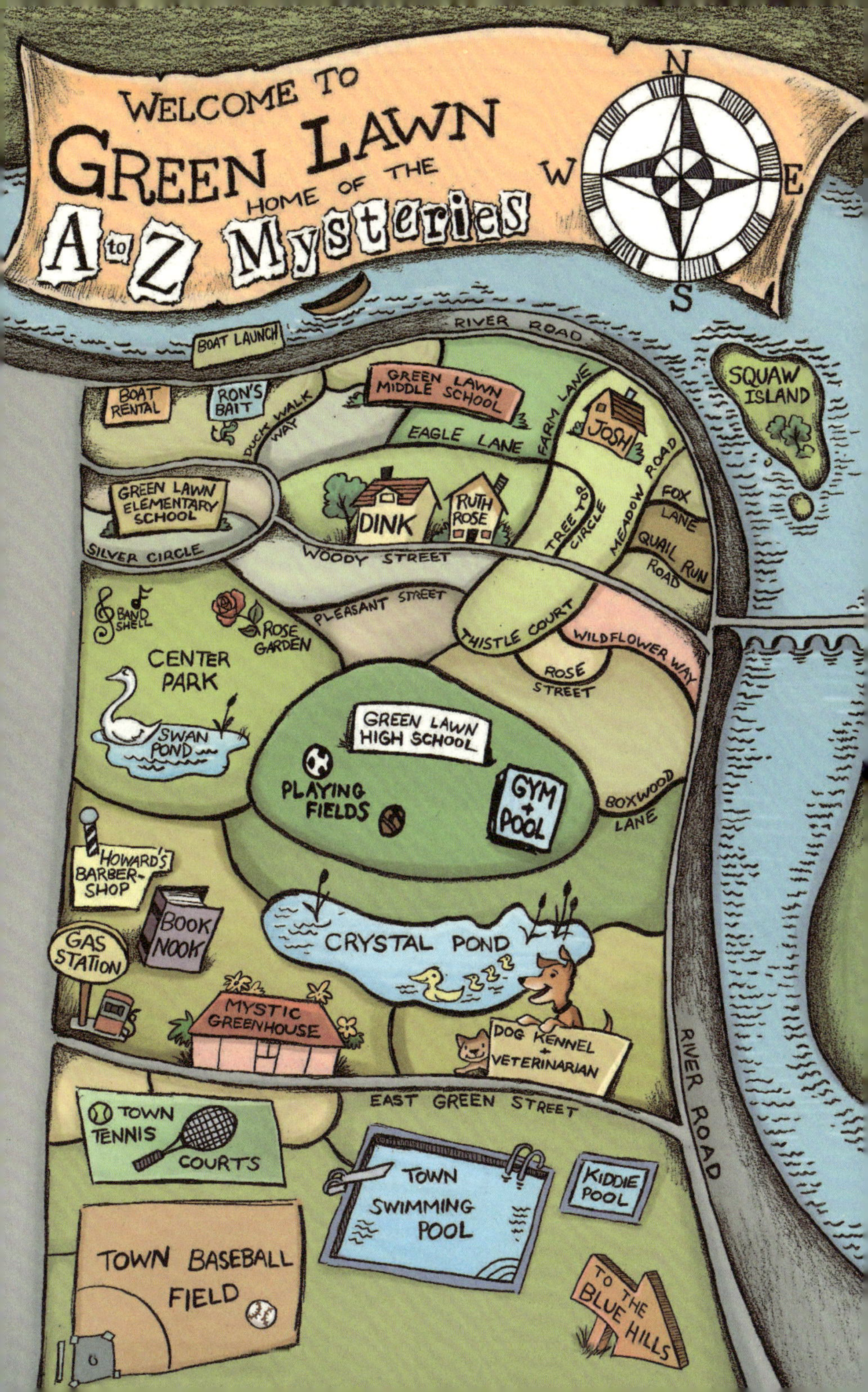

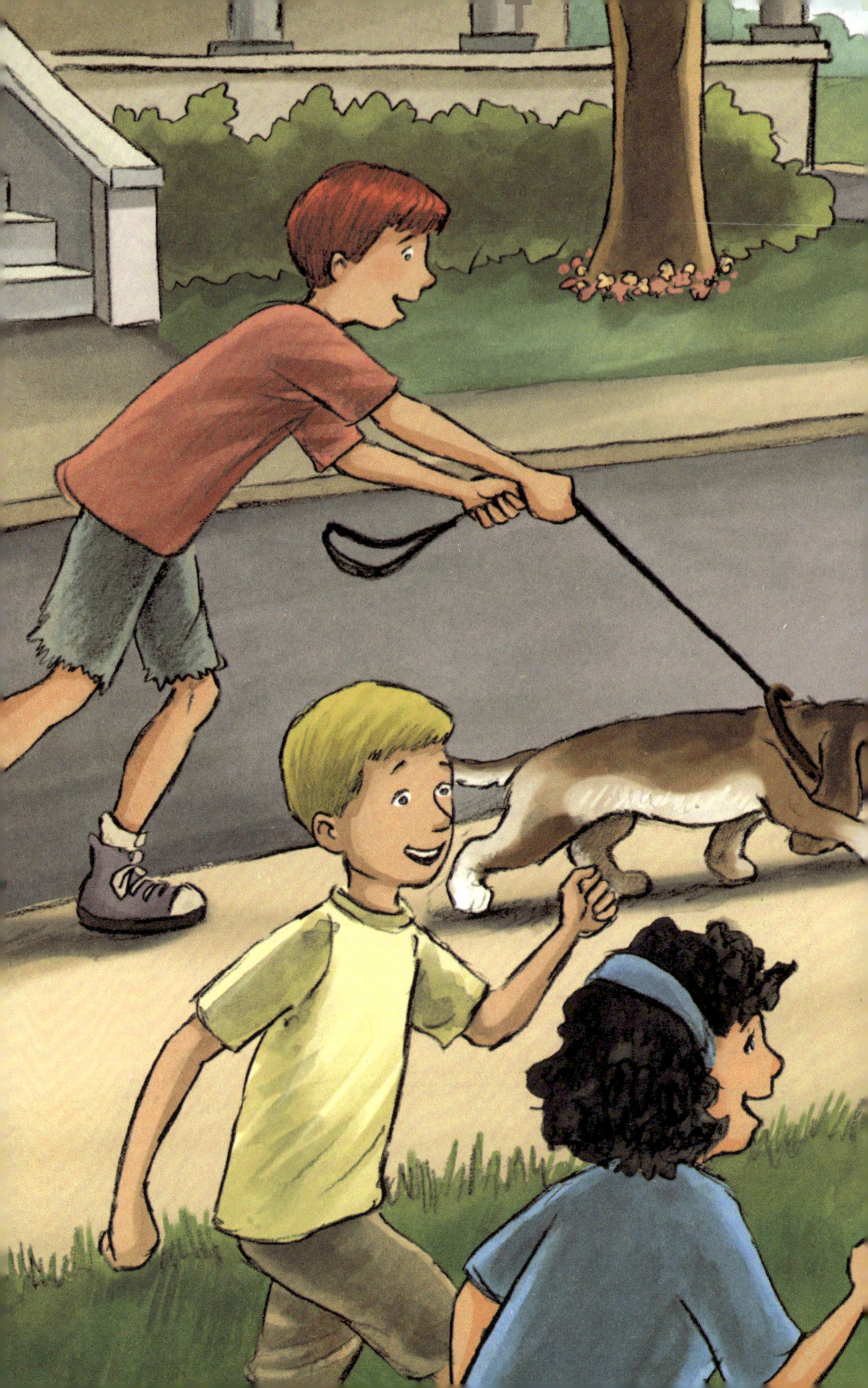

Chapter 1

Dink, Josh, and Ruth Rose hurried toward the high school. It was July 3, so they all wore shorts and T-shirts. Josh's dog, Pal, was leading the way on his leash. His floppy ears nearly touched the ground as he sniffed everything in his path.

"I can't wait to see Jud again," Dink said. Dink's full name was Donald David Duncan, but most people called him Dink.

The three kids had met Jud Wheat when they visited his parents' dude ranch in Montana. When Josh found a huge gold nugget there, he gave it to Jud to help pay for college. Now Jud was coming to Green Lawn for a visit.

"I wonder what the big surprise is that he mentioned in his postcard," Ruth Rose said. She liked to wear one color. Today it was dark blue, from her headband down to her sneakers. The color matched her sharp blue eyes.

"Read it to us," Josh said to Dink.

Dink pulled a postcard from his pocket. He read it out loud as they stopped at Pleasant Street:

Hi, Dink, Josh, and Ruth Rose,

    I'll be in Green Lawn on July 3 with a huge surprise. Meet me at the high school grounds at noon. Bye for now.

                        Your friend,

                        Jud

"Maybe the surprise is a large pizza," Josh said.

"You wish," Ruth Rose said.

"Look, there's Mr. Pocket," Dink said, turning toward Center Park. Their friend Thaddeus Pocket was standing in the town rose garden. He wore work gloves and held a shovel. His dog, Randolph, was gazing at the ducks in Swan Pond.

Josh dropped the leash, and Pal ran over to greet the fluffy little dog.

"Hi, Mr. Pocket!" Ruth Rose said.

"Well, hello, kiddos," the white-haired man said. "All set for the fireworks tomorrow night? I noticed workers setting up near the swimming pool."

"We're all going," Josh said. "Will you and Randolph be there?"

"I will," Mr. Pocket said. "But old Randolph prefers to stay home. He doesn't like the big booms."

"Pal is staying home, too," Josh said. "He doesn't even like birthday candles!"

Mr. Pocket started digging up a dead-looking rosebush that had no leaves or blossoms on it. In a wheelbarrow was a healthy bush, this one covered with shiny green leaves.

"Want to help me plant this new one?" Mr. Pocket asked the kids.

Dink looked at his watch. "Okay, but then we have to meet a friend at the high school. His name is Jud Wheat, and he's studying to become a teacher."

"He brought a surprise all the way from

Montana!" Ruth Rose said.

"This won't take long at all," Mr. Pocket said. He assigned tasks as he removed the old rosebush.

Ruth Rose poured a handful of fertilizer into the hole.

Dink shoveled in some of the loose soil.

Josh used the garden hose to fill the hole with water.

"Mother Nature may give us some rain by tonight," Mr. Pocket said, glancing up at the clouds. He lifted the new bush out of the wheelbarrow and placed it in the hole. He made sure the plant stood up straight.

"That looks splendid," Mr. Pocket said. "You three are super gardeners. Dink, if you'll return the wheelbarrow to the shed, I'll fill in the rest of the soil."

Dink handed Mr. Pocket the shovel and steered the wheelbarrow over to a garden shed. An old screwdriver held the door closed. Dink opened the door and guided the wheelbarrow inside.

There was barely room for the wheelbarrow in the packed little shed. The shelves were a jumble of pots, jars, bags of fertilizer, pails, books about gardening, and tools like the ones Dink's parents owned. On the clean brick floor were rakes, shovels, gardening stakes, and coiled hoses.

Dink left the wheelbarrow leaning against a stack of empty burlap bags at the rear of the shed. He replaced the screwdriver and left.

Just as Dink reached the others, a red car turned off Main Street and drove toward the high school. Steam escaped from under the car's hood.

"Is that your friend?" Mr. Pocket asked. "I hope he didn't drive all the way from Montana in that thing!"

"We'd better go," Dink said. "Want to meet Jud, Mr. Pocket?"

"Not right now," Mr. Pocket said. "Randolph and I need our lunch and a nap. Thanks for your help."

The kids took Pal and ran toward the red car. It stopped and a tall young man got out. He had dark, curly hair and broad shoulders. He was wearing a T-shirt, cutoff jeans, and red high-top sneakers.

"That's not Jud," Dink said as they approached the man.

Chapter 2

The man turned and waved. "Hi. You must be Dink, Josh, and Ruth Rose. I'm Scoop Raker. I work with Jud and his friend Dean. They should be here any minute."

Scoop raised the hood of his car, and more steam billowed out. He took a jug of water from the front seat, then unscrewed the radiator cap. Suddenly he yelled and stuck his finger in his mouth.

"You'd think I'd learn by now," Scoop said, shaking his head. He pulled a Band-Aid from his pocket, removed the covering, and wrapped the green Band-Aid around his finger.

会说话的霸王龙

Just then a long flatbed truck pulled up alongside Scoop's car. A brown tarp covered the truck bed, concealing something big and lumpy. The whole thing was tied down with ropes.

The driver's door opened and a tall, lanky guy hopped to the ground. He was wearing jeans, a short-sleeve shirt, and a cowboy hat. "Howdy," the man said, beaming at Dink, Josh, and Ruth Rose.

"Hi, Jud!" they all said at once.

A man stepped out of the passenger's side of the truck. He was short and wiry and had black hair tied in a ponytail. He wore work boots, baggy shorts, and a flannel shirt with the sleeves ripped off.

"Guys, I'd like you to meet my roommate and best friend, Dean Whitefeather," Jud said. "Dean, this is Dink, Josh, and Ruth Rose."

Dean walked around the truck toward the kids. He had a friendly smile and dark eyes. His shirt pocket was filled with pens. A ring of keys on his belt jangled when he walked.

The kids shook hands with Dean. Then Jud and Dean made a fuss over Pal, who gave them both big,

97

wet kisses.

"Well, what say we get busy?" Dean said, glancing at the sky. "Rain by midnight, I'll bet." He started untying the ropes.

Scoop climbed back into his car. "I passed the hotel on the way in," he said. "I'll go check on our room." He drove away, with only a little steam escaping from under the hood.

"Can we help?" Ruth Rose asked.

Dean smiled at her. "My three favorite words," he said.

"You guys can coil these ropes as we untie them," Jud said. "Just lay 'em on the ground."

Josh told Pal to stay, and the kids pitched in. After a few minutes, the ropes had all been removed. Dean and Jud yanked the tarp to the ground.

When Dink saw what had made all those lumps, he jumped back. He was staring right at the head of a Tyrannosaurus rex!

"Meet Tyrone the Tyrannosaurus," laughed Jud. "He looks even better when he's not in pieces."

Dink gulped. "Where did you get it?" he asked.

"We bought him," Jud said.

Josh grinned. "From a dinosaur store?" he joked.

"No, from the man who built Tyrone," Dean said. "He planned to start a dinosaur theme park, but he lost interest. He put an ad in the paper, and we saw it and bought Tyrone and the truck."

"Um, why do you need a dinosaur?" Ruth Rose asked.

"To raise money," Jud said. "Dean and I want to teach kids about the dinosaurs that used to live in Montana. We've decided to build a little museum on a piece of land behind the dude ranch."

"And Tyrone will be the star attraction," Dean added.

"When we first saw Tyrone, he was in the guy's barn all in pieces like you see him now. I developed a computer program to make him move and talk. We make money by taking him around the country and collecting donations."

"Is Scoop a teacher, too?" asked Dink.

"No, we met Scoop in Wyoming. He was looking for work, so we hired him," Jud said. "He's in charge of hotel rooms, getting permission for us to set up outside schools, making the flyers, stuff like that.

Scoop wants to work at the museum once it's built."

Dean climbed up onto the truck bed. "Let's put this guy back together, Jud," he said.

"How do you put him together?" Dink asked.

"Easy, like building a model with an Erector set," Dean said. He pointed to a box of large nuts, bolts, and cables on the truck bed.

"What's Tyrone made of?" Ruth Rose asked. "Is he heavy?"

"Not really," Jud said. He took the Tyrannosaurus's tail from Dean and laid it gently on the ground.

"Tyrone's mostly fiberglass and rubber. His bones are aluminum. The teeth, toenails, and eyes are plastic."

The kids gently touched one of the six-inch-long teeth. "It looks so real!" Josh said.

"Careful, some of those edges are sharp," Dean said. He grinned and wiggled a finger that was wrapped in a green Band-Aid.

They all looked over when Scoop's red car zoomed up. Scoop parked the car and climbed out with a stack of papers in his hand.

"How'd you kids like to help out?" he asked. "Can you take these flyers around town?"

Scoop handed the flyers to Ruth Rose. She looked at the top one. Beneath a picture of a Tyrannosaurus were the words:

COME MEET TYRONE THE TALKING TYRANNOSAURUS!
BEHIND THE HIGH SCHOOL, JULY 4, AT NOON.
ONE-DOLLAR DONATION PER CUSTOMER REQUESTED!

"You three will get in free, of course," Jud said, looking over Ruth Rose's shoulder.

"Cool!" Josh said.

"Who should we give them to?" Dink asked.

"Anyone and everyone," Scoop said. "Stores, friends, anyone who likes dinosaurs."

Ruth Rose divided the stack of flyers into three smaller piles. They each took a pile.

"Will you guys watch Pal?" Josh asked.

"No problem," Scoop said.

The kids headed toward Main Street with their

flyers.

An hour later, the kids were back. "The whole town is coming to see Tyrone tomorrow!" Dink said.

"Excellent! So what do you think of him now?" Jud asked, pointing to Tyrone.

Tyrone stood balanced on his thick rear legs and tail. His body and tail stretched out longer than a school bus, and he was nearly as tall as Dink's house. His back feet were as long as Pal, who was sniffing a giant plastic toenail.

"It's . . . it's . . ." Dink couldn't find the right words.

Jud and Dean laughed.

"Tyrone isn't full-sized," Dean said. "An adult T. rex would be even bigger. Come on, I'll show you what's inside this guy's belly."

He unclipped his keys and inserted one of them into a little hole in Tyrone's side. When Dean turned the key, a small metal ring popped out. Dean pulled on the ring and a door swung open on hinges.

"Awesome!" Josh said. "It was totally hidden!"

Dean picked up a rubber wedge from inside

and used it to hold the door open. Then he reached through the doorway and pulled down a set of folded, hinged steps. "Have a look," he said.

The kids kneeled on the stairs and peered inside the dinosaur's belly. Aluminum bars supported the walls. A row of hooks held tools and coils of rope and wire. There were no windows, and it was hot inside.

The floor was partly covered by a piece of carpet. A laptop computer sat on a small table in the middle of the carpet. A bunch of gray computer cables snaked across the floor. A few of the cables climbed up the dinosaur's chest and disappeared inside its neck and head.

"The computer does everything," Dean said. "I can move Tyrone's tail, mouth, and front feet just by clicking the mouse."

He squeezed by the kids and stepped inside Tyrone's belly. "I've put a loudspeaker up in Tyrone's head," Dean explained. He showed them a small microphone. "I speak into this, and it sounds like the voice is coming from Tyrone's mouth."

"Can you make him talk now?" Josh asked.

"That'll have to wait till tomorrow," Dean said. "We've been on the road since about five this morning, and I'm pretty whipped. I need about ten hours of sleep!"

Dean and the kids climbed out of Tyrone's belly, and he closed the door.

"Are you all staying at the Shangri-la?" Ruth Rose asked.

"Jud and Scoop are," Dean said. "I'm going to bed down out here." He pulled a sleeping bag from inside the truck and dropped it on the ground.

"Why do you sleep outside?" Dink asked.

Dean grinned. "Those two snore," he said, gesturing toward Scoop and Jud. "Besides, I like sleeping under the stars. Plus, I guard Tyrone. In the morning I'll go to the hotel and use their shower."

"Where can we get some good burgers?" Scoop asked the kids. "And breakfast tomorrow?"

"Ellie's Diner!" all three kids said.

Ruth Rose pointed toward Main Street. "It's between the pet shop and the fitness center," she said.

"Thanks for your help. We'll see you tomorrow," Jud said.

The three men climbed into the red car and Scoop drove off toward Main Street. A rumble of thunder over their heads sent the kids running for home.

Chapter 3

Thunder woke Dink during the night. He lay snugly in bed, watching the storm through his window. As lightning flashed, he thought about Tyrone, standing out there in the dark and rain.

The next day Dink got to the high school around eleven-thirty. He gazed up at Tyrone. The dinosaur was tall and silent under a blue sky. His mouth was closed and his eyes stared into the distance. The grass was still wet from the storm, and mist rose as it dried in the sun.

Jud, Dean, and Scoop were nowhere in sight. Dink walked over to the truck and looked in the window.

Dean's sleeping bag was spread across the seats.

A few minutes later, Ruth Rose showed up with her little brother, Nate. She was dressed in orange, from her headband down to her socks and sneakers.

When Nate saw Tyrone, his mouth fell open. He walked up to one of the rear legs and touched it. "It feels like a rubber dinosaur toy," he said.

Josh and his brothers, Brian and Bradley, came loping across the playing field. Pal was tugging on his leash.

The twins stopped in their tracks. "It's a Tankosaurus!" Brian yelled.

"No it's not!" Bradley argued. "It's a Trainosaurus!"

Josh laughed. "Guys, it's a Ty-ran-no-saur-us."

"It's not real, is it, Josh?" asked Bradley.

Josh let Pal off his leash. "No," he said. "It's just a big action figure."

Scoop pulled up in his red car and parked next to Tyrone. He hopped out and walked over to the kids.

"Morning," he said. "Some storm last night, huh? The thunder nearly knocked us out of our beds."

Scoop sat on the ground and pulled on a pair of

sandals. His wet sneakers were tied together, hanging from the car's antenna.

Dean and Jud came walking through Center Park.

"Hi, kids," Jud said. "Scoop, you missed a great breakfast. That Ellie makes amazing waffles!"

Scoop nodded. "I couldn't seem to wake up," he said.

Jud looked at Nate, Brian, and Bradley. "Do you guys like dinosaurs?"

The three little kids beamed and nodded.

"T. rex is my favorite!" Nate said.

People from town began arriving and stood around gaping up at Tyrone. Dink waved to Mr. Paskey from the Book Nook. He saw Mr. and Mrs. Spivets, who owned the Shangri-la Hotel.

Dink saw his mom show up with Josh's and Ruth Rose's mothers. Josh's mom carried a picnic basket.

"Guys, go sit with Mom, okay?" Josh asked the twins.

"Can we take Pal?" Brian asked.

Josh handed the leash over to Brian. "Okay, but don't let him off. And take him home when Mom leaves, okay?"

"Why does Brian get to do everything?" Bradley whined.

Josh sighed. "You two can share the leash, okay?"

Nate, Brian, and Bradley led Pal toward their mothers.

"This is great," Jud said, watching the crowd increase. "Dean, why don't you get Tyrone ready while Scoop and I collect money?"

While the kids were picking a place to sit, Dink saw more people he knew from town. A bunch of the O'Leary kids showed up, and Dink waved at them. Some people brought chairs or blankets to sit on. The high school playing field was filling up.

Jud and Scoop passed through the crowd, collecting a dollar from each person. When their hands were filled with bills, the men walked over to the truck and locked the money inside the cab. They each did this two or three times.

"They must make a ton of money," Josh said. "I'll bet there are two hundred people here!"

Jud climbed up onto the truck bed with a cordless

microphone. "Thanks for coming, folks!" he said to the crowd.

When everyone was quiet, Jud went on to explain why they were raising money. "Our museum should be built by next summer, and I hope some of you will come for a visit," he said.

Jud pointed his mike at the dinosaur. "Now I'd like you all to meet my friend Tyrone. Tyrone, why don't you tell these good folks about yourself?" he said.

Nothing happened. Tyrone stood silent and still. He didn't say a word.

"I guess Tyrone is shy this morning," Jud said. Then, in a louder voice, he said, "Tyrone? Can you say hi to all our friends out here? Wiggle your tail if you hear me."

This got a few laughs, but Tyrone still didn't move.

Some of the kids in the audience began to fidget. A boy sitting behind Dink muttered, "I wonder if we can get our money back."

Then, suddenly, Tyrone's tail moved to the right, then to the left. His small front arms waved up and down. His mouth opened and Tyrone said, "Hi!" in a deep voice.

"HI, TYRONE!" the crowd yelled back.

"How many of you know what kind of dinosaur I am?" Tyrone asked. Dink recognized Dean's voice coming from Tyrone's mouth.

Every kid and adult raised a hand. "Tyrannosaurus!" Nate hollered.

"That's right, I'm a Tyrannosaurus rex," Tyrone said.

"Now, how many of you remembered to eat a good breakfast this morning?"

Most people raised a hand.

"Well," Tyrone said, nodding his massive head, "about seventy million years ago, I ate other dinosaurs for my breakfast!"

Everyone laughed.

Jud hopped off the truck and sat with Dink, Josh, and Ruth Rose.

"Dean's good with the crowd, isn't he?" Jud said.

"You'd swear Tyrone is really talking," Dink said.

Jud nodded. "Yeah, Dean's a genius with anything mechanical. He had me scared at the beginning,

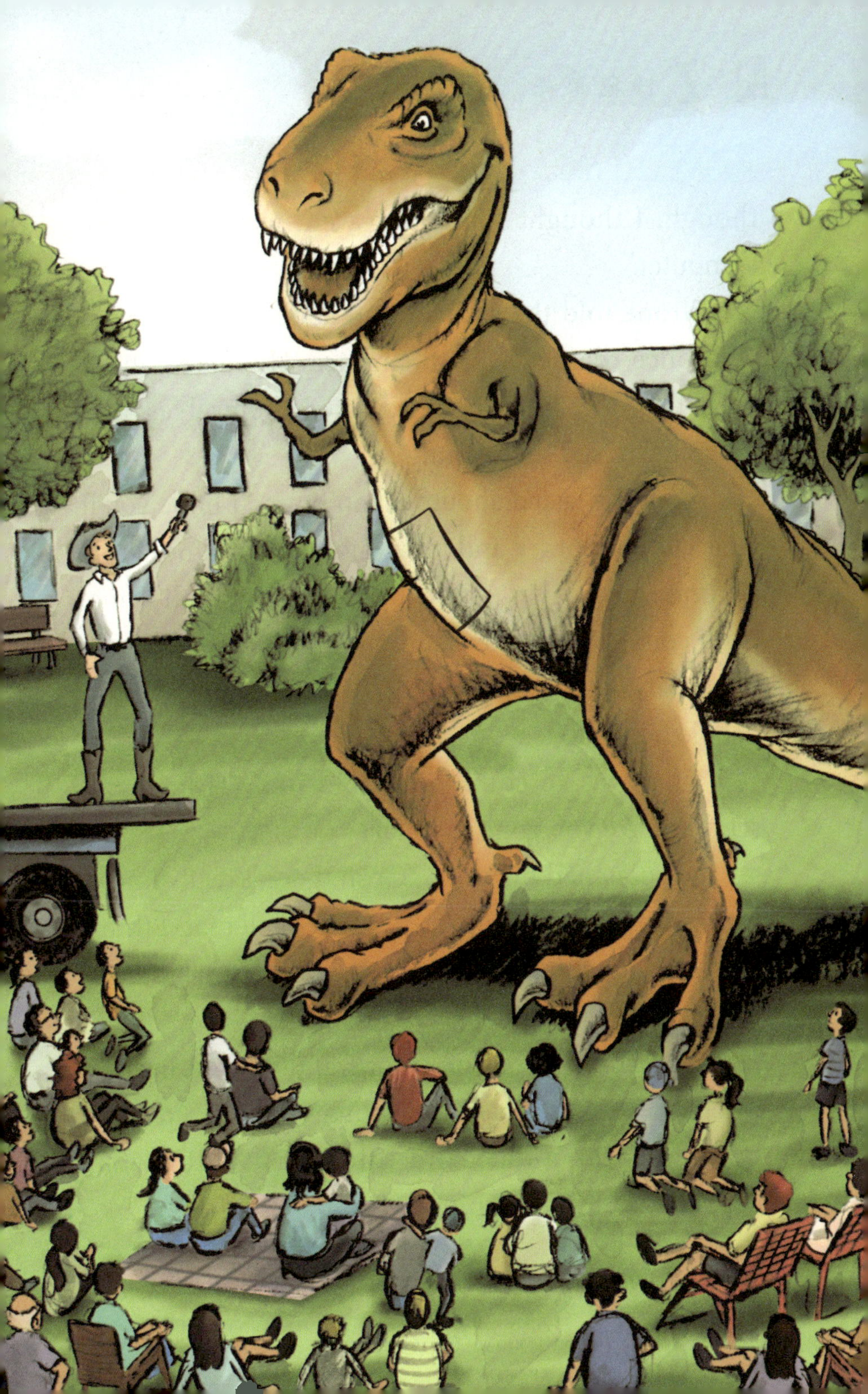

though. I thought something went wrong with the computer."

Tyrone told the audience all about the dinosaurs who once roamed North America. He talked about what they ate, how they protected themselves, and how they raised their young.

The show lasted about half an hour. "I hope you'll all go to the library and learn more about dinosaurs," Tyrone said, waving good-bye with his small arms. "And come visit me next summer in Montana!"

A lot of the kids yelled, "Bye, Tyrone!" as the people began to leave.

"That was so cool!" Josh told Jud. "How many schools have you gone to so far?"

Jud scratched his head. "Gosh, I don't really know, maybe fifty or so. Scoop keeps track of all that. I think he's lined up about twenty more before we head back to Montana."

Dean climbed out of Tyrone and walked over to where the kids and Jud were sitting.

"That was great," Jud told Dean. "But what happened at the beginning?"

Dean shrugged. "I couldn't get the laptop to boot up," he said. "One of the cables was loose."

"Well, at least you fixed it," Jud said, standing up. "It's getting warm," he added. "I could use some ice cream. After we clean up, why don't we meet at Ellie's? Tyrone is treating!"

"You just made Josh happy," Ruth Rose said. "What can we do?"

Jud pulled a plastic bag from his pocket. "If you'll go around and pick up paper, that would be a great help," he said.

While Jud walked toward the truck, Dink, Josh, and Ruth Rose spread out and began collecting litter.

Dink was leaning over to grab a crumpled flyer when he heard a shout. He looked up. The yell had come from near Tyrone. Jud, Dean, and Scoop were huddled in front of the open door.

Even from a hundred feet away, Dink could hear Jud yell, "I don't believe it!"

Chapter 4

Dink, Josh, and Ruth Rose ran toward Tyrone. "What happened?" Dink asked.

"Our money got stolen—that's what happened!" Scoop said.

"The money you just collected?" Josh asked.

Jud shook his head. "No, I still have that." He held up two thick stacks of bills with rubber bands around them. "I was going to add it to the rest of the money, but it's gone!"

Dean pointed to the floor inside Tyrone's belly. The table, chair, and carpet had been moved. Where the table and chair had stood was a square hole cut

会说话的霸王龙

into the flooring. A hinged door was open, revealing a compartment. It was empty.

"I built that as a hiding place," Dean said. "That's where we kept the money, in a duffel bag. We've been putting it in there since we left Montana."

"How much money was there?" Josh asked.

Jud's face was white. "All the money we've made so far," he said in a shaky voice. "Almost five thousand dollars."

Six pairs of eyes stared into the empty compartment.

"I don't see when anyone could have gotten in there," Scoop said.

Jud closed his eyes for a second. "I put the duffel bag in there yesterday," he said, "after we got Tyrone all set up."

"So someone stole it between yesterday afternoon and this morning," Dean said. "And it couldn't have happened last night, because I slept out here."

"I'm going to get Officer Fallon!" Ruth Rose said. "He's the chief of police."

"What can he do now?" Jud asked. "The money is

会说话的霸王龙

long gone."

"Officer Fallon catches a lot of crooks," Dink said.

Josh glanced down at the ground, dry now from the sun. "He might find some clues around here."

"They're right about bringing the police in, Jud," Dean said. "We have to do everything we can to find our money."

"I'll be right back!" Ruth Rose said as she took off running.

"Well, no one's getting this money," Jud said. He opened his shirt and stuffed the bills inside.

Dink felt Josh pinching his arm. When Dink looked at him, Josh motioned with his head for Dink to walk away with him.

He followed Josh away from the three men.

"I hate to say this," Josh whispered, "but I think one of them stole the money." He tipped his chin toward Jud, Dean, and Scoop.

"Why would they do it?" Dink asked. "Jud and Dean really want to build the museum. And Scoop's going to work there. They wouldn't steal their own money, Josh."

119

"But who else has a key to the door or knows about that hiding place inside Tyrone?" Josh insisted.

Dink shook his head. He kicked a small stone. "No one can make me believe Jud would do such a rotten thing," he said.

Just then Ruth Rose and Officer Fallon came hurrying across Center Park. Dink and Josh walked back to the dinosaur.

Officer Fallon introduced himself and pulled his notebook and pen from a shirt pocket. "Ruth Rose told me what happened," he said. He looked at the three men. "May I have your names, please?"

He wrote down each name. "Scoop?" he asked. "Is that a nickname?"

Scoop grinned. "Yeah, I was the editor of my college newspaper. I got the name because I was always first with a news scoop. My real name is Michael Raker."

Officer Fallon wrote it down. "Can you show me where the money was when you fellas last saw it?"

Dean pointed through the door at the empty compartment. "It was in there, except when we were on the road. Then we kept it with us in the truck."

"I put the duffel inside that compartment yesterday afternoon," Jud said. "That's the last time I saw it."

"Wouldn't it be safer to keep your money in a bank?" Officer Fallon asked.

"We thought the money was safe inside the dinosaur," Jud said. "No one but us knew about the hidden compartment. And I was planning on taking the money to my bank back in Montana."

"Was that compartment locked?" the police chief asked, writing in his notebook.

Jud shook his head. "No, but we always keep this outer door locked."

Officer Fallon examined the keyhole. He removed the rubber wedge and swung the door back and forth on its hinges. "Who has keys to this door?"

"I have one," Dean said. He tapped his key ring.

Jud held up his keys. "And I have the only other key," he said.

Officer Fallon made another note on his pad. "So Mr. Wheat put the money into that compartment yesterday afternoon," he said. "Then this morning, after the show, Mr. Whitefeather looked for the money and discovered that it was gone. Is that correct?"

"Actually, no," Dean said. "I did the show, but it was Jud who found out the money was missing."

"Could the money have been stolen last night?" Officer Fallon said. "Where did you fellows sleep?"

"Scoop and I slept at the hotel," Jud said. "We left the money in the compartment. We always do. Dean sleeps outside. He likes to guard Tyrone."

Officer Fallon looked confused. "Who's Tyrone?" he asked.

"That's what we call the dinosaur," Scoop explained.

Officer Fallon glanced at Dean. "You slept out here all night?" he asked. "Even during the rain?"

Dean smiled. "No, when it started to rain, I took my sleeping bag into the truck."

Officer Fallon made more notes on his pad, then turned to Jud. "Could anyone have snuck into your room and taken your key while you slept?" he asked.

Jud shook his head. "The door was locked."

Officer Fallon looked at Dean. "How about your key, Mr. Whitefeather?" he asked. "Where was it while you slept out here?"

Dean held up his key ring. "Clipped to my belt, inside my sleeping bag with me."

Officer Fallon swung the door wide and looked at the computer. "Who makes this thing work?" he asked.

"I do," Dean said. "And my computer."

"So as far as you knew, the duffel bag was still hidden under the floor this morning," Officer Fallon stated.

"That's right," said Dean.

Officer Fallon peered inside Tyrone. "And you would have been sitting right over the money at your computer, right, Mr. Whitefeather?"

Dean nodded. "But I figure it was already stolen by then," he said. "After the show, when Jud moved the table and pulled the rug back, the duffel bag was gone."

Officer Fallon placed the wedge so that the door

remained slightly open. He looked at the three men. "Gentlemen, let's walk across the street to my office. I'd like you to think about everything that's happened since you pulled in here yesterday. I want you to write it all down—even the tiniest details, no matter how unimportant they seem."

"How long will that take?" Scoop asked. "We have a lot of other schools to go to. We're supposed to be in New Haven tomorrow."

"Then we'd best get busy," Officer Fallon said.

Chapter 5

Dink, Josh, and Ruth Rose watched the men follow Officer Fallon toward the police station. Above their heads, Tyrone's big plastic eyes stared.

"This is great," Dink grumbled. "Jud comes to see us, and his money gets stolen."

"I just don't see how anyone did it," Ruth Rose said. "We were all here yesterday afternoon, and Dean guarded Tyrone last night. Plus, he was locked inside Tyrone during the show."

"So maybe Dean is the thief," Josh said. "He could have taken the money last night or even during the show. No one saw what he did after that door closed."

125

"But we know what he did," Dink said. "He was working on the computer. Otherwise, Tyrone wouldn't have moved or talked."

"That's just it," Josh said. "Tyrone didn't move for the first few minutes, remember? Maybe that's when Dean was snitching the duffel bag!"

Dink shook his head. "I don't believe Dean would steal from his best friend," he said.

Just then Officer Keene pulled up in his cruiser. He climbed out with a roll of yellow tape and several wooden stakes in his arms. "Hi, kids," he said. "Little excitement, huh?"

He set the tape and stakes on the ground and walked over to Tyrone. The wedge was still in place, letting him open the door wider. He glanced inside. "Whew, you could bake a pie in there," he said.

Officer Keene began shoving stakes into the ground around Tyrone. Then he strung the crime-scene tape around the stakes, forming a big circle around the dinosaur.

"Can we go to Ellie's?" Josh said. "My brain needs a drink."

会说话的霸王龙

The kids started walking across Center Park.

"Do you really think Dean is the robber?" Ruth Rose asked Josh.

"Yes," he said. "He has a key, and he knew where the money was hidden."

"What about Scoop?" Ruth Rose asked. "Could he have borrowed a key from Dean or Jud?"

"If he had, they would have mentioned it to

Officer Fallon," Josh responded.

"Maybe the thief was someone else," Dink said. "Some stranger who knew how to pick locks."

"But Dean was sleeping outside the dinosaur," Ruth Rose said. "How would a thief get past him?"

"That's why I think it's Dean," Josh said as he pulled open the door to Ellie's Diner.

The kids slid into a booth near the windows. One of the Tyrone flyers was taped to the glass. Ellie waved, then came over.

"Hi, kids. Why aren't you at the dinosaur show?" she asked.

"It's over," Josh said. "But someone stole their money!"

Ellie slid in next to Josh. "Who stole whose money?" she asked with wide eyes.

Ruth Rose explained about the money that was kept inside Tyrone's belly.

"Those poor guys," Ellie said, standing up. "They were so excited when they came in for breakfast this morning."

"Officer Fallon is on the case," Ruth Rose said.

"Good!" Ellie said. "Josh, your tongue is almost hanging out. How about some fresh lemonade?" she asked.

The kids agreed, and Ellie brought three tall glasses.

Josh took a big slurp through his straw. "So, you guys agree that Dean is the robber?"

Dink stirred his lemonade. "I don't. Dean wouldn't be dumb enough to steal the money while he was guarding it last night," he said. "That would point the finger right at him."

Josh shook his head. "He could have taken the duffel bag during the show," he said.

"How?" Ruth Rose asked.

"Easy," Josh said. "He locks himself inside Tyrone. He moves the table and rug, grabs the duffel bag, then puts the rug and table back. It only takes him a minute."

"Then what?" Dink asked. "Where did he put the duffel bag?"

He and Ruth Rose stared at Josh, waiting for his answer.

Josh blinked at them. He took a sip of his lemonade. "Okay, here's what happened," he said. "Dean told us he built that little compartment inside Tyrone, right? So what if he built a second one that only he knows about? And that's where he hid the money!"

Dink looked at Josh over his glass. "You think the money is still inside Tyrone?"

"Why not?" Josh asked. "It's perfect. No one would think to look for it there."

Ruth Rose squinted her eyes at Josh. "Except someone with a sneaky mind like yours."

"I say we go search old Tyrone the T. rex," Josh said, finishing his lemonade. "If I'm right, Dean is planning to come and get the duffel bag as soon as he gets a chance."

"I hate to admit it, but Josh is making sense," Ruth Rose said. "It won't hurt to look inside Tyrone."

The kids left their money on the table, waved at Ellie, and headed back toward the high school.

A few minutes later, the kids stood looking at Tyrone surrounded by yellow crime-scene tape.

Officer Keene was gone. "No one's supposed to go past the tape," Dink said.

"We could say we didn't see it," Josh suggested.

"Right," Dink said. "It's broad daylight and we can't see bright yellow tape."

"But what if it was dark?" Ruth Rose said, looking at Dink. "We could come back tonight."

Dink shook his head. "Forget it, guys. We'll be at the fireworks with our parents tonight."

Josh draped an arm around Dink's shoulder. "Perfect," he said. "While they're looking up at the sky, we can sneak away."

Dink finally agreed. "But I'm only doing this for Jud," he said.

The kids heard a bark and saw Mr. Pocket and Randolph inspecting the rosebush in the park. They walked over to say hi.

"Did you hear about the robbery?" Ruth Rose asked.

"Yes, and I feel bad for those young men," Mr. Pocket said. "Any news?"

Dink shook his head.

A to Z 神秘案件

"But something might break tonight," Josh said, giving Dink a little nudge.

"Our bush looks fine," Mr. Pocket said. "But I have to get rid of this dead one. Dink, you want to get the wheelbarrow for me?"

Dink ran to the shed. The wheelbarrow was where he had left it, leaning on the burlap bags. As Dink was leaving, he noticed muddy footprints on the bricks.

He brought the wheelbarrow to Mr.Pocket.

"Thanks," Mr. Pocket said as he loaded the dead rosebush into the wheelbarrow. "I'll toss this into the school Dumpster." He walked away, with Randolph galloping along beside the wheelbarrow.

"Look, there's Jud and Scoop!" Josh said, pointing toward the dinosaur.

The two men were standing outside the crime-scene tape. Jud was talking and pointing a finger at the door in Tyrone's side. Scoop answered him, shaking his head.

The kids were too far away to hear their words. After a moment, the two men climbed into Scoop's car and drove away.

Dean wasn't with them.

"Officer Fallon must be holding Dean as a suspect," Dink said. The sweet lemonade in his stomach suddenly felt sour.

Chapter 6

As they walked home, the kids talked about the theft.

Josh stopped walking. A sly look shone from his green eyes. "I figured it out," he whispered. "I know who stole the money."

"Who?" Dink said.

"It was Tyrone!" Josh said. "While everyone was asleep, he walked to the bank and made a dino deposit!"

Dink shoved Josh, and Ruth Rose rolled her eyes.

Before splitting up, they agreed to meet and walk to the fireworks together. "Drop off your sleeping bags at my house," Dink said. "My folks said we could sleep outside after the fireworks."

"And wear dark clothes," Josh said.

At eight-thirty, Josh, Ruth Rose, and their families met at Dink's house. Dink, Josh, and Ruth Rose piled their sleeping bags on the picnic table. The adults carried blankets, bags of popcorn, and bug spray. Nate, Brian, and Bradley had each brought their favorite stuffed animals.

The three families walked to Main Street and turned left. They took another left at Holly's Gas Station. From there it was only a short walk down East Green Street to the swimming pool, where the fireworks were set up.

"Why are you three dressed in black?" Ruth Rose's dad asked. "You look like ninjas."

"We're hoping the mosquitoes won't see us in the dark," Ruth Rose said, glancing at Dink.

Dink, Josh, and Ruth Rose walked ahead, leaving the others behind.

"Good thinking," Josh said when he was sure he couldn't be overheard.

A few minutes later, they all arrived at the town pool. Hundreds of people were already there. Blankets and chairs covered the lawns near the pool, tennis courts, and baseball field.

The fire truck was parked nearby in case it was needed.

"I see Jud, Scoop, and Dean," Josh said. The three men sat leaning against the fence that surrounded the baseball field. "Let's go sit with them."

"We can't," Ruth Rose said. "If we do, they'll see us sneak away later."

"Well, let's at least go over and say hi," Dink said.

"Yeah, and we can see if Dean looks guilty," Josh commented.

The kids wove their way through the blankets and chairs. Jud noticed them first and stood up.

"Howdy," he said, waving. "You guys want to sit with us?" Scoop and Dean said hi, too, but didn't stand up.

"Can't," Josh said. "We have to stay near our parents."

"Officer Fallon is a nice guy," Jud said. "I sure hope he can find our money. We're taking Tyrone down tomorrow and leaving."

"Where are you going?" Ruth Rose asked.

"New Haven first, then a bunch of other towns," Scoop said. "We have a lot more money to earn."

Dean didn't join the conversation. His dark eyes stared straight ahead.

"Good evening," a voice said. It was Mr. Linkletter, the Shangri-la Hotel's manager. He was sitting on a lawn chair a few feet away. Everyone said hi.

"I hope your room is comfortable," Mr. Linkletter said to Jud and Scoop.

"It's great," Jud answered.

Just then a circle of blue light lit the sky over their heads. "Oooh!" cried hundreds of people.

"They're starting!" Ruth Rose said. "We'd better go find our parents."

"How about breakfast at Ellie's tomorrow?" Jud asked. "I don't want to leave without saying good-bye."

"Sure," Dink said. "What time?"

"We're getting up real early to load Tyrone onto the truck," he said. "So how about nine o'clock?"

"We'll be there," said Dink. The kids walked away toward their families. They picked a spot near the

137

tennis courts where they could still keep an eye on the three men by the fence.

"Guys, did you hear what Jud said?" Ruth Rose asked. "They're taking Tyrone apart tomorrow!"

"So if that's where Dean hid the money, he needs to get it before then," Josh said.

"Or whoever," Dink added.

"Trust me, it's Dean," Josh went on. "Did you guys notice how he just sat and didn't say a word to anyone? In my book, that spells G-U-I-L-T-Y."

Volunteer firefighters had built a low barricade around the fireworks. The police had placed detour signs on River Road to keep cars away. Firefighters in white T-shirts went through the crowd, handing out tiny American flags.

For a few minutes the kids watched fireworks bursting over their heads. The sky went from black to red, white, and blue. The crowd clapped and whistled and yelled.

"When the next really big one goes off, let's boogie," Josh whispered.

A second later, the sky blossomed into a giant

yellow flower. While every eye was looking up, Dink, Josh, and Ruth Rose slipped away in the dark.

They darted across East Green Street and raced to the high school lawns.

A nearly full moon cast the dinosaur's shadow halfway across the playing field. Behind the kids, the sky was still lit with fireworks. A breeze swept across the field, making the yellow tape rattle against the stakes.

"Now what?" Dink asked. "I really don't like being here, guys."

"I don't, either," Ruth Rose said. "But if the duffel bag is still inside Tyrone, we have to find it tonight!"

Chapter 7

"Let's just do it," Josh said. "It'll take us five minutes. If we don't find the money, we go back to watch the fireworks."

The kids crept under the yellow tape. They were concealed in Tyrone's dark shadow. The rubber wedge was holding the door open an inch. Josh removed it and swung the door open.

"I can't see anything!" Dink said. "How can we search in the dark?"

"Wait," Ruth Rose said. She pulled a small flashlight from her pocket. She flipped it on and aimed the beam past the folded steps, into Tyrone's belly.

The table and rug were still off to one side. The compartment lid was up, and the space was still empty. Then Ruth Rose shut off the light.

Dink pulled down the steps, and they scrambled up into Tyrone's belly. Dink folded the steps back while Josh eased the door shut.

They were in a dark, stuffy cave.

"It's roasting in here!" Josh's voice complained from the darkness.

Dink was on his knees. One arm rested against the small table. The compartment that once held the duffel bag was in front of him, but he couldn't see it.

"Let's get this over with," Dink said. "I'd like to get back to the fireworks before my folks know we're gone."

Ruth Rose flipped on her flashlight and shone it around the small space. "Okay, Josh, show us this secret hiding place," she said.

"It wouldn't be right out in plain sight," Josh said. "Look for someplace no one would think of."

On his knees, Josh shuffled around to face the rear

legs. They were attached to the rest of the body with large bolts. "I'll bet these legs are hollow," he said.

Josh felt around and, sure enough, was able to stick his arm down inside one leg. "Nothing down there," he said.

Dink examined the other leg, but there was nothing hidden inside that one, either.

"What about up inside his head?" Ruth Rose asked. Her light followed the cables up Tyrone's chest and neck. At the top, only a dark hole showed where the head was.

"Let's find out," Dink said. He stood up and tried to reach his hand up to Tyrone's head cavity. "I'm not tall enough."

"Wait a sec," Josh said. He lifted the laptop computer off the table and set it on the floor. Then he slid the table over to Dink.

Dink climbed onto the table and reached again. This time his arm was inside Tyrone's head. He moved his hand around in the space. "All I feel are the wires that come from the computer," he said. "But my arm isn't long enough to reach all the way."

"Could I fit in there?" Ruth Rose asked.

"Probably," Dink said. "The head is hollow."

Josh giggled. "Like yours," he said.

"Let me go up," Ruth Rose said. "I'll stand on the table, then you guys boost me."

Ruth Rose and Dink traded places. Josh held the flashlight in his mouth as he and Dink lifted Ruth Rose up Tyrone's throat. She disappeared into the head, with only her feet sticking out. Then her feet vanished and they saw her face peering down at them.

"There's nothing up here but a little speaker attached to those wires," she said. "And a bunch of teeth."

Josh flashed the light around the walls. "I don't see anyplace else you could hide a pile of money," he said.

"So what should we do?" Dink asked.

"First, get some air in here," Josh said. He handed Dink the flashlight and reached for the door.

Dink shut off the flashlight. "Don't open it too wide," he said. "I don't feel like getting arrested for breaking and entering a dinosaur!"

Josh shoved the door. It didn't move. "Help me, Dinkus. It's stuck."

Both boys leaned their shoulders against the door and pushed.

"The door must have locked when we closed it," Josh said. "We forgot to wedge it open with that rubber thing!"

Dink flipped on the flashlight and aimed the beam up at Ruth Rose. "If I hand this to you, can you shine it out through the mouth?" he asked. "If you yell, someone might hear you."

She shook her head. "The mouth is closed."

"We have to try something," Dink said, waving the flashlight around. "I'm not staying in here all night!"

"Got it," Josh said. "I think I know how to boot up Dean's computer. If I can make Tyrone's mouth open, we can yell for help through the microphone and speaker."

"No one would hear us over the fireworks noise," Ruth Rose said. "But you gave me another idea, Josh. If you can open Tyrone's mouth, maybe I can climb out that way!"

"Ruth Rose, Tyrone's head is too high off the ground," Dink said.

He looked at Josh. "Is there anything we can make a ladder out of?"

Suddenly Josh grabbed the flashlight from Dink's hand. He shone it around the walls until the beam fell on the row of hooks. "I thought so," Josh said.

"What?" Dink said.

Josh reached out and grabbed a coil of rope. "This," he said. "We can use it to lower Ruth Rose out Tyrone's mouth to the ground!"

Dink looked up at Ruth Rose. "Do you think you could?" he asked.

Ruth Rose nodded. "Tyrone's mouth is pretty big,"

she said.

"Like Josh's," Dink said, grinning at his friend.

"Very amusing," Josh said. He passed the flashlight to Dink, then sat in front of the laptop. He turned it on, then tapped a few keys.

Several icons appeared on the screen. One of them was labeled TYRONE. Josh clicked on it, and a window appeared showing a list of choices. One of the words was MOUTH.

"Bingo," Josh said. "Get ready, Ruth Rose!"

Josh clicked on MOUTH. A second later, Dink heard a grinding sound.

"It worked!" Ruth Rose yelled. "Tyrone's mouth is opening!"

Chapter 8

Dink set the flashlight on the floor and tied one end of the rope to the folding steps. Josh formed a loop in the other end, big enough for Ruth Rose to step in. He stood on the table and handed her the loop.

"Are you sure you want to do this?" Dink asked.

"It'll be easy," Ruth Rose said. "I climb down the rope ladder from my cousin's tree house all the time."

"We'll hold the rope till you're ready to go down," Josh said. He added, "Be careful of those teeth!"

"Okay, give me a minute." Ruth Rose's face disappeared. Some of the slack rope went with her. "All right!" she yelled. "Just lower me real slow."

The boys felt the rope tighten with Ruth Rose's weight. They let the rope slip slowly through their fingers. Dink felt the friction making his palms burn.

Then the rope went totally slack.

"Is she down?" Josh asked.

They both heard someone banging on the door in Tyrone's side. "I'll be right back!" Ruth Rose yelled.

Dink and Josh sat and leaned against a curved wall. Ruth Rose's flashlight was growing dim, so Dink shut it off.

"Wish this place had an air conditioner," Josh said after a minute. He wiped sweat off his face with his T-shirt.

"Why not wish for a full refrigerator while you're at it," Dink said.

Josh grinned. "Or a microwave and a pizza. But I'd settle for a big fan."

The boys sat in the dark. Dink felt sweat trickling into his eyes.

"I'm cooking," Josh moaned.

"Don't be such a baby," Dink said. "Imagine what

148

it would be like inside a real Tyrannosaurus!"

Josh giggled in the dark. "Did dinosaurs eat kids?" he asked.

"No, Josh, because humans didn't live then," Dink said. "Besides, if a T. rex got one taste of you, he'd spit you out."

Josh poked Dink in the ribs.

Dink poked him back.

Just as Josh put a wrestling hold around Dink's neck, they heard something thump outside.

Josh gulped. "Do you suppose it's Dean, coming to get the money?"

Dink crawled to the door and put his ear against it. The door opened, and Dink nearly fell on top of Jud. Behind Jud stood Officer Fallon and Ruth Rose.

"You sure get yourself in some pickles," Officer Fallon said, shining his flashlight in Dink's eyes. "Good thing I found Jud at the fireworks."

Jud lowered the steps so Dink and Josh could climb down to the ground.

"Thanks," Josh said. "We were melting in there!"

"I don't suppose you found the money," Jud said.

"Ruth Rose told us what you were up to."

Dink shook his head. "Sorry," he said.

"I'm afraid that whoever took that duffel bag disappeared with it," Officer Fallon said.

Jud nodded. "It must have happened last night after we went to bed," he said. "I just don't see how."

Officer Fallon shined his light at the ground. "It rained last night, so even if the crook left footprints, they'd have washed away."

Footprints, Dink thought. "I saw wet footprints in that garden shed," he said. Dink pointed through the darkness toward the rose garden. "I went in to get the wheelbarrow for Mr. Pocket."

"That means someone went in there after it rained," Ruth Rose said. "And that was in the middle of the night!"

"Maybe the footprints were left by our thief," Officer Fallon said. He put a hand on Dink's shoulder. "Show me."

Dink led the way across the dark lawn. "There it is," he said when they reached the small garden shed.

"You folks please stay out here," Officer Fallon

told Josh, Ruth Rose, and Jud. His flashlight beam found the screwdriver. He removed it and opened the door. He played the light over the floor. Dried muddy footprints led from the door to the back of the shed.

"Hold this for me," Officer Fallon said, handing his flashlight to Dink. "Stand by the door so I have light."

Officer Fallon stepped inside and kneeled to examine the footprints. Then he walked through the shed, checking inside, under, and behind anything large enough to hide a person.

At the back of the shed, he moved the wheelbarrow. He poked at the stack of burlap sacks with a toe. Then he peeled off several of the bags and set them on the floor.

Dink saw him bend over and pull something from under the remaining bags.

"Jud, would you come in here?" Officer Fallon yelled.

Jud stuck his head in the door.

"Is this what you've been looking for?"

Officer Fallon was holding a dark brown duffel

bag. It was fat, as if stuffed with something. A long zipper ran along one side.

Jud beamed. "You found it!" he said.

Officer Fallon carried the bag out of the shed and set it on the ground. Under the flashlight beam, he pulled open the zipper. Nearly filling the bag were thousands of dollar bills bound in rubber bands.

Officer Fallon looked up at Jud. "Is this your money?" he asked.

Jud nodded. "I hope it's all there."

"What's that?" Dink asked. He pointed to something pale green that was stuck to the side of the canvas duffel.

"It's a Band-Aid," Ruth Rose said.

"Don't touch," Officer Fallon cautioned. He pulled a small plastic bag from his pocket. Using the point of his pen, he knocked the Band-Aid into the baggie, then sealed it.

"I wonder who this came from," Officer Fallon said. He held his light on the plastic bag.

"Scoop put on a Band-Aid like that one yesterday," Ruth Rose said. "He burned his finger on his car radiator."

"I saw one on Dean's finger, too," Josh said.

"We all use them," Jud said. He reached into a pocket of his jeans and pulled out a green Band-Aid.

Officer Fallon held Jud's flat Band-Aid next to the used one in his baggie. The two Band-Aids were the same.

Chapter 9

"All three of you fellas wear these Band-Aids?" Officer Fallon asked Jud.

Jud nodded. "Working on Tyrone, we were always nicking our fingers," he said. "So I bought a box of Band-Aids, and we all keep a few in our pocket."

Officer Fallon glanced at the duffel bag. "Who handled that bag last?"

"I'm the only one who ever put the money in the bag," Jud said. "I must've been wearing a Band-Aid, and it slipped off my finger when I stuck the bag in the compartment."

"Or the Band-Aid could have fallen off the thief's

finger when he stole the bag," Officer Fallon said. "Whoever it was." He gave Jud a close look.

Jud thought for a moment before he spoke. "I know it looks like one of us stole the money," he said. "But I sure didn't take it, and I can't believe Dean or Scoop would, either!"

"Could the robber be someone else?" Dink asked.

"But who?" Officer Fallon said. "Jud, you told me only you and Dean have keys to your dinosaur."

"That's right," Jud said. "But Dean is my best friend!"

Officer Fallon slipped the baggie and his pen into a pocket. "Between Scoop Raker and Dean Whitefeather, who had more opportunity to get at that duffel bag?" he asked Jud.

Jud looked at his feet. "Dean, I guess," he mumbled. "He slept next to Tyrone last night."

Officer Fallon put his hand on Jud's shoulder. "I want you to wait in my office while I get Dean," he said. "Do you think he's still at the fireworks?"

"I guess," Jud said.

"Meanwhile, I'll put this money in our safe,"

Officer Fallon went on. "I'll see you at the station in a few minutes."

Looking embarrassed, Jud turned and headed toward Main Street. In a few seconds, he had disappeared in the darkness.

Officer Fallon looked at Dink, Josh, and Ruth Rose. "Your parents might be missing you by now," he said. "I'll take you back, okay?"

Dink, Josh, and Ruth Rose followed Officer Fallon to his cruiser and climbed into the backseat. Officer Fallon drove them to Main Street.

Colorful fireworks were still lighting the skies over the town swimming pool. Officer Fallon parked between the tennis courts and the baseball field.

The kids watched him walk toward the baseball field fence; then they went to find their parents.

"There you are!" Dink's mother said. "We thought you'd been abducted by aliens!" Looking at his watch, Dink realized they'd been gone nearly half an hour.

The kids sat where they could watch Officer Fallon. He walked over to Dean, and the two men stood talking for a minute. Then Officer Fallon led

会说话的霸王龙

Dean to his cruiser. The car pulled onto Main Street and disappeared.

"I can't believe Jud's friend robbed him," Ruth Rose said.

Josh lay back on the grass. "I wonder what will happen to Tyrone now," he said.

"I guess Jud and Scoop will hire someone to take Dean's place," Dink said.

"Where is Scoop?" Ruth Rose asked.

"Wasn't he by the fence with Dean?" Dink asked.

"No," Josh said. "Only Dean was there. Maybe Scoop went back to the hotel. He said he didn't get much sleep last night because of the storm."

Dink remembered the storm raging outside his window last night. He thought about Dean waking up in the rain and dashing for the truck. In his mind, he saw those muddy footprints on the shed floor. And that morning, Scoop's wet sneakers hanging from his car antenna.

"Guys, I think everyone's wrong about Dean!" Dink said suddenly. "I think Scoop stole the money, and I think he hid it in the garden shed!"

"But he didn't have a key," Josh said.

"I think Scoop knew that Dean wouldn't sleep outside once it started to rain. Dean moved into the truck cab to stay dry, and that's when Scoop got inside Tyrone."

"How? Scoop didn't have a key," Josh said again.

"Somehow, Scoop must have taken Jud's key while Jud was asleep," Dink said. "Scoop stole the duffel bag, hid it in the shed, then ran back to the hotel. He must have planned to return to the shed later to get the money."

Suddenly Ruth Rose gasped. "Maybe that's where Scoop is now!" she said. "He could sneak away, like we did!"

"Come on!" Dink said. The kids zipped past the Mystic Greenhouse, cut behind the Book Nook, and raced toward the rose garden. Out of breath, they crouched behind some rosebushes ten yards from the shed. A light flickered through the open door.

"Someone's inside!" Josh hissed.

The three kids crept close enough to see inside the shed. They saw a dark-haired figure kneeling in front of the stack of burlap bags. When the man stood up, they knew it was Scoop Raker.

"What should we do?" Ruth Rose whispered.

"The screwdriver is there," Josh said. "I'm gonna lock him in!"

"No!" Dink said. "Let's go get Officer Fallon!"

Josh shook his head. "Not enough time! When Scoop doesn't find the money, he'll take off!" He started to crawl through the rosebushes toward the shed. "Ouch!" he yelled.

"What happened?" whispered Ruth Rose.

"Darn thorns!" Josh whispered back.

Suddenly Scoop burst out of the shed. He turned his flashlight beam on Josh. Before anyone else could react, Scoop had grabbed Josh by the arm.

"Okay, kid, what did you do with the money?" he demanded.

"YOU LEAVE HIM ALONE!" Ruth Rose cried as she and Dink sprinted to Josh's side.

"Yes, leave him alone," a deeper voice said. Officer Fallon and Dean stepped out from behind the shed.

Chapter 10

An hour later, the kids were lying on their sleeping bags in Dink's backyard. They were gazing up at the stars.

"There's the Big Dipper!" Josh said, sitting up.

"I think I see Mars!" Dink said.

"There's a shooting star. Make a wish!" Ruth Rose said. "I wish I could be the first woman president!"

"I wish Ruth Rose could become president and put me in charge of desserts," Josh said.

Dink and Ruth Rose sat up and laughed.

"I wish Jud and Dean would leave Tyrone in Green Lawn," Dink said.

"Yeah," Josh said. "That would be so excellent. We could make him walk all over town."

"People would pay us to give them rides in Tyrone," Ruth Rose added. "We could send the money to Jud and Dean for their museum."

The three kids sighed and settled back on their sleeping bags.

"I still can't figure out how Scoop got Jud's key," Ruth Rose said.

"Oh, that was easy," Josh said. "I figured it out a long time ago."

Dink popped up and glared at his friend. "And are you planning to tell us?"

Josh let out a dramatic sigh. "Scoop heard Dean say it was going to rain last night. He knew Dean would probably move inside somewhere to stay dry. I think that's when Scoop decided to steal the money. He waited till Jud was sound asleep, then took his key."

"But how did Scoop get into Jud's room?" Dink asked.

"He didn't have to," Josh said. "They slept in the

same room."

"Joshua, how do you know that?" Ruth Rose asked.

Josh grinned. "Remember when Mr. Linkletter said hi to us at the fireworks? I heard him ask Jud and Scoop how their room was. Room, not rooms."

"It's a good thing Officer Fallon showed up at the shed," Dink said. "I wonder how he knew Scoop would go there."

"Dean might have convinced him," Josh said. "Dean must've figured out the only way the crook could have gotten a key was by taking it from Jud during the night. And Dean knew Jud and Scoop shared a room."

"Well, I hate to admit it," Dink said, "but you're pretty smart."

"I know," Josh said. "But thanks anyway."

"You're welcome," Dink said.

"Maybe I'll put you in charge of the FBI when I'm president," Ruth Rose said.

Josh yawned. "Naw. I'd rather be in charge of food."

The three kids smiled in the dark. Then, as the stars twinkled above them, they slowly went to sleep.

Text copyright © 2003 by Ron Roy
Illustrations copyright © 2003 by John Steven Gurney
All rights reserved under International and Pan-American Copyright Conventions.
Published in the United States by Random House Children's Books,
a division of Random House, Inc., New York,
and simultaneously in Canada by Random House of Canada Limited, Toronto.

本书中英双语版由中南博集天卷文化传媒有限公司与企鹅兰登（北京）文化发展有限公司合作出版。

"企鹅"及其相关标识是企鹅兰登已经注册或尚未注册的商标。
未经允许，不得擅用。
封底凡无企鹅防伪标识者均属未经授权之非法版本。

©中南博集天卷文化传媒有限公司。本书版权受法律保护。未经权利人许可，任何人不得以任何方式使用本书包括正文、插图、封面、版式等任何部分内容，违者将受到法律制裁。

著作权合同登记号：字18-2023-258

图书在版编目（CIP）数据

会说话的霸王龙：汉英对照／（美）罗恩·罗伊著；
（美）约翰·史蒂文·格尼绘；周丽娟译. -- 长沙：湖
南少年儿童出版社，2024.10. --（A to Z神秘案件）.
ISBN 978-7-5562-7818-3

Ⅰ. H319.4
中国国家版本馆CIP数据核字第2024UF2245号

A TO Z SHENMI ANJIAN HUI SHUOHUA DE BAWANGLONG

A to Z神秘案件 会说话的霸王龙

［美］罗恩·罗伊 著　［美］约翰·史蒂文·格尼 绘　周丽娟 译

责任编辑：唐 凌　李 炜	策划出品：李 炜　张苗苗　文赛峰
策划编辑：文赛峰	特约编辑：杜佳美
营销编辑：付 佳　杨 朔　周晓茜	封面设计：霍雨佳
版权支持：王媛媛	版式设计：马睿君
插图上色：河北传图文化	内文排版：李 洁

出 版 人：刘星保
出　　版：湖南少年儿童出版社
地　　址：湖南省长沙市晚报大道89号
邮　　编：410016
电　　话：0731-82196320
常年法律顾问：湖南崇民律师事务所　柳成柱律师
经　　销：新华书店
开　　本：875 mm×1230 mm　1/32
字　　数：91千字
版　　次：2024年10月第1版
书　　号：ISBN 978-7-5562-7818-3
印　　刷：三河市中晟雅豪印务有限公司
印　　张：5.25
印　　次：2024年10月第1次印刷
定　　价：280.00元（全10册）

若有质量问题，请致电质量监督电话：010-59096394　　团购电话：010-59320018